A WOMAN OF PASSION

The Life of E. Nesbit
1858-1924

·E·NESBIT·

A WOMAN OF PASSION

The Life of E. Nesbit
1858 - 1924

JULIA BRIGGS

NEW AMSTERDAM BOOKS

New York

© 1987 Julia Briggs

Published in the United States of America by

New Amsterdam Books/The Meredith Press, Inc.

171 Madison Avenue

New York, N.Y. 10016

by arrangement with Century Hutchinson Ltd.

Library of Congress Cataloging in Publication Data:

Briggs, Julia.
    A woman of passion.

    Bibliography: p.
    Includes index
    1. Nesbit, E. (Edith), 1858–1924—Biography.
    2. Authors, English—19th century—Biography. I. Title.
    PR4149.B4Z59 1987 823'.912 [B] 87–11215
    ISBN 0–941533–03–4

Photoset by Deltatype, Ellesmere Port, Cheshire
Printed and bound in Great Britain by
Butler and Tanner Ltd, Frome and London

CONTENTS

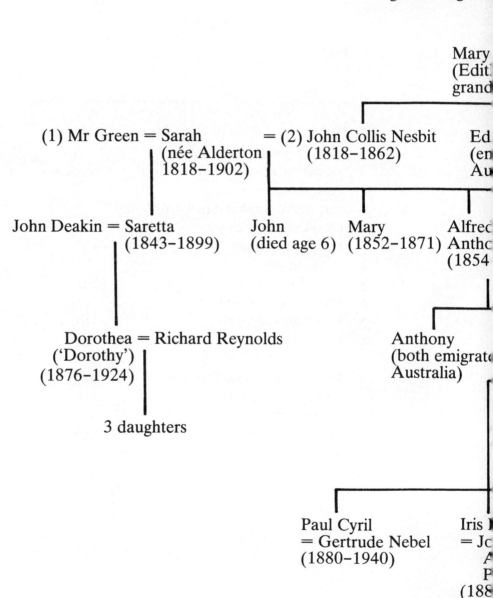

Jacob Planta
(Swedish surgec

granddaughter

Mary
(Edit
grand

(1) Mr Green = Sarah   = (2) John Collis Nesbit   Ed
            (née Alderton   (1818–1862)   (en
            1818–1902)   Au

John Deakin = Saretta   John   Mary   Alfrec
         (1843–1899)   (died age 6)   (1852–1871)   Antho
                                                  (1854

Dorothea = Richard Reynolds   Anthony
('Dorothy')   (both emigrate
(1876–1924)   Australia)

3 daughters

Paul Cyril   Iris]
= Gertrude Nebel   = Jc
(1880–1940)   A
                                        P
                                      (188

Pan
(190

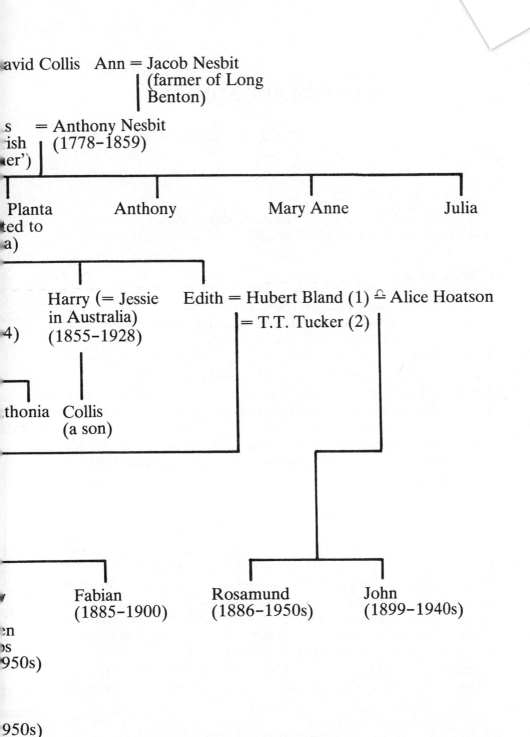

avid Collis   Ann = Jacob Nesbit
                    (farmer of Long
                    Benton)

s   = Anthony Nesbit
ish   (1778–1859)
er')

Planta   Anthony   Mary Anne   Julia
ted to
a)

        Harry (= Jessie   Edith = Hubert Bland (1) ⌒ Alice Hoatson
        in Australia)   = T.T. Tucker (2)
4)   (1855–1928)

thonia   Collis
         (a son)

        Fabian   Rosamund   John
        (1885–1900)   (1886–1950s)   (1899–1940s)

en
s
950s)

950s)

ACKNOWLEDGEMENTS

This is the second biography of Edith Nesbit to be written – the first was Doris Langley Moore's *E. Nesbit*, published in 1933 and, in a revised edition, in 1966. It was rightly regarded, then and later, as a reliable and finely written account. Mrs Langley Moore collected a mass of information from Edith's family and friends which she stored away with meticulous care, but she was unable to use a number of the more intimate details, and this in turn helped to obscure some of the essential outlines of her subject's life. With great generosity, Mrs Langley Moore passed on to me the material she had assembled, which included transcripts of letters to and by Edith, as well as many about her; from these a new and unfamiliar portrait of her began to emerge. In what follows the witnesses that Doris Langley Moore assembled speak for themselves, instead of being assimilated into the seamless narrative that biographers were formerly expected to provide. Yet though this account differs in most respects from its predecessor, it is often based on the same material, and could not have been written without the work so carefully carried out by Mrs Langley Moore. My largest debt remains to her.

The second collection of primary material that I have used belongs to Jocelyn Nixon, Mrs Paul Bland's great-niece, who generously loaned it to me for the several years that this book has taken to write; I am very grateful for her continued help and kindness. Many other people have contributed information, books and advice over the ten years since its inception. I would particularly like to thank Margaret Taylor of the Eltham Society, who first introduced me to Mrs Nixon and who is herself something of an authority on E. Nesbit; Doris Ker recalled conversations that she had had with Mrs Paul Bland; Christine Powell, who has worked on the Nesbit family tree and passed on valuable information about Edith's family as well as notes made in the course of her own archival research, and Mavis Strange (née Carter), who alone remembered E. Nesbit vividly, and gave me the woodcut reproduced on the jacket.

Some of the most exciting discoveries were made by John H. Davis at the Public Record Office. He also supplied me with copies of *The Weekly Dispatch*, guided me round Edith's South London and shared his expertise on the early history of socialism, as did Ross McKibbin. Further archival research was carried out by Jeremy Maule. Many others have contributed key pieces to the jigsaw puzzle; I would particularly like to thank the following for their help: Gillian Avery, for discussions about children's books over many years; C. A. Boardman, archivist to King Edward VI School, Birmingham, for material on Richard Reynolds; Mrs Colquhoun, for information about her father Hugh Bellingham Smith, and for showing me a letter from her uncle, Eric Bellingham Smith; Mike Dudley of the Ashmolean Museum for help with photographs; Roger Lancelyn Green, for valuable bibliographical details; Zoë Green, for reading and commenting on the typescript; Cathy Henderson, for research assistance; Michael Holroyd, for discussing, suggesting quotations and providing material on Shaw; John Jones of Balliol, for details of Richard Reynolds' career; Daniel Kirkpatrick, for advice on bibliography; Geoffrey Kitchener, for the history of Halstead; Sharona Levy, for material on Olive Schreiner; John Maddicott, for information about Bower Marsh; Roger Pensom, for his reading of 'The Town in the Library . . .'; William St Clair, for a crucial introduction; Louisa Smith, for information about H. R. Millar; Catherine Stoye, for showing me material belonging to her grandfather, H. G. Wells; Stephanie West, for help with Edith's irregular Latin; Helen White-house, of the Ashmolean Museum, for advice on Egyptology (again!); Sarah Wimbush, of the National Portrait Gallery, for identifying the woodcut artist Robert Bryden, and other advice.

Keith Thomas allowed me to borrow his little cache of books once owned by Bower Marsh, from which I have reproduced a manuscript poem and a photograph – the first fluttered out from the pages of one book, the second had been carefully pasted into another. E. Nesbit's books (and occasionally manuscripts) have been found for me or lent to me by Anne Excell, Margarita Reeve and Jeanette White, but particularly by Ruth Pryor and Gwen Watkins. I have drawn on Gwen's unique knowledge of children's books at a number of points;

she suggested several important sources to me and kindly read and commented on several chapters. The real bibliographical work has been carried out by Dr Selwyn Goodacre who assembled and checked the long list of E. Nesbit's publications. This was a major task, and I am most grateful to him for undertaking it.

Much research depends on the kindness of librarians and I would like in particular to thank Barbara Ludlow, archivist at the Greenwich Local History Library, Mycenae Road, SE3, which has its own collection of Nesbit material; also the staff of the Bodleian, the British Library, Nuffield College Library, and Angela Raspin of the Library of Political and Economic Science at the London School of Economics. I would like to thank the following librarians for their help, and their libraries for permission to quote material in their possession: Cathy Henderson of the Harry Ransom Humanities Research Centre at Austin, Texas, for Edith's letters to Richard le Gallienne and material from the John Lane Papers; Gene Rinkel, Curator of Special Collections at the University of Illinois at Champaign-Urbana for Wells's correspondence with Edith and her family; Lola Szladits of the Berg Collection, New York Public Library for Edith's correspondence with her agents, and Garnett's reports as reader to Fisher Unwin. I would also like to thank the Butler Collection of Columbia University for permission to reprint the Shaw letter on pages 94–5; the Yale Library for permission to reprint the Wells letter, pp. 299–300; the Fabian Society for permission to reprint material from the Fabian Papers; A. P. Watt, acting on behalf of the Executors of the Estate of H. G. Wells, for permission to use published and unpublished material by H. G. Wells; the Trustees of the British Museum, the Governors and Guardians of the National Gallery of Ireland, and the Royal Academy of Dramatic Art for permission to use published and unpublished material by Bernard Shaw. I am also grateful to the Mary Evans Picture Library, to Dr. M. J. Wells and the Fogg Art Museum at Harvard for Illustrations.

Finally I would like to thank Richard Cohen, ideal editor and publisher, for giving the book and its author his fullest attention at every stage, and Stephanie Darnill for her careful copy editing. I have had the best of readers in Malcolm Godden, whose contribution cannot easily be measured or repaid. My warmest thanks are due to my family, who have shown great patience with my long obsession, particularly my husband Robin who has read every draft and rescued chapters given up for lost – no thanks could be adequate; also to Jon who took photographs, and Simon who made the index.

FOREWORD

E. Nesbit is the first modern writer for children. She invented the children's adventure story more or less single-handed, and then added further magic ingredients such as wishing rings and time travel. Her books established a style and an approach still widely used today, yet she was forty before she produced her first great success, *The Treasure Seekers*, and had already tried her hand at many different kinds of writing – poems, plays, romantic novels, ghost stories, tales of country life, reviews, as well as her earliest and now long-forgotten writings for children.

Much of what she wrote, during her long and varied career, reflected current tastes and enthusiasms, from her adolescent love poems, Swinburne and Browning versions, to the late and largely uncollected naval yarns that she wrote with the help of her second husband, the Skipper. Between these limits she recorded her life with varying degrees of honesty in verse and prose, and while she seldom wrote entirely openly of her own experiences, she seldom wrote convincingly of anything else. Her best work is inspired by the ideas that aroused her, the books she had read, the people she knew, the places she loved, even when it seems furthest removed from everyday life. The houses she had lived in at Halstead, Lewisham, Eltham and Dymchurch appear again and again, as do her favourite locations – Fitzrovia, the Medway, Romney Marsh, the Sussex Downs above Eastbourne and the Seven Sisters. The dogs that bounce into the Bastable stories – Martha the bulldog, Pincher and Lady the deerhound – were all real and belonged to her, as did Max and Brenda, the helpful dachshunds of *The Magic City* (described by others as snappy, ill-tempered little beasts). Her family took part, her two elder brothers as Oswald and Dicky Bastable, while her own children figured as the

Five who found a psammead in a sand quarry near Rochester. Friends and lovers underwent various transformations: her husband Hubert Bland becomes Albert's unforgettable uncle, and she herself appeared as the writer Mrs Leslie and as the ideal mother of *The Railway Children*.

Any attempt to understand her inner life must begin with her books, where she orders her experience according to the impact it made on her, concentrating on certain people and events, while omitting others altogether, selecting, modifying and distilling what mattered most in the alembic of imagination. Much that she wrote about is only slightly altered, and some events are scarcely altered at all, though they are usually embedded in conventional fictions. If her books, taken all in all, are not uniformly well written, they nevertheless give an impression of a rich and vital inner life, of a response that was never less than passionate to her surroundings, family and friends, to her reading and the social milieu in which she lived. She and her husband were founder members of the Fabian Society, and she remained a committed, if distinctly eccentric, socialist all her life. The literary conventions of her day, reinforced by her own inhibitions, discouraged work that was too obviously confessional in tone, yet as she grew older she found herself able to write more directly about her deepest feelings: when her younger son Fabian died suddenly, she wrote with almost embarrassing frankness of her misery, guilt and her need to share her pain, as well as her bitter jealousy when her husband sought consolation for his grief with another woman, instead of turning to her.[1]

While her life, in its fullness, is richly present in her writing, there are few records elsewhere. Those who have begun research into it have encountered difficulties. Doris Ker, who assembled a radio programme about her in 1975 observed, 'Sooner or later, all trails run into the sand.' Although several of her contemporaries included pen portraits of her in their memoirs or autobiographies, and a substantial number of her business letters are available in various archives – letters to her agents, to publishers, to the Society of Authors or to the Fabian Society – little of her personal correspondence has survived. At one time her son Paul Bland kept sacks of her letters in his garden shed, but when he died, his wife, suspecting them of being both morally and physically unhygienic, made a bonfire of the lot. She also smashed to pieces her father-in-law's death mask, once treasured by Edith and kept on the drawing room mantelpiece wrapped in a silk scarf, to be unveiled only before trusted friends. Few objects connected with her writing or her personal emotions have survived: a birthday book, an address book, some books of manuscript poetry and a tortoise-shell tea caddy that she was fond of. Even one or two of her published books seem to have disappeared: none of the British copyright libraries contains a copy of her book of short stories, jointly written with Oswald Barron and intriguingly entitled *The Butler in Bohemia* (1894), nor have I ever seen a copy of her novel, *The Marden Mystery*, also published in 1894, but in Chicago.[2] Indeed were it not for the existence of Doris Langley Moore's very reliable and fully documented biography *E. Nesbit* (1933), compiled seven years after her death and drawing on the still vivid memories of her friends and children, there would be no key with which to unlock the inner chambers of her life at all. Without this essential source, it would be difficult to reconstruct more than the sketchiest outline. All later researchers have depended heavily on its thoroughness, accuracy and detail.

While there were evident advantages in writing her biography when so many who had known her were still alive, and so much of the material was still available, there were disadvantages, too. Although her family and friends were eager to help, their sensibilities and expectations inevitably shaped and limited what could be said. With characteristic foresight and the carefulness of a great collector, Mrs Langley Moore preserved all her correspondence, records of interviews and the transcripts of all the letters she had seen; her archive now provides much the fullest and most detailed source of information about E. Nesbit. The account that follows is largely derived from this material, though, since concepts of biography have changed substantially over the last fifty years, it is here presented in a very different form.

Yet even fifty years ago, E. Nesbit's life presented a number of baffling gaps to her biographer: no one seemed to know much about her childhood or adolescence, and it was particularly difficult to establish a definite chronology of the events leading up to her marriage in 1880. Soon after her biography appeared, a reader wrote to point out that E. Nesbit had contributed a series of memoirs to the *Girl's Own Paper* between October 1896 and September 1897 entitled *My School-Days*, and substantial quotations from these were included in a second edition.[3] Though they are somewhat self-dramatizing, dwelling alternately on horrors and delights, these reminiscences still provide the fullest account of a very obscure period of her life. They were to have a further importance for her as a writer: as her mind ranged over her childhood memories, she began to see how they might be worked into fiction, and a few months after completing them, the very first story about 'The Treasure Seekers' was published, in *Father Christmas*, the 1897 Christmas Supplement to the *Illustrated London News*; with these stories she had her first great success.

Edith Nesbit wrote and talked freely about her childhood, but she kept hidden from her closest friends the circumstances of her marriage to Hubert Bland in a City registry office, only two months before the birth of her son Paul. This was one of a number of discoveries that turned out to be thoroughly embarrassing for her biographer. Bernard Shaw, an old friend of the family, had, as it happened, warned her about difficulties of this kind at the outset: when Mrs Langley Moore first approached him, he replied via his secretary, Blanche Patch:

> Mr Bernard Shaw desires me to say that as Edith was an audaciously unconventional lady and Hubert an exceedingly unfaithful husband he does not see how a presentable biography is possible as yet; and he has nothing to contribute to a mere whitewashing operation.[4]

Shaw later relented – he had briefly been strongly attracted to Edith, and when Mrs Langley Moore mentioned some letters of hers in which she described him, he felt uneasy as to what they might contain and agreed to help. The first edition of the biography was nevertheless obliged to play down or even remain silent about a number of its discoveries. The thirties had their own ideas of what might be said or not said, and there is an interesting discrepancy between the out-spokenness of Edith's Edwardian friends – Shaw, H. G. Wells and Edgar Jepson, for example – and the reticence of her first biographer, a reticence imposed not only by contemporary tolerances and the susceptibilities of her surviving family, but also by the expectations of her readers. It was as a children's writer that E. Nesbit had made her reputation, and her public liked to think of her as the maternal figure she increasingly became in appearance, if not at heart, in her later years. The wilder escapades of a sexless tomboy were acceptable in her, but not those of a passionate and mature woman. Writers' lives were far less exposed to their interested readers at the beginning of this century than they are today, yet in her books, as in her correspondence with her admirers, E. Nesbit showed herself anxious to conform to their comforting picture of her; it would have been an awkward task for her biographer to have disillusioned so many hopes and wishes as to her character. Comparable impulses to protect her reputation from scandal or to deodorize it for consumption by the young are still apparent today. One old friend and admirer of hers from childhood told me that she felt 'very strongly about all the mud that has been slung, in my opinion absolutely without foundation' and that she would not contribute to a book that in any way substantiated scandal about her. The desire to smooth out the wrinkles remains strong: a critic in a recent preface to a selection of E. Nesbit's stories for children painted a glowing picture of her second marriage as a fairy-tale happily-ever-after.[5] In fact her last few years were spent in poverty and sickness in two converted huts on the edge of Romney Marsh. It ought, by now, to be possible to contemplate her love affairs without condemnation, and her last years without sentimentality.

If the expectations of her readers posed one kind of problem, the sensibilities of her family created another. Though Doris Langley Moore did not realize it immediately, her children were deeply divided, both by the circumstances of their birth, and also by her attitude towards them; family feeling was as partisan as if each member had been compelled to take sides in a divorce, and Mrs Langley Moore received two entirely different, and fundamentally irreconcilable accounts of Edith's marriage: for Paul and Iris, their mother was the heroic and self-sacrificing wife, the breadwinner and mainstay of the household whose financially dependent husband expressed his resentment of her in a series of adulterous adventures. Iris evidently disliked her father, and Paul was scarcely more fond of him; but for Rosamund and her husband Clifford Sharp, who had been a devoted admirer of Hubert's, Edith was flighty, an intellectual feather-weight anchored to reality by Hubert's wisdom and common sense. Clifford Sharp wrote to Doris Langley Moore:

> 'E. Nesbit' was *never* the dominating personality in her household until Bland's death in 1914 – whereafter she went to pieces . . .
>
> Bland had indeed a tremendous personality, ten times bigger than that of E. N., bigger than Wells's, bigger than anybody's who ever came [i.e. to their house] except *possibly* G.B.S. And E.N. always looked *up* to him and relied upon him to the day of his death. His mind was enormously bigger, finer and more powerful than hers *and it was within its range that she always lived* – and I am sure that she never for a second dreamed of even resenting, still less disputing its supremacy. She could not in fact do without it, it was the one thing that kept her sane and more or less steady.[6]

Clifford Sharp's view, that Hubert was the dominant partner, and that the marriage worked well most of the time, 'allowing E.N. to run about as she liked in her restless manner', was directly contradicted by the novelist Berta Ruck, a disciple of Edith's and a friend of Iris's from her Slade School days. She made the following criticism of Mrs Langley Moore's portrait:

> You make her too gentle! *colourless*, in comparison with what she was. Hubert was better liked by many people, but never, for one instant, did *his* personality outshine *hers*. *Hers often swamped his.* They were better apart.

She was unconsciously echoing Bernard Shaw's judgement on the Blands' marriage, that 'No two people were ever married who were better calculated to make the worst of each other.'[7]

It was almost inevitable that, in portraying their marriage, her biographer should have presented events from Edith's point of view rather than Hubert's. What later accounts there are have done little to redress the balance, partly because Hubert's achievements as a journalist (and some considered him the most forceful and influential columnist of his day) are difficult to appreciate in retrospect.[8] Those who came into contact with him often regarded him as a man of extraordinary, if unfulfilled, talents. Though children's books may be handed on with pleasure from parent to child, no one wants to read last year's newspapers. Bland's several volumes of essays have not worn well – a modern reader is as likely to be repelled by his rigidity on some issues (patriotism, imperialism, the role of women) as impressed by his eloquence, intelligence and wit on others.

These conflicting interpretations of Edith's marriage partly reflect underlying family resentments and, perhaps, unspoken assumptions about the position of women; she was nevertheless a woman who presented a mass of contradictions, and whose various roles, whether imposed or willingly assumed, were often difficult to reconcile. Her vitality and spontaneity made her adorable and difficult by turns. Berta Ruck dwelt upon her inconsistent and unpredictable nature:

> Among all the descriptions of E. Nesbit I don't find enough said of the vivid contrasts in her. She was wise – and frivolous; she was kind, . . . and so intolerant. She didn't dissect her aversions, but when she said of someone: 'Dear, I don't *like* them!' it was *finis*. She was a brave Socialist of pioneer views – and how artfully she included propaganda in her children's stories! But I have heard her complain that some illustration

made her characters look 'as if they weren't children of gentlefolk!' . . .

She could be morose as a gathering thunder-cloud. . . . When she emerged – a sunburst![9]

Such marked contrasts made her a constant source of surprise. When, many years after her death, her daughter Iris heard about her schoolgirl memoirs, with their emphasis on childhood terrors, she was sceptical as to how reliable they were on the grounds that she knew her mother to have been 'a most daring and fearless child.'[10] Yet a comparably unexpected mixture of courage and nervous sensibility is to be found in the adventures of the Bastables, inspired by memories of her own childhood. While her elder brothers appear as Oswald and Dicky, she presents herself as twins – the morally courageous and determined Alice and her vulnerable brother Noel, subject to fits of poetry, fainting and tears. As Alice staunchly defends her over-sensitive brother, she seems to be an image of E. Nesbit's energetic and dominating side, standing guard over a less confident but more creative inner self.

In order to become a children's writer, it is essential to remember what it felt like to be a child: Edith's many child-like enthusiasms, her love of parties, games, bicycling, boating, bathing and adventures of all kinds, are striking. Yet at the same time she was the mother of a growing family and often addressed her readers in the voice of a sympathetic and well-loved grown up. At her best, she resembled the most delightful of the adults who appear in her books, rustling up picnics, arranging outings and excursions and celebrating minor events with presents and poems, as Mother does in *The Railway Children*, or Aunt Edith in *The House of Arden*.

Her uncertainty as to whether in her own life she wanted to pursue the child's self-delighting freedom and irresponsibility or the adult's greater power to compass her own ends, to organize and advise, may reflect a deeper uncertainty about the nature of her femininity. Edith appreciated the attractions of the vulnerable and dependent little woman beloved of contemporary sentimental literature; but she herself was cast in a very different mould, accustomed to dominating any social gathering and used to having her own way – in a word, bossy. In later life, her young friends and disciples addressed her variously as 'Aunt', 'Madam' or even 'Duchess', with an allusion to that imperious character in *Alice*. While still very young, she had been forced to support herself, her child and her husband. Later she seems to have enjoyed her independence, financial and personal, as well as the rewards and authority that came with success. But in taking on such responsibilities, in constantly initiating rather than responding, in adopting what might be regarded as an essentially male role, she had contravened the unspoken assumptions of her day. Even the name she used to write under, E. Nesbit, intentionally gave no indication of her sex – if anything, it suggested a man. She sometimes spoke regretfully of having revealed herself to be a woman by writing a first-person poem in her own voice but most of her novels and many of her poems were written as if by a man. In the Bastable stories, though her own position in the family is occupied by the twins, Alice and Noel, it is Oswald who tells the story and whose flamboyant personality dominates and determines the voice. In her twenties, she emphasized an element of sexual ambiguity by cutting her hair short and smoking cigarettes. The young poet Richard le Gallienne was enchanted by her 'boyish-girl figure . . . her short hair, and her large vivid eyes'.[11]

But if E. Nesbit rebelled against the Victorian stereotype of 'the angel in the house', she was far from being the only woman of her generation, or indeed of her circle, to do so, and she soon found herself overtaken by women who were tougher, less conventional or more fundamentally committed to independence. As a socialist, she met and grew fond of Eleanor Marx, Charlotte Wilson and Annie Besant, women whose single-minded devotion to a cause made Edith look something of an intellectual butterfly. She also knew and admired the early feminist writers Olive Schreiner and Charlotte Perkins Gilman. Yet though several of her friends were actively engaged in the Women's Movement, with which she might have been expected to sympathize, she refused to be drawn into it and from quite early on regarded the women's vote as unnecessary and even undesirable, politically speaking. Her view on this matter, as on many others, had been strongly influenced by Hubert's. He believed that nature had allocated men and women different roles to play, and that political and economic equality was unnatural and undesirable, and would undermine family life. It is not surprising that she accepted his views on the subject so readily, even though they seemed to deny or diminish her own achievements. Bland's influence was hard to resist. He had a mind of unusual clarity and force; his views were dogmatically held and he spoke, as he wrote, both passionately and persuasively. It would have been difficult to have shared his life without absorbing many of his attitudes, some of which were movingly generous, compassionate and free from cant, while others, such as his views on the role of women, were defensive and self-interested.

E. Nesbit's political opinions permeate her work, sometimes surfacing as bubbles of high-minded propaganda – on the horrors of industrial disease, the cruelty of poverty and slums and (without any sense of inconsistency) the blight of urban development. *The Railway Children* blends romantic adventure with a raw anger at political oppression that comes out in Mother's account of the poor Russian's sufferings in Siberia, as well as in the Dreyfus-like conspiracy that has unjustly imprisoned Father. Yet the book is also permeated with the kind of class consciousness that allows Mother and the children, however hard up they are, to be respected by Perks and the villagers and even to patronize them mildly. But this particular social distinction may well have seemed crucial to a writer whose parents had worked their way up from lower middle-class origins by means of education, and who had herself been very poor, though she had always clung to a sense of herself as a 'lady', and devoted herself to the self-evidently middle-class profession of letters.

The injustice of the class system as a whole, and the exploitation of servants in particular, had always posed a problem for serious socialists. In 1889 Marjorie Pease, a young Fabian trying to set up house for the first time, admitted, 'I don't think we ought to have servants but that is an open question.' E. Nesbit occasionally recognized the resentments below stairs: ' "Don't you make any mistake, miss," the footman put in. "Nobody *enjoys* being in service, though they has to put up with it." '[12] But more often servants in her stories belong to some kind of sub-species. Though the nastiest of the children are punished for tormenting them, booby traps are normally expected to be taken in good part and servants are regularly portrayed in that comic, slightly contemptuous mode that exonerates us from sympathizing with them. Further down the social scale, however, the victimized slum child is depicted with compassion.

Such obvious inconsistencies of outlook are part of a larger blend of idealism and pragmatism which is closely connected to the sources of her power and originality as a writer. While predecessors like Lewis Carroll, or contemporaries like Kenneth Grahame or J. M. Barrie escape into self-contained fantasy worlds, golden ages or dream days where time stands still and delicate illusions can blossom, E. Nesbit's children struggle ineffectually with a series of recalcitrant or un-comprehending adults who always have the last word, in a context in which good intentions are guaranteed to backfire, and granted wishes seldom if ever deliver hoped-for satisfactions. However exhilarating adventures may be while they are going on, the heart's desire is to be restored safe and sound to your parents, with no further excitement in prospect. She never forgot that the best times of all are when nothing in particular is happening, though one never remembers that until afterwards. She never forgot that pain, embarrassment and anxiety are the usual accompaniments of all real adventures, nor – though her characters were so independent and enterprising – that all children, for better or worse, are ultimately at the mercy of all adults. She may even have helped to reverse the great tradition of children's literature inaugurated by Carroll, MacDonald and Kenneth Grahame, in turning away from their secondary worlds to the tough truths to be won from encounters with things-as-they-are, previously the province of adult novels or, at any rate, of the more sober children's writers, such as Mrs Ewing. Like Jane Austen's heroines, E. Nesbit's children start out with all sorts of misconceptions about life, usually derived from their reading. And while the transforming and enlarging powers of the imagination are constantly extolled, they are also forced to confront and respond to a gritty and prosaic reality.

It was E. Nesbit's peculiar achievement to hold romance – magic and adventure – in a vibrating tension with the reality principle, common sense and the harsh facts of experience. She created a loose synthesis that included inconsistencies as glaring as those within her own personality, and varied and rich enough to mirror those of life itself. The tones, attitudes and colourings of her work are constantly changing – she could be priggishly moralizing or as sentimental as the evangelical tracts she despised and derided; yet she also acknowledged how irresistible are certain forbidden actions, how compelling is the logic of desire. A comedy of deflation, subversion and demystification is always ready to erupt. On one page her children are held up for their exemplary honesty; a few pages later they are indulging in pointless bickering or the petty selfishness and spite of the nursery. In all this there is a range, a depth and energy which has often rendered criticism inadequate – narrow, partial or distorting. While her rapid shifts of attitude and mood, her wit and versatility, and her refusal to conform to a single approach or expectation make her writing difficult to analyse conveniently, they are also the source of its richly varied and wonderfully animated vision.

1

THE PANGS OF CHILDHOOD

'Oh! my Daddy, my Daddy!' That scream went like a knife into the heart of everyone in the train, and people put their heads out of the window to see a tall pale man with lips set in a thin close line, and a little girl clinging to him with arms and legs, while his arms went tightly round her.[1]

This moment from *The Railway Children* in which a father is restored to his daughter, beyond all expectation, is the most moving in all Edith Nesbit's fiction. It is a moment that shares its emotional intensity with some of the greatest discovery scenes in literature – Iphigeneia and her brother; Lear and Cordelia; Leontes and Hermione. It is as if the lost have been recovered, as if Bobby's father has returned from the dead. And, behind the story line in which he had been unjustly imprisoned, deep within its author's imagination, he had indeed returned from the dead. Edith's father died before she was four. She did not consciously remember a great deal about him and her memoirs of childhood are silent about her reaction to his death – he was away from home staying at a friend's house when he died. But the absent parent, the parent unavoidably detained elsewhere, is a pattern that recurs throughout her children's books. And, in several of her fantasies of wish-fulfilment, when the children achieve their heart's desire it is always to be restored to their far-away parents. Her exploration of wish-fulfilment and its psychological mechanisms ultimately becomes an exploration of her own deepest wishes, and the narrative stratagems of her children's books constantly resolve themselves into the recovery of the lost father, and the idyllic home from which the child has been shut out or disinherited.

'When I was a little child I used to pray fervently, tearfully, that when I should be grown up I might never forget what I thought and felt and suffered then,' wrote Edith in the introduction to her childhood memoirs.[2] And she never did. Her success as a writer for children is closely bound up with her peculiarly vivid memories of the joys, pains and passions of childhood. These were perhaps no more intense than many children suffer, but she remembered them from the inside in great detail, experiencing them as a series of violent contrasts. Some of these contrasts were produced by sharply changing circumstances, as the security of her earliest childhood was succeeded by a restless period of various boarding schools and foreign travel, in turn followed by a more settled spell in the Kentish countryside. But the contrasts were also an aspect of her character: a highly strung, imaginative and nervous child, she struggled to keep up with two elder brothers and not to be dismissed as 'only a girl'. Playing with them she developed an adventurous, tomboyish front that eventually became part of her. When she first began to fictionalize her childhood experiences through the adventures of the Bastables, she seems to have portrayed herself as twins – as the courageous, lovable Alice and her timid, highly-strung brother Noel.

Edith remembered her earliest childhood as an Eden before the fall and the coming of death. Its Arcadian setting was, surprisingly, an old house in South London:

> It was in Kennington, that house – and it had a big garden and a meadow and a cottage and a laundry, stables and cow-house and pig-styes, elm-trees and vines, tiger lilies and flags in the garden, and chrysanthemums that smelt like earth and hyacinths that smelt like heaven. Our nursery was at the top of the house, a big room with a pillar in the middle to support the roof. 'The post,' we called it: it was excellent for playing mulberry bush, or for being martyrs at. The skipping rope did to bind the martyrs to the stake.[3]

This house at 38 Lower Kennington Lane was pulled down within her lifetime and replaced by terraced villas, as London rapidly expanded southwards. Edith Nesbit was born there on 15 August 1858, to Sarah and John Collis Nesbit. She was the youngest child in the family, with two brothers, Henry (known as Harry) and Alfred, two and four years older than herself, and a sister Mary ('Minnie') seven years older. There had been another son, John, said to have been very brilliant, who died aged six, before she was born, and Mrs Nesbit also had a daughter Sarah ('Saretta') Green by her first marriage who was fifteen when Edith was born. The house at Kennington had about three acres of land attached to it, some of which was farmed. John Collis Nesbit ran a small school-cum-college where he instructed young men in agriculture and chemistry.

The agricultural college had belonged to the Nesbits for some seventeen years, having originally been started as a school by Edith's grandfather, Anthony Nesbit; he was still living there when she was born, but died in March of the following year. In his own line, Anthony was a remarkable man. Son of Jacob Nesbit, a farmer of Long Benton in Northumberland, he became a very successful schoolmaster, running schools first at Bradford (where his son John was born), then at Oxford Road, Manchester, and finally in Kennington Lane, where he opened a 'Classical, Commercial and Scientific Academy'. He was the author of several successful textbooks on arithmetic, measurement and surveying. His wife, Mary Collis, whom Edith liked to call her 'Irish grandmother', was descended on her mother's side from a Swedish surgeon, Jacob Planta, who had belonged to the Moravian Brethren.

Anthony Nesbit's several sons followed him into teaching or science: Anthony became an analytical chemist; Edward Planta became a schoolmaster, and at first he worked as an assistant to his father at Kennington Lane, but later emigrated to Australia, where Edith's brother Harry would eventually follow him. John Collis, the eldest and intellectually the most distinguished, was apparently his father's favourite. From the outset he was fascinated by the natural sciences: he studied chemistry under John Dalton, and also worked on electricity and geology and their application to practical problems, particularly to farming. He pioneered the use of artificial fertilizers – guano and natural phosphates – in agriculture. Gradually the school, which had taken the unusual step of teaching the natural sciences as part of its regular curriculum, was transformed into a chemical and agricultural college under his direction. He also provided soil analyses and advice on appropriate fertilizers for farmers. In December 1850 John married the widowed Sarah Green, daughter of Henry Alderton of Hastings.[4] Sarah Nesbit was a Kentish woman born and bred, and although she spent some years living in France, she gravitated towards London or Kent for preference. Her eldest daughter Saretta was born at Sandhurst (near Battle, where Mrs Nesbit herself had been born), and often stayed with her mother's family there until marriage took her to live in Manchester. Edith followed her mother's pattern, living most of her adult life in South London or in Kent, on the edge of Romney

Marsh. She knew the whole county well and particular Kentish towns and villages recur as settings for her fiction.

Edith, or Daisy, as her family always called her, was in her fourth year when her father was taken ill at a friend's house at Barnes, and died quite suddenly in March 1862, at the age of forty-three. She was too young to have many memories of the time before his death, but those that she did retain were recorded in several different ways. During her last illness, when she was in her sixties, certain childish memories returned – the pattern on a particular nursery carpet, for example, or her extraordinary christening, which does not seem to have taken place until she was a toddler. While waiting at the font with the sponsors, she managed to get her tiny kid shoes off her feet, and when the clergyman lifted her up to perform the ceremony, she dropped them into the font 'for boats'.[5] In 1896 the *Girl's Own Paper* commissioned her to write twelve monthly articles on her school days; since she hadn't much cared for school, these developed into a rambling, but very evocative series of early memories which provide the main basis for any account of her childhood. Many of these were of childish bug-bears; the college had a stuffed two-headed calf and a black emu skin hanging up as curios, and these used to terrify her until one of her father's pupils, a Mr Kearns, had the patience to persuade her to 'stroke the poor emu' and overcome her irrational fear. Another early terror was that of 'the mask'. In Dickens's essay 'The Christmas Tree', a catalogue of his nursery fears, he wrote of 'the mask', and his account may have jogged her own memory of the episode (her memoirs have a distinctly literary flavour). It appeared suddenly during a game of charades (later to become one of her favourite games): as the youngest, Daisy was cast as the high-born orphan who was to be abducted by an old gypsy woman, her sister Saretta in disguise. What she had not foreseen was that the loved familiar face would be concealed, in performance, by a big black bonnet and a 'hideous mask'. When she saw it, she screamed herself into some sort of fit:

> That old woman haunted my dreams for years – haunts them still indeed. I tell you I come across her in my dreams to this day. She bends over me and puts her face close to mine, and I wake with a spasm of agonised terror . . .[6]

For Edith, the terror of the mask came to be associated with her fear of death and mummies; the Ugly-Wuglies, dummies with faces made of paper masks, come appallingly alive in *The Enchanted Castle*.

Two particular early memories were so important to her that she used them in her children's stories – indeed, they provided the starting points for the first two Bastable books, her earliest successes. In fictionalizing these episodes, however, she dissociated herself from the role of passive victim that she had actually played in them in an apparently deliberate way. One day, when she and her brothers had been carefully dressed up for a party, they were sent out into the garden, like Tom Kitten and his sisters, to be good and keep clean. The boys decided that Daisy looked so pretty, so flower-like in her flimsy white dress that she ought to be planted out in a flower bed, like a real daisy. So they dug a deep hole beside a gooseberry bush and buried her so effectively that an adult had to be summoned to rescue her. In its earliest version, *The Treasure Seekers*[7] begins with the Bastables accidentally burying the wimpish Albert-next-door, dressed, as always in his 'Little Lord Fauntleroy' frilly shirt and velvet knicker-bockers. Albert's Uncle has to be summoned to dig him out. As a family, the Bastables strongly suggest the young Nesbits, with Mary a little old for Dora, Alfred and Harry translated into Oswald and Dicky, and the Alice/Noel twins standing for Edith herself. But in this episode it is Albert who is given Daisy's role: while the Bastables are digging for treasure in their back garden, he is accidentally buried, protesting that he doesn't want to dig and he doesn't like worms. Albert here takes the part of the victim, the muff, the outsider. Retrospectively, Edith sides with the adventurous spirit of her brothers, mocking and despising the timorous role she played in reality. Another story, 'The Twopenny Spell' (*Oswald Bastable and Others*), seems to dramatize this psychic transposition, since Lucy buys a spell which gives her her brother Harry's personality and he hers – with drastic results, since she is very nearly expelled from her school while he is beaten up by every other boy in his school. But the reason she bought the cheap spell in the first place was

partly to show him that she was not quite so much of a muff as he thought, and partly because she was naturally annoyed at being buried up to her waist in the ground among the gooseberry-bushes. She got into the hole Harry had dug because he said it might make her grow, and then he suddenly shovelled down a heap of earth and stamped it down so that she could not move. She began to cry, then he said 'muff' and she said 'beast', and he went away and left her 'planted there' as the French people say. And she cried more than ever, and tried to dig herself out, and couldn't, and although she was naturally such a gentle child, she would have stamped with rage, only she couldn't get her feet out to do it. Then she screamed, and her Uncle Richard came and dug her out, and said it was a shame, and gave her twopence to spend as she liked . . .[8]

Another replay that produced a comparable change of perspective involved a further early memory, one of the few associated with her father. In it her father is translated from the gentle and loving person he really was into a creature menacing and destructive. His ambivalent role anticipates her ambivalent feelings about him after his death:

> The first thing I remember that frightened me was running into my father's dressing-room and finding him playing at wild beasts with my brothers. He wore his great fur travelling coat inside out, and his roars were completely convincing. I was borne away screaming, and dreamed of wild beasts for many a long night afterwards.[9]

The Wouldbegoods, the sequel to *The Treasure Seekers*, begins with a wittily elaborated version of this incident: the Bastables, having just read Kipling's *Jungle Book*, decide to stage it as an elaborate game in the garden, with the hose as Kaa the rock python, and Dicky and Noel underneath the Indian Uncle's best tiger-skin rugs. Just as the game is at its height, their young visitor, Daisy, nicknamed 'the White Mouse' for her timidity, emerges from indoors. She turns a dreadful shade of green and faints away. The children's Indian Uncle returns unexpectedly and metes out punishments all round. Here the connection between the accidental victim of this piece of play-acting and the young Daisy Nesbit herself is made explicit by naming her Daisy. It is as if, as an adult looking back, Edith recognized that both incidents had been occasioned by fun and high spirits; in rewriting them, she now identified herself with her father and brothers, making fun of her original response of frustration or fear. Her stories often enact what she would have liked to have done rather than what she really had done; one aspect of their appeal is that they often reflect what children would like to be like, rather than what they really are like. The differences between the direct, if sometimes slightly self-pitying mode of *My School-Days* in the *Girl's Own Paper* and the adaption of the same episodes into fiction in the Bastable stories, written soon afterwards, is always revealing.

For the first few years after her husband's death, Sarah Nesbit stayed on at the Agricultural College with her family and continued to run it after a fashion, despite the loss of its director and star lecturer. With

Mary rapidly becoming a young woman, the nursery was now occupied by Alfred, Harry and Daisy:

> When I was a child in the nursery we had – there were three of us – a large rocking horse, a large doll's house (with a wooden box as annexe), a Noah's Ark, dinner and tea things, a great chest of oak bricks, and a pestle and mortar. I cannot remember any other things that pleased us. Dolls came and went, but they were not toys, they were characters . . .[10]

Daisy's favourite possession was 'a crockery rabbit, white with black spots, couched on a green crockery grass-plot', which she used to play with in the bath, and take to bed with her:

> I bought him with my own penny at Sandhurst Fair. He slept with me for seven or eight years, and when he was lost with my play-box and the rest of its loved contents, on the journey from France to England, all the dignity of my thirteen years could not uphold me in that tragedy.

She was also fond of her rag doll:

> She was stuffed with hair, and was washed once a fortnight, after which nurse put in her features again with a quill pen, and consoled me for any change in her expression by explaining that she was 'growing up'.

Nurse, backed up by an under-nurse, was in charge of the nursery, as in most middle-class Victorian households. Edith's scattered references to her make her sound loving, imaginative and sympathetic. From very early on, Daisy had been tormented by her fear of the dark:

> My nurse . . . never went downstairs to supper after she found out my terrors, which she very quickly did. She used to sit in the day nursery with the door open 'a tiny crack', and that light was company, because I knew I had only to call out, and someone who loved me would come and banish fear.[11]

The Nesbit children must have played regularly in the meadow beyond their home, but they also had all the amusements afforded by a great city close by. They were taken to the British Museum and to Madame Tussaud's, which in those days was still very much the creation of its founder, and thus greatly preoccupied with the French Revolution, displaying

> the waxen heads of kings and democrats, the very guillotine itself. And Madame Tussaud's daughter, with the breathing breast that seemed alive, and the little old woman in the black bonnet, Madame herself, who had seen the rise of republics and the death of kings.[12]

Edith retained her childhood affection for both the British Museum and Madame Tussaud's all her life. But perhaps her favourite outing was to visit the Crystal Palace, which, at Sydenham, was comparatively close; fifteen years after its opening it was still in its heyday:

> It is true that even in the palmiest days of the Crystal Palace you barked your shins over iron girders – painted a light blue, my memory assures me – and that the boards of the flooring were so far apart that you could lose, down the cracks of them, not only your weekly sixpence or your birthday shilling, but even the sudden unexpected cartwheel (do they still call a crown that?) contributed by an uncle almost more than human. It is true that the gravel of the paths in the 'grounds' tired your feet and tried your temper, and that the adventure ended in a clinging to bony fingers and admonitions from nurse 'not to drag so'. But on the other hand. . . .
>   Think of the imagination, the feeling for romance that went to the furnishing of the old Crystal Palace. There was a lake in the grounds of Penge Park. . . . How did these despised mid-Victorians deal with it? They set up, amid the rocks and reeds and trees of the island in that lake, life-sized images of the wonders of a dead world.[13]

Like the children of today, the little Nesbits were simultaneously terrified, intrigued and delighted by these mysterious dragons of the past, and not least because the great stone statues seemed so nearly alive. Their strange names and even stranger shapes exerted a powerful fascination – the giant sloth, clasping its tree, was remembered into middle age and put into *The Magic City*; but best of all was the great stone Iguanodon, so large that an inaugural dinner for twenty-one scientists had been held inside its nearly completed shell. These vast sculptures had been built by Benjamin Waterhouse Hawkins to the (thoroughly inaccurate) specifications of Richard Owen, a professor at the Royal College of Surgeons. The dinosaur park, opened by the Queen and the Prince Consort in 1854, caught and gripped the Victorian imagination as a whole:

> And the Dinosaurus . . . he had a round hole in his antediluvian stomach: and, with a brother . . . to give you a leg-up, you could explore the roomy interior of the Dinosaur with feelings hardly surpassed by those of bandits in a cave. It is almost impossible to overestimate the Dinosaurus as an educational influence.[14]

In *The Enchanted Castle*, Edith was to recreate the dinosaur park with its hollow Iguanodon, but she endowed it with the magic of imagination: after dark the stone monsters came to life and lumbered about the park.

In 1866 the tenor of life at Kennington was interrupted by the first symptoms of her elder sister Mary's illness – she was consumptive. Mrs Nesbit spent the next six years in an unsuccessful search for a healthier climate for her. Doctors customarily began by recommending sea air for weak lungs; the Nesbits accordingly took lodgings at Brighton, in Western Road, 'where there was a small gritty garden, where nothing grew but geraniums and calceolarias'. Here, for the first time, Daisy was sent to school, as a weekly boarder to a Mrs Arthur's. It was not a happy experience. She was tormented by another small girl who terrorized and blackmailed her; her horrid schoolfellow deliberately spoiled her dolls' tea set and her box of paints, acts of malice such as she had never encountered before:

> I remember the hot white streets, and the flies, and Brill's baths, and the Western Road, and the bitter pang of passing, at the end of a long procession, our own house, where always someone might be at the window, and never anyone was.[15]

Daisy's schooling at Mrs Arthur's ended, to her great relief, with the measles. Her recovery was marked by a rapt reunion with her mother and brothers, and then they all went to stay in

> a lovely cottage among the beech-woods of Buckinghamshire. I shall never forget the sense of rest and delight that filled my small heart when I slipped out under the rustic porch at five o'clock the first morning, and felt the cool velvet turf under my feet. Brighton pavement had been so hard and hot. Then, instead of the long rows of dazzling houses with their bow windows and green-painted balconies, there were lovely trees, acacias and elms, and a big copper beech. In the school walks we never had found any flowers but little pink bind-weed, by the dusty roadside. Here there were royal red roses, and jasmine, and tall white lilies, and in the hedge by the gate, sweet-brier and deep-cupped white convolvulus.[16]

But all holidays come to an end, and that autumn Daisy was sent to a 'select boarding establishment for young ladies and gentlemen at Stamford, and I venture to think that I should have preferred a penal settlement'. Mrs Nesbit probably selected this school in far-off Lincolnshire because a second cousin, Rachel Pariss, a year older than Daisy, was being educated there. Her presence does not seem to have made life very much easier for Daisy, however; a Miss Fairfield was the headmistress and although she was remembered as consistently kind and patient, her second-in-command seems to have persecuted Daisy – for her dirty hands, her untidy hair and her failure to understand long division. The punishment for these offences was to forfeit various meals, and to sit by herself in the unheated schoolroom: 'Day after day I was sent to bed, my dinner was knocked off, or my breakfast, or my tea . . . Night after night I cried myself to sleep.' She came to hate not only the school, but also Stamford and in particular Burleigh Park, where the children were taken each day for walks. The spring term went better, for her persecutor was away, and she gained a temporary popularity by showing the other girls how to make dolls' bedsteads out of matchboxes, but she was desperately wretched during the summer term and wrote home imploring her mother to take her away. Sarah Nesbit, normally the soul of kindness, was preoccupied – Mary was ill again – and she wrote back promising Daisy that she would soon feel better and be happy once more. This period of misery and even despair came to an abrupt end when her mother arrived unexpectedly to announce to Daisy her latest plans:

> Only when I heard that my mother was going to the South of France with my sisters, I clung about her neck, and with such insistence implored her not to leave me – not to go without me, that I think I must have expressed my trouble without uttering it . . .

Like most children, Daisy seems to have been unable to tell her mother just how unhappy she was at these two schools, despite Mrs Nesbit's ready sympathy: 'I have often wondered what it is that keeps children from telling their mothers these things – and even now I don't know,' she wrote as an adult.[17]

Something of her wretchedness at Stamford eventually found expression in a strange, slightly disjointed story called 'Lucy' (*These Little Ones*, 1909). It is related by an old gentleman as he re-reads his first diary, given him by his mother when she was going away. Her dress – 'violet silk flounces, and a white shawl with a Paisley border, and a lace veil, to her bonnet' – is precisely recalled, as precisely as the black moiré dress and Paisley shawl Edith's mother had worn when she came up to Stamford to see her. The little boy of the story is sent first to an aunt's, where he accidentally disgraces himself, and then back to school, now empty for the holidays. No one is there but a strange servant called Jane who takes him for dreary walks to Burleigh Park. In his desperate loneliness, he invents, or imagines, or even sees a silent child companion whom he talks to and plays with. But this secret friend, Lucy, has long been dead, and his mother returns to find him sick with that mysterious Victorian complaint, 'brain fever'. When he is better, he recalls 'being at Brighton, very jolly, with the others', presumably as Daisy was after her reprieve from Stamford. Here, as in Edith's memoirs of her schooldays (where holidays passed in deserted schoolrooms also feature), an understandable, if barely acknowledged resentment of her sister's illness comes through. In the next few years Mary's bad health was to result in Daisy's frequent banishment to unsympathetic relatives or unwelcoming schools. More than once she commented, as an adult, on the importance of familiar objects and surroundings to the child:

> I was bored with travel, as I believe all children are – so large a part of a child's life is made up of little familiar playthings and objects.

And

> It is a mistake to suppose that children are naturally fond of change. They love what they know. In strange places they suffer violently from home-sickness, even when their loved nurse or mother is with them. They want to get back to the house they know, the toys they know, the books they know.[18]

In the months that followed, Daisy found herself very far from all that had previously been familiar to her.

In September 1867 she carefully packed up her dolls' clothes in a miniature tin trunk, complete with a tiny padlock, and set out for France with her mother and sisters, the boys having been despatched to boarding school. Mary had been warned that it was unsafe for her to spend another winter in England. Mrs Nesbit had apparently been left well provided for, and she was only too anxious to find a healthier climate for her ailing daughter. The Newhaven–Dieppe crossing was very rough and little Daisy was violently seasick, but the family pressed on to Rouen, their first port-of-call. Here they admired the Gothic churches and 'the curious remnants of past days that we met in almost every corner of the charming old town', as Mary put it in an elaborate account of their travels that she wrote for her uncle Edward Planta Nesbit in Australia. From Rouen the family travelled on to Paris where they spent a fortnight, though they found the Great Exhibition disappointing. Daisy caught a glimpse of the Emperor Napoleon III, so soon to be deposed, driving in his carriage with the Empress and his little son, and she was amused and cosseted by her cousin Fred Collins, a former student of the college and now living in Paris. As the weather grew cooler, they pursued their journey southwards, through Tours, Poitiers and Angoulême to Bordeaux. Daisy was showered with new toys and little presents to compensate her for the sightseeing being rather above her head, and at Poitiers she had a tiny pair of blue kid gloves specially made for her. She also remembered picking up a small bone in the Byzantine church there which she decided was a human relic and treasured accordingly. Many months later, Alfred was to ruin her little fantasy by pointing out that it was only half a fowl's back. Bordeaux was holding its great annual fête when the Nesbits arrived, but the two elder girls thought the city lacked the life and gaiety of Paris, which it otherwise resembled, so they only stayed for ten days.[19] It was here that Daisy underwent what she always thought of as the most terrifying experience of her whole childhood.

She had all the nervousness characteristic of the imaginative child – she was easily frightened by the dark, by nightmares or unfamiliar sights. But although her longing for her father seems to have expressed itself as a morbid fascination with and horror of death, the years at Kennington Lane were not, but for his loss, remembered as notably different from her earlier years, and the two years of boarding schools after that were preoccupied with more immediate sources of distress. At that time

> I seem to have had a period of more ordinary terrors – of dreams from which to awaken was mere relief; not a horror scarcely less than that of the dream itself. I dreamed of cows and dogs, of falling houses, and crumbling precipices. It was not till that night at Rouen that the old horror of the dark came back, deepened by superstitious dread.[20]

When her family finally made the great break with the past and England, a familiar country and a familiar language, her isolation came home to her in the form of further terrors: death, her father and her fear of the supernatural became confused in a horrible nightmare that she had at Rouen, on her first night in France. Travelling from the station, exhausted after her seasickness, she noticed the words '*Débit de Tabac*' over a shop and felt 'seized with a horror of them', irrationally associating them with her father's tombstone – presumably because of the accidental resemblance between the words 'Débit' and 'Nesbit':

> I lay awake in the dark, the light from the oil lamp in the street came

through the Persiennes and fell in bright bars on the wall. As I grew drowsier I seemed to read there in letters of fire '*Débit de Tabac*'.

Then I fell asleep, and dreamed that my father's ghost came to me, and implored me to have the horrible French inscription erased from his tomb – 'for I was an Englishman,' he said.

Then I woke, rigid with terror, and finally summoned courage to creep across the corridor to my mother's room and seek refuge in her arms. I am particular to mention this dream because it is the first remembrance I have of any terror of the dead, or of the supernatural. I do not at all know how it had its rise . . .[21]

It was some two months later that Daisy was taken by her sisters to see the mummies at Bordeaux. She explained her eagerness to do so in terms of homesickness – they had 'cousins at home, in the British Museum, in dear, dear England', and those cousins had never seemed to her objects of terror. Rather, they were associated with 'plate-glass cases, camphor, boarded galleries, and kindly curators'. She was excited at the prospect of seeing them, and insisted on putting on her best blue silk dress. But the approach down the chill stone steps, the earthy smell and the glimmering blue light were daunting. And the mummies in the crypt of the church of St Michel were not comfortably inside a painted case but were corpses, preserved by some peculiar salts or chemicals present in the walls or earth about them. They were (and still are)

skeletons with the flesh hardened on their bones, with their long dry hair hanging on each side of their brown faces, where the skin in drying had drawn itself back from their gleaming teeth and empty eye-sockets. Skeletons draped in mouldering shreds of shrouds and grave-clothes, their lean fingers still clothed with dry skin . . . On the wall near the door I saw the dried body of a little child hung up by its hair.

That evening, left alone in the hotel room while her mother and sisters went downstairs for dinner, she grew terrified that a curtained alcove concealed, not beds, but mummies. When the young waiter arrived with her bread and milk, she flew to him and clung to him in terror. Though he spoke no English, and Daisy, as yet, no French, he understood the universal language of fear, soothed her, fetched more candles and sat with her until the others returned. Trying to describe the mummies' effect on her, Edith later wrote:

The mummies of Bordeaux were the crowning horror of my childish life; it is to them, I think, more than to any other thing, that I owe nights and nights of anguish and horror, long years of bitterest fear and dread.

All the other fears could have been effaced, but the shock of that sight branded it on my brain and I never forgot it. For many years I could not bring myself to go about any house in the dark, and long after I was a grown woman I was tortured, in the dark watches, by imagination and memory, who rose strong and united, overpowering my will and my reason as utterly as in my baby days.[22]

The crypt at St Michel is indeed very horrible, and a disastrously unsuitable place to take an impressionable child; in one sense, Daisy's reaction to it revealed no more than an entirely natural terror of death, especially when it took such a physically repellent form. But she herself presents the experience as a climax, as characteristic of a period of acute nervousness that lasted from around the age of ten through to her early teens; something more may lie behind it. Though her memoirs several times refer to her 'mortal terror of darkness', she never makes any attempt to explain it. The Enlightenment reaction to such bug-bears had been to regard them as a form of mental ill-health. But a number of evangelical writers for children considered them to have a divine purpose as a reminder of our own sinful natures. Several early Victorian books for children, most notably Mrs Sherwood's *History of the Fairchild Family* (1818), sought to instil virtue into young readers by confronting its child characters with terrible sights as part of a deliberate educational policy. When the children squabble, their father takes them to see a gibbet on which hangs a mouldering corpse of a man who raised his hand against his brother, and they are later taken to see a vault full of old coffins which is about to be bricked up:

'Ah! father,' said my brother, as we walked home, 'death, after all, is a very horrible thing.' My father answered, that death was sent as a punishment for sin, and was, and always would be, frightful to flesh and blood . . .

Daisy Nesbit, like most mid-Victorian middle-class children, had read *The History of the Fairchild Family*,[23] and her experience in the crypt may well have reminded her of their visit to the vault. While she offers no such pious explanation for her terror, she would have been familiar with the idea of death as a punishment for sin. Increasingly her imagination focused on the Gothic horrors of death and the awful animation of the inanimate – for had she not perhaps secretly wished for her dead father to come back to life, and if he had, would it not have been in this scarcely thinkable form? One way in which she later attempted to banish her terror was by making 'mummies', effigies or puppets assembled out of coathangers, bolsters, umbrellas and similar domestic objects. Their faces were painted paper masks, rather like the mask that Saretta had worn when playing charades. This game of 'making mummies' lasted a long time, perhaps was never really outgrown, since she was still playing it at twenty-one, and even in middle age. Yet the mummies thus made also retained the macabre nature of their originals, if we are to judge by *The Enchanted Castle*. Here the Ugly-Wuglies (as they are called) are brought horribly to life by the magic of imagination, along with the Crystal Palace dinosaurs; once animated, they reveal their true nature, being possessed by that hatred that the dead traditionally feel towards the living. Perhaps she had not wholly forgiven her father and so attributed to him the resentment that inevitably mingled with her longing for him.

After this terrible experience at Bordeaux, which may well have made little or no impression on her mother and sisters, the Nesbit family continued their journey southward. They made a two-day detour to visit Arcachon on its almost landlocked bay, finding little wooden cabins nestling under pine woods, and sandy, shell-covered beaches. From there they continued to Pau, at the foot of the Western Pyrenees, which had been a favourite resort for English visitors since the early nineteenth century because of its mild winter climate. The Nesbits settled into a comfortable *pension*, but Mrs Nesbit was anxious about Daisy: it was now November and, though travel was supposedly an education in itself, she had had no formal lessons since the summer. Moreover she was showing signs of restlessness and boredom: while the older girls actively enjoyed travel and sightseeing, and had friends to write to, books to read and resources of their own to fall back on, Daisy too often had nothing to do. Accordingly Mrs Nesbit asked around for a French family with whom Daisy could stay and learn French. She was put in touch with Madame Lourdes who had a little girl the same age as Daisy, called coincidentally Marguerite. The family seemed suitable in every way. Daisy herself was keen to embark on this new venture until the moment after her arrival, when her mother's carriage wheels began to roll away:

> Then I was left, a little English child without a word of French in the bosom of a French family, and as this came upon me I burst into a flood of tears.[24]

At this moment of desolation, Madame Lourdes took Daisy on her lap, and though she could not understand what was being said to her, she recognized the note of maternal kindness in her voice. Marguerite was also warm and companionable, 'the typical good child of the French story-books. She wore her hair in a little yellow plait down her back.' She and Daisy were cheerfully unpacking dolls' clothes and laughing at their attempts to understand one another, when her elder sister arrived back from work. Mlle Lourdes was a teacher, and knew enough English to help the child overcome her initial difficulties; Daisy was soon chattering away happily in French. She and Marguerite liked one another from the first. They shared a room, did their lessons together and played endless games. On one occasion, when they were being bandits (a favourite game in fact and fiction), they shut Mimi the cat, in the role of captive princess, in the cellar and forgot about her entirely. Two nights later, Daisy suddenly remembered what they had done, and the little girls crept down in their dressing gowns and out across a courtyard lightly powdered with snow to rescue the starving Mimi, and take her back to bed. As it was the Christmas season, they were asked to children's parties together, and it was a party invitation that occasioned their only serious quarrel: Marguerite asked Daisy not to put on her best blue silk dress as it made her own grey cashmere look shabby in comparison. But Daisy only had one other suitable dress with her, an old brown one which she hated. So she put on the blue silk and, prancing across the kitchen, slipped and fell straight into a tub full of washing. When Marguerite pointed out that the blue silk couldn't mock the grey cashmere any more, she flew into a temper and pushed Marguerite into the wash tub as well. Madame Lourdes, having learned what had happened from the cook, packed Daisy off to bed and, since Marguerite's dress was soaked, sent her to the party in Daisy's rejected brown one. Marguerite must have been a very tender-hearted child because later that evening she came to Daisy's bedside and said:

'You're not cross now, are you? . . . I did beg mother to let you come, and I've not enjoyed myself a bit, and I've brought you this from the party.'
It was a beautiful little model of a coffee-mill made in sugar.[25]

When, at the end of three months, a maidservant came to take Daisy back to her mother and sisters, she wept as bitterly at her departure as she had when she arrived. The routine of family life and the companionship of a child of her own age had been exactly what she had missed most on their travels.

Mrs Nesbit herself had stayed on at Pau for five weeks and had probably intended to spend the rest of the winter there, but Mary was ill again just before Christmas, and the doctor advised that the sea air at Biarritz would do her more good. There it was warm enough to play croquet on Boxing Day, and pick roses from a churchyard hedge. But the girls were eager, having come so far south, to see Spain, so they took a train and then a *diligence* (a stage coach) across the Spanish frontier to Irun and San Sebastian. The grubbiness and inefficiency of the Spanish inns upset Mrs Nesbit, however, and they retreated across the border once more and settled at Bagnères de Bigorre, a spa to the south-east of Pau, and rather higher up the foothills of the Pyrenees. Here hot springs from the rocks flowed into special swimming baths, while swift, icy streams ran down from the mountains, crossing the roads, running between the houses and even under them. Mrs Nesbit found a pleasant apartment in an old house built out over one of these little rushing streams. When Daisy rejoined them, she was delighted to be given the bedroom built out over an arch beneath which the foaming water disappeared; but its noise kept her awake all night, and next day she was in low spirits:

> My mother was busy letter-writing, so were my sisters. I missed Marguerite, Mimi, even my lessons. There was something terribly unhomelike about the polished floor, the polished wooden furniture, the marble-topped chests of drawers with glass handles, and the cold greyness of the stone-built houses outside. I wandered about the suite of apartments, every now and then rubbing myself like a kitten against my mother's shoulder and murmuring 'I don't know what to do.' I tried drawing, but the pencil was bad and the paper greasy. I thought of reading, but there was no book there I cared for. It was one of the longest days I ever spent.[26]

Mary was currently out of favour. The previous evening she had unintentionally hurt Daisy's feelings by laughing at some cuffs that she had painstakingly knitted for her mother while staying with the Lourdes family. Thinking the child out of earshot, she had remarked

> 'They would just fit a coal-heaver . . .'
> She never knew that I heard her, but it was years before I forgave that unconscious outrage to my feelings.

Saretta, who was much older, in better health and had more patience, was Daisy's favourite. When she saw how bored and depressed the child was, she asked her if she would like to see a shepherdess, and went on to make up a wonderful story about one:

> My sister had a genius for telling fairy-stories. If she would only write
> them now as she told them then, all the children in England would insist
> on having her fairy-stories, and none others.

Though Saretta wrote poems, she never wrote her fairy-stories down –
it was her little sister whose fairy-stories were eventually to become
famous, though when she wrote these memoirs of her childhood, she
did not yet know how famous they would become. After Saretta's
wonderful story, the visit to the shepherdess next day inevitably
turned out to be a bitter disappointment. Daisy had expected a figure
from a Watteau painting, all roses and pink ribbons; the wrinkled old
crone with her iron sheep-hook looked, she thought, more like the
fairy-tale witch.[27]

On 26 January 1868 Mary had written from Bagnères de Bigorre a
long letter to her uncle Edward in Australia describing their travels to
date and adding that her brother Harry, at school in England, was
apparently far from well. Daisy rejoined the others at Bagnères de
Bigorre in the following month. Looking back, Edith believed that her
mother had intended to visit Spain next, but from what Mary told her
uncle of her mother's disgust with their brief excursion across the
border, this seems unlikely. Probably Edith was remembering plans
spoken of earlier. In her memoirs she recorded that they began the
return journey north on hearing the news that the boys had contracted
whooping cough, but since the next thing that the Nesbits did was
some more sightseeing, and since they took a leisurely and indirect
route back, perhaps this news in fact only caught up with them later, or
else Mrs Nesbit had in the meantime been reassured that her return was
not urgently required. In any event, they now turned east and travelled
by *diligence* up into the Pyrenees, to the other, more fashionable, spa
of Bagnères de Luchon. As they climbed up into the mountains, they
passed a ruined castle, in the middle of which stood a square tower
without doors or windows, probably the old keep of Genost. The
driver told them that it contained buried treasure and that there was a
prophecy that one day a wind would blow the tower down, and the
local villagers would divide the treasure and all become kings of
France. He added that the tower was haunted. The Nesbits were
greatly intrigued both with the tower and the tale of its treasure, and
when they stopped at a wayside shrine soon afterwards, Daisy noticed,
close by, a stone with an iron ring set in it. This, she felt convinced, was
the entrance to an underground passage that led straight back to the
tower and its treasure. She fantasized about discovering the treasure

and all the presents she would buy with it for many years afterwards. In imagination, she finally revisited the tower by magic carpet, in *The Phoenix and the Carpet*.

The Nesbits spent several days at Bagnères de Luchon, going up into the mountains to visit the vertiginous waterfall known as the Cascade d'Enfer. Finally they turned northward and travelled on to the old town of St Bertrand de Comminges where they spent the night. From there they gradually made their way across central France, through the Auvergne, over the Cantal mountains. The older girls had read that one should see the mountains by moonlight, so they started out late in the afternoon. They were travelling, with all their luggage, in an open carriage, having agreed with their blue-shirted driver upon a price for the whole journey. Some miles out of Aurillac he stopped to pick up a ruffian who, he assured them, was a cousin of his; soon afterwards three more disreputable-looking men climbed on board, and similar excuses were offered. Mrs Nesbit began to fear that they were about to be robbed, even murdered. When they reached the half-way house, she carefully hid all her money, apart from the fare and the price of their supper, in a little canvas bag that she wore round her neck, intended for banknotes. She then appealed to the landlady, telling her what had happened and what she had feared. The landlady was indignant; she was, it turned out, the driver's mother and she added that he was now expecting twice the agreed fare to take them on to Murat. Mrs Nesbit emptied her (depleted) purse and assured her that the rest of her money was at Murat, and he should have what he asked when they got there. So they set out again across the bleak, moonlit mountains. For Daisy the climax of terror came when their carriage suddenly sped down between high cliffs into a seemingly endless tunnel, which lasted so long that she began to fear that they would never come out again – the driver's villainous friends, she supposed, must be waiting there in ambush for them. The driver, who may not have been such a villain as they all supposed him, relit the carriage lamps which had blown out as they entered and told Daisy that the tunnel would be 'something for you to remember and to tell your children about when you are old'. She was much relieved when they rattled out into the moonlight again. Eventually Murat was reached and they were set down at an inn so dirty that they could not bring themselves to lie down on its soiled bedlinen. They sat up for what was left of the night, and caught the first train out next morning.[28]

After this dramatic encounter – perhaps far more exciting in the retelling than in reality – the rest of the journey home made little impression. Back in England, Daisy was despatched to friends while Mrs Nesbit tried to sort out her plans. She stayed in

> a strange house in Sutherland Gardens – a house with large rooms and heavy hangings – with massive wardrobes and deep ottoman boxes. The immense four-post beds stood out about a yard from the wall, for some 'convenience of sweeping' reason, I believe. Consider the horror of having behind you, as you lay trembling in the chill linen of a strange bed, a dark space from which, even now, in the black silence something might be stealthily creeping . . .
> That was the torture of the first night. The next I begged that the gas might be left 'full on'. It was, and I fell asleep in comparative security. But while I slept, came some thrifty soul, and finding the gas 'burning to waste' turned it down. Not out – down.
> I awoke in a faint light, and presently sat up in bed to see where it came from, and this is what I saw. A corpse laid out under white draperies, and at its foot a skeleton with luminous skull and out-stretched bony arm.
> I knew, somewhere far away and deep down, my reason knew that the dead body was a white dress laid on a long ottoman, that the skull was the opal globe of the gas and the arm the pipe of the gas-bracket, but that was not reason's hour. Imagination held sway . . .[29]

The animating power of imagination, often figured as magic, is the central theme of her children's books, though her own experiences as a child never allowed her to forget its torments, as well as its delights. But when she came to write for children she controlled the elements of supernatural terror rather carefully, focusing instead on the courage and fearlessness that she aspired to but only later acquired.[30] To experience fear may well make one determined to master it. As an adult Edith wrote a number of ghost stories, and sometimes frightened herself in the process; she was still trying to exorcize her old terror of the dark.

Daisy's next school was a 'Select Boarding School for Young Ladies' run by a Miss Macbean, 'one of the best and kindest women who ever lived'. Daisy became very fond of her, and still went back to visit her ten years later.[31] 'If I could have been happy at any school I should have been happy there,' she recalled, yet even so she never forgot the ghastly shock she felt when she discovered that she was to be reunited with her family a few days later than had originally been promised. Mrs Nesbit, meanwhile, had returned to France where she was looking for a home for her little brood. At last the news arrived that she had found one, at Dinan in Brittany. Daisy, not yet ten, set off alone by train and boat to St Malo, where her mother and sister were waiting to meet her. The long tiring journey in the *diligence* was quite forgotten in the joy of going home – 'not to an hotel, not to a boarding-house, but home'. At the crossroads, Daisy's luggage was unloaded on to a cart, and she, her sister and her mother followed on foot:

> Up a hill wound the road, a steep wooded slope on one side, and on the other side a high, clay bank set with dainty ferns. Here and there a tiny spring trickled down to join the little stream that ran beside the road . . .
> The cart turned in at a wooden gate. We followed along the carriage-drive, which ran along outside the high red wall of the big garden, then through a plantation of huge horse-chestnut trees. To the left, I could see ricks, cows and pigs, all the bustle and colour of a farm-yard.
> Two great brown gates swung back on their hinges and we passed through them into the courtyard of the dearest home of my childhood. The courtyard was square. One side was formed by the house; dairy, coach-house and the chicken-house formed the second side; on the third were stable, cow-house and goat-shed; on the fourth wood-shed, dog-kennel and the great gates by which we had entered. The house itself was an ordinary white-washed, slate-roofed, French country house, with an immense walled fruit garden on the other side of it.[32]

The garden was full of fruit – peaches, apricots, nectarines, grapes, gooseberries, currants, figs, raspberries, cherries and strawberries – and the children were allowed to pick whatever they wanted; beyond the garden was an apple orchard with a swing and beyond that again lay meadows, lanes and streams, all waiting to be explored. There were the farm animals to be milked or played with, and – 'crowning happiness' – there was a pony of their own to ride:

> That summer was an ideally happy one. My mother . . . allowed us to run wild; we were expected to appear at meals with some approach to punctuality, and with hands and faces moderately clean. Sometimes when visitors were expected, we were seized and scrubbed, and clothed, and made to look something like the good little children we were not . . .[33]

The adventures of *The Wouldbegoods* owe much to the exploits of Alfred, Harry and Daisy at the farmhouse known as La Haye during the summer of 1868: they made forts in the haylofts and took the dogs up to join in the sieges – on one memorable occasion they even took the black pig up. They watched the great cider press being dragged round by the old, blind horse, and all the other interesting farm activities. There was a large pond in a neighbouring field for which they made a raft, and Alfred hollowed a cave out of the thick yellow clay on the far bank. They built dams and bridges across the nearby stream, caught tiny fish in its shallows, and pretended it was the Nile. One day they set out to find its source, taking special provisions for the expedition. They waded upstream, through meadows and a wood, then clambered through a tunnel which came out in the middle of a muddy swamp, lush with flowers and grasses. Over the next hedge, they finally found its source in 'a wayside well we had passed a thousand times'.

Edith's memories of La Haye were mainly of sunny hours, but one event was chilling, even though it took place in broad daylight. Once when she and the boys were exploring the little lanes at the back of their house, they came upon a ruined château, set well back from the road. Roaming all over it, they were intrigued to find a Bluebeard-like door that was boarded up, but the room glimpsed through the cracks seemed empty apart from a pile of straw on the floor. As they watched, the straw began to fly up into the air and spin itself into a kind of rope, stretching up towards the ceiling. The children fled, screaming with terror, and as they reached the gates of the drive, an old woman came out of a cottage and said to them, 'I can see, children, that you have seen the spinning lady.' When, in a calmer state, they went back to look for the château again, they were – as in all good ghost stories – quite unable to find it. La Haye itself was also supposed to be haunted, and a clattering noise as of coaches might be heard in the courtyard at night, but this seemed to have alarmed no one, not even the nervous Daisy.[34]

There were bright dewy mornings when the children crept down early to begin an adventure, and smoky evenings spent round a bonfire, being Red Indians and roasting potatoes in the hot ashes. There were special trips to the seaside at Dinard: 'A part of the infinite charm of those days lies in the fact that we were never bored, and children are bored much more often and much more deeply than their elders suppose.' School was the commonest source of boredom, and that autumn, when the boys went back to school, Daisy was sent to Mademoiselle Fauchet's 'select' school for girls at Dinan, and, since one of her family was ill, was sent five days before the other girls. Those five days with nothing to do, no books that she was allowed to read and only the empty schoolroom to sit in, were a very special kind of purgatory, which she later put into her books. Mlle Fauchet meant well but was entirely out of sympathy with small girls. She took her for a walk every day, however, and one day they walked to La Fontaine, beneath which ran her beloved stream, the Nile that she had so often explored with the boys. Daisy, quite overcome with homesickness, fled from her teacher and never stopped running until she had reached home and flung herself into her sister's arms:

> I know that I cried a great deal, and felt that I had committed an awful crime. I couldn't explain my feelings to myself, but I knew that in the same circumstances I should have done the same again, though I wept heartfelt tears of penitence for having done it at all.[35]

Daisy was not made to go back to Mlle Fauchet's; instead she became a pupil at the Ursuline convent at Dinan, where she remained, at least until November of the following year, 1869. This was one of the rare schools that she enjoyed, and looked back on with pleasure: 'I was so happy there.' In writing of singing and dancing games, she mentioned the Mulberry Bush, adding, 'A la claire fontaine, I remember as the French version, danced on wet days in the cloisters of the convent of my youth,' and she also learned Compagnons de la Marjolaine and Le Pont d'Avignon, 'a glorious game with its impersonations of animals, [that] has, as far as I know, no counterpart in this country'. She recalled crying a good deal at the prospect of leaving. The nuns, gentle and affectionate souls, were surprised and probably a little shocked at the passionate temper and high spirits of their small English pupil. Mère Marie Madeleine described her as 'a proper little devil, a holy terror' and thought of her as 'the mad English girl, capable of anything, but a good child'. A letter from Daisy to her mother, written from the convent, admits, 'The nuns are all very kind to me though I have been very naughty.' It goes on to enquire after

> that queen of dogs that splendid lady that estimable that lovely loveing loveable loved Trot. I hope Her Majesty is in bonne santé, that she has sufficiency of velvet cushions to support her royal feet, an abundance of daintys to please her royal palate, and a sprightly family of hippopotami to be a comfort in her old age. How is the old mother owl I hope she is not ill.[36]

A photograph of Mrs Nesbit in her glasses certainly makes her look rather like 'the old mother owl'. The middle of Daisy's letter is preoccupied with her marks in class. The last paragraph turns to more serious matters as she pleads to be allowed to become a Catholic, defending her request with an account of the mystery of transubstanti- ation which sounds as if it is parroting the phrases in which it had been explained to her:

> You say that you do not believe that our Lord is body and soul in the Holy Communion? Well, at the last supper when our Lord took the bread and wine He did not say This is the figure of My body this is the figure of My Blood. He said this is my body this is my blood. Do this in remembrance of me. What are you to do in remembrance of Him? What had he just done? He had changed bread and wine into his body and blood. The priests being the descendants of the apostles operate the change. I really have no more time so with love to you all.
>
> I remain,
your little Daisy[37]

Edith did not describe the convent in her account of her schooldays, but her romantic novel *Daphne in Fitzroy Street* begins with a fictionalized and romanticized version of life in the Dinan convent, though the girls in the novel are substantially older than Daisy was at this time. Daphne, in many ways a self-portrait, is presented as a natural leader among the other girls by virtue of her daring and organizational powers, shinning up and down trees and arranging wonderful midnight feasts in the attics. The novel gives a detailed account of the sweetmeats and goodies assembled for the secret party:

> There were little cakes of all kinds, *gaufrettes* and *millefeuilles* and cream *éclairs*; there were *petits suisses*, cool and white, on green leaf- platters. There were French plums, and *dragées*, and *sucre de pommes*. There were also candied fruits, Mandarin oranges, pitchers of water and the *sirop de groseille*.

Such feasts had a distant echo in reality, according to a letter about Daisy from Mère Marie Madeleine, written early in November 1869. It is in French, and addressed to Saretta, presumably because Mrs Nesbit did not speak French, though it is hard to imagine how she had got by for so long without it. The letter, occasioned by Daisy's imminent departure, refers to her violent tempers and hopes she will grow out of them. It goes on to add that the sisters have two pots of jam and two empty wine bottles of hers. The wine had been brought by her brother Alfred, who was just then at a school close by, and Mère Marie Madeleine guessed that he must have had the key to the wine cellar at La Haye and even wondered whether the wine might not have been responsible for Daisy's unreliable temper; certainly both children had been allowed to return to the farmhouse on occasions when their mother had not been there, so that they were comparatively un-supervised, though the farmer and his family were always on hand.[38] The nuns loved their young charges, mended their clothes and kept what watch they could over them; they were affectionate, unworldly, easily deceived and surprised, whereas most of Daisy's English school mistresses had seemed suspicious, reserved and disciplinarian.

Edith never fully recorded the sequence of schools that she attended after she left the convent, but for a while she and the boys were sent to schools in Germany in order to have an opportunity of learning a third language. Edith was sent to a school run by Moravian sisters, near Düsseldorf. Here she was more miserable than ever. After one particular scolding, she jumped out of a window and tried to run away to the school where her brothers were; but she knew too little German even to ask the way, and she was forced to turn back through hunger – she could find nothing but raw pumpkin to eat. Her misery there left her with a strong dislike of the Germans, and she and her brothers got into trouble by singing the *Marseillaise* in some public place at about the time when the Franco-Prussian war broke out, in 1870.[39] The war came as a liberation – it meant that she had to be sent back to her family. As they were then in France, she had to travel via neutral England, taking a boat to Southampton, and then another to St Malo. The boat to France was stranded in fog for more than three days. She was travelling alone, as she often had to, with no other female passengers on board and absolutely nothing for her to do. All the sailors could find for her to read were ship's timetables.[40]

Boredom loomed painfully large in her childhood, and at times it led her into mischief. She was sent to stay for a while with some relatives of her father's – a Dr Robert Bolton, his daughters and his wife Sarah (though she carefully omitted their names from her memoir since they were still alive when she wrote it). The Boltons were well-meaning but utterly unimaginative – he was a doctor and she and her girls were only interested in Court Circulars. Though the daughters sometimes played games with Daisy, they had very little idea of how to amuse their small cousin. They lived in a depressing square in Islington, and their home had little to offer a lively child by way of diversion:

> The dining-room was mahogany and leather with two books in it, the Bible and Family Prayers. They stood on the side-board, flanked on one side by a terra-cotta water-bottle oozing sad tears all day into a terra-

cotta saucer, and on the other by a tea-caddy. Upstairs in the drawing-room, which was only used on Sundays, were a few illustrated gift-books, albums, and types of beauty arranged on a polished oval walnut centre table. The piano was kept locked. There were a few old bound volumes of *Good Words*, which I had read again and again.[41]

One night Daisy went into the surgery where the doctor's prescriptions stood in their various bottles, waiting to be wrapped up and distributed. Idly, she poured the contents of the different bottles into a jug, mixed them all up and poured them back in the bottles, corked them up again and went to bed. In the night she realized what she had done, intending to own up next morning. But by next morning she had grown frightened that one of the patients who had taken the wrong medicine might die of it, so that she would be hanged for murder. She decided that it would be better to wait and see what happened, indulging in fantasies in which she nobly came forward at the trial to save Dr Bolton from the charge of having poisoned his patients. Between guilt and heroic daydreams another week passed, in which, if Dr Bolton's patients had met mysterious deaths, he certainly never mentioned the fact. At last she assumed, with some relief, that all his patients had survived her experiment, but she was now even more desperately bored than before. She wrote a frantic letter to her mother, begging to be taken away and saying that she was so miserable she wished she were dead. Having no stamps, she gave the letter to Mrs Bolton, who opened it and read it through before sending it on. She was outraged at the child's account of herself and added a note urging Mrs Nesbit to take Daisy back at once. Daisy was sent down to her mother at Penshurst in deep disgrace. She felt simultaneously guilty and furious with Mrs Bolton for having opened her letter, and secretly thought it served her right for prying. Mrs Nesbit's reproaches were characteristically mild, but Daisy's sister was angry with her, and told her that she had behaved ungratefully.[42]

The next morning I wandered up through Penshurst churchyard, and through a little wicket-gate into the park, where the splendour of a blaze of buttercups burst upon me. The may-trees were silver-white, the skylarks singing overhead; I sat down under a white may-tree. The spirit of the spring breathed softly round me, and when I got up to go back I was in love and charity with all men and women except Mrs Bolton.

'I am sorry if I have been naughty,' I said to my sister; 'I didn't mean to be, but –'

'That will do,' she said, skilfully stopping my confidences; 'now I do hope you are going to try and be a good girl, and not make dear mamma unhappy.'

'I will be good,' I said; 'oh, I will indeed!'[43]

The beauty of the natural world had the power to comfort and console her from childhood (when she peopled it with half-glimpsed fairies), until the end of her life, when she lay gazing out of the window at the 'little lovely hills of Kent' that she would never revisit.

Here, as elsewhere in her memoir, she does not specify which of her sisters it was who scolded her, but it could well have been Mary, who was inclined to adopt a high moral tone. Her mother, the original of all the loving, self-effacing mothers in her writing, could be ineffectual, fazed by her unruly family. In childhood, Daisy's behaviour was often of a type characteristic of the youngest – lively, self-willed, demanding, attention-seeking, and sometimes rebellious – the behaviour of a child who can afford to specialize in childishness, by contrast with more mature and dependable elder sisters. But the next ten years were to change her position in the family radically, taking Saretta and Mary away and revealing her two brothers as being, in their different ways, incapable of shouldering responsibility.

Naughty little Daisy found that her energy and creativity could be turned to good purposes, that she could grow up and take on adult tasks. Bobby in *The Railway Children* is a child at the crossroads. As 'little mother' to the others, she takes on herself adult responsibilities, sending for the doctor and turning to other adults for the help that her mother cannot admit she needs. Part of the poignancy of the restoration of her father is that it allows the little girl who has grown up too fast to be a child again. Edith had a special insight into that child's plight because it was her own. She learnt to provide for family and friends as *both* mother and father, but the irresponsible child lurked within her and, as her life wore on, was more and more inclined to assert itself.

2
CARELESS RAPTURES

A SONNET
To my Sister's Portrait
It is so lovely! Yet that portrait shews
But one half of her beauty, auburn hair
Falls o'er her shoulders and her throat, small fair
Soft hands, and a delicate Grecian nose!
Those eyes, those wells of truth and love and light
Speak volumes to a colder heart than mine
They are as tranquil those blue eyes of thine
As summer sea beneath a moonlit night.
Thy cherry lips make happy slaves of those
Who hear thee speak through them their *Christian* name.
Some love thee sadly without hope of love
Some give thee love while hoping for the same.
Some love thee with a love that cannot die
And, Maris Stella, such a one am I.[1]

If Daisy often behaved like a naughty child, she was undoubtedly precocious in her literary tastes and ability. She wrote this poem at the age of eleven for her sister Mary, and, if nothing else, it reflects wide reading and a quick ear for literary idiom. From then onwards she became a secret scribbler, hiding her writings from the boys who would certainly have teased her about them, and in this case even from the subject herself. Poetry in the Nesbit family seems to have been considered a feminine, even an effeminate interest. Mary enjoyed reading it and Saretta, under her whimsical pen name 'Caris Brooke', was beginning to have her verses published occasionally in various periodicals. But the boys regarded poetic sensibility as a mark of weakness, something to be laughed at or pitied. In order to maintain their high opinion of her, Daisy had acquired the habit of camouflaging her serious or heart-felt poems by writing verses that dealt with experiences they had shared, specially intended for them to read. Six lines of this kind on 'A German Household' are more sophisticated than they look, for their naïvety was surely meant to make her brothers laugh:

> I like the cat I like the dog
> And the red plums with the boiled hog
> I like the mountains and the Rhine
> And the apple sauce with the roasted swine.
> I like Jack Yorke and his father and mother,
> But not *Mr* Morsbach nor *Mrs* either.[2]

The poem sounds remarkably like the work of the fictional Noel Bastable. On the brink of adolescence, the contrasting personalities of the Bastable twins – Alice, the boys' boon companion, and sensitive poetry-writing Noel – were struggling for dominance within her.

Another inner tension evident in the sonnet to Mary is revealed in the persona it adopts, as conventional lover. In writing poetry, Daisy wrote in the voice most familiar to her from her reading, as a male suitor; as a strong and active personality, she enjoyed assuming a male role for the freedom to act that it conferred. But in time she too must grow up, become corseted and passive, a recipient of passionate addresses rather than an author of them. She never entirely accepted that role and this, the earliest of her adult poems, reflects a preference for being Mary's admirer rather than Mary, though her admiration was tinged with envy. From early on a degree of resentment was felt at the way Mary's ill-health had pushed Daisy out of the nest, from one hateful school to another, from bumpy stage coaches to dour relatives, from pillar to post. Now Mary was entering the charmed circles of literature and love, while her younger sister was only a schoolgirl and a hoyden.

When Mrs Nesbit was not worrying about Mary's cough, she was worrying about her social life, for if young girls were to make the right match, they must move in the right circles. Saretta was now in her mid-twenties, perhaps even regarded as 'on the shelf', but Mary at eighteen needed the kind of company that only London could provide. With Daisy settled at the Dinan convent and the boys at boarding schools, Mrs Nesbit took Mary back to London. 'How many balls has Minnie been to?' Daisy wrote to ask[3], but 'Minnie' had been introduced into the Pre-Raphaelite circle, and their discussions of

poetry and the possibilities of social change appealed far more to her
than the meaningless chatter at dances or the gallantries of the callow
young men she met there. She was now on visiting terms with
Christina Rossetti, and either through the Rossettis or perhaps
through Swinburne or William Morris whom she also knew, Mary was
introduced to a young blind poet, Philip Bourke Marston. He was a
year older than she, tall, with a slender, sensitive face and a serious,
intense, rather melancholic view of the world. One of her commonplace books has survived, and among the poems neatly copied out in
her fine, sloping copperplate hand, poems by Christina Rossetti,
Browning and Swinburne, is an early sonnet by Marston himself.[4]

Marston now fell deeply in love with Mary and a sequence of fifty-
seven love sonnets which formed the opening section of his first
volume of poems, *Song-Tide*, was largely written for her. Early in
1871 he and Mary became formally engaged; soon afterwards his book
was published and he gave her the first copy of it. Unlike everyone
else, Philip Bourke Marston could not see that Mary was daily growing
thinner and more hollow-eyed. In the autumn both of them went to
stay with some friends of hers in Normandy, at the Haute Motte,
Châteauneuf. Mary had finally and reluctantly warned her lover that
she had not long to live. It was nevertheless the most terrible shock
when, going into her room one day, he groped his way over to the bed
and discovered by touch alone that she was lying there dead. Others
came in later to find him in a wordless, tearless agony at her bedside:

> Here in this room there is no light of day,
>   Only dim light of funeral lamps is shed
>   Upon my past that lies here still and dead;
> Only love hears the words I have to say;
> Only he, watching, sees the gifts I lay –
>   Sad gifts, indeed – upon the silent bed.
>   Down distant passages I hear the tread
> Of feet that from this chamber keep away.

Mary had died on 30 November 1871. Her lover never really
recovered from her loss which had followed closely on his mother's
death. Impressively, he supported himself by his writing and latterly
learnt to use a typewriter rather than an amanuensis, but existence was
a continuous struggle for him. Mary's death was followed by that of
his favourite sister Cicely who had lived with him, and then by the
deaths of his elder sister and her children, and a series of close friends
including Rossetti and James Thompson. He himself died sixteen

years later, at the age of thirty-six, after one of the saddest of lives.[5]

With Mary's death, the search for a healthier climate was over and Mrs Nesbit gravitated to her home county of Kent. Earlier in 1871 the Nesbits had stayed for a while at Tonbridge; almost thirty years later Edith wrote to her mother recalling an occasion when she and the boys had got up to some delightful mischief there:

> There was the thanksgiving for the recovery of the Prince of Wales and I went out with the boys to see the illuminations, and we threw crackers into the gaping mouths of the trombone and cornopean – to the amazement and terror of the band.[6]

Mrs Nesbit eventually found a home for her brood in the village of Halstead, which lies to the south of Orpington, between Tonbridge and London, on the chalk of the North Downs – a wooded and hilly countryside more inviting to the painter than the farmer. The village itself was still very small at that time and, until the development of fruit-growing in the mid-nineteenth century, had been fairly poor. Today the older part of the village, clustered round the crossroads where Otford Lane crosses the Knockholt Road, is still much as it was then, with its two pubs – the Rose and Crown and the Cock – a row of picturesque cottages built of knapped flint, and several pleasant red brick houses. Beyond the crossroads stands the handsome Rectory, occupied in the 1870s by the Reverend Thomas Sikes and his family. Facing it was the old church, since demolished, with its sharply pointed tower and Norman arches. It stood in the grounds of Halstead Place, a large eighteenth-century house occupied by the local squire, only pulled down comparatively recently.[7]

Halstead Hall, the house Mrs Nesbit had taken, is at the crossroads, on the road now called Station Road, though the station had not then been built. It is easily recognizable from Edith's description:

> 'The Hall' it was called, but the house itself did not lend itself to the pretensions of its name. A long, low, red-brick house, that might have been common-place but for the roses and ivy that clung to the front of it, and the rich, heavy jasmine that covered the side. There was a smooth lawn with chestnut-trees round it, and a big garden, where flowers and fruit and vegetables grew together, as they should, without jealousy or class-distinction.[8]

Today, more than a hundred years later, the house looks rather less commonplace, with its pretty Regency porch and fanlight. Indoors the hall, staircase and individual rooms are low-ceilinged but pleasantly and comfortably proportioned – a very English house, with a great brick fireplace in the kitchen, shuttered sash windows, and a sense of space in quite a small compass – the sort of house in which one might picture a Jane Austen family. Since the 1830s the Hall had belonged to a family called Man. Harry Stoe Man, their founder, had fought in the Napoleonic wars and there were holes in his cheeks where a bullet had whistled through them. He was reputed to have been a ship's purser, cashiered from the navy for stealing blankets. He bought the Hall and later extended the frontage cheaply by adding a wooden frame building, tile-hung to resemble the original brick. He also attempted to extend the garden by enclosing the village pond. As this had been an important source of water for the villagers, a long and acrimonious lawsuit followed, which he eventually lost. Edith, describing the walled garden many years later, remembered that it 'ran round three sides of a big pond', the fourth side remaining accessible to the rest of the village. Harry Stoe Man was a thoroughly quarrelsome and litigious individual, and though he died in 1848, his troublesome spirit was supposed to haunt the Hall – the previous rector had even conducted a service of exorcism on the stairs.

Mrs Nesbit rented the Hall from Louisa Caroline Man, Harry's widow. She does not appear to have noticed anything amiss, so perhaps the haunting was only a family affair. Edith recalled their time at Halstead as 'uneventful, peaceful, pleasant', adding that the only real excitement was provided by the landlady's son who was regarded as either mad or eccentric. He suffered from the delusion that he was the rightful tenant, and every six months or so turned up with a carpet bag to announce that he had come to take possession. He was always persuaded to go away again, but on one occasion, while her mother talked to him, Daisy peeped inside his carpet bag: 'It contained three empty bottles that had held mixed pickles, a loaf of bread and a barrister's wig and gown.'[9] This strange visitor must have been Septimus, one of Man's several sons, who had at one time practised as a barrister. According to family tradition, Septimus had suffered from heat stroke in India, and was sent home, where he went down with brain fever and, having passed into a coma, was laid out for dead. The coffin had arrived by the time he eventually came round. It may have been this incident that gave Edith a morbid fear that her loved ones might accidentally be buried alive. After his recovery, Septimus behaved oddly, and his family made him an allowance, since he was no longer capable of earning his own living.

The years spent at Halstead were, for Daisy, the years of transition from childhood to young womanhood, and though she and her brothers still played, walked and picnicked, the carefree joy in their companionship that she had felt in the old days at La Haye was inevitably fading. Growing up brought with it those barely identifiable yearnings that separate the actable fantasies of childhood games from the more elusive adult daydreams of erotic success, requiring a wider social sphere. The boys were growing up and away from her, too. When Alfred, playing with a new gun, succeeded in shooting a fox, he asked his sister what he should do with it:

> 'Bury it, we can have a splendid funeral,' I said.
> 'You baby!'
> I was constantly forgetting that Alfred, at seventeen, was grown-up, and that our old games no longer interested him.
> 'Well, stuff it, then.'[10]

Alfred, always fascinated by practical experiments of any kind, actually took this suggestion seriously and attempted to do so.

One excitement that Daisy could still share with the boys, however, was the railway. If they ran down the field at the back of the house, they found themselves by the track, which cuts deeply through high banks of chalk, finally disappearing into tunnels in both directions. Walking along the sleepers, as the Railway Children were to do, the Nesbits could follow the line until it reached Chelsfield Station, though it was quite a tidy walk for them. Knockholt Station, mentioned in several of Edith's stories and used by her on her many return trips to Halstead, lies only a mile or so from the Hall, but it was not opened until 1876, after the Nesbits had moved back to London. Reading *The Railway Children* and knowing that it was partly written from her memories of Halstead, it is easy to imagine the young Nesbits going down regularly to wave to particular commuter trains, exploring the station and making friends with the porters and station master, being alarmed by a landslip close to the line (the cuttings are very steep round there), and perhaps watching a paper chase disappear into the tunnel, and wondering what they would do if one of the runners did not come out again. Certainly the red flannel petticoats which Bobby and Phyllis take off to stop the train before it reaches the landslip were worn by children in the sixties and seventies, but not in the Edwardian age when the book was actually written.

Daisy's room at Halstead was upstairs and faced westward, looking

out over the roses, shrubs and fruit trees of the back garden. She had an
old bookcase with a deep bureau drawer that let down to form a desk
top, and on this she wrote her poems, though the desk was kept
carefully locked so that the boys should not find out what she was up
to. In her verse she led a life crowded with the passion and events so
notably absent from her actual day-to-day existence:

> I don't know whether it was the influence of the poetry I read, or merely
> a tendency natural to my age, but from fourteen to seventeen all my
> poems were about love and the grave. I had no sweetheart in real life,
> but in my poems I buried dozens of them and wept on their graves quite
> broken-heartedly.[11]

Though she later joked about it, her imaginary inner life was surely
shaped by Mary's sad example.

The account of Halstead that Edith gave in *My School-Days* is
particularly concerned with places in which she could hide either her
possessions or herself. With the boys away at school, these retreats
conferred a newly-valued solitude. To her great relief she herself had
not been sent back to school and thus had only her elders to evade. One
refuge from them was provided by the raft that the boys had built for
the pond. Greater privacy was to be found in the dense shrubberies at
the end of the garden, or else on the roof. In the ceiling of Daisy's room
there was a trap-door – 'by turns a terror and a charm'. With the help of
a ladder, it was possible to climb up into the space between the roof and
the beams, and by squeezing between the beams, you could (and still
can) come out in a narrow passage that runs round the whole house,
under the eaves. From here another narrow wooden door leads on to
the flat centre of the roof, where all four tiled ridges slope down to
form a little rectangular area lined with lead, from which the rainwater
is carried away. 'This, until the higher powers discovered it, was a safer
haven even than the shrubbery.' It was the perfect hiding place: by
shinning up the tiles to the ridge, it was possible to look all round the
house unseen. Another trap-door beside the boys' room gave them
access to the roof as well. In the loft space, they all kept books and
some provisions – 'Happy, vanished days, when to be on the roof and
to eat tinned pineapple in secret constituted happiness.'[12]

To clamber up through the trap-door and out among the beams into
Daisy's secret place between the roofs is to be struck by how active she
must have been, and how little the stiff skirts and full petticoats of the
1870s hampered her freedom. Perhaps brown holland pinafores

helped, but it is not a particularly easy climb, even in the much less restrictive clothing of today. Though Daisy still played and hid and romped with the boys, her identification with them and with the freedoms afforded to their sex was gradually being undermined by a whole complex of physical changes that increasingly separated her from them – the unavoidable and irreversible changes of puberty, the alterations of the body that visibly began to define a girl's destiny as marriage and motherhood. The locked desk drawer, the depths of the shrubbery, the hidden angle between the sloping roofs all imply a newly-felt need for privacy, even as they represent and reflect the young girl's awareness of her body's strange and dangerous secrecies and secretions. Now there were things she could not talk to her brothers about, and dreams that she could not share with them. The strains and pains of childhood had ended when their travels and her schooldays were finally over; the stresses of adult life had not yet begun. She looked back on the years at Halstead with unalloyed pleasure, as a period of security and consolidation, and she revisited the village at intervals throughout her life.

If the physical changes of puberty can only be inferred, a rather different rite of passage was celebrated more publicly. According to her own account, when Daisy eventually showed some of her verses to her mother, Mrs Nesbit passed them on to Mr Japp, an occasional contributor to the *Sunday Magazine*. In a reminiscence of 1919, Edith recalled,

> The first poem I ever had published was a non-committal set of verses about dawn, with a moral tag. It was printed in the *Sunday Magazine*. When I got the proof I ran round the garden shouting 'Hooray!' at the top of my voice, to the scandal of the village and the vexation of my family.[13]

Whether these lines were published anonymously, as poems often were in those days, or whether she had simply forgotten the circumstances of her first publication, her earliest verses to have come to light appeared in *Good Words* for December 1876 after she had left Halstead. They were published under the title 'A Year Ago', though in manuscript they were more pretentiously headed '*Vies Manquées*':

> A year ago we walked the woods,
>   A year ago today;
> The lanes were sweet with black-thorn bloom,
>   The hedges white with may . . .

This year, oh love, no things are changed,
  As bright a sunset glows;
Again we walk the wild wet woods,
  Again the blue-bell blows.

Only – our drifted spirits fail
  Spring's secret springs to touch;
For now you do not care for me,
  And I love you too much.

It was signed D. Nesbit. A similar blend of sentiment and nature characterizes 'Love Song in May', published in the *Argosy* in May 1877, though the metre here is more ambitious. From her late teens onwards poems of hers, normally signed 'E. Nesbit', appeared from time to time in various magazines; she would be paid a guinea or a half-guinea for them. She secretly dreamed of becoming a great poet – 'like Shakespeare, or Christina Rossetti' – but in order to write verse at all, she had to imitate, and both the sentiments and techniques she used were usually rather secondhand. Commenting on her sonnet on Mary's portrait, she wrote, 'This was an attempt to write poetry like other people',[14] an acute analysis of what was to remain her major problem as a poet for the rest of her life: she could achieve a high standard of technical competence, but whatever she wrote sounded too much 'like other people'. It took her more than twenty years to find a distinctive voice of her own, and when she finally did so, it turned out to be prose and not poetry that she excelled at. She never really overcame the disappointment of that discovery.

As Daisy grew up, she began to need companionship of her own age, though at the time she may not consciously have realized this. Halstead was too small a village to offer much in the way of a social life. The Nesbits made friends with the Sikes family at the Rectory, and Daisy borrowed all Scott's novels from Mrs Sikes. A tennis lawn was laid out in the Rectory garden as the game became popular, and Daisy and her brothers played on it. But the Sikes children were too young to provide companionship – afterwards the little ones remembered only the delightful stories she had made up to amuse them – or else were away at school. Another clerical family, the Oakleys, came down every summer, and Daisy was to remain friendly with Violet for many years even though she was several years younger. In her novel *The Incomplete Amorist* (1906) the eighteen-year-old heroine Betty lives with her father near Sevenoaks, and walks each day through a chalky parkland that sounds very like the grounds of Halstead Place or

Chevening Park, a little further south. Betty dreams of becoming a painter, rather as Daisy dreamed of writing poetry. She is lonely and not a little bored, for she has nothing more demanding to do than to organize the village sewing circle, no girl friend in whom to confide and no young man to pay his attentions:

> [She] did indeed desire to fall in love. In all the story-books the main interest of the heroine's career began with that event. Not that she voiced the desire to herself. Only once she voiced it in her prayers. 'Oh, God,' she said, 'do please let something happen!'[15]

Predictably enough, what happened was not quite what Daisy had had in mind: her mother was obliged to move, either because the Mans wanted the house back or because Mrs Nesbit now found herself in financial difficulties. Her tenancy had apparently lasted from spring 1872 to autumn 1875, from Daisy's fourteenth to her seventeenth year. Detailed records have not survived, but the Kent Fire and Life Office at Maidstone listed insurance payments by Mrs Sarah Nesbit for Lady Day 1872, and then, in October 1875, a payment to insure her furniture and effects in the possession of the Reverend Hamilton.[16] This suggests that she had moved on the Quarter Day of the previous month, leaving her furniture in store behind her. Though their next home was to be in Islington, Mrs Nesbit gave her address as Manchester, presumably because she had not yet decided to settle in London, or if she had, had not yet found somewhere suitable to live. London certainly offered advantages in terms of the boys' careers and Daisy's social life. The Manchester address suggests that Mrs Nesbit went to stay for a while with her daughter Saretta, who earlier that year had married John Deakin, a former student of the Agricultural College, and was now settled there for good.[17]

Whatever the immediate reason for the move, Mrs Nesbit was no longer able to maintain her previous life-style. The years of travel abroad, and even the Maidstone insurance note (which listed 'stable, coach house, horse, cow, pigs, carriage, harness') suggest that she had been living comfortably off invested funds, but her situation now deteriorated rapidly. Family tradition blamed her sons, and particularly Alfred, reputed to be a spendthrift who could persuade his mother to give him whatever he wanted: 'He was a waster who got through two fortunes and always went back to his mother for money until she had nothing left', according to family legend. Yet the only record of Alfred at this date is a newspaper report of a lecture he gave on soils to the Sevenoaks Farmers' Club in 1875; here he is predictably described as 'following in his father's footsteps'.[18] Perhaps Mrs Nesbit's money was not well invested, or she was given poor financial advice, or unknowingly was running down her capital rather than the interest on it. Later, when neither Alfred nor Harry looked capable of supporting themselves, let alone anyone else, it was easy enough to blame them for a deterioration which may have had a less definite beginning.

For Daisy the move from Halstead could only be a painful upheaval, and she was later to write a number of stories in which a young woman somehow wins the right to live in a beautiful old house that she and her widowed mother are broken-heartedly obliged to leave. In one version of this story the heroine discovers a will in her favour concealed in a secret passage or a secret drawer. Of course, concealed wills are a cliché of Victorian plotting, and secret passages and drawers fascinated Edith all her life; at a deeper level, they may have stood for secret powers and capacities within herself. In the alternative version, a young man who is also the rightful owner falls in love with her and proposes marriage, so that she and her mother can stay after all – a myth which at once provides her mother with a spacious and carefree existence and herself with lasting personal happiness. Both fictions express the wish to ensure her mother's security and contentment by keeping the old home, though in dreams the old home may stand, more generally, for the past. Whatever such fictions imply about her wishes, reality was, as always, to prove less amenable.[19]

If the years at Halstead must be reconstructed mainly from the final episode of *My School-Days*, the next five years of Edith's life are the most scantily documented of any period; she later took good care that their social transgressions remained secret. Using those official records that are relevant, a manuscript book of poetry and the few letters that have survived from this period, it is possible to reconstruct in outline what happened next, though many of the exact dates and circumstances are now lost beyond recall. It was probably late in 1875 that Mrs Nesbit moved into lodgings at 6 Mount Pleasant, Barnsbury Square, Islington.[20] When Daisy had stayed near there with the Boltons some years earlier, she had hated it: 'If I went for a walk, the sordid ugliness of Islington outraged the feelings of a child who had always found her greatest pleasures and life's greatest beauties in the green country.'[21]

London had more to offer a young woman than a child, yet it was in

Manchester, rather than London, that Daisy made her first true friend. With Saretta married and settled there, both Daisy and her mother visited her regularly, and it was on one of these trips, probably in the late summer of 1875 when they were between homes, that Daisy first met Ada Breakell, described thirty years later as 'my dearest and oldest friend'. Ada herself was not at home when Daisy first met the rest of the Breakell family, but she later answered a letter that Daisy had written to one of her sisters while the sister was away. As soon as they met, Daisy and Ada took to one another. Ada thought Daisy wonderfully good-looking and was greatly impressed to learn that some of her poems had been published. The girls went roller-skating together, and when Daisy left, she asked Ada and her sister to pay her a return visit to London. They did so, and Ada met Daisy's brother Harry who, she remembered, was temporarily estranged from their elder brother Alfred. Some years later Ada was to become engaged to Harry. Thereafter the girls visited one another and corresponded affectionately; Daisy wrote several impassioned poems to Ada, poems that now sound more unconventional than they did then, when close friendships with one's own sex were less self-conscious.[22] It was during one of Ada's visits, in 1877, that Daisy first met Hubert Bland. Ada remembered her friend as being very attractive and inclined to 'light flirting'. Edith was, indeed, already engaged – to a young bank clerk called Stuart Smith, who was, a little surprisingly, eighteen months younger than she was. Ada recalled an occasion when they went to see him at his office: 'H. Bland was also working there, and one day, on our going in to change a note, Stuart introduced Mr Bland to us; that was the first time E. Nesbit saw H.B., as far as I know.'[23]

For a young girl given to indulging in literary daydreams, Hubert Bland must have seemed the very embodiment of them. At twenty-two, he was three and a half years older than she, imposingly tall, broad-shouldered and handsome, with dark hair, a distinctly military moustache and bearing, and those fine aquiline features characteristic of the English aristocracy. He had a forceful personality, a lively mind and a strong sense of humour, and what was more, shared Daisy's love of poetry, her hopes of making the world a better place, and, as it seemed, her sense of romance. Only his voice spoiled him – it was thin, and, when he became excited, inclined to rise to a shrill screech, 'like the scream of an eagle'. When Ada paid her visit in the following year, Daisy's engagement to the young Stuart Smith had been broken off, and she was instead engaged to Mr Bland, though her mother was not at all happy about this. Neither Mr Bland's manner nor his prospects recommended themselves as those of a suitable son-in-law.[24]

Had Mrs Nesbit known a little more about Hubert Bland, she would have been considerably more uneasy. Though Hubert looked such a gentleman, and in later life talked of landed relatives living in Yorkshire, he was in fact pure Cockney, born and bred in Woolwich, a depressed area lying behind the docks and around the Royal Arsenal. Here his paternal grandfather Cornelius had been a plumber and house-painter, his maternal grandfather had kept a public house, while his father Henry, now dead for many years, had been a reasonably prosperous commercial clerk. Hubert was the adored youngest child who lived at home with his widowed mother at 46 Samuel Street. He had been born round the corner from there at 22 Wood Street (now Wood Hill) on 3 January 1855. The census, taken four years earlier, records his parents, Henry and Mary Ann Bland, living at Wood Street with two sons, Henry and Percy, and a daughter Helen, aged nine, eight and seven, respectively. Like Daisy, Hubert was the youngest, and he was also something of an afterthought, receiving the special attention that often goes with that position in the family. His father owned the houses at Wood Street, Samuel Street, and a third one at 29 Frances Street, close by.[25] They were small but respectable terrace houses, either bombed or pulled down many years ago to make way for tower blocks. Samuel Street lies just behind the Royal Dockyard and close to the Royal Artillery Barracks; from an early age Hubert had admired and envied the uniformed cadets, and he later developed a passionate desire to go into the army. That there had not been enough money to buy him a commission had been the first and greatest disappointment of his life. It had left him understandably resentful of a social system which had baulked him of an entirely honourable ambition.

Bland had a quick and eager intelligence, and an analytical, if strongly prejudiced mind. He had made the most of his education at various local schools, but, with no connections or financial backing, he had been obliged to take a tedious job as a bank clerk. Always a keen reader and thinker, he had naturally been interested in the meetings of social protest organized in and around Woolwich by various communist and socialist groups. At these he had met figures such as the young Eleanor Marx, and Henry M. Hyndman, leader of the Social Democratic Federation. Bland was very much the type of disaffected young intellectual whose eagerness to change the world through political action reflected, in part at least, his own lack of opportunities. But what he lacked in opportunities, he more than made up for in personal attractions. Hubert was well aware of his gifts and abilities, and in particular of his powerful charm for women. His own daughter was to describe him as 'absolutely irresistible to the women he paid court to, not only before the event of capture but after.'[26]

Though Hubert Bland seldom recalled his youth in his essays, the one paragraph he did write about it is characteristically focused on his masculinity. The context is humorous (it occurs in an essay entitled 'If I were a Woman'), but the subject was one that he took only too seriously:

> I don't know why, probably quite without good reason, but I have from the very earliest age, cherished and petted the conviction that I was a particularly and peculiarly masculine person. I had my first love-affair at the age of eight (I have forgotten her name, but I still have a lively recollection of her side-spring boots and white stockings), and a year later I adventured upon my first cigar. At ten, I fought a prolonged battle with a drummer boy in the Royal Welsh Regiment, and, although it is true the credit of the British infantry was well maintained, I left my mark on the red-coated lad's honest face. At twelve I was formally engaged to the most charming of her sex.

When he met Daisy, Hubert already had an 'understanding' with Maggie Doran, his mother's paid companion. She was a lively girl, about a year younger than he was, whose father ran a dyer's business in Beckenham High Street. Indeed, Maggie was soon to bear Hubert a son. Mary Ann Bland liked Maggie, and was naturally anxious that he should marry her and regularize their relationship.[27]

Hubert was a delightful companion. He and Daisy spent as much time as they could together, and on one memorable occasion she took him to visit her old home at Halstead. Here the pleasure of rediscovering the past was combined with the lovers' excitement at discovering one another, of shared enthusiasms and mutual self-revelations. Many years later Edith wrote a short story, 'A Holiday', which recalls this occasion. A young poet and a school teacher he has met on the train spend an idyllic summer day together. Travelling in the same compartment from London, they get off at Knockholt Junction and walk through Halstead to Edith's favourite Chevening Park, where they picnic. The weather is idyllic and

She, too, had read her Keats and her Shelley and her Browning – and could cap and even overshadow his random quotations . . . Aloud, she said,

'There's a place under beech trees – a sort of chalk plateau – I used to have picnics there with my brothers when I was a little girl –' . . .

When lunch was over they sat on the sloped, short turf and watched the rabbits in the warren below. They sat there and they talked. And to the end of her days no one will ever know her soul as he knew it that day, and no one ever knew better than she that aspect of his soul which he chose that day to represent as its permanent form.[28]

At the end of the story they kiss and part for ever, for it is intended to illustrate the adverse effects of an over-developed 'literary sense'. Daisy's day at Halstead with Hubert, as she described it at the time in a letter to Ada, sounds charmingly ingenuous by comparison:

> Yesterday was awfully pleasant. Mr Bland and I went to Halstead and had no end of a 'nice time' – we went into the woods – and sat about – caught (and kissed) a chaffinch – had lunch in the kitchen of a funny old-fashioned Inn – came back to the station through the grounds of the Oakleys' house – home by train and a sumptuous drive in a hansom cab to conclude the most charming day I have ever spent. The country was fresh, young and jolly. So were we . . .
>
> I wish I could give you some faint slight idea of the jolly larks we had yesterday – T'were foine – we could not for a long time get *anything* to eat as a ghastly famine seemed prevalent for *miles* round Halstead – but at last we got into the queerest little 'Pub' – and having recd the usual answer 'Not a thing in the house, sir' – we felt despair gnawing chill at our vitals and I think our faces of woe softened the heart of that Innkeeper, for he relented and said 'If cold boiled ham – . . . ?' We pressed him to our bosoms (or felt like doing so) and fed – . At the risk of seeming 'young' I *must* reiterate. It was *fine!*[29]

Hubert's ability to 'talk like a book' when he wanted to amuse her, in an absurd parody of the pretentious literary language of the day (a trait inherited by Oswald, Albert's uncle, and many another young Nesbit hero) resonates through her letter. One can hear his voice behind hers. Yet delightful as that day must have been for both of them, what was Mrs Nesbit thinking of, allowing her young and attractive daughter to wander round the countryside, visit a 'pub' and sit about in the woods with a young man, and all unchaperoned? Did she, when her finances gave out, feel that she no longer had to live up to middle-class standards of watchfulness, or was Daisy's will already too strong for her mother? Daisy certainly seems to have enjoyed a degree of freedom exceptional among girls of her generation and class, at every stage, and she had an unusual self-confidence and self-reliance. She took good care, however, not to allow her own daughters a comparable freedom when they reached the same age. By then she had learned that young women seldom flout social taboos without paying a high price.

Daisy's letter to Ada describing her visit to Halstead was written from the Guildhall Library where she used to go to read, write or think while waiting to meet Hubert in his lunch hour, as she explains:

> I have not gone to Miss Macbean's after all, as circumstances over wh. no control prevented M[other] from going to Manchester, and I did not care to leave her alone at Mount Pleasant. I am spending the morning here as I am going to meet Mr Bland at noon . . .[30]

In a novel written thirty-five years later as a kind of tour of her own passional life, the hero leaves the heroine there to wait for him, telling her

> 'It's a beautiful place – very quiet, very calm. And the officials are the best chaps I've ever found in any library anywhere . . . Write your name in the book – . . . and go and sit at one of the side tables – they're like side chapels in a cathedral – and stay there till I come.'

When he rejoins her, they walk 'in silence down the gallery hung with Wouvermans and his everlasting grey horse'.[31]

Two other letters to Ada written at about this time (though unfortunately undated) struggle unsmilingly with some of the huge and intractable questions that trouble the young during the difficult business of growing up. Their tone is naïve; their author clearly took herself very seriously, and the total absence of the irony or self-mockery so characteristic of her later work helps us to understand why, in her early days, she feared her brothers' laughter. Later she was to build in such ironies, having assimilated and internalized their more robust, humorous and practical view of life.

> How different I was this time, last year! – Now I see the world through 'larger, other eyes,' – but the increased light brings with it infinitely increased sorrow. – Do you not find it so? – See – I am in a moralizing mood – do you mind? I wonder if it is *hard* to be *great*. It seems to me that all our lives we are trying *not* to be great – I fancy the real obstacle to human greatness lies in the backwardness of the human mind to conceive it. Greatness is around us on all sides, but we are mistrustful of the fact, and while its sun shines in upon us at every instant, we are for

ever shading it off with our timid hands. Greatness is easy – not difficult
– it is *giving up* ill – not acquiring good alone – but *oh*! to acquire is so
unutterably more easy than to *renounce*.

A truce to this –

Don't you think young men are very *soft* as a rule? – and yet most of
them seem to have *some* actual not *negative* good in them, which is more
than we say for all our own sex. Perhaps the men say that of us, though –
who can tell? – in wh. case it is more easy to account for the interest wh.
most of them seem to take in that 'saddest of sad sights, the
uninteresting faces of commonplace women' –

It's rather hard on you, is it not, to bore you with a letter like this. I
might treat you worse though. – as I treat Mr Bland sometimes – with
vicious and long expositions of one-sided views on every conceivable
subject of non-interest to humanity.

Another letter struggles defeatedly with similarly vast and nebulous
topics, perhaps 'because I feel rather dismal tonight':

I'm worried with trying to *understand* things. What good is my life to
me? What good can I do with it? *Can* I do *anything*?

Is life a dream and death a reality? – Or is *death* the substance? –

I think on – and on – I *nearly* get an answer and then – just as I think I
am attaining to what I so desire, it slips – and I lose my chance and then –
I have only to 'dry my eyes and laugh at my fall' and humbly begin my
train of thought all over again – I shall never be answered – I think still
and from my thoughts *gain* nothing – *attain* nothing, *see* nothing of all
that my soul longs to grasp

'Only I discern –
Infinite passion and the pain
Of finite hearts that yearn.'

I'd better stop, I think. I shall only sink into a veritable miry slough,
represented by my own ridiculous system of bad metaphysics – and, as I
don't want to drag you down with me I won't go on – on paper – In my
thoughts I sink or swim – alone . . .[32]

By the end of 1878 Daisy was deeply in love with Hubert. Both of
them were ardent admirers of the Brownings, as the letter just quoted
indicates – later they were to join the Browning Society – and she was
inclined to regard their relationship in terms of that greatest of poetic
love affairs. At Christmas she bought a little leather-covered notebook
and painted upon it a pretty sheaf of daisies. Inside she inscribed it 'To
Hubert Bland from Daisy Nesbit, for Xmas 1878' and copied into it
the passionate sonnet sequence that Elizabeth Barrett had written for

her husband, *Sonnets from the Portuguese*.[33] These included such favourite love poems as

> How do I love thee? Let me count the ways . . .

and

> If thou must love me, let it be for nought
> Except for love's sake only . . .

The effect of the inscription is to identify Edith, to some extent, with Elizabeth Barrett; it suggests that she now felt something of the open and passionate commitment to Hubert that Elizabeth there expressed for Robert Browning: 'these', it seems to say, 'are my feelings too'. An unfinished sonnet of her own may have been designed to accompany the little book:

> Go! little book – where I would gladly be
>   And take the chance which I would gladly take.
>   Be treasured for a while, for love's sweet sake
> And afterwards be cast by heedlessly –[34]

While copying out Elizabeth Barrett's sonnets, she was evidently struggling to write Hubert some love sonnets in a similar vein, but that rare combination of passion, spontaneity and mastery of form was harder to achieve than it looked – or so the following example would suggest:

> Now Fate has parted us a little space
>   And I, who yearn to hold you once again,
>   See meeting's pleasure through our parting's pain
> And dream, through solitude, of your dear face;
> But when I strive to teach my hand to trace
>   An image of my soul – I strive in vain,
>   And, ever striving, ne'er my end can gain;
> The lines my hand would form, my tears efface.
> Well is it that I fail, did I succeed,
>   I think so truly all your mind and heart
>   Are part of mine, as mine of yours are part
> That if the picture painted were, indeed,
> You would not find a new line in the whole,
> But, in a looking-glass, see your own soul.[35]

As a poetic model, Elizabeth Barrett's sonnets set too high a standard for the beginner. Nor were the Brownings' mutual raptures –

> O Lyric Love, half-angel and half-bird
> And all a wonder and a wild desire . . .

– really a suitable precedent for an inexperienced young girl, with too little in the way of protection and, in a society that punished the unconventional, everything to lose.

It is not difficult to guess what happened next, though exactly when it happened is less certain. Some clues may be found in the cheap black linen-covered notebook, into which her early poems are copied out in (fading) sepia ink in her large flowing hand. Inside the cover is written 'Daisy Bland, Aug. 27. 1879', and underneath, in darker ink and a later handwriting, are the words 'deeply regretted', underlined. The very first poem in the book is significantly titled 'Après' ('Afterwards'), and dated July 1879. It begins

> So now our bright brief love is done,
>   How sweet its dreams, my dear –
> The joy you coveted is won,
>   The end you chose is here.
> The end of all you cared to give –
> A love too weak to live!

A later poem, entitled *'Aimer – c'est être voue à la douleur, sans retour'* ('To love is to be condemned to endless sorrow') and dated 7 June 1879, is rather more explicit. It traces the course of a love affair, cynically concluding

> This is the end that has always grown
> From a woman's love, and a man's desire!

The second stanza expresses passionate physical love with an unusual directness, given the age and sex of its author:

> When you shewed me the depths and the heights of love,
> The passion of pleasure, and all its pain,
> With all the sweets and delights thereof
> My heart gave one sob, and was still again.
> Laid low in your arms, through your mouth's caress,
> A strong enchantment, a subtle power
> Shewed all life as small, – as a thing far less –
> Than the least light breath of that fleeting hour.

A third poem, dated July 1879, is addressed 'To Sophia (ever a virgin)'. Here she sneers at the prudential wisdom of the prude who has never been asked, demanding

> Do you think, if love lay at your feet
>   You would have the strong will to refuse it,
>   Would you still keep your character, sweet,
>   If you'd any inducement to lose it?[36]

Poetry, of course, cannot constitute proof, but the emphasis of these poems on the surrender to physical love, and the male lover's consequent lessening of interest does suggest that Daisy had recently experienced something of the kind herself. At any rate, the poems are no longer stale variations on themes from the Brownings' repertoire. They imply that, at some point in the recent past, Daisy had allowed Hubert to make love to her. By mid-summer, she was beginning to be afraid that, in doing so, she had lost him. The second of the poems quoted above anxiously asks

> *He* is my world, and does *he* reprove?
> *He* is my God, have I sinned to *him*?

That Hubert seduced her is certain; the evidence of the poems points to a date shortly before or during the summer of 1879. The resulting increase in tension between them might help to explain what followed.

The notebook poems make fascinating reading, but the book's inscription poses a further problem: what made Daisy Nesbit (who was not legally to become Mrs Bland for another eight months) begin her new copybook by signing herself 'Daisy Bland'? Into that book she copied out poems composed over the previous four years. What event could have made her feel as if she was beginning a new life, a life that finally committed her irrevocably to Bland and conferred on her the right to use his name? Young middle-class Victorian girls did not simply move in with their lovers and become common-law wives. Nor, given what followed, was this a mere try-out, like that of Catherine Earnshaw when she wrote out her name as 'Catherine Linton' and 'Catherine Heathcliff', in *Wuthering Heights*. In any case, the subscript 'deeply regretted' seems to rule out that particular explanation. Daisy had had her twenty-first birthday twelve days earlier, on 15 August; she was now legally independent, though she had nothing but her energy and talents to live on. Her mother had never liked Hubert Bland, or approved of their engagement and some kind of disagreement must have taken place, in which Mrs Nesbit in her usual mild way pointed out that Hubert looked no nearer fulfilling his promise of marriage, perhaps adding that she doubted whether he would ever do so. Daisy flew into a temper that was all the more passionate because her mother had voiced exactly those doubts that she herself now felt. She assured her mother that she was quite wrong, that Hubert was keener than ever, and that, since she had in any case attained her majority, she could marry whom she liked, and she would certainly marry Hubert. More than ever determined to prove her mother wrong, Daisy flounced out of the house, intending either to show how independent she was or even, by throwing herself on his mercy, to oblige Hubert to take pity on her cast-out state and repudiate her mother's unworthy suspicions once and for all. For she was now quite determined that he must.

Hubert's position was more complicated than she knew. Daisy was altogether a more interesting proposition than Maggie, being more intelligent, forceful and better connected, even though unfortunately she had no money of her own. For obvious reasons, he had not explained to his mother or Maggie that he had undertaken a second engagement, nor had he managed to tell Daisy that he wasn't as free to marry her as she supposed. So he did the best that he could, under these awkward circumstances. He helped her to find lodgings south of the river, well away from her old home at Islington and within comfortable walking distance of – but not inconveniently close to – his at Woolwich. The lodgings were with a family called Knowles at 8 Oxford Terrace, Greenwich, now 16 Dartmouth Row, on the edge of Blackheath. Today it is rather a grand address, but in the late 1870s the street had its shabby end. When Hubert settled her there late in August 1879, he gave her name as Mrs Bland, and the poetry notebook shows that she now felt she had a right to use it. This meant that he could spend the night with her, while she in turn had the satisfaction of being able to tell her family that he had been as good as his word.[37]

But, of course, he hadn't. It is impossible to guess whether he told her that a wedding would take a little while to arrange, or that the ceremony itself was of no legal significance, as long as they truly loved one another. Perhaps, like the French anarchist in their joint novel, *The Prophet's Mantle* (1885), he told her that his socialist principles would not allow him to marry:

> He had told her gravely and tenderly that he was at war with society and with most of its conventions, and that for him to marry in the ordinary sense of the word would be to compromise and deny every principle on which his life was founded. The true marriage, he had maintained, was fidelity and mutual love was more binding than could be a ceremony in which one of the performers did not believe. He loved her, he had said,

far too dearly to wish to deceive her in the smallest degree about his sentiments and so he felt bound to tell her that to him a legal marriage would be for ever impossible.

The novel's Russian philanthropist comments on these pious sentiments: 'I see that another life has been sacrificed on the altar of an abstraction.'[38]

Perhaps the whole subject of the delayed marriage was so embarrassing or painful to her, and so unwelcome to him, that they seldom or never actually discussed it. In any case, Bland did not move in as her husband, either then or later. Instead, he spent at least three nights a week at home with his mother in Samuel Street. He could have justified this to Daisy in terms of his duty towards his widowed mother, or else for business reasons, since at about this time or a little earlier, he had given up his job as a bank clerk and put what money he had into a small brush-manufacturing business. One reason he was anxious to get home regularly was, of course, to see Maggie, since he had made no attempt to explain his new commitment either to her or to his mother, nor to break off his love affair with her – it was to last for another ten years or so. Bland continued to spend several nights a week at Samuel Street until his mother's death in 1893. Until then, he used her address (Bowater Crescent, Woolwich – the lower end of Samuel Street was known as Bowater Crescent) for all his business correspondence. He did not tell his mother of his marriage for some time after the event. Effectively he was leading a double life.[39]

Meanwhile Daisy had told her family and friends that she was now married to Mr Bland. Ada, who had not been down to visit her since 1878, came to stay at Oxford Terrace during the winter of 1879–80 – she remembered that they had gone skating together at Dansent. Four years later, writing to Ada in Australia, Edith told her that she and Hubert were writing 'a delightfully weird story about a mummy and when we write I think of you. And the mummies we used to make of each other. Do you remember making one of that boy Frank at Oxford Terrace?'

In making mummies out of whatever domestic objects came to hand, Daisy was reverting to the childhood game that she had evolved to exorcise her terror of the mummies at Bordeaux. But now she had other, and more substantial problems to cope with. The Daisy of Oxford Terrace seems to have been half child and half woman, and there she would remain, caught between those two states, for the rest of her life. She must have felt all the adventurous child's excitement at her new-found freedom, yet there was the urgent problem of what to live on. Two poems of hers seem to have been accepted by the *Sporting Times* in September and October, and she dutifully toted her work round Fleet Street, but it was an exhausting and demoralizing business. And now the privileges of her new-found freedom were soon to be converted to responsibilities. It is impossible to tell whether she already knew she was pregnant when Ada came down to stay with her that winter, or at what stage and in what manner she found this out. Young ladies were commonly kept in a state of ignorance about their own bodies and Edith suffered from an embarrassment characteristic of her generation concerning all bodily functions. In the ordinary way, her mother would have been her natural confidant, but there may have been some residue of coolness between them after her precipitate 'marriage'. It's possible that she only discovered her condition by accident, like Alice Hatfield, the heroine of *The Prophet's Mantle*. When she collapses in a faint, everyone else suspects what is wrong with her, but it is left to the doctor to explain what has happened to her. The paragraph describing Alice's reaction to the news may embody something of what Daisy felt on a similar occasion. It includes several conflicting responses; perhaps, as women often do, Daisy felt something of them all:

> Alice had learned that that which she had feared, till a sort of hope had grown out of the very intensity of her fear – that which had seemed almost too terrible to be possible – was to be. She now had that certainty which is a spring of secret happiness to so many women, to some only a fresh care and anxiety, and to some, alas! the sign and token of social banishment – the warrant of disgrace and despair.[40]

The little black notebook includes no poems dated between September 1879 and 1881, and for what follows there are official records: Daisy's marriage certificate, dated 22 April 1880, the birth certificate of Paul Cyril Bland on 22 June and the census return for the following spring, 1881. Belatedly, Hubert led the seven-months pregnant Daisy to a registry office where they were married, with two strangers for witnesses:

> All that [she] remembered well. And what came afterward – the dingy house with the grimy door-step, and the area where dust and torn paper lay, the bare room, the few words that were a mockery of what a marriage service should be, the policeman who met them as they went in, the charwoman who followed them as they went out, the man at the

end of the long, leather-covered table . . . who wished them joy with, as it were, his tongue in his cheek. And the signing of names and dabbing of them with a little oblong of pink blotting-paper crisscrossed with the ghosts of the names of other brides and bridegrooms . . . and then they were walking down the sordid streets, she rather pale and looking straight before her and in her white-gloved hand the prize of the expedition, the marriage certificate . . . What a travesty of a wedding-day![41]

The marriage certificate is an odd document: Daisy, who forgot her father's Christian name in the stress of the event, gave her address as Oxford Terrace, but Hubert, always inclined to cover his tracks, gave his as 17 Devonshire Square. Devonshire Square is in the City, and at that time was mainly made up of lodging rooms over shops, so perhaps Hubert had once stayed there, or knew someone else who had, or perhaps it was his business address. It's unlikely that he was actually living there himself, or could have afforded to do so. They continued to live substantially apart. Later that summer, probably soon after Paul's birth, Daisy moved into a tiny house in Elswick Road, a newly built terrace off Loampit Hill, close to the Lewisham Road. The census taken in the spring of 1881 recorded 'Edith Bland, authoress' as living at 28 Elswick Road with her mother, presumably on a brief visit, baby Paul and two servants, the 'general' and a nursemaid (the younger servant was only fourteen). At the same time Hubert is recorded as living at 46 Samuel Street with his mother, Margaret Doran (described as a visitor) and one servant. Hubert gave his occupation as brush manufacturer, and his status as unmarried.[42]

3

NEW BEGINNINGS

The house at 28 Elswick Road where the Blands began their unconventional married life still looks like most young couples' first home, but today the street is patched and peeled and generally down-at-heel. In 1880, when the Blands moved in, however, the long terraces of stuccoed artisans' homes had only just been built. The houses were basically 'two up and two down' with several other very small rooms, and tiny yards at the back. They must always have felt crowded, once the ubiquitous living-in servant had been installed – and as narrow as a 'bandbox', which was how Edith later thought of it. Being both a practical and energetic girl, determined to make things work, she turned to and did what she could to make it more home-like: she ran up new curtains, tacked up deep chintz flounces around the mantelpiece and covered cushions to match, and she refurbished her mother's tatty cast-off furniture,[1] but a certain shabbiness lay behind and beneath the bright new coverings. One visitor remembered the cheap oil cloth on the hall floor, and the untrustworthy-looking chairs:

> The furniture was not all of one set . . . The carpet was very old, the sofa was concealed by a creton cover that hid it to the very casters, and the rest of the moveables were clearly spare pieces from the stock of [his] father or [her] mother . . .[2]

But despite her best and brightest efforts, things seemed to go wrong from the start. Not very long after Paul's birth that summer, Hubert caught smallpox. According to family legend, the maid had taken the baby to show off to her relatives, one of whom was already ill in bed with it, and the baby was thoughtlessly put down on the sick bed. Little Paul miraculously escaped infection, but his father somehow picked it up from his clothing. While the baby might have shared his mother's immunity, it seems unlikely that smallpox could really be picked up thus. That summer Hubert could actually have caught it almost anywhere, since there was a major smallpox epidemic in London, but the luckless maid became the scapegoat whose carelessness could be blamed for it. As always when things went wrong, Hubert went back to his mother, who nursed him with great care through this often fatal illness. Edith was not allowed, indeed did not dare, to go near him for more than two months. Eventually he recovered, but something of his good looks had gone – his face was now pock-marked. The strain of the disease that struck the city that year seems to have been peculiarly virulent. Thousands of Londoners fell ill, and temporary hospitals had to be set up to cope with them. In the face of all medical opinion, Hubert somehow managed to go down with it a second time.[3]

> Father was very ill . . . ; and while he was ill his business-partner went to Spain – and there was never much money afterwards. I don't know why. Then the servants left and there was only one, a General. A great deal of your comfort and happiness depends on having a good General . . .
>
> Then a great many people used to come to the door with envelopes with no stamps on them, and sometimes they got very angry, and said they were calling for the last time before putting it in other hands . . .
>
> And once a long, blue paper came; a policeman brought it, and we were so frightened. But Father said it was all right, only when he went up to kiss the girls after they were in bed, they said he'd been crying, though I'm sure that's not true. Because only cowards and snivellers cry, and my Father is the bravest man in the world.
>
> So you see it was time we looked for treasure . . .[4]

The opening of *The Treasure Seekers* recreates in a predominantly comic mode the Blands' desperate efforts to repair their fallen fortunes in the earliest years of their marriage. When Hubert recovered from his attacks of smallpox, his partner in the brush factory had apparently absconded with whatever funds there were, so that nothing was left.[5] Again this story includes a scapegoat element. While Hubert's partner may well have defrauded him, Hubert could never have had much money to put into the business in the first place; the eighties were years of economic depression, years when small businesses might well go to the wall without any help from greed or dishonesty. But however it happened, Hubert was now a man with responsibilities and no income. It was lucky for him that he had married a woman who was both determined and soon sufficiently competent to keep the household afloat by her own efforts.

Edith had already had single poems published in newspapers and magazines for some years before her marriage. Now the guineas or half-guineas she was paid for these, once merely pin-money, became a vital contribution to the family income, which could be further supplemented by writing short stories or sketches. Both poems and prose were accepted, on an occasional basis, by journals such as *The Weekly Dispatch*, *The Argosy* ('laden with golden grain'), *Longman's Magazine*, *Belgravia* and the fashion magazine *Sylvia's Home Journal*, in whose offices she was soon to meet her lifelong friend and companion Alice Hoatson. But hawking work round Fleet Street was exhausting and dispiriting, as even the cheerful Bastables found, when they tried to make their fortune by selling Noel's poetry:

> It was quite late in the afternoon when we got to Fleet Street. The gas was lighted and the electric lights. There is a jolly Bovril sign that comes off and on in different coloured lamps. We went to the *Daily Recorder* office, and asked to see the Editor. It is a big office, very bright, with brass and mahogany and electric lights.
>   They told us the Editor wasn't there, but at another office. So we went down a dirty street, to a very dull-looking place. There was a man there inside, in a glass case, as if he was a museum, and he told us to write down our names and our business . . . Then we waited on the stone stairs; it was very draughty. And the man in the glass case looked at us as if we were the museum instead of him. We waited a long time, and then a boy came down and said:
>   'The Editor can't see you. Will you please write your business?' And he laughed. I wanted to punch his head.
>   But Noel said, 'Yes, I'll write it if you'll give me a pen and ink, and a sheet of paper and an envelope.'
>   The boy said he'd better write by post.[6]

The miseries of trailing round Fleet Street, May's *Press Guide* in hand, were also recollected in Edith's novel *Daphne in Fitzroy Street*, where Daphne puts on her 'quietest hat and gown' and taking her little sister by the hand, 'went down into the City to call on editors. Someone had said . . . that the only way to sell your stuff for magazines was to call on editors yourself.'

She went out gaily, the child stepping beside her. She returned heavy footed with the child dragging after. And the brown paper parcel of sketches, whose string had been untied so often and so wearily, had grown strangely heavy to carry.

She can scarcely climb the stairs to her studio, and she tells her friend Claud, 'Oh, editors are hateful – even when you see them – and when you don't, and you generally don't – they're fiends, I believe.'[7] Nor did things go very much better when Edith followed the office boy's instructions and sent off her work by post. Mother in *The Railway Children* has a similar struggle to sell her work:

> Mother, all this time, was very busy with her writing. She used to send off a good many long blue envelopes with stories in them – and large envelopes of different sizes and colours used to come to her. Sometimes she would sigh when she opened them and say:-
> 'Another story come home to roost. O dear, O dear!' and then the children would be very sorry.
> But sometimes she would wave the envelope in the air and say:
> 'Hooray, hooray. Here's a sensible Editor. He's taken my story and this is the proof of it.'
> At first the children thought 'the Proof' meant the letter the sensible Editor had written, but they presently got to know that the proof was long slips of paper with the story printed on them.
> Whenever an Editor was sensible, there were buns for tea.[8]

As well as selling her writing, Edith had turned another talent to good account: she had discovered that she could sell greetings cards hand-painted with the formalized flowers and ferns then in vogue, flowers such as she had painted on the book for Hubert or on the cards she made for Ada; she then inscribed them with her own verses, thus commercializing one of the accomplishments nice young ladies might be expected to possess. This cottage industry, though more menial and less well-paid than writing, was also easier and less demanding, and at this stage of her life she was always glad to be given another batch of cards to paint. On one occasion, when she was two days late in delivering her painted cards to a firm of colour-printers in the City, the manager turned her away, telling her firmly that they never took in late work and her cards were no longer needed. She pleaded with him, and as he led her to the door, burst into tears. Thoroughly discomfited by this unexpected reaction, he relented, paid her generously for the cards she had done and gave her some more to be going on with.[9] No doubt her distress was real enough, but then and later this very emotional woman was inclined to use her emotions in a manipulative way. She was intensely self-willed, and the humiliation of weeping before a comparative stranger would have been far outweighed by the satisfaction of getting what she wanted. In a society which insisted upon women's weakness, a determined woman might well find herself obliged to exploit her frailties instead of her strengths.

The poetry notebook, silent for 1880, resumes with a darker ink and a thicker nib in 1881 with a series of 'farewell' poems: two are entitled 'Elle et Lui'. The third, called simply 'A Farewell', is dated June 1881. It begins

> How soon the ocean of dim distance rolls,
> Wave upon wave, between our parted souls!
> How little to each other now are we –
> And once how much I dreamed we two might be!
> I, who now stand with eyes undimmed and dry
>   To say Goodbye . . .
>
> I had no chain to bind you with at all,
> No grace to charm, no beauty to enthrall,
> No power to hold your eyes in mine and make
> Your heart on fire with longing for my sake
> Till all the yearning passed into one cry –
>   'Love – *not* goodbye'.
>
> Ah, no! I had no strength like that, you know,
> Yet my worst weakness was to love you so,
> So much too well, so much too well or ill –
> Yet even that might have been pardoned still –
> It would have been, had I been you, you I –
>   But now, goodbye . . .[10]

Edith could not, of course, bid a melodramatic farewell to Hubert, whatever his shortcomings as a husband. Psychologically more plausible in terms of their continuing to live together is a slightly later poem, 'Quieta non Movere' ('Let sleeping dogs lie'), rather precisely dated 'Oct. 1–10 1881'. Though the speaker is a man, the sense of a passion damaged yet liable to reawaken and even the images chosen seem to reflect her situation in one way or another:

If one should wake one's frozen faith
In sunlight of her radiant eyes,
Bid it forget its dream of death
In some new dream of Paradise;
Bid it forget the long, slow pain,
The agony, when, all in vain,
It fought for life, and how one swore,
Once cold, it should not waken more:

If from warm faith and hope set high
A lovely living child were born,
With eyes more clear than starlit sky,
And lips as pure as summer dawn;
Child-love might grow till one forgot
Old love, that was and now is not;
Forgot that far-off time of tears,
And all those desolated fears.

And yet of faith, hope, love – one knows
So well what end the years will make . . .[11]

These verses suggest that Edith had been through a period of disillusion, of psychological if not literal valediction. The image of rebirth in the second poem is only an image, but it gains a certain poignancy from the fact that Edith herself was pregnant for the second time when she wrote it.

A daughter, Mary Iris, was born on 2 December 1881. She was probably named after Edith's dead sister, though her grandmother had also been a Mary, and Hubert's mother was Mary Ann. At some point, Hubert must finally have steeled himself to tell his mother not only of his marriage, but also of the births of two further grandchildren, though Ada Breakell recalled that 'He did not let his Mother know . . . for quite a long time'.[12] At some point within the first year or two of her marriage, probably through opening a letter of his, Edith found out about Hubert's 'understanding' with Maggie, and that she had borne him a child – opening other people's letters was a bad habit of hers, noticed by Shaw and later greatly resented by her children.[13] If the verses just quoted are read autobiographically, they suggest that she may have made the discovery in the early summer of 1881, soon after she knew herself to be pregnant again. She was already more wary and may well have suspected that something of the kind was going on. Even so the discovery must have come as a shock. Hubert had, however, chosen *her* when faced with a choice between them, and armed with this confidence and determined to behave generously and avoid conventional self-righteousness, Edith visited Maggie and made friends with her. They remained friends, even though her love affair with Hubert was not yet at an end. Maggie later followed the Blands into the Fabian Society. What happened to Maggie's son, and even what his name was, remains mysterious. His birth certificate has never come to light, nor is he recorded as living at Samuel Street with his mother in the 1881 census entry, though Iris remembered that he was 'older than any of us and must therefore have been born some time before [1880]'. His absence from any records suggests an 'Oliver Twist job'.[14]

After the failure of Hubert's brush-making business, he had difficulty in finding work again – it was a period of rising unemployment. Eventually he found quite a decently-paid job as secretary to the Hydraulic Power Company, where he worked for four or five years until they decided that they wanted a professional engineer to do the job instead (or so they told him).[15] In the meanwhile he had begun to help Edith with the magazine stories she found so burdensome, sometimes finishing them off and sometimes taking stories she had started and developing them in new directions. He found writing a congenial occupation, and enjoyed the opportunities that fiction provided for generalizing about human nature. Hubert was probably responsible for the frequent epigrammatic or moralizing comments that occur in the stories they wrote together, comments imbued with a man-of-the-world air that he liked to affect – sometimes they came rather close to home: 'There is a good deal that Alice does not know. It is perhaps as well. Wives are none the happier for knowing too much of their husband's past.'[16] Although his earliest work was the fiction he wrote with Edith, Bland was later to become a celebrated columnist and for most of his life he earned his living as a professional reviewer and essayist.

In Edith's novel *The Red House*, the newly married husband and wife live in a 'bandbox' and are much given to finishing off each other's work, when they are not blissfully indulging themselves in domestic tasks better left to the servants – they are both inclined to prefer finding jobs around the house to getting on with their professional assignments. The novel paints a delightful if quite implausibly rosy picture of the early years of the Blands' marriage; the couple in the novel even use the same pet names for one another ('cat' and 'pussy') as the Blands did. By encouraging Hubert to take up writing, Edith had played the

role of midwife to his real talents, helping him to discover his true
métier. Her example showed him that journalism could provide a
respectable career in which one might nevertheless remain one's own
master. Neither of the Blands was at all suited to the routine of office
life. But the debts between them ran both ways, for if Edith pointed
Hubert in the right direction, he showed her the crucial importance of
tone of voice in establishing the authenticity of whatever was to be
said. All his writing depends on it, and it was only when she discovered
how to use it for her own purposes that Edith achieved her first real
success.

The early years of the Blands' married life are scantily recorded, but
by 1884 a vivid enough picture emerges from Edith's letters to her
friend Ada Breakell, who that January had sailed with her trousseau
for Australia, in the hope of marrying her fiancé, Edith's brother
Harry. Neither of the two Nesbit brothers had done at all well: Alfred
was married, and now worked as an analytical chemist at his own
London laboratory at 38 Gracechurch Street. He was particularly
interested in colouring and dyes: he patented a new ink for postmarks,
a method of preventing cheques from being fraudulently altered (never
used), and even invented the green carnation of the nineties;[17] but he
made very little money out of his discoveries, and when he died in
1894, he left his wife and two children practically destitute. Harry had
been even less successful at finding a niche for himself, so he emigrated
to Australia, as his uncle Edward had done. Ada decided to follow him
out there but something went wrong soon after she arrived and Harry
did not 'come up to scratch'. Either he had not yet found a job that
enabled him to support her, or else he decided it had all been a mistake
anyway; perhaps he simply lost his nerve, though he was eventually to
marry, some years later, and have a son, John Collis. Ada was left high
and dry. Edith's letters to Ada constantly urge her to write and say
how she and Harry are getting on: 'I wish I was Harry. I suppose he is
very happy now. I know some people in Blackheath who are just going
to be married – and whenever I see them I think of you and Harry.'[18]

For a while at least Ada felt too distressed or embarrassed to explain
her failure, even to her closest friend and confidante. Edith herself had
played a large part – perhaps too large a part – in promoting their
engagement. She was passionately fond of Ada and would dearly have
loved to formalize their relationship into sisterhood – indeed one letter
suggests that she would like to have married Ada herself! Edith always
wanted to make her dearest friends part of her family: Alice Hoatson

recalled Edith insisting that they were really distantly related to one another – nothing else could explain their resemblance. When Ada and Harry first became engaged, Edith could not have anticipated that this step might take Ada away from her for ever:

> No one [she wrote in April 1884] has loved you so long as I – (outside your own people I mean) – and I don't think anyone could love you *more*. It might be possible to love you *better* – and yet I don't know about that either. I think so often of those first few minutes in the bedroom at Dulwich. It was then I first felt and *realized* what it *meant* for you to be going away. If I live to be a hundred I shall never forget that evening. *My* Ada – my dear – my friend. I perceive that I am becoming very melancholy . . .[19]

Edith's letters to Ada record some of the small day-to-day events in her life; writing them out, Edith explained, made her feel closer to Ada:

> I am nearer to you when I am telling you even the little things of my daily life. Ada, I hope we shall never leave off telling each other the 'little things' – Life is made up of them – and nothing in either of our lives is too small to interest the other, I believe.[20]

Inevitably many of these 'little things' concerned the welfare and development of the children:

> Today Hubert and I and Paul went for a walk in the country. Hubert taught Paul to climb stiles, an accomplishment of which he (Paul) is very proud, as one always is of anything newly acquired. This afternoon we went to sleep, and this evening we have been diligently writing stories . . .
> Paul has cut his leg and had to have it sewn up. It was rather fearful for him, poor little chap . . .
> Paul is now learning to read . . .[21]

She tells Ada proudly about a dress she has made for herself:

> I have a new dress of terra cottery crushed strawberry mixture nun's cloth with dark velvet bodice and *trappings*. It does not suit me but is rather pretty, and fits me perfectly. I made it myself – ! – ! with a Butterick's pattern. I wore it last night.[22]

The difficulties of getting and keeping work are a recurrent concern in her letters:

> Hubert and I have just done a story for Longmans which has been accepted and will appear in the Christmas Number. Hubert wrote the

first part and we finished it together. £10. We have now finished *The Social Cobweb* [a serial that had run from January to March 1884 in the *Weekly Dispatch*], I am sorry to say it for £3.0.0 a week is not to be sneezed at. I suppose I shall go on writing poems for the *W.D.* . . .

April 11, 1884 I am not doing any painting just now, I am sorry to say – so I try to write as many stories as I can – but it is uphill work – writing when you don't feel a bit inclined. I hope the *Weekly D[ispatch]* will give me some more work later on in the year. We have just sent a joint story to *Belgravia* – of whose acceptance I feel some faint hopes. I still write poems for the *W.D.* . . . What seems to be the worst of my present life is that I have no time to do any *good work* – in the way of writing verse I mean. I want to write another longish poem or two and there don't seem to be any blank sheets of time lying loose round, to scribble it down on . . . If ever you think of any *plots* – mind you let me know. They are our great difficulty. The *writing* is a much more simple matter than the construction . . .

We are going to try writing a novel. Did I tell you I am writing nothing now by myself except poems. In all stories Hubert and I 'go shares' – I am sure it is much better when we write together than when we write separately . . .[23]

The letter to Ada just quoted was written over about a fortnight in April 1884; on Easter Sunday (13th), she drew for her friend a rather self-conscious portrait of herself as a devoted young mother:

Sunday – Easter Sunday. I am all alone in the house, 'alone' that is, as a far as grown-ups are concerned – for the bunnies are here. I have just got Iris to sleep, and laid her down and Paul is standing watching my scribbling pen – his quietness will not last long, so I will provide him with a box of bricks and then go on with this. It is so quiet – the *peculiar* stillness attaching only to Sunday *afternoons*. Especially from two to four. The maid has gone out for the day and I have just washed up the dinner things, and am sitting in the kitchen. The kettle is singing on the fire and the kitten purring before it. I sit here in my 'deck' chair, and my blue dress – and write to you. Charming domestic picture, isn't it. Paul and his bricks make a feature in it. His continual 'Look, mother, look' only *emphasizes* the silence – like the hum of bees and the stirring of trees, leaves undisturbed the silence of a June day in the country. The country – ah! I was there yesterday. Hubert and I went to Halstead, and had a long delicious time among the woods and primroses and dog-violets. But though Spring is well awake in these same woods, they are not *green*, only *grey*. The dead grass is *grey* – the birch stems are grey – the hazel stems where the light catches them are grey. The pale green of the budding leaves blends in a curious way with the brown twigs, so that

the trees look grey too – at a little distance, and the windflowers and
wood sorrel are thick enough to make the ground look white, as with
frost or snow. We had a delightful day – and brought home no end of
primroses. I got dreadfully sunburnt and am no end tired – but it was
worth it. The woods were near Bath's. Harry will remember them.
Where we used to picnic, in the old days. I seem to have lived three or
four lives *right through* since those old times – I wonder if your life
seems as long to you as mine does to me . . .

Saturday [April] 19th . . . Today I have washed my hair and have not
been out. I have done two sheets 'sides into middle' [cutting sheets in
half and sewing them up the middle was a piece of domestic economy to
make them last longer] – written some paragraphs for a newspaper –
cooked the dinner, nursed Iris for a whole hour – in the vain hope of
getting her to sleep. She persistently *waked* – and I eventually gave it up.
– I have also painted some cards. I am thankful to say I got some
yesterday. I do hope the supply will now be kept up. We have just
finished a story about a dream. I don't mind telling *you* that I feel an
inward conviction that it will be refused . . .

25th April 1884 . . . The children's characters are developing. Iris
ought certainly to have been the boy – and Paul the girl. *He* says '*You* do
it, mover' – *she* says 'I do it by *myself*' – with indescribable emphasis and
decision. They are very good children, I think, as children go – and if
only we don't add to their number I am satisfied. But that is a big
'if' . . .[24]

Ironically, though Edith could not have realized it yet, she had
become pregnant again at about the time she wrote this letter. Fabian
Bland, whose name should have been so auspicious, was born on 8
January 1885 and was the only one of the Blands' three children not to
reach adulthood. He was named after the Blands' great new
enthusiasm, the newly-founded Fabian Society, which now took up
much of their time and attention and through which they hoped to
effect changes in society. 'Fabian' was not, however, entirely unknown as a Victorian Christian name. The small hero of Mrs
Molesworth's *Carrots – Just a little Boy* (1876) had been christened
Fabian, though he was always known by his nickname.

Hubert had been interested in socialism from his days in Woolwich,
and as his financial problems became less desperate, he began to
involve himself in several idealistic groups that were just then coming
into being. In a paper read to the Fabian Society in 1907, 'The Faith I
Hold',[25] he light-heartedly sketched out his own intellectual development, beginning with his reaction against the pessimism and despair of

Schopenhauer's philosophy. From this, he turned to the activism of socialism, and in doing so, he was particularly influenced by three men, only one of whom could really be said to be a socialist at all. The first was the eloquent and enthralling American economist Henry George; the second was Henry Hyndman, the clever, prickly founder of the Social Democratic Federation (known as the S.D.F., and founded in 1883 – both the Blands joined); and the third was the mysterious and charismatic Thomas Davidson, whose Socratic method was designed to question catchphrases and lazy thinking, and to cast doubt on rigid systems of ideas that did not lead men back to the life of the spirit. Davidson was thus very far from approving the activist positions that some at least of his disciples would later try out, but by an odd twist of events, it was through Davidson's disciples that the Fabian Society was first founded.

In the same paper, Bland gave an amusing account of the kind of atmosphere in which the Fabian Society, and several other radical groups of the period came into being:

> The early eighties was a period of Movements, of coteries, literary, artistic, social ... and of Influences. Now Movements and coteries may be silly, pretentious, irrelevant; but at least they are interesting. It is gratifying to one's feeling of self-consequence, it engenders a satisfying sense of superiority, to shut oneself up, as it were, in a little mansion of one's own, and with a few eclectic spirits to think scorn of the world outside. So it was with some of us. We felt that we had had the misfortune to be born in a stupid, vulgar, grimy age, an age, too, that was getting stupider, grimier, more vulgar, every day, and so we turned away from it to a little world within a world, a world of poetry, of pictures, of music, of old romance, of strangely designed wall-papers, and of sad-coloured velveteen. Many of us (though I was not one of them) wore velveteen all day. I wore it only in the evening.[26]

Bland's references to wallpapers and old romances obviously suggest William Morris, who had belonged to Hyndman's S.D.F., but later broke away to form the Socialist League. Morris's presence at early Fabian meetings and similar discussion groups acted as a stimulus, and both his poetry and his idealized view of the past were to influence Edith strongly. Societies certainly seem to have been very much in the air at this moment, and when the Blands were not meeting their friends at political debates, they met them at the Browning and Shelley Societies, the Lewisham Literary Society, at various reading groups and even at societies for psychic research.

On 24 October 1883, a group of Thomas Davidson's disciples met at the rooms of a young stockbroker called Edward Pease who lived at 17 Osnaburgh Street. Their aim was to begin the New Life. Among those present were the socialist Harry Champion, Havelock Ellis, James Leigh Joynes and Frank Podmore. A fortnight later, a further meeting was held, and this time Hubert and J. Glode Stapelton, a well-to-do friend of the Blands, were present. Pease, as host, was asked to take the chair, but already Davidson's less worldly followers were alarmed at how things were developing, and thought that the socialist supporters like Pease and Podmore lacked 'inwardness' and were too 'mundane'.[27] On 7 December the group met again at the house of Dr Burns-Gibson and adopted the following draft constitution for the Fellowship of the New Life:

Object: The cultivation of a perfect character in each and all.
Principle: The subordination of material things to spiritual things.
Methods: (1) The supplanting of the spirit of self-seeking by that unselfish regard for the general good.
(2) Simplicity of living.
(3) The highest and completest education of the young.
(4) The introduction as far as possible of manual labour in conjunction with intellectual pursuits.

At this meeting Bland was in the chair, as he had been at an earlier meeting on 23 November. In the margin of the new society's Minute Book, an anonymous pencil annotation comments: 'The historical sense increasingly detects in this chairman appointed . . . the materialistic cuckoo who was to effect the dispersal of the Davidsonian brood of spiritual singing birds.'[28] A split between the spiritual followers who sought to remake themselves inwardly, and the activists – Bland, Pease and Podmore – was now imminent.

Bland also chaired the historic meeting on 4 January 1884 at which a group of members seceded from the Fellowship to establish the Fabian Society ('Cuckoo hatched', comments the same pencil). The new name was suggested by another stockbroker and friend of Pease, Frank Podmore: Fabius Cunctator, he explained, had been famous for delaying until the right moment, but when he struck, he struck hard, or, as Edith liked to say, 'straight from the shoulder'. Chubb, the leader of the New Fellowship, formally thanked Pease for his assistance as secretary during its formation and Podmore offered the new-born Fabian the Fellowship's good wishes for success. From this point on, although a number of members of the Fellowship regularly came to the Fabian Society, the idealists and activists began to go their separate ways, though then and later they were never wholly distinct. Edith, writing to Ada in the spring of 1884, described the state of tension between the two elements:

> There are two distinct elements in the F.S. The practical and the visionary – the first being much the strongest – but a perpetual warfare goes on between the parties wh. gives to the Fabian an excitement wh. it might otherwise lack. We belong – needs say – to the practical party, and so do most of our most intimate friends – Stapelton, Keddell, Watts, Estcourt, etc.[29]

Early in March, to her evident surprise and pleasure, Edith was elected to the Pamphlets Committee, no doubt because of her literary experience. There she joined Hubert, Stapelton, Keddell, Estcourt, a house painter called W. L. Phillips, and Miss Dale Owen (Robert Owen's daughter), and by 4 April they had prepared the first of the Fabian Tracts for publication. It had been drafted mainly by Keddell and Phillips and was entitled 'Why Are the Many Poor?'

> The Fabian Society takes up a good deal of my thoughts just now [she wrote to Ada in March 1884], I am also doing a good bit of serious reading – Among other things, Büchner's *Man*, Mill's *Subjection of Women*, Louis Blanc's *Historical Revelations* and an intensely interesting book which Harry would like called *Esoteric Buddhism* by Sinnett. You see my reading is rather mixed and miscellaneous – but it is the fate of most women only to be able to get a smattering, and I seem to want to read all sorts of things at once.[30]

Since many of Edith's surviving letters to Ada were written during that spring of 1884 when the Fabian Society was just beginning to get off the ground, they are often preoccupied with its meetings and members:

> On Friday evening we went to Mr Pease's to tea, and afterwards a Fabian meeting was held. The meeting was over at 10 – but some of us stayed till 11.30, talking. The talks after the Fabian meetings are very jolly. I do think the Fabians are quite the nicest set of people I ever knew . . .
> Yesterday Mr Pease came at 3. His people are Quakers and he has the cheerful serenity and self-containedness common to the sect. I like him very much. We went for a walk in the afternoon and got home about seven, supped and had a long evening of talk, which was very nice.[31]

Anxious that Ada should understand her latest enthusiasm, Edith devoted a long letter to describing what the Fabian was and who belonged to it, ending with thumbnail sketches of her new acquaintances:

> I should like to try and tell you a little about the Fabian Society – Its aim is to improve the social system – or rather to spread its news as to the possible improvement of the said S.S. There are about thirty members – some of whom are working men. We meet once a fortnight – and then someone reads a paper and we all talk about it. We are now going to issue a *pamphlet* – and the last meeting was devoted to the discussion of that same. I am on the 'Pamphlet Committee' – Now *can* you fancy *me* on a committee? I really surprise myself sometimes.[32]

Edith was alternately amused and intrigued by the new life-styles that she came across at the Fabian. Some of those who were in revolt against the dominant capitalist ethos of Victorian England had rejected more than its economics: the richly cluttered decor of the period, the mahogany and thick Turkey carpets were being replaced with distempered walls, scrubbed deal and coconut matting; the stiffly boned costumes gave place to flowing Liberty gowns and the heavy meals to 'plain living and high thinking'. Marjorie Davidson, who was to marry Edward Pease in 1889, raised an even more fundamental issue: 'We want to know what is the ideal Socialist home – I don't think we ought to have servants, but that is an open question.'[33] In *The New Treasure Seekers* (1904) Edith invented a Mr and Miss Sandal who exemplified many of the odd but worthy characteristics of the New Lifers – she may well have had a particular brother and sister in mind: James Leigh Joynes, an ex-Eton master, and his sister Kate. Kate married Henry Salt, another ex-Eton master who had also given up his teaching in favour of the simple life. The Salts took a cottage in Surrey, and their close friend Edward Carpenter would go down to stay with them. He used to make sandals which they all wore[34] – hence, perhaps, the name she gave them in the story:

> Father knows a man called Eustace Sandal . . . He is a vegetarian and a Primitive Social Something, and an all-wooler, and things like that, and he is really as good as he can stick, only most awfully dull. I believe he eats bread and milk from choice. Well, he has great magnificent dreams about all the things you can do for other people, and he wants to distil cultivatedness into the sort of people who live in Model Workmen's dwellings, and teach them to live up to better things. This is what he says. So he gives concerts in Camberwell, and places like that, and curates come from far and near to sing about Bold Bandaleros and the

Song of the Bow, and people who have escaped being curates give comic recitings, and he is sure that it does every one good, and 'gives them glimpses of the Life Beautiful'. He said that. Oswald heard him with his own trustworthy ears.

Later the Bastables go and stay in Miss Sandal's cottage at the seaside, and they can scarcely get over how bare it is:

> All the walls were white plaster, the furniture was white deal – what there was of it, which was precious little. There were no carpets only white matting. And there was not a single ornament in a single room! . . . There were only about six pictures – all of a brownish colour. One was the blind girl sitting on an orange with a broken fiddle. It is called Hope.[35]

Twenty years afterwards, Edith could look back on the Life Beautiful with detached amusement, but in 1884 she was impressed with the sincerity and dedication of her new acquaintances. Their search for a new way of living seemed to offer liberation from the stifling middle-class *mores* which – perhaps through no very deliberate act of choice – she had already flouted pretty thoroughly. In particular, she had failed to secure a husband capable of keeping her as an ineffectual angel in the house. Now, through her Fabian friends, she began to discover a new role for herself, one that was altogether better suited to an active woman of character and independence, who had been proud of being able to keep up with her brothers. A letter to Ada (who had now returned to England) describes her symbolic transformation:

> Now – Ada – I have something dreadful to break to you *gently*. – A certain friend of ours says 'When a woman becomes "advanced" she cuts her hair.' I don't know whether I am 'advanced' – but I have *Cut my hair off*!!!!!!!
> I retain the fringe – but at the back it is short like a boy's. I wonder how you will like it. – It is *deliciously* comfortable. Miss Adkin, Miss Hoatson and a few others like it. Others *don't*. I have also taken to all-wool clothing which is also *deliciously* pleasant to wear.[36]

The short haircut and less constricting clothing of the kind that Edith now adopted not only conferred greater freedom of movement, it also brought women a step closer to the condition of men, and a step further away from being glorified fashion dolls, whose elaborate coiffure and tightly boned and laced underclothing made it difficult for them to lead physically active lives or even dress and undress themselves. She had also taken up smoking, previously thought of either as a masculine prerogative or else as the hallmark of 'fast' women. Nora in the Blands' novel *Something Wrong*

> habitually smoked cigarettes. Not that she cared very much for the thing itself, but Nora in her way was somewhat 'advanced', and was very strong on the subject of the equality of the sexes. So she smoked as a protest against existing prejudices.[37]

Edith did not entirely share Nora's views on the equality of the sexes but she enjoyed several of the privileges that emancipation could confer. Suddenly, after four years of anxiety, drudgery and the demands of small children, she found herself mixing freely with clever and amusing men, and the more freely for being married. Through the Fabian Society and her new radical friends, she also met a new type of woman, an 'advanced' woman who wrote up her opinions in magazines, or spoke about them in public, and who expected others to find her views worth hearing: Eleanor Marx, Olive Schreiner, Clementina Black, Charlotte Wilson and Annie Besant were among the women who now entered her circle, and some of these were to become close friends. These women studied, wrestled with intellectual problems and enjoyed the peculiar freemasonry conferred by working in the British Museum Reading Room. It was exhilarating to be part of a new world struggling to be born, exhilarating to make new friends and find herself regularly in the company of young men once more, as she had seldom been since the long-lost happy days with Alfred and Harry.

'I really surprise myself sometimes,' she had told Ada, when she found herself on the Fabian pamphlet committee. She was now gaining confidence in public and a new friend, Marshall Steele, a professional elocutionist and public speaker, persuaded her to join him in giving public recitations in Working Men's Clubs, engagements that brought her a little money and a flattering sense of her own powers. Steele admired her poetry, and she wrote special pieces that they could recite together. Such performances ran counter to the traditional ideal of femininity, of mother as the serene hub of the household, the receptive ear for the rest of the family's activities: when Dinah married Adam Bede, in George Eliot's novel, she had to give up preaching. But the performing woman, celebrated in the previous century in Madame de Stael's novel *Corinne*, and for so long excluded from 'respectable' society, emerged once more in Edith's generation, and her appearances in Working Men's Clubs and on the Fabian list of speakers willing to lecture suggest that this was an area in which she felt confident of working alongside men.

But had Edith really become an 'advanced' woman, beneath her new haircut and all-wool clothing? Berta Ruck, a friend of twenty years later, described her as 'all for Women's Causes', but added that she used to give the following account of a houseparty for the Emancipated which she had attended when young:

> 'They talked and they talked and they talked for hours of Women's Rights. You never' – here E. Nesbit took out her cigarette, drew down her lips, and let that ineffable blank grimace widen her eyes – '*you* never heard so much about the Enfranchisement of Women. At last Miss – ' – a girlhood friend – 'and I were able to stagger up to our bedrooms and take out our hairpins and shake out our hair and I was just able to say faintly: "*Now* let's have a nice long talk ALL ABOUT YOUNG MEN!"'[38]

The tone of this anecdote is borne out by odd comments in her letters to Ada. In the long letter written between 11–25 April 1884, she recorded: 'On Monday we went to a Women's Rights meeting where I was *infinitely* bored. I saw and heard (for the first time) Miss Lydia Becker who is hideously like a *hippopotamus*.' Lydia Becker was one of the leaders of the Women's Suffrage Movement.

Nor did Edith immediately warm to the other 'advanced' women encountered at the Fabian. Charlotte Wilson, whom she later came to like, initially annoyed her; Edith suspected her of condescension, of assuming her own intellectual superiority to the less educated women around her:

> Mrs Wilson is the life and soul of the executive council . . . and she winds them all round her little finger. She was a Girton girl and is clever, and I am trying my very hardest not to dislike her. But it is difficult, as she is sometimes horribly rude, and will never speak to a woman if she can get a man to talk to. I don't mean that she is a *flirt* – she isn't, but I suppose women are not clever enough for her to talk to. She has a husband who is very nice, and a perfect gentleman.[39]

Edith was resentful at seeing Hubert apparently jumping to attention when Mrs Wilson spoke. Her force of personality, combined with her educational advantages, obliged her less-educated male colleagues to treat her opinions with respect. Edith was envious, possibly even a little jealous.

Charlotte Wilson was a passionate idealist, a woman who lived by ideas. Edith, however much she valued the freedom to behave unconventionally, was not. Charlotte Wilson's commitment to fight against social oppression and for women's rights lasted a lifetime. Edith hated injustice and suffering, but she preferred to believe that women were inferior to men, despite her own achievements. She was too humorous and down-to-earth to be able to take herself or anyone else seriously for very long. Though Edith shared the Fabian ideals, she tended to use the meetings as opportunities for drawing attention to herself (and obviously, but surely wrongly, suspected Mrs Wilson of doing the same). If she couldn't make an effective contribution to the discussion, she employed irritating little 'feminine ruses', pretending to faint, or despatching friends to fetch her a glass of water. At a meeting on 1 January 1886, Edward Carpenter read a paper on private property; the Minute Book describes the occasion thus:

> Awfully dull meeting. Wilson yawned like anything – No wonder! Infernal draught from the window, Coffin fidgeting – putting coals on the fire, distributing ipecacuanha lozenges, & so on. Miss Coffin sitting on the landing, evidently bored . . . Something making frightful noise like the winding of a rusty clock. Mrs Bland suspected of doing it with the handle of her fan. Wish she wouldn't. Two or three meetings like this could finish up any society.[40]

At the same time as the Fabian Society began to take off, so did Hubert and Edith's career as collaborators. From 1884 when Edith had told Ada that 'In all stories Hubert and I "go shares"', the Blands produced a number of short stories and two novels, working together until the late 1880s when Edith continued to write fiction while Hubert concentrated more on essays and political journalism. They wrote under the pseudonym 'Fabian Bland' and most of their fiction appeared in the radical London newspaper, *The Weekly Dispatch*, which did not pay particularly well but at least employed them regularly. From 6 January 1884 until 23 March it published under the title *The Social Cobweb* twelve episodes in which five different stories were unfolded, loosely linked to one another. It looks as if it had been written week by week, rather than conceived as a whole, and, like most of their fiction, it drew on familiar settings or situations to lend the narrative authenticity: the first story begins at Woolwich; the second is set at 'Bodhurst', i.e. Bodiam Castle; the fourth is set partly near Manchester and the last is set partly in Barnsbury Square, partly at a City stationer's like Raphael Tuck, for whom Edith painted cards.

Logically the next step was a novel and in the summer of 1885 *The Prophet's Mantle* was published, a well-thought-out book with a strikingly ingenious and complex plot that must have required elaborate advance planning. Its use of disguise, discovery and revelation, and its concealment of secrets from the reader reflects the influence of Dickens; as in *Our Mutual Friend*, the plot turns on a character who apparently dies in the opening pages. *The Prophet's Mantle* owes a great deal to its Victorian predecessors in its use of a fairly large cast and canvas, ranging over several settings and social contexts. It is still surprisingly readable, and the praise of contemporary reviewers ('well conceived and finely told', 'well written and good scenes', 'very thoughtful' and 'decidedly worth reading'[41]) seems quite justified. Although it was only published in a flimsy paperback edition by a downmarket publisher called Henry Drane (price: one shilling), its reissue in 1888 and 1889 suggests that it was selling steadily, if not well.

Interesting in itself, *The Prophet's Mantle* is indirectly informative about the Blands' current concerns and attitudes. Writing under pressure, they increasingly found themselves drawing upon their own experiences in creating character and situation. As *The Social Cobweb* had done and her later books would do, this novel takes as its starting point people and places Edith knew. In the end a great deal of her life got into her books, one way or another, though she would probably have been the last to admit it. When discussing her poetry, she firmly maintained that she put little or nothing of herself into it:

> All my verses were what Robert Browning calls *dramatic lyrics*. I imagined situations and wrote what I thought men and women would feel in these situations. And this I have done all my life. Of course, I have written scores of personal poems, to ease the heart, but the fire has been the only reader. Right or wrong, I could never bring myself to lay my soul naked before the public that reads books. My published poems are nearly all *dramatic lyrics*. Only my socialist poems are *real me*, and not drama.[42]

Though no one can know what the fire received, there is certainly an element of self-deception in this claim. She did publish some intensely personal poems, possibly because she needed the money they would bring her; and, leaving aside the genuine 'heart's outpourings', even those poems that purport to be narrative and dramatic are often indirectly revealing, in ways that she herself failed to recognize; they reproduce situations that, though disguised, are surprisingly close to her own.

What is true of the verse is much more obviously true of the prose, where the Blands were regularly casting about for subject matter. 'You remember Hamlin, the refined man in "The Copper Beeches?"' Edith asks Ada, in a letter. 'His real name is Podmore, and I think he is in love with Miss Hoatson;' ('The Copper Beeches' was a short story published in *The Weekly Dispatch*.) Another letter explains that the young stockbroker in *The Prophet's Mantle* was based on Edward Pease.[43] This habit of putting people and places she knew into her writing, altered but not beyond recognition, remained with her all her life. Her books can thus be read as a kind of extended commentary on her life, a guide to how she interpreted her experiences, as revealing as an intimate journal might have been, had she left one. Some possibly autobiographical elements in *The Prophet's Mantle* have already been touched on: the heroine, Alice Hatfield (whose name sounds as if it were suggested by Alice Hoatson's), has been left pregnant by her socialist lover, though she only discovers this when she is suddenly taken ill. At the end, he is persuaded to marry her, though, in the meantime, she has lost the child. The central theme of the book is socialism, or anarchism – in the mid-eighties, the two were not always clearly distinguished, and the battles had yet to be fought which would reveal their fundamental differences. There are scenes at the Sunday evening meeting of the Radical Club in Soho, and in a middle-class drawing room where a meeting of the 'Cleon' (i.e. the Fabian Society) is being held.

Nor is it merely the ideas and adherents of socialism that hold the stage – its causes are also shown: in Derbyshire, a mill is closed because the two brothers who own it cannot agree, or put the well-being of their workers first – the mill is later smashed up by the out-of-work mill hands, in impotent but justifiable fury. In London, the poverty and homelessness of the poor is much in evidence, though its presentation is obtrusively Dickensian in tone. Its hero, walking the streets, slackens speed

> to glance with a frown at the heaps of dirty rags that filled the corners of doorways and the embrasures of walls, and hid human flesh and blood: the flesh and blood of your brothers and sisters, my esteemed Royal Commissioners. These doorways and archways and out-of-the-way-corners are not, of course, to be included in any investigation into the homes of the poor; but perhaps they might be if these royal, noble and

eminent brothers realised that these are the only homes of a large proportion of the poor.

The pointed allusion to 'royal, noble and eminent brothers' refers to the members of the Royal Commission that was currently examining the problem of housing the working classes; chaired by Charles Dilke, it included the Prince of Wales and Lord Salisbury.[44]

The Prophet's Mantle is centrally concerned with Russian exiles in London who were to describe themselves as anarchists, anarchist-communists or sometimes nihilists; yet the term 'anarchist' is seldom used by the Blands, and was not to become familiar until the following year (1886). Mrs Charlotte Wilson, who as an influential member of the Fabian executive had irritated Edith, regarded herself as an anarchist. She had been converted to this ideology by reading the moving speeches made by Prince Kropotkin during his sensational trial in France in 1883. Mrs Wilson persuaded Kropotkin to return to London when he was released from prison, early in 1886. Here they jointly edited a journal called *The Anarchist*, and when this folded later that year, Mrs Wilson took over its successor, *Freedom* – 'an exponent of Anarchist Socialism'. The extraordinarily exciting and dramatic life of Kropotkin, his rare goodness and unswerving idealism provided the Blands with the model for Petrovitch, the Prophet of the title, who is endowed with the Prince's character and history. Either the Blands learned about Peter Kropotkin from his admirer, Mrs Wilson, or else they may have met him at Henry Hyndman's house in 1882.

Kropotkin had first visited London with his wife late in 1881, where he had joined his old allies, Nicholas Tchaykovsky and Sergei Stepniak, in a campaign to involve the workers in their cause, a campaign of the kind that they had previously found so successful in Russia. But in England they seemed to meet only with apathy. Kropotkin described his disappointment, and incidentally suggested how rapidly the socialist movement had developed in the mid-eighties:

> The year that I then passed in London was a year of real exile. For one who held advanced socialist opinions, there was no atmosphere to breathe in. There was no sign of that animated socialist movement which I found so largely developed on my return in 1886. Burns, Champion, Hardie, and the other labour leaders were not yet heard of; the Fabians did not exist; Morris had not declared himself a socialist; and the trade unions, limited in London to a few privileged trades only, were hostile to socialism. The only active and outspoken representatives of the socialist movement were Mr and Mrs Hyndman, with a very few

workers grouped round them. They had held in the autumn of 1881 a small congress, and we used to say jokingly – but it was very nearly true – that Mrs Hyndman had received all the congress in her house.[45]

The Blands' decision to base their socialist hero on Kropotkin was an inspired choice. He had had an extraordinarily varied and interesting life: born into the highest ranks, he had spent his early years at court in the 'corps of pages', had studied and visited Siberia on a scholarly expedition and was then converted to socialism by reading Bakunin and others. Returning to St Petersburg, he had worked with Tchaykovsky, printing pamphlets and preaching socialism, often disguised as a peasant called Borodin. When his second identity was discovered, he was arrested and thrown into the impregnable fortress of St Peter and St Paul. Here his health became so bad that he was transferred to a military hospital, from which he made a spectacular escape by more or less running straight out of the main gate. The theme of disguise and double identity had obvious fictional uses, and may have further had a particular appeal to Hubert, though Kropotkin's aliases had been intended solely for the benefit of mankind. In the novel, the Prophet has a double in the form of an unscrupulous and rakish secretary, the seducer of Alice Hatfield. The Prophet himself, Petrovitch, is a charismatic and philanthropic Russian, later revealed as the author of 'A Prophetic Vision', an account of what a socialist Utopia might be like. Anyone who reads this book or hears him speak is fired with his vision, and Petrovitch is endowed with all the warmth, genuine goodness and personal charm that Kropotkin apparently possessed. David Garnett wrote of him:

> It is difficult to describe his immense charm – it was due largely to his intellectual vitality, his unawareness of his own charm, and his infectious excitement about whatever subject cropped up. He listened to whatever anyone present might say and paid equal attention to all views – which was extremely flattering. The sweep of his mind, his capacity for seeing contemporary events in their relation to the general movements of history, was greater than that of anyone I have known . . .[46]

Petrovitch (later revealed as a certain Count Litvinoff in disguise) reminisces about his experiences which include an account of an imprisonment and escape obviously based on that of Kropotkin. Though Kropotkin was not to publish his adventures in book form for another fifteen years, he may have described them to a drawing-room group on his earlier visit to London, or the Blands may have learned about them from a mutual friend such as Charlotte Wilson or the Russian exile, Stepniak, who was in London attending Fabian meetings and writing for radical journals – he later contributed to the socialist magazine *To-Day* while Hubert was editing it. Stepniak lacked Kropotkin's personal charisma and impressive physical appearance, but he was a man of immense compassion, and in his way a powerful propagandist for his cause. It was not known until shortly before his death that as a young army officer, he had assassinated a senior police official in St Petersburg, escaping with extraordinary coolness and presence of mind. Both Stepniak, and Kropotkin, after his return to England in 1886, became friends of the Blands and cordial visits and letters were exchanged.[47] Through them, Edith came to regard the Czarist regime as profoundly evil and something of her reaction comes out in *The Railway Children* (1906) where the old Russian gentleman seems to be a portrait of Stepniak himself.[48]

Much of the excitement and drama of *The Prophet's Mantle* derive from the mood of active commitment to Russian revolution, but the book is mainly set in England, and in order to vary the scene from London a little, its authors made use of some Derbyshire locations. Some time in 1885, probably quite early in the year, Edith took Iris and went up to stay with Saretta and her brother-in-law, who had taken a cottage on top of a windy hill, right on the edge of the Peak District and just south of Manchester. The cottage stood between Hayfield and Mellor, and was not far from Marple, where Ada's family were then living. In the valley below lay the growing town of New Mills, the original of 'Old Mills', which had provided one of the settings for *The Social Cobweb*. The cottage, 'Three Chimneys', seems to have been named after a larger house near Mellor. Edith liked the name and used it in *The Railway Children* and elsewhere. Close to the cottage stood a large old house called Aspenshaw:

> It was a very pretty house, and somehow managed to escape, even at this dreary season, such dreariness as hung over Thornsett Edge, though it was built of the same grey stone, and had the same moorland background. There was a good deal of ivy about it, and the grounds were less regular and more full of evergreens and shrubs than the Ferriers' garden.
>
> As the two young men walked up the private road, they heard from the rear of the house a confused barking of dogs . . .[49]

At the real Aspenshaw lived the Woodcock family, who were

simultaneously dazzled, amused and amazed at their new visitor: tall, willowy and delicately good-looking, with her hair cut short, uncorseted and in her flowing all-wool gown, Edith would lie stretched out on the hearthrug to play with the dog. Provincial Derbyshire had never seen anyone so unconventional, so 'advanced'. Young Fanny Woodcock noticed how much all the men they knew admired her, as well as how much she enjoyed their admiration. Aspenshaw, its dogs, and even a son-in-law of the family, a lawyer called Bates (now renamed Gates), all find their way into *The Prophet's Mantle*, as did the satanic mills that lay below the house.[50]

The Blands wrote a second collaborative novel in the following year which was serialized in *The Weekly Dispatch*, but despite Edith's efforts it was never published in book form, and she later appropriated its title, *Something Wrong*, for a collection of horror stories published in 1893. Yet this novel was not entirely forgotten – Edith's obituary in *The Star* referred to it in preference to her children's books, describing it as 'a vivid and amusing picture of the inside of the [socialist] movement. Hyndman, Morris and other leaders appear as characters under very thin disguises.'[51] *Something Wrong* followed the pattern of *The Prophet's Mantle* (also surprisingly frequently mentioned in her obituaries) in weaving a fiction around the political groups and individuals that the Blands knew best: Hyndman becomes Gottheim, the genial, self-confident, somewhat bullying leader of the U.P.L. (the United Pioneers of Labour), and Morris appears as Dancer. The split between Gottheim and Dancer (Morris had seceded from the S.D.F. and formed the rival Socialist League), the 'Cleon' ('a society for drawing-room reformers') with Mrs Coburn (i.e. Charlotte Wilson) all contribute to form a convincing backdrop for the melodramatic love story that occupies the centre-stage; there is even a flattering little vignette of Hubert himself:

> Huntley in the flesh was better company than Marx in the spirit. Huntley was the object of much suspicion and dislike among the United Pioneers of Labour, who didn't understand much of him, and disliked the little they did understand. A Conservative by birth, education, and instincts, he was a Socialist of reluctant conviction and always liked to have a hit at the U.P.L. and their doctrines, as a sort of vengeance on the economic views which compelled him to adopt by reason a creed from which all his natural tendencies recoiled. He was a fairly good public speaker, and in that capacity always preferred to say unpalatable things, even if he had to go out of his way to do so, and his thrusts were

generally aimed impartially. The U.P.L. understood one thing about him well enough – that he liked his own way and generally got it. They hated him because he laughed at their cant phrases, and wore a single eyeglass. His almost complete freedom from sentiment, and his inability to get up enthusiasm to the call of Gottheim and Co., were other points which did not commend him to the U.P.L. All who knew him liked him except those who hated him.[52]

By 1886 the Blands' financial position must have looked a little more promising, what with regular requests for work coming in from *The Weekly Dispatch* and their first novel launched. They moved, probably in late March, from Blackheath and their 'bandbox' terrace house into a rather larger semi-detached house at 5 Cambridge Road (now Cambridge Drive) at Lee. Like their first home at Elswick Road, this house had been built only a year or two earlier, but it is prettier, as well as more spacious. The front door was (and is) panelled with milky glass in a fluid 'art nouveau' design; there was a steep pitched roof and a garden large enough for 'the bunnies' to play in, whereas Elswick Road had only a dismal yard. Edith was conscious of the children's need for space, and valued it herself. In the next decade, the family were to make three more moves: the first, six months later, was to 8, Dorville Road, just around the corner from Cambridge Road and similar in size (it has since been pulled down). Thereafter they moved to larger houses with more extensive grounds round about. The Blands' socialist principles and sympathy for the oppressed never prevented them from enjoying a thoroughly bourgeois affluence, reflected in their increasingly grand houses, growing numbers of servants and their practice of philanthropy in the best Victorian traditions.

4

ENTER G.B.S.

> The Society is getting rather large now and includes some very nice people, of whom Mr Stapelton is the nicest and a certain G. B. Shaw the most interesting. G.B.S. has a fund of dry Irish humour that is simply irresistible. He is a clever writer and speaker – is the grossest flatterer (of men, women and children impartially) I ever met, is horribly untrustworthy as he repeats everything he hears, and does not always stick to the truth, and is *very plain* like a long corpse with dead white face – sandy sleek hair, and a loathsome small straggly beard, and yet is one of the most fascinating men I ever met. – Everyone rather affects to despise him, 'Oh it's only Shaw.' That sort of thing you know, but everyone admires him all the same. Miss Hoatson pretends to hate him, but my own impression is that she is over head and ears in love with him.[1]

The tone of Edith's letter to Ada is not entirely transparent or self-deceiving, even though it somewhat anticipates the heroine's diary entry in Edith's novel *The Incomplete Amorist*: Betty, having just met and fallen in love with the Amorist, records: 'I do not like him particularly. He is rather old, and not really good-looking.' Nor does the letter to Ada sound quite as naive as its precise fictional equivalent: Daphne (of *Daphne in Fitzroy Street*) writes to her friend about the hero, a thinly disguised Shaw:

> I think he ought to have a lesson. All the girls admire him frightfully, and he's not really good looking at all, only very black hair with a hooked nose and a white face and eyes like smoked topazes – or do I mean cairngorms? I wish he would fall in love with *me*. I'd soon put him in his place. It would be a real pleasure to do it. But he's not likely to. I believe he hates me, really.[2]

A thread of self-deception and a cage of conflicting emotions were to characterize Edith's relationship with Shaw from the outset. Her

comment on her friend Alice Hoatson's response to him may reflect a
tendency to identify her own feelings with Alice's, or it may include an
element of wishful thinking, for Alice, at this moment, was beginning
to be 'head over ears in love', not so much with G.B.S. as with Hubert
Bland.

About a year earlier, the Fabian Minute Book recorded beside the
entry for the meeting of 16 May 1884 a special visitor: written sideways
in mauve ink in Shaw's own spidery handwriting is the comment, 'This
meeting was made memorable by the first appearance of Bernard
Shaw'. Looking back, Shaw recalled that he had been won over to
socialism largely by the arguments of the American economist Henry
George, as Bland and so many of those swept into the great socialist
revival of 1883 had been. But it was Bland himself who actually invited
Shaw to his first Fabian meeting. Earlier that month, on the evening of
4 May, Bland and Shaw met for the first time in the offices of *The
Christian Socialist*. Bland, who always enjoyed making converts, had
followed up their encounter with a letter and a copy of the first Fabian
tract 'Why Are the Many Poor?'[3] This had been published the previous
month and was the joint product of the Pamphlets Committee, of
which Edith had been a member. Bland's letter to Shaw explains:

> The Fabian about which I spoke to you last night is a new society of men
> and women.
>
>   Its object is to collect information on all social questions and to
> discuss such questions with a 'view to action' – we have no paid
> subscription but make a collection when funds are wanted – so that each
> member can give according to his means. The only rule to whose
> acceptance members are pledged is the following – 'that the members of
> the society assent that the competitive system ensures the comfort and
> happiness of the few at the expense of the suffering of the many and that
> society must be reconstructed in such a manner as to secure general
> welfare and happiness' – our meetings are held every fortnight at 17
> Osnaburgh Street and at 14 Dean's Yard, Westminster. I will let you
> know the date of the next meeting and the premises; and I hope we shall
> see you there. The enclosed is the only tract we have yet issued.[4]

Shaw, who was himself living at 36 Osnaburgh Street, was
impressed, not so much by the pamphlet itself, as by the name of the
society – he felt it could only have been chosen by just such a group of
educated middle-class men as he had been looking for. Attending his
first meeting, he saw that the society was small enough for him to make
an impact upon it, but potentially powerful, and that it was worldly

and realistic enough to complement his own curious blend of cynicism and idealism. It had gradually separated itself both from Hyndman's Social Democratic Federation, which was more avowedly political and addressed itself more directly to the workers, and also from Morris's breakaway Socialist League, which was becoming the party of the idealists, the anarchists and the disciples of Engels. Many individuals nevertheless belonged to more than one of these groups, and attended meetings of all three, as the Blands often did. Shaw himself became friendly with Morris and was attracted by his beautiful daughter May; later he ruefully claimed that he had considered himself 'mystically betrothed' to her.[5] At this stage of his life, Shaw was constantly playing with the idea of marriage, and proposing to any young women whom he felt confident would refuse him, while fleeing headlong from those who showed any interest in the idea.

Shaw threw himself into the Fabian Society wholeheartedly and was responsible for bringing into it a clerk from the Colonial Office called Sidney Webb, an earnest, undistinguished-looking little man with a Louis-Napoleon moustache and beard. Edith wrote to Ada that he had 'a face like a fat billy goat and a profusion of wild spots', but she admitted that he was 'no fool': in fact Webb possessed an invigorating grasp of the importance of statistics, as well as the need for first-hand knowledge and observation rather than impassioned blather. With Webb came another Colonial Office clerk, the darkly handsome, formidably intelligent Sydney Olivier. Speaking of how hard-up and careless of convention the Fabians had been in those early days, Shaw recalled an evening spent with the Blands at Elswick Road, when Olivier arrived in an old velveteen smoking-jacket of a chocolate brown. Meeting them in the tiny hall, Edith had noticed that the sleeve of Olivier's jacket was hanging on by a thread, so she promptly stitched it back on for him.[6] From the outset, these two civil servants showed themselves immensely capable, though temperamentally very different. Their energy and informed minds, in combination with Shaw's brilliant rhetoric, were to prove crucial to the later development of the Society, and arguably to that of English socialism as a whole. Shaw claimed that they all found Bland rather a trial, politically speaking, in the mid-eighties, because

> Olivier and Shaw were out and out communists and revolutionists. Webb was Liberal; but Bland was a regular Blackheath Tory. He went along with the others, and was always useful in keeping before them that particular point of view: but there were difficulties . . .[7]

Early in 1885 Shaw introduced to the Fabian Society its most celebrated, or perhaps notorious convert yet. This was Annie Besant, a powerful and impetuous woman who, after an unhappy marriage to a dreary clergyman, had joined forces with the atheist Charles Bradlaugh; the two of them had outraged public opinion by lecturing on birth control as a means of improving working-class standards of living. One result was that she lost the custody of her children in a much-publicized court case. Bradlaugh was widely condemned as 'bestial', an accusation that Edith reiterated in her letter to Ada of Easter 1884, where she gave her own account of the famous debate on 'Will socialism benefit the English people?', between Bradlaugh and Hyndman:

> Bradlaugh was weak and Hyndman was worse. Hyndman had a bad cold but there was no excuse for Bradlaugh – he is innately bestial – Forgive my strong language. I do so loathe the man. (I have been smoking too much and I feel quite silly.) The Debate was at St James Hall and I liked it because so many people I knew were there. All the Fabian lot.[8]

Though Bradlaugh was widely considered to have carried off the honours, so many of his followers were drawn into socialism thereafter that he was often said to have beaten himself. Early in the following year, 1885, Annie Besant invited Shaw to tell her more about the Fabian Society; she was soon to become its most dynamic member.

Shaw's acquaintance with the Blands dated from the summer of 1884, when he first started to attend Fabian meetings regularly. No doubt Hubert kept a paternal eye on his promising new convert. He was elected to membership on 5 September, while Edith's friend Alice Hoatson was elected at the following meeting. By Christmas that year, Shaw had joined Charlotte Wilson, Bland, Pease and Frederick Keddell on the executive committee.[9] In 1885 Shaw began to keep a diary in shorthand, and that year turned out to be an *annus mirabilis* for him, in more ways than one. In April his father died, leaving him a small life insurance policy. He had been living in great poverty, but now he went to Jaeger's and bought himself some new clothes. Although he looked, in his beige all-wool suiting, like 'a forked radish in a worsted bifurcated stocking', it was from this moment that he dated his extraordinary success with women: 'As soon as I could afford to dress presentably, I became accustomed to women falling in love with me. I did not pursue women: I was pursued by them.'[10]

1885 had begun with Mrs Besant's conversion to socialism. She invited Shaw to dinner and a long, intense friendship began between them that was ultimately to prove deeply painful to her. At the same time Shaw was enjoying a much less intellectual flirtation with another woman who, like Mrs Besant, was substantially older than he was – Jenny Patterson, an attractive and wealthy widow, was one of his mother's singing pupils and a close friend of hers. By the early summer, she could no longer hide her feelings for him, and, after a 'decidedly gallant' conversation and a 'declaration of passion', Shaw stayed at her house until three in the morning. His diary entry for 25 July records it as 'my 29th birthday which I celebrated with a new experience'.[11] Though Shaw's feelings for Mrs Patterson fluctuated wildly, their stormy love affair lasted for the best part of ten years. At the same time, he was visiting Morris and cultivating his friendship with May, as well as acting as friend and confidant to Karl Marx's gifted and unhappy daughter Eleanor. In the summer of 1884 Eleanor had finally decided to become the common-law wife of Edward Aveling, who was separated but not divorced from his first wife. Aveling was a committed socialist and a friend of Engels, but a difficult and unlikeable man, widely regarded as a scoundrel. He certainly behaved like one later, abandoning Eleanor to make an advantageous legal marriage, whereupon she committed suicide. Her decision to go and live with Aveling was a brave one because she knew that she risked alienating all her more conventional friends. Edith, who at this stage made close friendships with other women of her own age and interests, was one of these. Eleanor wrote Edith an affectionate, anxious letter, explaining and justifying her decision. This letter is almost the sole evidence for what must have been a particularly interesting friendship between two intelligent, forceful and highly emotional women. Writing from Derbyshire late in July 1884, Eleanor told Edith:

I feel it is only right that before I avail myself of your very kind invitation I should make my present position quite clear to you. The reason why I have not been to see you – and it required a great deal of self-sacrifice to keep away – and why I have not pressed you to come to me was simply that I would not do so till I could tell you frankly and honestly about the step that I have just taken. I am here with Edward Aveling, and henceforth we are going to be together – true husband and true wife, I hope, though I cannot be his wife legally. – He is, you probably know, a married man. I could not bear that one I feel such deep sympathy for as yourself should think ill of, or misunderstand us. I

have not come between husband and wife . . . on this question I have
always felt very strongly, and I could not now in act shrink from doing
what I have always felt to be right. I also feel that you and others may
think differently, and till you have thought over the matter I dare not
yet think of you and Mr Bland as among those friends whom we hope to
see when, four or five weeks hence, we return to London. That we
should be delighted to count you amongst our friends I need not tell
you . . .[12]

Her uneasy tone suggests that Eleanor fully anticipated the shock
she was about to give in socialist circles, in particular to those who set
great store by the proprieties, or who, like Bland (according to Shaw),
held 'the most severe and rigid sentiments in all sex questions . . . he
would take a violently condemnatory tone in denouncing everybody
who made any attempt at sexual freedom'.[13] Though some of the early
Fabians such as Edward Carpenter championed free love, and others
like the Blands would conduct their lives on 'Bohemian' lines, the
respectable and conventional marriages of Pease, Shaw, Webb, Olivier
and their socialist friend Graham Wallas were more typical. Considering these in her diary fifty years later, Beatrice Webb wondered, 'Have
there ever been five more respectable, cultivated and mutually devoted
and successful couples?' In her view, they were 'the utter essence of
British bourgeois morality, comfort and enlightenment'.[14] Perhaps
without thinking about it, she assumed that social reforms were more
likely to be brought about by those whose lives were outwardly
conformist, and who thus offered less obvious moral targets to their
antagonists. Despite the Blands' own rejection of convention at crucial
moments, in public they had so far preferred to maintain appearances.
The tone of Eleanor Marx's letter suggests that she expected them to
disapprove, and it seems likely that they did, if somewhat covertly. At
any rate, so thought the German socialist Eduard Bernstein, when, in
his reminiscences, he considered the English

predilection for the expedient of indulging in partial praise of a person,
in order to avoid telling the unpleasant truth about him, . . . a thing that
astonished me soon after my settling down in London. About the end
of the first year my wife and I received a social invitation from Mr and
Mrs Hubert Bland, who belonged to the inner circle of the Fabians.
They and their guests were interesting people, and the conversation was
very natural and spontaneous. But when in some connection or other I
spoke of the Avelings, there was suddenly a suspiciously unanimous
chorus of praise of them. 'Oh, the Avelings are very clever people.' 'Oh,

everybody must admit that they have been of great service to the movement,' and so forth, in the same key, so that it was at once clear to me that there was something in the air.[15]

Shaw did not suffer from bourgeois prejudice against common-law or free unions; indeed he found himself peculiarly at home in other people's marriages, acting as confidant to the wife, companion to the husband. He himself had grown up in a *ménage à trois*, and had learned to like and even admire his mother's entertaining friend, Vandeleur Lee, whom he preferred to his melancholy and alcoholic father. He played third party to the Avelings, as he did later to May Morris after her marriage to the inadequate Henry Sparling and for a while to the Blands, though he always insisted that he was never more than a 'Sunday husband' who 'had scruples, and effectively inhibitive ones too, about . . . cuckolding my friends'.[16] Certainly friendship with an attractive woman safely married to someone else looked like one way of enjoying her company without being required to make a deeper commitment.

Despite the Blands' implied disapproval of the Avelings (if that was what it was), it was at their house that Shaw's diary first records his meeting Mrs Bland, though he must have met her on a number of earlier occasions. With her was Philip Bourke Marston, the blind poet who had long ago been engaged to Edith's ill-fated sister Mary. Edith had kept in touch with Philip and always felt a great affection for him. The date was 6 March 1885. Three days later, visiting the Avelings again, Shaw found Edith there with Eleanor, and afterwards walked back with her to Charing Cross Station, where he kept her company in the waiting room until her train arrived. They were clearly on friendly terms, and a few days afterwards he sent her a copy of a magazine called *Time*, in which she subsequently published a poem. Later that month, he met both Blands at the Fabian Society and walked back to the station with them after the meeting. On five occasions that year, Shaw recorded seeing Mrs Bland 'at the Museum', that is, in the great domed Reading Room of the British Museum.[17] It was just beginning to be frequented by intellectual women such as Charlotte Wilson, Eleanor Marx and Constance and Clementina Black. One of Edith's motives for going, however, may have been to see Shaw. On 18 May, Shaw went back to Elswick Road with Bland, after a meeting of the Fabian executive, and spent the evening with them. He and Bland, discovering a mutual enthusiasm, 'put on the gloves and had a spar'. Though Shaw loathed all other forms of physical violence, he enjoyed the controlled aggression implicit in boxing; an early novel of his, *Cashel Byron's Profession*, is the story of a pugilist, and it was currently being serialized in the radical review *To-Day*. The contrast between the two men's characters came out in their very different boxing styles: both were unusually tall, but Bland was a heavyweight, dauntingly powerful and heavy on his feet, while Shaw was a middleweight, slender, lithe and always on his toes. Sometimes Edith asked them to have a spar 'out of pure mischief'.[18]

In mid-June, Shaw received a telegram from Mrs Bland asking him to tea that afternoon. As he had an engagement to review a concert the same evening, he went in search of Bland in the City, at the Hydraulic Power Company's offices, to make his apologies. On failing to find him, Shaw went down to Blackheath himself, returning in time for his concert. That year, Shaw spent several other evenings at Elswick Road, where their small rooms do not seem to have inhibited the Blands from entertaining regularly. He was there, in company with Alice Hoatson in July, and again in late August, when he had an energetic argument with the Blands as to whether or not children should be whipped, a discussion resumed after the next Fabian meeting. He next visited the Blands in early October and this time they argued about religion. A week or so later he met Mrs Bland by arrangement in the house of his friend and neighbour, Robert Ellice Mack.[19] If, as seems likely, Shaw was responsible for introducing Edith to Mack, he had, without knowing it, helped to turn her in a new and crucial direction. Robert Ellice Mack was an editor and publisher and it was through his commissioning that Edith began to produce books of verse, and later stories for children. The work she did for him was slick and vapid, but it paid the bills and in time she discovered how to parody its clichés and use them for comic effect.

For the next eight months or so Shaw was to see very little of Edith. In February 1886, pregnant again, she gave birth to a stillborn child, and not long after that she became seriously ill with measles, an occasion when Annie Besant thoughtfully came and took the two elder children, Paul and Iris, off her hands. On 22 March 1886 Shaw spent an evening at the Blands at Blackheath, in the company of Sidney Webb and Miss Hoatson, now acting assistant secretary to the Fabian executive. He and Webb missed the last train back and had to split the ten shillings for a cab between them. On 7 May, the Blands, Shaw and every other person in London who regarded themselves as cultivated, attended the Shelley Society's private production of *The Cenci*, with

Alma Murray playing Beatrice, the tragic victim of her father's incestuous desires.[20] Her performance was widely acclaimed, and Edith wrote her a particularly laboured poem:

> If he whom now for the first time we know
> Could have come back from nothing into being,
> He for the first time would have fully known
> How full a flame of genius was his own . . .
>
> In a vision
> He may have seen you, and have so forecast
> The triumph you should bring to him at last . . .
>
> Whose undreamed dream you are, as he your
> Art's heart is.

Shaw, of course, could not take the occasion at all seriously and used to describe how his great friend, the dramatic critic William Archer, having gone to sleep during the performance, 'fell forward flat on his nose with a tremendous noise, leaving a dent on the floor of the theatre which may still be seen by curious visitors'.[21]

So far Shaw had treated Mrs Bland much as he treated his other friends, enjoying her company, walking and talking with her as the opportunity arose, but in June 1886, according to the laconic diary entries, the pattern of their relationship changed. Before considering the entries themselves and the fictional accounts that each left of the other, it must be explained that where Shaw's biography was concerned, he showed himself determined to impose an authorized version upon events. He was only too friendly and helpful to his aspiring biographers, regaling them with vivid but carefully selected episodes from his past, so that they felt flattered by his confidences while entirely failing to notice that he had chosen his material with the utmost care, omitting anything that did not fit into his projected self-portrait. When Doris Langley Moore came to write of E. Nesbit, Shaw took good care to guide her hand in the composition of those sections in which he was involved.

When she first approached Shaw for help with her biography in the spring of 1931, he politely refused on the grounds that 'as Edith was an audaciously unconventional lady and Hubert an exceedingly unfaithful husband he does not see how a presentable biography is possible as yet; and he had nothing to contribute to a mere whitewashing operation'.[22] Knowing that many of the Blands' lovers were still alive and anticipating their reluctance to be mentioned, he ignored her further pleas for help. But by November Mrs Langley Moore had some further ammunition in the form of Edith's letter to Ada quoted at the beginning of this chapter and a couple of Shaw's letters to Hubert that remained unsold. None of these was in fact particularly revealing, but Shaw was not to know that. Realizing that Mrs Langley Moore was determined to write the book and fearing that she might have discovered some potentially embarrassing evidence, he agreed to see her at Whitehall Court on 10 November 1931. As always, he was friendly and forthcoming on a variety of topics, and, with a forethought born of experience, asked to see the Nesbit biography at proof stage. When she showed it to him, he carefully reworded several passages that she had based on his information, and repunctuated a long and perceptive letter to Hubert, which her book reproduced in full. He also reworded the sentence describing his relationship with Edith. Mrs Langley Moore wrote of the powerful impression that Shaw had made on Edith, and commented:

> She yielded herself to the luxury of being in love. Her sentiment, which she made no attempt to disguise, elicited from its object nothing of equal ardour, and was soon happily transmuted into a gay and untroubled friendship.

Shaw deleted 'of equal ardour' and substituted 'but a heartlessness which he knew how to make amusing'.[23] It was a characteristic piece of Shavian wishful thinking. Mature women seldom fall in love with men who offer them no encouragement, and once they have fallen in love, heartlessness is hardly amusing. Edith had fallen in love for the second time in her life with a philanderer as compulsive, in his own curious way, as Bland, even though his anxieties and inhibitions made him sexually undemanding. The experience was to be a searing one. She would never again trust herself to anyone as powerful as her first two loves; but then as powerful personalities they had few competitors.

The bare comings and goings of Edith's skirmish with Shaw are recorded in his diary. Since the few surviving letters are carefully guarded in tone, any evidence of their feelings is embedded in their writing: two, at least, of Edith's poems were written to Shaw, and nearly twenty-five years later, she turned the experience into a romantic novel, *Daphne in Fitzroy Street*. Shaw also wrote about their relationship, but in its immediate aftermath – a difference which may reflect the time it took each of them to get over it. Shaw, who was then working as a novelist and had not yet begun his career as a playwright, wrote two chapters of a novel about the Blands, and the ambivalent feelings that Edith aroused in him; and even within those two chapters, the viewpoint visibly shifts. He then laid the manuscript aside and totally forgot about it, turning from his struggles with it to write the revealingly titled short story 'Don Giovanni Explains'.[24]

The relevant entries in Shaw's diary begin on Saturday, 26 June, 1886:

> Mrs Bland at Museum. I did some German and read a little P[olitical] E[conomy] for my lecture; but on the whole the day was devoted to Mrs Bland. We dined together, had tea together and I went out to Lee with her, and played and sang there until Bland came in from his volunteer work. A memorable evening!

A note beneath reckons up the cost of all this – Shaw was embarrassingly poor at the time:

> Dinner (Mrs Bland and I) 2/- Tea (ditto) 1/2 Cab from Lincoln's Inn to Cannon St., 2/- Train to Lee 4d Extra fares 1st class 1/3 Train New Cross to London Bridge 3d Bus Mansion House to Tottenham Court Rd. 3d.

Shaw travelled first class only when he was particularly eager to enjoy the privacy it afforded; third class became preferable later when it was the woman's turn to be importunate. Shaw's 'friendships' regularly began with musical evenings, in which he and the lady in question would play and sing songs – these were often conveniently romantic, and though Shaw affected to despise all that sort of thing, he was actually quite as susceptible to pretty, clever women as they were to him. Bland came in from his volunteer work carrying his rifle; Shaw recalled that he 'could rest his rifle along the table on its heel and muzzle, and lift it with one hand by its grip to the perpendicular', a feat he must have performed that evening, on his return. Perhaps it was intended merely to impress; perhaps it implied a veiled threat. Bland seldom showed himself jealous, but one or two observations in Shaw's diary suggest momentary resentments. In the latter stages of the affair, Shaw seems almost to have cultivated his friendship with Bland as if he hoped to use it as camouflage.[25]

What Shaw had meant by the phrase 'a memorable evening' is enlarged upon in a small memorandum book in which he jotted down some notes for the year 1885. These included one on 'E.B.':

One of the women with whom the Fabian Society brought me into contact. On the 26th June 1886 I discovered that she had become passionately attached to me. As she was a married woman with children and her husband my friend and colleague, she had to live down her fancy. We remained very good friends.

This version characteristically plays down Shaw's own involvement, evident from his expenditure upon her, though ironically he had to borrow the money from Edith in order to spend it on her. On Monday 28, the diary records under expenses: 'Postal Order sent to Mrs Bland for florin borrowed from her on Saturday (2/1).' As it happened, she came to the Museum that day, so he need not have sent it.[26] Next day she wrote to him to thank him for the postal order:

Dear Mr Shaw,
    Your honest conduct provokes my reluctant admiration. I am glad you kept the moral course, and returned my 2/- though you still owe me something – and I suppose will remain always in my debt. I'll bring to Avenue Road [Annie Besant's house] tomorrow the story of mine you wished to see. Please read that lecture when you've time, and make fun of it as much as you like, to *me*. Did you ever return to me another *Longman* [the magazine] I once lent you – with a poem of mine in it (*Tekel*)? Really and truly that 2/- is partly yours as you paid my excess fares also. Out of it – but I shall not send you any back. One can't be *too* honest in this world or one would get no 'pennies for sweeties' – as the children say. By returning that 2/- you have done yourself out of quite a lot of chocolate creams – or whatever your special weakness is – what is it, by the way? *à demain* . . .[27]

Edith always believed that Shaw was in her debt, though later on the financial debts, at any rate, all ran the other way. And he never allowed her to find out what his special weakness was. Her anxiety to show him her poems and fictions assumes a wryly defensive note because he could be ruthlessly critical of her work. His harsh judgements are recalled in her novel where the heroine's drawings are dismissed as 'rubbish': 'You put that stuff in the fire, and never touch a pencil again except to do your accounts. What's the good of getting a little money if you can't look yourself in the face afterward?' demands Shaw's counterpart.[28]

On Tuesday, 30 June, the Blands and Shaw met for tea at Annie Besant's house and Shaw later had supper with Hubert at a favourite vegetarian restaurant, the Wheatsheaf. He wrote to Edith next day. A week later (8 July) he walked back from a meeting with her, Annie

Besant and a man called Tom Shore; he and Edith left the other two at Aldgate, and took a cab to Ludgate Hill and a train from there to Blackheath Hill, then walked the rest of the way to Lee, 'near her house' (the Blands had been living at Cambridge Road, Lee, since the spring). Afterwards Shaw walked back to Bloomsbury. It looks as if they must have parted some time after one in the morning, for Shaw notes that he 'walked home arriving at 3.30 a.m. after a walk of 2 hours'. Perhaps it was one of the three evenings a week that Bland still spent at his mother's. So far the impression is that Shaw was as responsive as Edith was encouraging. If Edith went to the Museum hoping to find him, he spent what little cash he had on taking her to lunch or tea, on a cab or a first class railway carriage. He had written to her, stayed out with her late at night and let himself in for a long walk home. St John Ervine, in his biography of Shaw, commented uncomprehendingly, 'the reader of the diary wonders in vain why he wasted his energy in such profitless activity'.[29] But if the stereotype of an innocent man relentlessly hounded down by tenacious women, the stereotype that Shaw created for himself, is discounted, it looks as though, at the outset of his relationship with Edith, he helped to set the pace, going out of his way to be alone with her and to please her and treat her. As she responded in turn with passion, he was to become evasive and to suggest that she was being unreasonably demanding. She was not the only woman with whom he played this cruel game; but his need to play it and to reassure himself through it of his own attractions was symptomatic of deeper anxieties and insecurities, as was his fear of dependence or commitment. He was the victim of a pattern of behaviour he did not recognize or understand, as much as were the women who loved him.

During July and August Shaw saw a great deal of Edith and he began to take her back with him to the lodgings he shared with his mother at Osnaburgh Street. The first occasion that he did so was on 22 July, when she had come to the Museum to meet Shaw's friend and her prospective editor, Robert Ellice Mack. Afterwards they walked back to Shaw's rooms together. More than twenty years later, this was how she recalled the occasion:

'[Edith],' he said again, in that voice that might well have been the life's music of some one else, '[Edith], kiss me –'

She could not speak; she could hardly breathe. His eyes still held hers. His face did not move, and yet their faces were drawing nearer together.

'Kiss me,' he said again. And he only needed to move his head forward a very, very little to take the lips she did not refuse. She drew back from that kiss and hid her eyes in his neck. His arm went round her shoulders. Almost at once he put her back into the embrace of the chair very gently, very definitely. Her eyes were closed.[30]

Memory and fiction both distort, and this passage has been moulded by both; but there is no reason to suppose that, in the telling, the tale was changed beyond all recognition.

When [Edith] looks back at that summer, it seems to her that the sun always shone. She sees always the glare of the glazed shop-fronts, the dry pavement that scorched one's feet, the fruit and flowers and barrows wheeled by hoarse-voiced, anxious-looking people, who sold everything very cheaply. She sees through the iron railings of University College the students sitting on the grass eating their lunch, or having inviting-looking tea-parties, the coloured pinafores of the girl students, the interesting attitudes and coloured neckties of the young men. She sees the women in the little by-streets that to them were home, and to her short cuts, combing out their hair on their door-steps. And everywhere little children playing in the dust.[31]

On the morning after he first took Edith back to Osnaburgh Street, she called on him there so early that he and his mother were still having breakfast; 'she lost her head a little, and instead of calling on him in the regular way . . . she sent up to say that Mrs Brown wanted to see him. He thought it was a charwoman and could not make out what reason she found for the ruse.' On discovering his mistake, he arranged to meet her at Portland Road (now Great Portland Street) Station and they walked in Regent's Park for an hour. Ten days later, on 3 August, she came to the Museum again; Shaw had tea with her, and afterwards they returned to Osnaburgh Street, where they went upstairs to meet his mother. Then they took a bus to Charing Cross and a train into the country, to Chislehurst, and walked all the way back to Lee together. The next day she did not reach the Museum until five, when they went for another walk in Regent's Park. Later in the month, on the 17th and 18th, the diary records 'Mrs Bland at the Museum', and on the latter, she went back to Shaw's rooms for tea. He walked with her to Cannon Street Station, and as the train was not yet due in, they walked down Dowgate Hill and sat for a few moments on the stalls beside the river. The diary comments laconically, 'pretty scene'. In all these walks, short or long, visits to Shaw's rooms for tea, sudden joyous glimpses of the river, there seem to be the elements of every love affair: the need to be together, to talk, to touch. For these two months, Shaw was clearly taking time from his writing to be with her, and enjoying her company – 'she was very attractive. I was very fond of her and paid her all the attention I could.' But the competition for his attention was keen. On Friday 20 August the diary records

> Mrs Bland at the Museum in the afternoon. Saw her to a bus at the corner of Chancery Lane. Gave her some tea at an Italian café on the way. J[enny] P[atterson] here when I came in. Got to Wildwood Farm [Charlotte Wilson's house, for a meeting of the Hampstead Historic Society] at 20½ [8.30 p.m.]. Mrs Besant there. Walked to her house door with her.[32]

A month earlier May Morris had sent Shaw a couple of photographs of Burne-Jones paintings, by way of a birthday present. As May was one of Burne-Jones's favourite models, and posed for the central figure in his painting 'The Golden Stair', one of these may have included a portrait of her. Shaw 'tried to write a few verses in acknowledgement', but verse was never a strong point. Perhaps he confided his struggles to Edith and she offered to help him out, for one of the two poems known to have been written for him is entitled 'The Depths of the Sea: for a picture by E. Burne Jones'. This takes as its epigraph the Latin words *Habes tota quod mente petisti/ Infelix*: 'Unhappy one, you have what you have sought with your whole heart'. But the quotation, from Book Four of Virgil's *Aeneid*, does not, in fact, include the extra-metrical word *'infelix'* (unhappy one).[33] The words are spoken by the goddess Juno to Venus, who has succeeded in making Dido fall in love with Aeneas; more colloquially, they mean: 'Now you've got exactly what you wanted'. Juno does not call Venus *'infelix'*, however; this is an adjective that Dido later uses to describe herself. It looks as if Edith was assuming the lines referred to Dido, and her unhappy passion. Shaw may even have suggested the quotation to her, for, though he claimed to find Virgil unreadable, he was to call an early play *Arms and the Man*, after Dryden's translation of the poem's opening lines. Edith herself may have learned a little Latin at school, or, like Maggie Tulliver, picked some up from her brothers' Latin grammar books. By twisting the line thus, the words can be made to imply that getting what you wish for may actually make you more 'unhappy' than not getting it. This was to become a favourite theme in her children's books, particularly those that deal in wishing magic; and though it is there treated comically, it had first been learned painfully, perhaps from the moment she had prevailed upon Hubert to marry her.

The mermaid, in Edith's poem 'The Depths of the Sea' 'deemed her soulless life was almost fair' until she saw the mortal man; thereafter she

> . . . yearned for him with all her body sweet,
> Her lithe cold arms, and chill wet bosom's beat,
>   Vowed him her beauty's unillumined shrine:
> So I – seeing you above me – turn and tire,
> Sick with an empty ache of long desire
>   To drag you down, to hold you, make you
>   mine!

The poem is made up of two sonnets; in the second, the mermaid succeeds in dragging the mortal down with her and drowning him (as she is doing in the painting):

> She shall find out the meaning of despair,
> And know the anguish of the granted prayer,
>   And how, all ended, all is yet undone.
> So I – I long for what, far off, you shine,
> Not what you must be ere you could be mine.
>   That which would crown despair if it were won.

The verses seem to accept the impossibility of the union between man and mermaid, or, perhaps, Shaw and herself, and to acknowledge that she could only possess him by making him into something other than the being she loved. Its perception is an unusual and a painfully honest one, and Edith thought well enough of the poem to include it in her first book of poems, *Lays and Legends*, published later that year.

In the meantime, Shaw was beginning to manifest all the perversity of mortal men reluctant to drown in love. By September, when Edith had come to expect him to invite her back to his rooms, the characteristic second stage had set in, and he started to find excuses to put her off. If she now showed herself to be tiresome and demanding, he had given her good reason to think that he wanted her company and that she mattered to him. The tone of the diary entries begins to change. Though Shaw was still prepared to put himself out for her (on 10 September, he arrived late at Lee, missed the last train, and had to walk all the way back to town), a note of resentment has crept in:

September 15: Finished review. Worked slowly and with difficulty. Mrs Bland came to the Museum in the afternoon and would not be denied coming here to tea. Drove her to London Bridge and walked back . . . Cab to London Bridge 2/6

The cab fare, more than twice the price of his lunch, was an extravagance that Shaw could ill afford, but he was probably assuaging conscience for having upset her, or so at least the equivalent scene in her novel suggests:

> 'Don't cry,' he said, very gently and aloofly. 'Don't cry. Believe me I'm not worth it.'
>
> 'Oh, yes, you are,' said [she], no longer mistress of herself. 'Oh, I *have* been so miserable.'
>
> Her head leaned toward him behind the rain-streaked window of the hansom. The splash of the horse's feet in the wet road emphasised the silence.
>
> 'Let's have the glass up,' he said; 'it's stopped raining. I should like to point out to you the beauties of the landscape.'[34]

Edith continued to haunt the Reading Room – she was there on the 3rd and 6th September, and again on the 13th and 15th, and three days after this, Shaw 'began to compose a song to Mrs Bland's words'. Early in October, on a wet Thursday morning, he went for a long walk with Hubert, going westward from Lee to Bexley and Foots Cray, but the entry does not say whether they discussed matters more personal than Fabian politics. On the 18th, Edith wrote to ask Shaw whether he would review her forthcoming book of poems, *Lays and Legends*, for *To-Day*, the socialist journal which had been serializing his novels. Through an act of Shavian patronage, this was now edited by the team of 'Fabian Bland', though in practice mainly by Hubert. 'Do you feel inclined to review my book of verses for *To-Day*? I want it reviewed of course – but equally can't do it myself as I mustn't do it favourably and *won't* do it otherwise.'

> Your request for a review [Shaw replied] came on the heels of a petition from Mrs Wilson for a review of 'Scientific Meliorism' for *Freedom* [an anarchist paper edited by Charlotte Wilson]. I have pointed out to her the impossibility of my writing anything this month for anybody. I even said that if I wrote in *Freedom* after pleading 'no time' to Fabian Bland when asked to contribute to *To-Day*, I should be morally dethroned. I cannot do anything for next month's number: that is certain; for *The U[nsocial] S[ocialist]*, which has cost me a month's hard work, is not finished, and I have only provided two shillings for the whole of November as yet, which is an appalling state of things. However, the December number might contain a review by me, if I were hard pressed for it. But it is much as if I were a dentist, and you asked me to pull out one of your teeth without gas. What is the use of

getting me to write down my secret opinion that your poetry is not as good as Shelley's. Here is the review for you, straight off.

'We have received "A Garden of Verses" by E. Nesbitt. The cover is decorated by a flower, slavishly copied from a broken-down Covent Garden product, stuck in a jar in the middle of the table. The author has a fair ear, writes with remarkable facility and with some grace, and occasionally betrays an incisive, but shrewish insight. On the other hand, she is excessively conventional; and her ideas are not a woman's ideas, but the ideas which men have foisted, in their own interest, on women. It is needless to add that she is never original; and it is probable that if she ever writes a sincere poem, she will suppress it. As a poetess she is of the school of Mrs Barrett Browning. Fully as morbid and sentimental as her exemplar, she is shrewder and less conscientious: she has not the scholarship, the thoroughness, the fearlessness of the author of *Aurora Leigh*, and not having the qualities, she has not the faults of the qualities. Thus she does not gush, as Mrs Browning undeniably did; and she is bitter where Mrs Browning was only sad. If the genius of Charlotte Brontë were compounded with that of Mrs Browning, and attenuated with vinegar, an E. Nesbitt might be the result. But it is by no means impossible that so clever a writer may be cured of her defects by the intellectual vigour which such delicate and kindly but firm criticism as the present is calculated, by its virtue as a nerve-tonic, to inpart. We may perhaps have something to add when we shall have had an opportunity of reading the book, which up to the present we have not had time to open.'

This is all I would say. Better send it on to Pease, and let me read the book for pure pleasure.[35]

Shaw's characterization of Edith's poems is painfully, as well as comically just. She was always hurt when friends did not admire her poems as much as she thought they deserved, though she was not so hurt as to destroy his characteristically brilliant letter. Despite this salvo, Shaw *did* write a review of the book, generously entitled 'Found at Last – a new poet' and offered it to the *Pall Mall Gazette*, but unfortunately they did not publish it.[36]

Shaw was now in full retreat. A week later, on 25 October, he and Edith spent a miserable evening together, an evening on which he deliberately avoided the privacy that he had previously sought out with her. As always when her company grated on him, he was particularly busy:

Wrote a batch of reviews. Mrs Bland at Museum. She lunched at Wheatsheaf with me and Joynes. She asked me to meet her at Kings

Cross in the evening and go for a walk. It rained. She insisted on going to Enfield. I insisted on going third class for the sake of company. There was no room in that class at Kings Cross, so we went second to Finsbury Park where we changed carriages. When we got to Enfield it was very wet. I got her some hot whiskey to prevent her catching cold. We returned first class. Got out with her at Kings Cross Underground and saw her to Pentonville where she was staying. Got home just after 1 in the morning.[37]

There was more rain on the evening of Sunday, 31 October, when Shaw met Mrs Bland at Portland Road Station at ten that evening:

We went for a walk along Camden Road, Caledonian Road and Barnsbury Square, where we went to look at the house she lived in as a girl. It rained heavily toward the end of our journey. Left her at Claremont Square and walked home.

Edith always loved taking close friends to visit her old homes. From then on Edith seems to have gone to the Museum when she hoped to see Shaw, and sometimes he walked back with her to her bus or to Cannon Street. On 18 November they took another of the evening train journeys that seem to have been one of their favourite ways of spending time together. When Shaw saw her at the Museum, they arranged to meet at Kings Cross at eight that evening: 'went with her to Highbury New Park. Left her at London Bridge.' Although Shaw noticed Bland looking 'rather sulky' when he came to the Museum and found the two of them there together on 6 December, Hubert was given little ground for jealousy thereafter. The difficulties of extricating himself from his involvement with Edith seem to have taught Shaw a lesson, though not immediately, since in January 1887 his relationship with Annie Besant 'threatened to become a vulgar intrigue'. At the end of that year, however, he and Annie returned each other's love letters and Shaw confided to his diary, 'Reading over my letters before destroying them rather disgusted me with the trifling of the last two years or so about women.'[38]

Although he continued to see Edith at the Museum and to talk to her, he was now obviously determined to limit the demands she made on him, and when she overstepped the bounds the outcome could only be a row. In March 1887, Shaw took rooms in Fitzroy Square, for the house at Osnaburgh Street was going to be pulled down. On 10 May,

Mrs Bland came to the Museum. We had tea at the Austrian Café. She insisted on coming to Fitzroy Square. My Mother was out, and she went away after an unpleasant scene caused by my telling her I wished her to go, as I was afraid that a visit to me alone would compromise her.

It says something for Shaw's equanimity that two days later he took Edith and her companion Alice Hoatson to the Wheatsheaf for lunch, and that he and Edith then went on to an art gallery to look at a Millais painting.[39]

But it was precisely that equanimity that made him such a maddening and frustrating lover; when he was no longer deeply involved, he conducted the relationship with a degree of good temper that at once expressed his detachment and made his partner appear the more unreasonable. The pattern of a cool man pursued by an 'impossible' woman is, of course, a recurrent situation in Shaw's plays – it is particularly evident in *The Philanderer* (1898) – but the plays never reveal what has driven the huntress to close in so relentlessly upon her prey. The opening phase of male desire which had initiated the relationship is seldom shown, or if it is it has been translated into some other less personal or more altruistic motive, such as Professor Higgins's ambition in *Pygmalion* to teach Eliza to speak 'properly'. Both in his plays and his accounts of his own life Shaw omitted the initial phase of male pursuit, not because he didn't pass through it but because he felt ashamed of being driven by sexual desire, or even by the desire to make a conquest. The role of pursuer seemed to him undignified, even a little ridiculous; he preferred to regard that role as essentially feminine, and he appropriated the idea of the powerful and sexual 'Life Force' in order to explain what drove women on thus:

> 'We went to *Man and Superman*,' she said. 'I do think it's silly.'
> 'Didn't you like it? Most young ladies rave over Mr Bernard Shaw.'
> 'Oh, it was clever,' said [she], 'much cleverer than anything I ever saw. But –'
> 'But?'
> 'People don't run after people like that in real life. It's simply caricature!'
> 'Don't they?' said he. 'You think that all that about the life-force is nonsense?'
> 'I don't know,' she said; 'anyway, even if it isn't, people don't behave like that.'
> 'I wonder,' said he. 'Well. I wonder. You think it's always the men who do the running?'
> 'Isn't it?' said she.
> 'Yes,' he said, 'in books.'

Suddenly, for no reason that she could have given, she wished her stairs clear of him.[40]

This dialogue between Daphne and Mr Henry, from Edith's novel *Daphne in Fitzroy Street* shows how far Mr Henry has been imbued with Shavian characteristics, while being carefully dissociated from the 'real' Bernard Shaw, author of plays.

Edith took some trouble to disguise Mr Henry's identity, making him a painter instead of a playwright, but he is nevertheless a *socialist* painter, and when he decides to paint Daphne dressed in a Salvation Army uniform and playing a tambourine, as a woman transfigured by love, there seems to be a deliberate allusion to *Major Barbara*, perhaps even a suggestion that the character of Major Barbara was in part inspired by Edith herself – though she seems to have been the only person who ever thought so. Shaw's preface to *Major Barbara* indicates that the play's concern with poverty owes a great deal to the old Fabian debates on the subject. Had not Shaw first been drawn to the Fabian by their earliest tract, 'Why Are the Many Poor?', and had not Edith herself helped to bring that pamphlet into being?

The title of *Daphne in Fitzroy Street* links it with Shaw's home territory, for he had lived in that street at number 37 in the early 1880s, and after five years at Osnaburgh Street was to move to 29 Fitzroy Square and live there for another ten. The book's heroine, Daphne, is a young girl just out of a convent, but her situation is brought a little nearer to that of her author in 1886 by giving her a much younger sister, Doris, only a year or two older than Iris had been at that time. Daphne, a little like the young Edith, looks on as her two lovers fight it out, and, rather more like Edith, pretends to faint at a crucial moment. Several of the book's characters seem to be portraits of real people – the Russian, Vorontzoff, strongly suggests Stepniak, a friend of Shaw's as well as of the Blands'. When Beatrice Dunsany read the book, she said how much she loved this character, adding perceptively, 'I think you must have known him.'[41] The dilettante, Seddon, sounds like the wealthy D'Arcy Reeve, who was later to act as Edith's patron, and was also known to Shaw. Although Daphne is courted by two devoted and charming young men she perversely falls for the exacting and contemptuous Mr Henry, in part because he has a determination that matches her own:

'Have you ever wanted anything frightfully and not had it?'
'No,' said [she], 'I always get what I want.'
'So,' he said very slowly, 'do I.'

Mr Henry fascinates women because he combines an unexpectedly frank ardour with an extreme independence that makes his behaviour unpredictable. As he falls in love with Daphne, so he retreats from her, telling her that he cannot allow her to come between him and his work. Daphne, who shares her author's self-will, cannot accept his rejection of her:

> You see Daphne had always made her dreams come true. She had engineered all things as she chose, till this thing came upon her. It was not possible to believe that now there were two elements which she could not control, her love for Henry, and Henry himself. The love, she admitted, was stronger than she was. But Henry could not be stronger than she and her love together. She was certain of victory if only she could meet him face to face.
>
> All day she spent, in spirit, on that staircase of his. And all the time she was telling herself, over and over again, that of course she should not go.
>
> And of course she went.[42]

But for all her determination Daphne's author could no more make her dreams come true than Daphne had been able to. Only within her fiction could Edith write a happy ending to her hopeless love: the end of the book reveals and removes the last impediment to their union. Mr Henry had finally – and *wrongly* – supposed Daphne to be married. His discovery that she is not brings them together at last. It looks as if her author wanted to believe that, had she been as free as Daphne all those years before, things might have turned out differently. The real end of Edith's relationship with Shaw is also included in the book, but it is used to make a kind of false coda, a darker prelude that sets off, by contrast, their final idyllic reunion in Paris:

> Time and change were busy with Daphne, and in the full splendour of spring a day came when she could . . . say sincerely to a soul that suddenly felt free: 'It is all over. Thank God, I do not love him any more!'
>
> 'But oh,' she told herself, 'if only he would love me again, and try once again to make me love him! That is what I really want. That's what would make the world really good again. If only I could hurt him as he hurt me. What's the use of my not loving him when I can't tell him so?'[43]

Daphne is full of the conflict and pain that Edith's love for Shaw created in her, feelings she formalized into the Swinburnean rhythms of her poem, 'Bewitched'. Shaw recalled that the poem, as originally written, had included a reference to his 'white malign face' – he had the

pallid skin that goes with reddish hair. Together they had altered this
to 'dark malign face' in order to disguise his identity when the poem
was first published:

> Attracted, repelled and heart-sickened
>   By rhythmic delight and disdain,
> Succeeding each other like wave-beats
>   On the storm-broken shore of my brain –
> I hate you until we are parted,
>   And ache till I meet you again! . . .
>
> For the depths of the night and the silence,
>   Are alive with your dark malign face:
> Your voice drowns all solitude's voices,
>   And your eyes – oh, your eyes! – are all space; . . .
>
> And all would be nothing to suffer,
>   If once at my feet you could lie,
> And offer your soul for my loving –
>   Could I know that your world was just I –
> And could laugh in your eyes and refuse you,
>   And love you and hate you and die![44]

Edith had made little effort to disguise her feelings, but Shaw as
usual developed his own view of what had happened and when he came
to explain Edith's passion for him to her biographer, Doris Langley
Moore, he took care to underestimate its seriousness: 'She imagined at
one time she had fallen violently in love with him . . . He had no real
love affair with her, for he was never serious in his feelings . . .'[45] To
such disclaimers as these she might reasonably have replied, 'I was the
more deceived.' Yet if Shaw prompted conflicting emotions in Edith,
she too aroused unresolved feelings in him, feelings that he attempted
to exorcise in the opening chapters of an unfinished novel that he began
writing in June 1887. This account of the Blands and his relationship
with them conveys, as no more personal statement could have done,
his confused and ambivalent feelings towards Edith. Having completed two chapters, Shaw set it aside, recognizing that they were too
closely drawn from life. The fragment has no title, and, having picked
it up and put it down again several times, Shaw forgot about it until the
manuscript turned up again in 1928. In 1946 he presented it to the
National Library of Ireland with an explanatory preface:

> Of this fragment I have not the faintest recollection. I should deny its
> existence if it were not before me as I write, all the more energetically as

it is a complete throwback to the Victorian novel, with its triangle of husband, wife and lover, who reappear some ten years later in my play called *Candida*. But in the play marriage is triumphant ... In the following fragment the convention of ... *Middlemarch* still prevails: the lover is the hero and the husband only the wife's mistake.[46]

Even this preface is characteristically deceptive: Shaw's insistence that he had totally forgotten about its existence is undercut by his confident account of the relationship between the three main characters. It is not self-evident from reading the two chapters themselves that the book was to treat a love triangle along *Middlemarch* lines. The wife seems far too disagreeable to be a potential Dorothea, and the lover seems, predictably, too reluctant. Shaw told Doris Langley Moore that he thought 'no two people were ever married who were better calculated to make the worst of each other' than Edith and Hubert. His unfinished novel also makes the worst of them both, in its own fictional terms. The two chapters convey only too vividly the sense of a difficult couple living in an atmosphere of domestic tension and discontent. Though the story unfolds in a doctor's house in a provincial town, there are many details in the descriptions and domestic circumstances of the main characters, Dr and Mrs Maddick, that evoke the Blands. The house is obviously poor – the gas is turned down in the hall and there is oilcloth instead of carpet on the floor. The furniture consists of hand-me-downs, and cretonne covers and new curtains scarcely conceal their decrepit state. None of the chairs is steady, and the hero perches as lightly as possible upon one.[47] Shaw here provides a colder view of the shabby gentility that would later characterize life with the Bastables off the Lewisham Road. There are three small, lively children, as there now were in the Bland household.

Dr Maddick is particularly unattractive – vain, lazy and greedy. He dresses flashily and sports not a dark moustache but a fair one. He 'dressed at being a young, handsome and dashing man, and had neither youth enough nor character enough nor money enough to be more than a passable counterfeit'. He is also something of a womanizer, and to his wife's evident resentment devotes much time to cosseting his wealthy women patients; he cannot be bothered with the poor ones. About Mrs Maddick neither the hero, young Dr Kincaid, nor his author can quite make up their minds, and much of the chapters' interest lies in this uncertainty. Kincaid's first impression is of 'a young woman who was profusely freckled and did not look very strong', but when he looks at her again, he discovered, to his surprise, that she was better worth looking at than he had thought at first. Her nose and forehead were beautifully set and shaped; and she had large eyes of a tawny brown colour, with long dark lashes. A want of breadth at the root of the nose and of firmness in the nostril made her look weak and sensitive; but her broad mouth, almost lifeless, and tightly closed by a chin with an unmistakeable snap in it showed that she was deficient neither in will nor temper. Her normal expression was one of suppressed resentment and quick intelligence. Altogether a woman so interesting that she could afford to have freckles and a shrew's mouth – who would perhaps have looked incomplete without them.

Kincaid's response to her takes the form of a series of see-saw observations, such as 'if this were not a brave and clever woman, she was a quick-witted and reckless one'.[48] Shaw's own hesitations, his advances and retreats from Edith, are vividly conveyed.

In the first chapter Mrs Maddick deliberately ignores all Kincaid's delicate hints and thoroughly embarrasses him by complaining of her husband's neglect and his attentions to other women. When Kincaid comes down next morning, he is shocked to discover her opening her husband's mail, an invasion of privacy that he considers quite improper, as he takes care to explain to her. She flies into a temper with him and throws a tea cup at his head, which he fields: 'I am glad the cup is not broken, since it didn't hurt you,' she said. 'I wish it had. I did not believe that I could hate anybody so after seeing them only twice.'

If Mrs Maddick's reaction to Kincaid is a volatile blend of attraction and hostility, his to her is scarcely less confused:

He noticed that he was not sorry to see her. The afternoon sun just caught a corner of the dusty green tablecloth, on its way to her. Her eyes were brown, amber, green, all colours at once. But to Kincaid, who knew too much about eyes to lose his heart to them readily, the most interesting thing about her was her extreme sensitiveness. She changed every instant, and at every word. He had not known her long enough to exhaust a hundredth part of the possible combinations and formulations of her restless suspicion, her shyness, her audacity, her impulsive frankness, her insatiable curiosity, base jealousy and vulgar envy. He was by natural aptitude as well as by training a student of psychology; and he appreciated this new subject.[49]

Deficient, it seems, in any natural reserve, Mrs Maddick displays a bewildering variety of emotions. That afternoon, she asks him to walk with her to the village, and then beyond it, where she shows herself less and less of a downmarket Madame Bovary, and more and more of Edith herself as

> they criticised the scenery, sounded each other's tastes and accomplishments, and discussed Herbert Spencer, George Eliot, Browning, Turgenieff, Walt Whitman, socialism, spiritualism, and other subjects . . . He calculated that she had read six books to his one, with the result of completely disguising from herself the fact that she was very imperfectly educated and consequently disabled by a vulgarity of thought of which he, who was highly educated as education goes, was acutely conscious. He knew too much to be guilty of the folly of trying to set her right or to assert the greater comprehensiveness of his own views; but he kept as far as he could to discussing faults of conduct; for here he found her frank, funny, subtle, and happy in the full play of her egotism.

Before the end of their ramble, during which she has invited him to help her over stiles and gaze into her eyes, she informs him, to his annoyance, that the long walk she has induced him to take will already have compromised her seriously, and almost in the same breath demands whether he believes in love at first sight. In other words, the Mrs Maddick of these two unfinished chapters corresponds closely to the Mrs Bland of the diary – after Shaw's initial enthusiasm had worn off.[50]

Shaw abandoned these two chapters in part because the Maddicks were too transparently based on the Blands. In the retrospective preface to his first novel, *Immaturity*, he had written:

> I have used living models as freely as a painter does, and in much the same way: that is, I have sometimes made a fairly faithful portrait founded on intimate personal intercourse, and sometimes . . . developed what a passing glance suggested to my imagination.[51]

The unfinished novel seems to depict the Blands in fairly minute detail. But what, if anything, can be learned from it, other than how the Blands appeared to him in a mood of disillusion? Does the preface imply that its author had originally intended the Shavian Dr Kincaid to figure as Mrs Maddick's lover at some later stage? And was it to be a consummated love affair or merely a romantic passion? Behind such literary speculations lies the more intriguing problem of what exactly had taken place on the diary's 'memorable evening' at Lee, and later in the rooms at Osnaburgh Street? Was it simply 'much pathetic kissing and petting'?[52] In the five years or so after his sexual initiation by

Jenny Patterson, Shaw was physically more ardent and less inhibited than he was to show himself again. On the other hand, Mrs Patterson, both because of her age and her relationship with Shaw's powerful mother, was a protective figure in a way that the challenging Edith could never be, providing the bedroom for their love-making and making most of the overtures herself. In practice Shaw's announced inhibitions about making love to his friends' wives seem to have held good, even though, as he frankly admitted:

> All autobiographies are lies. I do not mean unconscious, unintentional lies: I mean deliberate lies. No man is bad enough to tell the truth about himself during his lifetime, involving, as it must, the truth about his family and his friends and colleagues.[53]

Shaw undoubtedly knew something about the sexual side of the Blands' marriage, however, presumably partly from Edith. He explained to Doris Langley Moore that 'Bland suffered physically from headaches and other disturbances when he could not have women . . . and he [Shaw] thought that Edith was rather glad to have some assistance in satisfying him.'[54] Though his language implies the characteristic assumption of his day, that men have 'needs' which women reluctantly satisfy, he was by no means narrow-minded. By contrast with Bland, Shaw and Edith were both inhibited and sexually shy, and they may have found this quality in one another mutually reassuring. Shaw may have been not only flattered but even satisfied, as some men are, to know that Edith was willing enough to be seduced, and left it at that. She may have been relieved to find him less physically demanding than Bland, even if she was ultimately disappointed. Relevant, too, is the prosaic question of opportunity: Shaw's rooms did not offer sufficient privacy for more than petting, though that they offered that much is suggested by her later eagerness to be invited up, and his evident reluctance to do so.

Edith's passion for Shaw was intense. At one time she proposed leaving Hubert in order to run away with him, as he privately boasted to Doris Langley Moore; the obsession, fictionally portrayed in *Daphne*, affects her body as strongly as it does her inner state:

> Anxiety, thwarted longing, the persistent consciousness of unspeakable disaster, induced in the girl a continued physical nausea. She was driven to the craftiest expedients to hide from her friends how little she could eat, and how seldom. But she did hide it, hiding with it all the rest.[55]

This degree of physical response seems more characteristic of a mature woman caught up in an unhappy love affair than of a young girl falling in love for the first time, the situation of the novel's heroine. There is, of course, no way of deciding how reliable *Daphne* is as an account of her relationship with Shaw nor how intimate they had been; yet it was after this that she began to have consummated love affairs with younger men. Her experience with Shaw seems to have caused her to abandon her inhibitions about being unfaithful – and these inhibitions were effectively far stronger at that time for women than for men. Bland's persistent infidelities must, in any case, have encouraged her to look for some way of restoring the balance between them. Shaw's own chapters present Mrs Maddick as deeply resentful of her husband's amorous pursuits, so that she allows herself 'the impropriety of . . . complaining of her husband to a stranger'. Shaw's anxiety to determine what Doris Langley Moore wrote about his friendship with Edith would in itself be more suspicious, if it were not that he habitually treated all potential biographers thus. It looks as if, during the months of July and August 1886, Edith gave herself in her imagination to Shaw, assuming that his close and sensitive attentions to her were unique, and his exploratory caresses the prelude to a passionate love affair. It never came. She later reproached him with infirmity of purpose – 'You had no right to write the preface if you were not going to write the book' – forgetful of what she must once have known, that he was really no more self-confident than she.[56]

Both of them possessed the enviable knack of staying on good terms with their old flames. Shaw was to remain a frequent visitor of the Blands for the next ten years or so, and even though they no longer met socially after his marriage (his wife, he explained, would have regarded Edith as 'a piece of his past'), he later helped her out financially from time to time. Hubert told those closest to him that if ever they needed help, they should turn to Shaw, and indeed it was Shaw who paid for his son John Bland to go to Cambridge, after Hubert's death.[57] Whatever had taken place between G.B.S. and Edith did not prevent him from becoming the oldest and most dependable of their friends.

THE MOUSE AND THE CATS

Jan. 22, 1882. Press Day for *Sylvia's Home Journal* published at Warwick House, Salisbury Square by Messrs. Ward Lock & Co. Present in the Editorial Office, the Editress, Miss Graham, furiously at work on the opening address to her readers, myself [Alice Hoatson], reader and reporter on manuscripts for its pages, Miss Lord making up 'The Milliner and Dressmaker' from the rubbish heap not worthy of appearance in the first named journal. 1.30 p.m. a knock at the door. 'Come in,' I called, expecting to see the printer's boy seeking copy. Enter a lady, very tall and robed in black, pale as a ghost and shivering with cold. I was squatted on the floor at the gas stove, making cocoa for our luncheon. It was just ready and I hastily poured out three cups, handed a chair to the ghost and the others (who always brought their own luncheon), opened my sandwich box and offered it to the poor shiverer, who took it with tearful eyes and thanks. I poured my own into the milk jug and still squatting, all chairs being occupied, began to feed. E.N. was quite upset to see me on the floor and wanted to give up her chair to me, but I claimed I had the warmest place and was happy to keep it, collected some of my sandwiches (my mother always made too many and very good they were so there was no lack of food). In a trembling voice E[dith] responded to Miss Graham's question 'What can I do for you?' said she had brought a story she hoped would be accepted for *Sylvia*. 'Give it to Miss Hoatson, please,' said Miss Graham, 'she is my reader and if she reports favourably I will take it, but it cannot appear until next month as this month's issue is filled and goes to print this afternoon. I will let you hear its fate next week after Miss Hoatson's report. I must bid you goodbye now, but do not hurry away; my colleagues will entertain you. Goodbye.'

Off she went at that and Miss Lord also said adieu, having filled up her journal, though she was supposed to remain until 5 p.m. E[dith] looked relieved and I asked if she would remain until I had filled up my share of *Sylvia* and that it was only mechanical arrangement of the illustrated portion and would be sent off to press in half-an-hour. She accepted with thanks and I moved her close to the stove, assuring her I would read and report on the story before I left at 5 o'clock. We chatted for an hour then she told me she had a six weeks' old little daughter but need not hurry home for an hour. She gave me her address and hoped I would come some day to see her. I liked all so much that I promised to take the first chance. 'Oh, can you come next Sunday? Do if you can and make my husband's acquaintance.' She left shortly after and I busied myself with *Sylvia*, got it done and took it down to Mr Bowden to send over to the printers. Then I left, there being no more to do. I took her story with me to read on the train (I was then living at Brixton) and found it so exceedingly good that I determined to write to her there and then that I was sure it would be accepted on my report.

When I got to the office next morning (my hours were 10 a.m. to 5 p.m.) I was told there was a lady waiting to see me in my room. I hurried up (four flights!) and arrived breathless to find E. walking up and down looking more ill and ghostly than the day before. 'Oh,' she said, 'could you give me back the story you had from me yesterday? We had another copy and my husband took it to *The Weekly Dispatch* and we had a letter of acceptance this morning and it is to appear in next Saturday's edition. We shall never get anything more accepted if they find it appearing in another place! I have brought another written by me only – can you possibly let it be submitted instead?' 'Give it to me,' I said. 'There is no entry in the MSS book and I shall not report it. This will go in its place – I will read it later and get it taken, if Miss Graham approves.'[1]

This was how Edith's intensest and most painful friendship had begun – in an atmosphere of warmth and cameraderie that is the particular prerogative of working women – a group much rarer in the 1880s, at least among the middle classes, than today. Alice Hoatson was six months younger than Edith, and came from Yorkshire. Her father had been an accountant in Halifax, where she was born, but she now lived with her widowed mother in Brixton and worked for *Sylvia's Home Journal*, a Victorian woman's magazine mainly filled with detailed illustrations of current fashions for its readers to show to their dressmakers.[2] There were also pages of correspondence from girls discreetly signing themselves 'Madge St Clair', 'A Scotch Lassie' or, more poetically, 'Bluebell' or 'Stephanotis'. There were useful articles on how to dress prettily and neatly on ten pounds a year, what to wear when in mourning, how to cook economical dishes, grow ferns and manage the servants. Melodramatic serials ran from month to month ('Esther's Sacrifice', 'Cousin Gussie'), but short stories appeared rather seldom. It would be reassuring if Alice Hoatson's circumstantial account of her first meeting with Edith could be corroborated by the appearance of a short story of hers in the March issue (presumably Alice was 'putting to bed' the February issue on 22 January). But, like Edith's earliest published poems, the story in question is elusive: only three short stories were published in *Sylvia's Home Journal* in the whole of 1882: two of these are not in the least like anything Edith is known to have written, while the third – 'Twas in a Crowd', published in November – is disappointingly signed 'M.G.', an unlikely pair of initials for her to have used.

Alice Hoatson kept her promise to visit the Blands at Elswick Road: 'It was in May 1882 that I first saw Hubert. He was curious to know the girl she raved about,' she confided in the long, rambling account of her friendship with Edith that she wrote for Doris Langley Moore. This is a fascinating and tantalizing document, not least for what it leaves unsaid: that Alice became Hubert's mistress in 1886, and remained so until the end of his life, and that Rosamund and John Bland, brought up as Edith's children, were actually Alice's. St John Ervine's biography of Shaw described Hubert, on Shaw's authority, as

> a Tory Democrat from Blackheath, who sported fashionable clothes, wore a monocle, and maintained simultaneously three wives, all of whom bore him children. Two of the wives lived in the same house. The legitimate one was E. Nesbit . . .[3]

Alice's memoir is hazy about dates – for example, the date she actually gave for her first encounters with Edith and Hubert was 1881, yet she also remembered that Iris was six weeks old – since Iris was born in December 1881, this must have been a slip for 1882. Nor were her feelings much less muddled than her memory for dates – her account of Edith is profoundly ambivalent:

> She was, I think, without exception, the dearest, naughtiest, most cruel, most kindly, affectionate creature God ever sent into this world. One had ever the conviction she was a law unto herself, neither to hold nor to bind, yet never able to sleep until she had made confession, and as far as possible, reparation for any unkindness or injustice she had shown during the day. And there were many such instances.[4]

Though florid in style by modern standards, Alice's memoir practises a thoroughly Victorian discretion on all the more delicate aspects of their complex relationship; the reader is confronted with a disjointed sequence of anecdotes as vivid and compelling as they are evasive and unreliable.

From the outset Edith had shown Alice something of the extravagant affection that had characterized her friendship with Ada. Friendships between women in the nineteenth century were often warmer, more physical, and less inhibited than they are today, when women enjoy a far greater degree of social intimacy with men, but are more alert to uneasy nuances in friendships with their own sex. There were a number of subjects, particularly those relating to the body and its functions, which young men and women never normally discussed at that time, just as they could not share physically intimate space unless married, while both might safely be shared with other women. Just as she had done to her sister Mary, Edith expressed the warmest affection for her girlfriends, particularly when she was very young. She wrote them love poems as if she were a man, as if she felt that young men might not sufficiently appreciate their charms and she was going to make up for their oversights. In the summer of 1879 she wrote some verses to a younger friend, Emilie Bailey, that begin

> Enchanting darling, love to you
> Makes all old thoughts as dreams to me!
> I only know you never knew
> Love so entire as mine will be.[5]

While poetry is traditionally licensed to exaggerate, Edith had voiced similar feelings in her letters to Ada, letters written after she herself was married and when Ada was expecting to be. Such poems and letters reflected Edith's passionate nature.

Alice Hoatson came into Edith's life when, despite marriage, she was lonelier and more isolated than ever before. With two small children, anxieties about Hubert and the need to provide financially, Edith was weighed down, and Alice's cheerful capable personality and sympathetic ear were exactly what she needed. Alice would come and spend the night with Edith when Hubert was at his mother's, helping her with the children, domestic chores or with her writing, or simply listening to her plans and problems. Edith, in turn, showed her sincere affection for her new friend in a number of different ways: she wrote her some verses, later included in the medley poem 'The Moat House', whose sentiments cast disturbing shadows of coming events:

My sweet, my sweet,
She is complete
From dainty head to darling feet;
So warm and white,
So brown and bright,
So made for love and love's delight.

God could but spare
One flower so fair,
There is none like her anywhere;
Beneath wide skies
The whole earth lies,
But not two other such brown eyes.[6]

Because she was so fond of her, Edith wanted to believe that their lives were somehow fundamentally linked, so she was intrigued to discover that, in the days when she herself had been living in Barnsbury Square, Alice had been teaching English in a German school close by; had Edith attended classes given by a Miss Ervine, who taught Alice's German pupils, they might have met several years earlier. Edith liked to dwell on their similarities and felt so at home with Alice's mother that she was convinced that they must all be related, and she used to ask the genealogist, Oswald Barron, to work out their joint family trees. By 1884 Alice had been persuaded to join the Fabian Society, and was Edith's favourite companion, both there and elsewhere. Although letters to Ada in the second half of 1885 suggest, perhaps mischievously, that Alice was in love with Bernard Shaw, and that Frank Podmore was in love with Alice,[7] there may have been an element of match-making in these observations. In the case of Ada's engagement to Harry, Edith had certainly promoted, even over-promoted the match. Was she anxious to find a man capable of appreciating Alice as she had done? In that case, the end of her search turned out to be one of life's sharpest ironies. If Alice Hatfield in the Blands' novel *The Prophet's Mantle* was in part inspired by the other Alice H., here was a further irony, for Alice Hatfield's fate – falling in love with a charismatic socialist and bearing him an illegitimate child – foreshadowed that of the real Alice.

For some time during the early 1880s Edith had been urging Alice to 'chuck' her ill-paid job on *Sylvia's Home Journal* and join them. The move to a larger house made this possible and late in 1886 Alice finally did so. A friend of many years later, Mrs Alphonse Courlander, provided Doris Langley Moore with the received version as to how this had happened: according to her account, the Blands advertized for help with their two children, and Miss Hoatson applied for the job. She was dressed in grey, and looked so timid as she stood on the doorstep that they decided to call her 'the Mouse'; she replied that she would call them 'the Cats'. It is, of course, far too neat a story to be anything but a *canard*, a joke invented by Hubert to satisfy inquisitive visitors. By 1886, when Alice eventually joined them, the Blands did not have two but three children. Edith had often urged her to go and live with them before, so she would hardly have waited to answer an advertisement. The 'cat' nicknames that Edith and Hubert used to one another when feeling affectionate dated from an earlier phase of their marriage, and baby Iris had been 'the pussy-kitten' or 'kitten-cat' even before Alice knew them. Edith loved nicknames, a trait Shaw picked up in *An Unfinished Novel*, where Mrs Maddick calls her husband Pelham 'Rip' – appropriate enough for Bland. Alice became 'the Mouse' because she looked so small beside the tall Edith and Hubert, and perhaps because of her reticence. The children always called her 'Auntie' and so did many of their friends.[8]

Alice moved in with the Blands late in 1886, and apparently somewhat unexpectedly, since a Fabian leaflet printed in the autumn of that year still gives her address as 1 Pelham Road, Wood Green.[9] Her explanation of how she came to do so was that Edith had

never relaxed her efforts to get me to join my lot with hers and in 1886 I gave in, being seriously ill at the time. I was on a visit to her at the time and she nursed me so tenderly through it I could resist no longer.

But Alice's 'serious illness' was a euphemism for the birth of her daughter Rosamund in November that year.

During the summer of the previous year, June '85, Alice had agreed to take over from Miss Robbins as assistant secretary to the Fabian. Both Alice and Edith attended the Fabian Society on 16 October, according to Shaw's diary, but there is no further mention of Mrs Bland until the third week of March '86. The reason was that Edith had become pregnant again, some six months after the birth of Fabian in January '85. Alice, like the devoted friend she was, came to nurse Edith through the birth in February '86. Either just before or soon after it, she gave Edith a fat volume of blank pages, bound in green and inscribed 'For Verses. Edith Bland from Alice Hoatson. February 18 1886.' Perhaps it was afterwards, and intended to console her, for the baby was dead at birth or died immediately afterwards. It was entirely unexpected. Edith was utterly distraught, and Alice quite unprepared for her violent reaction:

> E. went nearly mad about this. I was nursing her. The doctor [was] Adrian Stokes whom we had for many years. He had a great opinion of me. I hope I deserved it, but E. never forgave [him] for the loss of her baby: why she thought him to blame I have never been able to guess. This baby I prepared for burial and E. had made me promise to bring it to her while Hubert was digging its grave in the garden. I had got a long fish basket and dressed the poor mite, laid her in it and put flowers all around. Then I took it to E. She had promised to let me take it away in a quarter of an hour. By that time I ought to have known the worth of her promises! Well, I didn't. For one hour and a half I struggled to get it from her while Hubert came to know what happened to keep me. At last she let him take it; he looked so wretched, he could not hide his misery.[10]

The way that the narrative suddenly switches to focus on Hubert's suffering instead of Edith's unconsciously reveals all that the memoir otherwise passes over in silence. While Alice had been nursing Edith, or even before, Hubert had bent his powers of persuasion to seducing Alice. Few women could resist his sustained attentions. When he came to her room at night, she could not turn him away. Perhaps she even believed that she was helping Edith by acting as her surrogate, relieving Hubert's urgent needs while her friend was *hors de combat* – all Edith's friends thought of Bland as 'unusually hot-blooded' or needing more sexual outlets than was 'normal'. However it came about, Alice was now deeply in love with Hubert and sensitized to his reactions. As she struggled to wrench his dead child from Edith's grasp, she was, though she did not yet know it, already carrying his living child within her.

By 22 March 1886, Edith was sufficiently recovered to start entertaining again; Shaw and Sidney Webb spent that evening at the Blands' house, with Alice Hoatson and Miss Ellis. Edith, still depressed from her loss, then went down with a bad attack of measles, caught from one of the children, and another three months passed before Shaw first noticed that there was more to Edith than freckles and a shrew's mouth. That summer, Edith was entirely preoccupied with Shaw. By the autumn his interest was waning, though she refused to moderate her demands on him. Late in September the Blands moved from Cambridge Road, where they only had a six-month lease, to a similar house close by, in Dorville Road. November brought the excitement of seeing her first volume of poems, *Lays and Legends*, in print. Alice, meanwhile, had been obliged by her advancing pregnancy to withdraw from all public appearances – indeed Shaw's diary does not record seeing her after April.[11] When Edith discovered her friend's plight, she felt deeply sorry for her, imagining her miseries only too vividly, for six years earlier she too had found herself in just such a position. But what was Alice to do? How could the 'ruin' that traditionally awaited the unmarried mother be averted? The answer seemed obvious enough to Edith, who enjoyed dramas and taking charge of awkward situations. She had often enough asked Alice to go and live with her, to become her companion and housekeeper. The solution presented itself with a compelling logic: if Edith adopted the baby, Alice could avoid disgrace and effectively keep the baby too. After her own bitter loss earlier that year she could not bear the idea of separating mother from child. Her gesture was characteristically quixotic – warm, impulsive and thoroughly short-sighted. Alice at first resisted, only too painfully conscious of how she had wronged her trustful would-be benefactor under her own roof. She had not confessed, in so many words, who the baby's father was, yet felt certain that Edith must have guessed and silently understood – more particularly since she had earlier positively encouraged Alice's friendship with Hubert. And in any case, it was difficult for Alice to envisage any bearable alternative. She was now unmarriageable and potentially a social outcast. In offering her a home, Edith not only enabled her to keep both the baby and her reputation; she also enabled her to live under the same roof as the man she loved. He, in turn, would become the baby's guardian and bring it up as his own child – Hubert could be

an affectionate father, especially towards his daughters. Exhausted by
both physical and mental stress, Alice uneasily agreed to Edith's plan.

In order that appearances might be maintained, Alice took up her
usual social round as soon after the birth as she felt able. On 19
November 1886, after the Fabian meeting, Shaw walked down to
Charing Cross Station with a group of members who lived at or near
Lee – Miss Ellis, the Blands, Miss Hoatson and the Stapeltons.[12] In fact
Rosamund had been born two or three weeks earlier, but she had no
birth certificate and her birthday was always celebrated on 19
November, the day that, as Shaw's diary shows, Alice resumed her
social life.

When Edith urged Alice to let her adopt the baby, had she, as Alice
assumed, really guessed who its father was? Did she, indeed, feel
partly responsible for what had happened, since she knew Hubert's
propensities well enough, none better, and she was later to admit, 'It
was my own fault. I might have prevented the opportunity. I didn't
and I deserved the consequences.'[13] She must have had more than an
inkling of the truth, but she probably rejected it from her conscious
mind, dealing with it as most of us deal with intolerable knowledge, by
hiding it from herself. There are two rather different accounts of how
she came to find out. The first occurs in a letter from Rosamund herself
to Mrs Langley Moore, written in an attempt to correct the latter's first
draft account of the episode:

> [Edith] discovered that A.H. was going to have a child but she did not
> know who the father was and A.H. steadily refused to tell her. After the
> child was born she befriended A.H. and took her into her home.
> (Before that she had often begged A.H. to live with her altogether). And
> then six months later made the discovery that the father was her own
> husband. By this time she had grown to love the baby so much she could
> not part with it.
>
> Now my father's story to me was this (and I imagine I am the only
> person he ever told it to). When it transpired who was the father, there
> was, quite naturally, the hell of a scene, and I and my mother were to be
> ejected then and there into the street. Whereupon my father said that if
> we went, he went too. He said that he had never loved his other children
> as he loved me and that he was passionately in love with my mother.
> Finally the matter was thrashed out and the decision was taken that they
> should all remain together. This business recurred several times during
> the first years of my life. I mean, there were other occasions when A.H.
> was told to go and take me with her, but my father prevailed and the
> situation continued until it became permanent. (This I had from

A.H.) . . . One thing I feel you do not take into sufficient account and that is the importance of my father's place in E. Nesbit's existence, and then also you probably underestimate his powers of fascination. Make no mistake about it: – he was absolutely irresistible to the women he paid court to, not only before the event of capture, but after. He had a tremendous hold on anyone he had ever possessed. And why? Partly because he took infinite trouble to please and partly because he never looked upon a woman as a light o' love. He was no he-man, dominating by sheer obvious sexual impulses. He had the sense never to let it *look* as if it were purely a physical urge on either side. He endowed every affair with the romance of his own imagination. This was a far more deadly lure and a far more efficient trap than the method of the modern cave-man with his snatch and grab stunt, with its intervals of brutal outspokenness and indifference. That doesn't last through a life time with *any* woman, but the other can. Chiefly through fantasy, perhaps, but what more powerful factor is there in a woman's life, and certainly at that period, than that of fantasy?

I don't feel that [your] phrase 'though, or because, she still loved her husband' is at all adequate to express the tremendous hold he certainly had on her from the moment he met her until he died. It wasn't simply that she came nobly up to scratch over a big crisis. She could not have borne losing him and there was a danger of that. *He* didn't want to lose either of them and I've no doubt he used every art of which he was capable to keep them both. And through a lifetime of riots and jealousies he succeeded. After his death they parted, though I feel sure he believed they never would.

I think you will get the picture wrong altogether unless you manage to convey how very dominant he was throughout her whole life. One of the things to bear in mind is that he was absolutely the only person who had any influence on her moods and who could control her tantrums and bring her round to reason. And he took a lot of trouble to do it, too, though often it brought on a heart attack [Rosamund was here referring to Hubert's later years], and then of course she was overwhelmed with contrition and full of tenderness for him. How many incidents of this sort I remember. There would be a stormy scene at meals ending in a hysterical outburst, when she would rush from the table and retire into her study with a violent slam of the door, leaving a shattered family staring uncomfortably at their pudding plates. Daddy would say 'Oh, God!' and make for his study, also slamming the door. But always after a short while one would hear him go up to her room and beg to be let in. She would open the door and one could hear a murmur of affectionate phrases – 'Now Cat dearest, don't go on like that. Your old Cat loves you and you love your poor old Cat, don't you? There, kiss your old

Cat and come and have your pudding.' And so on. He comforted and cajoled her and he always stuck by her and excused her to us, however unreasonable and fiendish she had been. And more often than not they would come down the stairs arm in arm and she would kiss us all round and *eat* her pudding.[14]

Rosamund's bitterness against her adoptive mother and her devotion to her father are transparently clear from her account, concerned, among other things, to establish her as her father's favourite: 'He said that he had never loved his other children as he loved me.' She went on to write of Edith's resentment of her, and her sense of childish bewilderment at being treated differently from the others. Neither she nor anyone else could bring themselves to tell Mrs Langley Moore of Edith's divisive will, which had provided only for her own children, not for her adopted children.[15]

After the publication of her biography, Doris Langley Moore received a letter from one of Edith's oldest woman friends, Helen Macklin, the dedicatee of her second series of *Lays and Legends* (1892) and her novel *The Red House* (1903). Helen Macklin questioned the account of the adoption of Rosamund given in the biography, for which Rosamund's letter, just quoted, had been the primary source:

> I will tell you what Edith said to me [she wrote]. At some time (I think not long) after Rosamund's birth, she had a severe illness through which she was devotedly nursed by R.'s mother. (I avoid the name, though of course we both know it: I will call her R.M.) Edith felt affectionate and grateful to her: and when she was recovering, she begged R.M. to tell her the truth. (She had suspected it from the first.) She could forgive it, she told her, but she wanted it not to be still denied. She said to R.M., 'I *know* it is Hubert, only tell me.' – I well remember her words and tone and look. – Then R.M. admitted it. After this Edith went into no more details: I remember not her words, but the impression I received, which was comforting, not saddening like that of the version you have been given – an impression of reconciliation and peace.
>
> After that, could she have seriously wished to send away mother and child? It would be very unlike her. But, of course, with her varying moods and her complete temporary surrender to them, she might at some time have said in a flash what she so little meant that she never thought of it again: and to a hearer's mind it might have a different weight and emphasis. I can only guess . . .
>
> There is another thing I think Edith would wish me to say – not of her husband's sins in one matter but of his attitude towards them . . . She invariably assured me that however little he could resist those tempt-

ations when they came, they were followed by deep repentance and regret: that he could not so hurt her without deep pain afterwards. (That he really loved her in spite of all you know already.) She would not have accepted your adjective when you speak of his '*ruthless* self-gratifications'. She wished me to think of him as he was between the lapses: *that*, she said, was the real man: his heart and thoughts were sound at bottom, in spite of his acts, and all I ever saw of him went to confirm her belief.[16]

These two contrasting accounts reflect more than the teller's attitudes; they also reveal, even if at second hand, the different ways in which Hubert (as transmitted by Rosamund) and Edith (as transmitted by Helen Macklin) wished to see their roles during the major crisis of their life together, a crisis that for Edith had brought a double jealousy and a double loss. Yet if this was the first time Edith had acted as an intermediary of some sort in Hubert's love affairs, it was not to be the last, as Rosamund pointed out:

> As for whether H.B. expressed contrition, well, we don't know that, but knowing him, I bet he did and I have no doubt there were tears and heart-wringings all round at the time. A.H. suffered some tortures, I know. She was a little unsophisticated mouse (which was what she was called by E.N.) of a person, up from Yorkshire and she came into this brilliant company, was dazzled by it, and succumbed, first to E. Nesbit's charms and then to Hubert's. The tragic thing was that it was E.N. who first persuaded her to go about with him in order to get him to give up another lady whom E.N. loathed. It was really rather a curious trait in her character that persisted long after she must have known the dangers of handing any girl over to him or attracting his attention to anyone. I saw it done myself when I was growing up.[17]

Edith found it impossible to write herself into the script of Bland's love life without becoming his usual confidante, occasionally his accomplice, and always his audience.

At times, life with Hubert was more than she could bear: she had asked Shaw to run away with her even before Alice heightened domestic tensions by joining the household, and she was later to make the same request of at least two other lovers, though none of them was apparently willing to make the necessary social sacrifices.[18] It may be that she asked only because she knew in her heart that they would refuse her, for she too had much to lose by an impulsive action of that kind. The wife who ran away to live with another man, even the divorced wife (who had to prove her husband's gross physical cruelty) had no status in society. She would have lost her children and been rejected from every middle-class drawing room. Though Edith often expressed her contempt for convention, she valued the good opinion of friends and acquaintances too much to allow her passional life and needs to decide all her actions. That Hubert returned contrite after each affair is widely attested, and this must have afforded both consolation and reconciliation, perhaps even reassurance, though at least two of his love affairs – those with Maggie and Alice – had a more permanent character. How often new romantic episodes occurred is hard to judge. Berta Ruck, a contemporary of Iris's, commented that 'he made love to every young woman who came near him'. There is a story of Edith paying a call on a young married friend of hers only to find her reclining gracefully upon the sofa, while Hubert sat close beside her, reading her poetry; he was later to cause a minor imbroglio by seducing one of Rosamund's school friends. Yet his son-in-law Clifford Sharp saw his behaviour in a different light. He wrote to Doris Langley Moore:

> I hope no one has suggested to you that Bland was a philanderer. He was as far from that as possible. He was not a woman's man but a man's man par excellence. In spite of his many affairs he paid small attention to women in general. And numerous (for that time) as his affairs were they could certainly be numbered. The reason they loomed so large was that they were *not* mere philandering. He despised philandering utterly both in principle and in practice.

Sharp knew Hubert well, though he tended to idealize him. Hubert's self-portrait as 'Huntley' (in *Something Wrong*) always declined, on principle, 'to walk with a man if a woman was available'; this sounds rather nearer the mark.[19]

As time passed, Edith learned to recognize that, on the whole, Hubert's passions blew themselves out and he returned, perhaps with relief, to the open and established pattern of their marriage. These episodes provided her with occasions for self-dramatization that she seems positively to have enjoyed – role-playing and scenes had always appealed to her, and certainly Shaw had recognized an element of the 'poseur' in both of them. But as well as being deeply understanding, she was also capable of feeling genuinely and desperately hurt, angry and betrayed. Something of both attitudes is indirectly reflected in her verse of this period. Two narrative poems express aggressive and destructive fantasies built around the theme of jealousy: 'The Moat

House', from *Lays and Legends*, (first series, 1886), is the story of a nun who elopes with her lover, bears his child, and is then abandoned by him for a socially advantageous marriage to 'perfect, saintly Lady May'. When he returns with his new bride, the heroine throws herself beneath the wheels of his bridal carriage. Here jealousy becomes self-destructive, and aggression is channelled inwards, against the self. A later poem, 'Bridal Ballad', published in *Lays and Legends* (second series, 1892), has the bride poison her husband on their wedding night for his infidelity, while he, in dying, acknowledges the justice of her act. The narrative element in the ballad form seems to have encouraged her to indulge in self-dramatizing fantasies.

A much more explicit pair of poems, written in the more fluid and personal voice she picked up from Browning, show that, to some extent, she could enter into Hubert's feelings, as well as her own:

The Husband of Today

Eyes caught by beauty, fancy by eyes caught;
   Sweet possibilities, question, and wonder –
What did her smile say? What has her brain thought?
   Her standard, what? Am I o'er it or under?
      Flutter in meeting – in absence dreaming;
      Tremor in greeting – for meeting scheming;
Caught by the senses, and yet all through
True with the heart of me, sweetheart, to you.

Only the brute in me yields to the pressure
   Of longings inherent – of vices acquired;
All this, my darling, is folly – not pleasure,
   Only my fancy – not soul – has been fired.
      Sense thrills exalted, thrills to love-madness;
      Fancy grown sad becomes almost love-sadness;
And yet love has with it nothing to do,
Love is fast fettered, sweetheart, to you.

Lacking fresh fancies, time flags – grows wingless;
   Life without folly would fail – fall flat;
But the love that lights life, and makes death's self stingless –
   You, and you only, have wakened that.
      Sweet are all women, you are the best of them;
      You are so dear because dear are the rest of them;
      After each fancy has sprung, grown, and died,
      Back I come ever, dear, to your side.
The strongest of passions – in joy – seeks the new,
But in grief I turn ever, sweetheart, to you.

Edith deeply believed this last line, and when, many years later, their son Fabian died, she translated her misery into a play about King David and the death of Absalom; here Absalom's mother Maacah, one of David's several wives, turns to her husband in her grief, only to discover to her silent horror that he has summoned his new queen to console him.

'The Husband of Today' is answered by 'The Wife of All Ages',[20] making a pair of lyrics rather on the pattern of Browning's paired love poems, or else his 'Any Wife to Any Husband'. Despite its unexpectedly bitter complaint of the double standard of morality, it ends by reaffirming the wife's subjection to her husband:

> Suppose I yearned, and longed, and dreamed, and fluttered,
>   What would you say or think, or further, do?
> Why should one rule be fit for me to follow,
>   While there exists a different law for you?
> If all these fires and fancies came my way,
> Would you believe love was so far away?
>
> On all these other women – never doubt it –
>   'Tis love you lavish, love you promised me!
> What do I care to be the first, or fiftieth?
>   It is the *only one* I care to be . . .

The poem sadly concludes:

> Nay, after all I am your slave and bondmaid,
>   And all my world is in my slavery.
> So, as before, I welcome any part
> Which you may choose to give me of your heart.

But Alice's arrival in the household was by no means all loss. Alice was socially unassertive, which allowed Edith to shine unchallenged; she was also capable and dependable, quite content to play 'the humble satellite to a comet', as she herself put it. She relieved Edith of organizing or undertaking the dull routine household tasks, and dealt more effectively and consistently with the servants, her steady temperament acting as a foil to Edith's volatile nature. Alice was their 'young and pretty but useful "Auntie" who . . . made and mended for all the children', providing them with the daily affection and attention they needed, whereas Edith gave them sudden bursts of warmth, presents, treats and celebrations in the form of outings or specially written poems. If in emotional terms her presence was at times a strain and a source of irritation, in practical terms she was a godsend. She continued to act as Edith's regular companion on trips to town, at political meetings and on social calls, and soon no one could remember how they had ever managed without her.[21]

Alice had first made herself useful by nursing Edith, and mutual nursing played an important part in the unfolding of their friendship: Alice had nursed Edith through her stillbirth and the attack of measles that followed it, and Edith seems to have nursed Alice through the birth of Rosamund. According to Helen Macklin, Alice was nursing Edith through another illness when she was persuaded to make her confession. Nursing created an intimate physical bond, in which the patient was dependent on the nurse, and both were tied by certain unspoken obligations: the nurse accepted that she must do all she could to make the patient as physically and mentally comfortable as possible, while the patient, subjected to her nurse's care, was expected to recognize her debt, and show gratitude. The unspoken rules governing the conduct of the sick room are implicit in much Victorian fiction. Several of Edith's friends noticed how she changed when she was ill, becoming gentler, quieter, perhaps more mature. In this constraining and neutralizing context, the two women had some chance of discussing what they had done to one another with the minimum of bitterness. Nursing figured so importantly in people's lives of course, because there was more unidentifiable illness than today and less in the way of confident diagnosis or adequate treatment. It thus acquired a mystique that it has since lost. At a time when most dangerous illnesses seemed to require that the patient be carefully nursed through a 'crisis' and when so little was known of the nature or pattern of illnesses, recovery was very often attributed to good nursing. Alice was proud of the fact that the Blands' family doctor, Adrian Stokes, thought well of her abilities as a nurse, and she regarded it as one of her special talents; in her sixties she fell back on it as a means of supporting herself. It was one of the more valued accomplishments that women might hope to acquire. Virginia Woolf's mother, Julia Stephen, virtually made a career out of it, publishing her *Notes from Sick Rooms* (1883).

As a journalist herself, Alice could also help Edith with her writing, and in those early days Edith was always glad of a collaborator when she was working under pressure. During the mid-eighties, she was still painting Christmas and Easter cards for Raphael Tuck, and Alice used to help her out with these, though she lacked drawing ability, and Edith had to improve her cards by boldly outlining her wavering efforts.

Edith was now working for Robert Ellice Mack, an editor with a small publishing firm that went under the large name of Griffith, Farran, Okeden and Welsh, and produced booklets printed by Ernest Nister of Nuremberg, whose speciality was the new and rather oily colour-printing process of chromolithography. These booklets consisted of illustrations, commonly romantic landscapes or domestic interiors, accompanied by suitable poems, and roughly grouped round a theme. Some of the poems were selections from the classics, others were specially written by Edith, and sometimes by her sister Saretta (as 'Caris Brooke') to go with the pictures. There was much decorative lettering and wreaths of flowers were scattered everywhere; the booklets must have proved popular because many of them were produced, first by Griffith, Farran and Co., and later by Henry Drane, publisher of *The Prophet's Mantle*.

Before 1890 Edith contributed only suitably romantic poems, but after that she began to write her first poems and stories specially for children, both for Nister and also for Raphael Tuck, and that was how her career as a children's writer began – in a very small way. In the early 1890s, Alice too produced books of poems and stories for children, writing under the unlikely pseudonym of 'Uncle Harry'. Alice remembered that

> Sheaves of illustrations used to be sent down to us and we wrote stories and verse to these pictures. Most of it was done on the nights Hubert went to his mother. He used to go about 10.30 p.m. and then we began and wrote till far into the night. Our inspiration was weak gin and water – very shocking! One tablespoonful each, in water, was our allowance but sometimes E. would say, 'Oh Mouse, just one more and we can get this batch done. Mack wants it done at once.'[22]

Edith quickly became adept at turning out the kind of verse and tales then in vogue for children. The surprise is that she ever managed to shake herself free from ephemera of this kind and begin writing stories whose originality far outweighed their conventional elements.

Given the circumstances in which she arrived, Alice could not have been absorbed into the household without some ructions, yet she also conveniently filled a gap. Edith, like most working women, herself needed someone to occupy the role of 'wife', to cope with the household and care for the children, a role Alice was better suited to than she was. Though she had become Hubert's mistress, she was no rival in any other way, and offered no threat in terms of talent or self-assertion; she herself had fallen under Edith's spell before she fell under Hubert's, and admired Edith as frankly and generously as Ada had done. She was content to be housekeeper, secretary, satellite, to occupy those secondary and dependent roles that both Edith and Hubert believed to be most natural to women. Though Alice had earned her own living as a journalist and had a sneaking sympathy for the women's movement,[23] her succumbing to passion and even to pregnancy showed her to be a real woman in a sense both the Blands approved. Though Edith eventually came to like the feminist Charlotte Wilson, the term she contemptuously applied to her – 'Girton Girl' – was for Edith synonymous with the kind of women who wrong-headedly wanted independence at any price, the price usually being love.

A magazine story Edith wrote in 1895, entitled 'The Girton Girl', has its heroine swimming heroically to save the life of the man whom she cannot acknowledge that she loves and who has consequently swum out to sea in despair. In one sense, the story has it both ways, since in recognizing the power of her love for him, the heroine becomes 'as other women', but her life-saving swim is an act of masculine courage, power and endurance. The story thus begins by mocking the 'Girton Girl', but later identifies with her as she succumbs (as her author had done) to a passion she was prepared to fight for. Yolande, in Edith's novel *The Red House* (1902) is also a 'Girton Girl', who refuses to wash up or darn socks until she is brought low by love:

> 'We've been up since the middle of the night . . .' [admits the newly-married Yolande]. 'We're both involved in one common ruin. *He* lit the fires: *I* got the breakfast. Then he found he had no socks mended, and – and there were buttons . . . I darned his socks, but I did not sew on his buttons. *He* did that. I think he'll get shirts with studs for the future. The needle broke, and the end went into his finger. Fortunately I'd attended classes on – what do you call it? – "First Injuries to the Aided" or something, so I was able to bandage his wounds, but it all took time, and he's two trains late already. I am prostrate – a worm at your intruding feet, for you've no business to come here and see my disgrace. But since you *are* here – I'll confess – I almost wish I had learned to do things like this before.'

Yolande is even reduced to dismissing her favourite cause: ' "Oh, bother the Higher Education of Women," said Yolande. "Let's wash up." '[24]

Edith evidently thought that not only was it natural for women to

succumb to passion, as she had done, but that it was somehow right
that they should do so. Later she lectured to the Fabian Women's
Group on 'The Natural Disabilities of Women', pointedly refused to
support woman's suffrage, and even satirized militant suffragettes in
the character of the 'Pretenderette', the dream double of the bossy
nursemaid in *The Magic City* (1910). For her attitudes on this, as on so
many other issues, Hubert was in part responsible.

Hubert's thinking was neither subtle nor deep, but it was quick,
forceful and persuasive. He adopted a detached and humorous
outlook, a man-of-the-world air which suggested that his opponents
were somehow innocent or sentimental idealists, and that he knew
better. Shaw shared something of this wordly tone – it is apparent in
the early writings of both of them – and one effect of it was to make the
first Fabians seem more sophisticated than the presence of the cautious
Pease or the over-earnest Sidney Webb would suggest. The 'women
question' was one whose claims could comfortably be dismissed by
Hubert in this key as quixotic or charmingly absurd, though Shaw, of
course, did not thus dismiss them. Shaw did observe, however, that
'the Fabian vein was largely the vein of comedy, and its conscience a
sense of irony. We laughed at Socialism and laughed at ourselves a
good deal'.[25]

Still, it was natural enough for Bland to assume that what all women
really wanted was the undivided attention of a man, since all his
experience seemed to bear out such a thesis. He would argue in private
that 'every woman had a natural right to a child, whether she were
married or not', a piece of transparent self-justification posing as
altruism. Bland held strong views on women and their wants. He had
discovered early on in life that the ardent suitor is not, despite the
conventions of fiction, all that common among the phlegmatic and
inhibited English. Women, hungry for affection, responded to
passionate pursuit by falling deeply in love, far more often than a man
had any right to expect. Bland had the obvious advantages of being
unusually tall, broad-shouldered and handsome (though now heavily
pock-marked); yet he was honest enough to recognize that these
attributes were rather beside the point:

> One of the ugliest men that ever lived, and one of the most triumphant
> in gallantry, Wilkes the Radical, used to boast that, give him but half an
> hour's start of the handsomest man in town, and he would cut him out
> in the favour of the loveliest woman of her time. And he made his boast
> good again and again.[26]

Bland would not have acknowledged that he despised women – indeed he insisted that he greatly preferred them to men ('They are nicer to look at and to talk to, it seems to me'); but he never seriously wanted to believe that they could have any interest in life other than attracting men. Accordingly, the type of women he professed to revere were those whose lives were focused on the game of love, for him the most interesting game in the world. The notion that women might have other games they wanted to play made him definitely uneasy. In his essay 'If I were a Woman' (1898), Hubert set out some of his views on the opposite sex, and its appropriate role in life:

> Woman's realm is the realm of the heart and the afternoon tea-table, not of the brain and the intelligence. It is hers to bewitch man, not to convince him. . . .
>   Most of those [i.e. women] that I know do nothing at all for their livings; they are content merely to exist beautifully, thus realizing, apparently without the slightest effort, my own highest aspiration, my own loftiest ideal.[77]

This last sentence has a humorous turn, and the whole essay deliberately adopts a 'man-of-the world' stance. Nevertheless, the claim that most of the women known to the author do not work for a living was simply untrue, coming, as it did, from a man whose wife had worked to support the household during their early years, and whose mistresses had had no option but to maintain themselves. Hubert had been in no position to support either of them. Edith herself apparently saw no unintended ironies in these words since she specially selected this piece and included it in a posthumous volume of Hubert's essays. She tended to collude, sometimes in surprising ways, in Bland's self-deceptions. But a clearer-sighted friend like Bernard Shaw felt that Bland ought to be more honest with himself. In an amusing letter of 1889, Shaw tried to tease Hubert into seeing that he had in fact ignored what Shaw referred to as 'secondhand principles', those rigid conduct rules of the bourgeoisie. He thought that Hubert ought not only to admit this candidly, but should feel justified in having done so, and he compared Hubert's abnegation of responsibilities to his own with approval. Shaw argued that the exceptional man must learn to turn his back on

> the loaves and fishes, the duties, the ready-made logic, the systems and the creeds. He must do what he likes instead of doing what, on secondhand principles, he ought. And of course, there is a devil of a

fight to acquire the power to do what you like and to get fed and clothed for doing it. You and I, according to the most sacred secondhand principles, should be prosperous men of business, I for the sake of my poor dear mother, who in her old age, has to live on a second floor and eke out the domestic purse by teaching schoolgirls to sing, you for the sake of your clever and interesting wife and pretty children. In bygone days . . . I would absolutely go now and then to look after some opening which I had no real intention of taking, but which I still thought it necessary to find some external reason for not taking. I doubt you have done the same thing in one form or another. Now I have no faintest hesitation left. The secondhand system on which I 'ought' to have been a stockbroker has absolutely no validity for me. My one line of progress is from writing stories, reviews, and articles, more and more towards writing fully and exhaustively what I like. And of course, my mother, the victim of my selfishness, is a hearty, independent, and jolly person, instead of a miserable old woman dragged at the chariot wheels of her miserable son, who had dutifully sacrificed himself for her comfort. Imagine Mrs Bland as the wife of a horrible city snob with a huge villa, a carriage, and several thousand a year, which is exactly what, on moral principles, it was your duty to have made her. You and I have followed our original impulse, and our reward is that we have been conscious of its existence and can rejoice therein.[28]

Shaw's honesty is characteristically bracing and his desire to free Bland from cant, from offering his respects to a social system in which he did not fundamentally believe was as laudable as it was unsuccessful. Bland *was* a snob; he had always coveted money and social status. And though he invariably ignored society's rules when it suited his book, before his public he paid them a reassuring lip-service.

Bland's essays were often written about women and in praise of them, but the type of woman he holds up for our admiration is precisely the type of woman on whom the 'advanced' of the day were beginning to turn their backs – women as dolls, as products of their own art, as objects of worship:

Woman's *métier* in the world – I mean, of course, civilized woman, the woman in the world as it is – is to inspire romantic passion . . .

Romantic passion is inspired by the women who wear corsets. In other words, by the women who pretend to be what they not quite are.[29]

The constricting corsets, the pearl powder and carmine, the dresses hand-embroidered in East End sweatshops, and the childish narcissism required to be worn with these things were no longer what the sensible, the 'advanced' woman wanted out of life. But then Bland did not have much time or sympathy for the 'advanced' woman; his essay 'If I were a Woman' recommends earning the approval of Mrs Grundy whenever possible, cultivating religion 'in an amateurish sort of way' and adds:

> I should not be 'advanced'. I might now and then be forward, but I should never be advanced. I should not wear knickerbockers (at least, not obviously), or clamour for a vote, or advocate out-of-the-way views about marriage. Pioneers, proverbially, have an unpleasant time, and I regard the world as a place to be comfortable in.[30]

Hubert's homage to the pleasure principle predictably turns out to include larger elements of self-interest and smaller elements of personal conviction than Shaw's had done; he could comfortably ignore the fact that Edith herself had cut her hair short in the manner of the 'advanced' woman, wore knickerbockers when cycling, and, far more significantly, had supported them both with her own efforts. Such facts were too threatening to Hubert's sacred sense of his own masculinity to have been absorbed into his view of the world.

6
ADMIRING CIRCLES

One evening in 1887 Noel Griffith, a young man of twenty-three who was training to become a chartered accountant and not enjoying it very much, was travelling by train to Lee. As he glanced up from the book he was reading, a powerfully built, rather military-looking gentleman opposite caught his eye, and observed, 'I see you are reading Herbert Spencer. What do you think of him?' The humorous face, with its bristling moustache and eyeglass looked vaguely familiar and in a moment or two Griffith recalled having met his fellow passenger a couple of years earlier, when he had been working on the accounts of a hydraulics company. Hubert Bland, always happy to talk about socialism and make new converts, chatted amiably to Griffith for the rest of the journey, and when they reached Lee, he invited the young man to come round and see him so that they might continue their conversation.

On the following Sunday afternoon Griffith duly paid a call on the Blands at 8 Dorville Road, and the occasion was one that he never forgot. Hubert's political views he found liberating, even intoxicating – socialism was to become a lifelong passion of his; but even more exciting was his first encounter with Mrs Bland, whom Hubert took him upstairs to meet. She was sitting up in bed, recovering from a miscarriage, her eyes bright, her hair a mass of shining brown curls. He thought her a delightful and fascinating woman, and on his next visit took her some flowers. She was charmed by his gesture – the socialists she knew were far too earnest to indulge in pleasant conventional courtesies of this kind – and flattered by his evident attention to her.[1]

Despite her illness and the hack work necessary to keep financially afloat, Edith, in the early months of 1887, was flushed with pleasure and renewed confidence at the unexpected success of her first volume of poems: Longmans had published *Lays and Legends* in November 1886 on the recommendation of their reader, Andrew Lang. The volume included a number of narrative poems (among them 'The Moat House'), several social protest poems, the two poems of disillusion with love written in the autumn of 1881 when she was expecting Iris, 'The Husband of Today' and 'The Wife of All Ages', and 'The Depths of the Sea', written for Shaw earlier that year. Though Shaw pretended to dismiss her verses, several established men of letters of the earnest eighties had been favourably impressed with them; and though the volume sold slowly, it enjoyed something of a *succès d'estime*. The novelist H. Rider Haggard wrote to her admiringly about her early verse:

> I hope that you will forgive me for doing a thing (which honestly I never have done before), namely writing to you to express my admiration of your poetry and the great pleasure which it has given me to read it . . . As one who writes himself I do know what is calculated to stir our human sympathy, and I must say that for sweetness and strength and beauty of imagery I know no verses from the pen of a modern writer of poems which appeal to me so much as yours. This must be my excuse for writing to you as one very grateful for shade in the desert land of contemporary verse.[2]

Swinburne, himself an obtrusive influence on Edith's verses, had written to her old friend and Mary's former fiancé, the blind poet Philip Bourke Marston, from 'The Pines', where he lived with Theodore Watts, on 15 November 1886 (the day after their publication):

> My dear Philip,
>   Some days ago I called Watts's attention to what struck me as the remarkable merit of some of the poems in a volume I had lately received from the author – poems which reminded me, in some of their finer characteristics, rather of your own than of any other contemporary's. I am naturally much interested to hear of your connection with the author. I thought 'Absolution' certainly a powerful poem . . . very well conceived and constructed. I had read before (I forget where, but quite lately) 'The Singing of the Magnificat' and it had struck me as something quite out of the common in conception. It is a pity the closing couplet should be so flat – but that might easily be remedied. 'Baby's Birthday' is a charming little piece – and I am rather fastidiously exacting with respect to poetry on the great subject of 'Baby' . . .
>   Come and see me, if you can, on Friday next, and I will read you a

lyric made near Beachy Head while returning from a long walk thither. I
am very much in love with Eastbourne – do you know it?

A postscript adds:

> I had forgotten to mention the poem called 'Two Christmas Eves',
> which struck me as singularly powerful and original – the sort of poem
> that Charlotte Brontë might have written, if she had had more mastery
> of the instrument of verse.[3]

Swinburne's commendations were only outdone, in archness of tone,
by a letter from 16 Tite Street, also written in November 1886:

> Dear Mrs Bland,
>   Thank you so much for sending me your volume of poems. I have
> been turning over the leaves, tasting as one tastes wine, and am
> fascinated by the sonnets . . . but I am keeping the book as a whole for
> study in the Clumber woods next week. 'The Last Envoy' seems a really
> beautiful piece of work. You see I am getting to know you, petal by
> petal, but I will not touch the larger poems just now.
>   Any advice I can give you is of course at your disposal. With regard to
> your next volume – but you do not need to be taught how to tune your
> many-chorded lyre, and you have already caught the ear of all lovers of
> poetry . . .
>   Oscar Wilde[4]

Philip Bourke Marston passed Swinburne's letter on to Edith. By
late 1886 he himself was seriously ill with consumption, and he died on
14 February 1887. His last years had been so darkened by a series of
griefs that no one would have wished them prolonged, but Edith was
nevertheless shocked and distressed by his death, as she explained in a
note to Shaw written four days later:

> Never mind about Saturday. We'll defer it to a more convenient season.
> I'm sick and sad, and no fit company for lively Fabian members. –
> Philip's death is the best thing that could have happened to him, but it's
> saddening to come to the end of a fifteen years' friendship – and to feel
> that you can do nothing for your friend now, ever any more. I can't be
> quite reasonable about it yet – because I have been fond of him so many
> years – I went and saw him today – but I was sorry afterwards. 'It was
> not Philip, but a vacant thing that had always underlain him, and which,
> apart from him, was ghastly'. – Forgive my wandering on like this. I
> thought your note seemed as if you were sorry a little about him – but
> perhaps you did not mean it. – I'm going to Buxton next week to try to
> get well and cheerful again. No doubt I shall see you at the Fabian
> tomorrow, unless I get too ill to go.[5]

Her need to confide her distress to Shaw suggests that she may not yet have entirely recovered from her emotional dependency on him, but she was soon to find consolation in the intimacy gradually developing between herself and Noel Griffith, a reassuring relationship in which he admired her unreservedly and she played at being the princess who bestows her favours on the gardener's boy. Noel Griffith was the first of a group of lovers and admirers who were significantly younger than Edith, and whose sentimental education she undertook. After the débâcle with Shaw, and the earlier and different catastrophe of her marriage, Edith seems to have preferred the position of comparative power conferred by being the elder and more experienced – as well as the more interesting and forceful – personality. She could retain her dignity and self-possession – indeed she later came to accept homage rather more readily than the friendship of equals. Her young men enjoyed the blend of maternal, romantic and sisterly affection that she brought to the relationship, and their own lack of ties meant that they could drop everything and fall in with her plans. When they eventually left her to get married, as they always did, it was a progress she was usually prepared for, and in the case of Noel Griffith, she grew fond of his wife, too. Interestingly, the novel *Daphne in Fitzroy Street* awards Daphne two consoling secondary suitors of this type, but in the end she chooses the impossible Shavian hero in preference to their self-effacing admiration.

Griffith was at once surprised and intrigued by what he saw of life at Dorville Road. As 'Fabian Bland' had written, two years before they actually experienced it, 'A *ménage à trois* is not the most ideal life.' His impression was that the Blands themselves 'rubbed along very friendly', but Miss Hoatson found the situation difficult, to say the least, and she seemed to get on Edith's nerves. He was also conscious that Maggie Doran was still sleeping with Hubert at this period, perhaps as often as he went home to stay with his mother. Maggie was now a member of the Blands' social circle, and Shaw's diary records meeting her with them in 1888 and again in 1892. She showed how far she had adopted Hubert's views by joining the Fabian Society in March 1890. Noel Griffith's election in November 1889 reflects not only his personal endorsement of the Blands' politics, but the Society's success in attracting 'educated and cultivated but impecunious young men', in Hubert's phrase.[6]

In conversation with Doris Langley Moore, Griffith talked frankly about the nature of Bland's 'needs', justifying his behaviour on the grounds that he was very hot-blooded . . . abnormally sexual, too much so for the tastes of his wife – though she had her own lovers when she found him unfaithful. She was herself a mixture of sensuality and intellectuality.

He vividly remembered joining the Blands on holiday at Whitstable for a few days. Watching Edith and Miss Hoatson bathing, Bland admired Miss Hoatson's figure and complacently invited Griffith to admire it too. That he sought, on occasion, to impress other men with his sexual conquests was later observed by H. G. Wells, with the undisguised contempt of someone who suffered from similar compulsions. As money grew less tight, holidays such as this one happened oftener. Seaside holidays were usually taken with the children, at Deal, Sheerness or Whitstable, but Edith was also rediscovering her youthful pleasure in 'messing about in boats'.[7]

Either in 1889 or 1890 Edith invited Noel Griffith to spend a few days' holiday with them on the Medway. This was not the first time the Blands had enjoyed a holiday on that river: apparently Hugh Bellingham Smith, a young painter from Blackheath, had accompanied them the previous year. Edith first met Hugh through his parents, who were founder Fabians and lived at Lee. She had described them rather caustically in a letter to Ada in 1884: 'His father writes plays – interested in social questions and dried fruits – married – very much. Mrs H.B.S. *very* youthful and gushing (eldest son aged 19)'.

By the late eighties, their second son Hugh, a student at the Slade, was in his early twenties. He painted a full-length portrait of Edith that was exhibited at the Blackheath Art Club, and said to be good of its kind, though his family giggled over it and nicknamed it, 'I'm hungry, Mother!' Hugh also drew some illustrations for the poetry booklets that Edith was churning out at the time. In 1890 he left to study in Paris and moved out of the Blands' circle for good.

Hugh's youngest brother, Eric, born in 1881, had his first lessons from Alice Hoatson in the Bland schoolroom, along with Paul and Iris. He only recalled a single glimpse of Edith, swathed dramatically in a black cloak that reached from neck to ankle, clasped over a yellow dress. Hubert he liked, because he insisted on teaching the two little boys how to box and bought them special miniature boxing gloves to wear. Hubert liked people to believe that he had been 'heavyweight champion at the 'varsity for three years'. Eric also remembered the house at Dorville Road:

It was violently bedaubed with paint, round porch, front door, etc., and stood out between its brick coloured neighbours. Inside there was quite a nice bright little sitting room and round it as seats were square-covered boxes with colour cloth or cretonne on them. I lifted one of those covers and underneath was Tate sugar.[8]

The Medway holidays were to become a regular feature of the Blands' life for many years. Other young men were to accompany them later, but between 1890 and 1894 Noel Griffith was a frequent member of the party. The trips normally lasted a week, though sometimes for no more than a weekend. They took place any time during the summer months, but the favourite time was 'before the hay harvest when all the fields and flowers were looking lovely'. Noel Griffith wrote:

> This [first] trip and all those after followed certain rules. Start at Maidstone after buying stores. Take a double-sculling boat for a week. Row up to East Peckham (near Yalding). Stay at a little pub near the river for about a shilling a night each. Take out lunch and a can of four-ale and spend the whole day and sometimes late into the evening rowing, walking and swimming. A quiet sleepy river with only a few barges drifting down from Tonbridge. All locks opened by ourselves with a prodigiously heavy crow-bar. Much damage to the hands at first but a beautiful accuracy attained later on. (My God! What holidays these were, snatched from a Chartered Accountant's Office. Lots of laughter and lots of good talk.) In other years some few young men used to join us for a day or two but none of them became well known. The party was invariably the same. Bland and Miss Hoatson taking it in turn to row with E. Nesbit and myself.[9]

Their bathing was surprisingly informal: Edith and Alice did not take special clothes and would simply tuck up their shifts and swim in those. Edith was strong, lissom and athletic. She ran like a hare, and could bend backwards over a low gate until her head almost touched the ground. On one occasion she dived to the bottom of Yalding Lock to retrieve a crowbar that Hubert had dropped, despite being terrified of finding eels at the bottom. While they were on holiday, she would write verses and sing these and other songs to her own guitar accompaniment. Griffith remembered their talk as being 'very much of the socialist state of the future', but perhaps their lighter conversations had slipped from his memory.

Edith loved the Medway, and the pretty village of Yalding. She went back for holidays there year after year, and wrote about the river and its locks in two of her romantic novels, *Salome and the Head* (1909) and *The Incredible Honeymoon* (1916). She patronized both the Yalding pubs:

If you go to Yalding you may stay at the George, and be comfortable in
a little village that owns a haunted churchyard, a fine church, and one of
the most beautiful bridges in Europe. Or you may stay at the Anchor,
and be comfortable on the very lip of the river . . .

   At the Anchor you breakfast either in a little room whose door opens
directly on that part of the garden which is adorned by two round
flower-beds edged with the thickest, greenest box you ever saw – this is
next door to breakfasting in the garden itself, – or you *do* breakfast in
the garden. Once upon a time you used to breakfast in a hornbeam
arbour, but now that is given over to bargees. The landlord of the
Anchor is a just man, and apportions the beauty of his grounds fairly
among his clients.[10]

They also stayed at a favourite pub a little further up the river – the
Rose and Crown at Branbridges, just south of East Peckham.
   The river was idyllically beautiful in high summer:

The Medway just above the Anchor is a river of dreams. The grey and
green of willows and alders mirrored themselves in the still water in
images hardly less solid-seeming than their living realities. There was
pink loosestrife there, and meadow-sweet creamy and fragrant, forget-
me-nots wet and blue, and a tangle of green weeds and leaves and stems
that only botanists know the names of.[11]

   The gates to this paradise were the locks – 'the Medway strings them
quite thickly on her silver thread'. The first is Stoneham Lock, then
came two more whose names were evidently unmemorable, then
Round Lock and Oak Weir Lock. At this time, all the locks had to be
levered up by hand, using a crowbar and supporting the weight of the
sluice on an iron pin. If the job was done unskilfully, it was possible to
trap your hand underneath the pin, and have the whole weight of the
sluice come down on top of it. Edith must have seen something of this
kind happen at Oak Weir Lock, since she describes exactly this
accident taking place there in both novels.[12] Noel Griffith's reference
to 'much damage to the hands at first' suggests that he might well have
been the victim, but perhaps the same accident happened to others. In
both novels, the heroine behaves with great presence of mind,
retrieving the crowbar, and looking after the young man as he faints
with pain on putting his shattered hand into the cold running water. In
her fiction, and no doubt in life as well, Edith loved to reverse that
familiar fictional situation in which a capable young man rescues a
helpless woman. Her young ladies – or in the children's books, little
girls – are strong, resourceful and as competent in an emergency as

their creator liked to think herself.

Noel Griffith regarded the Blands and their circle as a major educational influence on him, and felt that his view of the world had been completely changed by his contact with them. In their different ways, both of them had taken him in hand, for both of them enjoyed the company of disciples. Already their way of life seemed markedly Bohemian to a young man who had been conventionally brought up. Since their initial encounter, Hubert had lost his job with the Hydraulic Power Company and was now making out as best he could as a journalist. He and Edith, as 'Fabian Bland', continued to contribute short stories to the radical London newspaper *The Weekly Dispatch* during the late 1880s; in 1886 Hubert, at Shaw's suggestion, had taken over as editor of the left-wing review *To-Day*, previously edited by the Marxist Ernest Belfort Bax and the 'New Lifer' James Leigh Joynes. The Blands occasionally published short stories there when they could not find a more profitable outlet for them. Editing *To-Day* could only have been rewarding as an expression of political commitment. Its price and format were liable to sudden fluctuations, but it certainly never made money for anyone, though it did publish a number of worthwhile contributions from Shaw, Stepniak and even from Ibsen.[13] None of this provided enough for the Blands to live on, and they could hardly have managed at all had not Shaw come to the rescue by passing on to Bland some literary work that he himself was unable to undertake, supplying regular articles or reviews for a weekly paper. Shaw's own career as a journalist was just beginning to get off the ground and he made rather a point of handing out work that he could not undertake to friends in difficulties. He liked to think that it was this job that had laid the foundations for Bland's subsequent success as a columnist, and was rather proud of his role in the matter. Perhaps he saw it as a way of repaying that ongoing debt that Edith had referred to in her letter to him; 'you still owe me something – and I suppose will remain always in my debt.'[14] Hubert still spent a great deal of his time and energy lecturing and writing for the Fabian, work that brought no more immediate benefit than did editing *To-Day*, but which was to prove indirectly valuable in helping him to define and express his views forcefully.

Though Henry Hyndman, the aggressive leader of the S.D.F., liked to refer to the Fabian as 'The Micawber Club'[15] and regularly made fun of its 'drawing-room' reformers, the dynamic presence of Annie Besant had stirred the society into fresh activity. She was an ardent advocate of direct action and loved the sound of controversy and the scent of danger. Bland was attracted by her energy and determination, though he could not take her eagerness for martyrdom entirely seriously, as is shown by a letter to Shaw written somewhat earlier, in 1885, when she was still very much a new force in the Society. There had been trouble between the East End radicals and the police at Dod Street in Limehouse, and on 20 September the police charged a tightly packed meeting and arrested a number of people, among them William Morris. On the following Sunday a massive protest march demanding free speech was to be held at the same venue. Shaw must have asked Bland if he intended to join them. Bland's reply was written from the Star and Garter at Deal, where he was on holiday and glad to be out of it:

> Yours to hand – as I am not returning in any case until Tuesday I cannot very well be in Dod St. on Sunday – but if I did go I now find I should pay the fine. In this case the fine is an alternative punishment. It is not a case of apologise or go to prison.
>
> By the way I am not as independent in the matter of holidays as you think – I have already had my holiday and the Hydraulic Power Co. would not stand a secretary who took two holidays in a year and spent one of them in Holloway Castle. I think in all struggles with the powers that be the order of stepping into the breach must be thus
> 1 unmarried men
> 2 married men without kids
> 3 married men with kids
> 4 unmarried women (without kids)
> 5 unmarried women with kids
> 6 married women without kids
> 7 married women with kids
> 8 infants in arms
>
> By this you will see that I do not think Mrs Besant should go until some of our men are locked up. I am a *little* doubtful of the advisability of her interfering *at all* just now . . . and it looks as though we were rushing in at the fag end of a battle. However I am content to leave the decision to the wisdom of my colleagues on the exec. My strong opinion is that if we cannot get young unattached men to go, women ought not to be allowed to do so.[16]

Bland's chivalrous anxiety about Annie Besant seems to be little more than a smokescreen for his own determination not to get involved, but his tone is so consistently ironic that it is hard to tell how much of his letter should be taken seriously. In the event, some 60,000

people overflowed out of Dod Street, but there were no further arrests
– a general election was expected in two months' time and the Home
Secretary was not prepared to risk further adverse publicity.

Annie Besant continued to push the Fabian towards greater political
commitment. As the society's Honourable (i.e. unpaid) Treasurer,
Bland was now permanently on the executive, where he often found
himself supporting her practical initiatives. It was she who put forward
the idea of organizing a nationwide series of local Fabian groups, and a
famous meeting of September 1886 resolved that it was desirable for
socialists to form themselves into a political party, though the main
line of Fabian thought always tended to favour 'permeation', the
gradual infiltration and conversion of other parties to socialist
principles. But the disastrous rough house of 'Bloody Sunday' in
November 1887, when the radicals' attempt to hold a mass meeting in
Trafalgar Square was brutally broken up by the police, showed how
very limited their strength and support really was. Mrs Besant and
William Morris were among the crowds that clashed with the police
that afternoon, as was a reluctant Shaw. After searching in vain for
Annie, he went home for tea, while she struggled ineffectually to set up
primitive barricades against the police baton charges.

A number of her friends and allies now decided that their tactics
needed rethinking, but Annie Besant continued her fight on behalf of
the underprivileged, and in the summer of 1888 she persuaded her
Fabian colleagues to support the match girls' strike at Bryant and
May's. The girls had endured appalling conditions, working a
fourteen-hour day for less than five shillings a week and suffering from
phosphorus poisoning. After a series of protest meetings, they finally
went on strike. Annie made herself responsible for publicizing their
cause, which she did very effectively, and several of the Fabians helped
out in practical ways: Sydney Olivier and the radical clergyman
Stewart Headlam did some of the girls' paper work, and Shaw,
Graham Wallas and Bland took down the money they had collected to
the factory gates, doling it out to the girls as strike pay.[17] This episode
and comparable campaigns against industrial disease made a strong
impression on Edith. More than once in her books for children the
discriminating heroes or heroines chose to live in another world, or
another time and place, in preference to modern industrial England.
Billy, in 'Billy the King', regrets that the Plurimiregians have tried to
feed Eliza and himself to the dragon, but feels obliged to add:

'I don't know that it's worse than people who let other people die of lead-poisoning because they want a particular glaze on their dinner-plates, or let people die of phosphorus-poisoning so that they may get matches at six boxes a penny. We're as well off here as in England.'

This insight, which virtually no child of the time could have achieved unaided, has been carefully prepared for, since Billy has already 'turned on a little tap inside his head by some means which I cannot describe to you, and a bright flood of cleverness poured through his brain'.[18]

In January 1888 *The Star* had been launched as a radical evening paper, and Edith, anxious to get it started along the right lines, organized all her friends into sending in letters from different parts of England on socialist topics, so as to give the editor the impression that this was the burning topic of the day; her tactics were later imitated unsuccessfully by the Bastables, when they sent in encomiums of Albert's Uncle's serial to the editor of the *People's Pageant*.[19] Perhaps some of the letters to *The Star* specifically mentioned G. B. Shaw's political column, but after only three weeks of disagreement over this, Shaw reconstituted himself as 'Corno di Bassetto', and quickly became well known as an influential music reviewer. Bland, too, was beginning to establish his reputation as an effective journalist. That April the Fabian executive – Annie Besant, Bland, William Clarke, Sydney Olivier, Shaw, Graham Wallas and Sidney Webb – decided that the autumn programme should feature a special series of talks on socialism, what it consisted of and how it was to be achieved. Each member of the executive would talk about one aspect of the topic – Bland would take the immediate political prospects, while Shaw discussed economics and Annie dealt with socialist production. Rather more than a year later these lectures were published as *The Fabian Essays*, with a success that surprised everyone: the first thousand copies sold out within a month. The Fabian lecturers found themselves famous almost overnight. Bland's contribution rejected the notion of 'permeation' in favour of the establishment of socialism as an independent political party. Both he and Annie Besant had consistently argued the case for this, though it had never been fully accepted by the Society as a whole. Now Hubert was about to lose his chief ally on the executive: a month before the publication of *The Fabian Essays* at Christmas 1889, Mrs Besant became a convert to theosophy and abruptly resigned her membership.

Meanwhile the Fabian's other powerful woman member, Charlotte

Wilson, had been gradually edged out by Annie Besant's determination that the Society should adopt an active political role; Mrs Wilson could not reconcile this with the gentle anarchy she had learned from Prince Kropotkin. At a meeting held at Anderton's Hotel on 17 September 1886 Annie's proposal that all socialists make common cause and organize themselves into a political party was seconded by Bland and carried, though the debate was so noisy that the Society was told to hold its meetings elsewhere in future. On 25 September Hubert wrote a long confidential letter to Shaw, who was apparently anxious because Mrs Wilson was now in a position to split the Society. He assured Shaw that, though he liked Mrs Wilson well enough personally, he expected her support to be negligible:

> You have written very frankly and I will as frankly reply. I do think we should pursue Fabian tactics in the matter of political action but Fabian tactics do not mean dawdling merely. Fabius struck hard sometimes. *Of course* the Executive will be forced by outside pressure to take up the question – what do you take me for?
>
> I do know what Mrs Wilson's strength is in the Society. It is nil. She has practically no influence and no following.
>
> I think you must have forgotten the 'impression she made when she read the Anarchist pamphlet'. The impression was such that it nearly wrecked the pamphlet and a committee of revision was appointed. I chivalrously fought against this appointment because I thought it a deliberate snub to Mrs Wilson – while my colleagues basely deserted me. No – Mrs Wilson will never *split* the Society – all she can do is break off a small projection which even now rather spoils its symmetry. I think you are mistaken in thinking that Mrs Besant and I cannot work cordially together – so far we have always been in entire agreement. It was I who suggested when to move the resolution the other day. As a matter of fact I am nearly always willing to bow to her larger experience – especially in the realm of politics – as for Webb's bad temper, Podmore's supersubtlety and Olivier's obstinacy – for all these I don't care a damn. Altogether those three only have about 8 votes which they can influence, Mrs Wilson about 3. Mrs Besant by herself has a personal following of about 10 and I can make sure of 23 on a question of 'political action'. You may rely on these figures.
>
> I like skating on 'thin ice'. The elasticity and the spice of danger make good sport.
>
> Personally I am attached to Mrs Wilson – I like her very much and am racking my brains to think how we can keep her – I have no doubt to have hit on a plan presently. The applause she got last Friday as far as it came from Fabians was given to her because she spoke well and looked

such a nice little woman. I was one of the loudest applauders. Make
your mind easy about her – the opposition won't count when the fight
comes off. I think you are quite wrong about yourself – we shall want an
anatomical demonstration when we come to measures. You will miss
taking your tide at the flood if you let this chance pass you. I agree with
what you say about my needing someone to 'hold me back' – I have no
ambition to be a leader and shall be quite content to be *servus servorum*
in the new party. If it wants a cavalry charge led I shall be proud of the
honour.

To conclude. You may rely on my not acting rashly or *forcing* the
question to the front. No resolution re 'political action' shall be moved
until the majority is safe and overwhelming. The matter needs grave
consideration and shall have it as far as I am concerned.[20]

At a follow-up meeting on 5 November a compromise was arrived at
by which those in favour of direct political intervention would form a
separate Fabian Parliamentary League, but membership of this would
be optional, so that those who disagreed with this development, such
as Morris and Mrs Wilson, would not feel obliged to resign. By April
1888 the Parliamentary League had dwindled to the Political
Committee, and the anarchists had either pulled out or been assimilated. Thereafter Charlotte Wilson withdrew from Fabian involvement, though the development of Fabian thought now owed much to
her Marxist reading group, the Hampstead Historic Society, which
had attracted so many socialist thinkers – Webb, Olivier, Shaw and
Wallas had all read papers there and debated the justification of
socialism in historical terms. Mrs Wilson regarded the Fabians as 'too
pugnacious' and lacking in 'an earnest spirit of truth-seeking'. She now
devoted herself to editing the anarchist periodical *Freedom*, but her
concern for independence and sympathy for the oppressed made her a
natural supporter of women's rights. She returned to the Fabian in
1908 as the energetic secretary of the women's group, a cause for which
Edith herself had scant sympathy. Four years older than Edith,
Charlotte Wilson remained politically active for most of her long life,
dying at the age of ninety in 1944.[21]

In many ways Charlotte Wilson was the antithesis of Edith – a
woman moved by idealistic convictions rather than personal passions,
and the dominant partner in her marriage. Edith had described her first
adverse reaction to her as 'a Girton girl'. In fact Charlotte Wilson had
been one of fourteen girls educated at Merton Hall where Jemima
Clough (the poet's sister) was Principal; only later did it evolve into

Newnham. In a letter to Ada Edith provided further details about Mrs Wilson and her way of life:

> She has a husband who is very nice, and a perfect gentleman. Did I tell you about their house? He is a stockbroker and they used to live in a very charming and rather expensive house at Hampstead, but she at last declined to live any longer on his earnings (which she tersely terms the 'wages of iniquity') and now they have taken quite a little cottage where she means to keep herself by keeping fowls! It is a charming and quite idyllic little farm. They have two rooms – study and kitchen. The kitchen is an *idealised* farm kitchen, where of course no cooking is done – but with a cushioned settle, open hearth, polished dresser and benches and all the household glass and crockery displayed, mixed up with aesthetic pots, pans, curtains, chairs and tables – a delightfully incongruous but altogether agreeable effect.[22]

Two or three years later Edith had come to like Charlotte Wilson very much, and in 1892 she dedicated the second series of *Lays and Legends* 'To Alice Hoatson, Helen Macklin and Charlotte Wilson, in token of indebtment'. In the later 1880s she often used to go and stay with Mrs Wilson at her Hampstead cottage, Wildwood Farm. Shaw's diary records her staying there from 29 February to 4 March 1888, and on other occasions that year he met Edith in the company of Mrs Wilson: in April he had supper at Gatti's with the Blands and Miss Hoatson, Sidney Webb and Mrs Wilson, and in August, he visited Wildwood Farm on the off-chance one afternoon and found Mrs Bland and Iris there with the Wilsons. It was through Charlotte Wilson that Edith kept up an intermittent contact with the South African novelist Olive Schreiner whom she had known at least since the autumn of 1885, when Olive had dined at her house in company with Sidney Webb and the radical clergyman C. L. Marson. Olive Schreiner had been in England since 1881 and had several close friends in the Fabian and the Fellowship of the New Life – notably Havelock Ellis and Edward Carpenter. She was particularly fond of Eleanor Marx, as well as of Charlotte Wilson. In 1885 she was at the height of her success as the author of *The Story of an African Farm* (1883), an attractive and vital woman, whose face was illuminated by intelligence and animation, and by large, expressive dark eyes.[23]

Only the briefest notes survive to record the friendship between the passionately unconventional Olive Schreiner, who wanted to rethink the whole nature of the relationship between men and women, and the Blands – who, though concerned with the topic in practice, did not

outwardly rebel against society's rules. The first surviving note from
Edith to Olive is headed 'Wildwood Farm, Hampstead' and was
probably written in the early summer of 1888. It was found by
Havelock Ellis among his papers. Olive must have passed it on to him
with a number of other notes and letters when she finally left England
later that year:

> I have written to my husband to send you the *To-Days*. Thank you for
> your letter: it is very pleasant. I want to come and see you again, may I?
> – You see I am partly on the way to you, here – and Hubert wants to
> come with me. If it's the least bit inconvenient please say so. You did me
> much good, the other day. You took me out of my world into another
> from which I came out with a sigh and a shiver, as the train took me
> away from you. But the remembrance of it does me good still.
>
> Yours,
Edith Bland

Olive wrote to her friend Edward Carpenter, either in response to
this or to a similar note, in July: 'You would love Mrs Bland very
much. She's quite genuine. She wants to come again and bring all her
children.' Olive seems to have been living at Harpenden when she
received Edith's note. She wrote across it: 'This is from Mrs Bland.
Bland spent many afternoons here.'[24] It is difficult to imagine Hubert,
with his narrow notions of sexual morality and his conviction that a
woman's place was in the home, getting on well with the visionary and
iconoclastic Olive, but this may be only the result of seeing him in two
dimensions – as a sexual hypocrite, a faintly absurd Lothario, instead
of as a human being, who was drawn to a passionately romantic
woman like Olive Schreiner, even though he found her opinions so
alien. Two notes from Olive to Edith survive; the first implies that she
was engaged in the task of explaining to Hubert what her views were,
and was predictably experiencing difficulties in making him understand them:

> The long letter was to Mr Bland, there was only a note to you.
> I thought I'd given Mr Bland a wrong idea, from what he wrote,
> about my view of marriage, that it was the *legal* marriage that I was so
> strongly in favour of and not simply the union of one man and one
> woman resting on their free will. I believe so firmly that this [i.e. the
> union of free will] is the ideal after which the highest part of the race *is*
> feeling, that I have no fear that freedom of sex union will lead the highest
> individuals to unite in any other form. That was all that was in the letter,
> and I asked if you would send me your photograph.

I'm going to Woking on Tuesday. If the air is stimulating I shall stay there a week or until I get away to the continent. Will you and Mr Bland come and see me there. It's rather nearer than this.

Olive Schreiner[25]

In October 1888, Olive Schreiner left England for Alassio, never to return. She was lonely, in poor health and very low spirits. She explained in a letter to her closest friend Havelock Ellis, written on the 22nd, how Edith had confided in her and helped her greatly at the very last:

> Mrs Bland ('E. Nesbit') was so kind to me before I left London. I don't think I should have got away without her. She came the last morning to finish packing my things and see me off. Do you know, she's one of the noblest women? I can't tell you about her life, because I mustn't, but it's grand. The last night she lay by me on the bed and drew me very close to her and pressed her face against mine, and, do you know, I have felt it ever since. I am going to get better . . .

A letter to Edward Carpenter, written a couple of months later, enlarges on Edith's qualities of courage and strength:

> . . . about Mrs Bland. If I *could* tell you about her you would love her so! It's not that she does a hard thing. All of us can do that; but then we break down in health like Mrs Wilson and some others, but she goes on so sweetly and strongly it seems as if she must be drawing her strength from some source which no one sees. You mustn't mind if you've no time to give her when you're in town. I mean she's one who understands how one's heart goes out much further than one's hands can reach in this short life.[26]

The admiration of a woman like Olive Schreiner, and the sense that she had indeed behaved with the selfless generosity of one of her own heroines must have buoyed Edith up in her darker moments. The last known correspondence to pass between the two was a postcard from South Africa, whose tone implies familiarity and affection; it also implies, more surprisingly, that the Blands had discussed the possibility of emigrating. Headed 'Matjesfontein', it is dated 17 May 1890:

> I am sending this line to Mrs Wilson because I don't know your address. It's just to tell you I never forget you. Please send me a line. Things in the business sense are very bad in the Colony just now. I would not advise anyone to come out. There is a reaction after all the gold speculations. Please tell me something of yourselves. Love to Iris and kiss that wonderful little Paul for me.

Olive[27]

Though the Blands may sometimes have thought of getting out altogether, by the end of the eighties their finances were on a firmer footing and when the three-year lease of Dorville Road ended in September 1889 they moved to a larger house. There is no very obvious explanation for this general improvement. They continued to support themselves by writing: Edith had recently begun to contribute sentimental stories for children to a series of books of verses and short stories for the young, colourfully illustrated and usually printed by Raphael Tuck or Ernest Nister. These deal mainly in the clichéd situations of the day – good children who give their pocket money to the poor, honest farmers' lads, naughty spoilt children, pets and fairies – only very occasionally does a note of sincerity break through, and that when she is writing of children who have been left behind by their parents.[28] Hubert was now producing regular book reviews for the *Daily Chronicle* and a series of short society tales for a stock exchange journal. While none of these commissions look particularly valuable in themselves, the Blands had grown used to turning work out fast and efficiently, were becoming better known as writers, and more regularly sold their stories to the more expensive end of the magazine market. Their new home at 2 Birch Grove stood on the farther side of Burnt Ash Hill, but was still only a few minutes' walk from Lee Station. Birch Grove is a wide street of substantial semi-detached houses. Quite recently the even-numbered houses were pulled down to make way for modern 'town houses', but the far side of the road still has its original buildings and these give some idea of their scale. Alice Hoatson recalled that:

> There was a long fine drawing room, a good dining room on the ground floor, . . . and a decent-sized kitchen, etc., on the same [floor]. Here E. started a debating society and we had nearly every literary man and woman we knew meeting here once a month. Sometimes we had a paper read for discussion but mostly it was just talk on any subject under the sun. We kept it up for the three years we remained there.[29]

Edith, who was inclined to laugh at pretentious names, had once commented tartly on the 'Lewisham Literary Society', 'I think if its name were shorter it might be a better thing – but all its strength has run to title and it has three secretaries who between them can never get a notice out in time.' Her own society was simply called 'It'. A dozen years later, she would use this capitalized pronoun to refer to the elusive and awkwardly named psammead, in *Five Children and It*.

Alice's memory was, as usual, at fault over the meeting place of 'It', which was held at various different houses or rooms, just as she had forgotten how long they lived at Birch Grove – it was five years, not three – and, according to Shaw and Noel Griffith, 'It' came to an abrupt end when one of the speakers scandalized his audience: Harold Cox, a clever young socialist whose sister Margaret had married Sydney Olivier, read a paper on 'Nudity in Art and Life'. During this he described the attractions of a young woman lying naked on a tiger skin in front of the fire (thus anticipating Elinor Glyn by some years). This so upset suburban notions of what was permissible for debate that the society had to be closed down. Griffith recalled that 'E.N. was very angry with him for this escapade,' but Shaw's account of the episode makes it sound as if the offence was given quite unintentionally, through Cox's blend of naïvety and idealism – he was merely advocating the modern cult of nudism to an audience not yet ready for it.[30]

This was by no means the first occasion on which the Blands had shocked their conservative neighbours, though most of the time they were scarcely aware of doing so. A young friend, newly married, who lived opposite them at Birch Grove recalled:

> They rode bicycles in bloomers, they were absolutely unconventional and careless, they outraged 'Mrs Grundy' in every way and were condemned and generally disliked by the very respectable neighbourhood of Lee. In fact no rumour nor gossip was considered too bad to be believed about them . . .
>
> Mrs Bland was a smoker of cigars at this time, I remember. In fact she just went her own way and was the centre of a group of people who did likewise. I shall never forget our Saturdays during the winter of 1890–1 (I think). We worked at all kinds of things for the very poor of Deptford for some hours, then a supper of, probably, herrings, cheese and bottled stout, followed by a dance. Always the spirit of originality, freedom and difference.

This particular young woman also remembered meeting Shaw ('in his Jaeger-coloured clothes, with shirt to match'), the artist Hugh Bellingham Smith and Oswald Barron (a journalist and historian) at Birch Grove. She wrote of the four children:

> Little Fabian . . . was the most amazing child – odd and tiresome and a terror. The youngsters used to go about bare-foot and Fabian loved to way-lay the 'City Gents' on their way to the station and beg for halfpennies. Imagine the disgust of the neighbourhood.

Rosamund (Rom) was easily the most attractive. She was a real darling with her soft dark eyes and pretty ways. Sitting on the knee of a man-visitor she said gravely, lifting her skirt, 'Do you know, I have real lace on my drawers.'

Mrs Bland was a tender mother and devoted to the children who were considered neglected but I doubt if they were. They ran wild.[31]

Edith was eager to allow her children the freedom that she herself had valued so highly as a child; but it was enjoyed more conspicuously within the narrow-minded proprieties of the London suburbs than it would have been in the country. The Blands' hospitality was by now well known. Long before they could entertain on a lavish scale, they had begun to have regular 'at home' evenings, and the drawing room at Birch Grove was big enough to hold dances as well as parties. Edith played the piano, and was very good at 'vamping', improvising the accompaniments to everyone's favourite dance tunes, a skill she must have acquired in the long years of adolescence. She delighted in generosity, and hospitality is one of its most rewarding forms. She would allow the butcher's and baker's bills to mount up to huge sums, and would then write some verses or stories to pay them off. She liked this functional way of thinking about her work so that each piece of writing was destined to pay off some particular household bill; it seemed to encourage her.[32]

From the Fabians she had learned that there were ways of circumventing rigid Victorian *mores*, without losing caste, and this was a particularly valuable discovery for someone who was by nature such an individualist, and even a rebel. She had started out on married life by trying to conform to the proprieties she had so recently transgressed, but she found it difficult to do so and follow her own impulses simultaneously, and by the time she came to live at Birch Grove, she was beginning to feel that she could do without the approval of the Philistines and the Bores. As long as she and Hubert were accepted by those whose opinions they really valued, the rest could tut as much as they liked. When all they could afford were parties at which herrings, cheese and beer were served, they gave those, and everyone was delighted with their charmingly simple way of life – the more so because heavy Victorian meals with a lot of red meat were the usual middle-class fare. Edith never became a proper vegetarian, but, according to Berta Ruck, she preferred 'succulently Soho-ish, eggy-risotto stuff, rich in home-grown vegetables'; 'she liked macaroni, vegetable-and-rice dishes, and well-stewed chicken better than English food'. Iris remembered what a good manager her mother had always been; even when they were hard up, she fed the children on lentils, beans and suet pudding, rather than cakes or pastry, so that they were always well nourished.[33]

The parties that their neighbour from Birch Grove remembered, when everyone worked at making things for the poor of Deptford, were part of an annual event that had begun in 1888, at Dorville Road, and continued for ten years or so, steadily growing in scale and elaboration – the Christmas treat for the poor children of Deptford. This entertainment made a gesture that was wholly characteristic of Edith – it was prompted by a generous impulse, a genuine concern for the slum children of Deptford, whose plight she was later to dramatize in *Harding's Luck* (1909). But the treats were also amusing for her, occasions when she summoned her friends and set them all to work, but then magically transformed their working parties into real parties. She loved playing the fairy godmother, feeling her power to confer happiness by doling out presents to the 'poor and indignant', in Oswald Bastable's apt malapropism. She roped in all her chief admirers for these occasions, when she became the centre of humming activity, and if a few of her friends resented the work involved, most of them would have agreed with Alice Hoatson, that 'It was very hard but glorious fun and we enjoyed every minute of it'.

The first treat began with twenty poor children coming to Dorville Road, but the following year the numbers had increased and thereafter the event was held at the Deptford Board School, St Hughes Fields. There was a tea, with bread and butter and cake, a Christmas tree, the performance of tableaux, and later plays by the Blands and their friends, and of course presents. Every child was given an orange or an apple, a bag of sweets, a toy and a 'useful' present, which usually meant dresses or flannel petticoats for the little girls; the boys were more of a problem. Most years they got knitted comforters, except for one when Edith's brother-in-law John Deakin, who had an interest in a Manchester cloth-manufacturing firm, provided yards of blue corduroy suitable for trouser-making. That year every woman who helped remembered sewing up interminable pairs of navy blue corduroy pants – for many of the poor children were inadequately clothed. These 'useful' presents were made by the Blands and their friends at working parties held every Saturday for three months beforehand, as their neighbour remembered. Mrs D'Arcy Reeve, perhaps the wealthiest woman in the Blands' circle, helped and also got her maids to help with making the presents. One reason the numbers of children increased so rapidly was that at first they were chosen according to merit, but Edith was unhappy when she found this out and justly insisted that both good and bad children should come since bad children needed treats just as much as good ones. Soon there were more than five hundred, and when they reached a thousand, it became too much and, according to Rosamund, the whole thing had to be given up. Alice Hoatson remembered it coming to an end when 'Rosamund somehow caught scarlet fever and everything had to be hurried out of the house to a nearby neighbour who ran the treat for us'.[34]

It was on the eve of one of these Christmas treats, perhaps in 1890 or 1891, that Fabian, who had inherited something of his mother's inquisitiveness and rebelliousness, stole some of the sweets intended for the poor children and, when interrogated about his act, denied it. Stealing was bad enough, especially from the poor, but lying was more serious: it is a secret vice, undermining the codes of society; it is deeply dishonourable. He was punished by being beaten on his hands and then shut up alone in the schoolroom all day. Edith remembered finding him there, at the end of it, surrounded by the cut-out paper figures and patterns he had made from scraps of paper and material left behind after the older children's present-making:

> [Your mother] found you asleep on the hearthrug, your face incredibly dirty with tears and coaldust, and beside you the hearthbrush on which with cotton-ends you had hung little screws of crushed coloured silk. It had been a magic tree to your last waking thoughts, and when your dreams brought you to an orchard of trees even more richly enchanted it had, its use ended, fallen from your hand. Your mother carried you to bed and undressed you. You did not wake. She did not wake you even to wash you. The white sheets seemed then not to matter so much as your sleep.[35]

After Fabian's early death, Edith remembered this incident with bitterness and remorse: she felt that from that day, a shadow had fallen across his face, as of a soul that had felt itself forsaken.

From the outset the Deptford Christmas treats had included some kind of entertainment for the children, as well as tea and presents. Charades, acting, and tableaux were, in any case, popular Victorian parlour entertainments, and the more literary or artistic the circle, the more likely it was to enjoy these various forms of licensed showing-off. Edith, who enjoyed artificial drama almost as much as the dramas of daily life, always seized any opportunity of improvising costumes or dressing up. In the first few years of the treats, the Blands and their friends staged tableaux, but by 1892 Edith was writing full-scale Christmas plays for them all to act. In that year, it was *Cinderella*, and there were two performances, one for the children, and another for their parents and relations. Play rehearsals were held once or twice a week for three months, so that everyone would know their words, though some of the busier actors such as Laurence Housman asked to be excused from this chore: 'I will come part perfect, given time,' he promised. Under mild protest, Housman played the King in *Sleeping Beauty*, probably in 1895, and the Slave of the Lamp in *Aladdin* in 1896:

> Hew me in pieces before the Deptford board-school children, and have done with me [he wrote].
>
> Songs? Two. One is 'God Save the Queen' (on the night of the performance) and the other isn't. . .

Rosamund remembered playing the fairy godmother in *Cinderella*, but she also recalled the plays being acted at the New Cross Empire, Deptford, where the Bland children took round collecting boxes, which suggests a rather more professional level of performance altogether.[36] Edith enjoyed these amateur theatricals enormously, just as she loved charades or any other game that gave her the opportunity to perform; she was good on stage, and sometimes gave lectures for the Fabian Society on literary topics.

Laurence was the younger brother of the poet, A. E. Housman, and when he first met Edith in 1892 he was twenty-seven. She wrote to tell him how much she had enjoyed his poem 'The Corn-Keeper', published that year in the magazine *Atalanta*, to which she herself contributed work from time to time. She was in the habit of writing to authors whose work she admired to let them know this, and perhaps to suggest a meeting; several of her friendships began that way, though had she not written to him, she might in any case have met Housman at one of John Lane's famous tea parties for fashionable artists and writers.[37]

In many ways, Laurence Housman (1865–1959) was very different from his shy and reclusive brother Alfred. He had no patience with social conventions for their own sake, and was openly in revolt against certain features of the existing system – he was an ardent supporter of women's rights, and after the Great War, of pacifism. Like his elder brother, he was homosexual by inclination, but unlike A. E. he was not at all secretive or ashamed of this: he actively campaigned for greater freedom for homosexuals, and particularly for law reform. His friends included Oscar Wilde *after* his disgrace and Edward Carpenter. Gifted, sociable and amusing, he lived with his elder sister Clemence who also worked as a professional writer and illustrator. Housman had a witty, mischievous face with a somewhat Mephistophelian beard, and his sense of fun and high spirits, much in evidence in his delightful letters and postcards to her, appealed strongly to Edith. They had a great deal in common in terms of work, for though Laurence initially earned his living as a line artist, he really preferred writing, and, like Edith, was at first obliged to write more or less what came to hand, whether it was poems, prose or fairy tales for children. Unlike Edith, he always had more ideas for stories than he knew what to do with, and his inventiveness provided her with much-needed starting points for her work: it was Housman who suggested to her that a phoenix and a carpet might somehow be used in a story for children. He himself had written an episode in which a phoenix laid an egg in a letter-box, but had subsequently put it aside from lack of interest. When, in 1904, she sent him a copy of *The Phoenix and the Carpet* with a note thanking him for his contribution, he courteously replied:

> It is delightful to find how fruitful small suggestions – mere pegs or stems on which to hang a story – become under the genial breath of your invention. It is so long ago since I proposed the carpet and the phoenix as properties for a magic plot to be woven around, that I had forgotten all about them. I can't decide whether the artist has been drawing Mr Lamert or me as the father of the family – but I hope it is me. There is a smartness and a smugness which suggests careful study of the libellous portrait you have of me . . .

He also believed that he had given her the idea for *The Wouldbe-goods*.[38]

The active phase of Housman's friendship with the Blands lasted about ten years or a little more. During that time, he performed in their plays, played badminton in the garden at Grove Park (on one occasion, he accidentally hit Edith with his racket, and cut her nose badly), attended dances and parties, and went down to stay with them at Dymchurch. He was also taken to occasional meetings of the debating society, 'It', where he remembered hearing the old Marxist, Belfort Bax, read a paper. Through the Blands he was introduced to further

social highlights such as the annual 'Crab and Cream' supper held in rooms at the Temple, at which everyone ate as much of both as they could possibly manage, accompanied by wine and followed up by Benedictine. Sometimes joke debates or mock-trials were held. On one such occasion, Housman, to his great embarrassment, was required to conduct, impromptu, the prosecution in a case of Breach of Promise of Marriage against Oswald Cox (brother of the socialist, Harold Cox, who had brought about the closure of 'It'). Oswald Cox

came dressed as a baby in bare legs with his hair tied up in ribbon, his defence being that he was an infant under the age of consent. I was quite incapable, in those days, of speaking, except conversationally; and I hated the job and did it badly. Sutro [a playwright and author] was defending Counsel. Oswald Barron was the judge.[39]

Later, after he became involved in the women's rights movement, Housman became an effective and indeed a well-known speaker. Predictably it was this issue that hastened his rift with the Blands:

After 1902 I saw less and less of her. I never liked her husband; and when my feeling toward him became active dislike, it was embarrassing to continue visiting the house. I fancy she understood the reason, and acquiesced. When the Women's Suffrage Movement started, she disappointed me by refusing to take any part in it when it took the form of Adult Suffrage. I felt that this was a dishonest excuse, put forward, I guess, because her husband was a violent Anti, and she wished not to annoy him. . .

There was always an element of discomfort for me in our intimacy – she thought a great deal more highly of her work – especially of her poetry – than I did. I was never able to give her all the praise she expected and thought she deserved. It hurt her, I remember, when she wanted me to say that, of modern women poets, she came about next to Christina Rossetti, and I insisted that Mrs Meynell, and Mrs Marriott-Watson – to name no others, were both her betters. In fact it was *not* as a literary woman that I liked her. I did not think that she 'counted'. I don't think so now. But I admired her fine generous character, and her enormous energy – also her wonderful faculty of joie-de-vivre.[40]

Housman's fastidiousness where his literary judgement was concerned, and his determination to keep this quite separate from his warm admiration for Edith as a person obviously created embarrassments. 'On one occasion', he recalled,

when she was asked for a Christmas story, I gave her the rough version of one which I had abandoned, and she used it so much as I had written it that she wanted to put my name to it as part author, and was rather offended when I refused – my objection being that as I had not thought it good enough to publish myself, I was not going to be dragged into putting my name to it as collaboration.

A few years after sending this account of his friendship with her to Doris Langley Moore, Housman seems to have revised his opinion of her work somewhat, for in his memoirs, *The Unexpected Years* (1937), he described her rather more generously as 'an able and energetic writer of stories for children, but her prose was better than her poetry, and this she did not know. It was, indeed, rather an offence to hint it.' He found it difficult '– she hungering for appreciation, and I liking her so much – to remain sincere without seeming to be unkind.' A page or so further on, Housman speculates on whether

I have been unfaithful in my friendships; so many have come and gone, not through any active breach or loss of kind feeling, but from the fact that we have each become different people; and as we become different our points of intimate contact have diminished . . .[41]

If Housman was a friend who came and went, Marshall Steele, another of the performers in the Deptford children's entertainments, remained loyal to Edith all his life. She had known him from the late 1880s or perhaps earlier, and they must have met through a south London literary or socialist society – Steele moved in both these circles, and seems always to have lived in south-east London, at Lee or Grove Park. Iris recalled how very poor the family was when she went to stay with them as a child. Steele was married, with three daughters of around the same age as Edith's children, and he supported himself by teaching elocution, indeed he liked to refer to himself as a 'Professor of Elocution'; the subject was genuinely in demand in a society which judged men – as Shaw pointed out in *Pygmalion* – according to their vowels. It was Steele who had first encouraged Edith to write verses for recitation and he used to perform these with her at Working Men's Clubs, and also at private functions, at the kind of parties and smoking concerts then in vogue, where performances of various kinds were an established part of the evening's entertainment. A note of hers from 1890, to the publisher John Lane, promises

> Mr Steele and I will come and recite for you. – We will do a dialogue called 'Un Mauvais Quart d'Heure' – by Fabian Bland – if you like. Miss E. Nesbit is my reciting name – and Mr Marshall Steele's name is here written out in full.

Noel Griffith also recalled her giving recitation evenings with Marshall Steele, consisting of duologues and solos: 'They did this professionally, and found it profitable. She did it well.' Griffith recalled seeing them perform together at a hall in London.[42]

Marshall Steele admired Edith intensely. He must have met her when he was already married and fallen in love with her without quite realizing that he had done so. He and his wife Theresa became family friends and his daughters Olive, Mildred and Enid appear in Bland family photographs. The duration and warmth of his friendship is reflected in several small acts of homage: he gave her two volumes of Emerson, specially inscribed, and each year he composed a special birthday poem for her, an idea he may have first picked up from her. Though not all of these have survived, there are several examples from the 1890s and others dated 1911, 1917 and 1918, which suggest that he kept up the custom for much of her later life. The poems themselves are written with a deep yet innocent affection – she is 'my dear, true friend' and the 'dearest friend I ever knew'. The evidence of his devotion suggests that this was no mere poetic exaggeration. She, in turn, evidently liked and trusted him and felt she could rely on his respect for her. She dedicated *A Pomander of Verse* (1895) to him and when, late in the nineties, she received a request for a summary biography she replied.

> I find I have not the heart to write my biography with 'personal details' – so I have asked my old friend Mr Marshall Steele to do it for me – and he will send it next week. I have asked Mr Steele to make the biography

short – but he may possibly warm to his subject, and make the thing longer than you wish. In that case, of course, cut unsparingly.

Marshall Steele was strongly influenced by Edith, and seems to have emulated her, not only in the matter of birthday poems, but more professionally: when she gave up writing political poems for *The Weekly Dispatch*, she passed the job on to him, and he also wrote some children's stories rather in the style of her own early work and for the same publishers.[43]

Another ardent admirer, while very far from being a family friend, was the elegant and modish poet Richard le Gallienne with whom Edith had a passionate though poorly documented love affair in the early nineties. Le Gallienne himself sent Doris Langley Moore a lively if less than frank account of what happened:

> Though it is so many years since I saw her, my remembrance of Edith Bland is as keen and beautiful as ever, and I can still see her, as though it was yesterday, as I first saw her at Hampstead, seated in an arm-chair with her two little children at her side. It was a romantic moment for me, for she was the first poet I had ever seen, and, a youth just come up to London from the provinces, I looked on her with wonder, and [was] captivated by her beauty and the charm of her immediate sympathetic response. I fell head-over-heels in love with her in fact. She was quite unlike any other woman I had ever seen, with her tall lithe boyish-girl figure, admirably set off by her plain 'Socialist' gown, with her short hair, and her large vivid eyes, curiously bird-like, and so full of intelligence, and a certain half-mocking, yet friendly, humour. She had, too, a comradely frankness of manner, which made me at once feel that I had known her all my life; like a tomboyish sister slightly older than myself. She suggested adventure, playing truant, robbing orchards and such-like boyish pranks, or even running away to sea. I was hers from that moment, and have been hers ever since. At that time I would be about twenty-three, and she, I think, would be about eight years older. The year must have been 1889, but I cannot be quite sure. I saw her frequently from then on for several years, and I owe her an enduring debt of gratitude for her sympathetic appreciation and criticism of my early work. For her own work I had an enthusiastic admiration, and one of the few poems I know by heart to this day is the poem beginning
>
> > If on some balmy summer night
> > You rowed across the moon-path white . . .
>
> and, only a few evenings ago, I was repeating it to some friends.
> But before long I left England for America, where till recently I have

continued to live; and so, I am unhappy to say, we saw no more of each other. But her memory has always remained one of my most treasured possessions . . . All I can do is to recall her as a beautiful inspiring vision and a loved friend.

He added, by way of a postscript:

The only figure I recall from her circle of acquaintance, mostly 'Fabians', was Mr Bernard Shaw. I have also a lively remembrance of the strong, fighting, talking face of her husband, Hubert Bland. He and Shaw used, I think, to box together.[44]

Le Gallienne was unlikely to have forgotten Shaw, who had savaged his *English Poems* in *The Star*. Shaw replied to a friend's puzzled enquiry as to why he had reviewed the book so harshly in imagery that suggests that he had relative boxing weights in mind:

Why all this fury against a poor little sensitive plant like Richard? Why, his fighting weight is not two and a half ounces: a rough word would drive him to suicide . . . He was horribly hurt when I took his valentines and love letters, over every one of which I have no doubt he dropped a tear of quivering sensibility, and crumpled them up in my horny fist; and I shouldn't have done it if I had not thought he was getting spoiled . . .

This sounds a little disingenuous. Shaw may have been put out, though no doubt unconsciously, by Edith's interest in a man he thought of as 'twaddly enough', and 'slight' in every respect. If le Gallienne was getting 'spoiled', she had played her part in spoiling him. It can scarcely have helped that his *English Poems* contained at least two, and possibly more, love poems addressed to her.[45]

Le Gallienne's letter was true as far as it went, but like so many of the documents relating to Edith, it did not tell the whole story. The young le Gallienne was brought up by well-to-do but Philistine parents in Birkenhead. His father persuaded him to study for a career in chartered accountancy, but he found it hideously boring and dreamed instead of becoming a writer or a poet, a new 'Sir Walter Scott'. By the spring of 1888 he had met the publisher John Lane who became a close friend of his. A letter to Lane written in May 1888 includes his first reference to Edith; her name had come up in connection with Philip Bourke Marston who had died the previous year:

I am glad to know you a fellow-sympathiser in the work of poor P.B.M. – and that you were pleased with my notice in last week's *Academy*. I too have wondered whether the Miss Nesbit of the *Lays and Legends* is related to Marston's love – tho' I know nothing of her poems beyond several she had contributed to the magazines. Her work seems to be very fine according to the critics . . .

Further notes to Lane in November and December 'look forward to meeting . . . Miss Nesbit' when in town, and during December it seems that he called on her one Sunday afternoon, when she was normally 'at home' to visitors. Le Gallienne now left Liverpool for good, having failed his accountancy exams, and came to London, where he stayed at first with his friend Lane, and later in lodgings.[46]

Richard le Gallienne was a beautiful young man, in every sense. His friend Arthur Bennett described him, without exaggeration, as

a handsome youth. Tall and slim, his frame was cast in a delicate mould, but the elasticity of health redeemed it from any suggestion of feebleness. His face, somewhat pale and long, was of considerable charm and refinement; and his hair, black and glossy, clustered in curls round his head. His brow was broad and high, his nose slightly aquiline, his mouth full, his eyes large and dark.

Edith liked him at once and was soon writing to John Lane asking him to send her Richard's address, which she had lost. In March 1889 he presented her with a copy of his first collection of poems, *Volumes in Folio*, which Elkin Mathews and Lane had published for the Bodley Head in a limited edition. He inscribed it 'To "E. Nesbit", Esq.'[47] This was not purely a joke about her professional name; as his letter to Doris Langley Moore reveals, he found the element of sexual ambivalence in her appearance arousing, suggesting comradeship or independence, qualities he had not come across among the lifeless drawing-room dolls of Birkenhead.

Edith responded to his gift with some well-meant motherly advice, which he misconstrued as 'Mrs B's anathema upon my work', for he was even more hypersensitive to criticism than she was:

Thank you for your book [she wrote]. I have not had time to read it yet but am looking forward to doing so as soon as I have a quiet hour. I will gladly do what I can for it with the *Star*.

If I were a mentor giving advice to young poets – I think I should say: 'do not publish too many *slight* books – but wait a year or two and then choose the *best* of your work – and give the world some thing worthy of your highest dreams.' – Mind I say this – your book being still 'unopened'. –

You expressed a wish to meet G. Bernard Shaw. We are asking him to

"Oh! my Daddy, my Daddy!

"Oh! my Daddy, my Daddy!"
as pictured by Charles Brock
for *The Railway Children*, 1906

Edith's father, John Collis Nesbit

Edith, aged three

Sarah Nesbit, "the old mother owl"

Edith at seventeen

Mary Nesbit, who died in 1871

The front of Well Hall. The Blands moved in during the early summer of 1899

Below: Well Hall, summer 1899: standing, Richard Reynolds and Hubert (in the hat). Seated, from left to right: Olive Steele, Iris, Charlotte Perkins Gilman (lying), Paul, Dorothea Deakin (with Martha the bull terrier), Mrs. Steele and Rosamund at the edge. (Edith may have been behind the camera)

Above: Punting on the moat. Douglas Kennedy on the left, looking at the camera. His friend Cuthbert Collins standing (centre) and Edith punting, on the right

Left: Well Hall, winter 1899-1900: Fabian with Lady, the deerhound

come to us next Friday. Will you come too? Tea at 6. – I shall then be able to get you to tell me all about your new opera. And we might get a par[agraph] into the *Star* about that and your book if you like.[48]

His next visit to the Blands was of a delicate and probably an unwelcome nature. Lane had had some discussion with them as to whether they might write a study of Meredith's novels, which they both admired, but now he wanted to withdraw from the project and get someone else (in fact it was to be le Gallienne himself) to do it. Le Gallienne was despatched to act as ambassador in this tricky situation, to find out where the Blands now stood in the matter; it seems that they blamed Elkin Mathews for going back on the terms arranged but had accepted the situation and were no more than 'mildly sarcastic'.[49] If further letters were exchanged, they have not survived, but in May le Gallienne moved to lodgings on Hampstead Heath at 12 Wildwood Grove, and from there a muddy track ran down to Charlotte Wilson's cottage, Wildwood Farm. It was surely here that Richard met Edith again, with two of her children, and here that he remembered seeing her 'first' – a figure at once maternal yet childish, 'like a tomboyish sister slightly older than myself'.

Edith was charmed by le Gallienne's classical profile as much as by his undisguised admiration of her work. The poem of hers that he singled out in his letter to Doris Langley Moore was called 'The Mermaid', and had appeared in her second volume of verse, *Leaves of Life* (1888). Though essentially a minor poet, le Gallienne had a better ear than Edith, and the poem he had remembered was one of her more technically accomplished performances:

> If on some balmy summer night
> You rowed across the moon-path white,
> And saw the shining sea grow fair
> With silver scales and golden hair,
> What would you do?

Its theme is a favourite of hers – the dangers and enchantments of love – here traditionally embodied in the siren. It ends:

> I might look back, my dear, and then
> Row back into the shore again:
> Or, if I safely got away,
> Regret it to my dying day!

That Edith was, for a time, passionately in love with le Gallienne is endorsed by a family legend to the effect that after a particularly distressing row at home, she announced that she was going to run away with him. It was left, as unpleasant tasks so often were, to Alice Hoatson to stop her: she found herself struggling on the stairs with a desperate Edith in an effort to prevent her 'doing anything silly', and persuade her to calm down. When this scene took place is uncertain, but it may well have been after le Gallienne's own marriage in October 1891 to the slender auburn-haired Mildred, with her 'pretty clinging habit of gazing eagerly up into your face as she spoke or listened'.[50]

What evidence there is concerning their love affair occurs in yet another novel, though not by either of the protagonists, and one that was only published in serial form. In his Liverpool days, le Gallienne had been chummy with a young journalist called Arthur Bennett who was later to publish, in the unlikely setting of Warrington, a progressive monthly magazine 'dedicated to civic improvement and the liberal arts' – *The Dawn*. During alternate years after the turn of the century this featured an interminable autobiographical novel by Bennett called *Harold Wolfgang*, set in the town of 'Mornington', with occasional forays as far as 'Yarnchester'. Le Gallienne figures largely, especially in the early episodes before he departs for London, 'to fling his handful of incense on the altars of the new priesthood of letters'. Alias Robert du Mervyn, he marries his sweetheart and seems all set for success. Meanwhile back in Mornington, his friends are attempting to 'grasp the inner heart of Fabianism from the gifted lips of Alfred Rusk' (Rusk being, presumably, the Blandest food that Bennett could think of):

> Joe had once told Harold [Wolfgang, i.e. Bennett], some months earlier, that Bob [du Mervyn i.e. le Gallienne], amongst his numerous gallantries, could boast a sentimental episode with Mrs Rusk – a clever poetess and a very charming woman – and Harold had, of course, passed on the tale to Walter. They were both much interested, in consequence, in meeting Rusk, and Harold had no doubt invited him to lecture partly as the outcome of a not unnatural curiosity.
>
> Just before Rusk left with Walter for the train, he suddenly observed upon the study mantel-piece a recent rather striking photograph of Bob.
>
> He started as he looked at it and eyed it curiously, affecting obviously an unconcern he did not feel.
>
> 'Do you know Du Mervyn?' Walter innocently asked.
>
> 'Slightly,' Mr Rusk responded in a frigid tone. 'Is he a friend of Mr Wolfgang?'
>
> 'Yes, they are old comrades and bosom chums!' said Walter wickedly. 'Tell each other everything!'

'Ah!'

From a sheer love of mischief Walter seemed disposed to dwell on Bob and to enlarge upon the friendship; but Rusk seemed strangely ill at ease and quickly changed the subject.[51]

What happened next provided the occasion for some gruesome moralizing on the part of Arthur Bennett, for Mildred, after bearing le Gallienne a daughter late in 1892, fell ill with typhoid in the spring of 1894 and died:

> We shall not probe into Bob's soul; we dare not dogmatise upon such themes; the best of us is strangely weak, and love is like the wind – it bloweth where it listeth, and one cannot tell whence it comes or whither it goes; and, if we understood everything, we should pardon every-thing, as George Eliot wisely says; but we do know that Bob had penned some passionate verses to the unintending interloper which had accidentally been seen by [Mildred], and had found her weeping over them as if her heart would break. Was this to be the punishment for his brief sin, so honestly atoned for? How vainly he reproached himself for this and every lighter infidelity; how empty all his fine-spun theories of free-love seemed as he watched that little golden head toss to and fro in the fierce fires of fever . . .[52]

If le Gallienne had seriously intended to prevent Mildred from reading his poems to Edith, he should not have published them as he did in *English Poems* (1892). The poem that upset her, if Bennett's fiction is to be believed, was one expressing strong sexual jealousy, though it was rather apologetically tucked away under the misleading heading 'Love Platonic':

Why Did She Marry Him?

Why did she marry him? Ah, say why!
  How was her fancy caught?
What was the dream that he drew her by,
  Or was she only bought?
Gave she her gold for a girlish whim,
  A freak of a foolish mood?
Or was it some will, like a snake in him,
  Laid a charm upon her blood?

Love of his limbs, was it that, think you?
  Body of bullock build,
Sap in the bones, and spring in the thew,
  A lusty youth unspilled?

> But is it so that a maid is won,
>   Such a maiden maid as she?
> Her face like a lily all white in the sun,
>   For such mere male as he!
>
> Ah, why do the fields with their white and gold
>   To Farmer Clod belong,
> Who though he hath reaped and stacked and sold
>   Hath never heard their song?
> Nay, seek not an answer, comfort ye,
>   The poet heard their call,
> And so, dear Love, will I comfort me –
>   He hath thy lease – that's all.

The 'bullock build' suggests Hubert's greater girth and height – le Gallienne was slender and delicately made. How long his love affair with Edith lasted is hard to tell, but his letter to Doris Langley Moore spoke of seeing her frequently from 1889 'for several years', so it may well have begun before his marriage in 1891 and continued after it, though Mildred's death in May 1894 would have formed a certain terminus. It threw him into a state of total despair and must have left him with at least some of the guilty feelings that Arthur Bennett was so anxious to attribute to him. His letter suggested, without stating in so many words, that he had lost contact with Edith when he went to live in America, but this was certainly an over-simplification. He visited America for a month in the spring of 1895, and again in 1897, but he did not leave England for good until late in 1903, after the break-up of his second marriage and many years after he had lost all contact with Edith.

Her love affairs with Noel Griffith and Richard le Gallienne established a pattern that was to typify many of Edith's subsequent relationships, both of friendship and of love: she enjoyed surrounding herself with younger men, often but not always aspiring artists or writers whose careers she attempted to advance. She liked to hold court, while her young men adopted the attitudes of subservient worship associated with courtly love. Something of this pseudo-medieval posture is caught in le Gallienne's second poem to her, though its title, 'The Lamp and the Star', is more redolent of Shelley than of the troubadours:

Yea, let me be 'thy bachelere',
  'Tis sweeter than thy lord;
How should I envy him, my dear,
  The lamp upon his board.
Still make his little circle bright
With boon of dear domestic light,
  While I afar
Watching his windows in the night,
  Worship a star
For which he hath no bolt or bar.
  Yea, dear,
  Thy 'bachelere'.[53]

Ex libris ஃ E. Nesbit.

HOUSEMAN'S BOOKPLATE MADE FOR E. NESBIT

THE TWO OSWALDS

Noel Griffith had been elected to the Fabian Society in November 1889 and by spring of the following year was helping to audit its accounts, no doubt at the suggestion of its Hon. Treasurer, Hubert Bland. In May and June of 1890 Richard Reynolds and Oswald Barron were elected to the Society, and in the February of 1891, Bland and Noel Griffith proposed Bower Marsh for membership. These four young men all met through the Blands or else knew one other from living in rooms in the Temple, which retained something of a collegiate atmosphere. Griffith, the eldest, had trained as a chartered accountant but later became a barrister. Reynolds and Marsh were Oxford men, two or three years younger: Reynolds had been an exhibitioner at Balliol where he read Classics, and went down with a First in 1890, subsequently training to become a barrister, though he actually seems to have earned his living as a journalist over the next ten years. Bower Marsh had held an open scholarship at Exeter College, where he read Modern History and gained a Second in 1889. After a year or so abroad, he returned to London to train as a solicitor. He may well have known Reynolds from Oxford days, and sought him out when he returned to England. Oswald Barron worked in the Public Record Office, and as a journalist, but he too had rooms in the Temple. The four friends shared a common admiration of Mrs Bland, and formed a little band of courtiers around her. Probably all four were, at one time or another, her lovers as well as admirers.[1]

While their personal devotion to Edith was never in doubt, how did they relate to one another? Were they rivals for her attention or did they also value one another's companionship, content to take turns in hers? Noel Griffith had been the first on the scene, and was ultimately the most faithful, the only one of them to attend her funeral. He recalled with amusement an occasion in 1891 when Bower Marsh came down for the day to Rottingdean, where he and the Blands and Alice were on holiday as a foursome: up on the Downs, Edith's dog ran away and Marsh, to his intense annoyance, was obliged to spend much of his time chasing after it, while Griffith complacently continued his conversation with Edith. The role of faithful squire is not always a rewarding one. Yet Griffith remained on terms of friendship with Marsh for the rest of his life, and it was he who passed on to Doris Langley Moore the news of Marsh's death, late in 1935. Bower Marsh in turn related several stories about Edith and Oswald Barron, and all of them, as well as other friends like Laurence Housman, attended the debates, parties and dinners that Barron in particular liked to give in his rooms at the Temple. Reynolds was, at first, the least obtrusive and the most mysterious – he is scarcely mentioned by the others – yet he fell deeply and passionately in love with Edith and was still in thrall to her ten years later, when Griffith, Marsh and Barron had all married and moved either wholly or partly outside her circle. Noel, Richard and Oswald were immortalized when their names were conferred on the Bastables – no doubt Bower's name was too unusual for her to use.[2]

Bower Marsh first met the Blands soon after their move to Birch Grove at the end of September 1889, when he had been down from Oxford for several months. He did not see them again for some time as he went abroad for a year or more, returning during the winter of 1890–1. It was in February 1891 that he joined the Fabian. From then on he spent a great deal of time with them, particularly during the next two or three years, when his friendship with Edith was at its height. He was married in 1901 and saw little of them thereafter. Like Noel Griffith, he regarded the Blands as something of a revelation, especially as he was fundamentally rather more conventional than Griffith. The whole life-style of Birch Grove made an enormous impact on him since, as he explained to Doris Langley Moore, he had never encountered Bohemians before. He remembered the Blands as comfortably off, though always living a little beyond their means. Hubert now had regular work as a book reviewer, mainly of novels, for the *Daily Chronicle*. During the summer of 1892 he made a particularly successful lecture tour of the Midlands, taking in Manchester, Bradford, Burnley and Warrington where he met Arthur James Bennett, as the latter recorded in his serial novel *Harold Wolfgang*. Bland was to make a number of such lecture tours in the mid-90s and as a consequence of the 1892 tour he was invited to

contribute a regular column to Manchester's *Sunday Chronicle*. This
brought him a wide and devoted following in the North and a secure
income for the rest of his life. The column was written above his own
name, 'Hubert', and used his own particular man-of-the-world
approach to discuss a large range of topics, from Hegel's theory of the
state to the use of the powder puff, from flirtation to the divorce laws,
from bad politics to good fiction. Iris recalled that these articles

> were written on Tuesday . . . the subject being discussed, very often at
> breakfast. If politics were not sufficiently thrilling at the moment, or
> there were no striking new books, or the newspapers having a silly
> season, an article about women was the last hope and always forth-
> coming.[3]

According to Bower Marsh, Edith herself had been thought of as a
coming poet when *Lays and Legends* was first published in 1886, but
by degrees her poetry had ceased to be highly regarded. He thought
her problem was that, with such facility in writing, she had never really
worked hard enough at it to become a good poet, a view endorsed by
others. Even in her own judgement, the result often fell short of her
aim. W. E. Henley, an editor and poet himself, later wrote to her
praising some poems she had sent him, but adding, by way of a
warning:

> I like the verses. If you can keep up to the level of them, by all means go
> in for a sequence. I believe that, if you write them with all your heart –
> above all, if you do not run the risk of breathlessly making too many –
> you will do a piece of notable work. Think, if ever you feel disposed to
> settle down into the market-woman's canter – think to yourself this
> stage-direction:- '*Enter the ghost of The National Observer*'. And then
> say to yourself: – 'No, I *won't*. I'll make these verses for myself and two
> or three friends,' as Mozart made *Don Juan*. The idea is so good, and
> you are so full of sympathy and insight and knowledge, that – *if* you
> look out for the ghost – I am sure you will do an excellent piece of
> work.[4]

Bower Marsh thought her concerned first and foremost with
keeping the household going and paying the bills, so that she was too
easily satisfied with the saleable second-rate. He remembered her at
that time as doing an enormous amount of work for illustrated
booklets and magazines, writing stories and verses to accompany the
pictures regularly sent over for her. She never turned work away. But
hard work was punctuated by fun, usually in the form of holidays or

entertaining, and Marsh readily joined in both of these. It was somewhat easier for her to please herself now that Alice was there to provide the children with day-to-day care and mothering, and the boys began to go to boarding school. Marsh, like everyone who knew them, recalled the Blands' extravagant hospitality – guests were always invited to stay to meals and both of them loved to have lots of young people around. On Sundays, Edith was regularly 'at home' to callers, or invited new friends to tea, and Bower Marsh encountered a mixture of writers and socialists at Birch Grove – among them, the then popular novelist Richard Whiteing, and the Fabians Sydney Olivier and Graham Wallas (whom Edith described as resembling the famous Discobolus when young). Sundays were largely given up to friends but on weekdays, when the pressure of work obliged her to, she often locked herself up in her study at the top of the house, with a notice on the door saying that she was not to be disturbed. When working, she took no notice of whether there were guests about or not, and somebody else would be deputed to receive anyone who called.[5]

Edith's friendship with Bower Marsh flourished in the early 1890s; one day she made a special train journey down to Halstead with him so that she could show him her old home and walk once again in the woods and parkland she loved so much. Nostalgic journeys of this kind were always a sign of her special affection, a sign that she was taking someone into her heart as she took him into her past. On his birthday, 25 January 1892, she gave him her latest volume of poems, the second series of *Lays and Legends*, and she continued to remember the occasion by giving him her books for some years. Into a copy of her second book of poems, *Leaves of Life* (1888), Marsh pasted two sepia photographs of her – in the second of these she has her hands clasped behind her head and looks kittenish and inviting – a mood captured nowhere else. A third book of poems, the reprint of the first series of *Lays and Legends*, was given to Marsh on 20 April, to mark her return from a long holiday in Antibes. When this was opened, a flimsy sheet of paper fluttered out: it was the manuscript of a rondeau which she had written and sent him while she was away. She also gave him a watercolour sketch of a stone archway that she had painted in Antibes. Marsh thought that, had she been trained as an artist, she might have done well for she had a painter's vision; when out walking with the Blands, one of them would be sure to exclaim, 'Oh, isn't that paintable!'[6]

The holiday in Antibes was one of the Blands' few ventures abroad, and it was quite a major upheaval. It came about through the patronage of D'Arcy Reeve, the wealthy Liberal who, in the early nineties, decided to take Edith under his wing. She could have met him through Shaw (he is probably George Seddon in her novel *Daphne in Fitzroy Street*) or else through the Fabian, to which he was elected at the same meeting as Bower Marsh had been, in February 1891. The previous year D'Arcy Reeve had come across one of Edith's poems which he greatly admired; wanting to read more of her work, he enquired after it, only to discover from Longmans that both her volumes of poetry had gone out of print and there were no plans to reprint them. He decided to have the first series of *Lays and Legends* reissued, and a second series published at his own expense. Edith was naturally delighted with the idea – she had been unable to understand why Longmans would not reprint *Lays and Legends* when a second edition had sold out and there were still enquiries after it, and she had been unsuccessfully trying to persuade John Lane, among others, to take her third collection of poems, when Reeve solved both her problems by his generous intervention. But when he called on his protégée in January 1892 to see how she liked the new volume with its portrait frontispiece, he found her seriously ill with bronchitis. It is the heavy smoker's illness and at this period she was smoking forty cigarettes a day, rolling her own and often lighting one from another. Reeve advised her to go abroad, to Antibes on the Riviera, where the milder, drier climate would hasten her recovery. She told him it was out of the question – she could not make a journey of that length alone and in any case she could not afford to do so. But Reeve continued to plead with her and when she agreed that Alice might go with her, he immediately wrote out a cheque for three hundred pounds to cover their expenses.[7]

Alice and Edith set out late in January, but Edith was not yet really well enough to travel, and they had a particularly difficult journey. At Paris she and Alice caught what they assumed was the overnight train to Marseilles. They had taken sleepers, so they got undressed and into bed, leaving their money, watches and clothes scattered about the compartment. At ten p.m. the train stopped at Dijon and a porter opened the door and ordered them to get out. The two women had been asleep, and when Edith awoke, she had no voice, and had to explain in a choking whisper (since Alice didn't speak any French) that they were going straight through. The porter replied that they had got to change – they should have been on the train for Lyons. They were just beginning to pull on whatever clothes they could lay hands on, and pick up their scattered belongings when the carriage light suddenly went out. As they groped around in the dark, the station master arrived. In a hoarse whisper close to his ear, Edith asked for the light to be put back on, and he started back as if she had tried to bite him. He told them that they were under a misapprehension, and they must hurry up because their train was on the point of leaving. Half dressed, and clutching whatever they could snatch up in the dark of their clothes, open suitcases and other possessions, they struggled on to the platform and were hustled, without further ado, aboard the Lyons train. There were no sleepers, and as the two women tidied themselves up and looked through their baggage, they realized that they had left purses, Alice's watch and a number of other essential items behind.[8]

They reached Marseilles at seven a.m. The air was damp and chilly, and they were shivering with cold and hunger, but Edith insisted that they must find the Consul and a doctor. As it was too early for either, they went to have breakfast in a café, but Edith petulantly refused to eat anything until they had found the Consul, who turned out to live two miles outside the town and spoke very little English. When he heard that they were planning to stay at Antibes, he told them it would be far too cold for them, and urged them to go to Toulon instead – indeed they would just have time to catch the ten o'clock train. When they told him of their losses, he suggested they consulted the Consul at Toulon. They never did find the Consul at Toulon, but spent four miserable days there in a seedy hotel with grubby curtains and furniture. Edith continued to play the naughty child, apparently thinking that her condition justified that role; she kept asking for whatever was unobtainable – hot milk or mulled wine – and refusing to eat properly, but when they reached Antibes, the weather grew warmer, and she began to feel a little better and more cheerful.

By mid-March, Hubert had come down to join them, bringing with him from Paris two young ladies, May and Leonora Bowley, friends of theirs who lived at Lee and worked as commercial artists, doing line drawings in a style inspired by Walter Crane; later they illustrated some of Edith's stories. Everyone enjoyed the last part of the holiday: the sun shone and both Alice and Edith were much happier once Hubert had arrived. He and Alice, whom the French hotel staff politely assumed to be his sister, shocked the locals by going for early-morning swims. Edith was now well on the way to recovery, and much cheered by the admiration of some young officers from the local garrison. May Bowley recalled how the local inhabitants had stared at

Edith and Alice in their loose, 'aesthetic' Liberty gowns, how Edith hired a guitar and wore it slung over her shoulders and how she allowed one of the French officers to stroll about with his arm around her waist, while Mr Bland did not appear to mind at all.

Edith remembered their daily picnics by the shore:

> We used to sit on myrtle bushes . . . and read pleasant books and look out across the sea to the little shadow on the skyline . . . that is Corsica. And when we were hungry and thirsty we ate and drank, French bread which is long, and French butter which is perfect, and little French oranges which they call Mandarins, and French galantine which is a mystery.[9]

At that time Antibes was still quite unsophisticated. Hubert in an article for the *Sunday Chronicle*, suggested that the novelist Grant Allen had given a somewhat misleading account of the place 'in a widely circulated English magazine', though it was probably this account that had encouraged the Blands to choose Antibes in the first place:

> Instead of the verdure-clad woods and multi-coloured acres of flowers, spoken of in the magazine, I found myself in a quaint little Mediter-ranean town – all white walls, red roofs, soldiers and smells. When I call the town 'Mediterranean', I have sufficiently indicated that it is not French or even European . . . [it] is much more like Damascus or Jerusalem than it is like Paris or Boulogne-sur-Mer. It is of the Orient, Eastern; and as it is, so are all towns of more than fifty years of age, whose square old towers, whose embattled walls look down on this sapphire sea.

May Bowley also thought it 'looked like Nazareth from a distance'. Hubert doubted whether Grant Allen, who was staying at the Grand Hotel du Cap on the Cap Martin, had ever really visited Antibes itself, and he added, 'I took him up the old Roman tower built two thousand years ago, and I introduced him to all the smells.' Unfortunately the smells only alarmed the novelist – like many Englishmen of his time, he was afraid that he would catch typhoid from them. May Bowley remembered Grant Allen coming to dine with them all one evening at the cheap Hotel du Commerce where they were staying for a mere five francs a day. Apparently he 'held forth, with rather bad taste, on the inferiority of women'.[10]

What with the admiration of the French officers, and a dance to go to at Nice, their stay ended happily enough. Edith wrote home to Bower

Marsh celebrating the charms of the Hotel du Commerce in a rondeau, a form often used by Austen Dobson, whose skilful *vers de société* were then very much in vogue:

[handwritten manuscript of the rondeau]

Five francs a day, five francs a day,
For *díner* and for *déjeuner*,
For little rooms whose windows high
Shew us blue hills, blue sea, blue sky,
And snowy mountains far away.

In Toulon and Marseilles our stay
Was bleak with bills – and life was grey.
But now we pay – the Mouse and I –
Five francs a day.

Here life flowers daily, glad and gay
With *citron*, *rose* and *oranger*;
We watch the bright blue days go by,
And think of you at home – Ah, why
Are you not also here, to pay
Five francs a day?[11]

'Wherever they went, . . . their own circle went with them,' observed the novelist Edgar Jepson. Though Bower Marsh had been left behind when they went to Antibes, he joined them on several other holidays, just as Noel Griffith had. He went to Whitstable with them, where they stayed on several occasions, though probably not in September 1890, when they were there with Noel Griffith and several other friends including the socialist William de Mattos, who helped Edith to improve her swimming. Prince Kropotkin had also been invited, but tendered his apologies in his not quite idiomatic English:

> Certainly it would be so pleasant to join you at Whitstable. But I am afraid that it was only a castle in the air. I am not yet ready with my work, and will not be before 8–10 days – so that I must sit and write! And you, in the meantime will already return home.

He sent kind regards to Mr Bland and Mr Barron, who seems also to have been one of the party. Bower Marsh also went on the Medway with them and he stayed at Brenchley Manor, D'Arcy Reeve's country house near Tonbridge Wells, which he lent to Edith for a fortnight; Oswald Barron stayed there, too. Noel Griffith kept a diary from 1890 until his marriage in July 1895, in which he recorded some of the holidays he spent with the Blands – several weekend trips to the Medway, as well as various outings elsewhere: at the end of February 1891 the Blands spent four days at Oxford, where Griffith was auditing college accounts, and while there Edith wrote a poem on 'New College Gardens'. That year he, they and Alice spent a week in March and another in November at Rottingdean – it must have been during one of these that Bower Marsh had come down and spent the day chasing Edith's dog across the downs.[12]

The following year Noel, Alice and the Blands took a week's holiday at East Dene, near Eastbourne, early in December. From here they hired a dog-cart and visited Battle (Mrs Nesbit's family had come from Hastings and Battle), Alfriston, Bodiam Castle (a great favourite of Edith's, it provides the setting for the picnic at the end of *The New Treasure Seekers*) and Hurstmonceux which, transformed and transported to overlook the sea, eventually became *The House of Arden*. Griffith recalled that the Blands sometimes visited Angmering where they met Basil de Sélincourt, and business letters show that they stayed at Sheerness in 1889, and in September 1894 took a cottage near Worthing for a couple of weeks. In July 1895 they were back on the Medway at their favourite pub at Branbridges, from where Hubert wrote back to the Secretary of the Fabian, Edward Pease:

Damn! If anyone wants me in the North – don't forget to tell them that I have retired to the country broken in health, enfeebled in mind and not undamaged in reputation after 10 years spent in serving Socialism. At the same time nothing but a sense of duty to my wife and children keeps me down here in this lovely weather when I might be bellowing from waggons to the I[ndependent] L[abour] P[arty].[13]

Edith still went up regularly to Manchester to visit her sister Saretta who by the early 1890s was living at Booths Hall, Boothstown, Worsley; seven miles west of Manchester, this was a curious house, with a pretty old-fashioned garden. On a visit in 1893 during a miners' strike, Edith helped with the local soup kitchens and with raising relief funds for the miners' families. She also gave a party for the children at the local village school. One small girl vividly recalled her

tall fine presence, her expressive, sensitive face and her sparkling eyes . . . I remember how very distinguished I felt, when, during the games following the tea, Mrs Bland chose me and bestowed the kiss to which the 'IT' was entitled![14]

1893 was also to be the year in which Edith found her favourite holiday spot – Dymchurch, which she fell in love with and which gradually came to oust the Medway in her affection as the place where the Blands regularly took themselves, their family and friends.

Paul Bland described how his mother first discovered Dymchurch. 1893 was a blazingly hot summer with a drought that lasted from April to August, so she took the two elder children, Paul and Iris, down to the seaside at Hythe, on the Kentish coast. But she did not like it very much – it was too straitlaced, too full of boarding-houses and holiday-makers. Disappointed, she set off with the children on an exploring expedition in a char-à-banc, a kind of bus or waggon pulled by four horses, specially laid on for summer excursions. The char-à-banc drove westwards along the narrow coast road and five miles further on they found themselves in Dymchurch. In those days it was not a seaside resort at all, but just a little village standing by the shore, its long history attested by the old windmill, the Martello towers and the numerous legends of smugglers. Before the coming of the motor car, Dymchurch was a remote and isolated spot. A bus, pulled by three or four horses, ran from New Romney to Hythe and Folkestone on Tuesday and Saturdays. There was no water on tap: it had to be drawn up at the pump or collected in a rainwater butt – though problems of this kind were more likely to affect the servants who had to do the fetching and carrying, and there always seemed to be plenty of these to go round. It was only later, and through an initiative of Edith herself that the village acquired a dust-cart. Previously rubbish had simply been dumped in the sea.[15]

Edith was enchanted with Dymchurch, so old yet so unspoiled, and with characteristic decisiveness, she immediately took rooms there, and sent for the rest of her family. Hubert may well have stayed on in town for a few weeks. At any rate, in the second week of August his mother died so he must have returned to town. It was a terrible blow to him. A letter to Edward Pease thanking him for his sympathy, admitted that 'the loss of my mother has been so far the greatest sorrow I have ever had to bear'. Hubert had always had a particularly close bond with his mother, a bond in which Maggie Doran had also played a part. For some weeks he was occupied with winding up her business affairs and closing down the house at Bowater Crescent (Samuel Street) which, ever since childhood, had been his home too for three days of every week. At this point, if not before, Maggie moved away – probably to Beckenham where her father ran a cleaning and dying shop in the High Street. Meanwhile, by the end of October, Hubert was finally free to relax and enjoy the pleasures Dymchurch had to offer; he sent back some receipts to Pease from 'Marine Terrace', with a note that he would not be at the Fabian on the following day: 'We are having a very good time down here, shrimping, eeling, swimming, etc.' From then on, Dymchurch became an important part of their lives, and later it began to figure in Edith's books, often as 'Lymchurch'. In the late nineties, a number of other writers had houses on or near Romney Marsh – among these were Henry James at Rye, and Ford Madox Ford and Joseph Conrad at Aldington (both of whom she knew slightly, though she was inclined to feel contempt for 'literary people'); in 1900 H. G. Wells built himself a house at Sandgate and used Dymchurch as a setting in his novel *Kipps* (1905), while Kipling's *Puck of Pook's Hill* (1906) included scenes on the Pevensey levels and a story about the departure of the fairies called 'Dymchurch Flit'.[16]

When the Blands stayed there during the nineties, they took lodgings in the Mill House, which is where the Bastables stay in *The New Treasure Seekers*:

> It is before you come to the village, and it is a little square white house. There is a big old windmill at the back of it. It is not used any more for grinding corn, but fishermen keep their nets in it.[17]

The windmill has long since fallen down – it was quite dilapidated even then, but the Mill House still stands in Mill Street, and with some ugly modern accretions has now become the Mill Stores. After about 1902, the Blands moved nearer the centre of the village and on to the main street, where they rented a little weather-boarded semi-detached cottage, the other half of which formed the old Post Office. They were now living in the palatial splendour of Well Hall at Eltham, so their new holiday home became 'Well Cottage', and it is still called that today. Sometime in 1904 they took a much larger Georgian house almost opposite the church, known as Sycamore House, though it has since become Dymchurch Rectory. It was conveniently close to the Old Ship Hotel, from where a 'fly' could be hired to take one to the station. For a short while so many friends came down with them that Edith kept both houses going together, so that Sycamore House was known as 'the Other House' (perhaps with some allusion to Henry James's novella of that name). It was a handsome red brick building of the kind she liked best, with Dutch gables and a steep-pitched roof that swept low at the back into a garden of old fruit trees. As it was let unfurnished, Edith filled it up with second-hand furniture supplied by a local dealer. The Other House was finally given up in 1911 when she took Crowlink Farm on the Downs between Seaford and Eastbourne, and moved the furniture there. But she had fallen deeply in love with Dymchurch and the Romney Marsh, its wide skies, glowing sunsets and sense of space. She returned for holidays there in 1915, 1919 and 1920, and in 1922 she moved to her last home at St Mary's Bay, between Dymchurch and New Romney, where she spent her final painful years.

During Edith's many summers at Dymchurch, she explored Romney Marsh and its little villages with their eccentric medieval churches, at first by bicycle, but more often, as she grew older, in a hired dogcart. A number of her short stories are set in such sleepy hamlets as Ivychurch and Burmarsh, and her best-known ghost story, 'Man-Size in Marble', is set at Brenzett, and may have been inspired by a curious seventeenth-century funeral monument in the church: it portrays two life-size figures, one flat on his back, the other propped up on one elbow, as if about to rise. But in her story, the monuments that come to life, descend from Brenzett Church on Hallowe'en and destroy a living woman are those of medieval crusaders, not cavaliers, and the crucial influence is a literary one – that of Prosper Merimée's horror story 'La Venus d'Ille', in which a bronze statue of the goddess comes to life and crushes her chosen victim to death in a bridal embrace. Edith's story reverses the sexes, so that a helpless young woman is raped by the stone statues, their inhuman coldness and hardness characterizing the rape itself, as experienced by the victim. Her unimaginative and over-rational husband returns to find his wife's body thrown back across a table, her hair dishevelled, her eyes staring upward, and clasped in her fingers, a stone finger.

'Man-Size in Marble' with its suggestion of the horror of brutal male sexuality, is the most disturbing ghost story she ever wrote. It appeared in *Grim Tales*, a collection of ghost and horror stories published in 1893, though most of the individual pieces had already appeared earlier in various magazines. Ghost stories were very popular with editors at this period, and the morbid imagination Edith had acquired during her childhood equipped her particularly well for writing them. Though she made fun of Annie Besant's credulity about theosophy, she herself was strongly superstitious, surprisingly so for such a practical and realistic person. She had been determined that her children should not share her terror of corpses and skeletons, and had kept a skull and bones lying about the house when they were young so as to familiarize them with such sights, but she had never fully outgrown her own nervousness, and sometimes when she was writing ghost stories, she frightened herself so much that she was afraid to go to bed.[18] Some of the elements in her tales of terror seem to have their origin in particular phobias of hers, for example being buried alive, but as often as not they borrow plot elements and settings from other writers. She was most effective when evoking a tense or creepy atmosphere, a talent that her children's books seldom allowed her to indulge. The exception is *The Enchanted Castle*, and it is here rather than in her ghost stories that she drew most successfully on her own childhood fears to create an original and powerful fantasy.

In the same year, 1893, Edith published a second collection of short stories in the same format as *Grim Tales* under the title *Something Wrong* – a title that the Blands had originally used for their socialist novel serialized in *The Weekly Dispatch* some seven years before. This was rather a poor collection, and lacked the unifying principle of *Grim Tales* and most of her later volumes of short stories. By this stage of her career, Edith had published three volumes of serious poetry, much of it skilful and capable, but showing few signs of any real development; an enormous amount of ephemeral verse and prose in newspapers and magazines, and many whimsical or sentimental stories and verses for children, usually packaged with other people's work in brightly-coloured books and annuals. But she continually aspired to write something more than mere pot-boilers and for some time she had been in negotiation with John Lane over the possibility of writing a book of poems for him. They were on friendly terms, and he, for his part, thought her one of the handsomest women he had ever seen.[19]

Lane was an enterprising publisher; he had gone into business with the bookseller Elkin Mathews, whose bookshop 'at the sign of the Bodley Head' in Vigo Street had provided the name for their publishing house. Lane was particularly interested in new poets. His list included, among others, Laurence Housman and Richard le Gallienne who had adopted Lane as his close friend and mentor, and in January 1892 had been appointed as reader for the Bodley Head. Lane was also responsible for publishing the magazine that seems to typify the literary mood of the nineties, *The Yellow Book*: it included work by most of the leading writers and artists of the day, as well as poems by le Gallienne and even by Edith, and some of Laurence Housman's most Art Nouveauish drawings of nymphs and fauns. Many of the contributions to *The Yellow Book* were whimsical or precious in tone, and Edith's own writing in the mid-nineties took on something of its 'yellowish' tinge. This is especially apparent in the first of the two books she published with Lane, *A Pomander of Verse* (1895). Whether consciously or unconsciously both the title of the book and its contents were very much of their moment, typically arty, indeed typically Lane. Its different sections were headed 'Myrrh', 'Amber-gris', 'Bergamot', 'Musk', etc., and might have been invented by Max Beerbohm in a satirical moment. Her second book for Lane was a collection of short stories, several of them concerned with the rivalry of two women over a particular man, and written largely in a Kentish dialect which provoked Bower Marsh's snide comment, 'she had a delusion that she could reproduce dialect'. Entitled *In Homespun* (1896), these stories were published in Lane's famous 'Keynotes' series, which had specially designed covers, frontispieces and lettering; the best of these (but not hers) sported decorations by Aubrey Beardsley. Though Edith dabbled slightly with aestheticism, as became a lady of 'advanced' views, she was never really at home with its preciosity. She made a further attempt to assimilate this mode, or something like it, to her own romantic fiction in *The Literary Sense* (1903), a collection of stories that aspire to a Jamesian self-conscious-ness; but though she was always acutely aware of 'literariness', and of how reading experiences can affect the way readers, both young or old, think and act, she worked more confidently within a tradition either of naturalism or of outright fantasy.

A letter from Edith to John Lane, undated but probably written during 1892, informs him that

> My friend Mr Oswald Barron, who collaborates with me in prose and verse, is anxious to make your acquaintance and has asked me to bring about this end.
>
> May I bring him to see you, some Saturday afternoon? He is learned in archaeology and things like that: and I think you will like him, and I am sure he will like you.[20]

Edith had always enjoyed collaboration: she was intensely sociable, and the solitariness necessary for the act of writing did not come easily to her. Now that Hubert had his own articles to get on with, she was delighted to find the charming and clever Oswald Barron ready and eager to work with her, and for a number of years they wrote ballads and short stories together. According to Bower Marsh's account, Barron was full of ingenious and amusing ideas for plots, but they came so readily to him that he could not be bothered with writing them all up:

> Bland used to write a story every week for the stock exchange journal and was always ready to pay half a crown for a plot. When he offered Barron half crowns for plots, E.N. would say, 'You are robbing the poor boy,' but Barron was extremely fruitful in ideas which he would never have carried out himself.

According to Marsh, Edith not only locked herself upstairs to work, she would lock Barron up as well, until he had produced something. No doubt this was during the period when they were writing together and she was trying to advance his career by selling his verse to editors such as W. E. Henley. But when Doris Langley Moore approached Barron for information about E. Nesbit, he was extremely reluctant to discuss his acquaintance with her. By the early 1930s he moved in ultra-respectable circles – he had been Gold Staff Officer at George V's coronation in 1911 – and had no wish to see the fires of his youth raked over in public. The length and comparative openness of his love affair with Edith meant that the outline, if not the finer details, were accessible to any researcher. Barron accordingly urged Doris Langley Moore not to mention his name at all in her account:

> Do not be vexed if I say that I do not love biography of private folk. As for me, I am annoyed to see my own name in print. When some busy

person digs out the unimportant secret of my name and explains my
pen-name with it [he wrote under the name of 'The Londoner'], I grit
my teeth. I think it well that anybody writing as much as I do should be
left to his anonymity.

When asked by Mrs Moore if she might use Bower Marsh's anecdote
about Edith locking him up, he became even more uneasy; he was
probably more alert than she was to the familiarity it implied:

> Pray do not tell that anecdote about me, more especially since I cannot
> avouch it. The tale, I think, must have sprung up from some jest about
> my idleness: I can remember nothing that would support it.
>   Indeed I speak the truth when I say that I love privacy above all
> things. You will see this by the fact that I have been at much pains to
> keep all mention of my name out of print, writing always with an
> alias.[21]

But it was not merely the stories of Bower Marsh that revealed
Barron's intimacy with the household as a whole, and with Edith in
particular. Letters to Edith from friends during the nineties refer to
Oswald as if he was a member of the family, as he virtually was at
times. When the Blands went to Whitstable or Dymchurch or D'Arcy
Reeve's house at Brenchley, Barron went with them. It was he who
visited nearby Scotney Castle with Edith, and pointed out to her that
the name of the cluster of houses a mile or two south-west of
Brenchley, 'Old Cryals', might well be a corruption of the Breton
name, 'Kyriels'. Only a few years earlier Hardy, in his novel *Tess of the
D'Urbervilles*, had interested his readers in the implications of ancient
names come down in the world. Scotney Castle, with its old and new
houses, its round tower standing on an island, and the curious
derivation of 'Old Cryals' provided the starting point for her elaborate
romance, *The Secret of Kyriels* (1899). Barron himself took a keen
interest in local place names, lore and history. His particular areas of
expertise were archaeology, heraldry and genealogy; he later became a
Fellow of the Society of Antiquaries, and edited articles on genealogy
and armoury for the Victoria County Histories.[22] His first publication
(in 1888) was an edition of the parish register of St Margaret's Church,
Lee. Barron was living in rooms in the Temple when the Blands first
knew him, but he had grown up in and around Lewisham and Lee, and
he may originally have come across them through his local connections.

Though Barron was ten years younger than Edith, his liveliness and erudition utterly charmed her, and his way of looking at the world came to colour hers strongly. With her other young men, Edith tended to dominate easily, for she had a wider experience of books and life than they had, and a more firmly established point of view. But Barron knew much that she did not; he had a vivid historical imagination and a fresh and individual outlook. He had the rare ability to draw from Edith her own experiences and show her what was original and valuable in them. He gave her back herself, as love sometimes can, and once she had found how to translate herself into her work, the important phase of her development could begin. Edith's career pattern is, on the face of it, puzzling: she worked away at her writing, including writing for children, for twenty years before she found what she was supremely good at. Virtually none of her earlier work is worth reviving except for its historical interest. While it is often true that women discover within themselves fresh creative energies in middle age, when the more demanding stage of motherhood is past, Edith's genuine change of direction seems to have been at least partly due to the impact of Oswald Barron, as muse or midwife. No one, apart from Hubert, influenced her writing more. From now on, Oswald became an active presence behind it. Even though he walked straight out of her life when he married in 1899, that presence was strong enough to outlast his own departure by many years; it is apparent in many of the books by which she is remembered.

In 1894 the five-year lease of Birch Grove ran out and the Blands moved once again, taking a larger detached house, the Three Gables, in the smart new suburb of Grove Park, a little to the south and east of Lee. Their new house stood on the west side of Baring Road, nearly opposite Cooper's Lane and adjoining the footpath that runs down to cross the railway. Like several of her south London homes, this one has since been pulled down to make way for a block of flats, Stratfield House. Then it stood among fields and had a large garden with a lawn big enough for badminton, which they took up enthusiastically. In 1896 or '97 Oswald Barron, with two friends – Olindo Malagodi, the London correspondent of the Milanese newspaper *Tribuna*, and a young novelist, Edgar Jepson – also moved out to Grove Park. In his *Memories of an Edwardian and Neo-Georgian*, Jepson described his friendship with 'The Londoner' (i.e. Oswald Barron), his impression of the Blands and his memories of life at Grove Park:

I made new friends, among them the Londoner of the *Evening News*, who was then writing his daily article for the *Sun*, an evening paper in which for a while I wrote a weekly, but unkind, article . . . A bachelor, the Londoner was a witty and amusing companion and an intimate friend of the Blands, and through him I came to know them.

Mrs Bland . . . was an uncommonly clever and often amusing woman and as generous a creature as I ever came across. Not only was her purse always at the service of her hard-up friends and all the distressed who crossed her path, but there was no end to the pains she would take to get them work and straighten out their affairs and keep them on their feet. She was masterful indeed, as was natural in a Nesbit of the Border, and she rather queened it over the young writers and painters she gathered round her and directed their lives with a ruthless precision, which I thought good for them . . .

It was in order to be near the Blands that two of their friends, the Londoner and Olindo Malagodi, and I took a house at Grove Park. I did not give up my rooms in the Temple . . .

The Londoner, one of the earliest and the most intelligent of Mrs Bland's young men, was an uncommonly witty and amusing talker and helpful to her in the matter of the stories of the House of Bastable – indeed the hero of them was drawn from him. But he collected old oak, a horrible practice, in which she aided and abetted him. So it came about that our house at Grove Park was furnished with old oak, some of it museum pieces, and to the best of my remembrance we even had a *refectory* table in our dining room.[23]

Edgar Jepson was deeply impressed with Edith: she was not only 'very handsome still', but also exceptionally generous. He had already begun writing fiction himself, but found her patient and helpful with regard to his work, and amazingly hospitable and kind to her young protégés, some of whom were less than grateful. Jepson contrasted Barron with the artist Gerald Spencer Pryse (whom she would take under her wing some years later) in this respect: 'Barron lavished affection on her but Pryse was different.' On one occasion, the Grove Park bachelors themselves became the victims of one of Edith's acts of kindness, when she installed as housekeeper a certain Mrs Tanner, whom she mistakenly regarded as a deserving case. The household obediently put up with Mrs Tanner's intemperance until one afternoon when Edith and Alice Hoatson were being entertained to tea in the drawing room, and Mrs Tanner came in, rather the worse for drink. She propped herself against the doorpost and began to explain in an interminable monologue why she could not cook supper that evening. No one knew where to look, but at least Edith could now see for

herself, between laughter and embarrassment, the difficulties her
generous intentions had created for them.[24]

Jepson's memoirs described the Bland household as a 'patriarchal',
but essentially harmonious one: 'Bland and Mrs Bland had arranged to
go their own ways – an arrangement not uncommon at the end of the
last century among both the fashionable and the advanced.' He was
amused, as their neighbour at Birch Grove had been, at the way the
Blands casually, perhaps even unconsciously, outraged the whole
suburb, and he commented, as many of their friends were to do, on
their exclusive interest, as they grew older, in young people:

> The Blands' was a very pleasant and stimulating house to go to, and they
> must have been the most hospitable creatures in the County of London.
> It was a house of youth: they seemed to have no use for the old; they
> seldom encouraged the middle-aged and never the dull . . . though civil
> to their neighbours they were never intimate with them; they believed
> that the native residents would bore them by a lack of understanding.
> The native residents did not understand them; but how they did gossip
> about them!
>
> The Blands' aloofness was the right attitude for people interested in
> ideas to assume when living in suburbs . . .
>
> And then there were the Bland children. I do not suppose that any
> children were better known than they, for they were, to an extent, the
> children of the House of Bastable, and also to an extent they took the
> children of that house as models. Rosamund, then aged eleven, was an
> amazingly pretty child, and I was immensely fond of her, and once she
> and her brother Fabian, aged ten, had the genuine Bastable happy
> thought: they made posies of flowers from their garden, took off their
> shoes and stockings, and in their shabbiest clothes sold the posies to
> native residents on their way to catch the business trains to London. For
> a while the two children lived happily in an affluence beyond all dreams.
>
> Then a meddlesome native informed the Blands that their two
> youngest had slipped into the sphere of Big Business, and the Blands in a
> furious annoyance stopped the enterprise. Their annoyance astonished
> me: it seemed so Victorian, and here we were in the Edwardian age, the
> age in which Big Business was beginning to get into its stride and press
> gallantly on to the Great War. But there you are: there are few things
> which the unconventional detest more heartily than a form of un-
> conventionality which they do not themselves practise, and Rosamund
> and Fabian were in disgrace.[25]

Edgar Jepson's account of the children's exploit is particularly
interesting because it shows once again how much Edith drew from

experience. His account of what happened was coloured by the fact that she later wrote this episode into *The Treasure Seekers*; but if his memory of the children's ages is reliable, their initiative may have actually preceded her account of it by a year or two: Fabian would have been ten in 1895 and it was just the kind of hare-brained scheme that he would have thought up all by himself; Rosamund was eleven late in 1897 (she was nearly two years younger than he was), but Edith did not publish the chapter of *The Treasure Seekers* in which this episode occurs until the autumn of 1899, when both were in their early teens and the Blands had already left Grove Park.[26] So it seems more likely that she based her fiction on their escapade than that they modelled themselves on her fiction. By the time the Bastables had established Edith's popularity, her children had all reached adolescence. The chapter in which the flower-selling episode was utilized was the last to appear in a magazine before *The Treasure Seekers* was published in book form for Christmas 1899. Entitled 'The Nobleness of Oswald', it rewrote Fabian's original naughtiness as altruism. Alice Bastable is tormented by guilt because she had used the 'lucky', bad sixpence to pay for a telegram summoning Albert's Uncle, when she was afraid that her twin, Noel, was terribly ill:

> Alice was very unhappy, but not so much as in the night: you can be very miserable in the night if you have done anything wrong and you happen to be awake. I know this for a fact.[27]

Oswald's act of nobleness is to take some flowers sent for Noel, now convalescing with Albert's Uncle at Hastings, and sell them at the station:

> He put on his oldest clothes – they're much older than any you would think he had if you saw him when he was tidy – and he took those yellow chrysanthemums and he walked with them to Greenwich Station and waited for the trains bringing people from London. He sold those flowers in penny bunches and got tenpence. Then he went to the telegraph office at Lewisham, and said to the lady there –
> 'A little girl gave you a bad sixpence yesterday. Here are six good pennies.'
> The lady said she had not noticed it, and never mind, but Oswald knew that 'Honesty is the best Policy', and he refused to take back the pennies. So at last she said she should put them in the plate on Sunday. She is a very nice lady. I like the way she does her hair.[28]

Though Fabian and Rosamund's lapse here becomes an act that can all

too neatly be summed up under its copybook heading, the light tone
and sense of comedy is delicately maintained by the shift from third to
first person in the final sentence.

The first tangible outcome of Edith's collaboration with Barron was a
farce entitled *A Family Novelette*, performed in a public hall at New
Cross in February 1894. The second was a book of short stories, *The
Butler in Bohemia*, dedicated to Kipling and published by Henry Drane
in 1894.[29] Drane usually brought out his books in paperback and he did
not always deposit copies of them in the main copyright libraries. This
alone among Edith's books is nowhere to be found. The title suggests that
it was intended to amuse, as Barron's writings as 'The Londoner' were,
perhaps in a vein that anticipated *The Story of the Treasure Seekers*; it
seems likely that he encouraged Edith to use a form of comic irony that
also came naturally to him, but the contents of both play and book can
now only be guessed at. Several other stories and verses that they jointly
contributed to magazines are historical and melodramatic in tone, larded
with archaic oaths and exclamations and general gadzookery.[30] The full
effect of Barron's influence is most evident in the books she published
after he had gone, though several of these seem to have been conceived
and discussed while they were still together. Among these must be
numbered *The Railway Children* (1906).

Barron's vital contribution to Edith's work was to help her acquire
something he himself possessed in abundance – a sense of the past. He
taught her to feel the imaginative appeal of history, the mysterious
glamour of what is continuously changing and being lost, and to try to
understand it from the inside, though its fascination was not to be fully
dramatized until her stories of time magic, *The Story of the Amulet*
(1906), *The House of Arden* (1908) and *Harding's Luck* (1909). The
two latter, which deal with English history, are as strongly rooted in
particular places and particular objects (for example, Dicky's coral and
bells, an heirloom and an agent of magic), as Barron's historical
imagination was. Family names, places and buildings and the heraldic
signs that, if you could read them aright, would reveal precise details of
a family's history, all fascinated him, and his concerns are vividly
mirrored in the structure of *The House of Arden*, where that heraldic
animal, the mouldiwarp, the badge and crest of the Arden family,
presides over the action. And the action is simply the recovery of the
lost past, its buried treasure, its fallen towers, and its lost heirs – for the
most important journey of recovery that the children make is to find
their lost father.

Barron's concern with the past was neither dry nor impersonal; in his view the recent and personal past was as interesting and as well worth exploring as 'the dark backward and abysm of time'. For Edith this was to be even more crucial than her discovery of the appeal of the historic past. Barron helped her to rediscover her childhood, and by doing that, helped her to find out who she was, and thus what she could do. Though his correspondence with Doris Langley Moore was stiff and formal, the one aspect of Edith that he did allow himself to enlarge upon was her childhood. In a sense it might almost be said to have been his discovery, too:

> She told me that part of her childhood had been spent in Brittany, where she learned to speak French with some fluency (although not very accurately). Her family were, as it seems, ever on the move. More of her education was given at a school in Brighton. She always hated the memory of the hot and dry days in Brighton, recalling her happiness when she was fetched away to Knockholt in Kent, her best beloved home.[31]

All this Barron could, of course, have learned from reading Edith's memoirs, 'My School-Days', which appeared in twelve episodes in the *Girl's Own Paper* from October 1896 to September 1897. But it is much more likely that he elicited these memories from her directly and encouraged her to make use of them, first simply as memoirs, but later as fiction in her stories of the Bastables. Many of the adventures with her brothers which she first described in 'My School-Days' were restructured and used in the second volume of their adventures, *The Wouldbegoods* (1901). Her first book about the Bastables, *The Story of the Treasure Seekers* (1899), seems to have been partly inspired by conversations with Oswald about their respective childhoods ('identical but for the accidents of time and space', she wrote in the book's dedication). Barron had grown up in Blackheath, where the first Bastable stories are set, and where Edith had lived in the early, impecunious years of her marriage. Lively and irrepressible, the real Oswald was somehow merged with her once adored elder brother Alfred, whose death in 1894 was probably another of the triggers behind these stories of a family so similar to her own. With Mary (Dora) and Alfred (Oswald) dead, and Harry (Dicky) in Australia, there was no longer anyone with whom she could talk over her memories of past joys and pains – no one, that is, except Oswald himself.

Talking about her childhood memories to an entranced listener enabled Edith to revalue and reappraise her past, but some of her conversations with Oswald did not bear fruit for a number of years. Her schoolgirl memoirs had ended at Halstead, and she had no further space to include the picnics and games beside the railway line that for a while had been such a feature of her life there. Barron had referred to Halstead as 'Knockholt' because that was the name of the local station, where he and Edith had alighted for Halstead but she never referred to it by that name for the station had not been built in her day. Another death in the mid-nineties must have prompted memories of the risks taken when she was young and had played on the line and around the tunnels: in 1896 Edith's old friend Stepniak was killed by an oncoming train as he was walking along a railway line. The guard had shouted to him, but he had not appeared to hear, and some of his friends assumed he had committed suicide. G.B.S. offered a characteristically 'Shavian' explanation, a curious blend of imagination and distrust of feeling: 'He was slain through pure dare devilry – wanted to perform the feat of bounding across before the train, and, being older than he thought, was caught, Achilles-like, by the heel.'

More convincing than either of these explanations was that of David Garnett, who remembered that, since his imprisonment in conditions of intolerable noise in Turkey, Stepniak had been able to make himself deaf to all outer sounds by a process of inner concentration, so that he would not necessarily have heard either the approaching train or the guard's warning shouts.[32] Though *The Railway Children* was not written until 1905, it brings together themes of unjust imprisonment and political repression, figured in the plight of the absent father, the children playing on the line, and the victimized Russian refugee. If the little revolution of 1905 gave these subjects a special topicality, their particular collocation must date from conversations with Oswald Barron in 1896. He was always credited by her family with having inspired *The Railway Children*, as well as the tales of the Bastables.

Between 1896 and 1899 her friendship with Barron continued to unfold, and his historical interests began to colour hers deeply, but their impact on her writing was not yet apparent. Her published work looked very much the same as it had always done, and it was not until the publication of *The Treasure Seekers* in 1899 that the new writing self he had encouraged her to become finally emerged from the long dormant chrysalis of her old writing habits. In the previous year, she had published a fifth collection of verses, *Songs of Love and Empire*, dedicated to Hubert – her dullest so far. Commissions for children's books were now coming in with some frequency, and she wrote a number of different types, but they were all hackwork, and lacked distinction: there were the whimsical *Pussy Tales* and *Doggy Tales* (1895), the more instructive *A Book of Dogs* (1898), *The Children's Shakespeare*, and *Royal Children of English History* (both 1897). This last was partly illustrated by the artist May Bowley, who had stayed at Antibes with the Blands and, with her sister Leonora, illustrated a number of Edith's fairy tales including some published in the magazine *Father Christmas*. None of these books, however, gave any hint of the great transformation that was imminent and would turn her overnight into a best-selling author for children.

The process of writing up episodes from her childhood for the *Girl's Own Paper* from the autumn of 1896 to 1897 brought a number of incidents from the past to the forefront of her mind and suggested the possibility of making more extended fictional use of them. At Christmas 1897, the very first version of 'The Treasure Seekers' appeared. The Bastables' grouping as a family and the kind of adventures they would enjoy had developed out of and yet at the same time had begun to strike away from their author's early memories: ' "We must go and seek for treasure," said Oswald boldly, "it is always what you do to restore the fallen fortunes of your ancient house." '[33]

So begins the ur-version, published in a long-forgotten children's magazine called *Father Christmas* which was issued as a supplement to the Christmas edition of the *Illustrated London News*. 'The Treasure Seekers', an early version of chapters I, II and VII of the final book, was ascribed to 'Ethel Mortimer', since E. Nesbit already had another story, 'The White Messengers', in the same magazine. She had been contributing fairy stories to *Father Christmas* for the last couple of years.

'The Treasure Seekers', mark one, describes the misadventures of that arch-muff, Albert-next-door, in his frilly Fauntleroy shirts and velvet knickerbockers. First he is accidentally buried while digging for treasure, and then he is forced to play bandits and held to ransom. The Bastables' opening 'council of ways and means' must have been intended to act as a prologue to a whole sequence of stories of different ways in which the children would look for treasure, most of which their author had not yet fully worked out. She deliberately used the children's proposals as an advertisement for the book she was now working on. Oswald explains, 'I can't tell you about that now, but it will all be printed in a book some day, and then you can get someone to buy it for you for Christmas.'[34]

It was, and they did. Even in this first version, Edith makes use of a complex narrative technique by which Oswald relates much of the story in the third person, and often in a self-congratulatory and 'literary' style, every now and then slipping back into the first person. Edith was always much amused by literary clichés, and Oswald's childish desire to sound 'grown-up' gave her ample scope to parody some of these. As narrator, he attempts to conceal his identity in the book version, though not very effectively:

> It is one of us that tells this story – but I shall not tell you which: only at the very end perhaps I will. While the story is going on you may be trying to guess, only I bet you don't.
>
> It was Oswald who first thought of looking for treasure. Oswald often thinks of very interesting things . . .[35]

Oswald's narrative shifts ingenuously between first and third person narration, between a chatty, informal tone and one of deliberate 'literariness' that simultaneously conveys his inexperience as a story-teller, sets him in an ironic perspective and also solves one of the most fundamental problems of children's books – the question of 'Who is speaking, and to whom?'[36] Oswald's transparent device means that Edith is not obliged to decide whether she approaches her reader as a child or an adult – she can do both. This does not merely produce a brilliantly comic effect, it is stylistically and psychologically utterly convincing – children commonly tell themselves stories in which they take the leading role (as do adults, for that matter). It was, however, a remarkably sophisticated technique for a children's story to use and when ten more Bastable stories appeared in the *Pall Mall* and *Windsor* magazines, either Edith or her editor felt some uncertainty as to whether they were aimed at adults or children. There had been a comparable uncertainty about Kenneth Grahame's original and influential book *The Golden Age* (1895), whose use of the child's eye view had helped to mould Edith's own narrative practice. One episode was published under the subtitle 'Passages from the life of Oswald Bastable, Esq., of Lewisham in the County of Kent',[37] and doubt as to Oswald's status (is he a child or an adult?) contributes crucially to the comic tone.

Oswald's vanity and complacency are evident throughout, continuously inhibiting too close an identification with him. For Oswald is the Victorian patriarch in short pants, and his sense of superiority to anyone except another gentleman borders on the outrageous: sisters, snivellers, servants – for Oswald, the rest of the world is to be wondered at and pitied. Edith's liking for him is continuously tempered by amusement at his condescension, for though he usually prefers to overlook it, as a child Oswald belongs to an oppressed and subordinate class himself. While Oswald always presents events from a highly subjective and even solipsistic angle, an almost Jamesian irony points the reader to those elements in the situation that Oswald has failed to grasp. The irony thus reveals events and attitudes both as Oswald sees them and as they really are. This effect is simpler and less obtrusive, in reading, than an explanation can be, but it involves a rhetoric of some complexity. Oswald's confident assumptions about the role of women, for example, at once reflect his naïvety, while mocking wider attitudes through him – possibly Hubert's attitudes, among them. Oswald explains why his sisters cannot be allowed to share the pipe of peace with the boys: 'It is not right to let girls smoke. They get to think too much of themselves if you let them do everything the same as men.'[38]

Oswald's cartoon versions of current Victorian attitudes parallel his comic treatment of current literary tastes. *The Treasure Seekers* is above all a book about books, for the children's literary expectations govern many, perhaps most of their adventures, which are themselves conveyed in parodies of contemporary literary clichés. The final published version begins with Oswald's exasperated reflections on the proper way of conducting a narrative:

> This is the story of the different ways we looked for treasure . . .
> There are some things I must tell before I begin to tell about the treasure-seeking, because I have read books myself, and I know how beastly it is when a story begins, 'Alas!' said Hildegarde with a deep sigh. 'We must look our last on this ancestral home' – and then someone else says something – and you don't know for pages and pages where the home is, or who Hildegarde is or anything about it. Our ancestral home is in the Lewisham Road. It is semi-detached and has a garden, not a large one.[39]

A sense of the way in which literature and journalism shape expectations, both of style and behaviour, particularly the expectations of the young and impressionable, is central. The children's treasure-hunting, like their other games and adventures, is directly inspired by their reading, and though Oswald sometimes makes fun of bookish clichés, as he does above, he is just as likely to emulate them. In one episode, the Bastables set to and write their own newspaper, an idea that Edith borrowed from Charles Dickens's *A Holiday Romance* (1868) and had used for a series of pieces that appeared in *Nister's Holiday Annuals* in the mid-nineties;[40] Noel, like his creator, is continuously engaged in writing over-ambitious poetry which the reader is invited to laugh at, as Edith's brothers, she feared, would have laughed at her own earliest efforts. Noel's comic and parodic verses are juxtaposed to Mrs Lesley's (i.e. Edith's) own grown-up poetry in such a way as to reveal the limits of her self-critical powers. Though the Bastables' father, like the young Hubert, struggles on in business, several of the other adults they encounter – notably their surrogate father, Albert's Uncle – write for their living, and the whole book is preoccupied with the fulfilment (or lack of it) of literary structures (much more successfully than *The Literary Sense* was to be); it ends with the comic acknowledgement that the fulfilment of literary expectations cannot really be avoided. Oswald apologises for the success of their quest and the happy Christmas party with which the book ends: 'I can't help it if it is like Dickens, because it happens this way. Real life is often something like books.'[41]

The Treasure Seekers keeps the relationship between life and books under continual scrutiny, and this is made possible by the use of children's play and games as central themes. The chapter 'Noel's Princess' provides a typical example of the pervasive yet always creative way in which Edith draws on her own reading, and makes something quite fresh out of it. It begins with the Bastables playing in Greenwich Park, pretending to be the characters from *Sintram and his Companions*. Oswald announces:

> 'I shall be Count Folko of Mont Faucon.'
> 'I'll be Gabrielle,' said Dora. She is the only one of us who likes doing girl's parts.
> 'I'll be Sintram,' said Alice; 'and H. O. can be the Little Master.'
> 'What about Dicky?'
> 'Oh, I can be the Pilgrim with the bones.'[42]

Sintram (1814), now entirely forgotten, was a strange Teutonic fantasy by the German romantic writer de la Motte Fouqué, better known as the author of *Undine*; it had been popular with mid-Victorian readers, among them Louisa M. Alcott and Charlotte M.

The earliest
available
photographs of
Hubert and Alice,
both taken in
middle age

Left: 2, Birch Grove, Lee, where the Blands lived from 1889-1894 and shocked their neighbours

Below: Three Gables, Grove Park (1894-99). Oswald Barron and Edgar Jepson moved to Grove Park to be nearby

Halstead Hall, Edith's favourite home (from 1871-5)

Below left: "The Bandbox" – 28, Elswick Road, Blackheath, today. The Blands lived here from 1880 to 1886

Below right: 5, Cambridge Road (now Cambridge Drive). The Blands lived here for six months in 1886, moving to a similar house in Dorville Road, until 1889

Above: G.B.S. (the photograph of him that Edith kept)

Above: Edward Burne-Jones: *The Depths of the Sea.* Edith wrote Shaw a poem about this painting

Right: Edith at twenty-nine (Bower Marsh pasted this photograph into his copy of her poems)

Yonge. The Bastables' game leads them to an unfamiliar corner of the park, where they find a dumpy and humourless little girl. Noel, now metamorphosed into a hero from the *Arabian Nights*, introduces himself as Prince Camaralzaman, and the little girl replies that she is also a princess. They assume that she must be playing at 'make-believe', as they are, until her nurse comes out and carries her off screaming, and it becomes apparent that she is really and truly a fifth cousin of Queen Victoria. As in some of the most original Victorian children's books, there is a level of parody or allusion involved, since this chapter re-works 'The Finding of the Princess' episode in Grahame's *The Golden Age*, but in a comic and prosaic rather than a sentimental vein. In Grahame's story, the narrator, playing truant, finds a pretty girl and her young suitor and assumes that she is a princess, an expectation that the couple play up to. In Edith's version, the children find a genuine princess, but she is quite as ordinary as princesses usually are in life.

The contrast between E. Nesbit and Kenneth Grahame is revealing: Grahame, here and in *The Wind in the Willows*, creates an ideal fantasy world – dreamlike, safe and largely scaled off from the disappoint-ments, embarrassments and sheer muddle of daily life, though paradoxically Grahame's writing is at its most powerful when it hovers on the edge of acknowledging its own evasions. E. Nesbit's fictional world never had the irresistible imaginative appeal that his has had, being at once less perfect and more vital. The world of her books is as elusive, confused, messy and absurd as the world of lived life. When she makes use of fantasy elements, whether in the form of a children's game or as some magic power present in her story, her characters are constantly brought up against the hard edge of things-as-they-are, often with hilarious, and always with informative consequences. Indulged sentiment, reach-me-down idealism, and common clichés are regularly knocked. The Bastables collect money to make a Christmas pudding for themselves, but after they have done so, they feel pangs of conscience because they had asked for the money for the poor and then used it for themselves. When they try to remedy this by giving their pudding away, they discover that the poor are not merely indignant at their condescension but disgusted by their bad cooking (they had misunderstood the phrase 'washed raisins' and washed the raisins in soap).[43] The whole episode is another parody, this time of the 'Ministering Children' genre, popular around the mid-century.

Good deeds invariably go wrong and Edith must have vividly

recalled childish disappointment when the best intentions misfired, for she often writes about them: when the Bastables rescue what they suppose to be a 'high-born babe' stolen by gypsies, it screams unceasingly at them: 'If you have never had to do with a baby in the frenzied throes of sleepiness you can have no idea what its screams are like,'[44] comments Oswald. The phoenix whose egg the five children hatch in the nursery fire later catches sight of the Phoenix Fire Insurance Office and insists that it is his temple and he must pay it a state visit. He also carelessly sets fire to a whole theatre, when the children take him to see a play.[45] Over and over again Edith presents her child protagonists in unmanageable confrontation with irate adults whom they are quite unable to cope with. She is realistically aware of the child's lack of any real power other than the power of imagination, so that when they are whisked away on magic carpets, through the arch of the Amulet into the past, or use a wishing ring, it is only the power of imagination that is thus symbolically exercised. Father's disappointment, cook's anger, mother's distress – these are the all-too-plausible consequences of such flights into the unknown. Unlike Kenneth Grahame, and many other children's writers, Edith was under no illusions as to the most likely outcome of exciting adventures: 'Albert's Uncle came in, and his face wore the look that meant bed, and very likely no supper.'[46]

It is her refusal to idealize either the child's actual – as opposed to imaginative – power, or the nature of the world that children inhabit that constitutes E. Nesbit's great strength and perhaps her most important contribution to children's fiction. In her artistic sense of realistic limitations, it is tempting to see her femininity reflected: not for her the fully-mastered recreations of new worlds, happily exempt from the confusions, contradictions, messes and shortcomings of our own. Instead her fantasy works to provide continual reminders of the vanity of human wishes, and the inherent dangers of indulgence in fantasy itself, for while the imaginative life, as exemplified by make-believe or magic, is felt to be the source of the intensest stimulation, pleasure and excitement, it is equally likely to prove a snare and delusion, promoting continual misinterpretation, misunderstanding or misreading of things as they really are – that is, humdrum and prosaic unless imagination amends them. Her simultaneous acknowledgement of the power of the life of the imagination and the irreduceable chaos of experience makes her work inconsistent at times, but also necessarily complex and convincing.

After the Bastables' debut over the unlikely name of 'Ethel Mortimer', the next six episodes were published in the following summer of 1898, mainly in the *Pall Mall Magazine*. At this stage Edith had seven stories altogether and began desperately casting about for a publisher who would agree to pay her a sum down (£50) plus a generous royalty (16½%). She offered it to one after another without success – to Frederic Chapman who worked for John Lane, to Constable, Heinemann, Dent and even to her old friend Robert Ellice Mack, now with Nelson's at Edinburgh. She refused to lower her sights for she knew how good a book they would make: 'Everyone likes the book so much,' she told her agent Morris Colles, and 'I am very much in love with [it].' Finally, early in 1899, Fisher Unwin accepted it on the confident recommendation of their reader, that famous talent-spotter Edward Garnett.[47] Unwin was to publish seven more of her successful children's books, but she remained deeply suspicious of him. *The Story of the Treasure Seekers* came out that Christmas, using Gordon Brown's illustrations from the *Pall Mall Magazine*. From the very first its success was on a different scale from

anything she had ever achieved before. She used the dedication to acknowledge her debt to the man who had given her the confidence to write her first wholly original book:

To

OSWALD BARRON

WITHOUT WHOM THIS BOOK COULD

NEVER HAVE BEEN WRITTEN

"THE TREASURE SEEKERS" IS DEDICATED

IN MEMORY OF CHILDHOODS

IDENTICAL BUT FOR THE

ACCIDENTS OF TIME

AND SPACE.

The Story of the Treasure Seekers has the longest and most explicit of all Edith's dedications; it must have come to Barron as a parting gift or even as a belated wedding present. In the context of his marriage, its warmth spoke silently of her loss and pain, and perhaps of his embarrassment.

While she was looking for a publisher for *The Treasure Seekers*, she was also trying to place her second novel, 'Kyriel's Bridge', written in 1897 and published as *The Secret of Kyriels* early in 1899. Of her first novel, *The Marden Mystery*, published in Chicago in 1894, very little is known, though it seems to have had episodes in common with *The Weekly Dispatch* serial *Something Wrong* (1886). Her second novel had been conceived when she and Oswald Barron had visited Scotney Castle together.[48] Moreover its hero, Christopher, with his scholarly temperament and professional interest in history and genealogy, was clearly inspired by Barron's academic interests, just as Oswald Bastable was inspired by his more extrovert and exuberant side. But *The Secret of Kyriels* had an even more fundamental significance for Edith than its connections with Barron. It is the novel in which she makes her closest approach to the forbidden topic of sexuality, largely avoided by the fictional conventions of her day. Through the symbolism of this novel she found a way of expressing what could not be expressed elsewhere – her sense of what it meant to be a woman in a world dominated by men – and consequently it abounds in images of female imprisonment. Whether the book's imagery is conscious or unconscious is impossible to tell: there is an obvious sense in which Edith firmly belonged to a generation that found all bodily functions embarrassing and demeaning. Because of a strongly inculcated sense of 'delicacy' (which younger friends sometimes thought of as prudery), she moved confidently within the safe confines of children's writing, from which the dangerous area of sexuality had been rigorously excluded. Several major writers for children deliberately sought out this protected playground, far from the sexual battlefield. The Victorian myth of childhood innocence was inextricably bound up with a myth of childish sexlessness. Children were thought of as unsullied, their hearts unshadowed by even the most latent erotic impulses; paradoxically and tragically, they were the more eagerly debauched and exploited because of this.

In accordance with the conventions of her day, Edith's children's books never touch on the subject, and adult love is usually treated as comically absurd, or occasionally endowed with a degree of sentiment. Nor did the adult fiction conventions of her day encourage the explicit treatment of sexual feeling, though great writers seldom allowed that to stand in the way of saying what they wanted. But for Edith to come to terms in her writing with her own sexuality, and the problems it had brought her, was at once essential and very difficult. She had managed to use the ballad form to present something of her more violent feelings in poetry, though the effect there was too often crude or clumsy. Now she adopted the romance mode, the mode of woman's fiction, with its speaking symbolism, its topography of the body, to express the painful secrets of her inner life – for that, in the end, was the secret of *The Secret of Kyriels*. She was to do something comparable in two later exercises in the romance mode, *Salome and the Head* (1909) and *Dormant* (1911). But this was the first, the most passionate and the most revealing. Writing it was an important process for her, and, judging by the freedom and power of the work that followed it, it was also a liberating and enabling one.

The most important single influence on the book, perhaps because it was the single most important expression of a woman's struggle for integrity and independence in nineteenth-century fiction, was Charlotte Brontë's novel *Jane Eyre*. From *Jane Eyre* came the theme of the locked-up lunatic wife, who first appears to the living as a ghost; a passionate woman called Bertha, from the West Indies; a heroine, Esther, with the courage and determination of a man, who will not be bullied or intimidated, and who recognizes the importance of her own selfhood. And we first see that heroine as a child, possessed – like Jane Eyre in the Red Room – by terror of the supernatural, something that Edith's memoirs of her girlhood and her ghost stories show that she understood only too well. In both books fear of the supernatural and fear of sexuality seem to be related. Esther is, of course, a self-portrait:

the courageous girl who fights like a boy, can swim to safety, nurses her broken mother, finds her long-lost father. The feelings Edith could not acknowledge – her own disturbing passions, her determined pursuit of men she found attractive – are located and isolated in Esther's friend and anti-self, Bertha, who surprisingly turns out to be no mere languishing Southern blossom but a person of some initiative and determination; at the climax, she appropriates a bicycle and rides off on it, her skirt hitched up over pantaloons, to save the villain whom she misguidedly loves.

If Esther is Edith, and Bertha her rejected self, it is the mad woman locked up in the New House, the real Bertha Mason figure, who is actually *called* Edith, and whose age and tragic experiences as a woman identify her with her creator at a deeper level. After an idyllically happy few years, her husband travels abroad, and a jealous maid shows her a love letter, supposedly written by him. In her distress she runs away with an old suitor, Nicholas Kyriel, Esther's supposed father, but she never in fact becomes his mistress. Instead she gives birth to her husband's child (Esther), and, on finding that her husband had been entirely innocent, goes mad and is shut away by Nicholas Kyriel. This story recapitulates crucial features of its author's own experiences – the idyllic early days with Hubert, the revelation of his infidelity, the turning to another man for support, the birth of a child; but the sequence has been altered and distorted, and the real sources of pain have been fictionally dissolved by the romance mode: though she believes her husband has betrayed her, in fact he has not, and though he believes the same of her, she has not betrayed him. 'Edith' has thus become the unfortunate victim of her own femininity, complexly trapped by love and misunderstanding, locked up behind the secret panel in the New House. She is discovered, wrapped in furs, sitting in the enclosed and hidden courtyard at the centre of the New House, invisible and inaccessible from outside, under a dying vine – a poignant symbol of rejected feminine sexuality.[49]

The house at Kyriel's Bridge, though inspired by the real Scotney Castle, is also a characteristic construct of Gothic fantasy, its elements all suggesting, in different ways, the female condition. Bridges and passages are key features: the Old House is on a promontory on the lake, and the bridge provides a covered passage to the New House, which stands on an island. The New House, with its hidden courtyard and secret passages, is at once female, and associated with the mysterious power of the id, while the Old House faces the outer world, and, with its library of authoritative books, is at once masculine and perhaps stands for the superego. The passage between the two is very ancient, and felt to be of crucial, if unknown, importance. There is a further layer of topographical symbolism in the second island on which stands a tall round tower, a dovecote, from the base of which a secret underwater passage leads to a subterranean entry to the New House. As children, Esther and Kit climb down the tower and Kit wants to explore the passage, but Esther implores him not to, telling him that her father wouldn't want him to do so. Predictably, at the book's climax, Kit finds that he must enter this secret passage in order to save Esther. He swims across the lake, naked, and forces himself to enter it: 'It required more courage than Christopher had expected to . . . press his naked body through the opening into the dark vaulted chamber that might hold he knew not what.'[50] The trap-door at the passage's end only yields to the greatest pressure, and after Christopher's forced but necessary entry, the sluice gates open and the passage is flooded.

The silliness of the plot, and the slightness of the characterization only serve to point up the dream-like nature of the topography, with its obvious – if unconscious – symbolic overtones. The New House is the feminine self, usurped first by the shadowy figure of Nicholas Kyriel, a false father who cruelly imprisons the woman he desires; then it is claimed by the fraudulent villain Bertram, whose lust for Esther and the house are never wholly distinguished. His attempt to force her is foiled, and Christopher's symbolic penetration is linked with the discovery of the will that leaves the house to Esther and to her husband, on condition he takes her name. She can now take rightful possession of the house that is also the female body, and remain mistress of it, as the keeping of her name indicates. Escaping the false claims of male oppression, whether presented as paternal or erotic, Esther discovers her own identity through an equal relationship with the man of her choice. Within the language of fiction, *The Secret of Kyriels* thus lays claim to a degree of feminine independence and sexual choice which Edith covertly practised in her life, but could never openly acknowledge.

8

WELL HALL

On 15 August 1898, Edith wrote to thank her mother, now nearly eighty, for a piece of jewellery she had sent as a fortieth birthday present:

> I had a very nice birthday. Fabian made a bonfire in the evening and decorated the garden with Chinese lanterns. I had some pretty presents – a moss agate brooch, a gold ring (fifteenth century), gloves, table centres, a silver watch chain, a book, a pair of little old flint-lock pistols and some beautiful flowers.

She added:

> I *am* forty, as you say: but I never *feel* forty. When I am ill I feel ninety – and when I am happy I feel nineteen![1]

Many women feel forty to be some kind of climacteric, after which the landscape of their lives must change, as they lose their looks and the special biological function that seems to justify their existence. Edith had kept her slender figure and good looks longer than most, but now she began to put on weight, and her mouth took on the harder, narrower look of a woman who is tired or dissatisfied. She was to become pregnant again, for the last time, at the end of that year, but this baby, like the previous one, was born dead.

With Oswald Barron's departure and marriage, another distinct phase of her love life was over. Barron was married in 1899, but she seems to have anticipated his departure early in 1898, when she wrote a sequence of five poems entitled 'Via Amoris'. Their theme is the rebirth, against all expectation, of love, but a love now transfigured by the funereal figure of the Angel of Renunciation:

If this were Love, if all this bitter pain
Were but the birth-pang of Love born again,
If through the doubts and dreams resolved, smiled
The prophetic promise of the holy child,
What should I gain? The Love whose dream-lips smiled
Could never be my own and only child,
But to Love's birth would come, with the last pain,
Renunciation, also born again.

The five poems of which this is the second were written in a white heat, late in February or at the beginning of March, and a copy was despatched to W. E. Henley, whose opinion she valued, and who immediately acknowledged their note of authenticity:

> These are quite the best verses of yours which I have ever read. Had I a journal I should be pleased indeed to print them. I do not think them faultless – far from it. But they are *vécus* – they have heart and passion; and I congratulate you.

She also sent them to her first, and apparently rather unsatisfactory agent, Morris Colles of the Authors' Syndicate, asking him to sell them as a group if possible, and explaining that she did not always produce so many poems all at once:

> You must be alarmed at receiving so many poems from me. The supply will not continue long. I always write verse by fits and starts, sometimes writing nothing for months – but when I feel the desire to write verse I write hard, and work the lode for all it is worth.[2]

In this instance the stimulus to write seems to have been the expectation that Oswald was going to leave her, and that she must renounce his love. He was a straightforward person and would have told her that he had fallen in love with a girl he hoped to marry, and that he could no longer go on seeing her. The admiring circle of the nineties had all gone their different ways, apart from the faithful Richard Reynolds, and though she continued to enjoy and cultivate the company of young men, her relationship with them was steadily growing more maternal. Several of her Edwardian protégés accepted whatever she was prepared to give while offering little or nothing in return.

Edith had always been moody, passionate and volatile. Now her moods became more extreme and less predictable than before. The novelist Berta Ruck, who got to know her well a few years later, described her 'dramatic storm-and-brilliance quality':

She could be morose as a gathering thunder-cloud. She could flash into a *prima donna's* rage. Having spread panic, blight and depression over the entire household of which one member had displeased her, she would withdraw behind an emphatically-closed door, and there stay, leaving those who loved her to the darkness that can be felt.

When she emerged – a sunburst! The entire landscape and population would bask in that genial all-pervading warmth, charm and sympathy that streamed from her – for one half-hour of which I would exchange the life-long friendship of any of your even-tempered, well-balanced, impersonal, tepid, logical Laodiceans.[3]

It was easier to take such a view as an occasional visitor than as a member of her household. She was always stimulating, but never restful, and living with a rumbling volcano can be a tiring, as well as an exciting business. Ever since childhood, Edith had been passionately self-willed, and though generous and loving, sometimes less than responsive to the needs or feelings of others. As she grew older, she does not seem to have acquired greater self-control, and she often behaved as if she thought such control scarcely worth having. She was quite conscious of this lack of restraint in herself, and tended to justify it, after her success as a children's writer, in terms of an essential childishness within her.

In *Wings and the Child* (1913), her book about the importance of play in children's development, she described the kind of adults who, despite the evident marks of time, have never really grown up, who 'are only pretending to be grown-up: it is like acting in a charade':

> Such people as these are never pessimists, though they may be sinners; and they will be trusting, to the verge of what a real grown-up would call imbecility. To them the world will be, from first to last, a beautiful place, and every unbeautiful thing will be a surprise, hurting them like a sudden blow. They will never learn prudence, or parsimony, nor know, with the unerring instinct of the really grown-up, the things that are or are not done by the best people. All their lives they will love, and expect love – and be sad, wondering helplessly when they do not get it. They will expect beautiful quixotic impulsive generosities and splendours from a grown-up world which has forgotten what impulse was: and to the very end they will not leave off expecting. They will be easily pleased and easily hurt, and the grown-ups in grain will contemplate their pains and their pleasures with an uncomprehending irritation.[4]

This description is not merely a self-portrait, it is a self-justification. It insists on its author's right to innocence in a sophisticated and complex world; and it implies an egotism that imposes happiness – or misery – on others, but is less capable of responding to needs or feelings that have their origin outside the self. As she grew older, the 'pussy-kitten' and the 'princess' gave place to the 'duchess', or 'madame'. Love increasingly became an act of homage, exacted from courtiers or place-seekers, rather than one of reciprocation.

How much of her hardening imperiousness was already latent in the spoilt and undisciplined youngest child, how much of it developed out of her success and prestige as a children's writer, is impossible to decide. During the next ten years, she worked harder and wrote better than ever before – these were years of intense creative effort which, at least in part, explain and excuse her self-absorption, and the un-expected displays of temperament and occasionally even cruelty to those closest to her. The artist has only herself and her experiences to work from, and it is inevitable that the self, and its urgent demands and satisfactions, should be respected and indulged in a way that other professions cannot so obviously justify. If Edith was an artist in a minor genre, she was a major figure within it, and her important children's books display that coherence and complexity to be found in more obviously major masterpieces.

The autumn of 1898 was a busy one for Edith, as she explained to her mother:

> Just a few lines, dearest, so that you mayn't think I am forgetting you altogether! . . .
>
> My new book [*The Secret of Kyriels*] will be out shortly – the very first copy of all will be sent to you. I hope you will like it. I am very busy doing stories, articles, verse and reviews [she had recently been appointed poetry reviewer for the *Athenaeum*]. I have an order for a short novel – but I can't get time to do it – and I am writing a children's book – called 'The Treasure Seekers'. I took Iris to a dance the other day. She looked charming in an apricot coloured Liberty silk . . . and was very much admired.

Her routine of hard work interspersed with fun was suddenly interrupted at the beginning of October when Paul went down with typhoid, a familiar enough illness and only too often a fatal one. While he was being looked after by two full-time nurses, Edith took the girls away so that they shouldn't pick it up as well. In any case they were in quarantine, and so not allowed back to school (they were now both at Blackheath High). She cast about for somewhere to take them; Richard Reynolds, who was becoming increasingly indispensable,

suggested that she borrow his rooms in the Temple, though they were
so tiny that one of the girls' beds had to be made up on the floor. When
the girls were pronounced safe, they were packed off to stay with
friends and return to school.

Paul, meanwhile, had pulled through and by 22 October his mother
celebrated his recovery with a comic dream-vision poem describing all
the delicious food he was not yet allowed to eat, for he was still on the
invalid's liquid diet:

> As I lay on my bed in the silence of night,
> A vision came to me – a dream of delight . . .
> The vision was glorious, consummate, complete,
> A radiance shone round it, unearthly and sweet,
> For I dreamed, oh I dreamed about
>   Something to Eat!

Not long afterwards Alice contracted an illness diagnosed as
rheumatoid arthritis, which effectively paralysed her, and for some
weeks she had to be spoon-fed by Edith or Rosamund, to her great
misery and humiliation. When she recovered, the joints of her fingers
and toes were crooked. The year ended badly for Edith too, who was
thrown out of a dog-cart, but was fortunately more shocked than
hurt.[5]

With Barron's departure from Grove Park, the Three Gables lost its
appeal for Edith – the very fact that he had moved there to be close to
her filled it with painful memories. Though she still enjoyed the garden
and worked hard at it,[6] she began house-hunting, perhaps unconsciously searching for something that might re-create the happy
homes of her childhood, now that expense was no longer a difficulty.
The Blands always rented rather than bought the various houses that
they lived in, whether in London or at the seaside. The anxiety to own
one's own home was, at this time, more characteristic of artisans than
of the middle or upper classes. Many people, at every level of society,
owned homes (Bland's father had owned three different houses in
adjacent streets in Woolwich) but they didn't necessarily feel that they
had to live in them. In the spring of 1899 Edith discovered the house
she had been searching for, whose red brick-walled gardens and shady
moat recalled the farmhouse in Brittany and Halstead Hall. Its
foundations sank deep into English history, and its state of dilapidation demanded restoration. She was always attracted by the idea of
restoring ancient buildings (it became the central theme of *The House*

of Arden) and she associated restoration with the recovery of the past as a whole, and perhaps with the recovery of lost childhood happiness. The house she had found was Well Hall at Eltham, no very great distance from her earlier homes, but north and east of Grove Park.

When she first saw the house, it stood among fields at the end of a country lane lined with hawthorn, chestnut and lilac blossom and Queen Anne's lace. It was very large and not especially pretty: built of red brick, it had an imposing, and even slightly forbidding eight-eenth-century façade, softened by a heavy mantle of ivy. At the front there was a large circular lawn surrounded by a drive and a tall holly hedge screened it from the road. Two enormous cedars stood near the house, and still stand today, though the house itself has gone, and the grounds have been turned into a small municipal park, the Well Hall Plesaunce. The cedar branches had once come up to the bedroom windows, and the trees were full of owls. At the back of the house hung a pretty, if rather rickety balcony, overlooking a garden full of old roses, with lawns long enough for tennis or their favourite badminton. A deep, dank moat, flowing between high brick walls, enclosed the back lawn and lent itself to swimming or boating in the summer and skating in the winter; Edith was to write many of her best books sitting in the old punt, or under the cedars.

The back garden enclosed by the moat had reputedly been the site of a much older house that had once belonged to the Roper family. Sir Thomas More's favourite daughter Margaret, who married William Roper, was supposed to have brought her father's severed head back there for burial. There were also a number of outbuildings, sheds and stables, and two cottages that went with the house, always known, rather grandly, as the North and South Lodge. Beside the moat stood a long brick Tudor barn, with high chimneys and gables, the only part of the outbuildings still standing, and the only corner never rented out to the Blands. Like all houses of respectable pedigree, Well Hall was haunted – according to Edith, by a ghost who played the spinet faintly and tinklingly, but always in the *next* room, and by another who came and stood behind you when you were working at your desk and sighed a quiet little sigh – or perhaps she invented these to amuse her listeners.[7]

The five-year lease of Three Gables did not end until September 1899, but Edith had money to spare and she could not wait – they moved in that May. She had fallen in love with Well Hall and wanted to live there as soon as possible, more particularly because she wanted the child she was expecting to be born in the new house, which obviously needed a considerable amount of repair work before it would be comfortable and ready for its new occupant. Perhaps she felt that nest-making instinct which comes so strongly during pregnancy. In the event the Blands underestimated just how much needed doing there and they were soon overwhelmed by a series of domestic crises that made amusing anecdotes afterwards but were stressful to live through. Even before they had managed to install the bedroom furniture, the great oak staircase that swept upstairs from the black-and-white tiled hall collapsed, and for some time everyone had to live on the ground floor. Fortunately there was lots of space – indeed the house had thirty rooms. Blocked gutters and broken leads produced floods in the parlour when it rained heavily, soaking favourite books and Turkey carpets, while the sheer size of the house, as well as its reputed ghosts made it difficult to find servants who would stay, though by this time the Blands could easily afford, and actually rather needed, quite a large staff. They also had trouble with a disreputable tenant living in one of the two cottages until they let the other to a policeman and his wife. Then a journalist friend, Sidney Lamert, moved into the first cottage and the policeman's wife used to go in and 'do' for him.[8]

When Edith first set eyes on Well Hall she had promised herself that she would write a novel about it, and the result was *The Red House* (1902), which makes an entertaining narrative out of some of these early disasters; it also figured as the Moat House in the second adventure of the Bastables, *The Wouldbegoods* (1901). Well Hall was to prove a constant delight to Edith – its flowering trees and singing birds, and the beauty of the cedars under snow comforted and consoled her for the many maintenance problems it posed, and perhaps for the real losses that closely followed upon their move there. She lived there for more than twenty years, and gave it up with the greatest reluctance, when it became evident that she could no longer lead an active life. The house itself was burnt down in the mid-thirties.

One friend who visited the Blands during their first summer at Well Hall was the American writer Charlotte Perkins Gilman, author of 'The Yellow Wallpaper' and a pioneering feminist. She had first come over to England in 1896 as a delegate to an International Socialist Congress. She was quickly elected a member of the Fabian, where she met Shaw, the Webbs and Edward Carpenter, who made her some sandals. The first Fabian meeting she attended, in July 1896, was a particularly dramatic one. Shaw had prepared a 'Report on Fabian Policy', known as Tract 70, advocating the Society's traditional policy of 'permeation' and political non-alignment; inevitably the members of the Independent Labour Party voted against it, but were hugely defeated. Reading through her old diaries, she recalled:

> At my first Fabian Society meeting I noted 'Very exciting. J. R[amsay] MacDonald moves to withdraw Tract 70. Animated discussion. The executive wins – Tract retained. Mrs Bland asks to be introduced and asks me to dinner.' This was the beginning of a most pleasant friendship with a delightful family. She was 'Edith Nesbit', a well-known author . . . there were several youngsters, all attractive; I had most enjoyable visits with them, then and in later years.[9]

Charlotte Perkins Gilman (or Mrs Stetson, as she then was) returned to England in the summer of 1898; a friendly note to Edith written the following May invites her to

> Behold me ensconced in 'The Hammersmith and Fulham District Nursing Association Supported by Voluntary Contributions' – and eked out by an occasional boarder! I am the occasional boarder at present. But I am meaning to move more nearly in town soon – by next Saturday I hope . . .
> Behold a nice little lecture list; and intentions on my part to do some work in that line if it opens before me.
> But mostly I intend to live quietly and write while here – up to about September 1st, that is . . .
> Perhaps I shall see you at the Fabian meeting next Friday? Which will be a pleasure . . .

In her autobiography she recorded:

> One delightful visit was with the family of Mrs Bland . . . at Well Hall, Eltham, Kent. The earlier mansion, built for Margaret Roper by her father, Sir Thomas More, had been burned, and replaced by this one which they said was 'only Georgian'. Behind the house, just across a little vine-walled bridge, was a large rectangular lawn, surrounded by thick-grown trees and shrubs, outside which lay the moat that once guarded the older building. Here, in absolute privacy, those lovely children could run barefoot, play tennis and badminton, wear any sort of costume; it was a parlor out of doors. We all joined in merry games, acted little plays and fairy-tales, and took plentiful photographs.

One of the photographs taken that afternoon shows Hubert and Richard Reynolds, Paul, Iris and Edith's niece Dorothea Deakin, two of Marshall Steele's daughters, Martha the bulldog (who with Lady the deerhound figured in the Bastable adventures) and, at the front, the long, intelligent face of Charlotte Perkins Gilman herself. Edith may well have been behind the camera; from about this time she became interested in amateur photography. One of the family, probably Paul, had acquired a camera, a 'box Brownie' and a number of snaps were carefully pasted into the family album; snaps of the dogs, and of Rosamund and Enid Steele dressed up and acting a play, probably date from that happy summer afternoon.[10]

Such idyllic interludes took the edge off the recurrent domestic problems, but there were heavier blows to come: Edith lost the baby born soon after their move to Well Hall – a disaster that she painfully rewrote in her novel The Red House, where the love story ends with a tiny 'pussy-kitten', pinkly sleeping in the old oak cradle that the Bastable children have found while exploring the cellar (and which Oswald privately thinks would be more useful as a rabbit hutch). Like the earlier one, this baby was probably buried in the garden. Edith's sense of failure must have been exacerbated by the fact that Alice Hoatson was also pregnant and gave birth to a healthy son some months afterwards: John Oliver Wentworth Bland was born on 6 October, 1899 (though his birthday was always celebrated on the 21st), and this time there seems to have been little argument about his fate. Edith adopted the new baby, at once a consolation and a reminder of her own loss. She grew fond of him and would pet and cuddle him, but Alice was always the one who looked after John, went everywhere with him and mothered him.[11] The other children were now growing up fast: Paul, a sad and curiously lacklustre figure and a great disappointment to his father, had begun work at the stock exchange, a career that had appealed to Hubert but did not suit Paul; Iris, who had inherited her mother's talent for drawing and making things with her hands, had just started at the Slade; Rosamund and Fabian were still at school, but were now in their teens. John was very much an 'afterthought', the spoilt baby in a family where the other children were virtually grown-up, always known as 'the Lamb'. Even Hubert, who could be severe with the older boys, was indulgent and warmly affectionate to this child of his middle age.

Edith's own family had gone their different ways – Harry had emigrated to Australia in the early eighties, and Alfred had died in 1894, leaving his wife and children, Anthony and Anthonia (named after their grandfather) virtually destitute. The Blands helped out financially and in other ways, too. Edith tried to find work for their mother, contributed to the children's schooling, and even bought them clothes from time to time. After she had kitted out Anthonia to go to college, Rosamund pointed out that her own 'combinations' were 'in such a state that she couldn't elope even if she wanted to'.[12] After the Nesbit cousins grew up, they eventually followed their uncle out to Australia, but at the turn of the century they were still frequent visitors. Edith had always kept in close touch with her mother, who was now living either near or with her eldest daughter Saretta, in Manchester. She regularly visited them up there, usually going to see Ada Breakell's family at the same time; sometimes she would fetch her mother back to stay with her, but Mrs Nesbit had never got on well with Hubert, and as she grew frailer, the journey became more of a strain. Ada herself was now living in London and when her sister got married, she moved into one of the Well Hall cottages, North Lodge, a year or two after the turn of the century, and remained there until Edith finally left.

Saretta died suddenly, a few weeks after John's birth, on 25 October 1899. Her mother (who had now buried four out of her six children) and Edith were both deeply grieved. Saretta had always been her favourite sister, had loved her and told her stories, and later encouraged her to write verse. The following year Edith wrote a long elegy for her, dedicating it to Saretta's daughter Dorothea, an attractive and clever girl whom Edith was particularly fond of. It was easy for Edith to identify with her niece's grief since for her too Saretta had been more of a mother than a sister. The poem speaks feelingly of the pain of loss and the problems of coming to terms with it:

> Here, in the night intolerable, wake
> The hungry passionate pains of Love still strong
> To fight with death the bitter slow night long.
> Then the rich price that poor Love has to pay
> Is paid, slow drop by drop, till the new day
> With thin cold fingers pushes back night's wings,
> And drags us out to common cruel things
> That sting, and barb their stings with memory.

Later published in *The Rainbow and the Rose* (1905), the volume of poetry dedicated to Iris and Rosamund, her elegy was dated 18 August 1900, and thus written three days after Edith's own birthday.[13]

She may have felt a degree of surprise and relief to have reached it at

all, since earlier that year she had been the victim of an alarmingly
wrong diagnosis, as Iris recalled:

> [Mother] had been in bed and in much pain for some days with lumbago
> – one Saturday morning the doctor came to see her about a new pain – he
> told her that she had cancer of the stomach, that she must have an
> operation at once and must go to town on the Monday to see a specialist
> about it. He also, idiotically, added that her chances of recovery were a
> hundred to one against. You can imagine the weekend we had! One
> curious result the shock had upon my mother – it cured the lumbago.
> She was up and dressed in half an hour – I was at the time making some
> dressing gowns for her. She cheered me up from time to time by
> remarking that one of them would do for a shroud! On the Monday she
> saw the specialist who said there was nothing the matter! . . . She
> suffered constantly in winter with bronchitis and asthma, but very little
> else.[14]

Laurence Housman also remembered that weekend, for he was
summoned to a special 'farewell' party given on the Sunday evening for
a few close friends:

> Some – but I think not all of us – were told that she was about to face a
> serious operation; and there was the possibility that things might go
> very wrong indeed.
>   Whatever her own apprehensions were in the matter, she carried us
> through the evening with colours flying, apparently in the happiest
> spirits possible. And of course we all played up to her example to the
> best of our ability.

Thought-transference was one of the games that evening, and Edith
took the part of the medium and, by an act of 'jubilant will-power',
'galloped' Housman to success – it was the only time in his life that he
managed to do it.

> The next time I saw my hostess, all was well over. Then she said to me,
> 'Well, anyway, I found out that I wasn't afraid of death!' And the
> discovery gave her great satisfaction. But I am quite sure that what also
> pleased her was the way in which she had 'played up' while possible
> doom hung over her. For she had a dramatic nature, and loved not only
> writing plays for amateurs to act, but acting the play of life in her own
> person – a little theatrically. Indeed she had so much of a 'presence', that
> a certain amount of 'pose' came naturally to her, and that without any
> insincerity.[15]

Her fondness for playing out drama was something that Shaw had noticed and many of her later friends commented on, among them E. M. Forster who found her histrionic gestures a little embarrassing, and H. G. Wells who, in discussing 'the dramatized self', incidentally observed:

> E. Nesbit, by the bye, did some short stories in which she dealt with this same unreality in the world as she knew it. She saw through herself enough for that. They are collected together under the title of *The Literary Sense*.

The novelist Berta Ruck quite independently made the same connection when she observed of Edith that

> She loved . . . to dramatize the details of daily life. She herself called this trait '*The Literary Sense*' and brought out a book of short stories on that *motif*. But it was more than literary in her; it was the love of a bit of 'good theatre'. 'Drama, drama keeps women *going*,' I heard her say once. Of her one feels it was perfectly true.[16]

But if 1900 brought its melodramas, it also brought a real and totally unexpected tragedy. Fabian, now fifteen, had been ill with a series of heavy colds so it was decided that his health would be improved by taking his adenoids out. The Blands had changed doctors on moving to Well Hall, as Adrian Stokes regarded it as outside his beat, but a date was arranged with the new doctor for the operation. In those days, it was regularly performed at home, on the kitchen table or equivalent, as it was regarded as relatively trivial, and hospitals were only for major operations or for the poor. The whole thing seemed so unimportant that everyone forgot about it: on the morning of Thursday, 18 October, the doctor and his anaesthetist arrived at eleven o'clock to find Fabian out in the garden in his oldest clothes, digging, and his mother not yet up. She hurriedly washed and dressed, sent for Fabian and told him to bathe and get into some clean clothes at once, so that the doctor could proceed.

At one o'clock Hubert came into the library where Alice was working, his face distorted with grief, and reached out for the whisky decanter: 'Mouse, they've killed him,' he blurted out. Alice rushed to the bedroom where the operation had been performed. The doctors had gone, leaving the family to wake the patient from the anaesthetic (which was usually chloroform); but Fabian could not be woken. As his body grew cold and his limbs rigid, it was only too plain that he was dead. No-one knew how it had happened, but he probably choked to death on his own vomit as he lay unconscious – no one had remembered that morning or the previous evening that he was not supposed to eat before the anaesthetic. Edith was quite beside herself, and kept saying over and over again to Alice, 'Oh, Mouse, I wish you'd told me what would happen.' As if refusing to accept the unthinkable truth, she surrounded his body with hot-water bottles and candles in a pointless effort to warm him back to life, but as the muscles of his face set, she sent for the undertaker, in stunned despair.[17]

John was only a baby, too young to take it in, but the other children were shattered. Iris remembered that her father came down to the station to meet her off the train as she got back from the Slade that evening, in order to break the news to her. Paul described his mother as 'absolutely distracted' and recalled that, so trivial had the operation seemed that Fabian's place had been laid for lunch that day, 'which made matters no better'. Rosamund overheard Edith scream at Hubert, in the course of a hysterical outburst, 'Why couldn't it have been Rosamund?' These words suddenly crystallized what the thirteen-year-old child had always instinctively known – that her mother had always treated her differently:

> I was aware of it all through my childhood and as I did not know the cause until I was eighteen it was always a source of bewilderment to me . . . It wasn't just that she did not feel for me what she felt for her own children. How could she? She actually, I think, always *sub-consciously*, at any rate, had a lot against me. She did not forgive my existence. To John she was quite different. Somehow she never felt he was in competition with her own children as I had been and it may have been partly that that made the difference. Anyway a difference there was . . .[18]

Rosamund's letter refers to her having learned the secret of her birth when she was eighteen, i.e. late in 1904 or 1905, but Mrs Langley Moore assumed from her having overheard Edith's bitter words that she had discovered it that night, and presented it that way in her biography. When her book was published, Helen Macklin, a very old friend of Edith's, wrote to tell her that she had been visiting the Blands at the time, and was utterly convinced that no such revelation had taken place:

> I was staying in the house when he died and for some weeks afterwards . . . I read with amazement that Rosamund learned the secret of her birth that evening. I should think it impossible . . . It is true that [Edith]

felt that pain with intense bitterness on that night – she spoke to me about it then and often after – but she believed that Rosamund knew nothing . . .

She told me the bare facts in a burst of grief on the night of Fabian's death. But the next day she said more and often afterwards – since I now knew – she gave herself the relief of speaking to me about it.[19]

Fabian's death was not only a violent shock, it became a source of bitter self-reproach for his parents, his birthday celebrated with remorse for all the sufferings he had undergone. Edith's illustrator, H. R. Millar, remembered her being late with a particular piece of work because it had been Fabian's birthday (8 January), which always upset her. Edith felt particularly guilty about the occasion when Fabian had stolen the sweets intended for the Deptford school treat, and she described her self-torment in a short story called 'The Criminal' (she, by implication, being the real criminal, or at least the one who had been most punished):

My son; my little son. The house is very quiet, because all the other children grew up, long ago, and went out into the world. The lamp has just been lighted, but the blinds are not drawn down now. Outside, the winter dusk is deepening the shadows in the garden where, in the days when the sun shone, you used to shout and play.

Do you remember, understand, forgive?[20]

That second autumn at Well Hall, the whole garden seemed to mourn for the lost child who had so recently played in it and cultivated it:

I look out of the library window [wrote Hubert] and see those big funereal cedars lords of all, the whole garden subdued to their sombre humour. Day and night the piteous leaves of all the other trees are falling, falling like slow rain-drops; and at twilight they sound upon the garden paths as the footsteps of ghosts might sound – creepy, creepy. This morning I picked a rose for sheer pity of it, and in half an hour its charm was gone; its very colour had changed, its pink shell-like petals . . . had turned livid as the lips of a corpse; it exhaled, not perfume, but an odou, of death. The birds flutter about aimlessly, they seem to feel there is nothing left for them to do in a world full of sadness, no nests to be builded, no broods to be reared; and they haven't the heart to sing.[21]

Rosamund, who had some grounds for resentment, noticed with the clear cool gaze of the adolescent that Edith, though genuinely grief-stricken, could not help dramatizing an emotion which cast her in a central and tragic role. In fact, she quite literally dramatized it in a verse play called variously 'Absalom' or 'In the Queen's Garden'. It was never performed in public because the censor did not normally licence enactments of Biblical subjects.[22] It is written for three women, the three consorts of King David. Maacah, Absalom's mother, desperately awaits news of the battle in which her son may be killed. She is seated on the ground, her hands clasped about her knees – an attitude Edith herself often adopted. The other Queens, Abigail and Bathsheba (Alice and some more recent conquest of Hubert's, perhaps) vainly attempt to comfort her, but end up merely quarrelling with her. The play ends bleakly with the announcement of David's return, implying Absalom's defeat and death. Maacah's hope is that, for a moment, David will turn to her for comfort in their mutual loss, but instead he sends for his new wife, Bathsheba. Perhaps it expresses Edith's own wretchedness if, after Fabian's death, Hubert did indeed turn to others for consolation, when she looked for it from him. Yet the choice of this particular Biblical story also implies an underlying acceptance of the situation: David's greatness is never questioned, nor is his right to the single-minded devotion of his three Queens. Though Maacah is full of bitterness, the others speak of the joys his love has conferred on them, and of the privilege of bearing his sons. The play forcefully voices the pains of loss, jealousy and even self-deception but it does not suggest that things should have been otherwise or that David's conduct might have been different.

One element strongly present in the Biblical legend is the antagonism between David and his son Absalom – Absalom was killed when he rebelled and fought against his father, though this intensified rather than diminished his father's subsequent grief. It is possible that it was the rivalry between the two that first made Edith think of using this particular story. Paul, the eldest son, was gentle, affectionate and weak, despised by his father and afraid of him, but Fabian had inherited his parents' obstinacy and high spirits. Though they had often found him tiresome, he resembled them far more closely than did his elder brother and sister, who had reacted against their extravert parents by becoming altogether more reticent and self-contained. Paul thought Fabian very much like Hubert. Though wayward and difficult, Fabian was also quick and clever, mischievous and full of rebellious energy – exactly the kind of personality to clash with Hubert in his role as heavy Victorian father. According to Rosamund, Fabian was brilliant, misunderstood and constantly in trouble with Hubert;

his parents had certainly had problems in finding a school that could cope with him. When he was sent to a local school (St Dunstan's, Catford), he had been nicknamed 'Bloodthirsty Bill'. In January 1899, on the recommendation of Sidney Lamert, they had sent him to Loretto School, near Edinburgh, at some distance and with a strong tradition of discipline, but this had not worked out either and they had taken him away (or been asked to take him away) six months later.[23] But if Hubert had sometimes punished Fabian in haste, he now had ample leisure for remorse and repentance.

Were the Blands good parents? The testimony of their friends and their children is largely in conflict. Outsiders tended to see them as devoted parents. Their neighbour at Birch Grove had considered Edith 'a tender mother and devoted to the children who were considered neglected but I doubt if they were.' Helen Macklin criticized Doris Langley Moore's portrait of Hubert: 'That he was a very affectionate father scarcely appears, I think.'

Others saw different characteristics: Bower Marsh thought Edith very fond of her children, but not above seeing their weak points, while Ada Breakell was surprised at her firmness with them, perhaps unconsciously contrasting Edith's treatment of her children with Mrs Nesbit's easy going ways.[24] These varied opinions reflect not only the limited view of family life that friends inevitably have, but also their individual assumptions as to how children *ought* to be brought up, which can vary a great deal even within a single generation. Though Edith's childhood had often been unhappy, what discipline and severity she had encountered had never come from her mother. Parents, it is usually supposed, tend to repeat their own parents' mistakes, but the warmth that both Hubert and Edith received from their own indulgent mothers (both fathers had died young) was more apparent to their friends than to their children.

When a neighbour of theirs at Dymchurch, Mrs Ringland, remarked to Rosamund that they must have had a delightful childhood with such an 'understanding' mother as Edith, she replied, 'Oh, Auntie was the only mother we ever knew; Mother was always too busy to attend to us.' Rosamund had her own reasons for not caring for her adoptive mother, but Iris also commented on how little they saw of their mother as children and how seldom she played with them. She also told Doris Langley Moore that

my mother was never really interested in girls, or in women for that matter. She herself, as a child, was more like a boy. She just didn't understand girls at all. I suppose I was her favourite child in many ways, but she never understood a thing about me when I was young, she herself having been so different.[25]

Iris's assumption about her mother was patently wrong – all through her life, but especially when young, Edith had made a number of very close friendships with women and was liked and respected by some of the most interesting women of her generation. Yet the fact that Iris made this assumption itself reflects the degree of distance between herself and her mother. Berta Ruck, with her novelist's eye, described Iris as 'dark and temperamental and nearly always very unhappy or resentful of something'. Her expression in photographs is often sullen and she was undoubtedly resentful of her father, whom she is said to have hated.

Only Rosamund and John seem to have cared for Hubert; the latter he indulged and doted upon, perhaps in the wake of his remorse over Fabian. But Rosamund was unquestionably his favourite, as she was everyone else's – she was, according to Berta Ruck,

> a real beauty as far as the head was concerned, richly coloured, dark-eyed, with a short resolute profile and a great deal of Hubert about her. A real flirt. By twelve and thirteen she had plenty of seed-leaf love affairs.

Ironically, Rosamund's resemblance to her mother was often remarked upon, for they were both high-spirited and loved playing to an audience. Mrs Ringland was surprised at the revelation that she was not really Edith's daughter since she 'seemed almost the favourite of the family and was really very like E. N. who showed her off and made her dance or sing little songs or do imitations.'

Berta Ruck, who knew the family rather better, regarded the news as 'a bombshell':

> 'You're so like her!' I told Rosamund. 'How could one have thought –! I should have said the most like of all her children.'
> 'I know. Convenient,' said Rosamund serenely. 'That we've all got these brown eyes.'[26]

It was for Rosamund that Hubert wrote his *Letters to a Daughter* (1906), in the course of which he examines with some directness a father's attitude of sexual possessiveness towards his daughter.

Both the Blands were often thoughtless about their children's feelings. Edith dressed Iris and Rosamund, when they were young, in 'aesthetic' clothes that made them painfully self-conscious, or simply shabby ones that she had not bothered to replace. For two years the girls had hideous grey coats which they hated, but these went unnoticed by Edith until she had been away for a few weeks; coming back, she took in how worn they looked and hurried them off to buy some decent ones at once. Alice, who was better at observing the children's feelings, used to make or give the girls clothes as they grew older, perhaps to allay their embarrassment at being 'different'. And Edith would thoughtlessly dispatch John to get her cigarettes from the supposedly haunted room at Well Hall, entirely forgetting, for the moment, what it meant to be a nervous and imaginative child – though her books evoke it well enough.[27] The Blands were not harsh by the standards of the day – they did not beat their children when they were naughty, preferring to send them to bed or to some other form of solitary confinement, but both of them had uncontrollable tempers and were capable of inflicting thoughtless cruelty when annoyed. Hubert is said to have slammed the piano lid down on Paul's hands when he was playing, on an occasion when the boy's practice disturbed his concentration.

Both Iris and Rosamund referred to their mother's cruelty and Rosamund wrote imaginatively about the problems of discussing this aspect of her character to Doris Langley Moore:

> There was a very distinct streak of cruelty which even those in favour of its suppression would not deny and without any mention of it naturally the kindness and generosity loom much larger and the tempers and torments she *could* inflict seem merely childish and pardonable in one whose likeableness and charm was undeniable. I can see that you have to omit the cruelty because even supposing you were prepared to include it, it would shock and offend too deeply. And also I believe it would be an almost impossible task to describe it without somehow getting the focus wrong. A very few examples would give an impression that it was worse than it was.

As her children grew older, Edith was inclined to interfere in their love affairs ('disastrously', according to Rosamund) and read their letters.[28] Both Blands appropriated their children's friends when it suited them to do so; Hubert was not above seducing Rosamund's school friends, while Edith was to make close friends of Iris's Slade circle – Berta Ruck, Ambrose Flower, Michael Carr and Arthur Watts. Yet if their children sometimes felt oppressed and hard done by, so did Edith herself. She once observed bitterly to Berta Ruck, 'Water runs downhill. The affection you get back from children is sixpence given as change for a sovereign.' And when Berta reminded her of that remark at the end of her life, she said with interest, 'Did I really say that? I think it very sad, rather brilliant and *quite true!*'[29]

However shattered she may have felt, in the immediate aftermath of Fabian's death, Edith had promises to keep: the *Illustrated London News* had commissioned ten more Bastable stories, beginning that November, with an extra one for their Christmas edition, to run on till July of 1901; these eventually became *The Wouldbegoods*. She had already written several more Bastable adventures for the *Pall Mall Magazine* just before Fabian's death. Laurence Housman had first suggested to her the idea of a society for 'being good in'; the mid-Victorian proliferation of 'improving' books for children, on the pattern of *Ministering Children*, or, at a more sophisticated level, *What Katy Did*,[30] ensured that the subject could be treated in the same self-consciously literary and even parodic mode that had characterized the Bastables' first appearance. With the advent of their wealthy Indian Uncle, the Bastables now moved out of the squalor of the Lewisham Road to spend the summer in the spacious 'Moat House', which, though here set down in the Kentish countryside, is still recognizably Well Hall:

> It is a very odd house: the front door opens straight into the dining-room, and there are red curtains and a black-and-white marble floor like a chess-board, and there is a secret staircase, only it is not secret now – only rather rickety . . . there is a watery moat all round it with a brick bridge that leads to the front door.[31]

The October episode written for the *Pall Mall Magazine*, entitled 'The Waterworks', gives a brilliantly comic account of how the children accidentally emptied the sluices of a nearby river before an angling competition (her familiarity with locks came, of course, from the Medway holidays); and then how Oswald's carelessness with a cricket ball precipitated a terrible flood through the bedroom ceiling. He had been playing with it (it was really Noel's, anyway) among the lead roofs, and had carelessly left it to roll away down the guttering which it then blocked up. At the next heavy rainstorm, the water had collected on the roof and flooded through the leads – one of the disasters that had befallen the Blands on first moving into Well Hall, though in their case the blockage had been caused by dead leaves, rather than a cricket ball. For the November episodes Edith turned back for inspiration to memories of La Haye and the circus that she and her brothers had organized in the farmyard.[32] *The Wouldbegoods* was completed and published in time for Christmas 1901, and was her greatest success, financially speaking. In one year she made £1100 on the royalties from it, and this was her record, at the height of her sales. Fisher Unwin, who published the majority of her children's books, realized that during her lifetime the Bastable adventures always sold significantly better than her fantasies, and offered her better royalties on them accordingly.[33] After the success of *The Wouldbegoods* she continued to write odd Bastable stories for various magazines, and in 1904 she wrote a dozen more for *The London Magazine* which became *The New Treasure Seekers*. Since it was the Bastables who had first brought her success, she allowed them to put in a guest appearance in her novel about Well Hall, *The Red House*, published in 1902.

The book describes, in what another novelist, William de Morgan, termed 'photographic detail', the house and the Blands' early mis-adventures there – the leaking roof, the collapsing staircase, the overgrown garden, the drunken tenant, as well as the furniture that the Blands had installed under the influence of Oswald Barron's passion for old oak – oak dressers and settles, the elm kneading-trough, carved chests decorated with candlesticks and green Flemish crocks – they can still be glimpsed in the background of surviving photographs of the house. But the details of the house, its furnishings and surroundings, are inevitably idealized, as are its owners. The middle-aged couple with their difficult adolescent children, and their Auntie-in-residence become, through the transforming power of fiction, what the Blands always wanted to be – young. They are virtually a honeymoon couple, in the first year of a love match, and their story is told by the infatuated husband. Andrew Lang was frankly embarrassed: 'The effect is to make me feel painfully shy,' he admitted, and he was 'a little alarmed by a salute of XXV kisses. I thought that people should kiss and not tell.' But Richard Whiteing, another popular novelist of the day, congratulated Edith on

> The bantering playfulness of the love scenes, for such they are from first to last, though they are post-marital, is not to be surpassed. This is another fresh and distinctive note. The way in which the love making usually ends with marriage in romance, as it is said to do in real life, is sometimes quite disheartening. Now what I like in your book is that you begin with a marriage. I have sometimes thought that every novel should begin in that way now, for of course it is the starting point of the

whole problem, the rest is more or less a matter of convention, but the game really begins with the rice and the slipper. I wish I had your lightness of touch . . .[34]

Edith's novels tend to rewrite the events of her life as she would have liked them to have happened. In *The Red House* she imagines what most women dream of and perhaps too often expect, a marriage invested in all the trappings of romance. Chloe, the wife, is unfocused but cloudily delightful, while the narrator, Len, is in a continuous state of enchanted attention. Edith herself admitted how important romance was to her by living in such a way that she could continue to experience it after marriage, as Hubert had done too, yet she could never write honestly about the romance a married woman might find outside marriage; instead she reintegrated her admirers' *Frauendienst* more acceptably into a marital situation. Hubert was more openly cynical: he thought romance flew out of the window with marriage and security and said so with characteristic downrightness in his *Letters to a Daughter*:

> Now marriage, as we know it, is the inevitable slayer of romance. Before the intimacy of marriage romance disappears like a mist wreath in the blazing sun.
>
> Mind, I do not say that in losing romance you lose everything: there are many other things that are worth having, perhaps even more worth having, but you lose romance, and lose it in something less than six weeks.
>
> And when you have lost romance you are no longer 'in love' . . . The very feelings which attracted you to start with, which brought you together, are gone, and gone for ever.
>
> That is the stupendous fact of marriage; it kills the thing that made it. It is the outcome of illusion. People in love imagine that marriage is a continuance of the feelings, intensified, which they have for each other before they enter upon it . . . It is the very opposite of that.
>
> . . . It is not, I am convinced, so much because married folk see each other every day that romance takes wings; it is rather because *they can make sure* of seeing each other every day. It is the sense of security that kills.[35]

The Red House is undoubtedly sentimental, but the sentiment is infused with humour and the effect is no more embarrassing than that of, say, Dorothy Sayers' *Busman's Honeymoon*, which, unlike *The Red House*, is still in print and read with pleasure today. In a reminiscence of the Blands' early collaboration, the writer-husband

and illustrator-wife secretly touch up and improve each other's work –
one of the book's themes is how much people enjoy doing whatever
isn't their designated work, and all her life Edith liked to put down her
pen and spend a day gardening, making jam or cutting out a dress. She
had a strong practical streak and was very good at making and doing
things with her hands. The arrival, at the end of the book, of the new
baby, the 'pussy-kitten' (Hubert's pet name for Edith and then for Iris
when she was a baby), reverses Edith's loss of the stillborn child, born
at Well Hall, as well as the death of Fabian. Into this complex
interweaving of fantasy and precisely observed detail bounce 'the
whole tribe of those astonishing Bastable children', disguised as the
Blackheath Junior Antiquarian Society. Len and Chloe, the book's
hero and heroine, are as forcibly impressed by them as Nesbit's readers
had been, and there is something almost self-congratulatory in Len's
account of the children, as if the narrator within the fiction and the
author who created it have been drawn into a momentary complicity.
Len describes the Bastables as Edith had intended them to appear,
rather than as they had actually shown themselves in their own books:

> What struck me was their confident assumption that now we knew them
> we could not help liking them, and the assumption was, I own, justified.
> This was particularly marked in Oswald. He evidently thought a good
> deal of himself . . . And they were very much funnier than they meant
> to be.[36]

Chloe is so taken with them that she makes them an 'A1 lunch', and
they set off to explore the Red House cellars where they discover
various pieces of antique furniture, including the oak cradle for which
Chloe has provided an occupant by the end of the book.

The guest appearance of the Bastables in *The Red House* provided
the opportunity for an interesting technical device which Edith had not
attempted before: in *The New Treasure Seekers* (1904) she rewrote the
children's visit to the Red House as seen from Oswald's inimitable
point of view. In doing so, she was partly prompted by that need for
economy apparent in the work of most commercial authors, the
economy that makes them repeat plots, names and ideas from time to
time. In Edith's case, it also made her draw on the people and places
she knew best to provide starting points for her fictions. But there was
also a special kind of literariness involved: from the outset the
Bastables' adventures had also used other books to provide initial ideas
– episodes from Charlotte M. Yonge's *The Daisy Chain*, Kenneth

Grahame's *The Golden Age* or Kipling's *Jungle Books* all become grist for the mill, though their material is always handled in an essentially re-creative way; her sources could always be openly acknowledged because her use of them was never merely derivative.[37] Now she reworked her own earlier fiction by shifting its viewpoint. The Bastables arrive at the Red House disguised as an antiquarian society and Oswald's attempts to read his historical paper are hampered by his 'not being able exactly to remember the distinguished and deathless other appellation of Sir Thomas Thingummy, who had once lived in the Red House.'[38] Five years later she was to write two books, *The House of Arden* and *Harding's Luck*, whose events overlapped substantially and interlocked in a fairly complex way, but which employed radically different viewpoints. Her adaption of *The Red House* episodes may well have suggested this device.

The early years at Well Hall also saw her first successes with a different kind of writing for children from the mock-heroics of the Bastables, and one that, in the end, turned out to be more fruitful for her. In January 1891 George Newnes had brought out an illustrated monthly magazine called *The Strand*. The magazine market was already overcrowded, but somehow *The Strand* established a distinct identity from the outset. It had a policy of publishing a wide range of material, so that wholly serious articles on Siberian prison camps jostled with 'Zigzags at the Zoo', photographs of curios and nature's wonders, interviews with celebrities and fiction of all kinds, from adult melodrama to fantasy to fairy-tales. There were always pictures on every page, and more photographs than was usual, but it was the quality of its writers that made it famous. Sherlock Holmes first appeared in *The Strand*, and writers with large followings like Conan Doyle, H. G. Wells, Kipling and F. Anstey regularly published there, since Newnes paid well and it had a very wide circulation. In 1899 Edith received her first commission for it: she wrote a sequence of modern fairy-tales under the title 'Seven Dragons' (later published as *The Book of Dragons*, 1900). An eighth dragon story appeared that Christmas, and *The Strand* took another fairy-tale in November, so she had stories in nine out of the twelve issues that year. Thus began her most important and enduring association with a magazine, and one that was financially very rewarding (*The Strand* paid her thirty pounds per story or episode – a small fortune for someone previously accustomed to ask fifty for a whole book). Her close association with the magazine took a couple of years to become established – she published only three stories there in 1900 and none at all in 1901, but in 1902 it took a new serial in nine episodes, 'The Psammead' (later *Five Children and It*) and every year after that it serialized a full-length story by her until 1912, when her energy and inspiration began to flag. Her last full-length children's book, *Wet Magic*, ran from December 1912 to August 1913.

The stories Edith wrote for *The Strand* were, from the first, quite distinct from her other writing for children in that they involved magic and fantasy – a mode that was beginning to be particularly associated with the magazine through the success of such serials as F. Anstey's *The Brass Bottle* (1900), or Wells's *The First Men in the Moon* (1901). She never published any of her naturalistic children's stories in its pages: *The Wouldbegoods* had been serialised mainly in the *Illustrated London News*, while *The New Treasure Seekers* came out in the *London Magazine*, where it was followed by *The Railway Children*. By this stage magic had become such an integral part of her writing for children that the rest of her books appeared in *The Strand*, and it was only odd short stories – a few more about the Bastables, and several about the family who figure in *Five of Us – and Madeline* (post-humously edited by Rosamund in 1925) – that were published elsewhere. *The Wonderful Garden* (1911) allows the possibility of magical explanations, rather than actually deploying them, but its predominant tone and style links it with the other fantasy stories written, as it was, for *The Strand*. One factor that lent her work for *The Strand* a degree of unity was that, from *The Seven Dragons* on, nearly all of it was illustrated by the young line artist H. R. Millar, whose name came to be linked with her books. When Edith began writing for *The Strand*, Millar, though ten years younger than she was, was already established as their usual illustrator for fairy-tales, and he had had a notable success with Anstey's *The Brass Bottle*, where his precise, detailed and dramatically posed drawings exactly suited Anstey's comically prosaic fantasy. Though occasionally another artist, such as Claude Shepperson, would illustrate one or two Nesbit stories, Millar did most to establish her popularity, and worked with her longest and most closely. Edith invited him to Well Hall in the spring of 1902, where she much amused him by sweeping in with a long corset box under her arm in which she kept tobacco, cigarette papers and some enormously long cigarette holders. He thought her delightful and surprisingly unaffected:

For a highly intellectual woman she took the most astonishing interest
in quite ordinary everyday things . . . There was sound basis for that
casual brilliance of hers: it was always so effortless – without the
slightest trace of pedantry. It was this, I think that endeared her to all
and sundry.[39]

Her first story for *The Strand* was 'The Book of Beasts'; it appeared
in March 1899 and is undoubtedly a key work, a parable expressing her
view of the power of books and the ambivalent nature of the
imagination. So lucid a fable is somewhat exceptional among her
writings: one afternoon messengers call for little Lionel as he plays in
his nursery, and fetch him away to be King. After his coronation he
discovers in the Royal Library the Book of Beasts, once the property
of an ancestor who had been accounted a wizard. When the sun falls on
the pages of the books, its pictures – first a butterfly and then a
bluebird – come alive and flutter away into the palace gardens.
Overwhelmed by curiosity, Lionel turns another page and releases a
terrible dragon which consumes Parliament, an orphanage and a
football game. He turns further pages and looses first a manticora
(which the dragon eats), and then a hippogriff – a winged horse, on
which he bravely lures the dragon into the Pebbly Waste. Here it is
forced to fly back into the book in order to find some shade, having
first conveniently disgorged its victims.

The story's symbolism is obvious; like *The Treasure Seekers*, which
she was to publish that year, it is concerned with the power of books to
release their images into the mind and the world with both delightful
and disastrous results. While the butterfly and bluebird delight the
senses, the dragon brings fear, destroys several communal amenities
and can only be defeated by intelligence, courage, and the help of the
hippogriff, itself another creature that emerges from the book.
Towards the end of her career, Edith redeployed the themes of 'The
Book of Beasts' in her full-length fable about creativity, *The Magic
City* (1910), where a hippogriff once more flies to the aid of the
deliverer. Later in that tale there is an apocalyptic battle of book
people: when the barbarian hordes are released from one book, Philip
opens another and releases Caesar and his legions to combat them. As
in the earlier fable, and in her last children's book, the too aptly named
Wet Magic (1913), the evil released from books through the magic of
imagination can only be fought with a counterbalancing good from the
same source. Her continuous awareness of the power of books,
apparent in everything she wrote, is an endorsement of the power of

imagination in life, and, in her best work, an acknowledgement of the writer's responsibilities. But if the subtext is serious enough, the surface is usually delightfully playful; her fairy-tales often depend for their humorous effects on amusing juxtapositions of tone. Lionel, though only a small boy, is treated with all the deference due to a king until he releases the bluebird, against his ministers' advice:

> The Chancellor gave the King a good shaking, and said:
> 'You're a naughty disobedient little King,' and was very angry indeed . . .
> 'Well, I'm sorry if I've vexed you,' said Lionel. 'Come, let's kiss and be friends.' So he kissed the Prime Minister, and they settled down for a nice quiet game of noughts and crosses, while the Chancellor went to add up his accounts.[40]

The droll effect of her fairy-tales derives from their combination of implausible or fantastic events with a thoroughly prosaic or familiar narrative texture.

In 1902 came a new commission from *The Strand* for nine episodes of a serial, to run from April to December and to be illustrated by Millar. Edith's first two successes had been with the Bastables, based loosely on her own brothers and sister, with an additional and archetypal youngest child, H.O., thrown in for good measure. She realized that for the new story she needed to invent a different family; to be authentic, they needed to be familiar so she decided to use her own children, who were now quite old enough not to mind. This wasn't the first time she had done so: among the entertaining stories in *Nine Unlikely Tales* (1901) is 'The Blue Mountain', woven around her nephew Anthony and her grandfather Anthony Nesbit, after whom both the young Nesbits had been named. The story begins: 'Tony was young Tony, and old Tony was his grandfather. This is about young Tony, and no human being believes a word of it, unless young Tony does.'

'The Blue Mountain' is really a little girl, and the officious inhabitants of Antioch all turn out to be ants, the phonic element omitted from the Tonys' names – so the whole story is a complicated fantasy woven around their names. An even better story, the labyrinthine 'Town in the Library in the Town in the Library', opens with a similar appeal for credence, and two familiar characters: 'Rosamund and Fabian were left alone in the library. You may not believe this: but I advise you to believe everything I tell you, because it is true . . .'[41]

The 'Five Children' of her new serial, *The Psammead* (later, *Five Children and It*) are closely linked with her own, both by their names and their natures: the eldest is Cyril, Paul's second name, and close to him in age is Anthea – like Iris, named from the Greek. Fabian and Rosamund become, less poetically, Robert and Jane. Robert's identity with Fabian was confirmed by H. R. Millar, who told Doris Langley Moore that Fabian was the younger boy in *The Psammead*, that he used to draw his own second son in this role and that, by a sinister coincidence, his own second son had also died an unnatural death.[42] 'The Lamb' was of course, the Lamb, the family's pet name for baby John, who was much cosseted and cuddled by the others, particularly by Rosamund. But the real gap between the Lamb and the others is greatly reduced, for the five children are not yet adolescent, as the real Bland children were when John was born. When Edith began writing *The Psammead*, John was an energetic and destructive toddler, in his second year. Both the book itself and its dedication to him present him with a familiar blend of affection and exasperation:

> My Lamb, you are so very small,
> You have not learned to read at all.
> Yet never a printed book withstands
> The urgence of your dimpled hands.
> So, though this book is for yourself,
> Let mother keep it on the shelf
> Till you can read. O days that pass,
> That day will come too soon, alas!

Though lively and amusing, the five children were less obviously eccentric than the Bastables had been; but given the fantastic nature of their adventures, such an adjustment was probably necessary, and even desirable. Anthea/Iris is consistently presented as the most gentle, thoughtful, truthful and unselfish of the children; Robert/ Fabian is quick-tempered and high spirited, and occasionally mulish. Rosamund/Jane is the literary one, the one who likes 'talking like a book', and the one whom strangers always take to, though she can be careless and fickle. The holiday house in which the story is set was inspired by a real house where Edith had once stayed, probably on a holiday with her own children, long enough to visit Kit's Coty House close by and to take in the surroundings and use them in her fiction. It was a solid, ugly stucco villa between Maidstone and Rochester, close to Bluebell Hill:

The White House was on the edge of a hill, with a wood behind it – and the chalk-quarry on one side and the gravel-pit on the other. Down at the bottom of the hill was a level plain, with queer-shaped white buildings where people burnt lime, and a big red brewery and other houses: and when the big chimneys were smoking, and the sun was setting, the valley looked as if it was filled with golden mist, and the limekilns and oast-houses glimmered and glittered till they were like an enchanted city out of the *Arabian Nights*.[43]

At the bottom of the gravel pit the children found sand (there are also quite a lot of sand pits in this area), and in the sand, they found a sand fairy. For her new invention, Edith coined a new Greek name, by analogy with 'dryad' and 'naiad': since the Greek for sand is *'psammos'*, it had to be the 'psammead'. And so it was, though the children occasionally refer to it, a little more familiarly, as the 'Sammyadd'. But in a book whose theme is that you never get what you expect, this fairy is no Victorian miniature, decked out with tinsel, gauze and butterfly-wings:

> Its eyes were on long horns like a snail's eyes, and it could move them in and out like telescopes; it had ears like a bat's ears, and its tubby body was shaped like a spider's and covered with thick soft fur; its legs and arms were furry too, and it had hands and feet like a monkey's.

"POOF, POOF, POOFY," HE SAID, AND MADE A GRAB.

The psammead was brilliantly realized in Millar's drawings. Edith found his pictures so uncannily close to what she had originally imagined that she sometimes suggested to him that he must be telepathic; Millar was amused but thought this merely showed how much she underestimated her own powers of evocation.[44] Though the psammead has been compared to the cuckoo in Mrs Molesworth's *The Cuckoo Clock* (1877), it is a great deal less sententious, and more like Lewis Carroll's caterpillar or Humpty Dumpty – a tetchy adult, with the sulkiness and thin skin of a child. Though it quickly finds the real children tiresome, it is small enough to be in their power, and thus vulnerable to their demands. For the psammead, by blowing itself up, can grant wishes. These do not last beyond sunset, when the wished-for objects turn into stone – and this, incidentally, turns out to be the explanation for fossils: stone-age families would wish for more megatherium or icthyosaurus than they could eat, and the left-over bits were turned to stone. Perhaps Edith was poking gentle fun at the expense of the more far-fetched 'explanations' of fossils, such as that of the fundamentalist Philip Gosse (who thought God put them there to test man's faith). In any case, she always enjoyed finding some wildly implausible explanation or rationalization for something quite familiar.

Of course, the magical granting of them only points up Edith's favourite moral of the vanity of human wishes – you had better be careful what you wish for in case you actually get it. This theme is particularly relevant to young children who intensely desire the gratification of all their wishes, and yet would be terrified by the consequences of wish-fulfilment, their passions being such that each would kill the thing he loved. The child's realization that wishes have no power in the real world is at once deeply disappointing and yet also reassuring, since it protects the ill-controlled self from the appalling consequences such power would confer. Thus, in dramatizing the magical fulfilment of wishes, both here and in later books and stories, Edith had chosen a subject which had a special urgency for the young; the book related light-heartedly discoveries that its readers had made experientially, reassuring them that their decision to grow up and abandon regressive fantasies was in fact the right one. Several traditional fairy-stories make the same point – for instance the story of the old man, his wife, and the black pudding that he wishes for: she wishes it on to his nose because his wish has been so silly, and they have to use the last wish to get it off again. Bruno Bettelheim has pointed out that in such stories, 'after all the wishing is done, things are exactly as they were before the wishing began', and this is part of the comfort such stories afford.[45]

There is nevertheless a dangerous edge to the wishing game which Edith's narrative points up: Robert, beaten by the baker's boy, wishes to be bigger than him but this doesn't bring him any satisfaction, since he is now quite big enough to kill the baker's boy with one blow, and far too big to beat him in a fair fight. Even more dangerous is Robert's impatient wish that the Lamb be 'wanted' by everyone else. The children spend a hair-raising day trying to prevent the Lamb's abduction. Edith suggests that there is a moral in this episode, and

> you might as well think of it next time you feel piggy yourself and want to get rid of any of your brothers and sisters. I hope this doesn't often happen, but I daresay it has happened sometimes even to you![46]

Her grasp of the nature of sibling relationships is at once entirely realistic (her children bicker incessantly), but also benevolently relaxed, forgiving and defusing. Many of the children's wishes are, of course, less threatening than these two, and more fantastic and literary – nearer to the world of children's make-believe inhabited by the Bastables: they wish to be beautiful, to have unlimited wealth, wings, or Indians in the garden. The wishes invariably backfire, bringing more trouble than pleasure, and this theme, plus the comic juxtaposition of fairy-tale magic with everyday Edwardian life, recalls F. Anstey's *The Brass Bottle*. Never one to be embarrassed by her borrowings, Edith makes the children remember Anstey's book and wish, at the story's end, that everything that has happened should be entirely forgotten:

> 'It's like the "Brass Bottle",' said Jane.
> 'Yes, I'm glad we read that or I should never have thought of it.'[47]

The more obvious features of *The Brass Bottle*, the London setting, the Arabian Nights' magic, were held over to the sequel, *The Phoenix and the Carpet*, serialized in *The Strand* from July 1903 to June 1904.

At this stage of her career, Edith's stories were essentially episodic in structure. Though she had some overall scheme or strategy, each chapter was effectively a self-contained unit that could appear by itself in a magazine, though at the same time forming part of a developing sequence. She always wrote them as much at the last minute as possible, smoking furiously, and sometimes with wet towels wound round her head. Berta Ruck recalled her suddenly appearing at mealtimes and feverishly eliciting help from anyone who happened to be on hand at the time:

The mistress of the house, a tall handsome richly coloured woman in an unfashionably waistless green Liberty robe, hand-embroidered at yoke and cuffs, might drift in, after the meal had begun, from the top-floor study where she had been producing, against time, perhaps the next instalment of her serial *The Railway Children*. She would gaze around as if wondering who all these people were. Then, in a dazed voice, she would appeal to them, 'Can anybody tell me a plot to do next? . . . Rabbit?' (addressing her daughter Iris) 'Cat?' (her husband) 'Mouse?' (and other nicknames) . . . A sigh for our lack of helpfulness. She would then pick up the small child of the party (John), cuddle him on her lap, smile, and join animatedly in the general conversation.[48]

In order not to hold up Millar's complex and beautiful drawings (and there were far more of these made for *The Strand* than ever appeared in the book versions), she used, if she were very behind, to send him outline instructions as to what he should be drawing in advance of her text, assuring him that if they didn't work out right, she could always change the text to fit his pictures. One or two of these instructions survive, for illustrations to *The Wonderful Garden* (1911). But as Edith became more experienced at writing fantasy, her work grew more disciplined and pre-planned, and the episodic structure so evident in the Bastable stories and *Five Children and It* was gradually abandoned. Instead of a series of comparatively discrete adventures befalling the same group of children, she used something much closer to a single story-line, sometimes involving complex and initially puzzling time sequences (as in *The Enchanted Castle*, 1907). Her later work has a darker colouring than the books written around the turn of the century, even though this had been a period in which she had more obvious external causes for unhappiness. The books grow more serious as they grow more complex, and their sense of the insoluble nature of individual as well as social problems increased as their author grew older. There are new depths and subtleties in her later work, but the shimmering high spirits, and sense of exhilarating freedom that characterize the Bastable stories and the first two books about the 'Five Children' are the price paid for that gain. Though *Five Children and It* had taught lessons about self-knowledge and forethought, there is none of the social criticism that was to provide such a sustaining element in her later work. Only the psammead is allowed some ironic comments on the (very different) fantasies of adults who

wouldn't wish silly things like you do, but real earnest things . . . they'd ask for a graduated income-tax, and old-age pensions, and manhood suffrage and free secondary education, and dull things like that; and get them and keep them, and the whole world would be turned topsy-turvy.[49]

So much for the current socialist platform!

The summer of 1902, when Edith was writing her early episodes of *The Psammead*, is recorded in the family album with snaps of everyone on the balcony at Well Hall, in the garden and on the beach at Dymchurch: the camera, like the sundial, only numbers sunny hours. There are many familiar faces – Edgar Jepson, now married, with his little son Selwyn, who was the same age as John, the Steele girls, and Edith's nieces Anthonia Nesbit and Dorothea Deakin. John, a sturdy toddler in a smock, or simply naked, is lifted into the air by Alice or Rosamund, or plays by a breakwater at Hubert's knee. Paul looks shy, Iris melancholy or sulky and Rosamund is always dressing up. In the garden Iris's friends – Cuthbert Collins and the faun-like American, Michael Carr, whom she knew from the Slade – adopt dramatic attitudes: Carr is cavorting about with roses in his hair, while in another snap, Edith punts Cuthbert and his friend, the crippled Douglas Kennedy, round one of the corners of the moat.

In June Edith had sent Douglas Kennedy, who was a friend of Iris's, some verses inviting him to join them on their annual Medway holiday:

> How can I work? The stupid task
> That heartless publishers may ask
> Is all too hard for me to do,
> Dear Medway, since to you, to you,
> My thought flies, falling like an arrow,
> Amid your meadowsweet and yarrow . . .
>
> Dorothy, dearest of my nieces –
> Her dearness breaks one's heart to pieces;
> Iris, most aged of two dear daughters,
> Shall dream beside the Medway waters;
> And there with Esmond gay will be
> Reynolds and Kennedy and me!
>
> But ah, this joy that we were made for
> Must in hard coin be duly paid for –
> So I must whet my wits, and add
> A chapter to the Psammead . . .
>
> Dear Douglas – work like billy-oh
> That to the Medway we may go . . .[50]

Though the delights afforded by the Medway had not changed substantially, the Bland party that went boating that year was now larger and rather differently constituted. Alice stayed at home to look after John, and Hubert was occupied elsewhere, his place as the active man of the party being taken by Richard Reynolds. Iris was to join them, and so was Kennedy. Though confined to a wheelchair, he could be lifted into a punt and loved boating. Edith responded warmly at times to the needs and suffering of others, once they had engaged her imagination, and she seems to have pitied Kennedy and wanted to protect him. A note assures him:

> My dear Boy, my dear child, I wish God had let me have you for my own when you were little: but even if I had had you from the beginning for my very own I could not love you more. Be of good courage!

Kennedy told Doris Langley Moore that he had 'hundreds of letters' from Edith of which 'a great number are of an extremely private nature and unless one knew the circumstances which prompted them and to which they refer, they would be almost unintelligible . . .' Edith's letters to Kennedy were certainly not love letters, though he may have chosen to see them in something of that light. Iris's account of her mother's attitude to him was 'as usual, half-kind and half-cruel'. [51] Edith may have been imaginatively interested in his disability and sense of deprivation. Her own favourite among her children's books was *Harding's Luck*, the story of little lame Dicky of Deptford, while *Salome and the Head*, written in the same year (1909) includes another cripple, the passionate musician, Denny, who lives with and hopelessly worships the dancer, Sandra, in a house that stands on the banks of the Medway.

The fifth member of the boating party was a favourite of Edith's, her niece Dorothea Deakin, a handsome girl whose face suggests a strong and serene personality. Edith helped her to establish a career for herself as a romantic novelist. This was by no means the first occasion that Richard Reynolds had met Dorothea, but he was, then or later, to fall in love with her and want to marry her. A couple of terse private notes in Doris Langley Moore's card index record what she had heard from various members of the family on that subject: 'She appears to have had a love affair with Richard Reynolds, who later married her niece Dorothea Deakin.' And, on another card: 'He is said to have been deeply in love with E.N., and it is known that she prevented her niece's marriage for several years – with very regrettable consequences.'[52]

What those consequences were is nowhere spelled out, though it may have been that, through her delayed marriage, Dorothea's three daughters were born rather later than was considered ideal. Richard and Dorothea were married late in 1910 and Dorothea herself died shortly before her aunt, in 1924. It was a cruel twist of fate that the niece that Edith was so fond of and the last of her young lovers should have thus been drawn together, for though Edith had attempted to embrace renunciation in her farewell poems for Oswald, such self-sacrifice became even harder for her when it was clear that there was no successor to step into Reynolds's shoes; there was less of Hofmanns-thal's Marschallin about Edith than she liked to think. She probably convinced herself that her interference was carried out with the best of intentions, that Reynolds was not good enough for her beautiful niece – she was, after all, in a position to know his failings only too minutely.

In mid December 1902, Edith's mother died – she was eighty-four. Paul remembered going up to Manchester for her funeral.[53] Edith was staying with her niece and brother-in-law. She was very upset by the event; she had been deeply fond of her mother, though in many ways she had been a rebellious daughter, and had certainly never adopted her pliant, affectionate mother as a role model. Indeed Sarah Nesbit was very unlike her daughter – where Edith was determined or self-willed, her mother had been gentle and yielding; where she was demanding, her mother had been self-effacing and where she was flamboyant, her mother had been quiet, almost shy. Between them, there had been none of that clash of strong personalities that can make a mother-daughter relationship tense, and full of potential rivalry. When mothers do appear in Edith's fiction they usually seem to be based on Edith herself rather than on her mother (like the mother of *The Railway Children*). Yet Sarah Nesbit had continued to run the Agricultural College after her husband's death, and had brought up her children in a foreign country where she could not speak the language: though she had not always understood her smallest daughter's feelings, she had been a model of patience and loving-kindness. Nowhere in Edith's writing are mothers regarded as anything less than domestic angels, and while that presentation had something to do with Victorian ideals of womanhood, it had more to do with Mrs Nesbit herself who had managed, so much of the time, to live up to them.

THE CROWDED YEARS

In 1900 Hubert took a step which he must have been contemplating for some time, though it was probably precipitated by Fabian's death: he was received into the Catholic Church. Edith was to follow his example a couple of years later; as Hubert's son John was to observe, she took her religion, as she took her politics, from him. She had been brought up an Anglican, but Bland's parents seem to have been non-conformists – Iris remembered them as Plymouth Brethren. The family burial plot was in the municipal (and non-denominational) graveyard at Woolwich and Hubert himself was eventually buried there beside his mother, though with Catholic rites and a priest officiating. Hubert's conservatism (at odds with his socialism, though he sought to reconcile them), his respect for tradition and his admiration for discipline and good order led him towards Catholicism, which was then becoming fashionable in certain intellectual quarters, in the wake of the Victorian crisis in the Church of England, the resulting Oxford Movement and the great Victorian Catholic apologists such as Newman. The old faith was also associated with some very ancient English families, and latterly Bland encouraged his friends to assume that he had been born a Catholic, and came from a good old family of Northern stock.[1]

Their conversion seems to have had little outward impact on the Blands' lives. It was less dramatic than it would be today, for at that time the Catholic Church regarded Anglican baptism as adequate and only expected its converts to take the tenets of their new faith seriously, to receive the sacraments and make confession regularly. Hubert's practical observances remained fairly minimal. Gerald Gould, who got to know the Blands well a few years later, once asked Edith point-blank what his religion meant to her husband:

It was at the time when I was spending most of my Sundays at their house, and it was obvious to me that Hubert did not, in fact, take part in any religious ceremony. E. Nesbit replied that he was a merely formal member of the Church, i.e. that he went to confession and Mass the minimum number of times necessary to keep him from actual expulsion from the fold.[2]

Alice Hoatson regarded Hubert as a practising Catholic, and Paul recalled that his father did not eat meat on Fridays, but he apparently made little or no effort to bring up his children in that faith, as the Church enjoins. The elder children were perhaps already of an age to decide for themselves, but John received no religious education to speak of, as he explained:

> [My parents] never made any attempt to influence my religious views. I was taken to church about five times in all when I was little, three times to Benediction and twice to Mass. I remember that when I was about ten or twelve a Catholic boy at school, learning that I was a Catholic and finding that I knew nothing of the faith, gave me several tracts and a medal. I disliked the tone of the tracts so much that I returned home in great indignation saying that some silly fool was trying to convert me to be a Catholic. My Father mildly replied that it was quite a good faith and after all there was nothing to be so indignant about.[3]

It seems to have been the underlying dogma of Catholicism, rather than its ritual, that constituted its main appeal for Hubert, yet here again what little is known of his views remains puzzling. In conversation, he told Gerald Gould that he had been brought up in that faith (this was no more true than his claim to have been a boxing blue at Oxford), that as a young man he had lapsed, and that his study of Hegel had convinced him once more of the truth of the Catholic faith. Gould commented: 'The statement seemed to me at the time to be nonsense, but he was not in the habit of talking nonsense, and apparently believed what he said.'

Hegel is a notoriously difficult philosopher, and Bland was particularly proud of having read and understood him – from time to time he would expound Hegelian thought from his pulpit in the *Sunday Chronicle*. In a paper he gave on 'Socialism and Orthodoxy' (in 1910) he took Hegel's theory that the possession of property is an essential for freedom and the development of individuality in order to argue for common ground between a non-Marxist socialism and Pope Leo XIII's condemnation of it.[4]

Hubert's Catholicism brought him into contact with a more famous convert, Father Hugh Benson, who became a friend and visited Well Hall; there he was given a bedroom on the top floor with a little closet leading off it, which he arranged as a temporary chapel for himself. In the wake of Father Benson came Frederick Rolfe, 'Baron Corvo', who in February 1906 sent the Fabian Society a characteristically curious note:

> Mr Frederick William Rolfe (v. Literary Year-Book) encloses a subscription of Five Shillings. He is not a Socialist; and his experience of socialists is entirely disagreeable. He is a Roman Catholic; and finds the Faith comfortable and the faithful intolerable: consequently he is not even on speaking terms with Roman Catholics. But he is a student; and as such he is not anxious to confuse the goodness of a cause with the badness of its agents. And so begging pardon for these explanations, he ventures to ask the Secretary of the Fabian Society to supply him with the 'Credo' of the Fabians, for purposes of study.
>
> He is led to make this request by his immensely excited admiration of Mr G. B. Shaw's article in the *Clarion* ...

A few months later Rolfe wrote to Hubert appealing to him as 'a man of the world' to invest several thousands of pounds in the development of some historical material involving the Borgias:

> R. H. Benson of Cambridge read your *With the Eyes of a Man* with me during the vacation, and we examined your picture; and we decided that you were as man-of-the-wordly as possible. So I should like to have you in this Borgia scheme if it is likely to be in your line.

Rolfe also stayed at Well Hall where he was greatly charmed by John, whose precocious and forceful way of expressing himself impressed all who knew him. He continued to write John long amusing letters on his birthday for several years.[5]

Another new friend (and Catholic convert) was Cecil Chesterton, Gilbert's younger and wilder brother, who had joined the Fabian in 1901 and rapidly became a devoted disciple of Hubert, attracted by his curious blend of socialism and imperialism; only Hilaire Belloc was to influence him more. Cecil was an enthusiastic Fabian and in 1904 was elected to the Executive, although he lost his place again in 1907, for his outspokenness had made him a number of enemies. He was actively involved in the Church Socialist League, to which Hubert also belonged. In an introduction to Hubert's posthumous *Essays*, Cecil was to write admiringly of Hubert's intellectual integrity, his respect for the young and his Catholicism.[6] His future wife Ada, a journalist, left a vivid account of the partying at Well Hall, the variety of the guests – 'enthusiastic youth, artists, writers, flaming socialists and decorous Fabians' – and the charm of their hosts:

> Mrs Bland . . . was always surrounded by adoring young men, dazzled by her vitality, amazing talent and the sheer magnificence of her appearance. She was a very tall woman, built on the grand scale, and on festive occasions wore a trailing gown of peacock blue satin with strings of beads and Indian bangles from wrist to elbow. Madame, as she was always called, smoked incessantly, and her long cigarette holder became an indissoluble part of the picture she suggested – a raffish Rossetti, with a long full throat, and dark luxuriant hair, smoothly parted. She was a wonderful woman, large hearted, amazingly unconventional, but with sudden strange reversions to ultra-respectable standards. Her children's stories had an immense vogue, and she could write unconcernedly in the midst of a crowd, smoking like a chimney all the while.
>
> Bland, detached and saturnine, sat apart on these occasions, a springtide of femininity fluttering around him, waiting for a sultan-esque sign to approach. There was always an inner group of devotees, mostly of the Victorian type. He had a great attraction for the ingenuous.
>
> With such magnetic personalities in the family, Paul Bland and his sister Iris were overshadowed, but Rosamund, the other sister, was too dominant to be obscured. Dark and comely, with a full figure and lovely eyes, she was very attractive and many of the older men completely lost their heads over her.[7]

Hubert sat apart because, according to Iris, he did not like his wife's 'playing and dancing parties' and only appeared under protest. Iris attributed this to meanness: 'He was not really a generous man in money matters, but he couldn't say anything against Mother using her own money as she might wish.' His dislike may also have been a reaction to her unqualified success as a hostess. There was an element of envy or competitiveness in the Blands' marriage – Bland needed to get even with his talented wife for her recent achievements, as well as for 'her wit and freaks and fantasies', as H. G. Wells observed. In the early years of the century, when her career as a writer was at its height and she was earning substantially more than he was, the tide of her life was altogether at the full; he felt subconsciously threatened by her access of power. Party-giving was one of her greatest talents; even Rosamund, often critical of Edith, admitted that she organized them delightfully and visibly enjoyed them; it was the only art that she continued to practise in the aftermath of Hubert's death. She conferred on parties that sense of exuberant fun that had given birth to the Bastables. And in some ways they were a little like children's parties: after a leisurely meal, taken at a long baronial table laid out in the hall, after the good food, wine and conversation, there would be singing and dancing, or else games of all kinds – cards or paper and pencil games, charades, forfeits or noisier and more rumbustuous games based on hide-and-seek. Laurence Housman remembered one party where, as a forfeit, he had to find a lady's shoe while blindfolded, in order to give it to someone else. As he groped in vain among rustling silk petticoats, he overheard H. G. Wells remark, 'It's no use looking for my wife's feet – she hasn't any; she goes on castors.'[8]

The Wellses first met the Blands in the summer or autumn of 1902. H. G. recalled Well Hall as 'a place to which one rushed down from town at the week-end to snatch one's bed before anyone else got it'. Its parties had become famous. Noel Griffith's wife Nina, who greatly admired Edith, described one such party in vivid detail:

> The Blands' parties were large and frequent, and played an important part in their lives. Many notabilities attended them. Often ten or more of us would band together for the tiresome journey from town to join the seven or eight inhabitants of the house for an evening's amusement which was usually kept up into the small hours. It seemed a long and tedious way to go, and on a foggy night, after waiting perhaps an hour for a train from Cannon Street, and then being shot out to wait again on a chilly platform at Blackheath to catch the Well Hall train, one wondered why on earth one had accepted one's invitation so readily.
>
> One arrived late without a qualm (for meals were invariably late there) to be greeted by a large placard at the principal entrance saying briefly 'The Front Door is at the Back!' This was because the front door opened directly into the long hall where we dined when there were a lot of us, and it was therefore undesirable to let in the cold air. Or the notice might imply that there was more chance of being let in at the back: with any luck a gardener's boy, a child, or even a maid might hear us. Generally, even when we had made our entrance the prospect of dinner seemed to be remote, and we wandered about feeling forlorn and neglected, and still wondering why we had come. Mrs Bland would be finishing a chapter, and Hubert his article for the *Chronicle* and we knew that nothing could happen until their work was done.
>
> Then at last Mrs Bland would appear on the stairway, radiant – in riotous spirits, perhaps, because she had just escaped premature death by not falling over a dustpan left on the stairs; and that was, of course, an omen that it would be a good party [E. N.'s superstitiousness was

notorious]. She always wore the same kind of dress, a long flowery silk one, probably with Turkish slippers, and certainly with many silver bangles. These reached nearly to her elbow and were never removed. They were presents [from Hubert, one for each book she had published] and she prized them as an Indian prizes his scalps. She bathed in them, and they got in her way often, but I never saw her freckled arms without them until I went down to Romney Marsh at the very last, and she showed me that her hands were so thin that she could slip them off easily.

Her companion, Miss Hoatson, wore the same flowing dresses, but hers had more form about them, and a waist line.

Hubert would at last crawl lazily out of his den in 'immaculate evening dress' with velvet coat and a monocle worn on a black watered-silk ribbon which hinted at foppishness, though the glass was a necessity.

The dinners themselves were always 'chancy'. If poems, articles and books were doing well, they were quite grand. At one time two Swiss lads did the cooking and were full of surprises. I remember once they made little chalets of white sugar with real lights inside as a sweet. In leaner times we had a huge soup-tureen of haricot beans, doled out graciously and gaily by Madame, a large block of cheese to follow, and delicious apples from the garden. There was always plenty of red and white wine in beautiful Venetian bottles and the table looked lovely. Hubert had passion and skill as a rose grower. In summer we (the guests) used to gather a wicker clothes-basket full of roses, picking them off short to save the remaining buds. We would make a thick mat of them from one end of the long table to another, setting in at intervals the silver branch candle-sticks that Mrs Bland adored.

The party never flagged once the Blands had appeared. A friendly atmosphere hung about them, an atmosphere of festivity. They were intensely *lovable*; and we were gay because we knew that our hostess was enjoying the large company, and thinking how lucky she was to have got so many 'darlings' together. The conversation was good, and everyone was given a chance to express his own ideas. Hubert was a brilliant talker, but he was also eager to listen, especially to youth. 'Remember the respect due to youth', was one of his favourite sayings. Edith herself would wind on for hours if she was in the mood, while the children of the house were never shut away, and gave their opinions as definitely and dogmatically as the rest of us.

Invariably, in the midst of the most distinguished gathering, one would find some weak or wounded creature who was taking shelter at Well Hall – a baby rescued from poverty or illness (who surprisingly appeared at late dinner), a poor relation waiting for a job, a painter seeking recognition, a timid girl whom someone there believed in and encouraged to write stories. No one who knew the Blands could resist seeking their comfort and their counsels in distress.

After dinner we danced in the cleared drawing-room, and there were games and more talk. Devil-in-the-dark caused the destruction of so much good furniture all over the house that it had to be stopped. Mrs Bland collected old glass lustres long before there was a craze for them, and there were fine chandeliers in the drawing-room, which contained many beautiful pieces, strongly expressive of the individuality of those who had assembled them.

The dinner and dancing and talk lasted so long that most of us missed last trains and slept where we could, the men usually finding accommodation in the garden cottages. Next morning it was considered in the best taste to depart by an early train without seeing our hosts. The house would be in an incredible muddle, and the most tactful procedure was to breakfast with Paul, the eldest son, who left early for the City, and then vanish unheeded.[9]

One weak creature who found shelter at Well Hall was Maggie Doran, Edith's earliest rival for Hubert's affection. She had remained on good terms with the Blands – Shaw had recorded meeting her at their house in the late eighties – and Edith, with characteristic generosity, now took her into the household. When Maggie fell ill with pleurisy, Iris nursed her herself, but she grew steadily worse and was taken to Eltham cottage hospital where, on 25 March 1903, she died.[10]

Work, of course, had to come first, because it was what made all the parties and holidays possible; even at this stage of her life, when the Blands were better off than ever before, supporting a large house and staff, they spent rather than saved their income. The next two or three years were the busiest and most productive of Edith's whole life: for much of 1904 and 1905, she was turning out not one but two monthly instalments of serials simultaneously – *The Amulet* and *The Railway Children* were among them. She was now at the height of her powers and writing with exceptional speed and facility. She would plan out an episode in advance, either in her head or else in summary. Then she would simply write sheet after sheet of manuscript, on cheap coloured paper; she wrote virtually without correction, throwing the pages on the floor as they were completed. She worked mainly in the mornings and late afternoons. She could polish off five thousand words by the early afternoon, and then play a game of badminton and spend the evening in animated conversation with friends.[11]

In July 1903 Edith began a new twelve-part sequel to *The Psammead* for *The Strand*. Back in London, the five children (now reduced to four) ruin their nursery carpet by letting off their fireworks indoors, and inside its replacement they discover a mysterious egg. They hatch the egg in the fireplace and a phoenix emerges; it tells them that their new nursery carpet can take them wherever they want to go. The idea of the phoenix had come from Laurence Housman, while the Arabian Nights' magic owed something to Anstey's *Brass Bottle* (remembered at the end of *The Psammead*), though their combination is ingenious and the total effect quite original. *The Phoenix and the Carpet* was dedicated to Edith's godson, Hubert Griffith. His parents Noel and Nina had remained in close touch with the Blands, and had also taken a holiday cottage at Dymchurch. In December that year, Edith began writing a new series of Bastable stories for the *London Magazine* which ran for most of 1904 and eventually became *The New Treasure Seekers*. With an effort she completed *The Phoenix* in the first two months of 1904 for she and the girls – Iris, Rosamund and her niece Dorothea – were about to set off to Paris for a three-month holiday.

They left on 9 March and returned in late May, though Rosamund had to get back somewhat earlier than the others because she was still at school. She probably travelled back with Hubert and Paul, who had come over to join them for a while. Alice stayed at home to look after John and keep the household running smoothly. Before they left, H. G. Wells offered Edith an introduction to his old friend Arnold Bennett:

> I know no one else in Paris now except Arnold Bennett, who's rather a lark in an irritating way. Shall I send you a sort of testimonial for you to present telling them what a thoroughly respectable person you are, or what?

Arnold Bennett's journal, however, suggests that he met the Blands by accident rather than prior arrangement: an entry for 6 May 1904, records that after dinner on the previous night

> at Miss Thomasson's studio, I met Hubert Bland and his Liberty-clad daughter Rosamund. Mrs Bland was too indisposed to come. I also met . . . Berta Ruck, and some other people.[12]

One justification for the Paris trip was to enable Iris to continue her art education, and in particular to attend Colarossi's celebrated life-classes, where an international group of art students, huddled over an enormous stove, were instructed by suave, bearded professors with the tiny red ribbons of the *Légion d'Honneur* in their buttonholes. Two more of Iris's Slade friends were already there, studying – Berta Ruck (whom Bennett mentioned by name) and Arthur Watts. Berta was a tall, angular Welsh girl, with a humorously round face, whose real name, Roberta, Edith appropriated for the heroine of her next book, *The Railway Children*. She was to give up drawing shortly after this and later became a prolific popular novelist, under the combined influence of her husband, 'Oliver Onions', and Edith, who spent hours listening and advising her about her work. Berta had not met Edith before her visit to Paris, but they took to each other at once – Berta's strong, outspoken nature greatly appealed to the older woman. It was Berta who first nicknamed her 'the Duchess': when Iris delivered her mother's triangularly-folded, pencilled invitations to come to tea in her rooms in Montparnasse, Berta would remark, 'Ah, an invitation from the Duchess to play croquet.'[13] Her new title was soon widely adopted by Iris's Slade friends, and it increasingly came to suit her grand manner.

Iris's other friend from the Slade was the dashingly handsome Arthur Watts, whom Edith re-christened 'Oswald in Paris', partly because his Christian names were Arthur Oswald, as Barron's had been, and partly because he resembled him a little; she had never really got over the loss of the special friend whose joie-de-vivre was only equalled by her own. Thereafter Watts obediently signed his delightfully illustrated letters 'Oswald'. Both Berta and Arthur were soon established favourites, later becoming frequent visitors at Well Hall and Dymchurch. Both eventually lost contact with her – Berta after a row in 1909 which was only made up during Edith's final illness, and Arthur on marrying, in 1910. Edith liked her new 'Oswald' well enough to take him alone with her on a boating holiday on the Medway during which they worked the locks themselves; but he was always careful to keep a degree of distance between them, so that their relationship remained comfortably companionable, rather than romantic. She was, after all, old enough to be his mother.[14]

Noel and Nina Griffith went over to Paris that April, and joined the Bland party to go to one of Isadora Duncan's first and much acclaimed performances, dancing to the slow movement of Beethoven's Seventh Symphony. As well as meeting old friends, Edith, as always, made some new ones: a day or two after their arrival, they heard coming from the next room in their hotel 'the pleasant whining of a mandoline'. Never one to forego an adventure for the sake of mere etiquette, Edith dispatched Rosamund to find out what the player was like, on the pretext of borrowing some matches. He turned out to be a nice young American painter, with slicked-down hair and a tooth-brush moustache, called Hermann Webster, but always known thereafter as 'Monsieur Trente-Sept' – that being his room number. Once an introduction had been effected, as it were accidentally, Edith greeted and thanked him as they passed on the stairs next day, and suggested that he come and play his mandoline for them that evening. Webster was immediately attracted by Rosamund, who had inherited her father's good looks and sex appeal, and he asked her out to a Sunday evening concert. There they encountered a friend and fellow American, the immensely elegant and good-looking novelist, Justus Miles Forman. Forman was thoroughly Anglicized and might have served as one of Henry James's heroes. He immediately began to flirt with Rosamund, and before the evening was over had asked when he could see her again. She told him that he would have to call on her mother, as he did. Inevitably Edith was much taken with his classical good looks and elegant manners. He was writing a novel about a haunted man, and they were soon eagerly talking shop, while Forman began a more intimate and discreet friendship with Rosamund.[15]

By mid-May Paris was growing uncomfortably warm. Edith, who had not been entirely well, and never liked Paris as much as she expected to, decided to wind up her holiday in the countryside. She invited her new friends to accompany her, and indeed paid Arthur Watts's expenses for him. A party consisting of Edith, Berta and Arthur, and the two Americans, Webster and Forman, set off for the picturesque village of Grez-sur-Marne, east of Paris. Iris, with Dorothea, either stayed on in Paris or perhaps returned to London for the summer term. Grez was exactly the kind of spot that Edith loved best, its old stone bridge spanning a river bordered with forget-me-nots, grey willows and sparkling green river meadows, bright with buttercups. They went for picnics in a donkey cart, bathed in the river and boated – Edith, like so many Edwardians, could never resist any opportunity of boating. With Rosamund returned to school, her mother had the attention of the delectably green-eyed Forman all to herself, and the two of them sat about for hours on end in a little rowing boat, discussing the novelist's craft. Edith herself was now working hard at a new romantic novel, *The Incomplete Amorist* (1906), which opens at Halstead, but is largely set in art-student Paris, with some scenes at Grez near the end. Forman's appealing green eyes

are given, in the novel, to the Amorist, who is also partly a portrait of
Hubert (though his eyes, like Rosamund's, were brown). The maiden,
but thoroughly modern aunt who, with her cigarettes, her sense of
humour and her sensible short skirts, is partly a self-portrait, tells the
fluttery lady in love with the Amorist, 'I was a fool myself once about a
man with eyes his colour . . . When I come to die, the thing I shall be
sorriest for was that he wasn't my – lover, as we agree to call it.'[16] Edith
was evidently thinking not only of Forman but also of Bernard Shaw,
and the greatest disappointment of her life.

The holiday at Grez was idyllic, days of sunshine ending with
supper on the terrace overlooking the river, in the long spring dusk.
Berta Ruck recalled that

> In the evenings we supped out of doors with a lamp on the table, round
> which the moths fluttered and blundered. I see us now – the Duchess,
> with her inevitable cigarette in its long holder, her elbow on the table,
> the Inn cat lying asleep on the trail of her sweeping, peacock-blue robe.
> Mr Webster strumming his mandoline. Mr Forman fastidiously, Arthur
> scare-crowishly, turned out, and myself dressed by the Duchess in a
> bright green silken tea-gown of her own – 'here's a picturesque rag,
> Berta,' she said. 'You have it. I hate blouses and skirts, especially in a
> place like this. And wear a red rose in your black plaits and look as much
> like a Mucha' [a then-admired poster-artist . . .] 'as you can.'

Only one small cloud appeared on the horizon. On the second
evening there, a drunk lurched up to them and was politely escorted
away by Mr Webster. But next morning, as they waited in the parlour
for the weather to clear up, he reappeared and reminded Edith that he
had once set one of her poems to music. To her embarrassment and
distress, he then proceeded to play his song on the out-of-tune piano.
It seems that he was an English musician whose work had gone out of
fashion; he was drinking himself to death on absinthe.[17]

The intrusion of darker realities into a holiday world can occur at
any time, but it was at this stage of her career that Edith began to allow
them greater play in her children's books. Her strong, though often
simple sense of social and political injustice – which had emerged
clumsily, didactically and sometimes mawkishly in her verse, and
forcefully if sentimentally in the novels and short stories she had
written with Hubert – now began to make itself felt in her serials and
fairy-tales for children. *The Strand* for July 1904 carried 'Billy the
King', the tale in which Billy chooses to remain in the magic world
because of the harsh working conditions of the real one (see above, p.

137). And *The New Treasure Seekers*, which she was writing that year for the *London Magazine*, though it made gentle fun of the reforming zeal of the Sandals, was increasingly concerned with real poverty – no longer the shabby-genteel variety that the Bastables themselves had suffered when they lived in the Lewisham Road. A visit to Camberwell reminds Oswald of the two best-known novels of another popular children's writer of the day, Hesba Stretton, whose vivid and compassionate accounts of slum children's lives affected many of her readers' social views.

Edith justly admired Hesba Stretton's poignant stories, and her influence is particularly evident in *Harding's Luck* (1909). Oswald, in *The New Treasure Seekers*, observes:

> The tram ride was rather jolly, but when we got out and walked we felt like 'Alone in London', or 'Jessica's First Prayer', because Camberwell is a devastating region that makes you think of rickety attics with the wind whistling through them, or miserable cellars where forsaken children do wonders by pawning their relations' clothes and looking after the baby.[18]

There is a characteristic tinge of irony here, but it is never allowed to destroy the point, however clichéd, that the other half of London lives very differently. Elsewhere in the book, the Bastables cross the river to Millwall in search of Pincher, their dog; there they encounter from the poor a hostility which they attempt to defuse by politely pursuing their enquiries:

> So we got on very well, but it does not make me comfortable to see people so poor and we have such a jolly house. People in books feel this, and I know it is right to feel it, but I hate the feeling all the same. And it is worse when the people are nice to you.[19]

The stylistic awkwardness here reflects middle-class embarrassment and guilt, feelings clearly associated with the liberal dilemma; Oswald and his author can identify but not escape it.

The New Treasure Seekers has moments of making both actors and readers thoroughly uncomfortable in a way that Edith had not risked before. There had been scenes in *The Wouldbegoods* (1901) – when the Bastables accidentally dug up Mrs Simpkins's vegetables or when they set up the unsatisfactory 'Benevolent Bar' – in which class tensions were painfully apparent, but such episodes had focused primarily on adult misunderstandings of the children's good intentions, rather than on the tensions themselves. *The New Treasure Seekers* is far more consistently concerned with the problem of poverty and the dubious value of charity, which makes the benefactors feel better while failing to solve the underlying social problems. Its final celebratory picnic at Lynwood (i.e. Bodiam) Castle is interrupted by the village children – 'poor little Lazaruses', Mrs Red House calls them. They are offered the remains of the Bastables' picnic, and invited to join in the games, though to Oswald, 'they did not seem to be very clever children, or just the sort you would choose for your friends, but I suppose you like to play, however little you are other people's sort.'[20]

The tone here is uneasy, perhaps even ambiguous, because Edith is conscious of Oswald's unconscious snobbery, but has no means of dissociating herself from it. The moral direction becomes more and more complicated as it emerges that one of the village children is being victimized by the others because his father is in gaol. This provokes a facile condemnation of the children's conventional working-class morality: ' "Father's always kep' hisself respectable," said the girl with the dirty blue ribbon. "You can't be sent to gaol, not if you keeps yourself respectable, you can't, miss." ' It also allows the Bastables to exercise that middle-class charity which Edith had mocked when it had taken the form of the high-minded mid-Victorian *Ministering Children*, yet which she herself here adapts and adopts. Her intermittent efforts to tackle the theme of poverty seriously in *The New Treasure Seekers* are too uncertain in tone to be successful, but they were taken up again in *The Amulet*, and with more concentration, in *Harding's Luck* of 1909.

The Railway Children, which followed *The New Treasure Seekers* in *The London Magazine*, beginning in January 1905, offered its own version of harsh realities, and looked harder at the plight of the child whose father was in gaol since its central theme is wrongful imprisonment in England and Russia, and the relentless machinery of law that, once released, is as dangerous and ineluctable as an express train. The story begins with Father's arrest and subsequent imprisonment for selling state secrets to the Russians, on the evidence of letters found in his office desk. With the difference that the secrets had been sold to Germany, this was exactly what had happened in the notorious Dreyfus affair. Dreyfus, a French army officer and a Jew, had been wrongly accused in 1894, and condemned to solitary confinement on Devil's Island until 1897, when the real traitor, Esterhazy, had been publicly denounced. A retrial was held in 1899, but Dreyfus was never fully exonerated, and an Appeal Court was set up in 1903 to reconsider the evidence. Its proceedings dragged on and on (and were thus still in the public eye in 1905); Dreyfus was not finally reinstated until 1906. Serious mistakes of this kind could always occur under Western noses, but in Russia injustice and persecution were built into the system – no one could become a friend of Kropotkin and Stepniak without realizing that.

Stepniak, himself a victim of the Russian system and, more recently, of a railway train, is remembered in the figure of the Russian gentleman. Mother tells the children how he had been imprisoned in Siberia because he 'wrote a beautiful book about poor people and how to help them' (both Stepniak and Kropotkin had written on the harsh Russian regime), adding:

'You know in Russia you mustn't say anything about the rich people doing wrong, or about the things that ought to be done to make poor people better and happier. If you do, they send you to prison.'
'But they *can't*,' said Peter; 'people only go to prison when they've done wrong.'
'Or when the Judges *think* they've done wrong,' said Mother. 'Yes, that's so in England. But in Russia it's different . . .'

The poor gentleman had endured solitary confinement for three years, and then had been sent as a member of a chain-gang to the mines in Siberia; he had escaped, when the war came, by volunteering as a soldier and then deserting. Peter is uneasy about this:

'But that's very cowardly, isn't it – ' said Peter – 'to desert? Especially when it's war?'
'Do you think he owed anything to a country that had done *that* to him? If he did, he owed more to his wife and children. He didn't know what had become of them.'[21]

By 1905 Russia was encouraging volunteers for the war against Japan. In *The Railway Children*, Perks the porter and the station-master are supporting opposite sides, and Perks (who is pro-Japanese) reckons that the station-master hasn't told him the sad story of the Russian refugee because it didn't cast the Russians in a particularly favourable light:

' 'E wouldn't want to give away 'is own side with a tale like that 'ere. It ain't human nature. A man's got to stand up for his own side whatever they does. That's what it means by Party politics. I should 'a' done the same myself if that long-'aired chap 'ad 'a' been a Jap.'
'But the Japs don't do cruel wicked things like that,' said Bobbie.

'P'r'aps not,' said Perks, cautiously; 'still you can't be sure with foreigners . . .'

Perks's view, that it doesn't matter which side you take, as long as you stick to it, seems comically inadequate. Yet the book's structure suggests an underlying similarity in the way that faceless authority can perpetuate injustice. Though the harshness and oppression of the Czarist regime is emphasized, the fate of Father and of the Russian refugee are implicitly compared when Mother asks the children to pray for God 'to show his pity upon all prisoners and captives'.[22] And Father does not appear to be vindicated by any of those due processes of law of which Western democracies are so proud, but rather by the personal intervention of that convenient and paternal *deus ex machina*, the old gentleman.

English poverty and class conflict, which had begun to impinge on the Bastables in her previous book, is largely avoided in *The Railway Children*. In indicting higher authorities, Edith represents the lower levels of society as artificially homogeneous, stable and respectful. Perks misreads the children's birthday treat and accuses them of 'coming the charity lay' over him, but he later swallows his pride, and the episode (chapter IX) is an example of one of Edith's favourite themes, the difficulties of doing good. Class distinctions in the countryside (the story seems to be set around Halstead, with 'Maidbridge' combining elements of Tonbridge and Maidstone) are reassuringly well regulated and rigid. However hard up Mother may be, she cannot lose caste; everyone immediately recognizes her for what she is – a real Lady. And when Peter is caught stealing coal by the station-master, he too is recognized and addressed as 'young gentle-man', instead of being hauled off to the police station as a common thief. Here the God-given hierarchy of village life acts as a protection for the family who are consistently treated with a friendly deference that is – it is implied – their due, and is apparently quite unaffected by father's disgrace; (though there is no evidence that the villagers know about this, they do seem to have heard about his release at the end).

In the spring of 1905 Edith took another holiday in Paris, only for three weeks this time, leaving in mid-April and returning on 6 May. A week later, two one-act plays which she had written jointly with her favourite niece Dorothea Deakin were performed at the Freemasons' Hall, Woolwich. These were *The King's Highway* and *The Philandrist* (an answer to Shaw's *Philanderer*?). Unfortunately their texts have not survived. That month, when she was half way through writing *The*

Railway Children for the *London Magazine*, *The Story of the Amulet*, third and last of the tales of the 'five children', began to be serialized in *The Strand*. Where *The Railway Children* had glanced at some aspects of contemporary politics, *The Amulet* examines the nature of the state, its powers and functions, on a much wider front, using the enormous perspective of ancient history from which to do so. Contemporary politics are no more than touched on: Father, apparently a war correspondent, has been dispatched to Manchuria (presumably to cover the Russo-Japanese war), but by the second chapter this has become South Africa[23] – it is obviously unimportant which it is; so there is nothing to correspond to the focus on the Russian regime in *The Railway Children*, although arbitrary imprisonment certainly recurs as a theme. *The Amulet* looks not at the present, but at the past: Victorian children's books or adventure stories were quite commonly written in the form of historical novels; but it is one thing to set a story in the past and quite another to take the children of today, with all their modern perceptions, back into yesterday; since then so many children's writers have borrowed this idea that it now seems quite familiar. There were several possible prototypes for it: F. Anstey had invented *Tourmalin's Time Cheques* (1891) but these had brought Tourmalin time out rather than time past. More to the point was Wells's time traveller who had cycled into the distant future on his *Time Machine* in 1895: if time and space were somehow interchangeable dimensions (or both 'modes of thought', as *The Amulet* suggests) travel in time might be regarded as a logical extension of the rather primitive space travel that the five children had previously enjoyed in *The Phoenix and the Carpet*. But while the precise origin of the idea of time travel is difficult to pin down for certain, the concrete agent of the magic – the amulet itself – got into the book via a clearly identifiable place and even person.

Edith had begun work on *The Amulet* before *The Phoenix*, though she did not finish it or publish it until afterwards. In search of a theme for a successor to *Five Children*, probably early in 1903, Edith had gone to look at her old friends, the mummies in the British Museum. While there, she knocked upon the door of the Keeper of Egyptian and Assyrian Antiquities since a notice informed her that he was available to answer enquiries at certain times of the day. The Keeper, it turned out, was Ernest Wallis Budge, a rather portly man of her own age, with a high colour, a round face, and a suggestion of John Bull about him. As she went in, he gave her an appraising glance, deciding at once that

she was a most attractive woman, with 'a charming figure'. He asked
her what she wanted and she replied that she didn't quite know yet, but
that she was a children's writer, looking for new material for a book.
So many of the usual ideas for children's books had become hackneyed
and stale; she wanted a new line to take and wondered whether there
was any side of his work which might be made interesting to the young
– perhaps something might be done with their stories? He explained to
her patiently that there was a considerable amount of Egyptian
literature: the Egyptians had loved stories, and several of their kings
and great men had employed professional story-tellers as members of
their households. But when she asked what kind of stories they had
told, he had to admit that they would not do at all for a children's
book, being mostly about sex, with a good dash of magic thrown in.
They usually related the misadventures of unfaithful wives, impassioned lovers and moon-faced maidens, with everyone taking
advantage of everyone else and no moral whatsoever. She agreed that
they sounded quite unsuitable but was interested in the elements of
magic that they employed, so he explained to her the use of amulets
and words of power, and told her that she had better go away and think
it over, and come back if she decided that she wanted to know more
about them. She returned a few days later, and having asked him some
further details of names and words, began to write the first chapters of
the book; they included a drawing of a particular type of amulet, and
the word of power, transliterated as 'ur-hekau-setcheh'.[24]

𓄿𓎡𓅱𓋴𓍯𓏏𓊪𓉻𓐍𓏛𓇋𓆑𓂝𓏤

The Amulet's details of Egyptian magic as well as its choice of
settings strongly reflect Wallis Budge's wide interests. He had spent
much of the previous decade in Egypt and Asia Minor, smuggling back
precious relics of early civilizations to the British Museum by a series
of dishonest ruses that had outraged 'the archaeological Pecksniffs', as
he dismissively termed them. He suggested to Edith that she should
use the 'Tyet' form of amulet, the Isis knot, which supposedly gave the
(dead) wearer access to the different regions of the underworld; he
even presented her with one. Amulets do not, as the plot requires,
come in arc shapes nor in two halves, but they do carry words of power
or *hekau*, though the inscription used in *The Amulet* was one that
Budge invented specially for her and carefully wrote out in hiero-

glyphics: it might be translated as 'Great of magic (*hekau*) is the Setcheh-snake' (a mythological serpent which featured in some early spells for the dead). He also suggested that her first episode might include the arrival and conquest of the copper-users in Predynastic Egypt, that a later episode might be set in ancient Assyria, that the Egyptian priest who pursues the children should be named Rekh-Mara, after a high official whose painted tomb at Thebes had been the subject of much study and speculation, and added that 'Pharaoh' might appropriately be addressed as 'Great House', since that was the significance of his hieroglyph.[25]

Edith took her early drafts back to Wallis Budge as she wrote them and he in turn gave her many hours of his time: he told her about the priesthood of Amen-Ra, read her a description of an Assyrian banquet (but advised against including Assyrian love songs), and pointed out in the Museum the relief of an eagle-headed god who, as Nisroch, would release the children from the Babylonian dungeon. It would be easy to assume that the Learned Gentleman who reads the children the words of power written on the amulet is a portrait of Wallis Budge, to whom her book was dedicated 'as a small token of gratitude for his unfailing kindness and help in the making of it'. The Learned Gentleman's room, with its huge mummy case and its clutter of papyri and cuneiform tablets, was certainly inspired by Budge's room at the British Museum, and the Gentleman has been endowed with Budge's wide-ranging knowledge of early cultures, but they have nothing further in common: shy and retiring, the Learned Gentleman is the epitome of the absent-minded professor, whereas Budge was worldly, forceful and ambitious. The Learned Gentleman's boyhood nick-name, Jimmy, rather suggests that he included elements of Arthur

Watts's great friend, the shy and gangly Horace Horsnell, always known as 'Jimmy'. Horsnell wanted to be a writer and took his first step in that direction by becoming Edith's secretary.

Wallis Budge does, however, make a guest appearance in *The Amulet*, in a cameo role of the type Alfred Hitchcock would have appreciated: he appears during a dramatic scene enacted on the steps of the British Museum. The Babylonian Queen, brought by the psammead's magic to Edwardian London, flies into a fury with the Museum officials when they will not let her take her own jewellery out of the glass cases. So she wishes for the Museum's Babylonian collection to fly slowly out of the main doors, under the very noses of its custodians, and so it does. The nicest and most level-headed of the officials is evidently intended to be Wallis Budge:

> All the angry gentlemen had abruptly sat down on the Museum steps except the nice one. He stood with his hands in his pockets just as though he was quite used to seeing great stone bulls and all sorts of small Babylonish objects float out into the Museum yard. But he sent a man to close the big iron gates.
>
> A journalist, who was just leaving the museum, spoke to Robert as he passed.
>
> 'Theosophy, I suppose?' he said. 'Is she Mrs Besant?'
>
> '*Yes*,' said Robert recklessly.

The event is duly reported next day under the headline 'Mrs Besant and Theosophy: Impertinent Miracle at the British Museum'. The absurd identification of the Babylonian Queen as Edith's old friend performing a theosophical miracle is an amusing touch.[26]

Wallis Budge, always the opportunist, enjoyed Edith's visits – he found her quick and intelligent, with a delightful sense of humour. She, in turn, was fascinated and excited by what he told her of ancient Egypt, its magic, religion and literature. Gradually their friendship became a love affair (he also was married) and, as they grew more intimate, she began to talk about her troubles – her anxieties about her children and the house, Bland's infidelities, her disillusion with marriage ('two animals mating for animal purposes,' she told him) and of her search for love – she left him with the impression that she had never really found it. He told Doris Langley Moore many years later that he thought her a pitiful, unfulfilled woman, emotionally starved. His account of her sounds odd, and indeed surprising considering how much admiration and love she had received: did he simply misjudge her, or did she, in certain moods, feel that she never really had found 'true love' (whatever that may mean)? Something he said or something in his manner may have encouraged her to indulge in an uncharacteristic self-pity, and he in turn may have remembered that aspect of her when he had forgotten others.

When she looked back on her life in company with her family or other friends, she would always say how interesting it had been and how much fun, and that she would gladly live it all through again; yet Wallis Budge's impression corresponds to something – a tension or disappointment – that can be glimpsed in her expression in later photographs. Though she was still attractive, her looks were beginning to coarsen, and though she still enjoyed the devotion of Richard Reynolds, she now had more platonic or patronizing friendships than love affairs. It is also possible that Wallis Budge adopted his distinctly condescending view of her in self-defence, because she had somehow made him feel threatened. She was certainly inclined to make demands that he could not or would not meet – for example, she wanted him to visit her at Well Hall, which he felt unable to do under the circumstances of his marriage and hers. Perhaps she had wanted to show him off to Hubert. At any rate he had not wanted to be shown. More alarmingly she asked him to go away with her – as she had done with Shaw and Richard le Gallienne, and perhaps others as well. When he told her it was out of the question, she wept bitterly. Apparently they met two or three times more after that, and then an archaeological expedition to Egypt took Wallis Budge abroad and terminated a friendship that was threatening to become an embarrassment.[27]

How serious had she been in asking Wallis Budge to take her away from Hubert, Well Hall and her family? Was it merely some kind of a love test? And if he had actually agreed, would she have risked the public disapprobation involved? How desperate was she to escape? That she toyed with the idea throughout her married life is evident, but was it much more than a fantasy that she indulged, always knowing in her inmost mind that it was safe to do so? Perhaps it was the request she made of the men she was least sure of. We do not know whether she put the same request to Richard Reynolds who, according to her family, was violently in love with her and might even have agreed. From childhood, her first reaction to unhappiness had been to want to run away from it, and she had run away from school on several occasions. Escaping or running away provides a recurrent element in her romantic novels, while the theme of imprisonment or entrapment, something many people become painfully conscious of in middle age, dominates the children's books written at this stage of her life: it was to be evident in *The Railway Children*, and *The Amulet* involved a number of hair's breadth escapes from tight places – a Babylonian dungeon below the Euphrates, Atlantis about to be engulfed by a tidal wave and a Phoenician ship heading for the rocks. Later in *The Enchanted Castle* Kathleen is imprisoned by being turned to stone, while in the two books that followed, *The House of Arden* and *Harding's Luck*, Father and Uncle Jim are imprisoned in the Andes, the children are imprisoned in the Tower and Dicky is imprisoned in a Deptford slum as well as within his own crippled body, from which he escapes into the past.

While escape is obviously a basic ingredient of many fairy-tales and adventure stories, the events of her magic books tend to conform to a particular sequence which, in turn, may reflect a particular experience pattern: the stories begin in the grey everyday world, which is then transformed by magic; sooner or later the magic itself becomes threatening, entrapping or imprisoning, and the protagonists are usually glad to be released from it, back into the old familiar world, which may not have changed, even though they themselves have done. Edith's marriage to Hubert could be regarded as a wish-fulfilment that had turned into an entrapment – perhaps there is an element of this particular sequence in every love affair or marriage in which love and demands are returned. Increasingly her children's books and stories found happy endings in the restoration of absent or missing parents, and especially that of the lost father. The children want to find the amulet because it will grant their hearts' desire, their parents' safe return. The ideal, the shadow lover that Edith had sought for in vain through Hubert and all the others may, at a deeper level, have been equated with her dimly remembered father.

If *The Amulet* ends with the fulfilment of a private happiness, the book as a whole is concerned to point the connections between the achievement of private happiness and a public life conducive to it. In chapter ten, 'The Little Black Girl and Julius Caesar', the children find a black-clad orphan in St James's Park, whose mother has died and whose father has turned to drink – a slum child straight from the heart-wrenching pages of Hesba Stretton. The psammead takes her back to ancient Britain where she finds a loving mother. When Anthea asks, 'But why *here*? why *now*?', the psammead crossly replies, ' "You don't suppose any one would want a child like that in *your* times – in *your* towns? . . . You've got your country into such a mess that there's no room for half your children – and no one to want them." '

The Queen of Babylon, arrived in Edwardian London, also makes some harsh criticisms of the state of its inhabitants, as the children take her for a cab ride:

> 'But how badly you keep your slaves. How wretched and poor and neglected they seem,' she said, as the cab rattled along the Mile End Road.
>
> 'They aren't slaves; they're working-people,' said Jane.
>
> 'Of course they're working-people. That's what slaves are. Don't you tell me. Do you suppose I don't know a slave's face when I see it? Why don't their masters see that they're better fed and better clothed? . . . You'll have a revolt of your slaves if you're not careful,' said the Queen.
>
> 'Oh, no,' said Cyril; 'you see they have votes – that makes them safe not to revolt. It makes all the difference. Father told me so.'
>
> 'What is this vote?' asked the Queen. 'Is it a charm? What do they do with it?'
>
> 'I don't know,' said the harassed Cyril; 'it's just a vote, that's all! They don't do anything particular with it.'
>
> 'I see,' said the Queen; 'a sort of plaything. Well, I wish that all these slaves may have in their hands this moment their fill of their favourite meat and drink.'

This passage voices the Blands' scepticism about democracy and the value of political rights; it also dramatizes the social criticisms of Ruskin and Morris who saw modern industrial workers as subject to a slavery, 'a thousand times more bitter and more degrading than that of the scourged African, or helot Greek.'[28] The comparison drawn here between modern London and ancient Babylon, where the masters had been concerned for their slaves' well-being out of the merest self-interest, is pessimistic, though ancient Egypt also suffers from the oppression of the workers. The Queen in her radical innocence finally commands her guards to massacre the gentlemen of the Stock Exchange, the creators and upholders of capitalism and the pillars of this unjust society. Among them, incidentally, would have been Paul Bland.

Both the Queen of Babylon and the psammead can voice criticisms of dingy, degraded Edwardian London with all the detachment and force of independent outsiders. Another kind of criticism is provided by the accounts of other, and more beautiful civilizations – Babylon, at the height of its empire 'was very different to London . . . There were terraces, and gardens, and balconies, and open spaces with trees.' As well as Babylon, the children visit Tyre and Atlantis, whose capital, according to Plato, was another great and well-ordered city with an elaborate system of walls and canals. From his Dialogues Edith took her detailed description of a city symmetrically laid out and gleaming with its special metal, 'oricalchum'. All three ancient towns provide a sharp contrast to dirty, noisy, smelly London, where everything 'seems to be patched up out of odds and ends'. Edith had begun *The Amulet* in 1903, but she did not set about completing it until it had been sold to *The Strand*, in 1905. One particular book published that year had dwelt on the filth and squalor of modern London, contrasting them with the vision of civic beauty that it might yet become; this was her friend H. G. Wells's *A Modern Utopia*. Here the narrator is translated into an alternative world, where there is justice and a good society, where people are no longer poor or sick or ill-dressed, and London has become a vision of cleanliness and beauty:

> We shall find ourselves in a sort of central space, rich with palms and flowering bushes and statuary. We shall look along an avenue of trees, down a wide gorge between the cliffs of crowded hotels, the hotels that are still glowing with internal lights, to where the shining morning river streams dawnlit out to sea.[29]

In the twelfth chapter of *The Amulet*, 'The Sorry-Present and the Expelled Little Boy' (first published in *The Strand* in February 1906), the children travel into a brighter future, which to some extent balances the ideal examples of civic order that they have encountered in the past. Passing through the familiar doors of the British Museum in the future, they find themselves in a beautiful public park whose sunlit greenery and marble fountains closely recall the last moments of Wells's Utopia, before the hero is abruptly transported back to the 'sullen roar' and 'filthy, torn paper' of modern London. In this chapter, Edith rewrites *A Modern Utopia* from the child's point of view, focusing upon the nature of schools and nurseries in this brave new world. Wells's influence on her account is gracefully acknowledged by naming the small boy whom the children befriend after him. Robert enquires of his mother:

> 'Why do you call him "Wells"?' . . .
> 'It's after the great reformer – surely you've heard of *him*? He lived in the dark ages, and he saw that what you ought to do is to find out what

Edith at forty-five, and at the height of her fame

Hubert at forty-five

Hubert with John at Dymchurch   Alice with John

Paris 1904: standing from left to right, Berta Ruck, Rosamund, Edith, Hubert, Miss Gleistein. Arthur Watts kneels in front of Edith. Iris seated, left, with an unidentified friend and Dorothea, right

Edith with her grand-daughter
Pandora, c. 1918

Edith at a wedding in 1915 (it
was for Harry and Adelaide
who worked at Well Hall)

"Skipper" (T.T. Tucker, Edith's second husband)

Her grave at St. Mary's in the Marsh

you want and then try to get it. Up to then people had always tried to tinker up what they'd got. We've got a great many of the things he thought of . . .'[30]

If Edith had borrowed from Wells (and a few months earlier she had written to him, 'I've read your Utopia again. I don't disagree as much as I thought'), she had done so openly and boldly. Although she had reworked his vision in the obviously different (though equally Wellsian) context of time travel, her book's central theme – the search for happiness, signified literally by the complete amulet, and meta-phorically by a just society – makes Wells's Utopia particularly relevant since his book had been concerned to show how the achievement of personal happiness depends on living in a society which permits and even actively promotes personal fulfilment. In a symbolic moment near the end of Wells's *A Modern Utopia*, the botanist's unhappy and inappropriately possessive passion interferes with and finally actually destroys his vision of Utopia itself.[31] The link that Wells perceived between personal fulfilment and civic and social improvement made his vision dovetail neatly into the whole scheme of *The Amulet*, even though Edith did not read *A Modern Utopia* (which was first serialized in the *Fortnightly Review* and then published in 1905) until after she had written the early instalments of her own book.

The question of Edith's borrowings is a complex one, because while she drew on other books extensively and usually very openly, she bitterly resented it when she suspected other authors of plagiarising from her. In January 1906, alongside the ninth episode of *The Amulet*, *The Strand* published the first chapter of Kipling's *Puck of Pook's Hill*, 'Weland's Sword'. It was illustrated by Claude Shepperson, since H. R. Millar was currently working on *The Amulet*, though he later provided the illustrations for the published book. For four months, the two serials ran side by side, and Edith who until then had been an ardent admirer of Kipling, now privately accused him of pinching her ideas and even her treatment of them. She wrote indignantly to H. G. Wells, 'I say – do read Kipling in the January *Strand* and read my *Five Children and It* – will you?' She cited his own verses in support of her accusation, regarding them as an explicit confession on his part:

> When 'Omer smote 'is bloomin' lyre,
>   He'd 'eard men sing by land an' sea;
> An' what he thought 'e might require,
>   'E went an' took – the same as me! . . .

They knew 'e stole; 'e knew they knowed.
They didn't tell, nor make a fuss,
But winked at 'Omer down the road,
An' 'e winked back – the same as us!³²

Edith's admiration for Kipling's work dated back at least as far as the 1890s when she and Oswald Barron had dedicated their volume of short stories, *The Butler in Bohemia* (1894), to him. Two years later she had written to him to ask whether he would be willing to contribute to a children's magazine that she was planning at that time, though the project never really got off the ground; she also invited him to one of the 'crab and cream' dinners given in Oswald Barron's rooms at the Temple. Kipling was evidently one of the many enthusiasms she shared with Barron. But his reputation rapidly declined after the turn of the century, and by 1910 Hubert could chart 'The Decadence of Rudyard Kipling' in his newspaper column; Edith subsequently included the piece among Hubert's posthumously published *Essays*. Though John Bland thought he remembered Kipling having visited Well Hall, he was misled by a memory of one of Kipling's old school friends, George Beresford (M'Turk in *Stalky and Co.*) who had become a Fabian and, according to Shaw, had been a friend of the Blands from Blackheath days. In fact Edith never actually met Kipling, who was deeply shy, and had his social life very carefully organized for him by his wife.³³ But he clearly reciprocated her admiration: two long and characteristically whimsical letters written to her in 1903 and 1904 describe the pleasure given by *The Psammead*, and later by *The Phoenix and the Carpet*, of which she had sent him a copy.

The first was written from South Africa on 11 March 1903 in response to a letter from her:

Your letter of the 15th Feb. comes out to me here, but not *The Red House*. I will go into Cape Town and get it from the bookseller.

It has been on the tip of my pen to write you again and again – on the *Wouldbegoods several* times because I laughed over them riotously; but more particularly about the Psammead yarns.

My kiddies are five and seven (they can't read, thank goodness) and they took an interest in the Psammead stories – a profound and practical interest. Their virgin minds never knew one magazine from another till it dawned upon Elsie that 'a thing called the Strand' 'with a blue cover and a cab' was where the Psammead tales lived. Since which, as the advertisement says, I knew no peace.

I have been sent for *Strands* in the middle of the month, I have had to explain their non-arrival; and I have had to read them when they came. They were a dear delight to the nursery and they were discussed and rediscussed in all possible lights. You see *we* have a sandpit in our garden and there was always a chance of a Psammead!

I wish I could tell you what joy it gave them and how they revelled in the fun of it. A kiddy laughing at a joke is one of the sweetest sights under heaven and our nursery used to double up and rock with mirth. They were very indignant when the stories came to an end . . . They liked best the magic gold and the attempt to buy horses and carriages, and next to that the growing up of the baby.

In another year I shall give 'em the *Wouldbegoods* again. They've had bits of it, but it doesn't appeal, like the Psammead, to their years. If it isn't impertinence to say so I've been watching your work and seeing it settle and clarify and grow tender (this sounds like a reviewer but it isn't) with great comfort and appreciation.[34]

In October 1904, Edith sent Kipling *The Phoenix and the Carpet*, and received an even more mannered thank-you letter from him; he was now settled at Bateman's, his home in Sussex for the rest of his life. 'The nursery' has been elevated to 'the schoolroom':

I take the present of yr book about Carpets in a kind spirit though it has not done me much good personally and the trouble and fuss in the past on account of forgetfulness when I was ordered to buy serial *Strands* at the Station which is all of three (3) miles uphill you should have known to have appreciated. My orders were that any time I went that way to bring back a *Strand* and you know owing I presume to Sir G. Newnes's stinginess the Publication only comes out once a month but that didn't matter to them worth a cuss on account of their Innocence and I had to explain that too. Besides they couldn't read and though I said they might begin Education by reading out of the stray numbers as I bought them they wouldn't do that either but they got the Governess to read to them and me afterwards (not more than three times) and their mother just all the time and it came to fighting over looking at the pictures and splitting the *Strand* down Sir George Newnes's back cover so when the book came all in one piece I didn't say much in their direction but took hold of it on purpose to read and admire . . . but I no sooner had got it than both the two of them found out by watching the Post I suppose and they have Jumped it and took it off already and God knows I am sorry for the Governess first and me after and their mother too because it will all have to be read over again. They done just precisely the same about the Psammead whose title should not have been Five Children and It because everyone calls him by his own Christian name. I forget if I wrote you this on its appearance. It is criticism and I trust you will not be vexed: but a name is just as important to a Book as a Baby as it is born more frequent.

The consequence is they are highly delighted in the School Room though they say they knew it all before and they want a lot more of the same sort quick. I am to tell you this and I am to send you their love.

I am, Yours respectfully,
        Rudyard Kipling

P.S. If next time you publish you could run it off in a weekly it would be handier for me fetching it from the station as keeping them quieter between times.

P.P.S. The one they liked best was about the Cook and the Burglar. Children are given to crime from youth up.[35]

A final and much briefer note thanks Edith for the collection of stories *Oswald Bastable and Others* which she had sent Kipling in November 1905, two months before *Puck* appeared:

Many thanks for the more Oswald. I have got it under lock and key because of the children. They are going to have it not before Xmas: though I think they know some of the stories. They have been following the Psammead in the *Strand* and I think Mollie and the Missing will have by that means come in their way. But I've enjoyed it all, every word of it . . .[36]

Her assumption that in *The Amulet* she had hit upon a highly original idea in sending her children into the past by magic was surely justified. Fictional children had tumbled down rabbit holes, visited fairyland, or gone small or swift – her own five had flown on a magic carpet – but time travel was another matter. Wells's Time Traveller had explored the future, but not the past, and yet here was Kipling, some eight months after herself, using a sharp-tongued fairy not wholly unlike her own psammead to conduct two modern children into British prehistory. His timing, she felt, told its own story. Yet had she known more about Kipling's methods of work, she would have realized that it was precisely the closeness with which his serial followed hers that exonerated him: Kipling was, by this stage of his career, a very slow writer. Edith often composed her episodes for *The Strand* at the last possible minute; Kipling, on the other hand, though he had written with a comparable speed when young, now worked slowly and painstakingly. He is thought to have started *Puck* as early as September 1904 and to have written at least half of it before it began to appear in *The Strand* in January 1906.[37]

The other crucial evidence of independence is Kipling's very different method of introducing the past. In Edith's stories of time magic, the children travel directly into the past, which can give rise to metaphysical problems as to whether their appearance there can actually affect the course of history: for example, did the children's encounter with Caesar persuade him to invade Britain just at the moment when he seemed to have decided against it?

> 'And if you hadn't told Caesar all that about how things are now, he'd never have invaded Britain,' said Robert to Jane as they sat down to tea.
> 'Oh, nonsense,' said Anthea, pouring out; 'it was all settled hundreds of years ago.'[38]

Kipling uses a more tactful as well as a more traditional method, for his Puck brings people from the past to relate their experiences to Dan and Una in a dreamlike present. Swift had made use of a comparable device in Book Three of *Gulliver's Travels*, where the necromancers of the magic island of Glubbdubdrib called up the ghosts of great men of the past and engaged them in conversation, and long before Swift, Homer's Odysseus had summoned up the dead from Hades to speak. Though Kipling entirely suppressed the sinister aspect of the process, he had evidently started *Puck of Pook's Hill* with the idea that recognisable figures would emerge from the past to tell their stories. This is born out by Kipling's own account, in his autobiographical memoir *Something of Myself*, of the several false starts he had made during the book's composition:

> I wrote a tale told by Daniel Defoe in a brickyard . . . It turned out a painstaken and meritorious piece of work, overloaded with verified references, with about as much feeling to it as a walking-stick. So it also was discarded, with a tale of Doctor Johnson telling the children how he had once thrown his spurs out of a boat in Scotland, to the amazement of one Boswell. Evidently my Daemon would not function in brickyards or schoolrooms.[39]

If Kipling did conceive *Puck* entirely independently of *The Amulet*, as seems probable, their similarities are striking, though a few of these can be attributed to a common source in the (now wholly forgotten) novels of Edwin Arnold: in *Phra the Phoenician* (1891) and *Lepidus the Centurion* (1901), the past is explored through reincarnation. The influence of *Phra* is apparent in the extraneous last chapter of *The Amulet* where the children and Rekh-Mara find themselves at Tyre and then on board a Tyrian trading ship bound for the Cornish silver mines. Kipling, like Edith, had read Edwin Arnold, and their common interest in Phoenician galleys and Roman centurions is the result of Arnold's impact on them both.[40]

Edith may have been feeling somewhat over-wrought when *Puck of Pook's Hill* began to appear in *The Strand* in January 1906, for she had been working on *The Amulet* and *The Railway Children* simultaneously for the last eight months and the strain of keeping the two serials going through the summer and autumn of 1905 had been intense. She had never been in the habit of turning work away, but now she had more than she could comfortably manage. At this period of her life, when her creative efforts were at their height, she was more than ever inclined to fly into a temper or make a scene, although afterwards she would always be full of remorse for what she had said or done. The worst rows, when she retreated furiously to her room and banged the door, were known in the family as 'spreading blight', and had, by then, become a not uncommon domestic hazard. They were often precipitated by the unexpected absence, for example on a walk, of one of her favourites. Her children were now grown up and leading lives of their own; sometimes they wanted their friends to themselves; they would all slip away from the Duchess's dominating presence, and so provoke a 'blight'.

Berta Ruck recalled one such occasion during the summer of 1905:

There was one epic example of it at the Blands' holiday home (the 'Other House'), at Dymchurch . . . Generally it was house full as at Well Hall. Iris, Mr Richard Reynolds, and I had disappeared immediately after lunch for a long walk *without telling the Duchess*. She was 'involved' (i.e. writing). I don't know what kept us. Maybe we had found our way to what we flippantly called 'some haunt of gilded vice' such as an A.B.C. shop in Folkestone. We returned to find that Blight had spread, and thickly. The Duchess gave us one withering glance, and went silently back into her work-room. We were miserable.

After an hour, perhaps, that felt endless, she came out waving a sheet of paper which she put into my hand. The verses described the anxiety which we had made her suffer from three until half past six:

A Forgiveness

The Other House has curtains straight and red
 Like lashes fringing eyes set far apart;
It looks attractive: no one would have said
 To look at it, it held a breaking heart.

Yes so it was – from three to half-past six,
　　An anxious heart – which same belonged to me
Beat heavily: my mind refused to fix
　　On anything. I went without my tea.

My wandering thoughts perceived my Iris dear
　　Upon her head stand moveless in some dyke.
I saw my Reynolds overcome with beer,
　　My Berta in convulsions – or the like . . .

Repent! 'Tis all I ask! I don't insist
　　On tears, apologies or grovellings vain:
By red Remorse I would not have you kissed –
　　　　I merely ask, in a humble spirit, that you
　　　　will kindly let me know next time you are
　　　　going out to tea – (then I won't have any got
　　　　ready for you) and don't cause me such
　　　　agonies of anxiety *again*.[41]

The verses reveal a subtle mixture of annoyance and embarrassment at having made such a fuss about nothing – the absurd fates she imagines for each of them only thinly conceal the silliness of supposing that anything at all had happened to a group of adults out for a walk, other than mere forgetfulness. A similar scene took place a year or so later when the young Hester Radford went for a walk with another of Edith's favourites, the artist Gerald Spencer Pryse, and they did not return in time for the next meal. In both instances Edith's anxiety seems to have been little more than an excuse to cover up her resentment at being left out of a party of which she always wanted to be the life and soul. She was still the spoilt youngest child, asserting her right to the full attention and thought of everyone else. At the same time she had some excuse – she was under great pressure and understandably felt hurt when, after an afternoon of hard work, she came down to find that everyone had gone out and forgotten all about her – especially when it was her work that made the holiday possible in the first place. Her admirers, Berta Ruck amongst them, recognized that her 'blights' were merely the reverse side of a temperament that could radiate sunshine, warmth and charm, whose brilliance justified the black as well as the bright moments. And she was always full of remorse afterwards. When she was in a calmer frame of mind, she was capable of being unusually thoughtful about other people's feelings: sensing that Berta Ruck's mother was slightly jealous of her (quasi-maternal) friendship with Berta, she accepted an invitation to stay with

Berta's parents for a week at the end of October 1905. Colonel Ruck was Constable of Caernarvonshire, and while she was there, he took her on a prison tour. She rather upset the prison Governor by talking to the inmates, and, after engaging one in conversation for some minutes, parted from him with the tactful and friendly words, 'I wish you well'.[42]

Though Edith enjoyed the success her children's stories had brought her, she also resented it somewhat, disliking the way they threatened to eclipse her achievements as a poet and a novelist, rather as Conan Doyle had resented the success of Sherlock Holmes. Since children's books (and detective stories, for that matter) had no status as serious literature, to earn popularity in such a genre could be regarded as more of a slight than a compliment. She wrote to her agent, J. B. Pinker, 'I wish you could get me an order for a serial for grown-up people – something like the *Red House*. I don't think it is good for my style to write *nothing* but children's stuff.'[43]

In 1906 she published four books: in addition to *The Amulet* and *The Railway Children*, there was the romantic novel that she had begun work on in Paris, *The Incomplete Amorist*, and another book of romantic short stories, *Man and Maid*. *The Amulet* was dedicated to Wallis Budge, who had helped her so much with it. *The Railway Children* was dedicated to Paul, who had always enjoyed train spotting, and had supplied her with details about different types of engines. *The Incomplete Amorist* came in two editions, the first dedicated to Berta Ruck, while a subsequent one was jointly dedicated to Justus Miles Forman and Richard Reynolds, whom she may have had in mind as the prototypes of the Amorist and his reliable friend. *Man and Maid* was dedicated to Ada Breakell who had recently moved to Well Hall to be near her old friend once more. Though she loved making new friends, Edith showed loyalty and constancy to the old ones. Having worked so hard, she realized that she must have some respite from the monthly demands imposed by serial-writing, so from June till December 1906, when the first episode of *The Enchanted Castle* appeared in *The Strand*, she took a break from writing her usual monthly instalments for them; it was the last she would take for another five years.

During the summer of 1906 the young poet, Gerald Gould, first made the acquaintance of E. Nesbit, the well-known children's writer. Four years earlier he had come across some of the Bastable stories in old magazines while convalescing from a serious illness and had been enchanted by them, so he was excited when his friend, Clifford Sharp, offered to take him down to Well Hall to meet her. The two young men found her in the garden where she spent so many long Edwardian summers:

> I can see her now as vividly as I saw her then. She was sitting in a comfortable chair on the lawn of Well Hall – a majestic, ample figure, clad in a flowing robe of green, and festooned with a long and tangled scarf; her arms heavy with bangles: on her knee the inevitable box of tobacco, out of which she spun an endless chain of cigarettes: in her mouth the longest cigarette-holder in the world; at her feet, in an attitude of easy indolence, a delightfully but austerely handsome young man.

Gould, then only twenty-one, thought her – at forty-eight – charming and still attractive; though she looked her age, she did not seem to be in the least self-conscious about it. She, in turn, quickly discovered that he wrote poetry and had published a book of poems, *Lyrics*, earlier that year; she asked to see it and at once appointed herself his literary adviser and patron. Privately, he thought her inclined to overestimate the work of some, at least, of her young protégés, the weakest of whom had little or no talent.

She increasingly needed the stimulus of lively and creative young people around her, and encouraging them or helping them to sell their work provided a framework within which she had something to offer and they had something to gain. She liked to influence and 'mother' them in a way that could be rather stifling. On one occasion, when she and Gerald Gould were waiting for an underground train and she was being unbearably maternal, he could take no more and simply crept away. But despite the occasional rift, he grew very fond of Edith, whom he greatly admired; and he was unusual among her admirers in being equally impressed by Hubert: Bland's handsome appearance, powerful intellect and forceful personality made a dazzling combination, he thought. He was impressed by Hubert's ability to interest his *Sunday Chronicle* readers, many of them North country artisans, in such unpromising topics as Hegel's philosophy of the state. Yet good though his journalism was, Gould thought that Hubert's real talents came out only in conversation, lectures and debates.[44]

In addition to their parties, the Blands still regularly held a Sunday evening symposium; wherever she had lived, Edith had always loved organizing debating societies and salons of various kinds. At the

symposium some interesting person would open an informal debate
before an audience of perhaps forty listeners – among those who spoke
were H. G. Wells, G. K. and Cecil Chesterton, Hilaire Belloc, Shaw,
and the young Fabian, Clifford Sharp, who had first introduced Gould
to Well Hall. For Hubert, who cared less for parties, these occasions
provided an opportunity to show off his paces at his favourite
competitive skill, for Edith an opportunity to assemble all her clever
and delightful friends around her.

10
RECONSTRUCTING THE PAST

In 1893 George MacDonald wrote in his essay on 'The Fantastic Imagination': 'To be able to live a moment in an imagined world, we must see the laws of its existence obeyed. Those broken, we fall out of it.'[1] Whether Edith, who admired MacDonald, had read this essay or whether she knew it by instinct or observation, all her best work acknowledges its truth: fantasy, to be persuasive – and certainly to be comic – must be structured by rules: not the rules of everyday life but its own equivalent limits and taboos. *Five Children and It* was a carefully regulated fantasy in which the children's wishes had operated rather as the liberating aspirations and adventures of the Bastables had done – closely held in check by the laws of daily existence. *The Phoenix and the Carpet* was more loosely controlled and had included episodes set in India and on a South Sea island, recreated from books rather than from experience. *The Amulet* had taken the children considerably further afield but the imaginary past they visited was at least informed by historical knowledge. Her next serial for *The Strand*, *The Enchanted Castle* (1907), showed the reins on her imagination slackened as never before. The result was a story that has often captivated its readers, though it disappointed its author. Allowing imagination free play meant allowing childhood memories and traumas to surface, and this book more than any other reviews and re-engages with the darker experiences of childhood: the children, Kathleen, Jimmy and Gerald, have been left at school during the holidays (an experience Edith always recalled with misery); in the park of the castle the children come upon the huge stone dinosaurs from the Crystal Palace, as well as the classical gods that she had first fallen in love with in the Greek Court of the Great Exhibition; the dummies the children make to provide an audience for their play are identical with those Edith had made to exorcise *the* mummies; magic brings them to fearful life.[2] *The Enchanted Castle* becomes an exposition of the dangers of imagination in free flight; its central motif is the story of Beauty and the Beast (or Cupid and Psyche),[3] a fairy-tale particularly concerned with the power of fear, as well as the power of love to heal and restore.

Though it had not always brought her happiness, Edith still cherished an intensely romantic, not to say sentimental view of love as the binding force of the universe, the force that can outface even death itself. Her novels and stories for adults are mainly love stories, but, in keeping with the conventions of romantic fiction, these could not deal with her actual experiences as a wife seeking love outside marriage. Adultery in fiction could never be condoned or seen as consoling and even delightful or inspiring, as it had been for her in life. Instead her stories conformed to the patterns expected of current romantic fiction by presenting young girls and their problems in choosing the right husband and settling down to marriage and a happy-ever-after. Sometimes, as in *The Red House* or *The Incredible Honeymoon*, she wrote of the earliest days of a happy marriage, yet here as well, her adult fiction embodies rather too directly the fantasy of being a love object, worshipped and idolized by a devoted admirer. It is surprising how often she succeeded in reproducing this situation in real life; her preferred modes of address – 'Madame' or 'Duchess' – successors to the 'Princess' of her youth, tell the same story.

Unlike her poetry, much of her adult fiction reflects something of her characteristic charm and energy, and can still be read with pleasure and amusement, but its refusal to treat adult passion except within severely cramping limits amounts to a fatal weakness since its central concern is with exactly those feelings it cannot plausibly present. In writing for children, however, such constraints became insignificant; her children's books widened the range of themes available, rather than operating inside existing boundaries. Yet even here sentimental love was not entirely neglected – *The Wouldbegoods* had related the love story of Albert's Uncle and his Long Lost Grandmother, while confining it within Oswald's impatience with such adult absurdities. But as her children's books grew steadily more serious in tone, more complex in structure and more ambitious in scope, she increasingly turned to major themes – social injustice, civic reform, love and reconstruction – for inspiration; the theme of restoration or recovery of what had been lost, forgotten or destroyed came to dominate these later books. In them, terror, death and loss intrude in a way that they had not done before, and their magic is of rather a different kind – it carries religious overtones and might even be termed 'numinous.'

The Enchanted Castle returns to the earlier theme of the danger of granted wishes, elaborately counterpointing make-believe and reality. The book begins with the most complex switchback of magic and games that she had yet invented: one minute the children are playing 'let's pretend', the next their pretence has come true and they are caught up in a sequence of transformations that symbolically enact the dangers as well as the pleasures of the imagination. The author seems to have drawn a distinction in her own mind between 'magic', which was either good or neutral, and 'enchantment', which was in some way sinister. In *The Enchanted Castle* all the usual barriers between reality and imagination are down, and the children are confronted by an uncontrollable world in which fantasies are acted out. There is no longer the saving truce at sunset, when the wishes granted by the psammead dissolved. Here, things grow worse after dark: the stone dinosaurs and statues come to life by moonlight, and a ghost appears with his head under his arm, yet another unwelcome response to a spoken wish. The dinosaurs are, of course, identical with those that Edith had climbed inside as a child, as Kathleen does in the story. Part of the pleasure in doing so was the reassurance it offered that they were no more than hollow stone, a reassurance here denied since after dark the monstrous statues awaken and lumber down to the lake to drink. The book consists of a series of alarming swings between the familiar and the world of nightmare, a nightmare always threatening to become reality.

The terror of the inanimate suddenly starting into an appalling life was a favourite theme of Edith's fiction: in her most memorable ghost story, 'Man-Size in Marble', the evil Crusaders on a stone tomb descend from the church on Hallowe'en to destroy a helpless young woman. In *The Enchanted Castle*, Phoebus tells the children:

> 'In your beautiful temples, . . . the images of your priests and of your warriors who lie cross-legged on their tombs come alive and walk in their marble about their temples, and through the woods and fields. But only on one night in all the year can any see them.'[4]

But the worst of the book's terrors are the Ugly-Wuglies, the scarecrows assembled out of bolsters, umbrellas, broomsticks and coat-hangers, held in by hats, coats and gloves, with painted paper masks for faces. Made up to provide an extra audience for the children's play, they are brought to a shuffling, zombie-like life by yet another ill-thought-out wish. They are that ultimate in childhood terror – the not-person, the shape that looks alive but isn't, the dressing gown on the back of a door or the dress draped over a chair that terrifies the sleepy or delirious child.

Mrs Ringland, a friend from Dymchurch, remembered Edith making some Ugly-Wuglies as part of a game of charades, and carefully kept one of their painted paper masks as a memento. She assumed that Mrs Bland had invented them for the occasion and subsequently introduced them into this story,[5] but in fact the Dymchurch dummies were only the most recent in a long line of 'mummies' that Edith had made; their predecessors had been intended to exorcise memories of the crypt at Bordeaux. These coat-hangered, skeletal constructions, parodies of their originals, bones covered with rags of decomposing clothes and flesh, were created in an effort to master their terror through familiarity, as were the skull and bones that she kept around the house as an adult, ostensibly to familiarize her children with them. That the 'mummies' nevertheless retained something of the horror of their originals is evident from their appearance in *The Enchanted Castle*, where they fill both the children and onlookers with irrational terror. Their well-modulated voices, asking politely for a good hotel, come from paper faces, and they have no roofs to their mouths. This vividly horrible detail suggests not only the emptiness of the puppet ('the speaker had no inside to his head'), but of the hollow skull that inspired it. The Ugly-Wuglies are also the dead, and when the children try to shut them up in the tunnel behind the Temple of Flora (a tunnel strongly suggestive of the unconscious), they become angry, vengeful and genuinely dangerous. Previously they had been appalling but harmless; once shut away, a change comes over them: they manifest the traditional malevolence of the dead towards the living, and strike down the adult who releases them. At the same time the Ugly-Wuglies seem to symbolize a very different kind of horror – the emptiness of the bourgeoisie, uttering meaningless noises, remaining thoroughly respectable and anxious to find a good hotel, reliably recommended, and displaying, in their search, a complex mixture of credulity and suspicion. The most respectable of them all turns out to be 'something big in the city', a well-known stockbroker and rival of Jimmy, the little boy who becomes a repulsive elderly gentleman when he thoughtlessly wishes to be rich. The book ends with a newspaper announcement of the mysterious disappearance of Mr U. W. Ugli; the suggestion that, beneath the spell of appearances, stockbrokers are no more than empty bundles of clothes, or else greedy little boys, recalls the Babylonian Queen's ruthless massacre of members of the Stock Exchange in *The Amulet*.[6]

But if the imagination is self-affrighting, it is also self-delighting; the magic ring which, like stepping into a dream, makes awesome things seem familiar, enables the children to attend a feast of the gods. At the last, unbearable terror is transformed into unbearable beauty and both are finally subsumed in love. The children, Lord Yalding and his long-lost sweetheart find themselves in the Hall of Psyche. When the children had visited the hall earlier, it appeared to each one of them to be built in a different architectural style, thus embodying further memories of the courts at the Crystal Palace – Moorish, Egyptian and Greek. The Greek courts had included the statues of Venus and Hermes which inspired the banquet of the gods that the children attend. Here they meet Phoebus, Hebe, Aphrodite Urania ('with a voice like mother's at those moments when you love her most') and Eros ('a really nice boy, as the girls instantly agreed'), as well as Psyche herself.[7] Though the story of Cupid and Psyche is never directly referred to, elements of it seem to recur throughout – the motif of invisibility, of the lost loved one, the combination of terror and love that accompanies divine visitations, even the enchanted castle itself, while the nursery version of the myth, Beauty and the Beast, is the subject of the play acted before the audience of Ugly-Wuglies. How far Edith was conscious of this underlying motif is hard to decide; some of the writing here is so careless and perfunctory as to suggest that at moments she had altogether lost interest in her narrative. It nevertheless embodies with a special clarity and force the theme that prompted so much of her best writing and was especially appropriate to childhood – the inextricably mingled dangers and delights of the imagination.

In January 1906, as the first episode of *The Enchanted Castle* appeared in *The Strand*, romance was in the air at Well Hall. Rosamund had always had men buzzing round her, but now Iris had at last acquired a serious suitor: Austin Philips was a civil servant some six years older than herself, the son of the Postmaster of Manchester; she probably met him through her cousin Dorothea, who had grown up in Manchester, though Austin himself, after serving in South Africa, was now Postmaster at Droitwich.[8] Iris had been ill before

Christmas with suspected appendicitis; when she was better, Edith wrote to H. G. Wells and his wife, in reply to their invitation to Sandgate, explaining that she had to take Iris to visit him instead:

> You know my dears, I can't help it about Droitwich. Chaperoning lovers is 'no cop' as Miss Ruck would say. But of course when Iris *can* go away I must do what she would like best, and she wants to see her sweetheart.

Iris was married just over a year later, on 5 February 1907: 'Mother was not much engrossed in wedding preparations. There were very few,' she recalled. A year after that, she returned to Well Hall where she gave birth to a daughter, Pandora, on 27 January 1908, Paul having been despatched for the doctor at three in the morning. The baby was noisily healthy from the first, but Iris was quite ill and took a month or so to recover.[9] Her marriage was not, apparently, a success and she did not stay long in the new *ménage*. Back at home, she began work as a dressmaker, calling herself 'Madame Iris'. By 1912 she was running a small business from a flat in Rathbone Place, off Tottenham Court Road – the rent was shared with her mother. Berta Ruck recalled a conversation about her, many years later:

> I said to E.N. about Iris: 'Isn't it amazing, when she was a girl at the Slade having a good time she never seemed happy. Now, when she's had a perfectly hellish time, very hard up and very ill, she seems so much happier than she was then.'
>   E.N. said: 'Can't you see why? She has something to love now. The adored child, Pandora takes all her time and energy and fills her life.'

If Iris thrived on difficulties, she certainly had her fair share of them. Though her letters to Doris Langley Moore have the truthteller's asperity of tone, she was, when young, the most affectionate of the Bland children, and her mother's favourite.[10] The gentle Anthea and Roberta of *The Railway Children* are both to some extent portraits of her.

A month before Iris's wedding, on 14 January 1907, Maskelyne and Devant staged a fairy play that Edith had written around their conjuring tricks: *The Magician's Heart* was put on at St George's Hall, Langham Place. David Devant played Taykin, the wicked magician, whose heart was boiled to soften it, and he stage-managed several spectacular appearances and disappearances.[11] A few months after the wedding, the Blands paid another visit to Paris, this time taking Alice Hoatson, Arthur Watts ('Oswald in Paris') and Ambrose Flower, a

"THE MAGICIAN'S HEART,"

AN ORIGINAL FAIRY PLAY.

By E. NESBIT,

Author of "The Treasure Seekers," "The Wouldbegoods," "The Amulet," &c.

Scenery by SIGNOR TONDI.

PERSONS OF THE PLAY:

Princess Carina ..	.. Miss CASSIE BRUCE
Nurse ..	Mrs. HENRY BEDFORD
The King ..	.. Mr. J. B. HANSARD
The Prince of the Diamond Mountain	Mr. EDWARD MOREHEN
The Diminished Magician	Mr. F. TERRY
Gnome ..	Mr. A. BOOTH
Jester ..	Mr. E. ARNOLD-MUSSETT
James (Apprentice) ..	Mr. CHARLES GLENROSE

and

Professor Taykin (a Wicked Magician)	.. Mr. DAVID DEVANT

Ladies and Gentlemen of the Court, Guards, Slaves and others.

SCENE I.	**A Room in the Magician's Tower.**
(Five Minutes' Interval),	
SCENE II.	**The Palace Kitchen.**
(Five Minutes' Interval).	
SCENE III.	**The Throne Room.**

Stage Manager .. MR. NEVIL MASKELYNE.

Performances for Private Entertainments.

Maskelyne & Devant's Entertainment Bureau provides any class of Refined Entertainment. Send for list of Latest Novelties to

THE SECRETARY, ST. GEORGE'S HALL, W.

tall, slightly precious young man from Iris's Slade set, whom Edith had nicknamed 'Florizel'. Her combination of grandeur with a genuine contempt for authority and convention greatly amused Flower. He remembered visiting Versailles on a particularly hot day, and beating a retreat from the heat of the buildings:

It was in vain we looked for cool green carpets. We were, I remember, a gasping party of five – Miss Hoatson, Mr Bland, Arthur Watts, me and the Duchess – some of us youngsters used to call her that. Always she had the grand manner, the air, democrat though she was, and no Duchesse of the *ancien régime* was ever more in harmony with those terraces and parks and fountains of the Louis than she – although we had eaten our little yellow omelettes on rough white china, and drunk the sharp Vin Ordinaire that turns bright blue when spilled on the coarse white table cloth, in the little *auberge* beyond the gilded gates. Thirsting for the shade, we crossed those sandy plateaus and found at last a lovely place of cool dimness, great trees around and large fountain splashing in its wide basin. We sank on the marble seats, and the cool grass – yes, grass at last – was refreshment. But there were richer pleasures to be found: 'How wonderful to paddle in that fountain,' said the Duchess! And in the next breath, 'Let's!' In less than a minute she and I were in! Paddling in the 'Eaux de Versailles', my trousers turned up, her skirts about her knees as if it were Margate ...

This escapade was soon interrupted by the gendarmerie who came and hauled them out, though in quite a kindly fashion, out of consideration for the inexplicable follies of the English.

Ambrose Flower remembered Edith crossing swords with authority on another occasion when, on a very hot night, they visited the Comédie Française. In the intervals of a Victor Hugo melodrama, they hastened down the corridors of the theatre in search of some fresh air, but every time they tried to open a window, an officer on duty ordered them not to. They climbed higher and higher until they reached the Grand Foyer, where Edith, gasping for air and staging the fainting fit that had once been such a feature of Fabian meetings, finally persuaded some officers to open the two largest windows for her.

> But with her, we always had fun like that. More than anyone ever met she could create out of ordinary day-by-day affairs, incidents of fun, of romance, of beauty, of poetry.[12]

According to the young Fabian, Clifford Sharp, she had 'an altogether fascinating capacity for enjoying doing absurd things. *Any* adventure appealed to her.'

Such high spirits and sense of occasion in a woman old enough to be their mother appealed to several of Iris's Slade School contemporaries, especially to the poor but delightful Arthur Watts. From his flat in Fitzroy Square he wrote pleadingly to her:

> Heaven forbid that I should seem forward – but Jimmy [Horsnell] being here – and it being a very glorious evening and I having work to do that could only be done (I feel) at Dymchurch and Dymchurch alone – I make so bold as to suggest that you, he and I should spend another week like the one of a month ago. Oh Madame, Madame, London is no place for us in the spring – think of driving together to Aldington Knoll where the woods are all turning golden green! – and think of the great open sky and then London – and the S[outh] E[astern] R[ailway] and yes, you'll have to change at Blackheath.
>
> If we may come, wire to me here; if you have only eyes and ears for London, wire us our doom just the same, but in any case, forgive me for my cheek![13]

Arthur Watts introduced Edith to his friend Gerald Spencer Pryse, who had trained at the Central School of Art as a lithographer. With Arthur Watts, Spencer Pryse would cycle down to Dymchurch during the night, arriving unannounced next morning and without even a change of clothes: 'She always took it well,' Watts recalled; indeed she was childishly pleased by unexpected arrivals, and flattered that her young friends felt they could always rely on a welcome. Watts was struck, as Ambrose Flower and Berta Ruck had been, by her inconsistencies – her breadth of vision, combined with a physical primness that to his generation looked like prudishness, and her curious mixture of unusual tolerance and petty irritation.[14]

On one occasion, Arthur Watts and Spencer Pryse, with some other friends, built a raft out of old fencing, tarred it, set a wicker chair on it and invited her to go for a voyage across the moat. She accepted gracefully, climbing on board in her beautiful Liberty gown. The raft predictably capsized a few minutes later under the weight of its passengers, entirely ruining the gown. Yet she was the most amused of the whole party. On another occasion, she decided, in the earliest days of motoring, that it would be a great adventure to hire a car for the return journey from Dymchurch to London. She set out with her two tiresome dachshunds Max and Brenda, Arthur Watts and his bull terrier and Spencer Pryse and his two greyhounds, all packed in behind the driver. On winding and potholed roads, the journey took most of the day, and the dogs fought incessantly. Spencer Pryse nearly came to blows with Arthur Watts because his bull terrier kept attacking the greyhounds. Throughout she remained not only undaunted, but apparently enjoyed the excitement of it all. Yet Watts noticed that if a parcel cost seven pence when she had expected it to come to five, she would fly into a violent rage. Her sudden anger could strike at any time, and was not limited to friends and family – she was quite capable of making scenes in shops, with complete strangers. Watts put it down to too much smoking and continual anxiety about the work she should have been doing and wasn't. He noticed that she disliked writing and never worked systematically or regularly, but was always willing to be distracted: 'She always lived by instinct and acted on impulse.'[15]

There were faithful squires still eager to punt her round the moat, or play badminton at Well Hall, to walk along the breakwaters at Dymchurch, smoking and talking, or to play rounders on the beach with her. Though most of her young friends were enchanted with her freshness and unconventionality, others were less impressed, and one or two remained in her circle for what they hoped to gain from her friendship, rather than because they had fallen under her spell. Gerald Spencer Pryse accepted hospitality and patronage readily enough, but made little attempt to behave pleasantly in return, and in the end came to be thoroughly disliked by her family because he was so often

careless of her feelings. She, however, remained deeply fond of him
and did everything she could to advance his career and get his work
better known. In 1908 he drew seven pictures to accompany her poem
'Jesus in London' for a specially lithographed edition, and in the
following year he illustrated her novel *Salome and the Head*, and a
book of short stories, *These Little Ones*. In 1910 she made an
unprecedented break with tradition by persuading *The Strand* to let
him illustrate her serial, *The Magic City*, instead of Millar, though
Millar was to provide the drawings for the published book.[16]

During the summer of 1907, Spencer Pryse drew her into a new
venture that he had become involved with: several of the masters at the
Central School of Art were interested in the possibilities of using
lithography for reproducing text as well as drawings, and there was a
proposal to publish a magazine printed at the School which used this as
the sole method of reproduction. There would be no hand-set printing
at all, the contributions being written out in fine calligraphy instead.
The chief proponent of the scheme was Ernest Jackson, who taught
lithography and could supervise the whole reproduction process,
while another master, Graily Hewitt, was to undertake the actual
calligraphy. The idea had already been discussed with several people
but nothing definite had emerged when Spencer Pryse suggested that
Edith might be approached to help with the literary side. A meeting
was held at Well Hall at which her enthusiasm for the project fired
everyone's spirits. She had always fancied herself as an editor and she
had earlier been involved in schemes for starting children's magazines,
the first in the mid-nineties, and again in 1905, but each time they had
fallen through. A strong individualist and a habitual procrastinator,
she was not really suited to organization or office routine: 'un-
businesslike by nature, and yet scrambling through somehow',
recalled Hewitt. But the meeting at Well Hall was a success and it was
decided to go ahead with the magazine which was forthwith named
The Neolith. Jackson was to supervise the technical side, Hewitt
would carry out the calligraphy, Edith would be literary editor and
Spencer Pryse art editor. Each of them put ten pounds into the kitty
and their initial float paid for circulars advertising the magazine to
possible subscribers, as well as providing down payment on the rent of
a flat in Dean Street, to be used as an office. Later Edith took on the
cost of the rent herself, and she retained the flat as a convenient
pied-à-terre for several years after the magazine had folded.[17]

The flat was in Royalty Chambers, a building on the northern side of the old Royalty Theatre in Dean Street. In her novel *Dormant* (1911), Edith invited her readers up the uncarpeted stairs and into the magazine's office:

> If you mount the steps of the Royalty Theatre under the glass roof where the pink geraniums and white daisies make a light that you can see from the end of the street, you will find between the box office and the pit entrance a door, and beside it the legend 'Royalty Chambers'. When the theatre is closed, as it quite often is, the ragged children of Soho play about the entrance, and on the lower steps of that staircase elderly little girls sit nursing heavy babies and scolding their little brothers, and the door of Royalty Chambers serves them as shelter, ambush, and hiding-place. It is an untidy doorway, through whose door, mostly open, the wind blows dust and straws and scraps of paper. If, picking your way through the clusters of infants, you go up a flight of stone steps, you pass, on your right, the fine rooms where the Management does its business, when it has any. Still ascending, you pass another plate on the door of Mr Ben Burt, where to his name are added the significant words 'Correspondence only'. On the floor above you find a brown door on which is whitely painted the word [*Neolith*], and below it ['E. Nesbit], Editor'.

Once inside the office, there were books everywhere, and the furniture suggested a room in a farmhouse – it was

> old and solid and heavy, from the settle that stands out from the wall at right angles to the fireplace, the gate-legged table, the oak church-table on which [E. Nesbit] keeps [her] pens and inks and papers. A tall clock ticks near the door. It has a silver face, and a painted moon and sun mark the hours of day and night. There is a round mirror over the mantelpiece, and there are some comfortable round-bodied Windsor chairs, shaped cunningly to support the back. The divan with the leopard skin looks like a happy accident. The windows are curtained with cotton fabric of a pleasant green colour, and on one window-ledge a blue-lustre mug stands, and in it, all the year round, a few cheap flowers. On the floor is a Persian carpet. A door opens from this room into a dining room, white walled and furnished with beautiful simplicity. A dark dresser holds pleasant red and blue crockery and Nuremberg glass: the chairs are of apple-wood, rush-seated and ladder-backed; the floor is covered with a pale India matting. On the mantel-shelf are brass candlesticks and crockery greyhounds with crockery hares in their mouths.[18]

Inevitably *The Neolith* was launched with a party: about twenty contributors and friends dined at the *Villa Villa* restaurant nearby and then returned to the flat to play games and sing songs, while Edith strummed on a guitar borrowed from the restaurant proprietor, who had been invited to the party in exchange for the loan. Graily Hewitt remembered Spencer Pryse and the artist A. S. Hartrick being there, as well as Hubert and G. K. Chesterton, who held forth on the brilliant promise shown by the young Gerald Gould. One person who did not attend was the moving spirit behind the magazine, Ernest Jackson. He was a somewhat dour character who did not get on with Edith and found her difficult to work with – indeed, there was constant friction between them: when he became impatient with her lack of organiz-ation, her response was to burst into tears, which only irritated him further. Though he claimed to like her, his view of her was unsympathetic:

> She would weep whenever anything went wrong. She seemed . . . to have little artistic taste. She was headstrong and would not easily suffer contradiction. She was not self-critical in any respect . . . She had quite definite opinions but they were usually wrong.

Jackson congratulated himself on remaining calm in the face of feminine sobs and sighs, but he clearly thought Edith a silly and headstrong woman. At nearly fifty, the helplessness and fears that she had so often exploited to get her own way seemed merely embarrassing or pathetic.[19]

Graily Hewitt, the calligrapher, was gentler than Jackson, but he too was discomfited by her displays of helplessness. She struck him as 'one of those very flustered ladies. Her clothes never seemed quite right, and she was always losing scarves and things.' Later he admitted that 'those beads and bangles and incessant cigarettes' (she still rolled them herself) had inhibited what sympathy he might have had for her. Like Jackson, he found her difficult to deal with: but at the same time he admitted that it was her energy and enthusiasm which had got the magazine off the ground in the first place: 'She was a stage-managing person.' Hewitt had what was in many ways the most demanding task, that of copying out all the literary contributions on to specially prepared transfer paper in a regular italic script, and at the same time arranging them on the page, usually at a stage before he knew what other work was coming in. He remembered it as a 'nightmare of struggle', and thought that this method of reproduction was too slow and difficult for the magazine ever to have been an unqualified success.[20]

Edith did not have the patience or the persistence to make a good editor. Her concept of the magazine was at once vague and intensely idealistic. A letter to the socialist writer Evelyn Sharp soliciting a contribution of not more than 2,000 words, promises:

> You may say *exactly what you like*. It seems possible that there may be something that you *want* to say, something that you would not easily place in a Harmsworth or Pearson publication. I want all the literary contributions to be in the most beautiful English and they may be as plain spoken as they will. The only thing I bar is Yellow Book suggestiveness, and that, I know, your own fine taste would, of itself bar.

A postscript adds:

> I want the *Neolith* to present, both in art and literature the *truth*. Almost everything that's printed now is *lies*, in one form or another. I want the plain naked unashamed truth.[21]

Evelyn Sharp did not rise to the occasion.

The first edition of *The Neolith* appeared in November 1907. Its pages were exceptionally large (folio size), and its beautiful flowing script looked imposing and unusual. In the first edition, Edith published her painful memories of Fabian ('The Criminal') and work elicited from past and present friends: G. K. Chesterton contributed a stirring poem, 'The Secret People'; Shaw sent a short story, 'Aerial Football', about a bishop and a charwoman trying to get into heaven; there was a weak ballad by Graily Hewitt himself (though Edith admired it so much that he seriously contemplated trying for a literary career) and a slightly better poem by Gerald Gould. Later contributors included Laurence Housman, Andrew Lang, Father Hugh Benson, Cecil Chesterton, Edgar Jepson and Oswald Barron, who supplied some ballads under the pseudonyms 'Oswald Bastable' and 'Oliver Basingstoke', ballads that Edith had fruitlessly attempted to persuade W. E. Henley to take ten years earlier. The last edition of *The Neolith* to appear included her long verse drama 'In the Queen's Garden'. As well as poems and prose, each magazine carried half a dozen full-page lithographs on a wide variety of subjects – sometimes buildings, dramatic scenes, portraits and even architectural drawings. Frank Brangwyn and A. S. Hartrick, Sickert and Charles Shannon contributed artwork; Shannon drew a design for a fan.

The Neolith ran for four issues and then folded, without having made a significant profit or loss for its joint editors. It had been run as a

co-operative venture, with those involved giving their time and work
for nothing and only the printer taking payment. The immediate
reason for its closure was that Jackson, in particular, could no longer
spare the time for it. From the outset it had been a deeply un-
commercial scheme, since so much energy had to be expended in
writing out all the literary contributions by hand; and though the
standard of illustration was high, there was never any attempt to link
the pictures and the texts, or to organize the texts around some central
theme, so that at best it could never be more than a high-class scrapbook of discrete contributions from particular – and rather limited –
literary and artistic circles. But the Royalty Chambers remained a
positive asset, providing a conveniently central base from which to
excurse and entertain. As always, new ventures brought Edith new
friends, and through editing *The Neolith* she had made two who were
to be important to her and were loyal to the last.[22]

One was Lord Dunsany, author of fantasy novels, fairy tales and
romances of a type more popular today than when he wrote them.
Gerald Spencer Pryse had loved his book *The Gods of Pegana* (1905)
and showed it to Edith. Dunsany was an Anglo-Irish peer, a man of
about thirty who had turned to writing as an escape from the
apparently insoluble political problems around him. He used to claim
that at this period, his reading public consisted of four people, of
whom Spencer Pryse was the first and Edith the second. She wrote to
him at once to ask for a contribution to *The Neolith*. He sent her a
story that he had just completed, *The Sword of Welleran*, which she
admired but knew at once to be much too long for the magazine, so she
persuaded him to write something on a smaller scale altogether. In the
end, some short stories of his appeared in two issues of the magazine.
She asked him to lunch with her at Royalty Chambers, and they liked
one another immediately. Dunsany remembered the occasion vividly
because, by coincidence, the hands of her grandfather clock suddenly
whirred round and round, as if it had gone quite mad: 'it almost
seemed odd that I, who had written so much about Time in my *Time
and the Gods* [1906], should have been so greeted,' he observed. Later
he invited Edith to meet his wife at their London home in Cadogan
Place, which she visited several times. On one occasion, she met the
poet W. B. Yeats there; he had also moved in socialist circles in the
early nineties and so asked her whether she was still involved in the
Fabian: she protested that she was still an active member. Later she
compared Yeats to a very handsome raven. The Dunsanys, in their

turn, visited the Blands at Well Hall, where they remembered playing hide-and-seek on the evening of their arrival, and a game of charades in which John Bland took the part of Endymion. They also visited the Other House at Dymchurch, and in 1910 Edith and John travelled to Ireland to stay at Dunsany Castle for ten days or so.[23]

The other new friend she made through *The Neolith* was Edward Andrade, later a distinguished physicist. It says a great deal for her vitality, gregariousness and personal charm that at fifty she could still make lasting friendships with men twenty or thirty years younger than she was, and as gifted, yet as different from her earlier friends as were Dunsany and Andrade. She first met Andrade when he submitted some poems for the magazine, though they were never actually published – perhaps they came in too late to catch the last issue. He liked her at once, and kept in touch with her until her death. He was probably the most intelligent and analytical of her many clever friends, Shaw always excepted; his impression of Edith, given in a letter to Doris Langley Moore after reading her biography, is thus particularly interesting:

> Looking back, it seems to me to be both true and remarkable that although many admired her very deeply, found her a wonderful companion and a sympathetic and shrewd friend, a generous hearted woman with a touch of genius, no one ever loved her or felt tender about her as distinct from pityful and sympathetic. Perhaps tender is not quite the word I want – I mean an emotion which has something of love in it even if not quite love. There was in her that something of hard and shrewish – so well developed, to the exclusion of nearly everything else, in Iris – which you have brilliantly suggested, without being unkind. A woman who has maintained husband and home as she did in her early years, has a right to be imperious, but, although myself the most faithful of drudges, I understand to some extent Hubert's flings.[24]

As soon as he had written it, Andrade felt that he had been unguarded, and hastily added, 'Don't for Heaven's sake ever quote this. It may be all wrong.' His observation that she did not invite tenderness or a certain kind of intimacy may have been partly the result of his angle of vision, as a much younger man. Yet his suggestion that the absence of a quality of vulnerability may have driven Bland to look for it elsewhere interestingly parallels Wells's view, that Bland's affairs were prompted by the need to get 'even with her'.[25] Both men saw Bland as having some justification for his infidelities; in Wells such a response may have been no more than an uneasy male reflex, but

Andrade's choice of words suggests a more flexible and self-critical stance. In point of fact, Hubert had no such justification for his behaviour towards Edith: he had been engaged to Maggie Doran before he met Edith and had made no effort to break off that love affair even after marriage. Andrade's feeling that Bland was provoked by the absence of some yielding or responsive quality that Edith lacked may embody a psychological truth about the Blands' relationship, even though it does not in fact explain Bland's infidelities; rather some element of hardness in Edith may have developed in response to them.

Andrade met Edith in 1908, at much the same time as she began to be drawn into the 'Baconian' movement, whose object was to prove that Shakespeare's plays had actually been written by his contemporary, Francis Bacon. Andrade's impression was that some relative of Oswald Barron's had 'first started the whole thing, but very soon she was in touch with a monstrous regiment of quacks'.[26] She was fascinated by the whole complex of ideas that Baconianism opened up, and the mysteries upon which it claimed to throw light: not only had Bacon written all Shakespeare's plays, he was also a prince of royal blood, and the author (perhaps with others) of Burton's *Anatomy of Melancholy*, the Authorized Version and Spenser's *Faerie Queene*, to name but a few. These and further revelations were supposedly embedded in a series of complex ciphers which Bacon had built into his writings, trusting to the wisdom of future generations to unravel them. In addition, informed readings of his *New Atlantis* revealed Bacon's connections with Freemasonry, while from *Sylva Sylvarum* his role as a key figure in the Rosicrucian mysteries could be inferred. The founding mother of this movement was an American, Delia Bacon. Writing in the mid-nineteenth century, she regarded herself as a descendant (even though Bacon had left no heirs). Her extravagant theories had captured many late Victorian imaginations – Mark Twain's conversion was often cited. More commonly, the Baconians themselves were regarded as a lunatic fringe, but there was some sympathy for the view that 'Whoever wrote *Hamlet*, that frowsy money-grubbing provincial never did', as Edith put it. A substantial number of well-established literary figures sympathised: Henry James voiced his doubts about 'the clown of Stratford' in his own inimitable manner: 'I find it *almost* as impossible to conceive that Bacon wrote the plays as to conceive that the man from Stratford, as we know the man from Stratford, did.'[27]

Edward Andrade's mathematical skills ensured that he was soon participating in Edith's attempts to master the various ciphering systems which she believed would reveal the truth of the Baconian claims; but despite his best efforts, she never really grasped the mathematical implications of the methods she was using. She had become convinced that Napier's system of logarithms was involved, perhaps had even been invented by Bacon, but Andrade never succeeded in making her understand how logarithms actually worked. She struck him as having 'no mathematical capabilities at all', and he was all the more embarrassed because he thought the whole theory a complete waste of time:

> I was in a very awkward position about the B[acon] S[ociety] business. I never saw anything even faintly exciting, no matter on what grounds deduced, come out of all this labour, but I was very fond of E. Nesbit, and could not bear to hurt her feelings. I discouraged the 'research' in every mild way I could, but I could never bring myself to tell her that it was, in my opinion, all nonsense. I used to argue with her, but this kind of madness feeds on argument.[28]

A late novel of hers, *The Incredible Honeymoon*, written in 1915, includes a visit to Stratford-upon-Avon that provides the occasion for a full review of Baconianism. Three different characters express their different reactions to it. The heroine, Katherine, initially voices lay resistance to the whole notion: 'You aren't a Baconian, are you? . . . But you can't be, because I know they're all mad.' After she has looked at the Birthplace, she says that she'd prefer to believe the Stratford claims because 'It's such a very big lot of lies, if they are lies'. The book's hero, Edward Basingstoke, occupies an advanced position in which certain Baconian premises are accepted, perhaps close to his creator's own position. His first name – Edward – was Andrade's, while his surname recalls the pseudonym Oswald Barron had used when publishing his verses in *The Neolith*, 'Oliver Basingstoke'. Edward reassures Katherine: 'Don't be afraid. I'm not a Baconian, for Baconians are convinced that Bacon wrote the whole of Elizabethan and Jacobean literature off his own bat. I only think there's a mystery.'

The third speaker is a genuine Baconian freak – 'a tall, gaunt man in loose, ill-fitting clothes with a despatch-case in one hand and three or four note-books in the other.' He explains to Katherine:

> 'It *is* interesting . . . There's nothing like it. I've spent eighteen years on it, and I know now how little I know. It isn't only Bacon and Shakespeare; it's a great system – a great cipher system extending through all the great works of the period.'[29]

It quickly emerges that Edward is not merely open-minded – he has also dabbled in the subject, and a learned and eclectic conversation ensues. The Baconian, whose name is Vandervelde, lives only for his research, which he sees as a quest for truth:

'There's nothing else worth looking for. The truth, whatever it is. To follow truth, no matter where it leads. I'd go on looking, even if I thought that at the end I should find that that Stratford man did write the plays.' He looked up contemptuously at the smug face of the bust.

So far Vandervelde has financed his investigations from his own money, but it has now come to an end and he is on the point of having to take 'a situation' and abandon his study of the ciphers. Edward, however, has unlimited supplies of money (the strict rules that controlled and limited the fantasy elements in her children's books were abandoned in her romances) and he tells Katherine, 'I can very well afford a small endowment for his research, if you say so.' And of course, being a warm-hearted open-minded heroine, she does.[30]

Edward shared with his creator the desire to support the learned Baconian and his research, but what in him appears a splendid and generous gesture looked rather different to Edith's own family and friends, when she did exactly the same thing. Edward Andrade explained to Doris Langley Moore:

She had a long-haired man whom she maintained at her expense in Dean Street, who was by way of being a great expert on the Baconian aspect of the Droeshout portrait and the Baconian title pages. I don't think he ever did any work for his money, and fancy that he vanished when the Dean Street chambers were given up.

But Iris remembered him living in the flat that Edith had moved to after Royalty Chambers, in the autumn of 1912, and from which she herself had run her dressmaking business:

He had one attic room in a flat that I shared with mother in Rathbone Place – whether he paid rent or whether mother let him have the room I don't know – it is quite likely that she only met him at the Bacon Society – the whole subject so infuriated me that I never troubled about anyone connected with it.[31]

Iris, like the rest of Edith's family, bitterly resented her mother's act of patronage and regarded its beneficiary as being at worst a charlatan and at best a wastrel; yet at one moment it looked as if her endowed research was about to bear fruit: in July 1909 the Bacon Society's journal announced 'A Great Baconian Discovery':

Mr E. V. Tanner will shortly publish the result of fifteen years' labour on an arithmetical cipher of Francis Bacon, which he discovered in the lines addressed 'To the Reader', placed opposite the engraving by Martin Droeshout, forming the counterpart to the title-leaf of the 1623 folio edition of Shakespeare's plays.

An inspection of Mr Tanner's work justifies the opinion that his is the most remarkable discovery of cipher which has yet been made in connection with the printing of those priceless dramas. The cipher is arithmetical and can readily be verified by 'the plain man'. It points to the fact that Bacon chose the year 1623 for the publication because of the peculiar powers of the figures constituting it.

But this is not all. Mr Tanner, upon evidence that is almost eerie in its characteristics, but which is both ample and easy of verification, propounds the theory that Francis Bacon was the re-organiser of Free Masonry . . .[32]

There is much more in the same vein. Predictably, the book never appeared.

Though Edith's family suspected Tanner of deliberate deception, he was a sponger by accident rather than by design. He seems to have been constitutionally unable to hold down a job or sustain any activity for very long. When Edith first met him, he was middle-aged, four years younger than she was. Born Edmund Vivian, but always known as 'Max' (Edith named her dachshund after him), he was the fifth son of a speculator, John Tanner, whose sixth child, Beatrice Stella, born ten months later, became famous under her married name of Mrs Pat Campbell. Stella seems to have inherited more than her fair share of the family's vitality and initiative, while from the outset Max was considered too weak and sensitive to go to work. In 1875 he travelled with his father and elder brother to Texas, where John Tanner had hoped to recover his lost fortunes, but Max was soon sent back to England as too frail for that harsh climate. At home he was cosseted and left to amuse himself by playing the piano or chess, and though he later married and even fathered a daughter, he never worked anywhere for long. After her own success, Mrs Pat Campbell made him a small allowance, but no doubt he was glad of any further support he could get in the stressful business of surviving. He eventually outlived Edith and spent his last years in the Papworth TB settlement, outside Cambridge.[33]

Her family's exasperation focused particularly on Tanner, but they were more generally uneasy about the amount of time and money

Edith was now devoting to her new obsession. She would spend hours on end working out a particular cipher until she had converted, by some complicated and often inconsistent mathematical process, a few lines of Shakespeare into the message 'I am F.B.' or 'I am hog' or 'F.B. is W. Sha.' Reluctant friends would be dragged in, as Andrade had been, or argued with, if they remained sceptical. She built up a substantial library of rare and valuable books on early ciphers, logarithms and related subjects, and she borrowed from Bernard Shaw his facsimiles of the Shakespeare folios to work from. As her hobby grew more expensive, it increasingly annoyed her children. Only her second husband, more generous and detached than they, recognized that her deciphering games seemed to soothe her, and even to answer some inner need. She herself referred to them as 'a mental narcotic – such as some people find in playing patience'.[34]

How was it that such theories, regarded by her most intelligent friends as 'dreary nonsense', caught and held her imagination for the rest of her life? The answer must lie in their promise of hidden revelations, of wonders inaccessible to the uninitiated, sudden illuminations and mystic truths such as are momentarily glimpsed in her books for children. Iris described her as enormously interested in secret societies, magic and mystery of all kinds. Baconian theories appealed to her through their supposed connection with Rosicrucianism and also because they represented an alternative to established views, and she was an instinctive rebel. In its trivial way this new interest paralleled her earlier enthusiasm for Fabian socialism, which had offered an alternative to traditional party politics;[35] she had then rejected many of the tenets associated with socialism, tenets characteristic of alternative life-styles such as vegetarianism, women's emancipation or free love. Like many of its adherents, she only accepted socialism insofar as it was compatible with her sense of herself as a lady, and with the type of life she wanted to lead. Baconian theory was at once safer and less demanding than socialism in that the alternative it offered was academic or intellectual, rather than social or practical. It did not even entail attendance at meetings or active campaigning; as a hobby it could be pursued in the privacy of one's own home, and was thus better suited to the decreasing activity of later years. Yet, as socialism had seemed to do, it held out the promise of some wonderful instant solution to an inadequate and muddled state of affairs. Blinding illuminations, truths about all literature were just around the corner. In the later phases of her life, books began to occupy that place in her imagination that life and social conditions had once held: *The Magic City* (1910) and *Wet Magic* (1913) make literal this retreat of the imagination, so that characters are released from books to fight battles that will save the ideal city. Baconian theories seemed to hold out the hope that the magic of the imagination, its projected ideals as well as its strategies of concealment, might yet be proved true in some world beyond themselves.

Her most rational friend, Bernard Shaw, was predictably appalled that she had sold out to unreason, not least because, as well as borrowing his first folio facsimiles, she had begun to borrow money from him as well. The first time she asked him for help, he gave her a cheque for the then large sum of a hundred pounds. When, after an interval of a year or so, she returned with a similar request, he gave her the money but told her that this was the last time and in future she must sort out her financial affairs for herself. She left, feeling angry and humiliated. She made at least one attempt to convert Shaw to her new creed, in May 1910; his response on one of his famous postcards may stand as the last word on the subject:

> Have you ever considered (this is a belated reply to yours of the 8th May) how utterly impossible it is that Shaw of Dublin could have written his wonderful plays. Is it not clear that they were really written by Sidney Webb, L.L.B. Shaw was an utterly ignorant man. His father was an unsuccessful business man always on the verge of bankruptcy, just like old Shakespear or John Dickens. Shaw had a very narrow escape from the police for setting fire to a common. He was a disgrace to his school, where he acquired little Latin & less Greek. He got no secondary education & came to London an unknown & obscure provincial. And this is the man to whom people attribute the omniscience, the knowledge of public affairs, of law, of medicine, of navigation &c&c&c which informs the plays and prefaces of G.B.S. Absurd! Webb, the L.L.B, the man who carried all before him in examinations in his boyhood, the upper division civil servant of the Foreign & Colonial Offices, the author of Industrial Democracy &c, was clearly the man. I could pile the case much higher if there was room.
>
> G.B.S.

Edith had too lively a sense of humour not to see the funny side of it all. Indeed she introduced Mr Bacon-Shakespeare into *The Magic City* as the gaoler, and had Mr Noah explain to the children that he

> has written no less than twenty-seven volumes, all in cypher, on this very subject [i.e. how to unravel a magic mat]. But as he has forgotten

what cypher he used, and no one else ever knew it, his volumes are of but little use to us.[36]

The Baconian in her novel *Dormant* (1911) is simply called William Bats.

Late in 1907, when Edith was working on the second issue of *The Neolith* with its conscientious calligrapher, Graily Hewitt, she shocked him by remarking that the first chapter of her new serial for *The Strand* was due in a day or two and she hadn't yet thought of anything to write: 'Never mind', she said. 'I'll write a non-committal chapter or two in an hour or two.'[37] The serial thus dismissed was *The House of Arden*, appearing in January 1908, and her conversation with Hewitt was no more than bravado. Though an element of improvisation is evident in all her children's books, they usually begin by establishing the book's central theme, and *The House of Arden* is no exception: the first episode provides a description of the house and its inheritors, and by the end of it, Edred and Elfrida have found the mouldiwarp, the heraldic white mole that is their family's badge, and have even begun to look for the treasure which will restore the house to its former glory.

In the second chapter of *The House of Arden* her Aunt Edith gives Elfrida 'a red book with gold pictures on back and cover – and it was called *The Amulet*', an indication of important continuities between these two tales of time travel. Like its precursor, *The House of Arden* is concerned with the possibility of reconstructing an ordered society in the midst of the social chaos and injustice of Edwardian England. The search for an ideal society underpins the book, though this only becomes apparent near the end, when the children rescue their father and Uncle Jim (Aunt Edith's sweetheart) who are missing and assumed dead, from a South American Utopia. It stands on a plateau as inaccessible as Conan Doyle's *Lost World*, and is inhabited by a people older than the Incas, who know neither fear nor sorrow. Father and Uncle Jim acknowledge that this prison of theirs is also a paradise and, were it not for their loved ones, they would never want to leave. They also realize that, whatever happens, they must ensure that its secrecy is preserved and it is not contaminated by modern capitalism, exploitation or commercialization.[38] The historical and geographical unlikeliness of this unearthly or otherworldly kingdom points up its imaginary nature. At another level, this unreachable plateau stands for death, or even heaven, from which loved ones can only be recovered through the magic of imagination. Until its final chapter, the book is concerned less with the recovery of the lost father than with restoring the fabric of society as figured in Arden castle and its lost estates – these two aspects are not, in any case, unconnected since the recovery of the past is, symbolically speaking, the recovery of the lost progenitor, and the search for the past and the search for the father are one.

The discovery of the family's lost treasure is deferred to a sequel (*Harding's Luck*, 1909), and the absent father is seen as the real, the lost and buried treasure, just as he had stood for the heart's desire in *The Amulet*. His reunion with Elfrida on the very last page reiterates the climax of *The Railway Children*, and reflects how central this act of restoration had become to her writing:

> And then a great wave of love and longing caught at her, and she knew that . . . the treasure was hers, and in one flash she was across the room and in her father's arms, sobbing and laughing and saying again and again –
> 'Oh, my daddy! Oh, my daddy, my daddy!'

Since the lost father is arguably always Edith's own, it is not surprising to find that Elfrida includes elements of her author's tomboyish girlhood, and that she and her brother Edred contradict most traditional gender stereotypes: Elfrida is naturally courageous and dominates him, partly as the elder, but mainly as the better. In every way more worthy, she is nevertheless wholly debarred from the inheritance. It is Edred who becomes Lord Arden, while she can't even call herself Lady Arden;[39] yet what discoveries they make and adventures they have are consistently due to her persistence, courage and creative powers – it is *her* poetry that first summons the mouldiwarp. This acid little beast, which arranges the time magic for them, speaks in broad Sussex dialect and rules over white things – daisies, pigeons, swans, and all white creatures, their whiteness emphasizing that this is 'white' magic.[40]

The mouldiwarp takes the children back into English history, but no longer as conspicuous strangers, as they had been in *The Amulet*; so not only must Edred and Elfrida put on the clothes of children from the past, but they must assume their identities as well. The housekeeper at Arden, Mrs Honeysett, observes when she first meets them that 'There was always a boy and a girl' in the Arden family. In this way they are provided with forebears whose roles they can assume, although what becomes of those earlier children during the time their places are occupied remains mysterious. In the sequel, *Harding's*

Luck, the witch-nurse explains that the Jacobean Ardens have gone back to Julius Caesar's time, but this shifts, rather than solves the problem.[41] The process of changing places with identical children from an earlier time allows Edred and Elfrida to experience the past at first hand and with great directness, yet they take back with them their modern speech habits as well as their modern knowledge. Sometimes this doesn't amount to a great deal: when the Napoleonic invasion is expected imminently, Elfrida tries unsuccessfully to remember from her lessons whether it had taken place or not – she had never got beyond Edward the Fourth in history, on account of always having to go back for the new girls. But when they travel back to James I's time, her knowledge has unaccountably improved and she not only recites 'Remember, remember, the fifth of November' but also provides the names and details of the various conspirators just in time to give away the Gunpowder Plot and be imprisoned for treason. Later still she is distressed at meeting Anne Boleyn a-maying, because she knows what will become of her ('Oh, do be careful . . . Your darling head!').[42] As in *The Amulet*, the children puzzle over the question of whether their visits to the past have really affected or could have affected the course of history, but they do not find an answer.

The Arden family goes back a long way, and, with its castle, comes partly to stand for English history itself. Edith was always moved by the historical associations of old buildings – apart from Well Hall itself, Scotney Castle had contributed to *The Secret of Kyriels* and Bodiam figures in several of her books. Arden includes elements from a number of different castles, but she had one in particular in mind while writing – Hurstmonceux on the Sussex Downs. Moated and once elaborately fortified, it had been allowed to fall into decay and between its old walls a more modern house had been built.[43] This is exactly what has happened at Arden, providing an apt symbol for the reduced scale of modern life, sheltering within the larger, finer shell of the past; or else, in a more personal interpretation, an aging exterior which nevertheless harbours a continuing life deep within itself. And since Cliffville, where Edred and Elfrida live, seems to be Eastbourne, Arden Castle or Hurstmonceux, at nine or ten miles off, is about the right distance away. The imaginative importance of Hurstmonceux for Edith is evident from its appearance elsewhere in her fiction: it provides the setting for an early story, 'Hurst of Hurstcote' as well as for the penultimate chapter of *The Incredible Honeymoon*, written in 1915, where it appears under its own name.[44] But in *The House of*

Arden two features have been altered: its characteristic Tudor red brick becomes grey stone, the usual building material for castles. And its position on the thyme-covered slopes of the South Downs has been altered so that it can overlook Pevensey Bay, and smugglers and shipwrecks can be included in the story.

With the ruined castle Edred and Elfrida inherit the burden of its restoration, which poses two problems for them: it cannot be properly restored until they can find out what it was like originally, and they must also find the means to restore it – in this case, the buried treasure. The power of time to conceal and destroy, and the capacity of the imagination to restore and recover thus stand at the centre of the book. But whereas *The Amulet* had explored remote civilizations, *The House of Arden* examines English history, and the earlier book's vision of a brave new Wellsian tomorrow gives place to the reconstruction of a former beauty and order, since lost. To some extent, such a plot suggests a failure of confidence in the present and its potential for positive change, and a consequent idealization of the past. There is no attempt to disguise its cruelty and suffering – a witch is persecuted; the children are imprisoned in the Tower for treason, and pursued by Henry VIII when their warnings upset his queen; yet the people they meet there display a kindness and dignity associated with an 'organic' and pre-industrial society. The debate about the relative merits of past and present societies surfaces at the end of the book in the form of an argument between Edred and Cousin Richard; he too has travelled back from the present into the past, and he voices a much more adult and critical view of the present:

> 'Why don't you want to come with us to our times?'
> 'I hate your times. They're ugly, they're cruel,' said Richard.
> 'They don't cut your head off for nothing anyhow in our times,' said Edred, 'and shut you up in the Tower.'
> 'They do worse things,' Richard said, '*I* know. They make people work fourteen hours a day for nine shillings a week, so that they never have enough to eat or wear, and no time to sleep or to be happy in. They won't give people food or clothes, or let them work to get them; and then they put people in prison if they take enough to keep them alive. They let people get horrid diseases, till their jaws drop off, so as to have a particular kind of china. Women have to go out to work, instead of looking after their babies, and the little girl that's left in charge drops the baby and it's crippled for life. Oh! I know. I won't go back with you . . . in *your* time nobody cares.'[45]

Three-quarters of the way through writing *The House of Arden*, Edith suddenly saw the possibility of providing a sequel by introducing a third child who travels back from the present to the past – a child who travels independently of Edred and Elfrida, and whose response to the past contrasts with theirs because his experience of the present has been far more painful. He will be identified with their Jacobean cousin Richard. In the first two *Strand* episodes in which he appears (for July and August), Richard is presented as if he belongs to Jacobean England and is entirely at home there; unlike Edred and Elfrida, he talks in an imitation of its more formal and antique idioms. But in the ninth episode, he is suddenly revealed as different. He has been totally reconceived and now he shows himself to be entirely familiar with Edwardian technology, and even with its schoolboy slang: when Edred shows him their Kodak camera, he replies, 'Oh, stow that . . . I know now it's all a silly dream,' adding that he is quite familiar with '. . . railways and steamboats, and the Hippodrome and the Crystal Palace. I know Kent made 615 against Derbyshire last Thursday . . .' Edred jots this last detail down, and takes it back to his own times for verification. He writes it on the back of a bill from Gamages (then a famous department store) for three ships' guns, a compass and half a dozen flags, made out to Mr R. D. Arden of New Cross, which Cousin Richard must somehow have taken back with him into the past.[46]

Although, in *The House of Arden*, Cousin Richard uses twentieth-century slang, it may not have been until Edith began work on her sequel that she decided to make Richard more than merely critical of modern times, and less than middle class. The Richard Arden who lived at New Cross, bought materials from Gamages to make ships in bottles, and knew of the Hippodrome and the Crystal Palace, resembled her usual readers and characters. Dickie of Deptford, whose imaginative needs must be satisfied by an empty rabbit hutch, is a rather different figure. By the bold stroke of recasting Cousin Richard as a slum child, she could show him not only as a critic but as a victim of modern times. The wretched plight of pauper children was all too evident, yet Edwardian London closed its eyes to the miseries at its own back door. Edith followed Ruskin and Morris in regarding such apathy as symptomatic of a wider social degeneration. Although the plight of poor children lay largely outside the experience of the protected middle-class audiences whom she regularly wrote for and about, it had been gradually emerging as an important theme in her

children's books – exemplified by the 'little Lazaruses' at the picnic at
the end of *The New Treasure Seekers*, or 'the little black girl' of *The
Amulet* who finds a happier home in prehistoric Britain. Slum children
were more directly and painfully portrayed in her stories for adults:
'The Ashpits' is about a small boy with nowhere to play but a rubbish
tip, who accidentally poisons himself by drinking from a brightly
coloured bottle that he finds there. Originally published in *The
Neolith*, it was reprinted in *These Little Ones* (1909), a collection of
short stories, several of which are concerned with slum children and
the physical and emotional privations they endured. In another story,
'How Jake went home', a boy is knocked down by a cab and taken to
hospital, which appears to him as a kind of heaven. This incident was
briefly rehandled in *Harding's Luck*.[47]

Several stories in *These Little Ones* show imaginative adults
intervening to adopt, or attempt to adopt a slum child. In *Harding's
Luck*, though Lady Talbot tries to adopt Dickie Harding, he runs
away, and later Dickie himself takes responsibility for an adult, the
tramp Beale, and his childish loyalty and devotion succeed in
reclaiming the tramp from a life of petty crime. In using such a plot
formula Edith was reverting to the type of story which the evangelical
writers for children, and in particular Hesba Stretton, had first made
famous: her story, like theirs, showed how a particular slum child,
through qualities of innate virtue, came to reform and redeem the life
of a beloved adult. It was a sentimental pattern, but, as in the best
paintings of this period, the sentiment was rendered more acceptable
by a high degree of accurate observation. Hesba Stretton herself wrote
knowledgeably about the poor and their living conditions and she
recognized the childish capacity for love, the sense of justice and
longing for a better life. Edith knew far less about low life than did
Hesba Stretton, who had taken an active interest in slum conditions,
but she remembered exactly how it felt to be a child: Dickie's misery,
when the empty rabbit hutch is taken away in the opening pages, is one
of the most inward and memorable passages in her work.

Ultimately the plot structure, according to which the child becomes
in some sense the protector and teacher of the adult, and thus takes on
what are essentially adult responsibilities, can be traced back to
Charles Dickens, whose novels Edith enormously admired and
virtually knew by heart. Dickens's influence is particularly evident in
the plot of *Harding's Luck*, which reworks a number of events from
Oliver Twist. Like Oliver, Dickie is an orphan, deprived of his

inheritance; like Oliver, he climbs into a house as part of a burglary, fails to escape and is befriended by the kind lady who lives there; like Oliver, Dickie has been born into the gutter, but is eventually recognized as a boy of good family, in token of which both he and Dickie are allowed to speak that other, less limiting language of the literate middle classes. Edith explains this by asserting that 'most children can speak at least two languages'[48] but, as with Oliver, Dickie's command of English seems to be largely due to the fact that he is the hero, and thus one of 'nature's gentlemen'. In order to transform the aristocratic-sounding Richard Arden into a slum child, Edith altered his name to Dickie Harding. Hardy's novel *Tess of the D'Urbervilles* had popularized the link between old families coming down in the world and the phonetic corruption of their names, and in *The Secret of Kyriels*, the rare and aristocratic family name has been corrupted to 'Cryall'. But it is not only Dickie's name that has come down in the world; he himself has become a cripple in Edwardian England. His lameness gives symbolic expression to the maimed society that refuses to make adequate provision for its motherless and superfluous children; it is also the direct consequence of inadequate child care. Both symbolically and literally the damaged child serves as a reproach to his society.

Although Dickie is a cripple in his own times, when he travels back into the past he is sound, and this contrast between present sickness and past health underlines the book's social message. The opening paragraph of *Harding's Luck* establishes a contrast between the London of today and yesterday:

> Dickie lived at New Cross. At least the address was New Cross, but really the house where he lived was one of a row of horrid little houses built on the slope where once green fields ran down the hill to the river, and the old houses of the Deptford merchants stood stately in their pleasant gardens and fruitful orchards.

Such contrasts were frequently drawn by idealistic socialists: in William Morris's lecture on 'The Lesser Arts', for example, he described how Londoners had once dwelt among 'fair gardens running down to the broad river', but these had since been replaced by 'a whole county or more covered over with hideous hovels, big, middle-sized, and little'.[49] In his prophetic vision, *News from Nowhere* (1888), he imagined London restored in the future to what he considered to have been its former state, as a kind of garden city. For Morris, Victorian

London was a place of squalor and meaninglessness, dehumanized by the Industrial Revolution and, before that, by the long bleak process that had begun with the rise of capitalism, and had brought about certain fundamental changes in working conditions, completed by the late seventeenth century: before that, 'the workman of the sixteenth century worked still as an individual with little co-operation, and scarce any division of labour'.[50] Although Morris regarded the late fourteenth century as the optimum moment of English history, he also thought that society retained for a little while longer its essentially organic nature, and a sense of the dignity and beauty of labour that accompanied it – these were aspects of the past that Edith emphasized in depicting Jacobean London. In an episode reminiscent of Millais's painting 'The Boyhood of Raleigh', Master Richard finds the old seaman Sebastian on the quay; he has carved for the boy a perfect miniature of his own old ship *The Golden Venture*, in which he had sailed with Raleigh against the Spanish. Sebastian teaches Richard how to carve wood, and when he returns to the twentieth century, he is able to use that skill to earn an honest living. Edith's newly acquired interest in Bacon and his contemporaries gave her a further impetus to attempt an imaginative re-creation of his moment.

One of several ways in which the past is here shown as superior to the present is in its sense of established, and therefore unquestioned and accepted hierarchies; by contrast twentieth-century servants are often spiteful or grudging: Lady Talbot's maid resents her mistress's plan to adopt the crippled child burglar and so is willing to help Dickie escape. Servants in Edith's books are divided into two stereotypes: there are the old-world retainers, full of natural respect for their superiors, like Mrs Honeysett or Old Beale, or the villagers in *The Railway Children*; the old values, it seems, survive in the country, while being eroded in town. The other type is urban, pert, flouncing and short-tempered, fair game for bribes and booby traps. These, just as much as the doggily faithful, are clearly relegated to a lower species. Though occasionally in earlier books their unremitting servitude is briefly pitied, it is not until *The Magic City* (1910), her next, and in many ways her most imaginative book, that the harsh nursemaid, the city's destroyer, suddenly turns round to remind a baffled Julius Caesar

'You don't understand. You've never been a servant, to see other people get all the fat and you all the bones. What [do] you think it's like to know if you'd just been born in a gentleman's mansion instead of in a model workman's dwelling you'd have been brought up as a young lady and had the openwork silk stockings and the lace on your under-petticoats.'[51]

If the unattractive race of nursemaids have feelings, so, as Shylock pointed out, have Jews. Edith's anti-Semitism parallels her treatment of the servant classes in that her prejudices reduce individual characters to despised stereotypes. *The Treasure Seekers* depicted the lisping, ironically-titled Generous Benefactor, in reality a grasping money-lender who returns obsessively to the theme of interest rates, while in *The Amulet* the Queen of Babylon's guard carry out an energetic pogrom of Jewish stockbrokers in the City. *Harding's Luck* includes a lisping Jewish florist, a Mr Rosenberg, as well as a rather more sympathetic Jewish pawnbroker who presents Dickie with his family seal out of sheer kindness; his unexpectedly ready response to Dickie's request for a loan is the occasion of a curious, and embarrassingly didactic apologia:

> The sense of romance, of great things all about them transcending the ordinary things of life – this in the Jews has survived centuries of torment, shame, cruelty, and oppression. This inherited sense of romance in the pawnbroker now leapt to answer Dickie's appeal. (And I do hope I am not confusing you; stick to it; read it again if you don't understand. What I mean is that the Jews always see the big beautiful things . . .[52]

Perhaps Edith had consciously undergone some change of heart: the Jewish bookseller Mr Abrahamson in *Dormant* (1911) is also kind and well-meaning, though like all her portraits of Jews, something of a caricature, and closer to literature than life.

The Jewish pawnbroker in *Harding's Luck* is a good example of the way in which, at this stage of her career, Edith's books for children developed as she wrote them, steadily growing more complex in structure as they progress. On the pawnbroker's first appearance in the first chapter he had no Jewish characteristics – indeed he was referred to as a gentleman, something no Jew could ever be, however kindly. His change of race is an afterthought. The plotting as a whole, according to which the red-haired burglar and Dickie's 'aunt' attempt first to steal a letter and subsequently to kidnap Dickie himself, as heir to the Arden title, is never remotely plausible, in part because the narrative keeps rewriting previous events from different, and less convincing angles. But the lost heir and the stolen evidence of his birthright are such ancient and potent romance ingredients that there is little point in scrutinizing them too closely. The book also includes many powerfully simple effects which counteract and minimize its logical inconsistencies. Yet there is a sense of defeat implicit in its ending: *The House of Arden* had retreated into the private satisfaction of the longed-for reunion with the father. In *Harding's Luck* the treasure is recovered which will enable the castle and estates to be restored and rebuilt so that the Ardens can now set their own house in order, but the misery of the Deptford slums, and the emotionally crippled children they bring forth cannot be cured so easily; in acknowledgement of defeat before this insuperable problem, Dickie surrenders his twentieth-century existence and chooses to make his home in the past. The reason he gives for doing so is altruistic: his 'death' will restore the title to Edred's father. His action suggests that the search for a solution to modern social problems has been abandoned; it also anticipates the end of Edith's own creativity, for she was gradually losing that sense of buoyancy and light-heartedness on which, as she recognized, so much of her success as a children's writer had depended. Yet despite its retreat and its obvious technical flaws, *Harding's Luck* was widely admired for its moral message and even provided the basis for a famous sermon;[53] she felt proud and pleased to have written it.

Edith had never before put a crippled child at the centre of a book, though such children had occasionally appeared in marginal roles in her earliest fiction. Interestingly, a romance for adults written the same year as *Harding's Luck* (1909), *Salome and the Head*, portrays the hopeless love of the crippled flautist, Denny, for the dancer, Sandra; it eventually drives him to commit a murder. This book is set partly on the Medway, where Sandra has a house; she first encounters the hero when, out boating, she discovers him with his fingers trapped in a lock that he was trying to open. The title of the book refers to Sandra's most famous performance as Salome, presumably inspired by the overnight success of the Canadian dancer, Maude Allan, who danced the role to Richard Strauss's music. At the book's climax, Sandra finds herself dancing, not with her usual stage prop, but with the bleeding and severed head of a murdered man.

As in her earlier romance, *The Secret of Kyriels*, buildings seem to take on an important symbolism of their own. In America the book was retitled *The House with No Address* because Sandra lives in a London house totally invisible from the outside world: it is set at forty-five degrees to the other houses in the terrace, and all its windows open on to a secret inner square of garden. It has no external point of access – entrance is by a lift from below. These curious architectural features at times suggest not only the topography of the female body; they correspond closely to Sandra's intense need for privacy, her determination to evade the importunities not only of the 'stage-door Johnnies' who vainly solicit her favours, but also of her sinister husband. Sandra's sexual innocence is strongly emphasized because the dancer's display of her body seems, on the face of it, to be deliberately provocative. The narrative insists that she is 'straight', that is, sexually pure, while not entirely exonerating her from the charge of narcissism, implicit in the imagery of the inward-looking windows. In addition to her stage admirers, she is also persecuted by her husband, a mysterious and coercive figure from the past; it is actually his head that she dances with, though she does not know this. Her dance nevertheless suggests a degree of self-celebration and unconscious hostility, even aggression against men in general and her husband in particular, which is reinforced by the Salome motif. The aggression that, as heroine, she cannot be allowed to display has been displaced on to Denny, her sickly accompanist, who plays a murderous Noel to her Alice. Though Sandra is entirely innocent, entirely 'straight', she seems to reflect an element of surprising violence within her creator, rather as the early ballad of a vengeful bride had done.

If the dancer Maude Allan had provided one starting point for *Salome*, Well Hall and the legend that Margaret Roper had brought the severed head of her father, Thomas More, back there for burial, provided another. Edith later told her brother Harry that she had written the book in exactly thirty days and been paid two hundred pounds advance for it, but she thought it had ' a few nice things in it'.[55] She must have agreed to such terms in order to solve an urgent need for money. The financial difficulties of this period may partly explain why that particular year, 1909, was such a productive one for her: she also published *Daphne in Fitzroy Street*, the novel that describes her unconsummated affair with Shaw, and a book of sentimental short stories about children, *These Little Ones*, dedicated to Alice Hoatson, perhaps in secret token of their joint motherhood. In October that year, Rosamund's engagement to a young Fabian journalist Clifford Sharp ended in their marriage, conducted by the radical clergyman, Stewart Headlam, whom Edith had introduced into *Salome* as one of Sandra's fans; Headlam's notorious interest in dancing and dancers provided justification for doing so.[56]

In the midst of wedding preparations, Edith wrote to Lord Dunsany to thank him for a book he had just sent her:

> It is a beautiful book and I sat down on a packing case amid waves of straw and tissue paper that surge round us at this time – because my daughter is going to be married and life seems all packing and unpacking – and read in your book for a half hour which I ought to have spent on seeing to wedding things. It is good of you to send it to me, and I thank you very much.
>
> We, too, remember with pleasure the day you came to Well Hall; and I often think of you both, and hope that I may soon see you again. I suppose there is no chance of your being in London before the spring? The country must be very beautiful now. Even Well Hall garden is wearing splendid clothes. But I hate the autumn.[57]

The Dunsanys responded with an invitation for her to go and stay with them at Dunsany Castle, which she did in January of the following year, 1910. She felt freer now that Rosamund was finally and safely settled into married life, for only the year before she had been snatched at the eleventh hour from the jaws of that small, bad wolf, H. G. Wells.

11
THE ROW WITH H.G.

H. G. Wells and his second wife Catherine were first introduced into Fabian circles by their friend Graham Wallas in 1902. They were soon on good terms with the Webbs, the Shaws and the Blands, though Wells did not actually join the Society until February 1903. His reputation as a writer was by then well established and he had recently built Spade House for himself at Sandgate, along the coast from Dymchurch, between Hythe and Folkestone. Though Wells found Spade House a congenial place in which to work and play with his two young sons, he was easily bored and always glad to have friends close at hand. The Wellses' first recorded visit to the Blands took place at Dymchurch that autumn, and Mrs Wells wrote to Edith in November 1902, enclosing some photographs taken that afternoon:

> I send these with a quaking heart, fearing indeed they may make an end to our friendly relations. But please don't be angry with us, and put them in the fire if you feel like it. The amateur photographer must be the best hated of all creatures. Well, we at any rate treasure them as being mementos of a most delightful afternoon. I suppose you have abandoned Dymchurch.

Another undated letter urged Edith and Hubert to spend a night with them at Spade House:

> We hear suddenly from the Hicks that you've left Dymchurch, and I gathered from your son that you were staying on some time. We are much unstrung by your departure, because our plan was to induce you to come here for a night on your way home.[1]

Henry Hick was Wells's doctor, and a mutual friend. These two letters came with affectionate regards from 'Catherine Wells', but a later and more intimate one is signed 'Jane', the pet name H.G. had given her.

Their friendship developed over the next year or two, while retaining a comparative formality, with both the Wellses addressing Edith as 'Mrs Bland'. A letter from H.G. written in the autumn of 1903 congratulates Edith on her collection of short stories, *The Literary Sense*, with a warmth that includes a degree of politeness, but is also perceptive about their tone:

> The stories are good and gay and I've liked the book immensely. They are a game and a very pretty game and all sorts of people will do their little talks more carefully on account of them, and with little plagiarisms more or less carefully handled. They hang queerly and pleasantly between the illusions of the schoolgirl and the blood and racket of this sensual life. They are not the heady stuff of Romance nor that reality that cuts to the bone, but they are quite delightful Young Fancies.

A less strained and more spontaneous enthusiasm is evinced in a letter written the following winter, December 1904:

> 'Steamed Lady,
>   I never told you how we like the *Phoenix and the Carpet* and how extraordinarily more than the late Mrs Ewing who was once first we now esteem you. The Phoenix is a great creation; he is the best character you ever invented – or anybody ever invented in this line. It is the best larking I ever saw. Your destiny is plain. You go on every Xmas never missing a Xmas, with a book like this, and you will become a British Institution in six years from now. Nothing can stop it. Every self-respecting family will buy you automatically and you will be rich beyond the dreams of avarice, and I knock my forehead on the ground at your feet in the vigour of my admiration of your easy artistry.

This was one of Wells's prophecies that, exceptionally, came true. It sounds more heartfelt because Edith's comic fantasies appealed far more to Wells's taste than did her adult writing. He genuinely admired her children's books and many years later told Doris Langley Moore that he considered them underrated.[2]

Their friendship was now on a more relaxed and intimate footing, and a few weeks later Edith wrote to Wells from The Other House at Dymchurch, into which she had recently moved:

> I will, with your kind leave, come on Thursday, bringing with me Miss Ruck and Mr Reynolds. The latter you know. Miss Ruck is a young woman who has just begun to write . . . Of course she admires your

work immensely, and wants to see whether *you* are as nice as *it*. She doesn't believe anyone could be. And doesn't take any notice of what I tell her about you. Thinks. . . . But I haven't room to finish the compliment. I will hire a big expensive carriage for the pilgrimage to your temple. But its on the distinct understanding that we are to get you both here afterwards for at least 28 hours. This is such a pretty house. I do want Madame to see it.[3]

A letter to Wells a month later begs him to contribute something to a magazine for children she was planning, preferably illustrated by himself (Wells was an engaging cartoonist), adding:

Directly I got home the horrors of housekeeping clawed me, and I've lived in a wild whirl of misery ever since. So that I can't even remember whether I wrote a proper 'bread-and-butter letter' to the Lady Jane. If I didn't, will you beg her to 'love and understand' – It is most horribly hard on women who work; that they should have, as well, to constantly fight with beasts at Ephesus – I mean in the kitchen. Don't hastily curse me and say 'No' to my request for the story. It means a great deal to me, and to the success of my venture.[4]

Edith and H. G. got on very well. They were both extravert and full of fun – both of them loved long walks and arguments, parties, games of all kinds and charades. Edith borrowed a number of ideas from Wells's books – at first openly and, after their estrangement, covertly, while he may have learned from her something of the art of party-giving. Both had marked childish streaks in them, characteristic of the privileged youngest child who has not fully consented to grow up. Shaw recognized this trait in Wells, describing him more than once as a spoilt child, but it was also evident in Edith. During 1905 Wells published *A Modern Utopia* and *Kipps*, which was partly set at Dymchurch. Edith enjoyed *Kipps* unreservedly but her initial reaction to the *Utopia* was less enthusiastic, though it was to have a substantial influence on the serial she was currently writing, *The Amulet*. That summer Wells made plans to join the Blands on the Medway; she wrote him a note telling him where to find them:

My dear Sir,
    I can't remember whether you were told that our Inn at Yalding is 'The George' – It would be dreadful if you were to seek us vainly at the 'Bull' or the 'Anchor'.
    I've read your Utopia again. I don't disagree as much as I thought. And I think it is a splendid book. I wish I could write books like that. You must be very very glad of yourself when you think of that book.[5]

One afternoon towards the end of July H.G. turned up at Well Hall entirely without warning, carrying his valise and announcing, 'Ernest, I've come to stay'. He called Edith 'Ernest' because he had first supposed that the bare initial stood for a man's name, and what, after all, was more important than being Ernest? (Coincidentally, an early Bodleian cataloguer made the same assumption.) Edith was delighted with Wells's confident expectation of her hospitality, and immediately set about organizing entertainments in the form of tableaux and charades to celebrate his arrival and amuse him next day. These were based on the titles of his books and he had to guess what they were: for *Love and Mr Lewisham*, Paul sat at a table, studiously reading, while little John, got up as Eros with a bow and arrow, shot at him. Wells stayed about a week, on this occasion, and while he was there completed the draft of his novel *In the Days of the Comet*, writing in the garden as Edith herself did; it was not finally published until the following year. He and Edith sat up talking until two or three in the morning, but he also went out of his way to be pleasant to the rest of the family, telling John fairy-tales, talking politics with Hubert and flirting mildly with Rosamund.

It was remembered by everyone as a delightful visit, and Wells's letter of thanks (or 'roofer') touched on some of the pleasures of his stay:

Dear Lady,
  A roofer! The thing cannot be written! Jane I think must take on the task of describing the departure of a yellow, embittered and thoroughly damned man on one Thursday and his return on the next, pink – partly his own and partly reflected from Enid [Steele] – exultant, with a beautifully hand-sewn wreath in one pocket and a programme in the other and his manner – full of the most agreeable memories. If – as I have always said – the gratitude of a lifetime. . . .
  Remember me to Bland whose state seems better than it was, to Iris – I think repeatedly of those last beautiful moments – to the charming lady whose name I have never been able to grasp but whose work I dread and admire – to Miss Hoatson and the lady I invariably beat at Badminton. I've sent *The Country of the Blind* to Rosamund and my respects to Enid enclosed. Paul (who is Paris), greet for me and Jimmy (who is Pan). Remember me to Reynolds, my fortunate supplant – there he is a-clicking among you all! Remember me to Eros as was John. Yale I fear is too light-minded to recall me and the older dog too old. (The jackdaw never loved me.)
  Fine impalpable threads of agreeable association trail from Lodge to

stair way, hold me to your upstairs and your downstairs bedrooms, take me under the trees of your lawn, and to your garden paths, to the green seat in the garden and all about you.

It was a bright dear time.[6]

Back at Spade House both Wells and Jane wrote to Edith begging her to go and stay with them; Jane's letter simply urged that she stop on her journey down to the Other House (the train took Edith to Folkestone, from where she hired further transport for the luggage and herself):

> *Do* break your journey here when you come to Dymchurch. You know it will be much nicer for you to do that than to go hurtling on to Dymchurch the same day. Dearest Mrs Bland, we want you to, so much. You will, won't you? Please say yes.

H.G. sent a charming letter in which he invited the Blands to visit them in relays, since Spade House was too small to hold them all at once:

> Dear lady,
>   This fickle heart is still distributed in palpitating portions among the inhabitants of Well Hall and Jane (Mrs Wells) joins with me as ever in such regards. We want to get a lot out of you all when you come to Dymchurch. We want you all to come over in ones and twos and threes and be affectionate, first some of you and then others, and play the pianola too, and even, it may be, read at times. Who are coming and when? We have appointed one room with two beds in it for all September (except for the 9th when Edward Clodd is here and one occasion of Garnetts) as the Well Hall Room, and other accommodation can be arranged for. Jane says, *you* are coming, you personally, on your way. Is that so? Bland might like to come over when Clodd is here and help me to put the fear of God into him. But for Bland and me there is always Philosophy. With Rosamund I have really to go thoroughly into the sorrows of an incipient literary career. Iris – I never *have* talked to Iris. Gyp ever values the riper experience of a man like John. Miss Hoatson has never even so much as looked at Spade House. I hope you begin to see the advantage of regarding Dymchurch as a sort of circulating library of you; and me coming over to change you. For them as like games it is proposed to erect a sort of badminton, but there we are open to advice.
>   Yours ever,
>   H. G. Wells
> Good accomodation for Bicycles – TEAS

I have also a very high-class game of soldiers that is not to be sniffed at even by Paul.
Miss Ruck and Enid [Steele] and Reynolds count as *Blands*.[7]

Edith could hardly fail to be charmed by such an appeal. Replying to Jane, she said she hoped to come on 30 August and stay for a couple of days, while a less formal note to Wells tells him:

> It was very good to get the two kind letters from Spade House this morning. Because my life-light is practically out at the moment. My pet niece [Dorothea] is very mizzy at her father's dangerous illness – my other (next pet) niece [Anthonia?] is ill – I've lost a hundred pounds through the incredible imbecility of an American, and Pinker [her agent] – Well, you know what *he* is!
>
> You know, if you see much more of us you will 'get through' us – and we don't wish that.
>
> Don't, please don't discourage Rosamund. She *must* earn her living. If Hubert and I were to die she'd have to earn it at once: I want her to be able to earn it by writing – and not have to go into a shop or be a humble companion.
>
> Yours in real dejection – but very glad of those two letters.[8]

Rosamund had taken her first hesitant steps in the direction of a literary career by writing *Cat Tales* (1904) for Ernest Nister, with Edith's help, and following it up with *Bill R.N.* (1905), *Moo Cow Tales* (1905) and *Bunny Tales* (1906) written by herself. These little coloured books were hack work in the old Nister style that Edith herself had long ago abandoned, after the success of *The Treasure Seekers*. Rosamund was undoubtedly talented, but this empty form gave her no opportunity of distinguishing herself and afforded little or nothing in the way of artistic satisfaction. Edith's feelings towards Rosamund were complicated, the more so because Hubert was so fond of her, but in affectionate moods she wanted to make Rosamund into a version of herself, something the intransigent Iris had wisely refused to become. This created a burden from which Rosamund was tragically unable to escape. Her one piece of creative writing, *The Man in the Stone House* (1934), is a novel about a young girl's need to elude parental legacies and impositions. Her desire for freedom and H.G.'s notorious sympathy for the plight of bright young women locked up within oppressive familial and social conventions would soon bring them together.

Visits and books were exchanged with the Wellses in September. Edith gave H.G. an earlier book of romantic short stories, *Thirteen*

Ways Home (1901), and was disappointed when he didn't like them:

> The *Thirteen Ways Home* are fairy-tales. Yes: so's *The Red House*: but in the same sense as your *Utopia* is a fairy-tale. Love is not always the detestable disintegration that you pretend to think it. Sometimes, and much oftener than you admit, it is 'nice straight cricket'. Anyhow, one wishes it to be that – you do, too – and why should you have a monopoly of Utopias? All the same, I'm not very proud of *Thirteen Ways Home* ... I'll grant that they're too sentimental. But it's a dreadful thing, and one of the curses of middle age to forget how to be sentimental at all.
>
> We enjoyed your being here very very much: and we expect you on the 21st October. But I hope we shall see you at Dym before that. Thank you for the kind things you say of the Blands: even if the things are ironical, they're very nice.[9]

It was inevitable that they would disagree over the presentation of love, as soon as Wells felt confident enough to do so. With increasing openness H.G. came to celebrate the importance of physical passion in love; this was precisely the area that Edith could not cope with and carefully evaded in her romantic short stories, regarding it as a 'detestable disintegration', a degrading and bestial aspect. Wells observed with interest her 'strain of anti-sexual feeling' and 'a certain essential physical coldness' in her.[10]

Half a dozen more letters from Edith to the Wellses, written over the next three months, have survived; it is probably pure chance that they have done so since a number of other letters she sent them have apparently disappeared – a few because they gave offence, most by accident. The Wellses stayed at Well Hall on 21 October 1905, as she had asked, though Edith was obviously preoccupied during their visit. After they had gone, she wrote to them in high good humour:

> Oh my dears – oh my dearie dears! Virtue must have gone out of you both during this good week-end, for quite unexpectedly, and with a most thrilling suddenness I find that I have finished *The Railway Children* which have sat on my bent and aged shoulders for nearly a year!!!!!!! Thank you so much! This, as you perceive is a *roofer*. I am writing to thank you for having been here. It was very good ... I enjoyed every minute of the time that you were here – in one way or the other. Your own devoted
>
> Ernest[11]

Edith must have been writing up the November episode (the eleventh of the series) of *The Railway Children* for the *London Magazine* when she suddenly saw how to wind up the whole book, and did so, though there were two further episodes to be published. It must have been a relief to have finished it, since she was simultaneously writing *The Amulet* for *The Strand*, and was scarcely more than half-way through with that. A note written a week or two later asks the Wellses to a dance and to dinner beforehand with Beatrice and Sidney Webb. Jane, meanwhile, had sent a letter to Jimmy (Horace) Horsnell via Edith. It was an invitation for him to go down to Sandgate and help her with typing up H.G.'s work. Though Horsnell worked, on and off, for the next eight years as Edith's secretary (a substantial number of her business letters are in his neat, tiny handwriting), he also acted for part of that time as Wells's secretary.[12] Two further letters, one to Jane and one to H.G., written at the end of November, indicate that Edith was finishing her play for Maskelyne and Devant, *The Magician's Heart*, though to her disappointment it was not performed until the following year. She was very busy over Christmas and deferred an invitation to go down to Sandgate until the end of January. Early in December Iris was taken ill with suspected appendicitis, which upset Edith very much; as Iris recovered, the visit looked as if it might have to be postponed again so that Iris could be taken to Droitwich to see her young man, but in the end Edith did go down, in the last week of January, taking the girls with her.[13] All three sent the customary 'roofer' of thanks, but Edith's sounds dejected; instead it is Rosamund's note that captures the humour and observation that usually characterized her mother's letters. Edith wrote:

> This is the roofer that I ought to have written on Thursday. Please forgive me – there was such a lot to do – and I have been very much worried. I was worried too, all the time I was with you, and I know I was a dull guest. You'll forgive that, too, won't you?

Rosamund's letter to Jane was sent from Lee, where she was staying with Marshall Steele and his large, noisy family. She was there for a week, but regretted not being at Well Hall for the following Saturday, since Jane and H.G. were expected that weekend:

> This is a bread-and-butter letter written under exceedingly trying circumstances. I am staying with the Steeles and three of them are playing 'Table-croquet', one is asking me questions, another is tuning the banjo, and another is talking to the parrot. My head is in a whirl, and my pen is leaking. (They have begun to play the banjo in good earnest now.) I believe what I set out to say was 'Thank you very much for everything in the past week, not excepting Frank [the younger son].' I was truly very happy and absolutely the only thing I have to look

forward to is my visit in April. I'm awful sorry I shan't see you on
Saturday, but I shan't be back. Since I was given permission to stay until
Monday-week I think it as well to take advantage of it, although I really
want to come back on Saturday. Please will you give my love to Gip [the
elder boy], and my heart to Frank. I'm going to see a lot of him in April,
I hope.

Iris's letter followed two months later (she had been unwell since
before Christmas). It was full of warmth, assuring Jane, 'I have never
been in any house where I enjoyed myself so much, or felt every one to
be so sympathetic', but a postscript suggests that shadows had already
fallen between the two families:

Will you be offended if I ask you not to answer this? I am so much
disliked at head quarters now-a-days that my every act must be careful
and I cannot risk being asked questions about my correspondence for I
should surely 'answer back'. Please don't hate me.[14]

And here the letters end. The Wellses and the Blands had been on
terms of close friendship, paying each other regular visits and keeping
in touch through frequent notes. Over the next three years that
friendship was to be dissipated by ideological disagreements, suspicion
concerning H.G.'s intentions towards Rosamund, and finally by a
major but well-concealed row, followed by mutual recriminations and
denunciations; their long shadow falls across Wells's account of the
Blands in his *Experiment in Autobiography* (1934). The first steps in
their estrangement came about through Wells's efforts to reform the
Fabian, to turn it 'inside out and then throw it into the dustbin', in his
own phrase.[15] Such a process meant unseating the 'Old Gang', the
executive of fourteen, which still included Pease (its permanent paid
secretary), Shaw, Webb and Bland (as honorary treasurer); they had
run the Society since its earliest days and, twenty years later, showed
no signs of stepping down.

Clifford Sharp, who had first introduced Gerald Gould to Edith,
was one of a group of young socialists who founded the 'Fabian
Nursery' in 1906 – he acted as treasurer, Rosamund as secretary; Cecil
Chesterton, G. K.'s younger brother, was also a member. The
Nursery was divided between an almost excessive respect for their
elders (Clifford Sharp and Cecil Chesterton were both ardent disciples
of Hubert) and a sense that the Society was due for some kind of
change. The Webbs had encouraged Wells to join the Fabian in 1903,
and though he had threatened to resign with Graham Wallas in 1904,

he finally settled down to a determination that the Fabian – piddling little middle-class club that it was – must have something made of it: its membership must be opened up, its finance put on to a practical and businesslike basis; it would have to give up its easy toleration of a wide range of ideas and abandon its policy of permeation in favour of putting up candidates for Parliament and generally becoming more politically effective. Wells brought a zeal for reform and efficiency such as Annie Besant had shown twenty years before, and, like her, he was doomed to exhaust his initiatives in the face of the Society's loose organization, its protean structure and its determined and experienced rejection of left-wing sectarianism.

Wells's unheralded visit to Well Hall during the summer of 1905 may have been no more than the impulse of a moment; his assiduous cultivation of Edith that year a reflection of how much he liked her personally and the charm that her quirkily unconventional and Bohemian household had, at first, held out for him ('it had seemed so extraordinarily open and jolly'); but he was also eager to consolidate support for his projected reform of the Society, which included the eventual overthrow of the Old Gang, and with them Bland himself. To have Edith and Rosamund on his side in the coming struggle would be particularly valuable, for the Blands and their friends, acting in concert, still constituted a powerful pressure group within the Society. Even though for the last few years Edith had stopped attending meetings regularly, she still retained her own circles of influence and her various young admirers (Cecil Chesterton, for a while, among them).[16] Wells saw his campaign as particularly addressed to the intelligent and independent women in the Society whom he rightly identified as a restless and active group. His campaign for its reform began in 1906 with two lectures delivered in January and February, 'This Misery of Boots' and 'The Faults of the Fabian'. The latter criticized the Society for its failure of nerve, its lack of ambition or larger aims, and particular members of the Old Gang were mocked for their narrow outlook (the Webbs) or their inappropriate levity (Shaw). Though Wells was a notoriously poor public speaker (always addressing the floor or the ceiling and frequently inaudible), his speeches were pointed and hard-hitting, and they went down well with an audience eager for change, though unable to formulate exactly what changes they wanted. The executive agreed to set up a special committee to consider the Fabian's present structure and future activities. Wells, pleased with the effect of his opening moves, left for the United States at the end of March, pausing only to leave Shaw a warning note:

> You leave my Committee alone while I'm in America. If I'm to satisfy
> myself with 'us'; who's us? I'm not going to identify myself with your
> damned executive nohow, but I'm always open to a deal that will give
> results.[17]

Once he had gone, the Webbs and Bland began to question his
seriousness and commitment; Beatrice recorded in her diary her dislike
of his 'odd mixture of underhand manoeuvres and insolent bluster'.
Shaw who genuinely liked and admired Wells and always relished the
prospect of a good fight, recognized that he had voiced a discontent
that was widely felt within the Society, a sense that the Old Gang were
played out. He advised Wells to conduct his campaign with tact and
conciliation but Wells rejected any suggestion of a compromise; if the
existing executive would not make way for his grand new plans, then
he would force them to stand down altogether.[18]

In September 1906, *In the Days of the Comet*, the novel that Wells
had completed the previous year at Well Hall, was finally published. It
was not well received. The book's ending, with the passing of sexual
possessiveness under the good influence of the comet, encouraged
adverse critics to read it as a plea for free love, and Wells's next lecture
to the Fabian, on 12 October, seemed to take a step further in the same
direction. In it he attacked 'private ownership' as an element in
marriage, suggesting that the economic and sexual exploitation of
women were related issues. Women wanted freedom and their
discontent made them a 'a huge available source for socialism'. He
wound up with a plea for the state endowment of motherhood. The
suggestion that free love might become part of a socialist platform
upset many of the Society's more conventional members who feared
that Wells's arguments might bring them into disrepute. Hubert
Bland, in public a great stickler for the proprieties, wrote Pease a note
saying:

> I am inclined to think one might do worse than force this 'sex and child'
> question to an issue as amongst Fabians. We had to do that with the
> Anarchists and we may have to do that with the Free Lovers.[19]

Wells's committee (as he saw it) presented its report for discussion to
the Fabian on 7 December to a packed Essex Hall – a third of the entire
membership had turned out; Wells's activities had in any case attracted
many new members. The special committee proposed that the
Society's Basis should be rewritten, its name changed, its executive

enlarged, more recruits made and candidates put up for Parliament – in other words, it must drop its drawing-room exclusivity and become a popular socialist party. Wells might still have pushed his proposals through had he not insisted that their acceptance would constitute a vote of no confidence in the executive; his ambitious and large-minded schemes were thus yoked with what began to look like a petty personal vendetta. Wells spoke at great length and very poorly; he seemed bent on losing his cause single-handed.

The meeting lasted so long that a vote was postponed until the following week. Shaw was now confident of winning but anxious that the executive's supporters should attend and that the executive should appear unruffled, generous and good-tempered. A note to Bland urged:

> No: on the whole, don't speak. Wells has said 'We must have a speech from Mr Bland'; and as his method of obtaining it is one which leaves no practicable alternative to dignified silence except retorts of a nature impossible from so big as man as you to so little a man as he (except with pistols), I think you had better leave the job to me . . .
>
> What I propose to do is to take the weight of the debate on myself . . . and demand an unconditional surrender – that is, a withdrawal of the amendment. I have all the points of detail noted, and can smash him to atoms on every one of them. I will play the moral game on them in an eye-opening manner. With luck, I believe we can get a smashing victory . . .[20]

In the event, Shaw achieved just that. Bland insisted on speaking, but merely observed that this challenge to the Old Guard had come 'not from the young but the elderly and middle-aged members of the special committee', and his claim was reinforced when Clifford Sharp, Cecil Chesterton and many other members of the Fabian Nursery came out for the executive. Shaw wound up the meeting with a cunning tactical device: he teased Wells into agreeing that he did not intend to resign if defeated, and then pitched into him with characteristic comic malice: 'Wells was squelched by a joke', it was said. No vote had taken place and very little discussion of the committee's report. Many people, among them Beatrice Webb, thought that, if Wells had not pressed for the overthrow of the Old Gang, he would have succeeded in getting his policies accepted.[21]

A week later Shaw wrote to Wells assuring him that all was not lost: 'You can easily retrieve the situation if you will study your game carefully, or else do exactly what I tell you.' Wells never did anything he was told; he could hardly resign immediately, having just agreed not to, but he had been publicly defeated, and his hopes of using the Fabian as an organ for implementing his dreams of world reform began to fade; he was no longer interested in its proceedings and grew lazy about attending committee meetings. But he was still angry with what he regarded as the hypocrisy and the rigidly patriarchal attitudes of the executive, and still anxious to help its discontented womenfolk find freedom, though he now pursued his goal on a more personal basis. One result of this was that some socialists assumed that his motivation had, from the first, been no more than his own sexual gratification. His row with the Fabian, according to R. K. Ensor, was caused solely by 'his misconduct. Any attempt to cast an ideological veil over it is quite ridiculous and after the event.' He instanced Wells's long drawn out love affair with Amber Reeves. But first there was the little matter of Rosamund.[22]

Rosamund had been a great focus of admiration in the Fabian Nursery, and had many suitors, including two particular admirers of her father, Cecil Chesterton, quick, clever but physically repellent, and the handsome fair-haired Clifford Sharp. He had read engineering at University College, London, but had not bothered to work and had gone down without his degree, determined to become a journalist. Beatrice Webb, who thought highly of his abilities, observed that he was 'not a sympathetic or attractive personality, he has little imagination, he is quite oddly ungracious in his manner'. Hubert also considered Clifford a serious and indeed a gifted young man and Rosamund, who enjoyed a very close relationship with her father, was also willing to be impressed, and even to contemplate becoming engaged to him.[23] For Wells, meanwhile, Bland had come to stand for all that he found most intolerable in the attitudes of the executive – he was the personification of male complacency and sexual hypocrisy; and Rosamund as Bland's favourite possession was also his chief victim. Wells conceived a passionate desire to emancipate her from her voluntary servitude and her blind admiration for her clay-footed father. A quarter of a century later he wrote of his affair with her as

a steamy jungle episode, a phase of coveting and imitative desire, for I never found any great charm in Rosamund. I would rather I had not to tell of it. But in that damned atmosphere that hung about the Blands, everyone seemed impelled towards such complications; it was contagious . . .

Yet in March 1907 he wrote to Violet Hunt: 'I have a pure flame for Rosamund who is the Most – Quite!' At some point that year Wells elicited a promise from Rosamund that she recalled many years later:

I remember I gave you a promise on the seashore at Dymchurch twenty-two years ago that I would tell you if ever I was stranded. You told me that Clifford would be no good to me. How horribly, terribly right you were![24]

The details and dates of Rosamund's love affair with Wells remain mysterious. Rosamund herself told Doris Langley Moore that their friendship had been interrupted and never resumed when her parents went through her correspondence and discovered that Wells had 'amorous designs' upon her; she put this at 1906, but she did not always remember dates accurately, nor does she seem to have been entirely frank about the events and feelings involved. A letter from Rosamund to Jane Wells written on 4 March 1908 implies that, although relationships between the families were strained, they were still superficially amicable, and the final break had not yet taken place:

Dear Mrs Wells,
    Of course you have an invitation to the Nursery lectures. I wouldn't think of sending you a ticket. It never occurred to me to write and ask you because I thought you would understand that you were to come if you wanted to. I'm so sorry you aren't coming to our dance on the 20th. I thought I might have had an opportunity of talking to you a little bit. You know, I suppose, that Iris has been frightfully ill. She is really better now and is well on the way to getting quite well. The baby, who is to be called Rosamund Philippa [in fact, Pandora], is very healthy and howls a great deal. I am going back with Iris when she goes home to stay for two months and help with the baby.
                    With much love . . .[25]

What happened next is uncertain: Iris may not have gone home for a while, or Rosamund may not have stayed with her for as long as she expected. However it came about, within a month or two of writing this letter, Rosamund and H.G. were caught at a London railway station in the act of running away together. The whole episode is obscure since all the protagonists felt compromised in one way or another and would not talk about it – though everyone else did. Even the date is uncertain, though it is virtually impossible that Jane Wells would have been asked to a dance at Well Hall after the event. According to Fabian gossip, Hubert and Clifford had caught up with

Rosamund and Wells at Paddington Station where they found the lovers already on the train. Hubert took hold of Rosamund and threatened Wells with a public scandal. According to the more highly-coloured family version, Rosamund had agreed to go to Paris with Wells for the weekend as 'a lark', and was dressed up as a boy (a not implausible detail given her passion for dressing up and Wells's celebrity); Hubert hauled Wells off the train and did not pause to waste words on him. He simply did 'what any gentleman would have done', and thumped him, there being no horse whips to hand; Hubert wasn't, after all, an amateur boxer for nothing. If this version is true it is curiously anticipated by a passage in Bland's *Letters to a Daughter*, written for Rosamund two years earlier:

> I remember you, when you were in your cradle, punched me with one fist while you clung on with the other to a woolly red ball that you would cram into your mouth. Well, just so, but more effectively would I punch a man who tried to take you away from me. And at the root the motive for the punching would be the same. So, . . . unless the man be quite of the right sort let him look to himself, for I still keep my punching muscles in trim.[26]

Paddington was a less unlikely venue for lovers leaving for the continent than it would be today. A boat train to Plymouth linked with the transatlantic liners on the last lap of the journey from America to France. But how did Hubert and Clifford discover their where-abouts? Were they simply embarking on a naughty weekend for the fun of it, or was it an elopement, Wells's last determined effort to release Rosamund from the clutches of her father and her engagement to his acolyte, Clifford Sharp? Was it precipitated by a panic in the wake of her parents' discovery of their correspondence? Their being followed to Paddington suggests a betrayal of some kind (by Alice, perhaps?) or even self-betrayal, some infirmity of purpose on Rosamund's part, some deep wish to be reclaimed. She could have left an assignation note behind her, or else, like Wells's own Anne Veronica when she wanted to go to the forbidden dance, she may have simply announced what she was planning to do – after all, she was now twenty-one and legally above the age of consent. She returned with her father, but when he got her home and began to preach a sermon on the laxity of Wells's morals, she replied that he was hardly in a position to adopt a tone of moral superiority since, according to Wells, he was a 'fearful roué' himself. Bland, already infuriated by her attempted abduction, now felt that Wells had not only contaminated her innocence but also alienated her affection. He could understand and even forgive her being taken in by 'the little cad', but that she should have had her mind poisoned against him was more than he could bear. It did not occur to him, then or later, that Rosamund, highly intelligent as he knew her to be, might well have corroborated Wells's criticisms of her father from personal observation, for example when he was engaged upon seducing her schoolfriend; nor that her affair with Wells was, if only at a subconscious level, an act of deliberate rebellion against his authority, an attempt to escape from his oppressive influence by transferring her allegiance to his most powerful rival.[27]

For a brief moment Rosamund had attempted to exchange her real father for a surrogate, a man who shared Bland's questing sexuality but instead of upholding traditional domestic values, sought to overturn them. The shift of feeling involved, from Bland to H.G. and back again, is, perhaps, implied in a curious little story that she related to Doris Langley Moore many years later, in the course of illustrating Edith's failure of generosity towards her:

> When my father died I was the only one of his children who received nothing of his. She gave various personal possessions to each of the others but not a thing to me. It wasn't until she married again and was leaving Well Hall that she gave me a silver-handled stick he had liked to use in the house after he went blind. And that stick had been given me years before by H.G., only I had left it for my father because he liked it particularly! When he died she had said to Auntie that she hoped I would not ask for it because she couldn't part with it, so naturally I didn't.[28]

The symbolism of the stick received from H.G., surrendered to her father and then appropriated by her mother seems almost too transparent. Rosamund emerges from all this as a young heroine such as Ibsen or Chekhov might have drawn, the vulnerable victim of selfish and self-seeking adult passions. She continued to cherish a love for Wells that he did not return, and perhaps never had, and her subsequent marriage to Clifford Sharp was, as Wells had warned her, an unhappy one.

The row that followed Rosamund's unsuccessful elopement was, predictably, of epic proportions. According to Wells, Edith 'wrote insulting letters to Jane denouncing her tolerance of my misbehaviour – which came rather oddly from her.' Shaw, who enjoyed being a busy-body and undertaking the role of peace-maker, tried to reconcile the injured parties and was savaged by Wells for his pains:

> I think you do me an injustice – I don't mean in your general estimate of my character – but in the Bland business. However you take your line. It's possible you don't know the whole situation.
>
> Well, I had some handsome ambitions last twelve-months and they've come to nothing – nothing measured by what I wanted – and your friendship and the Webbs among other assets have gone for my gross of green spectacles. Because it's all nonsense to keep up sham amiabilities. I've said and written things that change relationships and the old attitudes are over for ever. On the whole I don't retract the things I've said and done – bad and good together it's me. I'm damnably sorry we're all made so.
>
> And damn the Blands! All through it's been that infernal household of lies that has tainted the affair and put me off my game. You don't for one moment begin to understand, you've judged me in that matter and there you are![29]

Shaw may have understood better than Wells supposed, but his well-intentioned interventions merely incited Wells to more furious denunciations:

> The more I think you over the more it comes home to me what an unmitigated middle Victorian ass you are. You play about with ideas like a daring garrulous maiden aunt, but when it comes to an affair like the Bland affair you show the instincts of conscious gentility and the judgement of a hen. You write of Bland in a strain of sentimental exaltation, you explain his beautiful romantic character to me – as though I don't know the man to his bones. You might be dear Mrs Bland herself in a paroxysm of romantic invention. And all this twaddle about 'the innocent little person'. If she is innocent it isn't her parents' fault anyhow.
>
> The fact is you're a flimsy intellectual, acquisitive of mind, adrift and chattering brightly in a world you don't understand. You don't know, as I do, in blood and substance, lust, failure, shame, hate, love and creative passion. You don't understand and you can't understand the rights or wrongs of the case into which you stick your maiden judgement – any more than you can understand the aims in the Fabian Society that your vanity has wrecked.
>
> Now go on being amusing.[30]

But it took more than Wellsian venom to make the downy old Shaw lose his temper. In a piece on Fabian politics, he summed up Wells and his efforts to save the Fabian with high good humour:

He was the most completely spoilt child I have ever known ... the faintest shadow of disapproval threw him into transports of vituperative fury in which he could not spare his most devoted friends.

... H.G. had not an enemy on earth. He was so amiable that, though he raged against all of us none of us resented it. There was no malice in his attacks: they were soothed and petted like the screams and tears of a hurt child ...

Nothing could abate his likeableness ... H.G. was honest, sober, and industrious: qualifications not always associated with genius ...[31]

The seduction of Rosamund was, in one sense, a symbolic re-enactment at chamber level of the challenge that Wells had thrown out against the Fabian Old Gang on the public stage; the struggle for possession of her repeated in miniature the struggle for control of the Society, with Shaw trying, unsuccessfully in each case, to mollify both parties. Wells's self-justification was that he was trying to protect Rosamund from Hubert's unhealthy interest in her:

In that hothouse atmosphere of the Bland household at Dymchurch and Well Hall ... I found myself almost assigned as the peculiar interest of Rosamund, the dark-eyed sturdy daughter of Bland and the governess, Miss Hoatson. Rosamund talked of love, and how her father's attentions to her were becoming unfatherly. I conceived a great disapproval of incest, and an urgent desire to put Rosamund beyond its reach in the most effective manner possible, by absorbing her myself. Miss Hoatson, whose experiences of life had made her very broad-minded, and who had a queer sort of liking for me, did not seem to think this would be altogether disastrous for her daughter; but presently Mrs Bland, perceiving Hubert's gathering excitement in the tense atmos-phere about us, precipitated accusations and confrontations.[32]

Wells's feeling that Alice Hoatson looked favourably on his seduction of her daughter may have been no more than self-deception; there is, on the other hand, some evidence to support his impression that Bland's affection for Rosamund was unusually intense. Her photograph, looking artificially serene, provided the frontispiece for Hubert's *Letters to a Daughter* (1906), and the text is suspiciously insistent that

His daughter is the only woman in all the world for whom a man five-and-twenty years her senior can feel no stir of passion, no trace of ... sex-love; the only woman from whom he cannot possibly evoke passion in return. That fact of itself gives his daughter a chamber all to herself in the man's heart, a chamber guarded by an angel with a flaming sword ...

His daughter is the one young woman to whom a man can talk of love
quit of the faintest fear of being led into making it.

Wells characterized Bland as a man fascinated by the idea of sexual
transgression, who would have 'thought it a crowning achievement to
commit incest or elope with a nun'.[33] Bland's attitude to sexuality,
according to Wells's account, was fundamentally opposed to his own:

In company, in public, Bland talked and wrote of social and political
problems and debated with a barrister-like effectiveness, but when I was
alone with him, the fundamental interest insisted upon coming to the
surface . . . He would give hints of his exceptional prowess. He would
boast. He would discuss the social laxities of Woolwich and Blackheath,
breaking into anecdotes, 'simply for the purpose of illustration'. Or he
would produce a pocket-worn letter and read choice bits of it – 'purely
because of its psychological interest'. He did his utmost to give this
perpetual pursuit of furtive gratification, the dignity of a purpose. He
was, he claimed to me at least, not so much Don Juan as Professor Juan.
'I am a student, an experimentalist,' he announced, 'in illicit love.'
    'Illicit love'! It had to be 'illicit' and that was the very gist of it for
him . . .
    There was no real inconsistency therefore between Bland's private life
and his enthusiasm for formal conventionality and it was perfectly
logical that though we were both disposed to greater freedoms by the
accepted standards, we were in diametrically antagonistic schools. He
thought it made a love affair more exciting and important if one might be
damned for it and I could not believe these pleasant intimacies could
ever bring real damnation to anyone. He exalted chastity because so it
meant a greater sacrifice . . . He was sincerely disgusted at my
disposition to take the moral fuss out of his darling sins.[34]

In the immediate aftermath of their failed escape,

Rosamund was hastily snatched out of my reach and, in the resulting
confusion, married to an ambitious follower of my party in the Fabian
Society, Clifford Sharp – and so snatched also out of the range of
Hubert's heavy craving for illicit relations.

Wells's account foreshortens events considerably. Rosamund did
not, in fact, marry Clifford until September of the following year,
1909, and Wells himself, in the immediate aftermath, began a far more
serious love affair with another young Fabian, Amber Reeves. By the
spring of 1909 Amber had become pregnant by him and accepted an
offer of marriage from an old admirer, but Wells continued to visit her
and make love to her after her marriage. The Blands now gossiped

freely to their friends about the events of the year before, and Wells found his allies evaporating. Beatrice Webb recorded in her diary that August:

> The end of our friendship with H. G. Wells. A sordid intrigue with poor little Amber Reeves ... apparently H.G. tried to seduce Rosamund Bland. If the Reeveses had known of that, they would not have allowed Amber to stay with him for a month at a time.[35]

At this critical juncture in his fortunes, as it seemed to him, Wells became convinced that the Blands were deliberately mounting a whispering campaign against him. Perhaps he was right, perhaps mildly paranoiac: the Blands may simply have enjoyed adding their own contribution to the current pool of gossip, enjoying the newly available sympathy for parents of Wells's victims and a general indignation that more than justified Hubert's earlier aggression. Wells's now notorious treatment of the luckless Amber had, after all, provided them with the perfect opportunity to say to Rosamund not only 'I told you so,' but also 'There, but for your loving father's interference . . .'

In 1910 Wells set about transforming his bitterness over the Fabian débâcle, his humiliation at Bland's hands and his lost hopes of a new life with Amber into the consoling and triumphant fiction of *The New Machiavelli*. He had some initial difficulty, however, in getting the book published, not only because of its frank treatment of the 'sex question' but because of its potentially libellous characterisation of real people: there is a full length and deeply ambivalent portrait of Beatrice Webb as Altiora Bailey, as well as a thumbnail sketch of the Blands as the Booles, the spiteful and interfering couple who ape the Baileys and deliberately spread scandal about the hero's love affair at a point of crisis during his career. That the Booles, rather than the Baileys, are made responsible for the scandal-mongering, suggests that Wells still hoped to salvage something of his former friendship with the more respected and influential Webbs, while, in the case of the Blands, there was nothing to be salvaged and he allowed his venom free rein – he had yet to get even with Hubert:

> These Booles ... set themselves industriously ... to disseminate a highly coloured scandal against me. It was almost entirely their doing, I am persuaded; at the worst the Baileys were guilty only of a passive acquiescence. But the Booles certainly needed no help. Boole, I found, was warning fathers of girls against me as a 'reckless libertine', and his

wife, flushed, roguish, and dishevelled, was sitting on her fender curb after dinner, and pledging little parties of five or six women at a time with infinite gusto not to let the matter go further.[36]

Mrs Boole is spitefully characterized as 'a person of literary ambitions', while her husband is presented in recognizable physical detail:

I've still the odd vivid impression of his fluting voice, excusing the inexcusable, his big, shifty face evading me, his perspiration-beaded forehead, the shrugging shoulders, and the would-be exculpatory gestures – Houndsditch gestures – of his enormous ugly hands.

Bland's high voice and huge shoulders and large hands were all too easily recognizable.[37]

One curious and apparently gratuitous detail, as to how the Booles came to know the well-hidden secret of the hero's love affair, suggests that a third individual is also being pilloried:

For a time I couldn't for the life of me discover [Mrs Boole's] sources. I had, indeed, a desperate intention of challenging her, and then I bethought me of a youngster named Curmain, who had been my supplementary typist and secretary for a time, and whom I had sent on to her before the days of our breach ... He was a tall, drooping, sidelong youth with sandy hair, a little forward head, and a long thin neck. He stole stamps, and, I suspected, rifled my private letter drawer, and I found him one day on a turn of the stairs looking guilty and ruffled with a pretty Irish housemaid of Margaret's, manifestly in a state of hot indignation. I saw nothing, but I felt everything in the air between them. I hate this pestering of servants ...

This precise description of Curmain tallies exactly with what photographs show of 'Jimmy' (Horace) Horsnell, who was still working as Edith's secretary and had for a time also worked for Wells. The portrait here given of him is a peculiarly unpleasant one, and must have hurt, as it was intended to; being in the public domain and yet unchallengeable, it must have seemed hard to live down. This passage may be one reason why Horace Horsnell later refused to acknowledge that he had ever worked as Edith's secretary, a refusal that entirely mystified his friends and her children.[38]

If the Blands appeared in *The New Machiavelli* in an entirely unfavourable light, one might expect Rosamund to have been treated more generously. Nina Griffith believed that the novel included a portrait of Rosamund; if so, it has – at least in the later stages – been merged with that of Amber Reeves. But the hero's first impressions of the heroine Isabel would certainly fit Rosamund, both in terms of her behaviour and even, to some extent, of her colouring:

> My first impressions of her were of a rather ugly and ungainly, extraordinarily interesting schoolgirl with a beautiful quick flush under her warm brown skin, who said and did amusing and surprising things. When first I saw her she was riding a very old bicycle downhill with her feet on the fork of the frame . . . and on the third occasion she was for her own private satisfaction climbing a tree. On the intervening occasion we had what seems now to have been a long sustained conversation about the political situation and the books and papers I had written.[39]

The New Machiavelli ends with a retreat into fantasy; the hero, Remington, has joined Isabel and her baby on a remote and symbolic island, having abandoned his brilliant career in politics to live with her as a social outcast. In reality, Wells agreed to give up Amber and the baby daughter she had born him. Yet for a writer retreat or escape need not signify defeat so much as retrenchment.

Wells never really forgave Bland for humiliating him in public, and the account he gave of the household in his *Experiment in Autobiography*, though written twenty years after Bland's death, is still animated by bitter resentment and contempt, while being full of brilliant perceptions. Wells was particularly disgusted by Bland's sexual hypocrisy and Edith's tacit complicity in her husband's love affairs; he saw Well Hall as 'a world of roles and not of realities':

> E. Nesbit was a tall, whimsical, restless, able woman who had been very beautiful and was still very good-looking; and Bland was a thick-set, broad-faced aggressive man, a sort of Tom-cat man, with a tenoring voice and a black-ribboned monocle and a general disposition to dress and live up to that. The two of them dramatized life and I had as yet met few people who did that. They loved scenes and 'situations'.

Wells was struck, as so many people were, by Edith's love of drama and role-playing, but Bland's posturings seemed to him both more serious and more sinister: not only did they go far beyond mere self-dramatization into the realm of outright dishonesty, but Bland himself was at once more committed to them and more deceived by them than she was. Wells was not, of course, the first to identify Bland as a poseur – Shaw had done as much twenty years earlier in his *Unfinished Novel*. But Wells's hatred sharpened his powers of observation and he

recognized Bland's poses as aspects of a need to get even with a wife who was cleverer, more capable and socially superior to himself:

> It was I am convinced because she, in her general drift, was radical and anarchistic, that the pose of Bland's self-protection hardened into this form of gentlemanly conservatism. He presented himself as a Tory in grain, he became – I know of no confirmation – a man of good old family; he entered the dear old Roman Catholic church. These were all insistencies upon soundness and solidity as against her quickness and whim. He was publicly emphatic for social decorum, punctilio, the natural dependence of women and the purity of the family. None of your modern stuff for *him* . . .
>
>   She acquiesced in these posturings. If she had not, I suppose he would have argued with her until she did, and he was a man of unfaltering voice and great determination. But a gay holiday spirit bubbled beneath her verbal orthodoxies and escaped into her work. The Bastables are an anarchic lot. Her soul was against the government all the time.[40]

Wells's shrewd guess that Bland's self-presentation was a way of dealing with his wife's superior abilities is persuasive, and he was quick to see exactly what was most phoney in Bland: his pretensions to come of a good family, his military appearance, and the uniform of the successful businessman suggested authoritative roles that Bland had never, in reality, achieved:

> The incongruity of Bland's costume with his Bohemian setting . . . might have told me, had I had the ability then to read such signs, of the

general imagination at work in his *persona*, the myth of a great Man of
the World, a Business Man (he had no gleam of business ability)
invading for his own sage strong purposes this assembly of long-haired
intellectuals.[41]

Brilliant though Wells's analyses of Bland, his marriage and his
household undoubtedly are, there is nevertheless something distinctly
disingenuous in his account of them. He too adopts a role, ironically
the role of the innocent abroad, the simple man coming, for the first
time, into a world of sophistication and pretense, the man of
authenticity, with no previous experience of role-playing. More
disturbingly, both in his *Autobiography* and in the account of his
love-life appended to it, he describes himself as having been affected by
the atmosphere of intrigue that radiated from the Blands: 'It was like
Alice . . . you discovered with amazement that you were changing
your own shape and stature.'[42] He must have felt uneasy about his
treatment of Rosamund to need to justify it to himself and his readers
thus – as the result of some uncontrollable change within him brought
about by the spell cast by Well Hall. In their own way, Wells's
assertions of his own innocence, his own naïvety were just as much
self-selected fictions, deliberate posturings as were Bland's absurd
personae. Wells's adopted role, on this occasion as on others, was
carefully chosen to defuse criticism of the part he had actually played;
Shaw's account of him as a spoilt child shows just how successful he
was in the role of *enfant terrible*. In reality, Wells had played a part
which only too closely echoed that of the detested Bland, the part of
the experienced seducer. Bland's unforgivable crimes were not his
hypocrisy nor his dogmatism but his vanity and sexual susceptibility.
He shared too many of Wells's own weaknesses – it was their
similarities, not their differences that were the real source of Wells's
hatred and anger.

Both Edith and Rosamund had been deeply fond of Wells and both
attempted unsuccessfully to renew contact with him after Hubert's
death; but he was as great a man as ever while they had become no more
than unimportant moments in his past. Edith, always a great believer
in 'kiss and make up', wrote late in 1915 to ask, 'Don't you think there
ought to be a time-limit for quarrels?' Wells must have replied, for a
second letter begins 'My dear Sir', the mode of address she had
regularly used to him in the heyday of their friendship. Rosamund
wrote him a love-letter, occasioned by seeing a reproduction of his
portrait by William Orpen; it is a love-letter eloquent of her

unrequited love for him and the emptiness of her later life:

> Clifford came home the other night and thrust a page of *The Tatler* under my nose, saying, 'There's H.G. for you.' And it really was! You cannot imagine how glad I was to see him again. Orpen is awfully clever. He has put down all that is essentially you, and nobody ever did that before. They put the unessential and obvious. But this is the real H.G., the H.G. who writes unforgettable, and darling things, the H.G. one loves, and always loved and couldn't misunderstand. This was once my H.G. and I think in some deep place in me is still my H.G. Now that I have put that down it seems rather cheek because really it is the other way round. Last winter I made a discovery. I was ill in bed for five months, fairly sure I wasn't going to recover, and during the better times I re-read your earlier books – all that I read at nineteen and twenty. I found then that what I had, for years, thought of as 'Rosamund' was simply something made up of bits of H.G. Wells. It was a shock to find there was no 'I' at all, that thoughts and feelings that I had supposed my own were all to be found in you. It put me on the track of myself and by going further back still, and then following the scent later, up to present-day I discovered that I was simply a conglomeration of about five different men. Yes, *men*, dash them! And certainly you had supplied more pieces than anyone else. By degrees I got used to this idea that I don't exist except simply as a thread on which all sorts of odds and ends are strung together. What still worries me is that I see there is no choice about what things hang there and stick, and what don't. And that I can't alter a *thing*. Yet I am glad so many of your bits stuck and that is my excuse for writing.[43]

WELLS, AS HE PICTURED HIMSELF

12
RECONSTRUCTING THE CITY

In 1909 Edith read E. M. Forster's novel, *A Room with a View*, and admired it so warmly that she wrote to tell him so. When he thanked her, she invited him to lunch at Royalty Chambers. He remembered the occasion as one of acute embarrassment because she asked him to open or close a window, and, in clambering to his feet, he overturned a large pile of plates on the floor. Seeing his stricken expression, she said, 'Sit down and I'll tell you what those plates cost', and proceeded to explain that they were a bargain from the Caledonian Market. Thereafter they kept in touch, writing to one another from time to time and exchanging books, and in 1911 she invited him to visit Well Hall. He liked her and admired her energy and versatility. She played him Beethoven's Seventh Symphony on the pianola and they strolled through the orchard together discussing books, but she occasionally embarrassed him by a sudden histrionic gesture: as they walked, she would adopt a melodramatic manner to relate some story or other, and he could not tell whether it was a joke or whether she expected him to take her seriously. At the end of that day, as the sun went down, a strange little ceremony took place in the garden: Edith produced some models of factories and suburban villas made out of cardboard and brown paper, and everyone ritually set fire to these effigies of urban encroachment.[1]

Eltham had changed in the decade or so that the Blands had lived there. The rows of workmen's cottages now came up to the very walls, and trams drove backwards and forwards along the main road beyond the gates. On one occasion when Hubert was grousing about the invasion of cheap houses, Harold Millar, Edith's illustrator, pointed out that, as a socialist, he ought to have been in favour of them: 'You've been calling for them long enough, and here they are.' His remark annoyed Hubert, but Edith laughed and agreed. E. M. Forster, too, was painfully conscious of the hideous sprawl of housing along arterial roads, and the development of new towns that was obliterating the beloved countryside; but he also realized that to condemn their spread might be inconsistent with a concern for better living conditions and slum clearance. More than thirty years later, in his essay 'The Challenge of Our Time' (1946), Forster described how a town was to be built on the farm lands around his earliest home:

> 'Well,' says the voice of planning and progress, 'why this senti-mentality? People must have houses.' They must, and I think of working-class friends in north London who have to bring up four children in two rooms, and many are even worse off than that. But I cannot equate the problem. It is a collision of loyalties. I cannot free myself from the conviction that something irreplaceable has been destroyed, and that a little piece of England has died as surely as if a bomb had hit it.[2]

Edith could not equate the problem either, but unlike Forster, she could scarcely see that a collision of loyalties was involved. In *Harding's Luck* the 'horrid little houses' which have been built over the former gardens and orchards of Deptford are slums, so that any potential conflict between urban development and overcrowded housing is averted. The spread of ugly modern villas appears as a theme in her writing for children from comparatively early on, but at first it is treated with her own inventive humour: 'Fortunatus Rex & Co.' is a complicated little story that begins at Miss Fitzroy Robinson's select boarding school for the daughters of royalty. When all her pupils vanish, one royal father is so distressed that he goes into commerce to take his mind off his loss:

> The King floated a company, and Fortunatus Rex & Co. became almost at once the largest speculative builders in the world.
>   Perhaps you do not know what a speculative builder is. I'll tell you what the King and his Co. did, and then you will know.
>   They bought all the pretty woods and fields they could get and cut them up into squares, and grubbed up the trees and the grass and put streets there and lamp-posts and ugly little yellow brick houses, in the hopes that people would want to live in them. And curiously enough people did. So the King and his Co. made quite a lot of money . . .
>   The ugly little streets crawled further and further out of the town, eating up the green country like greedy yellow caterpillars . . .[3]

Twelve years later she was still using the metaphor of yellow caterpillars, but the note of humour had been replaced by one of impassioned denunciation:

> Once there were nightingales that sang in the gardens on Loampit Hill. Now it is all villas. Once the Hilly Fields were hilly fields where the children played, and there were primroses. Once the road from Eltham to Woolwich was a grassy lane with hedges and big trees in the hedges, and wild pinks and Bethlehem stars, and ragged robin and campion. Now the trees are cut down and there are no more flowers. It is asphalt all the way, and here and there seats divided by iron rods so that tired tramps should not sleep on them. And the green fields by Mottingham where the kingcups used to grow, and the willows by the little stream, they are eaten up by yellow caterpillars of streets all alike, all horrible; . . . everything is getting uglier and uglier. And no one seems to care.

This passage from *Wings and the Child* (1913) is itself a distant echo of Ruskin's lament for the rape of Croxted Lane in Dulwich, where he had once walked with his mother among flowers and flowering trees: 'No existing terms of language known to me are enough to describe the forms of filth, and modes of ruin, that varied themselves along the course of Croxted Lane.'[4] Edith had grown up at a time when Ruskin's reputation was at its height: his social criticism had provided the foundation of her own socialist beliefs, and phrases and titles of his are deliberately redeployed throughout her work. The elegiac rhythms of his prose must have resonated through her memory as she wrote. South London had indeed spread steadily outwards, despoiling the green fields and country lanes in a triumph of raw red and yellow brick. Ruskin, living at Herne Hill in the 1820s and 30s, like Edith in Lower Kennington Lane in the 1860s, had grown up in a semi-rural landscape soon to be buried forever.

H. G. Wells, whose early home was further south in the (then) village of Bromley in the 1870s, described in similarly Ruskinian terms its urbanization, in *The New Machiavelli* (1911). At the beginning of the novel, the hero Remington is living with his lover and her baby in exile on a remote island. Yet even though he is now far from the seats of power, he is still preoccupied with the crucial political question of how society should be ordered: the opening pages invoke Machiavelli's instructions to his Prince (which Remington intends to rewrite), as well as Plato's schemes for his ideal Republic, (earlier discussed in *A Modern Utopia*). From here the narrative leads directly into a description of the elaborate cities and empires that, as a child, Remington had built upon the nursery floor, implying that, even then, he was already unselfconsciously concerned with the construction and reconstruction of society:

> It is the floor I think of chiefly; over the oilcloth of which, assumed to be land, spread towns and villages and forts of wooden bricks; there are steep square hills (geologically, volumes of Orr's *Cyclopaedia of the Sciences*) and the cracks and spaces of the floor and the bare brown surround were the water channels and open sea of that continent of mine.

This passage must have been written by the end of 1909 for the book's manuscript was with his publishers by February 1910, though it was not actually published until 1911.[5]

In January 1910 the first episodes of Edith's new serial *The Magic City* appeared in *The Strand*. It describes the building of an elaborate miniature city, a game she was currently obsessed with. In the middle of that month she and John had crossed the Irish Channel to stay for a week or two at Dunsany Castle near Dublin. There the Dunsanys joined in her latest game, building fantasy cities all over the drawing room floor out of the bric-à-brac that littered the Edwardian parlour – ashtrays, fingerbowls – anything that might be redeployed as exotic architectural features.[6] In *The Magic City*, the building takes place on a table-top rather than on the floor, but many of its details nevertheless recall Wells's elaborately described childhood game. The row between the Blands and the Wellses had, of course, been far too bitter for Edith to acknowledge that she owed Wells any sort of debt especially since she had been invited to build a 'magic city' as part of the Children's Welfare Exhibition at Olympia at the end of 1912.[7]

Like Edith, Wells was particularly fascinated by miniature buildings and battles and when he lived at Sandgate, he had spent hours playing with his two sons on the nursery floor, building railways and cities and conducting wars with toy soldiers. His graphic account of these games in *The New Machiavelli* led to a suggestion that he should write a book about them – the result was *Floor Games*, published in December 1911. It included a number of ideas that had already contributed to *The Magic City*, for Wells's floor games had been played out with his children and friends several years before either her story or his was actually written. Common to both are islands, islanders and temples – the earliest version of *The Magic City* was entitled 'The Temple City'. Wells asserts as a general principle that 'a large part of the fun of this game lies in the witty incorporation of all sorts of extraneous objects', an aspect that particularly appealed to Edith, who loved any exercise demanding ingenuity and inventiveness. Inevitably, they shared the same building materials – wooden building blocks, plasticine, twigs from the garden potted up in cotton reels, and miniature animals, employed as architectural or sculptural features.[8]

There are some characteristic differences: Wells's games commonly involved wars. Indeed he wrote a sequel to *Floor Games* entitled *Little Wars* (1913), which lays down some of the principles for modern war gaming, while adding, in a sad little postscript written under the shadow of approaching war, how much better it would be if all wars could be confined to nursery floors. Another characteristic difference between the two is reflected in their contrasting attitudes to machinery: Wells's floor games invariably featured a miniature railway, complete with stations, a scenic route and a clockwork train. Edith had inherited from William Morris a fundamental distrust of machinery of any kind, so that it figures in her Utopian city only as a threat: there is a law that anyone who asks for machinery must keep on using it (though the children enjoy a ride in someone else's motor car). *The Magic City* continued the debate as to how to reconstruct society that had been pursued through several of her earlier children's books. The antithesis or shadow of the magic cities were the cardboard villas and factories made of brown paper with identical slit windows whose ritual burning Forster had witnessed. In *The Magic City* E. Nesbit's concept of a socialist Utopia was still bound up with that of Wells and his presentation of it, just as it had been in *The Amulet*, five years earlier. Yet if *Harding's Luck* (1909) reflected her loss of confidence in the future in terms of its hero's retreat into the past, *The Magic City* took this process a stage further by reducing Utopia to a child's model of order, easily broken up by an officious and unimaginative adult who unjustly dismisses its maker as a 'naughty, wicked boy' and a liar – Plato's claim against all fiction-makers.[9]

While the idea of building an elaborate miniature city as a figure of Utopia, as well as particular constructional features, owe something to Wells, the plot of *The Magic City*, that of creating an imaginary world and somehow becoming the right size to enter one's own creation, was Edith's own, if such a widespread childhood game or fantasy may be said to belong to anyone. She unequivocally claimed the idea as her own in *Wings and the Child*, where she described how she helped Fabian to make an Eastern fort to accommodate some beturbaned toy soldiers he had been given: she took 'brass finger-bowls and lustre

basins off the dresser in the dining-room' to make domes, with
chessmen on brick pillars for minarets, and supplemented the limited
supply of building bricks with small books.[10] This account is born out
by a remarkable story, written a year or two before she met Wells,
which involved Fabian and was evidently inspired by just such a series
of buildings – 'The Town in the Library in the Town in the Library'
(*Nine Unlikely Tales*, 1901). It begins:

> Rosamund and Fabian were left alone in the library. You may not
> believe this; but I advise you to believe everything I tell you, because it is
> true. Truth is stranger than story-books, and when you grow up you
> will hear people say this till you grow quite sick of listening to them:
> you will then want to write the strangest story that ever was – just to
> show that some stories can be stranger than truth.

What follows is a brilliant fantasia of fact and fiction: Rosamund,
Fabian and Mother are recognizably themselves, and the library, the
bureau and the children's Christmas presents probably corresponded
closely to their actual equivalents. It is a magical occasion, Christmas
Eve. The two bored children, in quarantine for measles, break up the
familiar surface of things through an act of transgression in the form of
disobedience: though Mother has specifically forbidden them to do so,
they open the bureau drawers and discover their Christmas presents
hidden inside. They then pull the drawer on to the floor and build a
town inside it with bricks, picture blocks and books. 'The Beauties of

THE GUARD-ROOM

Literature in fifty-six fat little volumes' is used to make a set of steps and a gateway which the children climb and pass through into an interior world:

> Rosamund and Fabian simply walked up the steps into the town they had built. Whether they got larger or the town got smaller, I do not pretend to say.[11]

Once inside the town, the children are pursued by the toy soldiers that they had found among their Christmas presents. In flight from them, they come upon their own house. They run inside and upstairs to the library where they proceed to break open the bureau drawer, knowing that they will find inside the dried figs and crystallized fruit for Christmas. Armed with these, they can feed the hungry soldiers:

> You see the curious thing was that the children had built a town and got into it, and in it they had found their own house with the very town they had built – or one exactly like it – still on the library floor.

Making another gateway of books, they find themselves trapped in an apparently infinite regress of towns and houses and libraries, in a startling modern image of the endlessly mirroring series of literature, imagination and experience. As a story, it impressed E. M. Forster,[12] and must also have appealed to the Argentinian writer Jorge Luis Borges, self-confessedly an admirer of her contemporaries, Wells and Chesterton. Yet while the particular combination of library and labyrinth lend this tale a modernist twist, all Edith's children's stories are preoccupied with the effect of reading upon the child, even though only a small number of them actually allow books as objects, with their contents, to be reified and figure significantly in the narrative. Curiously, this process occurs most often at the beginning ('The Book of Beasts', 'The Town in the Library . . .') and at the end (*The Magic City*, *Wet Magic*) of her career as a successful writer for children.

'The Town in the Library . . .' appeared in *Nine Unlikely Tales* in 1901, but there are several reasons for thinking that it may have been written a year or so earlier: seven of the tales in that collection are known to have appeared previously in periodicals (four in *The Strand*), and six of those seven were published before Fabian's death in October 1900. The relaxed and unsentimental treatment of Fabian in the story strongly suggests that 'The Town in the Library . . .' was also written before that date, since after it, she could only write of him with guilt and misery. An incident in which he and Rosamund discovered their

Christmas presents while Mother was busy with her charity activities might well have taken place, or else there may be a recollection of that other Christmas Eve incident when Fabian had stolen the sweets intended for the Deptford treat – an event which, in the aftermath of his unexpected death, had come to seem intensely distressing (she described it in her short story 'The Criminal'). The open question of when 'The Town in the Library . . .' first appeared has a further interest because, though it looks so startlingly original, a story by another children's writer, Evelyn Sharp, seems to resemble it in several respects. Evelyn was the sister of the folk-song collector Cecil Sharp, and was herself active in the Fabian and in women's suffrage; being in the same line of business, she was certainly known to Edith who had approached her in 1907 as a possible contributor for *The Neolith*.

Evelyn Sharp's story, 'The Palace on the Floor', appeared in her collection *The Other Side of the Sun* in 1900, a year before *Nine Unlikely Tales*. This story and 'The Town in the Library . . .' have sufficient features in common to suggest that one might have influenced the other. Evelyn Sharp's treatment of the friendship between a little girl and boy is written in a style so arch as to make any modern reader cringe; its winsome sub-Dickensian sentiment about childhood sweethearts is something Edith carefully avoided. In 'The Palace on the Floor' Prince Picotee builds a castle for his toy soldiers. His friend Dimples laughs at how seriously he takes them, but in the night, the Captain of the toy soldiers comes and frog-marches her down to the nursery where she finds that Picotee's palace has grown big enough for her to enter. Here she is given a meal of plaster dolls' house dishes, and she and the Prince, now King, explore the palace together. Next day they discuss whether or not they simply shared the same dream, and whether it might even come true when the little prince grows up. Though there are links with 'The Town in the Library . . .', some features of the story are closer to *The Magic City*, in particular coming downstairs at night to find that the toy building has grown; also the character of the bossy Captain, and the plaster meal which the children must pretend to eat.[13] It is possible that Edith came upon Evelyn Sharp's story while she was casting about for material for her next *Strand* serial.

Part of the framework for *The Magic City* was adapted from another of Edith's own stories, the negligible 'Cinderella' (*The Literary Sense*, 1903): Charling runs away from home when she overhears some careless servants gossiping about her father's remarriage. She comes upon Harry who is also running away because his beloved elder sister is marrying some chap he doesn't know, but already hates. Harry befriends Charling and takes her home where they discover, inevitably, that father and sister are getting married to one another. In *The Magic City* the focus falls not on the girl's feelings but on the boy's, and the far-fetched coincidence of their meeting is removed, since the boy has been sent to stay with the girl, whom he cordially dislikes, during his sister's honeymoon. An important theme here is the difficulty, yet the necessity of learning to share one's loved ones – something that Edith, like most people, found easier to recommend than to carry out. At the book's climax, the boy, Philip, must give up his claim to possess his older sister Helen exclusively by symbolically handing over to the homeless islanders the island refuge on which only he and she could live, and the only place where Helen can enter the magic city world. Philip's intensely possessive relationship with Helen is unlike any other sibling relationship in Edith's fiction apart from that of the 'Cinderella' story. It was probably inspired by Hubert's devotion to his sister Helen, eleven years older than he was, an age gap similar to that between Helen and Philip in the book. The 1861 census records Hubert, aged six, living with his parents and his seventeen-year-old sister, his elder brother Percy having apparently already left home. If Helen later became a schoolteacher, as family tradition has it, she may well have taught Hubert his first lessons and played the kind of delightful imaginary games that Helen plays with Philip in the book. Edith, herself devoted to her older sister Saretta, would have sympathized.

Once Edith had decided upon the outline of her story, she or her secretary made some typewritten notes; in the earliest drafts Philip is called 'Haldane Philip Haldane', his name recalling that of Lord Haldane, the Liberal politician, currently engaged in reforming the army. Hubert was said to have had an almost excessive admiration for him.[14]

> Haldane's sister is married to Lucy's father. They are all to live together at Well Hall. The children are left in charge of Lucy's nurse who takes Lucy's part in everything and foments natural dislike. Lucy is a white rabbit of a child, delicate and shy. She has been left to the care of a trained nurse, and is suppressed. Haldane has lived with his sister, who has played imaginative games with him. Nurse called away and Lucy taken to an aunt's. At parting with the nurse Haldane says 'May I play with Lucy's bricks?' The nurse says 'oh yes anything you like'. So

Haldane takes everything he wants for a city such as his sister has built, and builds the city. The servants scold him and say they shall clear it all away in the morning along with the other rubbish. So at night he creeps down to have another look at it. The room grows small [for 'tall'?] or he grows small and he gets into the city. He should be there some time before he realises it is the city which he himself has built.

These working notes, along with some textbook details concerning the Megatherium or Great Sloth, a cancelled chapter, and the manuscript of the book itself are among the few of her working papers to have survived. Today they are kept in a branch of the Greenwich Public Library because in 1913 a Woolwich public librarian, Philip Bursill, was sufficiently farsighted to accept them. Initially he sent her an appeal for his local collection. She replied by asking him

Is it a collection of books only, or would you like a manuscript of one of my books? This will probably be more interesting to the next generation than to this. You see, like W[illiam] S[hakespeare] I can't believe that my work will die with me!

When he replied in the affirmative, she sent him copies of *Daphne in Fitzroy Street*, *The Incomplete Amorist*, and *Rose Royal* (the American title of *Dormant*), and the manuscript of *The Magic City*, adding:

If anyone ever should be interested in this M.S. the most interesting thing will be the comparison of the notes with the finished work. The comparison will show how a story develops itself, and how far it sometimes travels from the author's original intention.[15]

In the cancelled second chapter, Philip is arrested by the guards for trespassing and taken before the city's judge – not Mr Noah but a Chinaman with a black pigtail. He is condemned – trespassers, Philip remembers, must be persecuted – but the judge explains that it is only 'prosecution', not 'persecution' that he is condemned to, and he is despatched as a first-class prisoner to the Red Tower with the kind gaoler (Shakespeare – or rather Shakespeare-Bacon, in the final version). Here a kindly professor of history (an earlier note suggests the gaoler's daughter) explains to him the traditions of the city, and the myth of the deliverer. Philip is told that he can stay on if he becomes a citizen. Notes then suggest that he would have had to perform three kind acts to qualify as a citizen, so he must help a child who cannot learn its lessons, mend a broken tree and rescue a fish out of water. On qualifying, he goes to live with the gaoler because he had liked his daughter, and at this point the notes and the narrative peter out. The most obvious difference between this earlier draft and the later text is that Philip here performs his task alone; he has not yet been joined by Lucy, though in one place in the cancelled chapter some lines for Lucy have been written in over the top; the various mentor figures – the Chinaman, the professor of history – are later combined in the familiar toy figure of Mr Noah, and the three kind acts are commuted to the altogether more ambitious notion of seven tasks which will designate their performer as 'The Deliverer'.

It was appropriate that the manuscript that Edith sent Philip Bursill in the belief that it would interest the next generation was that of a book peculiarly concerned with creativity and the permanence of works of art. At the centre of *The Magic City* lies the fantasy of an alternative world where everything made in this world has an independent existence, even after it has been destroyed and dismantled by the hateful nurse. Mr Noah explains to Philip, 'Everything people make in that world goes on for ever.'[16] Philip finds not only the city (or rather, the City, for it is not only his creation, but a blueprint for a better world), but his earliest efforts at building – a sandcastle (threatened by the sea) and the island that he and Helen had designed for their private delight. All this he must reclaim by performing the tasks, and to do so, he must accept Lucy's help, which at first he finds very difficult to do – after all, she is only a *girl*, and a particularly unwelcome one at that. But she knows some secrets that he does not, such as how the (now giant) crochet mat was made, and she is quick-witted and courageous, as Edith's heroines so often are.

Though building or making is the main mode of creation, the less literal 'making' of books underpins the story at every point. It's not merely that books make up the physical fabric of the city, as they had done in 'The Town in the Library in the Town in the Library'; they also provide some of its contents. In addition to the Noah's Ark animals, there is the magnificent Hippogriff: 'He came,' Mr Noah explained, 'out of a book. One of the books you used to build your city with.'

Ariosto's winged horse is only one of several creatures that quite literally 'come out of books', as the animals in the earlier story, 'The Book of Beasts', had done. Barbarians are released from Caesar's *De Bello Gallico*, and they can only be fought by legionaries, led by Caesar himself, summoned from the same book by Philip and Lucy. In the final chapters the city is threatened first by the power of inertia or decay, represented by the punningly named Megatherium or Great

Sloth (another book escapee), and then by the pointless destructive-
ness and vandalism of the barbarian hordes. In order to overthrow the
Sloth, the children set out on their yacht, shoot over the edge of the
waterfall and find themselves making a long, dark underground
voyage, an episode Philip suddenly remembers as deriving from yet
another book, *The Last Cruise of the Teal*, which 'Helen gave . . . me
just before she went away. It's a ripping book, and I used it for the roof
of the outer court of the Hall of Justice.'[17] But the long water-filled
underground passage is something more than an allusion to an obscure
adventure story: recalling the passage behind the Temple of Flora in
The Enchanted Castle where the Ugly-Wuglies were concealed, and
anticipating the underground passage that leads out into *The Wonderful Garden* where the imaginary panther lurks, it is also a symbol of the
dark and subterranean workings of the unconscious itself, as in
Coleridge's 'Kubla Khan'. Out of it the children will suddenly emerge
into the daylight of conscious thought, bringing order and meaning
into a society threatened by entropy and violence.

The Magic City is full of other books, whether as part of the
structure or merely glancingly referred to – even the parrot insists on
reciting Dryden's Virgil ('poetry of a rather dull kind that went on and
on'): ' "Arms and the man I sing" ' it began, and then something about
haughty Juno'. And there are less obvious allusions, as when Philip,
having built a new doorway for his city, finds himself, like Alice, the
wrong size to pass through it and, like Alice, weeps. But though there
is an insistent concern with the relationship between books and
imagination, the primary act of imagination is that of love, and of
identification with others. Before Philip can deliver the City, he must
learn to love Lucy and forgive Helen, while the destroyer is
characterized by her failure to love. As Caesar explains to her:

> '. . . life has pronounced on you a sentence worse than any I can give
> you. Nobody loves you.'
> 'Oh, you old silly,' said the Pretenderette in a burst of angry tears,
> 'don't you see that's just why everything's happened?'

The Pretenderette, swathed in her disguising motor veil, turns out to
be Lucy's repressive nurse, literally the city's destroyer, since it was
she who dismantled Philip's miniature city in the first place, leaving
Lucy trapped inside it and obliging Philip to build a new entrance in
order to get back in again to rescue her. In the same way, Caesar, in the
last pages, is also revealed as Lucy's father: '. . . Lucy cried out in a

loud cracked-sounding voice, "Daddy, oh, Daddy!" and sprang forward.'[18]

The mysterious 'veiled lady', later revealed as the nurse, designates herself by the suggestive title 'Pretenderette' during a scene where Philip and Mr Noah are discussing the killing of the dragon:

> 'If there isn't a princess it isn't fair,' said the veiled one; 'and I shall consider it's my turn to be Deliverer.'
> 'Be silent, woman,' said Mr Noah.
> 'Woman, indeed,' said the lady. 'I ought to have a proper title.'
> 'Your title is the Pretender to the –'
> 'I know,' she interrupted; 'but you forget you're speaking to a lady. You can call me the Pretenderette.'

In calling the nurse 'the Pretenderette' and making her the enemy, or even *the* enemy, of the city, Edith must have intended a mocking allusion to the suffragettes, who by 1910 had become very active on the political scene. The implication is that suffragettes were a threat to social order – aggressive, unfeminine women who had sacrificed love to self-seeking demands for power – for the Pretenderette is a pretender to the crown. And given Edith's sense of the primacy of romantic love, it is quite possible that she actually believed something of the sort. Hubert certainly disapproved of suffragettes, preferring to consider that women's function was to be supportive, comforting and decorative – an idea he clung to all the more because Edith's independence tacitly challenged such an assumption. Their young friend Gerald Gould differentiated between the Blands' attitudes to this political issue, suggesting that their approaches actually contradicted the received view of gender roles – 'he, hard-brained and logical; she, intuitive and emotional':

> E. Nesbit's attitude towards Woman Suffrage, for instance, was a reasoned one; she favoured Adult Suffrage, but refused for political reasons to support the Conciliation Bill [this would have allowed the vote to about a million women]; whereas Hubert's contribution to the controversy was to exclaim, with the manner of one swallowing an emetic: 'Votes for women? Votes for children! Votes for dogs!'[19]

Yet Hubert's irrationality on this issue also coloured his wife's view of it. In 1908 Edith's old friend Charlotte Wilson, who had gradually isolated herself from the Fabian Society through her commitment to anarchism, rejoined it and founded a women's group with a strong commitment to the cause of women's rights – indeed they claimed to

be 'the only socialist body to take part in the suffrage agitation', and
they joined demonstrations against the government later that summer,
carrying a banner that announced 'Women's Will Beats Asquith's
Wont'. It was natural for this newly founded group to turn to such
senior and experienced women as Beatrice Webb and E. Nesbit for
advice or support, and Edith accordingly agreed to read them a paper
on 'Motherhood and Bread-winning', a subject on which she was
well-qualified to speak. She must then have lost her nerve – at any rate,
she changed her mind about what she wanted to say, for her paper was
re-titled 'The Natural Disabilities of Women', and given on 29 May
1908. What she was actually talking about becomes clear in the
subsequent minutes: the executive committee decided to devote their
July meeting to

> a lecture from a medical woman upon one point raised by Mrs Bland in
> her lecture . . . i.e. is the normal action of sex function in healthy
> women a serious and insurmountable hindrance to vigorous, sustained
> activity . . . ?

Later minutes gradually become more explicit, and another reference to 'the natural periodic fluctuations in the physiological life of
normally healthy women' is finally elucidated when Dr Constance Fry
came to talk about 'the effects of menstruation'. A further letter on the
subject from Miss Alice Gardner, tutor at Newnham College,
Cambridge, was also read out; both would have repudiated any claim
that this 'natural function' constituted a genuine disability.[20] It is a
little surprising that the ultra-fastidious Edith actually elected to
lecture on this topic, even though she was speaking to an audience
entirely composed of women; less surprising that the point that she
had raised was thought to require authoritative medical rebuttal. Edith
may have found in the notion of natural disabilities an explanation that
accounted for the inferior status accorded to women in society; after
all, she knew herself to be as clever and capable as any man. The
reaction of the Fabian women's group to her lecture may have served
to increase her distrust, or even dislike of their political activities.

The veiled lady in *The Magic City* was not transformed into the
Pretenderette until the fourth episode published in the *Strand* in April
1910. In June of that year, Edith wrote to Evelyn Sharp to explain why
she would not become a signatory of a 'memorial' sent by authors to
the Prime Minister, requesting him to put through the Conciliation
Bill:

I am sorry I cannot sign the enclosed memorial as it does not embody my views. I am for adult Suffrage, but primarily my political interest is all for Socialism, and I do not wish Socialism to be endangered by an extension of the franchise to Conservative women.

Rereading her note, she deleted 'women' and inserted the words 'a class of women mainly [Conservative]'.[21] This particular line of argument was commonly used by socialists who did not want to see the vote extended to women: it looked intellectually respectable, merely privileging one serious set of principles over another; Gerald Gould had described it as 'reasoned'. But it could also be an evasion; coming from a woman who had enjoyed some of the freedoms usually reserved for men, as well as the homage and indulgence allowed to women, it surely glossed a little too lightly over underlying tensions and inconsistent commitments.

Evelyn Sharp's role, both as a writer for children and a well-known advocate of women's suffrage, is also suggestive. It was, after all, her story 'The Palace on the Floor' which stood in such a curious relation to Nesbit's own 'The Town in the Library . . .' The Pretenderette may include a reference, conscious or unconscious, to Evelyn Sharp herself, both as suffragette and as literary plagiarist: Edith was always annoyed by plagiarism, as her resentment of Kipling revealed. But if Evelyn Sharp is somehow connected with the Pretenderette, the relationship is an ambivalent one, for the charge of plagiarism could have operated in either direction – Edith may have been the borrower. And while Edith opposed women's suffrage, she had in practice enjoyed the benefits of independence, both financial and sexual. The 'veiled lady' stood for aggressive political demands and the selfish appropriation of what rightly belonged to others, stances that Edith consciously rejected as alien. But the disguising veil conceals a painful identity with her author, as the rejected self. She herself loved motor cars, and swathed herself in veiling to keep off the dust thrown up by unmade roads. She herself could be demanding and domineering, carelessly appropriating what belonged to others. Her most thought-less behaviour was often prompted by the fear, so memorably expressed through the Pretenderette, that she was unlovable and unloved.

The Magic City's central lesson is the need to love and share love. Philip must give up his exclusive relationship with Helen and learn to care for the mild and gentle Lucy, while the bullying and destructive nurse is condemned to make herself beloved to the characterless Halma men. The book seems full of topical advice in a year when Edith was finally forced to accept Richard Reynolds's love for her niece Dorothea, and his determination to marry her. Reynolds was the last and most faithful of her young Fabian admirers: one by one, Noel Griffith, Bower Marsh and Oswald Barron had married and gone their various ways, but Reynolds had outlasted them, had been her lover through the difficult years between. She had known for some time that he wanted to marry the mild and gentle Dorothea, and she seems to have done what she could to prevent him doing so, despite her own fondness for Saretta's daughter.[22] On 21 December 1910 their marriage finally took place. For Edith, only too conscious of her greying hair and thickening body, this event must have felt like the beginning of old age. Early in the following year, restless and desolate, she looked for a new seaside home – Dymchurch was pervaded by painful memories of Richard, who had so often hurried down to stay with her there during the school holidays – since 1901 he had been working as a schoolmaster at King Edward's School, Birmingham.

In April 1911, she found a house called 'Crowlink' at East Dene, high above the Seven Sisters on the cliffs of West Sussex: 'an old farm house near the sea – very lovely. Part of the house is Tudor and part earlier. It used to be a smugglers' retreat,' she wrote to her brother Harry in Australia. She loved its old chimneys and dormer windows, its brick path and lichened tiles, its hall paved with black and white chequered stone, its wide, polished staircase and slender, shapely banisters. Beyond lay cliff and sea, and she was exhilarated by the salt air, the wide sky and the sense of space. She stayed at Crowlink as often as she could during the next five years – and the house is still there today. Like all her favourite homes, it was haunted, and her very first action on moving in was to go round pinning up charms over the doors to ward off evil spirits – to little avail, as it seemed.[23]

It was at this stage of her life that a young admirer, Mavis Carter, first got to know Edith. With her younger sister Kathleen and their cousin Cecily, Mavis decided to write to tell her how much they had all loved her stories, but their first letters went unanswered. They wrote again, perhaps a little reproachfully, and received a characteristically contrite reply:

> My dears, I *did* write to you, in answer to your other letters. I wonder what became of *my* letter? Perhaps it perished in one of those conflagrations caused by bad boys who drop lighted fuses into pillar boxes. Or perhaps it was delivered at your house and was put in a

drawer and then slipped over the back edge into the house the drawer lives in, and when the house maid found it at spring cleaning time she thought it was an old letter and put it in the dustpan. But I suppose we shall never know. Its fate will remain forever a mystery like that interesting affair of the Man with the Iron Mask, or that never-really-solved question 'What became of the little Dauphin?'

I am very pleased to have your letters, and to know that you like my books. You are quite right to like Kingsley and Dickens and George MacDonald better than you like me, my dear Cecily. There is one other person whose books you ought to like better than mine – and that is Mrs Ewing. Oh – and Hans Andersen is another. If I had a magic carpet I would lend it to Kathleen for a month. Then you could all come and see me on it, and that would be jolly for all of us. I wish Mavis could have magic adventures like my children: the best I can do for her is to call the next child I write about Mavis. I like your drawings very much. Letters are much more interesting when there are drawings with them . . .[24]

Edith's claim to have answered the children's first letter was certainly justified by her general practice with regard to fan mail. Now at the height of her popularity as a children's author, she regularly received large numbers of admiring and enquiring letters from her child readers – sometimes they were even addressed to 'Oswald Bastable'; she conscientiously replied to them all. Paul, who occasionally helped her out with answering them, remembered that he had often written as many as thirty letters at a time. 'Jimmy' Horsnell continued to work for her intermittently until 1913, though in 1912 he was replaced for a while by a young man called Charles Bastable – a coincidence in which life seemed bent on imitating art.[25] Edith's friendly and humorous response to the Carter girls established a correspondence with them that lasted for the rest of her life and when Mavis was sent to boarding school at nearby Folkestone, she and her mother were invited to have lunch with Edith at Dymchurch.

Mavis's schoolgirl diary for 12 March 1910 recorded her mother coming to fetch her from school and 'something . . . that at the time seemed so like a dream I could hardly believe it':

Mother looked awfully excited. 'Mavis' she said, 'we are going to see E. Nesbit and have lunch with her now!' We got into a carriage and had a 10 mile drive to Dymchurch on the way I beseiged Mother with questions and she told me how it had happened. She had sent my photo to E. Nesbit and told her how happy it made me to be at school in the E. Nesbit county the answer was a wire reply paid, 'Can you all come to lunch with me tomorrow 1-30?'

Poor old Kay [her younger sister, Kathleen] didn't go she was so afraid she might feel faint cause she has felt faint lately. So when we got there oh! well She *was* a dear rather stout, jolly brown eyes and brown hair and a funny old fashioned house. Of course I felt rather shy at first but one dosent [sic] feel like that long with Her.

We had dinner with a dear Puppy scrambling all over the place and then we went a walk; Mother and E.N.'s Secretary went on the sands. E.N. and I talked; she was glorious she gave me one of her books and wrote in it and sent Kay a photo. At last we had to go and we drove away blowing kisses and I the happiest girl in the world.

[Things E.N. said to me]

There are two kinds of naughtiness one is being mean, and the other is carelessness.

I like the Amulet very much I was reading it the other day and found it quite amusing.

Looking back, Mavis Carter recalled Edith's appearance that day:

I see her now as she stood in the door-way of that Other House at Dymchurch ('the house with the red blinds'), her untidy brown hair pinned up in curls that were always coming down – the eternal cigarette – the trailing Liberty frock of some lovely faded colour – and her true brown eyes looking at you over the spectacles – looking you through and through . . .[26]

In November of 1910 Hubert became seriously ill. He had suffered from chronic heart trouble for some years, but now he had a major attack and was prescribed complete rest. At the beginning of January 1911, when he was well enough to travel again, Edith took him down to Cornwall in the hope that the mild air would do him good. They stayed at the Headland House Hotel at Looe for the month, and Hubert gradually convalesced. While there, Edith wrote Mavis a long letter about the various moral problems that troubled the child, problems they had first broached on the March day she had visited Dymchurch. In those days, middle-class children were encouraged to examine their consciences and develop a strong and effectively inhibiting sense of duty:

Mavis dear,

Thank you for your letter. Mr Bland has been ill, and we are down here for him to get better. And he *is* getting better, thank God.

My dear, I know what it is to have a temper: I've had a long and hard fight with my own. One thing I think one can do is always to say one's sorry directly one *is* sorry. Because some times, right in the middle of a quarrel one feels 'How silly!' or 'What a beast I'm being' and yet one goes on quarrelling because one doesn't know how to stop. Stop at once: say 'I'm sorry.' If the other quarrelling person hasn't reached the being-sorry stage it will perhaps say 'oh yes – it's all very well – you always *are* sorry when it's too late' or something like that, which makes one long to say every disagreeable thing one ever thought of in one's life. But it's better not to say them. It's better to say nothing. And take what the other person may say, in *its* temper, as a little penance for losing your own.

Losing one's temper is a sort of madness, and the moment you are sane again *stop the row*, no matter how nasty the other person may be about it. I know all this is easy to say, and jolly hard to do. But you have to try, and to try every day. I find it helps if you just say in the morning, 'Dear God, I don't want to lose my temper today, and you're going to help me, and I'm not going to lose it – am I?' And at night – if you haven't succeeded as you meant to succeed, own that you've failed – and tell yourself that tomorrow you aren't going to fail.

About your Mother and doing things for her – I can only say that since my Mother died things come back to me from years ago – little things that I might have done for her and did not do. And I would give the world if I had done those little things. On the other hand Mothers understand a great deal, and make enormous allowances.

Sometimes, I know, one tries to be extra nice, and then everything goes wrong, and the people one is trying to be nice to misunderstand and don't appreciate. But God understands and He is pleased.

You know, when people are very clever and very athletic everyone admires their feats. And people don't mind saying 'I took a first class at Oxford' or 'I won the two mile handicap' – but no one thinks of saying 'I have been good' or 'I am good' – the only person you can say that to is God. – It's a great mistake to think that one ought only to talk to God about one's sins, or when one wants something. He is our Father, and He is pleased and proud of us when we come to Him and say 'Dear Father, I have tried to be good today, and you have helped me, and I think I have been good. Thank you dear Father' –

You *did* ask me, didn't you? If you hadn't, of course I wouldn't have written what looks very like a 'preachy' letter.

I am so glad you like the *Magic City*. You don't say whether you liked the *Railway Children*, but I hope you did.

I haven't time to write much more, because I have given all my time to the serious part of your letter. But I like your drawing . . . We are in a house on the cliff and I see the sea as I write. It is quite warm and sunny, very beautiful. There is an island about half a mile out. An American owns it, and nobody lives on it but a caretaker. It seems a pity, doesn't it?

My niece has just married a Birmingham man, and I expect I shall be coming to Birmingham some time in the summer. If I do I shall come to see you . . .

The letter ended with a sketch of the island and a note that 'The island sits on the sea as cosily as an eider-duck on her nest.'[27]

Like Alice, Edith gave herself very good advice, even though what her family remembered were the occasions when she did not follow it. The particular note struck in her letter to the child – the determination to improve oneself – is most evident in the character of Bobby, in *The Railway Children*. Mavis Carter and her family were living at Edgbaston at this time, which explains the promise to go and see her there when Edith visited the Reynoldses in the following summer, but the allusion to an 'Oxford first class' (Reynolds had taken one) suggests that her mind was still running on the 'Birmingham man' as she wrote.

She was as good as her word, and that summer Mavis, Kay and Cecily spent a long, delightful day on an excursion with her and Richard:

> There was another lovely time when she came to Edgbaston in 1911 . . . and stayed with her niece Dorothea Deakin – whose husband took us all out in his car 'The Green Lady'. It was blazing summer – and there was much discussion as to appropriate garb for the occasion. We three children eventually went in bright coloured linen frocks – and sun bonnets to match – which delighted E.N. who deplored for the rest of the drive the fact that while *we* were all in sun bonnets *she* was in a little motor bonnet bought for the great event and which she didn't like at all. We went to Leicester's Hospital and Warwick Castle and Guy's Cliff and Stratford, where she thought it very wrong that one had to pay sixpence to see Shakespeare's church. We all had a picnic tea and certainly the day remains one of the happiest I've ever known. She often talked about it after.

It was an important day for Edith, too. She described the visit to Warwick Castle and Stratford in some detail in *The Incredible Honeymoon* (1916), though here the two young lovers are un-chaperoned by three children. In a letter to Mavis written during her last illness she sent her love 'to the three who went with us to Warwick that day. Do you remember?' and at their final meeting, shortly before her death, she talked nostalgically of it, recalling how much nicer the children's old-fashioned sun bonnets had been than her own motor veil. Mavis also remembered, but did not mention, her own embarrassment at not having the money to pay the entry fee for Warwick Castle.[28] For Edith it had been just the kind of jolly expedition she loved best, surrounded by a group of admirers, new and old. There were to be few such occasions left to her. But whether it was the company of three happy children or that of her old lover, his full attention briefly restored to her, that made that day so memorable, who can tell?

When Mavis Carter wrote of Edith, it was with a glow of unclouded admiration, but in conversation she recalled her imperiousness and old-fashioned insistence on 'deportment'; and though the puppy at Dymchurch was a delight, she also remembered how much she had disliked her snappy little dachshunds Brenda and Max. Rosamund remembered how dreadfully spoiled these two were, how they would rush all round the table and jump up on her lap. Edith herself adored them and kept them leashed to her chair during meals, often forgetting they were there and falling over them as she got up at the end of it. She had, of course, put them into *The Magic City*, along with the parrot, to help Philip and Lucy perform their tasks. Brenda was characterized by her endless complaints: ' "I knew how it would be," she kept saying in a whining voice; "I told you so from the beginning. I wish we hadn't come. I want to go home. Oh! what a dreadful thing to happen to dear little dogs." ' The presence of Max and Brenda in *The Magic City* (Edith had always put her dogs into her children's books) is obscured since, surprisingly, both the book's illustrators drew them as dalmatians instead of dachshunds.

Gerald Spencer Pryse had done the original drawings when the book was first serialized in *The Strand*. As Millar had always illustrated Edith's serials there, this change must have been at her own request and part of her exertions to get his work better known. Spencer Pryse was a dog-lover – he kept greyhounds himself and drew the cocoanut-bearing greyhounds of chapter two with energy and grace. He must certainly have known Edith's Max and Brenda, so the mistake is a particularly odd one; possibly he thought dalmatians looked more like Noah's Ark dogs, which is what they are, though they are also clearly described as 'dachshunds, very long and low'.[29] In general his lithographs for *The Strand* are effective, though he ran into difficulties with the Megatherium; and sometimes they are intensely evocative, conveying a sense of space or distance rather as a dramatic camera shot does, something that Millar's detailed, precise and slightly flat line illustrations seldom achieve. The book's publisher, Macmillan,

MILLAR'S VERSION OF THE APPROACH TO THE MAGIC CITY — THE DALMATIONS
ARE VISIBLE IN THE BACK OF THE CAR

nevertheless wanted Millar as illustrator and he produced twenty-seven new drawings for the published volume. Either because he was working very fast or else because he remembered Spencer Pryse's drawings unconsciously, he took over a number of his subjects and in several cases treated them from the same rather unusual angles, with the paradoxical result that these are some of his most powerful and memorable illustrations. He adopted Spencer Pryse's dalmatians without a second thought, but his Megatherium looks rather more like a horse, and less like a soft toy.

Millar was reinstated as the illustrator for her next serial in *The Strand – The Wonderful Garden* (1911). The early sections of this were, as usual, written under great pressure. She very seldom presented Millar with a complete chapter to work from. Instead, she would write out brief summaries of the episodes she was planning, often accompanied by little sketches and suggestions as to what scenes might make suitable pictures. In the case of *The Wonderful Garden*, one such summary and some of her instructions to him have survived. Typically her letters would wind up with the reassurance that if the drawings didn't fit the text, she could easily alter it:

> I am very much behindhand with this number, and I think it best to write and suggest subjects for two or three drawings so that you can be getting on with them. So I enclose a *précis* of the next chapter. The curate was mending the churchyard wall, himself laying the stones, when they found him.
>
> I will let you have the full chapter as soon as I can.
>
> If any little details in your pictures don't agree with the story I can make that right . . .
>
> Then [the children] think they will do something useful, to make up for whatever it was that they did wrong, and they set to work to arrange the books on the shelves according to *colour*, which seems to them a better arrangement than according to size or subject. They get all the books out on to the floor. (This might make a picture) . . .[30]

It looks as if Edith wrote herself into *The Wonderful Garden* by beginning with some familiar elements: the three children, the three C's (all named after their Uncle Charles), are staying with the Sandals from *The New Treasure Seekers*, here renamed Percival and Emmeline, but otherwise living in the same palely distempered house, its walls adorned with Watts's *Hope* ('a blind girl sitting on an orange'). The children's adventures begin when the sad little dress-maker who has been crossed in love (and who first appeared in 'Miss

Peckitt's Pincushion' in *Thirteen Ways Home*, 1901) gives Caroline 'The Language of Flowers' for her birthday. When the Sandals have to go away, the children are sent to their Uncle Charles, whose house contains the walled garden of the title. Here they are joined by the runaway Rupert, and what follows is a series of incidents which the children believe they have brought about by magic, although the older and more sceptical Rupert sneers at their credulity: while there are no events that cannot – just about – be explained in rational terms, the atmosphere of the book is imbued with that sense of imminent transformation that Edith remembered so vividly from her own childhood. The children's faith is unexpectedly supported by their uncle, who seems to be a portrait of E. V. Tanner. He is actually writing a book about magic and what Caroline calls 'the Rosicurians', while engaged in a search for his ancestor's two volumes of magic lore. After a number of adventures, the children find the books for him and plant the seeds of the flowers of heart's desire in the garden. When these finally blossom, their uncle announces that he is taking them to India to see their parents, their true heart's desire (as in *The Amulet*). *The Wonderful Garden* is not the most complex or well constructed of her books, but it has been greatly loved by readers for its detailed and imaginative recreation of that childhood sense that magic may, after all, be made to operate in the workaday world.

Edith's other book of 1911 was a romantic novel, *Dormant*, which has several links with *The Wonderful Garden*. Its heroine is named 'Rose Royal', which became the title of the American edition. The three C's had formed a society, 'the Royal Order of the Rose', called 'Rose Royal' for short by their uncle. Both books include adults who seriously believe in magic: the hero of *Dormant*, William Bats (who lives in Edith's Dean Street flat and is the former editor of the *Monolith*) is also an ardent Baconian, while his friend, Anthony Drelincourt, is studying alchemy in order to re-create with the precision of modern chemical processes the elixir of life. The book draws on fantasy elements that are more characteristic of her children's books, as if she could no longer work within the everyday world and was instead exploiting possibilities of fiction to transform reality. Events begin when the young people answer advertisements from a newspaper, an episode adapted from *The Treasure Seekers*; and just as *The Enchanted Castle* had included elements of the tale of Cupid and Psyche (or, more familiarly, Beauty and the Beast), *Dormant* is underpinned by the story of the Sleeping Beauty. Bats refers deprecatingly to Anthony's 'twaddling fairy stories about Sleeping Beauties',[31] while the book's title and the heroine's name also seem to allude to it : in French this tale is known as 'La Belle au Bois Dormant' i.e. the Beauty in the sleeping wood – 'dormant' describes the wood rather than the princess; its alternative titles, 'Briar Rose' or 'Sweet Briar', make further references to roses.

Rose herself is not, however, the enchanted sleeper. Her lover, Anthony Drelincourt, restores to life his uncle's fiancée who has been 'dormant' – that is, in a state of suspended animation for more than fifty years; she assumes, when he wakes her, that he is his own uncle, her lost lover, and because he has fallen in love with her in return, he does not immediately disabuse her. The three main female characters are all different versions of their author: Rose is Edith's usual heroine – lovable, capable, confident, generous and independent, Daphne of Fitzroy Street or Esther of *The Secret of Kyriels*, the beloved 'fairy princess'. Lady Blair is 'the fairy godmother'; she is seventy-two but looks 'like a Dresden shepherdess grown old', 'wonderfully girlish in a large hat and white veil', 'any age you please down to thirty'. She tells Anthony

> 'What I'm now going to say is rather in the nature of a love declaration. I wish that I were twenty so that I might marry you.'
> The charade feeling was overpowering as Anthony answered – 'I wish you were.'

She too had loved Anthony's lost uncle, fought his fiancée for him and lost. While she has aged, however beautifully, the fiancée Eugenia has been rendered immune from time by the elixir, freed from the ageing process to be young and loved for ever, a state all women must wish for – or must they? Like Elina in Çapek's play *The Makropoulos Case* (1922), Eugenia finds the thought of immortality unbearable and longs, when she knows the truth, for death as a release. Her 'dormancy' may be a figure for the young girl hidden in the ageing woman, the fairy princess tragically buried within the fairy god-mother. But as in *The Enchanted Castle*, the magic of imagination pierces the dull, material surface of things, as Anthony explains: 'How do you know what strange actions and interactions follow, when once, ever so little, you pierce the thin veil that divides the material from the spiritual world?'[32]

At the climax of the Cupid and Psyche story, Psyche, gazing upon her sleeping lover, discovers that he is not a monstrous phallic serpent but a being of flesh and blood, vulnerable as herself; this reverses the climax of 'The Sleeping Beauty' where the male lover gazes upon a woman asleep. As if conscious of this relationship, Edith had already introduced the Sleeping Beauty motif into *The Enchanted Castle*, which begins with the tomboyish Mabel pretending to be the Sleeping Beauty, under the wondering gaze of Kathleen and the boys. Though *Dormant* was written for adults, its structure and symbolism belong to the world of her children's writing, and its closest resemblance is to the complex interweaving of fact and imagination on which *The Enchanted Castle* and *The Wonderful Garden* depend. Its use of fairy-tale motifs allowed its author to find, in the elixir of life, a wish-fulfilling solution to the problem of her younger lovers who had all turned away to look for life-partners in women of their own age. But Eugenia and the novel as a whole finally acknowledge and accept that, for better or worse, we are only at home in our own moment, and with our own generation. Edith's fantasies are powerful precisely because in her best writing she retained a healthy distrust of the impulse towards fantasy and wish-fulfilment.

If *The Wonderful Garden* and *Dormant* explore the meaning of transformation, they do so at a time when bleak necessities increasingly determined her life. The next few years were lonely and unhappy, darkened by Hubert's heart trouble and failing sight. He had always been very short sighted in one eye (the monocle was a necessity rather than an affectation). Now the retina of his good eye became detached, apparently as the result of a bad fall, and he was expected to lose the sight of it altogether. Alice Hoatson became his eyes. In addition to her housekeeping duties, she read to Hubert and wrote at his dictation, working as his amanuensis as well as his secretary. Ill health had forced him to give up lecturing and finally he was obliged to resign as the Fabian's first honorary treasurer, but he still wrote his famous weekly column for *The Sunday Chronicle*, and continued to review some novels each week for the recently founded *New Statesman*. Clifford Sharp, his son-in-law, had been appointed as its first editor. Alice now spent long hours working with Hubert, closeted in his study, and he became increasingly dependent on her. This arrangement scarcely pleased Edith but there was no obvious alternative, and since a row might bring on a heart attack, self-control, or at any rate toleration became essential. The household – which still consisted of a fairly extended family – was now artificially peaceful, uneasily quiet. Edith's oldest friend Ada Breakell had for some years been living in the North Lodge, one of the two cottages that flanked the entrance to Well Hall. Paul was still at home, travelling up to the City every day, where he toiled away rather unsuccessfully at being a stockbroker. Iris lived with her little daughter Pandora, but she too worked in town, running her dressmaking business from the flat in Rathbone Place. John, the baby, once everyone's favourite cuddle, was now growing tall, though he retained the amusing precocity characteristic of late-born children. Edith felt increasingly excluded from her family's lives, and would retreat to Crowlink whenever she could, taking her secretary or John and his friends down with her, lest the solitude became unbearable.

Some time during 1911, Edith received a long letter from her brother Harry in Australia. He had finally married a girl called Jessie, and had a son, Collis. Edith sent a copy of *The Magic City*, saying

> I have no good news this time. Hubert's eyes have gone wrong – at least one of them has, and the doctors fear he may lose the sight of it altogether. But there is still hope.
>
> I wish things would turn out so that you *could* come back to England.

She asked him which of her books he had, so that she could send some of the others, and signed herself, as ever, 'your loving sister Daisy'.

Harry had evidently changed very little, and in the spring of 1912 he wrote asking her to invest some money in a newspaper he planned to start in Brisbane. She answered:

> I ought to have written before, I know, but I have been very busy and rather ill and we have been away. We are awfully hard up at present, so I can't take any shares in your paper, but I send you a poem which you can use if you like. It has not been published. If you don't care for it send it back, please. I wish your paper every success. And I will send you something else for it, if you like, later on.
>
> I wonder whether you would care for me to send you Baconiana – are you a Baconian or a Shakespearian? I have been investigating the question of ciphers in the works of Shakespeare – and have found several – but I don't know enough about figures to get very far. I wish you were here to help me.
>
> Have you heard that Alfred's son Tony is going out to Edward Nesbit [his great uncle] in Adelaide? Edward is paying his passage – which I think is jolly decent of him.
>
> I have had a one-act play accepted by a London manager, but it won't be performed till the autumn . . .[33]

The play she referred to was a comedy, *Unexceptionable References*, licensed to Vedrenne and Eadie of the Royalty Theatre in Dean Street, her old landlords. It does not seem to have been a great success and as it was never published, the text has not survived. It had been written in January and February 1912, when she had more free time than usual to work at it since, as she explained to Harry, *The Strand* had failed to commission her regular serial:

> It was a great blow to me when, owing to the muddleheadednesses of an agent, *The Strand* did without me last year. It made me very hard up, and added considerably to the worry of life. But next year there will be a story in *The Strand*.[34]

By 'last year', she meant that *The Wonderful Garden* had finished in November 1911 and, exceptionally, she had not contributed to the Christmas issue that year. Her next contribution – a Christmas story and the first episode of her last serial, *Wet Magic* – appeared, after a twelve-month gap, in December 1912. It was her longest absence from the magazine since April 1902, when *The Psammead* had begun to appear. Since December 1906 she had provided an episode or a story for them for every monthly issue. The loss of income was substantial since they paid her £30 or more per story – five or six guineas per thousand words, but she regularly received almost as much again on American rights, so that she might make up to £50 out of a single story and then resell it twice over as part of a book. The loss of a potential £500 a year or more could not easily be compensated for. She had become accustomed to having money to spend: since 1907 she had run three homes – Well Hall, with its fleet of servants, a London flat at Dean Street (and later Rathbone Place), and the Other House at Dymchurch, which was succeeded by the handsome old farmhouse, Crowlink. She was not prepared to adjust her standard of living, but she was no longer able to maintain it. She had never entirely lived within her income and had always borrowed money on her prospects, from her agent, J. B. Pinker (whom she blamed for the loss of the *Strand* commission), and probably from others too. But in 1912 she could no longer pay off her debts; it was around this time that she started to borrow money from Bernard Shaw, and her family began to blame her insolvency on the mysterious fascination of the Bacon-Shakespeare cipher.

But why had *The Strand* failed to commission a serial from their most popular children's author? Was there some further explanation than her agent's 'muddleheadednesses'? She herself tended to be quarrelsome and sometimes even paranoiac over questions of money and copyright. Few authors changed their publisher with such regularity – her best-known children's books alone were published by seven different companies, and she seems to have dealt with nearly thirty different publishers in all. In her correspondence with publishers or with agents, she regularly assumed that she was being cheated – 'Uncle' Fisher Unwin, who had bought up the rights of most of her best-known children's books, was regarded as particularly suspect, and in the end her intense distrust of him resulted in a massive row. Her business dealings tended to be conducted in a plaintive, resentful or peevish tone that must have been trying for her correspondents.[35]

Another explanation for her loss of *The Strand* commission in 1912 may lie in a more fundamental psychic exhaustion: during the last ten years, she had written an enormous amount of fiction both for adults and children. Her creative energies flagged as she missed the excitement and admiration that had once buoyed her spirits up. Lonely and tired, her year's respite from *The Strand* must have felt like a liberation, as well as a deprivation. In December 1912 she contributed to it the first episode of a new serial, *Wet Magic*, and a short story, 'The Sleuth Worm', which was largely a reworking of earlier ideas; and when *Wet Magic* came to an end in August 1913, she never wrote for *The Strand* again. Its literary editor, Greenhough Smith, set high standards, and anyway she had lost the impulse to work.

In the autumn of 1912 the five-year lease on Royalty Chambers fell in, and she moved to 42 Rathbone Place, where E. V. Tanner continued to pursue his arcane research in an attic room. The move was a major upheaval but 'the British workman is a wonderful being', she declared. Soon afterwards she wrote another long letter to her brother Harry, who had apparently made some carping comments on the poem she had sent him for his newspaper:

> Do just what you like with the poem – and if you get any money for it give the same to Collis as a little present from his Aunt. I think the *idea* of the last verse is all right, but I agree with you that it might have been more poetically expressed. On the other hand I felt it needful to *condense* at that point . . .
>
> We live very quietly now that the girls are married and Hubert's eyes are so bad.
>
> I am *frightfully* busy. Rehearsals of my play every day. It will be performed next Tuesday. In addition to this (bother this pen!) I have

undertaken to build a 'magic city' of bricks and dominos and odds and ends at Olympia for the Children's Welfare Exhibition. And in order that it may be advertised beforehand I have had to build a part of it – about 10 ft. by 6 – in the flat which I share with Iris (she does dressmaking; and has a work room and reception room at Rathbone Place, close to Winsor and Newtons, and I have the other rooms). The bit of the city which I have built looks jolly nice, but it is a most awful fag to do. I will try to send photographs of it when they come out. I am to have a 'stand' 32 ft. by 20 which will be like a room, open on one side, and lining with blue (to show like sky). Millar's illustrations are also to be shown. The tables on which the city will be built will be about 18 ft. by 8, so you see it's no light job to cover all that space with towers and bridges and palaces and gardens, all made of common objects of the home such as biscuit tins and bowls and chessmen and draughts and dominos and tea-kettle lids . . .

I had no idea when I undertook this Magic City building what a bother it would be, or I should never have undertaken it – but they say it will be a good advertisement. I am also to read fairy tales at Olympia . . .

I will send you *The House of Arden*. I'm glad you like *Harding's Luck*. I am extremely fond of it myself. I am sending you *The Incomplete Amorist* and *Daphne*. If there are any others you want let me know.

It is a good thing for you that the thick of the world's between us, or I should certainly insist on your teaching me how to deal with logarithms, because the Shakespeare cipher I am after involves the use of Logs, not Briggs but Napiers. I can get no books dealing with Napier's Logs . . . And I am quite incapable of learning such things from books even if there were one, which I don't believe there is.[36]

The production of her play, *Unexceptionable References*, offered one kind of distraction, the city-building at Olympia another – both were welcome alternatives to contemplating the empty pages she could not fill. *The Magic City* had not sold at all well and the idea of making one to advertise the book had come to her during the summer. She approached the book's publisher, Macmillan, with the suggestion that she might hold a small exhibition at Selfridge's, the famous department store. Various arrangements were made for her to do so and she began setting the city up but, according to H. R. Millar who went along to help, she used so many of the toy department's bricks that the manager refused to supply her with any more. Growing impatient with his meanness, she packed up her own materials and walked out. The possibility of transferring the scheme to another department store such as Debenhams, Hamleys or Gorringes was discussed, but then she came up with the much better idea of putting it on at the Children's Welfare Exhibition to be held at Olympia at the end of that year. Here she could have a larger stand, with space for Millar's drawings and for her books to be displayed and sold. The exhibition, sponsored by the *Daily News*, was to be visited by royalty. Sir Frederick Macmillan obligingly agreed to pay for the bricks, while she was to receive an appropriate proportion of the gate money.[37]

Her book *Wings and the Child* (1913) describes in careful detail how the magic city at Olympia was constructed, though its larger subject was the role of imagination in children's play, and 'the science of building a magic city in the soul of a child':

> Let me remember how many good friends I found among the keepers of stalls, how a great personage of the *Daily News* came with his wife at the last despairing moment, and lent me the golden and ruby lamps from their dining-table, how the Boy Scouts 'put themselves in four' to get me some cocoa-nuts for roofs of cottages, how their Scout Master gave me fourteen beautiful little ivory fishes with black eyes, to put in my silver paper ponds, how the basket-makers on the one side and the home hobbies on the other were to me as brothers, how the Cherry Blossom Boot Polish lady gave me hairpins and the wardens of Messrs. W. H. Smith's bookstall gave me friendship, how the gifted boy-sculptor for the Plasticine stall, moved by sheer loving-kindness, rushed over one day and dumped a gorgeous prehistoric beast, modelled by his own hands, in the sands about my Siberian tomb, how the Queen of Portugal came and talked to me for half an hour in the most flattering French, while the Deity from the *Daily News* looked on benign.
>
> . . . My big magic city at Olympia showed me . . . that the building of magic cities interests practically every one, young or old.[38]

The tone of this account is one of affectionate reminiscence, and she undoubtedly enjoyed meeting the many admirers who came to wonder at the fantastic miniature city, to buy her books and listen to her explanations as to how she had designed and made its various different features; but her correspondence with Macmillan tells a rather different story: they had displayed leaflets for children's books by other writers, but not for her; they expected her to pay for the watchman's overtime – 'As to my time and expense – I have done practically nothing since the third week in October except work for the success of the City, and spend money on it and its attendant expenses.'

Conscious that she was behaving like a spoilt child, she excused herself to Mr Ratcliffe of Macmillan, explaining and justifying her behaviour in terms that anticipated those of *Wings and the Child*, as well as other more personal apologies that she found herself making in later life:

> I am still not at all well: the failure of *The Magic City* has quite knocked me over. You know, really, I am a person who has never quite grown up, (that is why I am able to write for children!) and I feel this blow as though I were a disappointed child.

But Macmillan had had enough, or she had had enough of them. At any rate she did not publish with them again. In April 1913 she wrote regretfully to Sir Frederick, as she sent in the bill for the bricks:

> As I have just had the enclosed from Selfridge's it is evident that something happened to their account – suffragettes perhaps, and that you never received it . . .
>
> I am sorry the venture did not turn out more profitable for you and for me, but I still hope the advertisement will not be thrown away. By the way, it is a long time since I had any statement of accounts from your firm . . .[39]

Her last children's book, *Wet Magic*, serialized in *The Strand* from December 1912 to August 1913, gives every sign of having been written under strain. The four children are lifeless (the girls were duly called Mavis and Kathleen, after the Carter sisters) and their Mermaid guide is at first acid-tempered in the manner of the psammead or the mouldiwarp. There is one moment of genuine imaginative power at the outset as the children recite Milton's invocation 'Sabrina fair, listen where thou art sitting . . .' and glimpse something move in the depths of their aquarium; but the under-sea adventures that occupy most of the book are too distantly related to daily experience to be compelling. Whereas the large element of fantasy in *The Magic City* had been sustained by the replay, on an imaginary level, of tensions existing in the familiar everyday world, no such compensating human drama operates in the outer story of *Wet Magic*. Edith makes the children suffer under the regime of the unsympathetic Aunt Enid ('much older than a real aunt and not half so nice' – all but her early work had extolled the devotion and 'unsung heroism' of aunts, and she herself had proved a generous one to Alfred's children). Aunt Enid rather implausibly reveals just how old-fashioned she is by imposing the hated books of Edith's own childhood on the children – *Eric, or Little by Little* (1858, by F. W. Farrar) and the apparently imaginary and parodic title, *Elsie, or Like a Little Candle*.[40] The theme of books, good and bad, is still central: a range of literary water spirits are conjured up, from Milton's Sabrina and Heine's Lorelei to Undine, from Kingsley's *Water Babies* to Arnold's 'Forsaken Merman', and at the extraordinary climax, the good and bad 'book people' slog it out in a battle for possession of the undersea world, itself a figure for the imagination. But though the idea of the good and evil influences of literature literally fighting for possession of the caverns of the mind is a promising one, the terms of the struggle are curiously and uncharacteristically muddled, as if its author lacked the energy to work out its rationale.

The Mermaid explains to the children that the people in the books

'are always trying to get out of the books that the cave is made of; and some of them are very undesirable characters. There's a Mrs Fairchild – we've had a great deal of trouble with her, and a person called Mrs Markham who makes everybody miserable, and a lot of people who think they are being funny when they aren't – dreadful.'[41]

Mrs Fairchild is from Mrs Sherwood's harshly evangelical *History of the Fairchild Family*, which, like most Victorian middle-class children, Edith had long ago read and been frightened by, though as a character Mrs Fairchild is undoubtedly gentler than her husband. But Mrs Markham isn't exactly 'out of' a book at all: she was the author of a series of history text books which Edith must have used at school and grown to hate. The confusion of unpleasant fictional characters (Uriah Heep, Caliban, Giant Blunderbore, grumpy Aunt Fortune from Elizabeth Wetherell's *The Wide, Wide World* and Mrs Randolph from the same author's *Melbourne House*) with real and thoroughly well-meaning authors like Mrs Barbauld who, by the mid-nineteenth century, had merely come to seem boring, blunts whatever point the battle might have made and suggests that, at a deeper level, its author was no longer confident of mastering or ordering the disruptive elements of wish-fulfilment, imagination and magic. Like Caesar in *The Magic City*, real historical figures join in, and victory goes to the book heroines, disciplining mothers led by Boadicea, Joan of Arc and Kingsley's Amazon, Torfrida, who carry off Mrs Markham, Aunt Fortune and Miss Murdstone under their large and capable arms as if they were so many naughty children.

Writing to her brother Harry late in 1913, Edith could find no good news to give him; she was overwhelmed by depression and a sense of utter defeat:

I am very glad that things are looking brighter for you, and that your health is better. Things are pretty black for us – Hubert has practically lost his sight – he is undergoing a very expensive treatment which *may* do some good, but so far has done very little, if any. I am getting very tired of work, and the expenses of life don't seem to get less. I wish everyone had a small pension at 50 – enough to live on. I have had a novel in hand for some time, but I have been too worried to get on with it.

   I am now going into the country for a few weeks, in the hope of getting some work done.[42]

The novel she had begun work on, *The Incredible Honeymoon*, was not to be completed for another two years, years that saw Hubert's death and the start of the Great War. In the meantime Edith took refuge at Crowlink, and from there wrote to Lady Dunsany on the large sheets of coloured paper that she normally used for her professional writing because, she explained, she had used up her letter paper and 'Eastbourne is not reached under two hours':

I am very glad you like *Wings and the Child*. I enjoyed writing it. Indeed I am getting very tired of writing stories, and wish I need only write verse, and set down the things I think. Any success my stories have had is due I think to a sort of light-hearted outlook on life – and now that Hubert's eyes have failed him a steam-roller seems to have gone over all one's hopes and ambitions, and it is difficult to remember how it felt to be light-hearted.

   I am down at Crowlink trying to get well and to do a little work. It is a lonely little house on the Downs, not a sound all day but the wind and the sea, and on sunny days, the skylarks. The quiet is like a cool kind hand on one's forehead. There are no flowers now, except the furze which as you know only goes out of flower when kisses go out of season – so I have cut two standard furze trees and put them in pots. They look exactly like Japanese dwarf pine-trees – only they are covered with the sweet-scented yellow furze-flowers. They are a great solace. I am alone here except for the dogs, and my new secretary, a quiet youth who types what I write and in the evening plays chess with me. We neither of us are chess-players, so it is quite a pleasant amusement – and not the weighty business that your real chess-player makes of the game.[43]

The silence and space were at once soothing and disorientating. While down at Crowlink, on this occasion or some other at about this time, Edith seems to have lost her sense of humour, proportion and even, for a while, her reason. She wrote to her new agent, A. P. Watt (she had dumped J. B. Pinker in 1912, after the loss of the *Strand* commission), urging him to drop everything and come down at once:

> I know it sounds mad, but I have found out the Shakespeare cipher. I
> have told no one but you. The discovery ought to be worth thousands of
> pounds. I can't leave my work. Do trust my word. I have imagination
> but I am not a fool or a liar. *Come and see.* You will be very glad if you
> *do* come. It is wonderful yet simple and you can work it yourself. I am
> willing to trust you with the secret, and I think you will come at once
> and receive it . . .
>
> *It comes out as definitely as the result of an addition sum.* You will see.
> You will see . . .
>
> Try not to think about history or literature or the *improbability* of
> cipher being there. It *is* there.

Her delusion seems to have induced a state of mild paranoia – the
several letters are postscripted 'Please tell no one', 'Please keep all my
letters locked up. I don't want your staff to know anything about the
matter.' She proposed to Watt that she should write some articles
giving samples of her results – 'Then let Sidney Lee [the Shakespeare
scholar] and Miss Marie Corelli attack my results. Then produce the
cipher key.' The 'discoveries' themselves amount to several short
fragments of verse and prose, some of which even she regarded as
virtually incommunicable – another postscript warns that 'Mary
Fitton's is so scandalous that I'll keep it to myself till I've gone over it
to see if I can make anything more decent out of it. Perhaps I've made
an error in the working.'[44]

The fragmentary notes reveal that Elizabeth I had been secretly
married to the Earl of Leicester and had born him two sons – Francis
Bacon and the Earl of Essex. But the Queen could not love them
because 'F. Bacon was born out of wedlock by nigh a week'. The
theory that Bacon was the son of Elizabeth by Leicester was already
accepted by a few of the more extravagant Baconians, but Edith's own
version of this fantasy endowed it with several painfully personal
twists:[45] seeing herself as Elizabeth, the seven unmarried months of
her own first pregnancy were here telescoped to seven days and offered
as an explanation of her failure to love her elder son; and the guilt of
that first sin was associated with the failure to love and therefore to save
her ill-fated second son, for in this version the rebellious Fabian
becomes Essex, whom Elizabeth had condemned to death, just as
Edith feared she had condemned Fabian to death by permitting the
fatal operation. In unravelling the 'secrets, Mysteries and so on' of the
Bacon-Shakespeare cipher, she had revealed her own deepest and most

unspeakable fears. She had moved into the world of her own most
secret fictions, and what was hidden there now presented itself to her
as 'facts', revealed in the external, 'objective' world by means of a
cipher as rigid, invariable and capable of proof as 'the multiplication
table'. In such a state she could no longer write about the dangers of
wish-fulfilment or its hidden terrors, since she was living them; she
was no longer the master but the victim of her imagination, and the
apparently solid building blocks of reason itself had betrayed her.

13

IN THE SHADOWS

'I wish I could write some more about Roberta and Phyllis and Peter [the Railway Children] –' Edith replied to an enquiry from Mavis Carter, 'but I feel sometimes as though I should never write anything again – worth reading or writing, that is.'[1] In such moods, she would retreat to Crowlink, in the hope of making some progress with her novel, or perhaps merely to lift her spirits slightly. At the beginning of 1914 Hubert had lost what little was left of his sight and was now more than ever dependent upon Alice: with her constant help, he managed to continue to write his weekly column and do a little reviewing. A spell of balmy spring weather in early April encouraged Edith to set out for Crowlink once more, taking with her Cecil Gould, Gerald's younger brother, who had recently assumed his brother's role as admiring disciple: John Bland and his great friend Stephen Chant had gone with them. One mild evening, as they were finishing supper, a telegram arrived. The message, scrawled in thick lead pencil, read: 'Come at once Hubert very ill'. Edith told the others and at once ordered a car from Eastbourne. The long drive back to Well Hall was passed in total silence. Edith could not trust herself to speak. She alone realized what the telegram had meant – that the partnership of more than thirty-five years had come to an end. The journey into oncoming darkness, through an indistinct and unidentifiable landscape, seemed to anticipate her own future.[2]

Back at Well Hall earlier that afternoon, Hubert had been working with Alice in his study. He was now obliged to dictate his famous column for *The Sunday Chronicle*, a column followed each week by more than a million readers in the north of England. It was a Tuesday, so he began by writing a letter to the editor to ask whether there was any particular topic that he wanted him to deal with that week; then he went on to dictate a review for the *New Statesman* of some novels that Alice had read him a few days earlier. As he finished, he rose unsteadily to his feet and announced, 'Mouse, I feel giddy.' Alice jumped up from the desk, alarmed at his expression, and ran to the door, shouting to Ada Breakell, who was downstairs, to telephone for the doctor. She ran back and tried to support his swaying, massive frame, but he would not let her; instead he slowly lowered himself on to his knees on the hearth rug. As she tried to take him in her arms, he murmured reassuringly 'It's all right – I'm not hurt' and, in the minutes that followed, grew still. She sat there, as the light of the spring evening faded, until two doctor friends arrived (their own doctor had gone up to town for a lecture that evening); between them they lifted Hubert's heavy body on to the couch. In her state of shock, all Alice could think of was that the review and the letter to the editor that Hubert had just dictated must catch the next post, but the doctors reminded her that her first duty was to telegraph Edith, at Crowlink, to return immediately. Coming to herself a little, Alice also telephoned Clifford Sharp who arrived soon afterwards with Iris – Rosamund was staying in Dymchurch, convalescing after an illness. Clifford took the review and posted off the now pointless letter for her, adding a further note of his own.

Edith and the others arrived at about two in the morning. Though she had understood the import of the telegram well enough, when she actually saw Hubert lying on the couch, as he had so often done, she could not believe that he was really dead and rushed round trying to warm his body back to life, surrounding the corpse with hot-water bottles and swathing it in eiderdowns. Alice begged her not to, knowing quite well that the body must be kept cool, not warm, and the more so since Clifford, who had always regarded Hubert as one of the great pioneers of socialism, had arranged for a death mask to be taken. Edith called the doctor out; he arrived in the early hours of the morning, opened a vein to convince her that Hubert was really dead, sent away the wraps and explained to her as if to a child that the room must be kept as cold as possible. 'It was a time of horrible misery,' wrote Alice. Now that Hubert had gone, Edith seemed to be behaving like a mad woman, and with Hubert gone there was no one left who could calm her. Alice was uneasy as to whether the funeral arrangements were what he would have wanted, remembering that he had been a Catholic, but on this score at least her fears were unjustified: Hubert had died on 14 April; he was buried on the afternoon of

Saturday the 18th beside his parents in the family plot at Woolwich Cemetery. The service was conducted by a Catholic priest, the Reverend Francis Jeffrey, and there were about forty mourners. Among them was his elder sister Helen Craig who, three years later, was herself buried beside him.[3]

On the day after the funeral *The Sunday Chronicle* announced Hubert's death – 'Sudden End to a Great Writer's Career' accompanying this with a 'pen picture' of him written by a young journalist (later a playwright), St John Ervine. Clifford Sharp had suggested his name to the editor because he had belonged to the Fabian Nursery and had been an admirer of Hubert's. Ervine, researching the article in haste, had interviewed Marshall Steele's daughter Enid. She was a close friend of the Bland girls and had been very fond of Alice, but had never got on with Edith and the dislike had been mutual – indeed, only the previous year, Edith had borrowed her name for the unpleasant aunt in *Wet Magic*. The outcome of Ervine's interview was an article that devoted two paragraphs to extolling the virtues of the Mouse, while failing to mention Edith at all. Ervine recalled his first sight of Hubert walking down Walbrook towards Cannon Street Station:

> It was not, however, his appearance that attracted my attention, though that was remarkable: it was his manner. He was striding down Walbrook, talking loudly in his curious, thin, tinny voice to a lady whom I afterwards learned to know as his devoted friend and, when his eyes failed him, secretary, Miss Alice Hoatson. He did not appear to be in the least self-conscious, or to know that people were turning to gape at him. He simply went along telling Miss Hoatson very loudly 'all about it.' . . .

The article went on to describe Hubert's gifts as a public speaker, and the subsequent failure of his eyesight, which he bore 'very philosophically':

> Just what one would have expected of 'Hubert'.
> He found that he could dictate his articles, and Miss Hoatson helped him, reading to him, and then taking down his comments as he made them. I do not think that anyone ever guessed that his reviews of books were written by a man who had not read one of the books, but had sat patiently in his study while a woman friend read them to him. His style remained as firm and as acute as ever, although his sight had disappeared.
> He was a wise man in his way; a normal man with a very well-defined

view of a normal man's needs, and he was able to express those needs more ably than any other man of his day.

It ended by quoting Hubert's last words to Miss Hoatson. There was no indication anywhere in it, or in the *Sunday Chronicle*'s preliminary announcement, that 'Hubert' left behind a widow, herself a famous writer, and four children. The omission seemed to be more than just a matter of bad taste – it looked deliberate. Alice Hoatson described the article as 'the most insulting and impossible laudation – meant as praise, no doubt, but dreadful to me, and to Edith too'.[4]

It is not difficult to imagine Edith's fury: she had always feared that Alice had privately supplanted her in Hubert's affections, simply by being the little 'mouse' of a woman that she was by nature, and thus exemplifying all Hubert's confident theories that the role of woman was to comfort and support, and that they found ample fulfilment in so doing. But Edith knew that, in public at least, the respect and sympathy due to a widow was hers as of right: Alice, in whose arms Hubert had died, should properly have nursed her griefs in private; illicit love affairs were under some obligation to observe a decent discretion. That Hubert's own newspaper, with whom he had so long been associated, should so publicly and pointedly have linked his name with that of his mistress, while flagrantly ignoring the respect due to Edith's feelings as his widow, his acknowledged partner of more than thirty years' standing, was deeply wounding. Nor was that all – Hubert's will left the household effects to Edith, but the balance of his estate (valued at £900) was left in trust for his favourite son John on the grounds that 'my wife is happily able to earn a good income and my other children are provided for'. As if reasserting her rights in him, Edith set about editing a new selection of his articles from the *Chronicle*: they were published later that year under the simple title *Essays by Hubert*.

The row over St John Ervine's article set relations between Alice and Edith on a difficult footing for a while, though Edith must have known perfectly well that Alice had always shunned the limelight, found it dreadful, and would scarcely seek it for herself at such a moment. Hubert had, of course, often acted as a buffer between them, precisely because, as the main occasion of their mutual hostility, he had had to be. His death folded them in a terrible bond, since for both of them he was irreplaceable. For both, though in very different ways, he was the only man – his body, mind and personality altogether larger than those of any other. Though Hubert's infidelities had tormented Edith, they had shared a lifetime of one another's passions and companionship, through bad times into success. No one would ever know her or understood her as Hubert had done. He was her first lover and no one had ever succeeded in supplanting his particular place in her heart, even though at times she had sought to escape from their often painful complicity. In the years after his death, she kept his death mask wrapped in a silk handkerchief on the mantelpiece, a sacred relic. When she liked or trusted someone, or as a special sign of favour, she would take it down and unwrap it.[5]

After she had recovered a little from the immediate shock – for Hubert's death had come without warning – and the most urgent business arrangements had been put in hand, Edith's instinct, as always, was to run away from the house of grief. She decided to go to Paris, a city at once familiar but not haunted, taking John with her. For some years, now, she had known and liked a young journalist called Alphonse Courlander. He was currently writing a Parisian gossip column for the *Daily Express*, and living in the rue de Rivoli with his pretty, plump wife Elsa, a fashion artist, and their small daughter. Early in May, the Courlanders welcomed Edith to Paris, settled her in a hotel in the rue des Pyramides and accompanied her on various expeditions. Elsa remembered a visit to a cinema where the film was so bad that she and Edith collapsed into loud giggles. A bossy official came up and told them that they must not laugh there, and sat down nearby, to keep an eye on them. This set them off again, and Edith demanded, 'If we may not laugh, may we cry?' and burst into noisy simulated tears.[6]

She had not been in Paris long, however, when the shock of Hubert's death caught up with her, and she was seized with violent stomach pains. She lay in her hotel, living on bowls of bread and milk and wrote to her family, begging them to fetch her home. Characteristically, it was Alice who volunteered for the job: Edith instructed her to leave the housekeeping to look after itself and come to Paris at once. When it was a matter of making herself useful, Alice never let anyone down, and least of all Edith, to whom she still felt guiltily indebted for her share in Hubert's heart and home. She went over at once and found Edith lying in bed, fretting that John had scarcely seen anything of Paris since his arrival. Alice obligingly took John on a lightning tour of the parks and museums, to Versailles and the races, and then they set out on the homeward journey, arriving home by mid-May.[7] Soothed by the familiar surroundings, and the loveliness of summer in the garden, Edith recovered to some extent and turned to deal with urgent affairs, not the least of which was John's education: at thirteen, he needed some coaching to get him into a good school. A temporary classics tutor was advertised for.

George Seaver, a young man of twenty-four, applied for the post and vividly recalled his first sight of Well Hall and its mistress:

> I found myself on a day in the golden summer of 1914 . . . before the hall-door of a huge mansion clothed in thick ivy from base to massive gabled summit; and was ushered into an enormous upstairs drawing room whose windows overlooked large lawns including a badminton court, old-world flower borders and an ancient well-filled moat complete with barge, all overhung with weeping willows, wild briar roses, columbine, honey-suckle, berberis and many another flowering shrub. A desk overflowing with manuscripts filled the space below the central window . . .
>
> Presently the door was flung open and a tall lady in a trailing black silk gown and somewhat careless disarray stepped – or rather swept – into the room. Her countenance was round and ruddy, her bird-like eyes and curly hair were brown, her freckled wrists jingled with silver bangles, other trinkets hung from necklaces about her dress; she carried a long cigarette-holder in one hand and under her arm a tobacco-tin and papers; with nimble fingers she rolled her own cigarettes and smoked incessantly. She might have been a gipsy queen.[8]

For his pupil, John, much that impressed an outsider was inevitably taken for granted. Edith's children were harsh critics of her books, and John remembered hating their more didactic moments. Though she was always hospitality itself to his friends, her unreliable temper and occasionally prim standards of deportment and behaviour, applied without warning to anyone, could create embarrassment. She was annoyed whenever anyone was late for a meal, and she was inclined to give unwelcome or inconsiderate orders: sometimes John was despatched to fetch her cigarettes from one of the reputedly haunted rooms; sometimes the children were sent down to the main road with the roses left over from party decorations, with instructions to give them away to passers-by – a source of deep embarrassment. She liked to organize her family and was inclined to treat them like extra servants, rather than as individuals with wishes of their own: one perfect summer's afternoon she insisted that John and his friend Stephen Chant should rebuild a pigsty which she herself had once put up, and in which she had just decided that she was going to install some pigs – though, of course, she never did.[9]

In August war broke out. Edith, meanwhile, had twice written to the Society of Authors, asking whether they thought she had any chance of getting a pension from the government: 'I wish I could get a pension! ... If I had a *certain income*, however small, I could contentedly spend what's left of my life in making it do. And I can't write. The spring seems broken.'[10] She had not fully recovered from the illness that had begun in Paris.

Towards the end of the month her stomach pains suddenly became acute once more and the doctor had to be called in. He diagnosed a duodenal ulcer. Explaining that she must have an operation at once, he arranged for her to be admitted into Guy's Hospital. Alice now found herself suddenly left to cope, with neither Hubert nor Edith to tell her what to do, and she scarcely knew which way to turn. The most urgent task was to get Edith taken to hospital. Uncertain as to how she should set about this, Alice asked Shaw if he would lend them his car for the afternoon. Hubert had left Alice and Rosamund with clear instructions to go to Shaw, as his oldest and most trusted friend, for anything they needed. Shaw politely refused, saying that his car was being repaired, and enclosing £5 to pay for a substitute. Alice hired a car – it cost £1.8.0. – and conscientiously sent back the change. Edith, who had grander ways of doing things, scolded her when she heard about this, saying that she ought to have kept the difference since Shaw's secretary would merely put the money back into the petty cash, and Shaw himself would be none the wiser.[11] Edith had never had any scruples about accepting money from Shaw, either because she thought he still owed her something on account of all the feeling she had lavished on him or else because she knew she would have done the same for him in good times – had, indeed, done the same for others.

The operation was a very serious one, and when Iris visited her the next day, her temperature was very low and the surgeon who had operated on her warned Iris that there was little hope of recovery. Edith herself was insisting that all she needed was food, which the doctors had expressly forbidden her to have. Iris, feeling that if her mother was really dying, she might as well have what she wanted, went out and bought a jar of invalid food, Brand's essence of beef, and fed her half a teaspoonful an hour, all through that day. By the end of it, her temperature had risen and she was a little better. Iris left, feeling gratified at an improvement that she attributed to her treatment, even though it had been strictly against hospital orders. Edith's fondness for breaking rules was highlighted during her stay in hospital. Alice wrote, with a blend of admiration and disapproval, that 'she was quite the naughtiest patient they ever had but they all loved her and she was the life and soul of her ward'. She remembered Edith presenting the hospital matron with a cheque for £7 when she left, in a grand gesture of generosity.[12] Alice's tone when writing of her old friend was one of indulgence, such as an adult might extend to a child: while Edith's tempers and uninhibited 'naughtiness' shocked her, she was somehow proud of her ability to get away with it, to charm people and win them over as she had once won over Alice.

As she grew older the plea that she was 'a child at heart', and thus could not help herself was increasingly offered by way of mitigation or self-justification. She whispered it to John during her last illness, and he thought that she possessed both the good and bad qualities of a child – the energy and unreflecting delight, the generosity and sense of fun, but also the tempers, jealousies and injustice of a child; he found it difficult to regard her as an authority figure. In *Wings and the Child*, written the year before, she enlarged upon her conviction that inwardly she had remained a child in a grown-up world, offering it as an explanation of her success as a children's writer and describing it in an image taken from one of her favourite games:

> For a middle-aged gentleman with a beard or a stout elderly lady with spectacles to move among other elderly and spectacled persons feeling that they are still children, and that the other elderly and spectacled ones are really grown-ups, seems thoroughly unreasonable, and therefore those who have never forgotten [their childhood] do not, as a rule, say anything about it. They just mingle with the other people, looking as grown-up as any one – but in their hearts they are only pretending to be grown-up: it is like acting in a charade. Time with his make-up box of lines and wrinkles, his skilful brush that paints out the tints and contours of youth, his supply of grey wigs and rounded shoulders and pillows for the waist, disguises the actors well enough, and they go through life altogether unsuspected . . .
>
> They will be easily pleased and easily hurt, and the grown-ups in grain will contemplate their pains and their pleasures with an un-comprehending irritation.[13]

Edith recovered from her operation, and was out of hospital by the second half of September, but she was left very weak and in a state of deep depression, and after a further six weeks of more or less constant pain, it was discovered that the wound had not fully healed. Nursed lovingly by Elsa Courlander and Alice, she made a very gradual recovery. Three months later she wrote, 'Even now [I] am only able to get up to crawl about the house for part of the day'. Though inwardly shivering in the absence of Hubert's sustaining affection and encouragement, she began to look a little more like her old self again. But the coming of war had changed the pattern of life at Well Hall for good. Many of the young men whose company she had once so much enjoyed had joined up and some, like Cecil Gould, would not return. Alice and Ada Breakell had stayed on, and Elsa Courlander and her daughter Rosemary had taken refuge there when Elsa's husband had died suddenly in October 1914. Paul was still living at home and working at the Exchange, but he had undertaken special constabling duties and these often kept him out late. Iris and her daughter Pandora had also moved back to Well Hall and John, the most academic of the Bland children, was studying classics at the City of London School, and, inevitably, training in the school O.T.C. Most of the servants had left: younger men joined up, and everyone else who could went to work in the nearby munitions factories at Woolwich, as their contribution to the war effort; even Iris took a job there as an overseer.[14]

Edith was appalled by the war, and was constantly torn between her early, and ultimately Gallic, hatred of the Germans, and the painful recognition that they were human beings too. Her initial reaction was one of violent patriotism – she edited an anthology of *Battle Songs* (1914) and she wrote an article attacking the Germans: 'I felt it my duty . . . It was a horrible thing to have to do, but I did it,' she told her brother Harry. In a letter to E. M. Forster she voiced such violent anti-German sentiment that he was quite shocked, and though he replied to it, he found its tone so unsympathetic that he let their friendship lapse. Yet at the same time she was also taking active steps to prevent an old German friend of hers from being interned, and she rebuked Alice sharply when she shouted and clapped at a German Zeppelin shot down in flames, sternly demanding whether she realized 'that there are people being burned alive over there?' Joan Evans, then a small child living at Well Hall, remembered weeping with Edith 'as we saw the first Zeppelin that came down in flames and watched the black human shapes fall from the burning wreck'. Perhaps this was the same occasion.[15]

During the last year Edith had been wishing, and indeed voicing her wish, for a pension. In 1915 Maurice Hewlett, the well-known historical novelist, arranged for her to receive a Civil pension of £60 a

year for her services to literature. She was gratified by the compliment
and the financial help was very welcome though, characteristically, she
was indignant at having to pay income tax on it. It did not, however, go
very far towards alleviating her financial problems. In the past she had
always spent whatever money she had earned before she earned it and,
apart from a legacy of £500 from an uncle, received about ten years
earlier, she had always worked for every penny. Without the
substantial payments she received for her *Strand* serials, she was hard
put to maintain the upkeep of Well Hall, which was large and
expensive to heat and run. Now her friends began to urge her to give it
up, but she was determined not to do so. She had been in tight places
before and was a born fighter. Like her own Bastables, she held a
council of ways and means to consider how Well Hall might be made
to pay for itself. Even before the war, when money had first begun to
get tight, she had sold some of the excess garden produce to the local
working people, though she had never really managed to do so on a
strictly business basis: when a poor old woman came to ask for some
cheap flowers for her daughter's funeral. Edith had made her a special
wreath of narcissi and white lilac and written some verses specially for
her, but refused to take any payment. Now she set to, selling garden
produce to the munitions workers on their way into the Arsenal, as
well as, on a larger scale, to two local military hospitals; she had also
begun to take in 'pigs' – i.e. paying guests. In February 1915 she wrote
to her brother Harry describing her new life:

> I am much better in health – but I do not find I can take much interest in
> life. Without Hubert everything is so unmeaning. I don't do much
> writing, though I am always hoping I shall be able to again. I have taken
> in paying guests since last October. – If I could get a few more I should
> get on all right. Also I sell flowers out of the garden, and apples and
> vegetables. In the last eight weeks I have made by that alone 25/- a week.
> Then there is the pension. If I could live without writing I should like
> never to write another line. The war makes everything more miserable.
> It seems too horrible to be true.[16]

A month or so later she wrote to her old friend, Edward Andrade,
now an officer fighting at the front:

> The garden is beginning to look like Spring –
>   'The stream of the Kidbrooke runs fuller and deeper,
>   Bronze buds in the lilac, red buds in the creeper . . .'
> We have torn our hands and arms with tying up the roses, and Mrs
> Courlander digs and weeds and sows seeds which will grow to flowers

which you will see, please God, when Summer comes. And they say the war will be over before Summer is. When I say the prayers for you I think of you and all the happy times we have had together – particularly Dymchurch. I remember the great Water Row – and the Bridge where we were always in the soup, and how you tried to explain logarithms with matches and sand and how I sometimes thought I understood, and never really did! I still go on with Bacon Shakespeare, and it goes much better. But I think he means by logs a sequence of numbers not necessarily Briggs' or Napier's reckoning on logs. However!

I went to a concert at Queen's Hall the other day, the Fifth and the Emperor: and there, too, I thought of you and wished you well. I can hardly believe that this hellish war is *real*. It seems too horrible to be true . . . I am still not able to work – but I hope to go to Crowlink soon, and perhaps then I may have an inspiration. But with this war going on the world seems so unreal that doing any writing seems futile. It feels like beginning an epic on the morning of the Last Day, with the last trumps sounding in your ears . . . I have put your badge in front of St Anthony, so that he may keep you in mind, and I will burn a candle for you when I go to church on Easter Sunday.

As for so many others, her religion became more important to her during the war, and her letters to Andrade are full of prayers said for him, yet she seems to have fallen back on it in an effort to offset her even stronger sense that nothing held meaning for her any more. Her next letter admitted that 'Nothing seems worth while, somehow. It is like doing work on the sea shore when you know the tide is coming in that will wash away you and your work together.' Though she had hoped to find inspiration at Crowlink that spring, it turned out that the owner himself had decided to re-occupy it and would not renew the lease. So in May she returned to her other favourite holiday spot, and took rooms at 'Sea Breeze', Dymchurch.[17]

But the Crowlink house continued to haunt her, and it worked itself deep into the novel she was trying to finish: *The Incredible Honeymoon* begins in the nearby village of Jevington and ends with the happy pair installed in 'Crow's Nest Farm', alias Crowlink itself. The rest of the book sends its young eloping couple on an escapist tour through a series of places that had meant a great deal to her, as if her imagination itself was in flight from an unbearable present. She had always loved revisiting places where she had been happy. Starting, as she had started in her imagination, from the cliffs high above Eastbourne, the lovers visit the Guildhall Library and a dingy Registry Office in the City, as she and Hubert had done so many years before. They take a boat on the Medway and after an idyllic day, drop the crowbar in the water while trying to raise Oak Weir Lock. They visit Warwick Castle and Stratford, as Edith had done with Reynolds and the children on that not-to-be-forgotten day, and at Stratford they meet the Baconian who sounds so like E. V. Tanner. They visit Caernarvon and are taken round the prison by Colonel Bertram (i.e. Colonel Ruck), and the heroine wishes the poor prisoners well, just as Edith herself had done on a similar occasion. Finally the hero returns to his London flat in Montague Street (close to Dean Street), and then, after meeting the heroine at Folkestone, he drives her through Dymchurch, New Romney, Rye and Winchelsea, to end with a picnic lunch at Edith's favourite ruined castle, Hurstmonceux; they have dinner in their own new (yet old) home at Crowlink. The significant omission is, of course, Well Hall, darkened by the shadows of Hubert's death and the war. As if to compensate it for this temporary neglect, her last novel, *The Lark* (1922), places the beautiful 'Cedar Court' firmly at the centre of the action. *The Incredible Honeymoon*, a sentimental journey through her own past memories, appeared in America in 1916, but had to wait until 1921 to find an English publisher.

During the summer of 1915 the sale of garden produce got fully under way, and, once it began to run smoothly, Edith decided it was time to branch out and start a chicken farm on the site of the old stables and the back yard. She had been vaguely interested in poultry-rearing for some time, and was determined that hers should be run by thoroughly modern methods, using artificial lighting to stimulate the hens to lay more – in other words, an early battery farm. Several outbuildings were converted for the purpose, at some expense, and a person competent to run it was sought for. A Mrs Evans answered the advertisement. She was the wife of a West Country doctor with four children, but she was now separated from her husband and had some experience of running a farm of this type. In the autumn of 1915 she packed her children off to boarding schools, and arrived to look after the chickens. For a while, all went well and in the summer of 1916 Edith wrote to Edward Andrade in a more optimistic tone:

> The garden and egg business goes well. We sold 1100 eggs last week. And I stand all Friday and Saturday making up bundles of flowers to sell to working men. It's a queer life, but I think it's the best that could befall me just now.

But soon there was a shortage of chicken food, followed by its rationing; the artificial light failed to produce the high laying rates expected, and rats or foxes killed the hens and stole their eggs. Finally an outbreak of fowl disease put an end to the whole project and the surviving chickens had to be killed, plucked, trussed and sold off. Like everyone else, Mrs Evans found work at Woolwich, filling shells.[18]

During the war years Well Hall evolved into a small community with most of the adults contributing in one way or another to the war effort. As a mode of life it had simplicity and direction, and offered certain kinds of consolation, as Edith began to recognize. Mrs Evans's four children came to join their mother during the holidays as P.G.s, and her elder daughter Joan retained vivid impressions of life at Well Hall. She recalled their first night there at the beginning of the Christmas holidays, late in 1915; their mother met the girls at Liverpool Street and they crossed London to catch a train to Blackheath and a further train to Well Hall Station:

> That first night we assembled for supper in the dining room, the old Hall, where a long oval table was placed lengthwise in front of a roaring fire. The table looked gay; there was the smell of food and the chatter of voices; everything radiated warmth. But we were bewildered. Grown-ups gathered; there were other P.G.s beside ourselves, and we children, seven to nine strong, as always, congregated at the far end of the table. And then E. Nesbit appeared on the stairway. She was fifty-seven at this time, rather stout, and dressed in a flowing sort of dress not unlike today's Caftan, with a kind of longish oriental coat. She wore Turkish slippers and quantities of jangling bangles – she always wore those – reaching almost up to her elbows. Her face was small, her voice warm and soft. Her wispy hair was parted in the middle and knotted in a kind of bun at the back. She wore large spectacles and carried under her arm a box – she was seldom without it – in which was a tin of tobacco, cigarette paper, and a long quill cigarette holder.

On that first night, little Joan decided that John Bland looked sulky and disagreeable, and when he dropped a log from the basket he was carrying, she shied it at him. He turned to chase her and in the ensuing scuffle, the ice was broken. Later they became the best of friends: 'John would often carry my little sister on his shoulders, give his hand to his niece, Pandora, and tell me to hang on to his coat tails while he took us all over London to see the sights.'[19]

Joan Evans remembered with pleasure the children's involvement in adult conversation and games, for 'nearly always there was something exciting after dinner, in which all ages participated on equal terms'.

Edith had always loved games, and the household still continued to play 'Devil in the Dark' (a screamy, scary version of hide-and-seek), charades, dumb crambo and a great variety of word games, particularly rhyming or the 'noun and adjective' game in which a noun and two adjectives are drawn from a hat and a verse must be made from them; in a simpler game you have to find an adjective for a noun beginning with one particular letter. She also liked drawing games (she had always drawn well), including one in which squiggles had to be turned into different kinds of 'Madonnas' – on one occasion, Stephen Chant remembered, she had drawn an Eskimo madonna. She also enjoyed more conventional games such as chess, whist, piquet and patience. During air raids, everyone congregated in the hall to play 'racing demon' – a fast and furious version of patience in which you try to palm your cards off on everyone else – by the light of a single flickering candle. Sometimes there were sing-songs round the piano, with Edith or Ada Breakell playing. Everyone joined in with old favourites or sang some of Edith's own words, such as 'Rolling down the Medway'; sometimes there would be a fancy-dress party as a special surprise for someone; often the carpet would be rolled back for dancing. As a little girl, Joan suffered from asthma and bronchitis, as did Edith herself. When she was ill, Joan was sometimes invited to sit with her and listen to stories, or help her sew a dress or mend a sheet; once she participated in the great Bacon hunt, having been 'handed a large magnifying glass and told to see if I could find a pig in some old engraving or print of Shakespeare'. In the summer there was badminton and the inexhaustible pleasures of punting round the moat.[20]

The day-to-day organization of the household was complicated not only by the presence of the P.G.s, but by the wartime system of ration books:

Food rationing required that we each have our own coloured jar with our ration of sugar, and the same for butter or margarine. A certain amount was taken from each ration every week for cooking purposes. No swapping was allowed until Thursday; then the bargaining began. Cooking, whenever possible was done in a hay-box cooker. This was a large insulated box with two round, deep holes. The food, after having been brought to the boil in special long, round casseroles, went into the box between preheated iron discs; the lid was sealed tightly, and the casseroles left to cook for hours.

How the whole domestic running of the household was managed, I just don't know. Help came and left; the maids' sitting room became another bedroom, occupied by another P.G. I do remember a boy of about eleven, a cook's son, called Pelham, walking backwards and falling into a large crock of hot marmalade. His knickers were scraped and the marmalade, made with everybody's precious sugar, was reboiled and served. After that, when the marmalade was passed around at breakfast, one said politely, 'Have some Pelham!'

Domestic management was Alice Hoatson's province:

> This diminutive, vivacious, and competent little woman, with her big brown eyes and mop of grey hair, was, when we arrived, the pivot of all the functional and complicated household finances at Well Hall.

Mrs Evans and Alice hit it off at once, and later they began to cook for one another and took their meals together, either in the hut in the garden from which the garden produce was sold or in Ada's North Lodge, to Edith's annoyance. Some years later Mrs Evans took a flat in Blackheath and Alice joined her there for a year or two.[21]

For part of the war, Rosamund and her husband Clifford Sharp were abroad, despatched on a secret government mission to Sweden and the Baltic Provinces. Meanwhile in 1916 Paul became engaged to be married, to a young woman who taught at a Woolwich primary school, Gertrude Nebel. She was of German descent, but like most people in that situation, anxious to live it down. She may well have agreed to their engagement on condition that Paul join up – at any rate, he did so soon afterwards. He became a sapper with the London Electrical Engineers and was stationed at a garrison at Newhaven, where he worked as an engine driver for the rest of the war. Newhaven was 'a wearisome hole – and miserable for *him* because there's nothing for him to do in his off-time,' as Edith explained in a letter to Edward Andrade. She went down to join him there for a week or two soon after his initial posting, fearing that he would shortly be sent abroad. She sent a lively account of her depressing surroundings to her 'dearest Edward Edward':

> I came down here on Monday with the Englishman's '*sang froid habituel*' and I really thought, that first night, that I should have coughed my worthless life away. But I have worked a marvellous cure (or mitigation) of my cough with *Worcester Sauce*. The only warming thing I could find on a midnight raid of the Coffee Room. As First Aid in a bronchitic emergency it has its points. This is a horrid inn. My bedstead is enormous, modern and made of brass and iron – but I think

the bed dates from one of the earlier Ptolemys. It has a pyramid in the middle and slopes to the sides so that you can only remain in it by curling round the pyramid and holding on to the one pillow with your eyelashes. The sitting room is what William Morris might have seen in a nightmare. It is difficult to understand how so much plush and walnut and of such a quality could have been brought together in one *real* room.[22]

Though several of those who lived at Well Hall during the war looked back on their time there as a kind of idyll, and Edith herself was to romanticize it in her final, delightful novel *The Lark* (1922), there were inevitably tensions and difficulties, partly because she could never decide whether or not the 'pigs' should be treated as old friends; they were certainly invited to join in the various evening games, dances and activities. As a result, they were inclined to impose on her in ways which made her resentful, and her family even more so,. Among the P.G.s was the novelist F. N. Butterworth who wrote under the pen name 'Peter Blundell'. He was then holding down a safe job in munitions and both he and his wife were inclined to take advantage of their hostess's unstinting hospitality. They were hated by the gardener because they were in the habit of going out into the garden after dinner and helping themselves to the best fruit which was being kept for sale. But by the summer of 1916 her various domestic problems suddenly became quite bearable, for Edith had found herself an unexpected protector, someone who was ready and willing to fight her battles for her: Thomas Terry Tucker, always known as 'the Skipper', was a marine engineer, currently Captain of the Woolwich ferry for the London County Council. He looked 'like a little fat Cockney robin', was a keen socialist and had first met Edith through Hubert, whom he had visited regularly during his blindness, bringing him items of local socialist news. Tucker's first wife had died in January 1916, and as the year wore on, he made no attempt to disguise his admiration for Edith, and his eagerness to help her with her problems around the house or garden, whenever he was free. It was he who suggested that they sell the produce from a hut in the front garden, probably because he had noticed how cold it was for Edith standing outside in bad weather – such thoughtfulness was very characteristic of him. He organized a special team of men to bring the hut down one Sunday, and helped install a gas fire, so that it was warm and comfortable inside.[23]

Having the hut seemed to establish the sale of produce on a more businesslike basis. Edith wrote an excited letter to Paul at Newhaven in June 1916 describing the success of their first day with it:

We opened the hut-shop today, and did splendidly, taking nearly £5 for eggs and vegetables and flowers. I am sure we shall be able to sell everything we can rake together out of the garden. We got a drainpipe and set a jug of lilac and flags on top so that it showed from the road, and had a hen coop with 3 hens and a cock to attract customers! We are very comfortable now, with Louise [the cook] and a woman who comes in. I do not have to do so much house-work. We make our own bread: it is a fair treat, after the baker's stuff which is making everybody ill . . .

I was on my feet today from 8.30 to 8.15 so I am pretty tired: but I am very well. And Mr Tucker keeps up my spirits and prevents my worrying over trifles.[24]

Edith had always needed uncritical admiration in order to flourish. Mr Tucker, as everyone observed, was a very different figure from the clever men of Oxford and London, who had formerly provided it, yet his devotion warmed her back to life, and as her existence became important to him, so it regained value for her once more. His version of what happened next was that he found her one day in tears and low spirits and remarked, 'It looks to me as if you could do with a tug around here.' Her version, given in a letter of February 1917 to her brother Harry, was rather different:

I have had a horrible three years since Hubert died, shivering in a sort of Arctic night, and about six months ago I had an offer of marriage from a marine engineer, the best man I have ever known. I said 'No', and he then said he was very sorry I could not care for him, but that would not prevent his devoting the rest of his life to me and that if ever I needed a friend's help he would be there. He has been very, very kind and helpful ever since Hubert died, and after I refused him he quietly devoted himself to my interests in every way – helping with the poultry farm, finding men to work for me – and so on. Presently I found he had refused an appointment with £100 rise in salary. I asked him why and he told me that it was because he would not leave the neighbourhood where I was. So then I began to think it was rather a one-sided arrangement, and that perhaps life would be less wretched if one joined hands with a good friend and chum who believed that one could make him happy. And after a good deal of hesitation I talked it over with my son Paul, and at last said Yes – and I was married last Tuesday. I am very happy. He is the soul of goodness and kindness, and he never blunders in matters of sentiment or emotion. He doesn't blunder in anything, for the matter of that, but you know in those matters how fatally easy it is to go wrong. After the cold misery of the last three years I feel as though someone had come and put a fur cloak round me. Or like one shipwrecked on a lonely island, and I have found another shipwrecked mariner to help me to build a hut and make a fire. He is a widower and I knew his wife and he knew Hubert, so we can talk about *them*. His name is Thomas Terry Tucker and his whole life seems to have been spent in doing good. Also he is fond of laughter, and likes the same kind of jokes that please me. I am very, very happy. I feel as though I had opened another volume of the book of life (the last volume) and it is full of beautiful stories and poetry. I am staying for a short time at his little house and then he will come to live with me at Well Hall. He will keep on his engineering job till the end of war and then I hope he will retire. He is 60. I send you his photographs. He does not really look so like Bluebeard as his pictures suggest. You might write to him and wish him luck, will you, dear?

She signed this letter with her new name, 'E. N. Bland-Tucker'.[25]

A week or two earlier she had written to Edward Andrade, recently married himself, to justify the step she was about to take; the message is the same but the manner of telling it rather different:

Everyone is very much surprised at my marrying Mr Tucker – but no one more surprised than I am. I told you that he is the best man I have ever known. Further, he is (as you are, and as I am) the child of the Comic Muse, and by the same Father – who? Apollo? Bacchus? Perhaps Vulcan – but no scandal about Queen Elizabeth! He likes, and makes, the same kind of jokes that we make and like, and my chemical, or physical, sympathy is such that I like to be near him. The other day we were both very much tired with the labour of re-furnishing his little house, which we shall use as a *Refuge*, and we sat on a sofa with my head on his shoulder, and fell happily asleep, both of us. This means lots as you know. It is extraordinarily rum that I should have found someone who suits me like this. It is like a consolation prize for all sorts of failures. And the knowledge that I have a friend and comrade to sit on the other side of the hearth where life's dying embers fade is incredibly comforting. The fact that he isn't literary makes everything possible. I couldn't have married anyone who came anywhere near to competing with Hubert. But this man is different: his only points of resemblance . . . are his sane Socialist view of life, his sense of humour, and his love for me. I feel fur-wrapped from the cold of old age. Wrapped, indeed, in furs of price, for he is (as my gardener said of him) an 'only' man. There is no one like him. I grow fonder of him every day.[26]

Delightful though these two letters are, the need to justify her decision tells its own story. One reason that she felt she must prepare the ground so carefully was because her family had reacted to the idea of her remarriage with shocked surprise: while the Skipper was unquestionably kind and well-meaning, the moment he opened his mouth, it was immediately evident that he was not 'a gentleman'. He never wore a collar in the house, dropped his aitches and had the vowels of a London waterman, however genuine his feelings and amusing his way of expressing himself. Edith had always prided herself on disregarding class boundaries: at Dymchurch, Arthur Watts recalled, she had made a close friend of a Mrs Fisher, an old village woman, the mother of a large and dissolute family who looked after the house for her. She and Edith were like sisters; on her arrival they would kiss, and talk and go about arm in arm. Such relationships were fine, as long as it was clearly established that she herself was a lady, with advanced views. But for her children to accept the Skipper into the family as their stepfather was altogether another matter. Paul was particularly distressed, and the more so because his in-laws to be, the Nebels, were rather prim and proper, and the Skipper was not at all the sort of person they would normally have invited into their drawing room. Iris, too, was upset and uncomprehending. Only Rosamund unexpectedly supported their mother, perhaps because she had absorbed Wells's socialism at a deeper level than the others. Edith, having encountered nothing but opposition so far, burst into grateful tears, telling her, 'You are the only one who has been kind to me about this.' Rosamund couldn't resist teasing her a little: 'He's not *Tommy Tucker*, I hope?' Between laughing and crying, Edith replied, 'That's the worst of it. He *is*!' Rosamund instinctively liked and trusted the Skipper, and when he was left alone, some years after Edith's death, she went to live with him for a while.[27]

Paul's reaction reflected his conformism, the quality that made Iris say of him that he 'was never really of the family – all the queer strained atmosphere caused by our various stormy temperaments passed over his head'.[28] Iris's own reaction to her mother's announcement reflected her natural pessimism – her own experience of marriage had been unfortunate. Yet the Skipper's respectful homage evidently answered to a deep-seated need in Edith which had previously found expression in her romantic fiction, as well as in her cultivation of the almost courtly devotion of a group of younger lovers. She had always enjoyed power, being the centre of admiration and attention, being addressed as 'princess' or as 'madame'. In her fairy-stories it is quite often the under-under gardener who falls in love with the princess, while her love stories regularly featured heroes in attitudes of ardent and selfless idolatry: the exception – Mr Henry, the Shaw figure in *Daphne* – proves the rule because his lacerating contempt for love contrasts him with the two more conventional worshippers of the novel. Several of her short stories play out the inverted Victorian fantasy of 'The Poor Man and the Lady'. The Skipper approached her with exactly the kind of deference that pleased her best ('he never blunders in matters of sentiment or emotion', she had told Harry), so that she had the constant pleasure of conferring valued favours on him.

Edith's second marriage took place on 20 February 1917 at St Peter's, Woolwich. It is a Catholic church, and this seems to have been the first and only major ceremony of her life to have been conducted in one. The Skipper was 'C. of E.' so the choice had been hers. Religion had become more important to her during the early years of the war, though Iris remembered her mother's anger at the Pope's neutrality, especially when the Germans invaded Belgium. Several of those who met her at this stage of her life were struck by what they felt to be a strong spiritual strain in her. The Skipper himself remembered how she would kneel down and pray when she visited the room that had been occupied by his first wife, hoping that she would look kindly on their marriage. Yet this attitude of reverence suggests a moral simplicity which, in practice, the Skipper possessed, but Edith had long left behind. Berta Ruck described the Skipper as having

> the rigid morality of his class. [He] would have considered it unforgivable, he told me, that any woman even contemplated belonging to anybody but her husband, ... was the antithesis of all the brilliant intellectuals with whom she had associated, most of them sophisticated, several of them physically attractive – and yet, yet, he made a success of it, with this fastidious, petulant, exacting, mature, and even spoilt woman who was, snobbishly speaking – by many degrees his social and cultural superior.[29]

Under such circumstances, whole areas of her past life must have remained concealed from him; what may have made this easier for her is that she had, for so long, almost concealed them from herself.

February 1917 was notoriously cold. 'Clifford has congestion of the lungs, and Miss Hoatson has the beginnings of neuritis. In these dismal circumstances I can't have a party,' Edith explained to Edward Andrade; yet despite these unpromising auspices, she told him, she was contemplating with pleasure this sudden late flowering of her life:

> My own future – what there is of it – pleases me more and more. I am

growing very fond of Mr Tucker, and I am never dull with him. And it is a great happiness to feel that some one else thinks that you are the happiness of his life. He deserves all the happiness in the world, for he is as good as gold. I am sure you will like him. He has a very little house near here, and I have been refurnishing it with the Crowlink furniture, and we shall keep it on so as to have a little refuge from P.G.s. How lovely when the war is over and you and your Kitty can come and have tea with Mr Tucker and me in the kitchen of The Hutch![30]

Edith's problems did not vanish with her second marriage – Well Hall continued to be a burden financially, and the P.G.s continued to overstep the bounds of hospitality – but the Skipper enjoyed protecting her and she felt cherished as never before. Elsa Courlander observed a marked change in her after her second marriage – she seemed twice as 'human' and much less 'frightening'. The Skipper himself was easy-going, cheerful and philosophical and his mood of relaxation rubbed off on her; the passion, intolerance and fiery temper that she had shared with Hubert gave place to a more tranquil frame of mind. As she told Harry later that year:

I feel peaceful and contented in my new life with him. He is the best man I have ever known, and he has a philosophy of life which makes all things easy to him. He never worries and he never lets me worry – so, though we are pinched for money, and hard put to it to keep going I am quite at ease. He cares absolutely nothing for material things and *possessions*, though he enjoys life and is very merry and jolly. He has been all over the world as ship's engineer and is a born *observer*. Also he has words to clothe his thoughts and observations. If we had time I am sure we could do some good writing work together. I send you a paper with a sketch in it I wrote with Mr Tucker's help, and an article about a *ship*![31]

One reason why she was now happier and more relaxed than ever before was that 'for the first time in my life, I know what it is to possess a man's whole heart'. At times she found herself wishing her mother had lived to see her so loved.[32] It was not merely that Tucker's single-minded devotion contrasted with Hubert's roving eye; it also contrasted with the inward reservations of her young admirers, the most faithful of whom had, in the end, turned from her to marry younger women, a process in which she saw all too painfully reflected her gradual loss of attractions. Even Richard Reynolds, who had been most deeply in love with her, had eventually left her to marry and have a family of his own. But the Skipper was sixty, a year or two older than she was; for him she was no mere stopping place on the way to some other more legitimate or more permanent relationship. He wanted nothing else. Edith fully realized that they might not have long together – in a moment of prescience she guessed that there were perhaps five years of happiness left to them – but these were unclouded, 'the happiest years of my life', she told Elsa Courlander.[33]

Though she did not consciously realize it, her heavy smoking had seriously damaged her health: the bronchitis and asthma that she had suffered from every winter for so many years gave warning of the weak state of her lungs. When she was unwell, she would be seized by fits of uncontrollable coughing, such as she had experienced in the hotel at Newhaven. Yet it was the Skipper who was first taken ill: soon after their marriage, he caught pneumonia and it was, as always, Alice who nursed him through it. Once he had recovered, it was made quite clear that her services were no longer wanted at Well Hall – Edith had become impatient with finding Alice at the Skipper's bedside, however useful she had been in the immediate emergency. Alice went up to stay with her sister in Yorkshire, and when she returned to London, took a flat at Blackheath, where she supported herself by working as a nurse. Her long, close, painful years with Edith had finally come to an end.[34]

Touched by the trust and love that he had shown her, the one-time 'Duchess of Dymchurch' set herself to become the Skipper's 'mate' and sea-cook (he loved to use nautical terms, and they greatly amused her). When he stayed up late working at the ferry, she would keep his supper warm and wait up for him till he got back, sometimes until two or three in the morning. Then he would eat, and they would talk about the events of the day and the events of days past, until the sun rose. If he knew in advance that he was going to be late, she would go with him and cook beef steak and make hot coffee in the galley of the ferry boat, delighted with this new game. She had always loved to please, but tended to expect warmth or gratitude in return; never before had her kindness given so much pleasure or been so warmly received.[35]

Paul's marriage to Gertrude Nebel had taken place two months after his mother's, on 23 April 1917. Like many wartime weddings, the couple were soon parted again, but Paul took leave from the garrison at Newhaven whenever he could. Although Edith told Edward Andrade that her prospective daughter-in-law was 'very pretty and very nice', when she came to know her better she found her disconcertingly cool and reserved. Some verses she wrote for Gertrude might be regarded as a charming gesture if they did not have a faintly reproachful undertone:

Gertrude, holding Paul's dear hand,
Do not call me 'Mrs Bland'. ⁻
Call me 'Jane' or 'Bet' or 'Sue',
Anything but what you do!

Your own Mother holds the right
To be 'Mother', yet I might
Beg from you, dear girl, dear woman
Some alternative cognomen.

'Mater's' not so dusty, and,
Dear, 'Mama' deserves a hand;
'Maman', 'Mutter', 'Madre', all
Make their own appeal and call.

And, if none of these appear
Just the thing, there's still 'My dear' . . .
Call me something that will prove me
That you really truly love me.[36]

Appeals for love, even when written in verse, are usually unsuccessful. The immediate problem was solved when Edith, having briefly
tried out 'M2' or Mother 2, decided that she was 'MIL' (mother-in-
law) and Gertrude 'DIL' (daughter-in-law) or Dill, with an extra 'l' for
love. Had they really liked one another, such name-finding would,
perhaps, have resolved itself, or at any rate not have constituted an
embarrassment. Edith distrusted Gertrude and did not think her good
enough for Paul or sensitive enough to her own feelings. Gertrude in
her turn preferred not to get too deeply involved with her difficult and
demanding mother-in-law. She was, in her own way, a domineering
woman herself, and in marrying her, Paul was partly replacing his own
powerful mother, as Edith must unconsciously have recognized. Their
marriage was not an entirely happy one. Because Gertrude's demean-
our was more placid and more conventionally decorous than that of his
own family, Paul made the mistake of thinking that she was genuinely
calmer and easier to get on with, but her feelings were no less
passionate – merely more repressed and unexamined. She made Paul
feel as inadequate as his own family had done, but in rather a different
way.

In the meantime Edith continued to write sketches, articles and
occasionally short stories in a slightly desultory way; many of them
were published in the *Saturday Westminster Gazette*, but sometimes
they appeared in the Chestertons' *New Witness* or in Clifford Sharp's

New Statesman. Several of those that she had written just before or during the early years of the war were dialect stories, set in Romney Marsh, rather in the vein of *In Homespun*, the volume she had written for John Lane nearly a quarter of a century earlier. She probably intended to assemble them in a book, though she never actually wrote enough of them to do so. She also began to write up some of the Skipper's yarns about life at sea and on the river and a number of these were published but only one of them ('Tammy Lee's Jack' in the posthumous *Five of Us – and Madeline*) ever got into a book. She had always loved dialect and local colour, had used it both in prose and verse, and so the Skipper's nautical language and stories appealed strongly to her. But she was probably mistaken in thinking she used it well; her best work had exploited a range of different tones and was often characterized by irony, wit and a degree of sophistication and multiple awareness that was alien to the Skipper's reassuring simplicity of vision.

'My darling daughter, Thank God for this day! Now our boy is safe! I tried to come and see you today, but trams were too crowded.' So runs Edith's most affectionate note to her daughter-in-law, dated Nov. 11. 1918 – a little melodramatically, perhaps, since the only thing Paul was likely to die of in the Newhaven garrison was boredom. But now he would be discharged, and John, who had been doing so well at school, could take up his scholarship at Cambridge. Another young man who had escaped the war and gone on to Oxford joined the Well Hall household as a P.G. a couple of years later: Russell Green lived there for three months in the early autumn of 1920 and found himself greatly intrigued by Edith and her entourage. She in her turn immediately took to him, granting him all kinds of favours. But her family suspected him of taking advantage of her kindness, and he was soon cordially disliked by all of them, so that when the Skipper lost his temper and went so far as to swear at him in the garden, it was felt that Green had rather asked for it. Edith was writing up some of the Skipper's yarns at this time, though not working on very much else. Now that Alice had finally gone, she was greatly preoccupied with housework, which she apparently rather enjoyed, though she was assisted by several vaguely defined 'helpers' acting under her general supervision.

Russell Green was particularly struck by the way in which the household seemed full of bizarre and incongruous elements, 'a psychological kaleidoscope' which nevertheless all somehow fitted into the gaunt and weathered old house, standing deep in the massed foliage of late summer. Edith herself looked like 'a motherly George Sand'. Green was delighted by 'her fairy godmother charm', but, as Shaw had done so many years earlier, noticed 'a hint of hardness in the pressure of her lips which suggested a very strong and unrebuttable will'. In his view, her forceful personality provided a strange contrast to 'the bluff timidity' of the Skipper. At weekends Paul ('the middle-aged business man') and Rosamund (described by Edith as 'a dark and dangerous woman') would come down, and there would be 'a continuous series of amiable tea-parties' attended by little girls with bright hair ribbons in their pigtails around the small mahogany tea table; later there were dinner parties round the larger oak dining table, attended by a variety of people who were 'more or less friends of the family'. Edith still kept open house, and her P.G.s were never entirely distinguishable from her guests.[37]

Well Hall itself seemed to him beautiful but, like its châtelaine, enjoying an Indian summer. When he arrived, he was shown upstairs to a tiny room at the top of the house, possibly the old 'maids' sitting room' – certainly the sort of room that had formerly been occupied by servants. It looked out over the back lawns through a balcony of crumbling iron railings. Far below, the moat was overgrown with briar roses and brambles as if it were the veritable *bois dormant* of the fairy-tale, and beyond lay the rambling old orchard where Edith liked to walk, and where she had composed so many of her books. The house itself was crowded with the valued possessions of a lifetime, and these served to disguise the underlying dilapidation – her bed, for example, was covered with a sumptuous fur rug, but the carpets on the floor were threadbare, and in the bathroom was a large zinc bath with a sagging bottom, boxed in with wood, of a type that had been obsolete for many years. With no money to spare for repairs or replacements, the household had to manage as best it could. If the bathroom was not up to date, at least it should be tidy: leaving the bathroom as you would wish to find it is, of course, an unavoidable concern for landladies, but instead of pinning up humourless orders, Edith composed an ode, 'The Order of the Bath', urging, 'Hygeia's votaries' to refrain from 'pouring libations on the temple floor', invading its precincts with muddy boots on, leaving the windows closed and the soapy water in the bath:

Miscreants, repent! And sin this year no more!
With reverent heart approach the bathroom door;
Thus shall Hygeia's blessing still attend
Upon you till one-nine-two-one shall end.

But the trials of the landlady were not to last much longer.[38]

Life at Well Hall was not growing any easier, although Edith had recently acquired a new housekeeper, helper and friend in Olive Hill. Miss Hill wrote stories for children and had first approached Edith to ask for advice about her work. She fell in love with Edith from the first and was soon invited to join the extended family. She was the last of those women such as Ada Breakell and Alice Hoatson who had dedicated themselves to Edith in self-effacing admiration. She became indispensable in the last years of her life, and was with Edith when she died. The Skipper was struck by Edith's ability to attract loyal women friends, and observed that, while some women attracted the male sex and others attracted their own, she attracted both to an extraordinary degree. But even with Olive Hill lending a helping hand, Well Hall had now become an overwhelming financial burden: the heating bills alone were enormous – £100 a year, the Skipper said, and there was very little money coming in that did not have to be paid out again. Though there were her royalties (paid at 20 or 25 per cent on the reprints of her most popular children's books) and she was writing odd sketches and occasionally poems for newspapers, these produced nothing like the substantial sums that she had earned in her heyday.[39] Selling the garden produce was necessary but itself involved further expense, since the gardener and whoever manned the hut had also to be paid; in addition the P.G.s had to be fed, the house heated, and the cost of rates and helpers met. John had won a scholarship to Cambridge, but it didn't cover his expenses; Shaw, at the request of Rosamund, had put his hand in his pocket to pay whatever was necessary for John's education, though he later told Doris Langley Moore that he considered it 'astonishingly little'. Edith herself had been reduced to selling various odd items – some letters from Kipling and postcards from Shaw – and finally even to borrowing small sums of money from Edward Andrade.[40] The Skipper's answer to insoluble problems was usually to say 'To hell with it!', but he now realized that some more fundamental change must be made.

Though Crowlink had long passed out of her hands, Edith had kept her ties with Dymchurch and had gone down there for occasional holidays both during the war and after it: she had taken the Skipper when he had been convalescing from an illness in July 1919, and in the following year she was there with John in September. So it was quite logical that when, in 1921, she and the Skipper began to look for a new home that they could afford to buy outright (Edith and Hubert had always rented), they began their search at Dymchurch. Near the little village of St Mary's in the Marsh, between Dymchurch and New Romney, and just off Jefferstone Lane (known as 'Jesson' to the locals) they found a pair of brick-built huts put up for the Air Force during the war. They were long and low and had been used to house a photographic laboratory and some stores – the lab was rectangular and thin, the storehouse shorter and wider. Joined by a passage, and made comfortably habitable, it seemed that they might be transformed into a permanent and even comparatively spacious home for them both, with rooms for the family and even for one or two helpers as well. Though her beloved Well Hall had to be abandoned, Edith would have all the fun of master-minding the substantial conversion necessary to remake the huts into a home. The rebuilding would be paid for by selling much of the old Well Hall furniture which would in any case never have fitted into the 'Long Boat' and the 'Jolly Boat', as the huts were quickly christened. The passageway that joined them became the 'quarterdeck gangway'.

In the end Edith found leaving Well Hall a terrible wrench. So much of her life had been passed there and so many of her dearest friends and deepest feelings were bound up with it. She wrote to Berta Ruck a couple of years later, recalling the old partying days there:

> When you were at Well Hall I used often on summer evenings to slip away from the table and go and look through the window at the rest of you finishing your desserts and your flirtations and your arguments amongst the flowers and fruits and bright glasses and think 'This is how I shall see it all some day when I am not alive any more.' Well, it won't be Well Hall I shall go back to now when the time comes for it died before I did and it is quite dead.[41]

Yet it was also darkened by memories of pain and loss. In November 1917, she had published 'The Haunted Garden' in the *Daily Mail*:

> Autumn is here; and the garden is still gay in purple and gold: the leaves are not all yellowed, but they are fading and fading fast. Soon the golden-rod and the Michaelmas daisies will have gone where rose-leaves go and it will be winter here: the rose-thorns will lie bare to the last of the wind, and the rain will fall on the garden like tears that are never dried.

> Let the winter come. This garden has no more need of summer . . .
> The haunted beauty of the summer garden is harder for us to bear than
> the desolation of autumn when we walk among the dead and drifting
> leaves. We who are old and lonely, who know that our days cannot
> return to us – we feel that the autumn is our own, and that winter sleep
> comes soon. But they – the summer was theirs . . .[42]

Ostensibly her essay is a lament for the young people whose lives had
been lost or ruined in the war, but the elegy extends to include Well
Hall and her own sense of the loved dead who had walked there and
would not come back.

Symbolically, perhaps, the last thing she did before leaving Well
Hall was to make her will – on 2 February 1922. It was witnessed by
the Elliots, a couple who had for a while been P.G.s, and who took the
house over after she left. In it, she made the Skipper her executor and
left her property – now chiefly the Long Boat and the Jolly Boat –
between him, Iris and Paul, while ensuring that Ada Breakell and
Olive Hill should retain the right to stay on there if they wanted to. In
the event, Ada remained in London, but Olive accompanied the
Skipper and his Mate to their last home. Nothing was left to John or
Rosamund, on the grounds that 'Rosamund is well provided for by her
marriage and John had his full portion of his family's money in legacies
from his father and aunt.' This self-exculpating sentence suggests a
reference back to Hubert's will in favour of John, which must have
hurt her very much. Though John had been left money by his father
and, presumably, by his aunt, Helen Craig, it was not apparently
enough to see him through Cambridge, since Shaw had to be asked to
help out. And when, later, Clifford's alcoholism destroyed his earning
capacity, Rosamund was left apparently destitute. But both Hubert
and Alice had finally passed out of Edith's life, and she felt that she had
already paid their children whatever was owing to them and more,
much more.

Leaving was itself a kind of death, and it probably hastened her own,
as great life changes are thought to do; but during the previous summer
she had had a curious, and apparently unconscious presentiment of
death, which formed the subject of a letter, published in the *Saturday
Westminster Gazette* on 25 June 1921:

> Sir, I have three times awakened with verses in my mind made during
> sleep. In each case I was convinced at the moment of waking that the
> poem in question was a masterpiece. The first was this:

Bachelor bears compare combine
  To cheat me out of my mortal span:
They've had their dinner, and I want mine, –
  That is the difference, said Timothy Bann.

I awoke with the distinct and strong conviction that Timothy Bann was an important but unconventional person – a kind of Mark Rutherford or Theophrastus Such.

The second poem was longer. I thought as I woke that it would be beautiful, set to music. The air 'Coming Through the Rye' did not occur to me:

Mr Oddy
Met a body
Hanging from a tree;
And what was worse
He met a hearse
As black as black could be.
Mr Oddy
Said, 'By God, he
Ought to have a ride!'
Said the driver
'I'd oblige yer,
But we're full inside.'

In my waking hours I should not have conceived, much less executed, this piece of work. Nor could I have rhymed 'driver' and 'oblige yer'.

Much more distinctive than her sense that these were masterpieces (since a feeling of elation or mastery is quite common in dreams) is the concern with death apparent in both verses. In the first the bears combine to 'cheat me out of my mortal span', in other words to shorten her life, while in the second the living 'body' of the traditional song has changed its meaning and become 'body' in the sense of a corpse; this introduces a hearse and a driver, so that the parody transforms the erotic encounter of the original into an encounter with charioted death. Such an analysis of what are merely nonsense verses risks sounding heavy-handed – and Edith herself strongly disapproved of psycho-analysis[43] – yet the play of the dreaming mind is often revealing. Death seems to have been an unconscious preoccupation both at the beginning and the end of her life.

In the spring of 1922 Edith wrote to Mavis Carter:

My good child, know this – that we have left Well Hall and gone (I mean come, for I am there) to live in the middle of Romney Marsh. And we

are in the thick of the removal. And our bungalow is only half built. So
that where I should be sleeping, workmen are building their nests – I
mean their chimneys. Most of the rooms are mere plane [sic] surfaces
indicated by chalk lines on a cement floor. The rooms that *are* done are
filled to overflowing with battens and quartering and matchboards and
planks and doors and 'horses'. Shavings are knee-deep everywhere, and
where there is nothing else there are carpenters' benches of *far* more
than three dimensions.

So you can see I can't ask you to tea at Well Hall, don't you? Nor
Cecily either, who *might* have come to see me again and again and again
in the months that are now dead and gone and lost beyond recall.

Still, if she, or you, or both, turn up here we'll find you a plank-bed
and an eiderdown of shavings, and the sound of the sea and the skylarks,
and the forever changing beauty of the marsh and the sky.

My serial [*The Lark*, 1922] is not a fool serial – but jolly good stuff –
so all the young men I know tell me – rather to my surprise. For I
thought it was a girls' story – and that Mavis, though aged 62, would
have liked it. But you never know, does you?

Mr Tucker, I may tell you is much attached to Mavis, and wishes to
assure her of a special welcome when she comes to the Long Boat.[44]

The wit and energy are still there, even though the tone is occasionally
peevish, as in the suggestion that Cecily ought to have gone to see her
and didn't, or in her defence of her new serial, *The Lark*.

It did not need defending: this last of her novels is among her most
readable – a pure romance full of happy improbabilities pegged down
by telling concrete details, rich with her own passionate enthusiasms
and prejudices. It is, among other things, a farewell to Well Hall, a
kissing cousin to *The Red House*. When she had first seen that house,
she had promised herself that she would write a novel about it. Cedar
Court in *The Lark* is its final appearance, and the book is immediately
inspired by her own recent efforts to make a living out of it by selling
the garden produce and taking in paying guests – the awfulness of those
'pigs' (there are identifiable sketches of Russell Green and the
Butterworths), the problem of finding and keeping a cook, the
excitement over the shop takings and the difficulty of adding them up
correctly are all there. It is a book filled with intimate personal
touches, and many of her heroines' activities – making overalls out of
Indian bedspreads, for example – reproduce her own. It provides good
evidence, if any were needed, that happiness was the only condition
she needed to write well, for the quality of writing here is consistently
energetic and humorous. But one curious and wistful episode recalls

the transformation at the heart of her earlier novel, *Dormant*. Lucilla, the more staid of the two heroines, at one point dresses up as an old lady – there is, perhaps, a glance towards Mr Rochester's disguise as a fortune teller in *Jane Eyre*, or towards Harry's disguise in Charlotte M. Yonge's *The Daisy Chain*; but its main point is that the disguise (and this was the metaphor she had used for old age in *Wings and the Child*) *is* only a disguise. Isolating though it is, it could eventually be pulled off – unlike the changes that had befallen its author:

> A very curious experience this, of Lucilla's: to sit in an armchair, with the weight of old age on her bowed shoulders and on her brow the wrinkled indiarubber brand of seventy years; to be with these young people and not of them; to feel their glances meet hers – not with the hopeful give-and-take of youth and youth, but with the impersonal, distant, half-pitying tribute of youth to age, Curious, very.
>
> Not that the young people were neglectful of Miss Lucas. Far from it. They were kind, they were attentive, they were deferent and courteous, they were everything that young people should be to old ladies. A really old lady would have found these manners charming, but to Lucilla these manners were intolerable. Her only comfort was the reflection that Dix and Rochester knew that under the wig and the wrinkles was hidden the real Lucilla, whose acting they must be secretly admiring. But the Thorntons did not know, and, though they were kind, they were not interested. Yes, that was it. Lucilla was accustomed to being found interesting – and no amount of kindness or courtesy can make up in our fellow-creatures for lack of interest.[45]

No wonder that Lucilla could scarcely wait to take off her disguise.

Though living permanently at Jesson St Mary's must have felt a little like exile, Edith still had a number of close friends around Dymchurch dating from the days when she had gone down to the Other House each year. Several of these were theatrical families: Athene Seyler had a cottage along the sea wall, and vividly remembered a boating trip with Edith on the Royal Military Canal at Hythe, and being bullied into playing charades (which, as a professional actress, she loathed); but she was also struck by Edith's seriousness and her concern with religious and spiritual matters. Mrs Thorndike was another very old friend, and her two children Russell and Sybil had always been fond of Edith. Russell had been much amused to discover that the sand pit near Rochester in which they had played as children was exactly the same one that she had used for the setting of *Five Children and It*. By 1922 Sybil herself was married and had children of her own: her eldest son

John enjoyed Edith's company as much as his mother had done and remembered that they had called on her often during the summer of 1922. He was greatly impressed by Captain Tucker ('a tiny stocky man with a beard'), and his manner, which was

almost a caricature of an old sailor.
'Avast there, me hearties!' he would shout as Anxious Annie [their car] drove up to the bungalow. 'Come aboard. Tea's ready in the Long Boat, but Madam's titivating herself in the Jolly Boat.'[46]

Even at this final stage of her life she still displayed her remarkable capacity for making new friendships – perhaps the warmest of these was with Noël Coward. He had borrowed Athene Seyler's cottage earlier that year and had at once made up his mind to live on the Marsh, taking a cottage next to the Star Inn at St Mary's which he shared with his mother. As a child – indeed, for the rest of his life – he adored Edith's stories and enjoyed her particular sense of humour. On his way to school, he used to pass a second-hand bookshop where they sold off old copies of *The Strand* at a penny a time. He saved up all his pocket money until he had a shilling, enough to buy a whole story all at once. On one occasion, some numbers turned out to be missing, so he stole a coral necklace from one of his mother's friends, pawned it and bought the book outright from the Army and Navy stores – an escapade which greatly delighted Edith when he told her. On discovering that she was living close by, he went to call on her and tell her how much he admired her work. She was, of course, utterly charmed by him, and they became friends at once. He showed her some of his plays, and she discussed them with him, treating him as a serious writer (though he was still only twenty-one) and making criticisms of their characterization which he thought valid. He particularly liked her tough-mindedness, her astringent view of the world. She made no pretence of being a sweet old lady: one day when he was late for tea, she was thoroughly annoyed with him; on another occasion, he took his mother and Edith took an instant dislike to her, but he thought all the more of her for showing her feelings so openly. For him, she was a real Bohemian, 'the most genuine Bohemian I had ever seen'. He wrote of his meetings with her

[I] found her as firm, as nice, and as humorous as her books had led me to expect. The Skipper, her husband, was a grand old man who loved her and guarded her devotedly through her last sad years.
    The friend, Miss Hill, was a wispy creature, with an air of vague

detachment, which inspired Athene Seyler to christen her irreverently, 'The Green Hill Far Away'.[47]

Another writer whom Edith got to know for the first time in the summer of 1922 was the novelist G. B. Stern. In July she had gone down to St Mary's with her shell-shocked husband, Geoffrey Holdsworth, to visit Noël Coward, but on arrival they discovered that he was away. They stayed at the Jesson Country Club, but Holdsworth found its atmosphere oppressive. When they discovered that E. Nesbit, whom both of them had read and admired, was living close by, they introduced themselves and soon found refuge in the Long Boat. Edith was kind and motherly to the edgy young couple, allowed them to wander about the house at will and provided all their meals for the several days of their stay. G. B. Stern bathed in her warm and reassuring presence, and, being an intense egotist, felt slightly resentful when her granddaughter Pandora arrived – Edith played the piano while Pandora and the Skipper danced a hornpipe.[48]

The summer of 1922 was a happy one, but it was to be the last that Edith was well enough to enjoy. That autumn and winter her asthma and bronchitis returned, her cough grew bad, and she began to lose weight rapidly. During the following summer Berta Ruck, who had lost touch with Edith a dozen years earlier through a trivial quarrel, bumped into Iris in London. Iris said that her mother was very ill and urged her to write at once. Berta wrote a rather stiff little note, enclosing her latest novel, and received a warm but worrying response:

Yes – I always took an interest in your work and believed in it and thought you would do great things. And I was always fond of you, my dear. *The Arrant Rover* has come and I have read it. I like it best of any I have read of yours. And amid the thick tide of new fiction how pleasant to meet girls who are *like* girls and not like. Full stop.

I am glad to hear that your mother is safe anchored again for a while after the storm of her bad illness. I shall never forget her kindness and my stay with her. I put some of Caernarvon in my *Incredible Honeymoon*.

I suppose I shall not get well again. But like Charles II I take an unconscionable time over the business. You would not know me – I am so thin. Once a Rubens Venus in figure but now more like a Pre-Raphaelite St Simeon.

I suppose you have thousands of stately motor cars? Why don't you get into one of them and come and see us? We can put you (and the motor) up . . .

You are right. When I saw Pandora in her 1872 frock I see my own ghost: but I had less nose and not quite such big eyes.[49]

When Berta Ruck finally arrived at Jesson, she was greeted by the Skipper,

a short, hatless, collarless, unmistakably sea-faring figure, bearded like Captain Kettle.
'Are you Berta? Come aboard,' was his brisk greeting. 'Madam's waited tea for you.'

He took her into the drawing room, full of the familiar Well Hall furniture and pictures, where Edith lay on the sofa – her brown hair turned grey at last, her ruddy face colourless and her once sun-tanned arms now dead white, and spotted with the dark freckles that Shaw had noticed so long ago. Berta had missed her train and the Duchess's first words were 'You're very late, girl!' To which Berta replied, 'Fifteen years . . .', a little piece of melodrama that seemed to gratify her.[50]

It was clear enough that Edith was terribly ill, but what was wrong with her? Iris said that she had an internal illness that was never identified by the doctors, and that even specialists were quite unable to explain why she had grown so terribly thin and was often in such violent pain that she had to be treated with small doses of morphia. The Skipper referred to it vaguely as 'her old trouble', as if he thought it was either connected with the duodenal ulcer she had suffered from in 1914, or else her chronic bronchial troubles. The latter was nearer the mark, since her symptoms would be easily diagnosed today as those of lung cancer, now associated with the heavy smoking that she had indulged in for a lifetime.[51] For most of her last two years she was desperately ill; eating little or nothing, often too weak to talk or hold a pencil, she lay propped up in bed looking out at the flat lines of the Marsh, stretching away to places that she would never revisit. Her family visited her frequently; she was now too weak to pursue the bitter quarrels that had latterly marred her relationship with John. Noel Griffith, the most loyal of her old lovers, went down to see her, as did Edward Andrade, and Ada Breakell stayed with her for nearly a month; Mavis Carter, on holiday near Folkestone, paid a surprise visit in August 1923 – no one had warned her of Edith's illness and she was terribly shocked at the change in her:

She talked for long all about that happy day in the Green Lady riding down the Warwickshire lanes. A touch of the old shrill sharpness because I sat on my chair all huddled, inelegant, feet tied in an inartistic knot – no satisfying her until I'd assumed a Queen Mary attitude – straight back, hands clasped and quiet in lap, feet crossed at ankles! Then a sudden cry – 'Forgive me, dear, you must allow me a sick woman's privilege to be disagreeable – and I *am* very ill.'

She insisted, to Mavis's distress, on getting up and accompanying her to the gate, leaning heavily on the Skipper's arm. When Mavis had kissed her and waved the last goodbye to the frail figure at the gate, she walked down to the beach, flung herself full length on the sand and sobbed uncontrollably.[52]

By December, Edith could no longer get out of bed and had had enough. She wrote to Mavis:

> It is a long business and I am getting very tired of it. But just when I hope the end may be in sight I get a little better and realise miserably that I've got to go on with it a bit longer.
>
> I have everything to make me happy except health, kindest and most loving nursing and care.
>
> My bedroom is 20 feet by 15, a four-post bed like a golden shrine and a view of about 8 miles of marsh bounded by the little lovely hills of Kent.

During those last months Edith gratefully accepted the letters and other little services of her old friends. Mavis was asked if she would prepare a special scrapbook, intended for the Skipper's birthday, into which a number of photographs, and most of the articles and sketches that Edith had written during the last decade were to be pasted. Her instructions were detailed and minute, and poor Mavis worried herself ill over it.[53] Berta Ruck wrote regularly and in the early spring of 1924, in a hard frost, travelled down with boxes of hot-house flowers from Harrods – carnations, red roses, freesias and scented narcissus. She and Olive Hill unpacked the boxes slowly, close to the bed so that Edith could watch them:

> Finally when they were all out, she said with a little greedy sigh: 'I should like to pack them all up again, and unpack them, just for the fun of it.'
>
> 'Shall I do that?' asked Miss Hill.
>
> 'No! Of course not! Put them in water.' Then she turned and pointed accusingly at me with a hand on which the freckles stood out as they do on the pale lining of a fox-glove. 'Berta! Those flowers. You bought them now, really, instead of for my funeral? You thought, why not let her have them while she can enjoy them? Didn't you?'

'Yes,' I snapped, 'I did.'
'So sensible,' she said, satisfied, and sniffed at her red carnations.[54]

Even at this stage, her mind within her failing body was as active as ever. She wrote some charming verses for Mrs Thorndike who had sent her a special gadget for raising the bed so that she could look out of the window more easily, and she dictated several long, reflective letters to Berta that revealed how little she had changed within:

I have been so very ill that my dear darlings have had so much to do with looking after me that they have not been able to do much else, and that is why I have been such a long time writing. I have got a little girl, the postman's daughter, from whom you probably received a squiggle the other day. She writes poetry, very gentle and ingenuous and quite open hearted. I tried to let her know, without revealing that I knew whom she was in love with, that if you write *only* about your heart's core, you give yourself away to everyone who reads a verse of yours, whereas if you write about indifferent subjects as well, your jewel soon becomes concealed among the pebbles on the beach. This, I told her, is the use of the dramatic lyric. She seems a gentle little thing with aspirations and quite good and pretty thoughts. She is the only new person I have seen lately. And I daresay she will not care to keep coming, for it is a long way from New Romney, and I cannot use her much at a time. The rest of the time she spends palely patching pillow-cases which I fear she thinks unworthy of one aspiring to the stars for his sake. Talking of poetry, I don't believe I have ever told you how very, very much I like Frances Cornford. I wish I could have writen 'The Watch' instead of only endorsing it . . .
[Frances Cornford's poem runs:

I am so sick, so sick, so sick,
O death, come quick, come quick, come quick.]

I have heard from Mrs Brownlow. I don't know whether I shall ever be well enough to answer her letter. It is a frightful exertion even to dictate. So will you please thank her when you see her for all the kind things she says? I'm so *glad* when anyone likes my poetry. It is really what I should naturally have done, that and *no* prose, if I had not had to write for a living . . .

I agree with you that for the people who keep their wits and their health, the human span of life is far too short. What things there are still to see and to do, and to think and to be and to grow into and to grow out of!

I am very glad your sister's baby is all right. It is nice to think of her being happy with a new baby. The loveliest moments of one's life are those. As for me, I do really get less and less alive, and say Frances Cornford's poem over to myself with more and more frequency and conviction.

I don't think it's any use to try and think of people at any particular hour of the day. Life surges in so. Far better to agree to think of them whenever you see or do some particular thing. When I was sixteen, I stood at a window with a girlfriend of mine and her brother whom I did not particularly care for [probably Violet and Frank Oakley]; and she said, looking out at the stars, 'Let us three promise always to think of each other when we see the Great Bear' and I have done so ever since.

The letter was dictated to Olive Hill, but a postscript, added in her own handwriting, bids

Good bye, my dear. Whenever you think of me do not forget to think how much happiness your loving kindness has given me and how you have helped my last, long months. I really think the door will open soon now and I may be able to scurry through at last. But I shall remember you wherever I wake.

That letter was dated 17 March 1924. A month later, on 21 April she picked up her pen and struggled once again to write to Berta. Despite intense pain and the numbing of morphia, she had a poem in her head which she was anxious to get on to paper:

I *will* try to write to dear Berta myself. It is impossible to get hold of anyone else. I am now supposed to be a little better. Changed the doctor, who now gives me morphia to take the edge off the pain, but I am still as sick as a dog – (or cat. I think a cat is sicker, don't you?) I have a poem coming with its form nebulous, but its content all arranged and a few really good lines done – it is for you when I have (if I ever have) done it. (I have caught the Skipper. The D[octor] has come. I hope I can hold the pencil till the D. has gone. Still got him!)

But her writing tails off here and the poem never reached the paper.

Though longing for release from pain, like many people of strong constitution her body clung to life and in her last four days she suffered terrible agonies. Her children were sent for and she died on 4 May 1924 in the arms of Iris, with Olive Hill beside her; the Skipper and Paul had crept away to have some lunch, and Iris did not call them back for Edith had been past recognizing anyone for some little while.[55]

She was buried, as she had wished, beneath a spreading elm in the quiet churchyard of St Mary's in the Marsh. She had asked for no memorial stone, but her grave is marked by two wooden pillars joined by a crossbar, a little like a bed-head, carved with her name, her clover leaf sign and the words 'poet and author' – it was made by the Skipper. The funeral was attended mainly by her family, and some of the villagers. Many of her old friends sent flowers – Marshall Steele, Bower Marsh, Berta Ruck, Elsa Courlander and the Dunsanys, and so did new ones like Noël Coward, but out of the 'old crowd' only Noel Griffith and Edward Andrade had kept closely in touch during her illness, and only they travelled down for her funeral. The service was conducted by the Anglican rector, the Rev. T. F. Cooke whom she had liked and trusted; she had had many long discussions with him about religion, theology and the Bible during her last two years. Towards the end she had decided that Catholicism was only an aspect of a wider faith, though an aspect that had attracted her since childhood, and that moment, half a century earlier, when she had written to her mother from the French convent to ask if she might join the Church of Rome. The service ended, as the Skipper had requested, with the final words from her novel *Dormant* which he believed summed up her faith, words that her brother Harry thought should have stood as her epitaph:

> 'It seems such waste, such stupid senseless waste,' said Bats. 'His great thoughts, his fine body that loved life, all the friendship, the aspiration, the love . . . all thrown away, gone, wasted for ever.'
>
> 'Who says that it is wasted?' said the Jew. 'It is his body that has served its turn and is cast away. The great thoughts, the friendship, the aspiration, the love; can we say that these die? Nay, rather, these shall not die. These shall live in the Courts of the Lord, for ever.'[56]

St Mary-in-the-Marsh
Romney Marsh

AFTERWORD

Seven years after E. Nesbit's death, Doris Langley Moore decided to write her biography: she had always admired the children's books, and she gained an entrée into her circle via Hubert Griffith, Edith's godson, to whom *The Phoenix and the Carpet* had been dedicated. Hubert introduced Mrs Langley Moore to his father Noel, Edith's early lover, and through him she gradually met the rest of the family. At this time the Skipper and Olive Hill were still living in the Long Boat and the Jolly Boat, which had been kept very much as they were when Edith died. Her study, latterly her bedroom in the Long Boat, the 'magic room', still contained her big four-poster bed, and the burnished glass witch balls that she had hung up there. In the dining room of the Jolly Boat were (and still are) the rush-seated ladderback chairs, made from apple-wood, that had once stood in the kitchen of the Dean Street flat; one wall was occupied by a huge dresser decorated with flowers in pokerwork, done by Edith herself – she kept a special set of tools for doing this. In the wide sitting room were sofas and tables from Well Hall, and the grandfather clock with a sun and moon on it that had once whirred round inexplicably when Lord Dunsany was lunching at the *Neolith* office; on the walls hung lithographs by Gerald Spencer Pryse, whose work she so much admired.

The Skipper had been enormously proud of Edith and was at first delighted that she was to be the subject of a whole book. He still had boxes and bags of her old letters, and he went through these trying to find interesting items for Doris Langley Moore to use. When she came down to visit them, he and Olive Hill tried to recall as much as they could of what Edith had told them about her childhood. Towards the end, she had been haunted by one or two vivid early memories – of a particular Turkey rug on her nursery floor, and of the little kid shoes that she had dropped in the font at her christening.[1] Many of her old friends were still alive. Some, like Noel Griffith and Arthur Watts, spoke unguardedly of their memories of her. Others were more circumspect: Shaw was initially reluctant and remained less than frank about Edith's passion for him. Marshall Steele's death had occurred a year or two after her own, and her brother Harry had died in Australia in 1928. Bower Marsh, still friendly with Noel Griffith, talked to Mrs Langley Moore but did not reveal how close he had been to Edith at one time. Oswald Barron refused to be mentioned by name. Sidney Webb, now Lord Passfield, insisted upon his 'very slight acquaintance' with the Blands, while having to admit that he had dined with them at Elswick Road and had later visited Well Hall ('a call necessitated by a business transaction'); he too preferred not to be mentioned in the biography. Richard Reynolds was a widower and had gone to live in Capri; his wife, 'Poor Dorothy', had died a few months before Edith herself, leaving three young daughters – 'after years of suffering. Seems hard that she should be taken from her three little children and I should be left a withered tree,' Edith had written to Berta Ruck.[2] Ada Breakell agreed to talk to Mrs Langley Moore, but failed to shed a lifetime's habit of discretion. Alice Hoatson was nursing a sick sister when Mrs Langley Moore first contacted her, but she sent off a long, rambling and deeply fascinating account of her years as Edith's closest companion. She was to live out a poverty-stricken old age in south London, maintaining the sad pretence that Rosamund and John were her niece and nephew, and fantasizing about the frequency of their letters and visits.

When the biography was finished, neither Paul nor the Skipper liked it. 'I didn't suppose that they would – they will have to bear it,' wrote Iris whose view of life was that there was much to be endured and little to be enjoyed. Edith had carefully concealed the humiliating circumstances of her marriage to Hubert, but Mrs Langley Moore's researches at Somerset House had turned up her marriage certificate, dated two months before Paul's birthday. Paul was distressed at this discovery, and his wife and prim in-laws were far from pleased. While the book tactfully passed over this, and various other scandals in silence, it was still evident that Mrs Bland had been a most unconventional lady. The Skipper was unhappy on rather different grounds: he thought Hubert had been presented unfairly, and Edith's first marriage had been contrasted unfavourably to her second; he felt too much had been made of his essentially marginal position in Edith's life, and feared that her old friends would think that he had claimed

more than his due. He was uneasy about the warm thanks he received
in the acknowledgements:

> 'I don't *like* all this sugar,' [he confided in Rosamund], 'I know the
> woman wants to make a contrast and all that, but it's not the right *thing*.
> I only came into the last years of your mother's life, and people will
> think I handed out all sorts of things I never mentioned and never *would*
> mention.'[3]

A few old friends entirely failed to respond to requests for
information: her secretary, Horace Horsnell, much to everyone's
surprise, utterly denied he had ever held such a position, while Gerald
Spencer Pryse characteristically did not bother to reply. When the
more intimate and awkward details of her life emerged, both
Rosamund and John seemed entirely relaxed as to what information
was given about their births. After reading classics at Cambridge, John
had trained as a doctor and was working as a bacteriologist at the
London Hospital in Whitechapel. He confidently assured Doris
Langley Moore that nothing she said about his parentage was likely to
affect his career prospects. Both Rosamund and John were inclined to
take their father's part, to some extent, both of them having felt let
down by Edith at different times, not least by her discrimination
between them and her own children in her will. Rosamund's
relationship with her adoptive mother had always been tense, and her
husband Clifford Sharp had been particularly concerned that justice
should be done to Hubert who, in his opinion, had always been the
dominant member of the partnership, and the more important of the
two. Iris had cordially disliked her father and did not agree; neither did
Berta Ruck. But by this time Clifford himself had become an alcoholic
and had been humiliatingly relieved of his editorship of the *New
Statesman*. Rosamund had endured his illness, and its disastrous
consequences, and was on the point of finally leaving him. He turned
up at the launching party for the biography and was so obviously
drunk that Noel Griffith persuaded him that he had come on the
wrong day; Doris Langley Moore chatted to him in the kitchen for
what seemed an interminable time, while Hubert Griffith fetched a
taxi; the noise of the party was going on in the next room. Clifford died
not long afterwards.[4]

Rosamund went down to stay with the Skipper in the Long Boat in
the autumn of 1932. When Miss Hill finally decided to move out early
in 1933, she realized that, though he didn't like being looked after, the

Skipper wasn't really well enough to live on his own any more. Rosamund herself was finishing work on her first and only novel: set on the Romney Marsh, *The Man in the Stone House* (1934) is essentially a romance, but like Edith's romances, it is permeated by her own experiences and dreams. It tells of a young girl between childhood and adolescence who falls deeply and passionately in love with a much older man, a writer living in complete seclusion since his imprisonment for a crime incited by a heartless mistress. The unmanageable tangle of parenthood is cut away altogether since the girl is brought up by a harsh and rigid clergyman who wrongly supposes himself to be her father, her mother having died at her birth. The man she loves is small and fair, and wonderfully attentive to her education, both of body and mind. He has an obvious physical resemblance to H. G. Wells, though the complex blend of erotic yet paternal love that he shows her may serve to conceal the physically very different presence of Rosamund's real father. In the end the unspeakable problem of sexuality comes between them as a village child is assaulted and murdered and only the heroine can identify her attacker. The book ends with the clergyman's death and the promise that she and the writer will share an indefinite future. *The Man in the Stone House* is a powerful, compelling and deeply revealing fantasy.

Rosamund probably stayed on at Jesson to look after the Skipper – at any rate she was with him, holding his hand, when he died in May 1935. She was the only one of Edith's family to display any creative ability, though her talent was not, of course, inherited from her mother. Her letters to Mrs Langley Moore have a quality of openness and honesty that is appealing; she seemed not to flinch from feeling, however painful. Paul and Iris led sad lives beneath the shadow of their dominant and energetic mother. Paul belonged neither to his parents' world of literary Bohemia nor to the surburban, conformist society of the Stock Exchange into which Hubert had pushed him. He had few ambitions of his own and liked to live at a slow and dreamy pace that somehow annoyed his wife. Too much had always been expected of him and he took refuge in mediocrity; cars, gardening and pub company afforded solaces that were disapproved of at home; he grew tired of his existence, and in a state of deep depression, poisoned himself in October 1940 at the age of sixty.[5] Iris was 'the survivor'; her narrow lips, exaggerating that feature of her mother's, were permanently clenched against the disasters that she had somehow anticipated from the first. Her daughter Pandora, Edith's only grandchild, became a successful dancer and worked for a time in Pavlova's company. She in turn adopted two children, Max and Fern, but was killed in a road accident in the 1950s. Iris, now an old lady, though still earning her living as a dressmaker, was left to bring up the two of them. Nothing survived of Edith but her books, and of these only her children's books are still read and reprinted today.

Why was she successful only in that one vein, rather than in the various others that she practised (for she had attempted most of the forms of writing then popular)? Why are *The Railway Children* and the Bastables and the psammead remembered, long after her novels and poems have been forgotten (though Philip Larkin included one in his *Oxford Book of Twentieth Century English Verse*)?[6] Something within her clearly responded and corresponded to the position of the child in her society: second-rate citizens, then as now, they practised a quiet subversiveness, an irony at the expense of the absurd world of adults which appealed strongly to her. She experienced all the child's primitive desires to control the world around her, yet she was conscious, as the children in her books are, of being a subject in a world where the rules are laid down by full-grown men – and where women, like children, are relegated to marginal positions and occupations. Then (as now?) the activity of writing children's books was not accorded recognition as a serious or worthwhile literary enterprise, however successfully it might be carried out. Her best work was enthusiastically received – it was 'delightful', 'graceful', even 'original' – but the genre was one that nobody took seriously. Frustrating though this was, it offered certain advantages: it left room for play and for experiment, for there was no literary establishment whose limited tastes must be gratified in order to succeed. She felt herself to be full of a spontaneous freshness, an innate adventurousness that challenged the stale routines of modern urban life, recapturing the careless joys of childhood, re-opening the locked doors of the past – it is a sense constantly present in her books, and intermittently present in her life.

At the outset of her career, Edith had proved herself a capable home-maker and mother, as well as a wage-earner. When obliged to, she had become the mother who holds the home together in adversity, supporting herself and her children, while remaining patient, loving and understanding – the sort of mother whose idealised portrait stands at the centre of *The Railway Children*, on whose self-reliance and resourcefulness the children's fragile world depends. But Edith grew bored with playing the tolerant parent to Hubert's sexually irrespons-

ible child, and began to compete with him in childishness, recreating
her tomboy relationship with her brothers in a sequence of love affairs
in which she played older sister to a younger man. By insisting that she
too could be a naughty child, she forced Alice Hoatson to adopt the
responsible and maternal roles she had abandoned, to look after the
immediate needs of Hubert and the children. The determined childishness of both the Blands, their desire to play the *enfant terrible*,
manifested itself in their preference for and praise of the young, and the
company of the young. Sometimes they seem to have usurped their
children's roles, playing every game more amusingly and energetically
than they could. Children need their parents to be parents, not rivals.
Edith wanted to share and sometimes even to monopolize her
children's friends. Her children do not seem to have found it easy to be
happy, and it may be that the mother who still wanted to be a child
stood in their light.

Edith had never entirely wanted to grow up nor fully accepted that
she had. Even when she found contentment in her second marriage,
she would say, 'Mr Tucker and I feel that we are old by mistake.'[7]
Being a child enabled her to ignore or justify breaking rules of social or
sexual conduct. As a writer for adults she was obliged to assume a tone
of responsible judgement which would not allow her to approve or
condone her own personal code of behaviour. As a children's writer
she could overlook it altogether: the accepted silence of children's
books with regard to sexuality as well as the anti-romanticism of
children's culture provided her with a convenient evasion, while
allowing her to write up the element of camaraderie in her love affairs
that served as a screen for the unacceptable elements of passion
beneath. With Oswald Barron, she could play at being Oswald and
Alice, replaying her old relationship with her brother Alfred, knowing
that beneath that level lay a more intimate and romantic scenario.
Through the Bastable stories, she recreated her intense involvement
with Oswald Barron in a new mode which simultaneously allowed
her, by writing in his voice, to identify with him and to praise him; at
the same time as mocking him gently. Her success with *The Treasure
Seekers* and its sequels was decisive in determining what direction she
would take as a writer.

Yet while she identified with children, in writing for them, as she
had identified with Oswald, her books only sold because they
appealed to adult buyers. And most of her later books are spoken by an
adult narrator, in a tone that is occasionally didactic, and usually

auntly. It was in this voice that she warned her readers of the dangers of
the inner fantasy world, of their own most atavistic wishes, as well as
of the outer world in which greed, social injustice and urban squalor
threatened the green and good places of the earth. The desire for
irresponsibility had, all the time, coexisted with a desire to be listened
to, to have a voice in a world where women were seldom heard. She
had been disappointed when her friends remained unimpressed by her
poetry, a genre that *did* command listeners, and she finally came to feel
that her poetic talents had been dissipated by the necessity of selling
her work in the market place. She cherished no such illusions about her
adult fiction, which was written in a popular romantic style: of *The
Red House*, probably her most successful adult novel, she told Nina
Griffith, 'If you like that sort of stuff, it's just the sort of stuff you'll
like. Don't read it because you know me. Try it on your cook.' Like
everything else, it was written primarily to pay the bills. Yet though
she knew the limited value placed on children's books, it was
nevertheless as a children's writer that she recognized her own
achievement. From its inception she declared of *The Treasure Seekers*,
'I am very much in love with the book, and I think it should be a great
success.'[8]

While the marginality of children's books kept them in low esteem,
it could also operate as a source of strength. Though some things could
not be said at all or only indirectly, the lack of fully developed rules and
patterns left children's fiction as one of the freest and most versatile
forms of the nineteenth century. The brilliant explorations of the inner
self expressed as fantasy by the romantic writers were later increasingly
found in marginal forms of writing – in folk tales, ghost stories or in
children's books: Lewis Carroll's *Alice*, Thackeray's *The Rose and the
Ring*, Kingsley's *The Water-Babies* and much of George MacDonald's
fiction make use of fantasy in daring and experimental ways that point
forward to more modernist freedoms. Edith's fantasy was to follow
their example, using magic and the supernatural to explore the buried
self and the unspoken rules, and allowing her to invent and deploy
powerful myths about the city, the past and the nature of creativity. By
using magic as a symbol for the power of imagination, she explored its
nature and capacity, and the meaning and implications of hidden
wishes and desires.

At the centre of Edith Nesbit's writing for children stands the
concept of imaginative play, with all its complex meanings. For play is
at once forward-looking and backward-looking, light-hearted and

deeply serious. Children use it as a way of learning to grow up, or of re-enacting what they have lost, and it combines the impulse to believe with the recognition that it is an indulgence in self-deception. A full understanding of the nature of play may even be the key to maturity, though it can scarcely be fully achieved by a child. Books themselves represent an important form of play. All her books bring about a confrontation between play and experience, though they often increase the power of the imagination within play by the use of magic. But much of the play itself derives from a range of other books, since the middle-class child's experiences are normally largely acquired at second-hand. Events are commonly shaped or determined by reference to a range of Victorian children's books, some of which have long since been forgotten: the Bastables' reading includes La Motte Fouqué's *Sintram* (1814), Dumas's *The Count of Monte Cristo* (1845); Captain Marryat's *The Children of the New Forest* (1847), Charlotte M. Yonge's *The Daisy Chain* (1856), Dickens, and, more recently, Kipling's *Jungle Books* and *Stalky*, Kenneth Grahame's *The Golden Age* and Sherlock Holmes, as well as books written in the mid-century evangelical tradition, such as *Ministering Children* (1854), and *What Katy Did* (1872), which only Daisy and Dora are prepared to read.[9] Nor are the references to such books mere glancing allusions: often an episode can involve an extended examination of a particular literary model that includes elements of parodic replay. Like a number of major nineteenth-century writers – among them Jane Austen and Flaubert – E. Nesbit presents her critique of life in terms of a critique of reading habits and the peculiar dangers and deceptions that reading can offer.

For better, and sometimes for worse, Edith's fictional children occupy a book-shaped world and it is probably this quality, more than any other, that has served to date them, for while they are constantly playing games based on their reading, most of today's children derive their imaginative worlds primarily from television and films instead. Their social milieu, largely dominated by school, is very different from that of Nesbit's children, enjoying long Edwardian holidays; this means that only more sophisticated readers can break through the shell of difference to recognize and identify with the feelings within. She has nevertheless had a decisive influence upon much modern writing for children, arguably stronger than that of any other single writer: adventure stories of the 'famous five' type, stories of magical happenings and visits to the past largely owe their existence to the models she established.

As well as influencing popular children's fiction, her best books have also been treated with great seriousness: two deeply religious novelists of the supernatural, Charles Williams and C. S. Lewis, were fascinated by the way in which she dissolved the barriers of time and space and created structures in which everyday appearances faded to reveal deeper truths beneath. C. S. Lewis borrowed a number of specific devices to use in his own fictions, most memorably the magical 'Bigwardrobeinspareroom' which opens into another world, but also the island in *The Magic City* which appears wonderfully beautiful to those who belong there, but physically repels invaders (borrowed in *The Great Divorce*). But it was *The Amulet* that excited Lewis most, as he pored over it as a small boy in a large house in Northern Ireland: 'It first opened my eyes to antiquity, the "dark backward and abysm of time." I can still re-read it with delight.' He remembered the sweetness of the voice of the Amulet when he described the song of Narnia's creation, and the alarming appearance of the Queen of Babylon in London, when he pictured Jadis's unwelcome visit in *The Magician's Nephew*; the terrible Assyrian god Nisroch appeared as the evil god Tash in *The Last Battle*. The *Amulet* also seems to have appealed to Lewis's friend, Charles Williams, for he jotted down from it, 'Knowledge that Time and Space are only modes of thought. Is not this the beginning of all magic?' and some such idea seems to govern the structure of his own fantasy novels. Yet, with characteristic self-mockery, the idea that so interested Charles Williams is comically misremembered several times by Robert and Cyril in the book:

> 'But will the Amulet work both ways?' inquired Robert.
> 'It ought to,' said Cyril, 'if time's only a thingummy of whatsits-name . . .'[10]

More recently a famous physicist, Freeman Dyson, has found in *The Magic City*'s distrust of machinery a profound image of our contemporary condition, stuck once and for all with wonderful or disastrous technological toys.[11]

While an element of comedy and conflict toughens and energizes her books, some of her keenest devotees have found in them an escape into an arcadia that somehow epitomizes 'the English outlook and ideal of life', a world of childhood which constitutes a permanent and precious alternative to the insistent or intractable pressures of adult life: shortly before her death, Edith received an admiring letter from the novelist Clemence Dane who asked:

I wonder if you quite realise what intense enjoyment you give – not only to children, but to people like myself who work very hard . . . You've given me pleasure and *rest*, real delight when I badly need to get right away from myself – over and over again.

Another great admirer, Noël Coward, continued to reread her each year; a copy of *The Enchanted Castle* lay beside his bed when he died. In 1956 he wrote home from Jamaica:

I am reading again through all the dear E. Nesbits and they seem to me to be more charming and evocative than ever. It is strange that after half a century I still get so much pleasure from them. Her writing is so light and unforced, her humour is so sure and her narrative quality so strong that the stories, which I know backwards, rivet me as much now as they did when I was a little boy. Even more so in one way because I can now enjoy her actual talent and her extraordinary power of describing hot summer days in England in the beginning years of the century. All the pleasant memories of my own childhood jump at me from the pages . . . E. Nesbit knew all the things that stay in the mind, all the happy treasures. I suppose she, of all the writers I have ever read, has given me over the years the most complete satisfaction . . .[12]

FOOTNOTES

A Note on Sources

The main primary sources I have used are the archives of Doris Langley Moore and Jocelyn Nixon, described below. In addition, the Fabian Papers at Nuffield College include letters from both the Blands as well as much other information about their involvement with the Society. Edith's letters to her agents Morris Colles and J. W. Pinker are in the Berg Collection, New York Public Library; her letters to the Society of Authors in the British Library (Add. MSS 56762) and to H. G. Wells among the Wells Papers in the University Library of Illinois at Urbana-Champaign. Her correspondence with her publishers (often on an acrimonious note) survives where their archives have been preserved, e.g. Macmillan's in the British Library (her letters in Add. MSS 54964), John Lane Papers in the Harry Ransom Humanities Research Centre, Austin, Texas.

Jocelyn Nixon's archive consists of several MS notebooks of poems (many cut out and pasted in from periodicals), a family photograph album (from which a number of snapshots are here reproduced), the scrapbook of Edith's late writings made up by Mavis Carter, some books of posthumous press cuttings and some miscellaneous letters and poems mainly addressed to Paul Bland or his wife. Material from this collection is referred to in the footnotes by the initials 'JNA'.

Doris Langley Moore's archive consists of four main items: typed transcripts of letters to and from Edith (these have been checked against the originals where possible, but they are now largely lost or destroyed); Mrs Langley Moore's correspondence with Edith's family and friends during the writing of her biography (1931–3); four notebooks of interviews taken down in shorthand, with the author's transcriptions of them; and a card index, largely based on material from the notebooks, but not entirely, since certain items of private or confidential information are stored only on the file cards. Mrs Langley Moore's archive is the source of the notebooks and file cards referred to in the footnotes, as well as of all letters not otherwise attributed.

FOREWORD

1 'The Criminal', *The Neolith*, no. I, November 1907, p. 22, reprinted in *These Little Ones* (1909), pp. 107–117; 'In the Queen's Garden', *The Neolith*, no. IV, August 1908, pp. 1–11.

2 *The Butler in Bohemia* was published, apparently in paperback, by Henry J. Drane who printed several of her early works. Bower Marsh had a copy of it and Noel Griffith took the collation from his copy, sending it to D.L.M., 5 December 1932. It has since disappeared. E.N. listed *The Marden Mystery* in her *Who's Who* entry; E.N. to Morris Collis informs him that it 'had a success in Chicago', n.d. [recd. 16 July 1898], in the Berg Collection, New York Public Library.

3 Sybil Ann Henderson to D.L.M., 17 April 1933; these memoirs have been reprinted under the title *Long Ago When I Was Young* (1966, 1974).

4 G.B.S. to D.L.M., 8 May 1931.

5 E. Nesbit: *Fairy Stories*, ed. Naomi Lewis (1977), p. xiii.

6 Clifford Sharp to D.L.M., n.d. [12 December 1931]; a postscript adds 'Iris always hated him and he never liked her or Paul. It was as if he was half-ashamed of them.' Rosamund regarded this as 'distinctly exaggerated' (R.S. to D.L.M., 15 December 1931).

7 Clifford Sharp to D.L.M., 17 December 1931; Berta Ruck to D.L.M., 13 January 1933; G.B.S. in interview, Notebook 4.

8 See, for example, Norman and Jeanne MacKenzie: *The First Fabians* (1977), pp. 67–8.

9 Berta Ruck: *A Story-Teller Tells the Truth* (1935), pp. 145, 147.

10 Iris Philips to D.L.M., 8 May 1951.

11 R.L.G. to D.L.M., 26 August 1931.

12 Norman and Jeanne MacKenzie, op. cit., p. 95; 'The Ring and the Lamp', *Oswald Bastable and Others* (1905), p. 220.

CHAPTER 1

1 *The Railway Children* (1906), ch. XIV, p. 307.

2 Introduction to *My School-Days*, twelve articles published in the *Girl's Own Paper* from October 1896 to September 1897, vol. xviii, nos. 875–924, hereafter referred to by part and page numbers.

3 *Wings and the Child* (1913), p. 144.

4 Information about the Nesbits from the *DNB* entry for John Collis Nesbit, and from Mrs Christine Powell. Anthony Nesbit may have first made the acquaintance of the Aldertons when, according to some satirical verses he wrote, a younger son of his (probably Anthony junior) died at Hastings – 'Character of Hastings', dated 27 December 1843 (MS in JNA). A Thomas Alderton, possibly Sarah's brother, was named as his executor in Anthony's will, dated December 1856. (Edith herself was sent to a school run by Moravian sisters, for a short time.)

5 Notebook 2, interview with T. T. Tucker.

6 *My School-Days*. Part IV, 'In the Dark', p. 264.

7 Notebook 2, interview with T. T. Tucker; 'What shall we Play at?' *The Daily Chronicle*, 23 April 1910, p. 7; 'The Treasure-Seekers' by 'Ethel Mortimer' (i.e. E. Nesbit), *Father Christmas*, 1896; *The Story of the Treasure Seekers* (1899), ch. II, pp. 19–26.

8 'The Twopenny Spell', *Oswald Bastable and Others* (1905), pp. 167–8.

9 *My School-Days*, Part IV, p. 264.

10 *Wings and the Child,* pp. 38–9.

11 On the crockery rabbit, see *Daphne in Fitzroy Street* (1909), p. 239; *Wings and the Child*, p. 39, 'Playing with Water', *The Daily Chronicle*, 18 June 1910, p. 7.; the rag doll, *Wings*, p. 40; her nurse, *My School-Days*, Part IV, p. 264.

12 *Wings*, p. 51.

13 *Ibid.*, p. 48.

14 *Ibid.*, p. 49. For details of the Crystal Palace dinosaurs, see Stephen Prickett: *Victorian Fantasy* (1979), esp. pp. 81–2.

15 *Ibid.*, p. 144; *My School-Days*, Part I, 'Stuart Plaid', p. 28.

16 *My School-Days*, Part I, p. 28.

17 *My School-Days*, Part II, 'Long Division', p. 106; Part I, p. 28.

18 *Ibid.*, Part VI, p. 375; *Wings*, p. 39.

19 Mary Nesbit to her uncle Edward Planta Nesbit, 26 January 1868; *My School-Days*, Part III, 'South with the Swallows', p. 184.

20 *My School-Days*, Part IV, p. 266.

21 *Ibid.*, Part III, p. 184.

22 *Ibid.*, Part V, 'The Mummies at Bordeaux', p. 313.

23 Mrs Sherwood: *The History of the Fairchild Family* (1818), pp. 282–3. See also *Wet Magic* (1913), ch. IX pp. 163, 184, 188, 197. (This episode is discussed on page 353).

24 Mary Nesbit; to Edward Planta Nesbit; *My School-Days*, Part VI, p. 375.

25 *Ibid.*, p. 375.

26 On Mrs Nesbit's visit to Biarritz, see Mary's letter, cited above; *My School-Days*, Part VII, 'Disillusion', p. 435.

27 *Ibid.*, p. 436. (This episode is compared to Mrs Ewing's tale of *Mrs Overtheway's Remembrances*.)

28 *Ibid.*, Part VIII, 'In Auvergne', p. 534.

29 *Ibid.*, Part IV, p. 264.

30 Iris Philips to D.L.M., 8 May 1951, insisted that her mother, far from being 'haunted by terrible fears' was 'on the contrary . . . a most dauntless and fearless child'.

31 *Ibid.*, Part IX, 'La Haye', p. 575; on her later visits, see E.N. to Ada Breakell, headed 'Guildhall Library', n.d. [c. 1879].

32 *My School-Days*, Part IX, p. 575.

33 *Ibid.*, Part X, 'Pirates and Explorers', p. 635. E.N. used to say that her mother had once let the house to Lord Kitchener's family, and that, as a child, he had lamed her pony, Punch.

34 Notebook 1, interview with John Bland; also file card 'Ghosts'.

35 *My School-Days*, Part XI, p. 711.

36 'I was so happy there' from 'Things to Eat', *The Daily Chronicle*, 30 April 1910, p. 7. For the convent games, see *Wings*, pp. 111–2; the nuns' names for Daisy from an undated letter she wrote to her mother from the convent (*'le bon petit diable, le brise-fer'*), and from *Daphne in Fitzroy Street*, p. 12 (*'la folle Anglaise, capable de tout, mais bonne enfant'*); quotation from a second undated letter from the convent.

37 Daisy to Mrs Nesbit from the convent, n.d.

38 *Daphne in Fitzroy Street*, p. 32; letter to Saretta from Mère Marie Madeleine, 3 November 1869.

39 Notebook 2, interview with T. T. Tucker; 'On Running Away', *The Daily Chronicle*, 25 June 1910, p. 7.

40 Notebook 2, interview with T. T. Tucker.

41 *My School-Days*, Part XI, p. 711. The Boltons' identity suggested by Mrs Christine Powell.

42 *Ibid.* (E.N. used this episode as the basis for a children's story, later included as chapter seven, 'The Madness of Madeline' in *Five of Us – and Madeline*, published posthumously in 1925).

43 *Ibid.*

CHAPTER 2

1 Quoted in 'When I was a Girl' by E. Nesbit, *John O'London's Weekly*, 15 November 1919.

2 *Ibid.*

3 E.N. to Sarah Nesbit from the Dinan convent, n.d.

4 Mary's commonplace book, dated December 1869 and numbered III (JNA). Marston's sonnet, entitled 'Desolate' ('I strain my worn-out sight across the sea, . . .'), was later published in *Song-Tide*, 1871.

5 The date of Mary's death from DLMA, filecard on 'Dates of Main Events'. Information about Philip Bourke Marston taken from P.B.M.'s *Song-Tide and Other Poems* (1888), edited with a memoir by William Sharp (though Sharp repudiates the story about P.B.M.'s discovery of Mary's corpse) and P.B.M.'s *Collected Poems* (1891), edited with a biographical sketch by L. C. Moulton. The stanza quoted is from 'The Watchers', *Collected Poems*, p. 120.

6 E.N. to Sarah Nesbit, headed 'The Rose and Crown, Branbridges', n.d. [c. 1899].

7 Details concerning nineteenth-century Halstead, the Hall and the Man family from Geoffrey Kitchener's history of the village, published locally in 1978.

8 *My School-Days*, Part XII, p. 788.

9 *Ibid*.

10 *Ibid*.

11 'When I was a Girl'.

12 *My School-Days*, Part XII.

13 'When I was a Girl'. The detail about Mr Japp is from *My School-Days* where he is wrongly described as the editor of *Good Words* (who was Donald Macleod) and the *Sunday Magazine* (this was W. G. Blaikie). The *Sunday Magazine* for 1874–5 published 4 poems by 'Caris Brooke' (i.e. Saretta) and one by A. H. Japp. In the 1875–6 volume, there are no signed contributions from either of the Nesbit sisters.

14 'When I was a Girl'.

15 Violet Oakley visited Edith in 1887 and 1888, according to Shaw's diary – Bernard Shaw: *The Diaries 1885–1897*, ed. Stanley Weintraub (1986), Vol. I, pp. 309, 389; *The Incomplete Amorist* (1906), p. 5.

16 This information supplied by Geoffrey Kitchener.

17 The 1861 census for the college records John Deakin of Liverpool, age 16, living there as a pupil. He was slightly younger than Saretta (RG/9/353,4,5).

18 Rosamund Sharp to D.L.M., 16 June [1931]; undated newspaper cutting from the *Mark Lane Express*, c. 1875.

19 Stories of this type are 'Yosodhara', *The Argosy* (1885), vol. 40, pp. 372–380; 'Thor and the Hammer', *These Little Ones* (1909); 'The Lie Comes True', *To the Adventurous* (1923); 'The Christmas

Pudding' *Thirteen Ways Home* (1901). 'The Garland of Oak Leaves', *Thirteen Ways Home*, is about providing for mother, and anticipates the treatment of this theme in *The Railway Children* (1906).

20 This address supplied by Mrs Christine Powell and confirmed by E.N.'s letter to Ada Breakell, headed 'Guildhall Library', n.d. [c. 1878].

21 *My School-Days*, Part XI, p. 711.

22 Ada is described as E.N.'s 'dearest and oldest friend' in the dedication of *Man and Maid* (1906). Information from Notebook 2, interview with Ada Breakell. There are three poems for Ada in E.N.'s book of early MS poems: 'To Adah' ('Awakened in the shadowy dawn . . .'), April 1879, p. 10; 'To Adah' ('Last Spring our days were full of ease . . .'), December 1878 (published in the *Union Jack*), p. 18; 'To Ada' ('When life held on her bosom . . .'), undated, p. 55 (JNA).

23 Ada Breakell to D.L.M., 23 October 1931, describes Stuart Smith as 'a very young man (17) in (I think) a money-changer's office (or Bank)'. This is confirmed by E.N.'s birthday book where Stuart Smith's birthday appears as 16 February 1860. The novelist Edgar Jepson said (in interview, Notebook 1) that he had been told by Edith that she had met Hubert on a picnic where they shared a plate of strawberries. I have preferred Ada Breakell's account – she was an eye witness and her memory proved consistently reliable.

24 The phrase 'like the scream of an eagle' is Shaw's, from a long autobiographical letter to Archibald Henderson of 3 January 1905. See Bernard Shaw: *Collected Letters 1898–1910*, ed. Dan H. Laurence (1972), p. 496. Ada Breakell's letter to D.L.M., cited above, asserts, 'Mrs Nesbit did *not* like Hubert Bland.'

25 Information from Hubert's birth certificate, census records for 1851, 1861 and 1871 and contemporary post office directories and rate books, collected by the Greenwich Local History Library, Mycenae Road, S.E.3.

26 For his intellectual development, see 'The Faith I Hold', *Essays* by Hubert Bland, (1914), pp. 212–233; on Hyndman, pp. 223–5. Rosamund Bland's comment on her father from her letter to D.L.M., 12 December 1931.

27 'If I were a Woman' in *Essays*, p. 203. Mary Margaret Ann Doran was born on 22 December 1855 and died on 25 March 1903.

28 'A Holiday', *The Literary Sense* (1903), pp. 108–9.

29 E.N. to Ada Breakell, headed 'Guildhall Library', n.d. [c. 1878].

30 *Ibid.*

31 *The Incredible Honeymoon* (American edition 1916, reprinted 1921), pp. 131–2, 134 (all page references to 1921 edition).

32 Two (apparently fragmentary) letters from E.N. to Ada Breakell, n.d. [c. 1878–9]. The quotation is from the last lines of Browning's 'Two in the Campagna', which is concerned with following (and losing) a particular train of thought, so that the letter partly paraphrases the poem, especially the final stanza:

> Just when I seemed about to learn!
> Where is the thread now? Off again!
> The old trick! Only I discern . . .

33 The book is in JNA.

34 MS book of early poems, p. 36. The fragment is dated 1879, but sounds as if it might have been intended for the book of *Sonnets from the Portuguese* (JNA).

35 MS book of early poems, dated November 1878, p. 16 (JNA).

36 *Ibid.*, pp. 1, 6–7, 9–10.

37 This reconstruction is speculative and based on three pieces of evidence: Edith's address on her marriage certificate (8 Oxford Terrace, located from a contemporary postal directory); E.N.'s letter to Ada Breakell, n.d. [c. 1885], cited on p. 49, includes a reference to Oxford Terrace; a letter from Ada Breakell to D.L.M. 23 October 1931, comments: 'What you tell me about the first child being born only two months after the marriage is news to me! [Ada was Paul's godmother] I remember Edith writing and telling me that she was married – but I do not remember that she told me *when* or *where* . . . If it is true that Paul's birth was so soon after the marriage, it was concealed from me, for I have no recollection that I suspected any irregularity about it.

'After my visit to the Nesbits in 1878 I don't think I stayed with E.N. again until after she was married. It must have been in the winter for I remember we skated on the ice at Dansent.' This is likely to have been the winter of 1879–80, before Paul's birth and E.N.'s marriage, since E.N. was probably obliged to move from Oxford Terrace when Paul was born (both letters in DLMA). E.N. always gave the date of her marriage as 1879, though it was actually 1880 (see, for example, her correspondence with Francis Galton, among the Galton papers in University College Library, London).

38 *The Prophet's Mantle* by 'Fabian Bland' (1885, reprinted 1889), p. 97 (all page references to 1889 edition).

39 Alice Hoatson's account of E. Nesbit (DLMA) provides information about Bland staying with his mother; Bland's marriage certificate describes him as a brush manufacturer; Bowater Crescent was the address used for all his Fabian correspondence until his mother's death.

40 *The Prophet's Mantle*, p. 63.

41 *The Incredible Honeymoon* (1921), pp. 146–7, 152.
42 Census for 1881, RG/11/733(3); RG/11/743(6).

CHAPTER 3

1 For the title, 'Bandbox', and the home-making details, see E.N.'s *The Red House* (1902), esp. chapters I, pp. 8, 12; IV, p. 84.
2 The 'visitor's' comments are, in fact, those of G. B. Shaw from his *roman-à-clef* about the Blands, *An Unfinished Novel*, ed. by Stanley Weintraub, 1958, p. 42.
3 Hubert's attacks of smallpox described in Alice Hoatson's memoir; see also Notebook 4, interview with G. B. Shaw.
4 *The Story of the Treasure Seekers* (1899), ch. I, pp. 6–7.
5 Alice Hoatson's memoir records 'all the money gone and much of the stock. The remnant, a few most excellent brushes. These he used to give as presents to his friends. I have one . . .'
6 *The Story of the Treasure Seekers* (1899), ch. V, pp. 66–7.
7 *Daphne in Fitzroy Street* (1909), pp. 140, 141, 142.
8 *The Railway Children* (1906), ch. III, pp. 53–4.
9 Notebook 2, interview with T. T. Tucker. The firm seems to have been Raphael Tuck, for whom she was later to write children's stories.
10 MS book of early poems: two 'Elle et Lui' poems, pp. 48, 51. 'A Farewell', p. 57 (JNA). A revised version of it was published in *The Argosy* for November 1883, vol. XXXVI, p. 416, and as 'A Good-Bye' in *Lays and Legends* (1886), p. 194.
11 *Ibid.*, p. 63. 'Quieta non movere' ought to mean 'Let sleeping dogs lie', but the normal (and correct) form of the proverb is 'Quieta noli movere'. Substantially revised, this was published as 'Possibilities' in *The Argosy* for August 1884, vol. XXXVIII, p. 160, and, with its title corrected to 'Quieta ne movete', in *Lays and Legends* (1886), p. 77.
12 Ada Breakell to D.L.M., 23 October 1931.
13 See Shaw's *An Unfinished Novel*, where it provides the occasion of an argument, pp. 77–9, and Notebook 1, interview with John Bland.
14 Maggie was still Hubert's mistress in 1887 – see interview with Noel Griffith, Notebook 3. On 11 March 1890 Miss Doran was elected to the Fabian Society (Fabian Papers at Nuffield College). Details of her death and her son's age from a corrective slip from Iris Philips to D.L.M., n.d. [early November 1932]. John Davis, who searched for the missing birth certificate, described this as 'an Oliver Twist job'.

15 See Alice Hoatson's memoir, and interview with Shaw in Notebook 4.
16 *The Prophet's Mantle* by 'Fabian Bland', published by Henry Drane (1885, rp. 1889), p. 242. Only the later reprints of 1888 (British Museum Library) and 1889 (Bodleian Library) appear to have survived. All page references are to the latter.
17 The *DNB* entry for John Collis Nesbit includes a final paragraph on his son Alfred.
18 E.N. to Ada Breakell, 30 March 1884.
19 E.N. to Ada, n.d. [11–25 April 1884].
20 E.N. to Ada, 2 March [1884].
21 E.N. to Ada, [? February 1884]; E.N. to Ada, 2 March [1884]; E.N. to Ada, n.d. [11–25 April 1884].
22 E.N. to Ada, 30 March 1884.
23 E.N. to Ada, 30 March 1884; E.N. to Ada, n.d. [11–25 April 1884].
24 *Ibid.* 'The wood near Bath's' must be Chalkhurst Wood – two brothers, Albert and Edwin Bath worked Colegates Farm, about half a mile north-east of Halstead Hall and this is the nearest wood (information from Geoffrey Kitchener). The weak story about a dream is likely to have been 'The Fabric of a Vision', subsequently published in *The Argosy* for March 1885, vol. 39, pp. 234–244.
25 Reprinted in *Essays* by Hubert Bland (1914).
26 *Ibid.*, p. 214.
27 See Norman and Jeanne MacKenzie: *The First Fabians* (1977), p. 26.
28 From the first Fabian Minute Book (Fabian Papers at Nuffield College).
29 E.N. to Ada, 'Sunday (later)' [6 April 1884].
30 E.N. to Ada, 2 March [1884].
31 E.N. to Ada, n.d. [? February 1884].
32 E.N. to Ada, 'Sunday (later)' [6 April 1884].
33 Norman and Jeanne MacKenzie: *The First Fabians*, p. 95.
34 According to Shaw – see *Shaw: An Autobiography 1856–1898*, selected by Stanley Weintraub, 1969, 'The Fabian Experience', p. 123.
35 *The New Treasure Seekers*, 'The Flying Lodger', pp. 209–10, 214–5.
36 E.N. to Ada, n.d. [after 23 August 1885].
37 *Something Wrong* by Fabian Bland, published in *The Weekly Dispatch* from 7 March–4 July 1886. Chapter IV, p. 12 (21 March).
38 Berta Ruck: *A Story-Teller Tells the Truth*, 1935, p. 145.
39 E.N. to Ada, n.d. [c. summer 1885].
40 Notebook 4, interview with G. B. Shaw who observed: 'She was a very restless woman and would not keep quiet. She would always make a sensation at every meeting . . . At a time when the others

were quite serious, her little drawing-room tricks were quite trying. She was a woman who would always make scenes and get up vendettas. When the society became a body that met in big halls, she no longer appeared.' The comments on the meeting of 1 January 1886 quoted from the first Fabian Minute Book are in Shaw's handwriting (Fabian Papers at Nuffield College).

41 Cited from the paper cover of the 1889 edition.

42 'When I was a Girl', *John O'London's Weekly*, 15 November 1919.

43 'The Copper Beeches' was published in *The Weekly Dispatch* on 23 August 1885 (p. 12); E.N.'s letter to Ada referring to it is undated but written after that. The reference to Edward Pease is from another undated letter [? summer 1885].

44 *The Prophet's Mantle*, ch. XIII, p. 89. It may be relevant that on 6 March 1885, Charlotte Wilson, Miss Edwards and Rowland Estcourt were instructed by the Fabian executive committee to report on the Poor Law, and particularly to disprove government allegations that distress was being overestimated (see F.S. executive committee minutes, 23 December 1885, Fabian Papers at Nuffield).

45 Prince Kropotkin: *Memoirs of a Revolutionary*, 2 vols. (1899), vol. ii, pp. 251–2.

46 David Garnett: *The Golden Echo* (1953), p. 20.

47 Notes from Peter Kropotkin to E.N. are dated 31 December 1888, 4 September 1890 and a third is addressed to Mrs [Charlotte] Wilson asking for her address, dated 14 April 1907 – he had obviously lost touch with her in the meantime. A note from Stepniak to E.N. is dated 7 December 1886, and there is an interesting undated [? summer 1885] letter from E.N. to Stepniak, asking him to 'please read *The Prophet's Mantle* first and let me have it again as early as you can, because I want to try and arrange to have it published in book form'.

48 *The Railway Children* (1906), ch. V, pp. 114–6.

49 *The Prophet's Mantle*, ch. XVII, p. 125.

50 Notebook 3, interview with Mrs V. Taylor (née Fanny Woodcock). The lawyer, Gates, appears in the first chapter of *The Prophet's Mantle*: 'It was his boast that he only had eight clients, and that he lived on them . . . He had a genial, hearty way with him . . .'

51 *The Star*, 5 May 1924.

52 The first climax of *Something Wrong* occurs when the hero and his girlfriend find themselves trapped by a fall of stone in the 'Brocklehurst' (i.e. Chislehurst) caves. A reader's report on an unidentified novel by E. Nesbit involves a similar cave ordeal, though it seems to have been rewritten from a different narrative viewpoint. This unnamed novel was probably *The Marden Mystery*,

published in Chicago in 1894. Marden is in Kent, near Maidstone –
E.N. country, but not very close to Chislehurst. The caves at the
latter provided the setting for a story called 'The Dene Hole',
published in the *Pall Mall Magazine* for April 1909, and included by
Rosamund (as 'The Dwellers') in *Five of Us – and Madeline* (1925).
Of 'Picnics' E.N. wrote: 'When we were little . . . our favourite
place was the caves at Chislehurst', *The Daily Chronicle*, 11 June
1910, p. 7.

CHAPTER 4

1 E.N. to Ada Breakell, n.d. [c. summer 1885].
2 *The Incomplete Amorist* (1906), p. 18. *Daphne in Fitzroy Street*
   (1909), p. 190.
3 The first Fabian Minute Book is among the Fabian Papers at
   Nuffield College. Shaw described his conversion to Fabianism on a
   number of occasions – see *Shaw: An Autobiography 1856–1898*,
   selected by Stanley Weintraub (1969), ch. 6, 'The Fabian Experience', esp. pp. 122, 128–135. Shaw's letter to Archibald
   Henderson of 3 January 1905, *Collected Letters 1898–1910*, ed. Dan
   H. Laurence (1972) is his earliest version of how he became a Fabian
   (p. 494) and includes an account of the Blands in their early days (p.
   496) similar to that which Shaw gave D.L.M. (Notebook 4,
   interview with G. B. Shaw). For Shaw's meeting with Bland on 4
   May, see Norman and Jeanne MacKenzie, *The First Fabians* (1977),
   p. 42.
4 H.B. to G.B.S., 5 May 1884, in the Shaw Papers at the British
   Library (Add. MSS 50557).
5 *An Autobiography 1856–1898*, pp. 167–8.
6 E.N. to Ada, n.d. [c. summer 1885]; Notebook 4, interview with
   G.B.S. This episode is also referred to in Shaw's letter to Archibald
   Henderson cited above, p. 496.
7 Notebook 4, interview with G.B.S. Shaw's letter to Henderson
   gives a vivid pen portrait of Bland as 'a man of fierce Norman
   exterior and huge physical strength . . . [he] never was seen without
   an irreproachable frock coat, tall hat, and a single eyeglass which
   infuriated everybody. He was pugnacious, powerful, a skilled
   pugilist, and had a voice like the scream of an eagle. Nobody dared
   be uncivil to him. He is now much mellower; but I still avoid sitting
   next to him at a meeting because his shoulders are so broad and
   massive that it is impossible for his next neighbours to sit upright.
   His individuality, his opposite point of view to Webb's, and his
   common sense, were of great value to us, and are still.'

8 E.N. to Ada, n.d. [11–25 April 1884].

9 Details from the first Fabian Minute Book, among papers at Nuffield College.

10 Bernard Shaw: *The Diaries 1885–1897*, ed. Stanley Weintraub (1986), vol. I, esp. pp. 78, 91 (19 April, 19 June 1885). The 'forked radish' phrase is quoted in *The First Fabians*, p. 50, but not attributed (though it echoes Falstaff's 'Forked radish', *2 Henry IV*, III. ii. 311). Shaw on women falling in love with him quoted from *An Autobiography 1856–1898*, p. 170.

11 *The Diaries*, pp. 95, 96, 99 (4, 10, 25 July 1885).

12 Yvonne Kapp: *Eleanor Marx*, vol. 2, The Crowded Years (1979), p. 17.

13 Notebook 4, interview with Shaw (who added, 'His position was fundamentally a little weak').

14 Beatrice Webb's Diary, 16 July 1935, quoted in *The First Fabians*, p. 411.

15 Eduard Bernstein: *My Years of Exile: Reminiscences of a Socialist*, trans. Bernard Miall (1921), p. 203.

16 *An Autobiography 1856–1898*, p. 169.

17 *The Diaries*, pp. 67, 69, 71 (6, 8, 13, 20 March 1885); Mrs Bland at the Museum, pp. 74, 78, 89, 102, 112 (1, 20 April, 5 June, 7 August, 18 September 1885).

18 *The Diaries*, p. 85. On his sparring with Bland, see Notebook 4, interview with Shaw, who recalled that Bland had once fought a gypsy at a race meeting, though as a pugilist he was hampered by bad sight. On Shaw as 'Pugilist and Playwright', see Stanley Weintraub: *The Unexpected Shaw* (1982), pp. 37–45.

19 *The Diaries*, pp. 90–91, 96, 108, 109, 116, 118 (15 June, 11 July, 29 August, 4 September, 5, 13 October 1885).

20 *The Diaries*, pp. 154–5, 167–8.

21 E.N.'s poem 'To Alma Murray' is included in her main scrapbook of poems (JNA). The story about Archer is related in St John Ervine's *Bernard Shaw* (1956), p. 183.

22 Postcard to D.L.M. signed by Blanche Patch (G.B.S.'s secretary), 8 May 1931.

23 D.L.M.'s correspondence with Shaw, her interview with him (Notebook 4), and a proof copy of her biography marked up by him (this passage occurs on p. 80) are in D.L.M.A.

24 These chapters are published as *An Unfinished Novel*, ed. Stanley Weintraub (1958). Professor Weintraub's introduction, in which he suggests that the central couple was based on the Blands, is reprinted in *The Unexpected Shaw*, pp. 24–36.

25 *The Diaries*, p. 179. Bland's trick with the rifle was described by Shaw in interview, Notebook 4, and included in D.L.M.'s biography.

26 *The Diaries*, pp. 34, 180.

27 E.N. to G.B.S., 29 June 1886, among the Shaw Papers in the British Library (Add. MSS 50511).

28 *Daphne in Fitzroy Street*, p. 145.

29 *The Diaries*, pp. 180, 181, 183; St John Ervine, op. cit., p. 156.

30 *The Diaries*, p. 186. *Daphne in Fitzroy Street*, p. 250–1.

31 *Ibid.*, p. 252.

32 Shaw, in interview, Notebook 4. *The Diaries*, pp. 186–7, 189, 192.

33 *The Diaries*, p. 187 (27 July 1886). 'The Depths of the Sea' was published in *Lays and Legends* (1886), pp. 153–4. St John Ervine connects it with Shaw, *Bernard Shaw*, p. 183. The Latin epigraph from *Aeneid* IV, line 100.

34 *The Diaries*, pp. 197, 198 (10, 15 September 1886); *Daphne in Fitzroy Street*, pp. 284–5.

35 *Lays and Legends* was published on 3 November 1886. E.N. to G.B.S., 18 October 1886, among the Shaw Papers at the British Library (Add. MSS 50511). Shaw replied the same day (*The Diaries*, p. 205). His reply, to which Michael Holroyd drew my attention, is in the Butler Library of Columbia University, New York.

36 The manuscript of the unpublished review is at Bucknell University – see Stanley Weintraub's note in *The Diaries*, p. 212 (10 November 1886).

37 *The Diaries*, p. 207.

38 *The Diaries*, p. 209; Edith visited the Museum on 1, 10, 18 and 29 November, pp. 209, 212, 214, 217, also 219 (6 December); comments on Annie are in preliminary notes to 1887, p. 230.

39 *The Diaries*, pp. 268, 269.

40 *Daphne in Fitzroy Street*, pp. 184–5.

41 Lady Dunsany to E.N., 6 July 1912: 'Yes, I agree that Daphne's prospects were distinctly uncertain even if she married him, but then even a book heroine need not expect more than average happiness and she had a fair chance of that. The person I loved was the Russian . . .'

42 *Daphne in Fitzroy Street*, p. 249; p. 371.

43 *Ibid.*, p. 404.

44 'Bewitched' appeared in *Leaves of Life* (1888), pp. 41–3, and is inspired by Swinburne's 'Dolores'. It must have been previously published in a periodical, for Shaw recalled that 'She wrote a poem to him and there was a line in it about his "maddening white face". When the question of the half-guinea she could get for it came up, they changed this to his "maddening dark face" to conceal his identity' (in interview, Notebook 4). Shaw had misremembered the exact phrase.

45 In interview, Notebook 4.
46 Preface to *An Unfinished Novel* (1958); see also Stanley Weintraub's textual note, p. 95.
47 In interview, Notebook 4; *An Unfinished Novel*, p. 42.
48 *Ibid.*, p. 52; p. 41; p. 42.
49 *Ibid.*, p. 78; p. 88.
50 *Ibid.*, pp. 90–91. Mrs Maddick recalls Edith's behaviour, as described in St John Ervine's *Bernard Shaw*: 'She was always insisting on something', p. 156.
51 Cited by Stanley Weintraub in his preface to *An Unfinished Novel* and reprinted in Weintraub's *The Unexpected Shaw* (1982), p. 34.
52 A phrase used in *The Diaries* (p. 169, 13 May 1886) with reference to Jenny Patterson.
53 *An Autobiography 1856–1898*, p. 1.
54 In interview, Notebook 4.
55 Interview, Notebook 4: *Daphne in Fitzroy Street*, p. 353.
56 G.B.S. to Molly Tompkins, 22 February 1925 in his *Collected Letters 1911–1925*, ed. Dan H. Laurence (1985), vol. III, p. 904; 'I remember a well known poetess (now no more) saying to me, when I refused to let her commit adultery with me . . .'
57 Shaw in interview, Notebook 4.

CHAPTER 5

1 Alice Hoatson's memoir written for D.L.M. She incorrectly gave the date of this episode as 1881.
2 Information from Alice's birth certificate shows she was born on 6 February 1859 in Gerrard Street, North Halifax, to Joseph and Ruth Hoatson (née Smith). Further information from her memoir.
3 St John Ervine: *Bernard Shaw* (1956), p. 123.
4 Alice Hoatson to D.L.M., 4 July 1932.
5 MS book of early poems, p. 11, dated July 1879. E.N.'s birthday book gives Emilie Bailey's birthday as 31 October 1862 (JNA).
6 From part I of 'The Moat House', *Lays and Legends* (first series, 1886), p. 22. D.L.M.'s filecard on Alice Hoatson links her with this poem.
7 Information from A.H.'s memoir; Alice was elected to the Fabian on 19 September 1884 (Fabian Minute Book, among Nuffield Papers); E.N. to Ada, n.d. [c. summer 1885, and after 23 August 1885].
8 Elsa Courlander told this story to D.L.M. in interview, Notebook

3. Both the young wife and her new baby in E.N.'s novel *The Red House* are called 'pussy-kitten'. Iris was called 'kitten-cat', and later 'rabbit':

> 'They often call me Bunny
> or sometimes kitten-cat,
> My proper name is Iris
> So please to call me that.'

Iris was often called 'that' by facetious friends on the basis of this verse – May Bowley to D.L.M., 11 November 1931.

9 A.H.'s memoir; Alice's Wood Green address from Fabian Society Leaflet, 1886–7 (Fabian Papers at Nuffield).

10 Bernard Shaw: *The Diaries 1885–1897*, ed. Stanley Weintraub (1986), vol. 1, pp. 118, 154. Scrapbook of E.N.'s verse, inscribed from A.H. (JNA); A.H.'s memoir. Stillborn babies were not registered at this period.

11 *The Diaries*, p. 161 (15 April 1886).

12 *Ibid.*, p. 214.

13 'It was my own fault . . . ', quoted by D.L.M. in *E. Nesbit* (1933), p. 159, without indicating source, though it was probably Rosamund. 'She [i.e. Rosamund] must have happened with Mrs Bland's consent,' wrote May Bowley to D.L.M., 11 November 1931.

14 Rosamund to D.L.M., 12 December [1931].

15 Her will, dated 2 February 1922 and proved on 12 June 1924, is discussed on page 384.

16 Helen Macklin to D.L.M., 9 June 1933.

17 Rosamund to D.L.M., 15 December [1931].

18 Shaw in interview, Notebook 4; Sir Ernest Wallis Budge in interview, Notebook 2; according to filecard on Richard le Gallienne, she wanted to go away with him, also.

19 Berta Ruck to D.L.M., 17 January 1933; the story of Edith's call, May Bowley to D.L.M., 11 November 1931 (she added, 'Mr Bland was good looking though marked with smallpox, tall and dignified and very conceited. If Mrs Bland wanted to leave him a note or attract his attention to a letter she would stick it in the frame of the looking glass – "where", she said, "he would be sure to notice it." '); Clifford Sharp, the last of several postscripts, to D.L.M., n.d. [12 December 1931]; *Something Wrong*, ch. 6, *The Weekly Dispatch*, 28 March 1886, p. 12.

20 In *Lays and Legends* (first series, 1886), pp. 80, 82.

21 A.H.'s memoir; description of Alice, May Bowley to D.L.M., 11 November 1931.

22 A.H.'s memoir. Her memory, as to details, may not always have

been very accurate. She described Mack as the 'manager for Nister', but he seems to have worked for the English publisher Griffith, Farran and Co., for whom Nister acted as printer. Alice Hoatson appears to have written two books for children under the pseudonym 'Uncle Harry' – *Holiday Hours in Animal Land* [1890] and *Playtime Picture and Stories* [1891]. She described them as having been written for 'a man named Drane', but they were in fact published by S. W. Partridge and Co., rather than by Henry Drane.

23 The Fabian Women's Group meetings of June 1913 recorded her donation to the 'Banner Fund' (Fabian Papers at Nuffield).

24 'The Girton Girl', published in *Atalanta*, vol. VIII, September 1895, pp. 755–759; *The Red House* (1902), ch. 12, pp. 268–9, 270.

25 *Shaw: An Autobiography 1856–1898*, ed. Stanley Weintraub (1970), p. 139.

26 May Bowley to D.L.M., 11 November 1931; 'The Fountain of Youth' from Bland's *With the Eyes of a Man* (1905), p. 212.

27 'If I were a Woman', *Essays* by Hubert Bland (1914), pp. 209, 205.

28 A copy of this letter from Shaw to Bland, dated 18 November 1889, was made by D.L.M., and, repunctuated by Shaw, was published in her biography *E. Nesbit* (1933), pp. 100–102. Reprinted from there, it appears in Shaw's *Collected Letters 1874–1897*, ed. Dan H. Laurence (1965), pp. 228–9.

29 'A Plea for the Powder Puff' in Hubert Bland's *With the Eyes of a Man* (1905), pp. 85–93; 'Fine Feathers' and 'The Honest Woman' from his *Essays* (1914), pp. 195–202, 253–259; quotation from the latter, pp. 255, 257.

30 'If I were a Woman', *Essays*, pp. 210–211.

CHAPTER 6

1 Notebook 3, interview with Noel Griffith.

2 H. Rider Haggard's letter to E.N., 5 September 1886, actually preceded the publication of *Lays and Legends*, but should be associated with her early success as a poet: 'The immediate occasion which prompts me to write this is the reading of your poem in this month's Longmans, but I have been a humble admirer of your poetic power ever since I read "Absolution", now some years ago'.

3 *The Swinburne Letters*, ed. Cecil Y. Lang, vol. 5, 1883–1890 (1962), pp. 173–4.

4 *The Letters of Oscar Wilde*, ed. Rupert Hart Davis (1962), p. 190.

5 E.N. to G.B.S., n.d. [18 February 1887], in the Shaw Papers at the British Library (Add. MSS 50511).

6 'Fabian Bland' quotation from *The Social Cobweb*, ch. II, *The Weekly Dispatch*, 13 January 1884, p. 12. Griffith's account of the Blands in interview, Notebook 3. Fabian details taken from Minute Books, among the Fabian Papers at Nuffield College.

7 Griffith in interview, Notebook 3. H. G. Wells: *An Experiment in Autobiography* (1934, 1984), vol. ii, p. 606.

8 Details about Medway holidays, Griffith to D.L.M., n.d. [soon after 26 November 1931]; Bellingham Smiths referred to in a letter from E.N. to Ada Breakell, 'Sunday (later)' [6 April 1884]. H.B.S.'s painting of Edith is mentioned in a letter from Mrs A. J. Moore to D.L.M., 1 July 1931. The booklets illustrated by H.B.S. are *Winter Snow*, selected and arranged by E. Nesbit with pen and ink drawings by H. Bellingham Smith (Henry J. Drane, undated, c. 1888); *All Round the Year* by E. Nesbit and Caris Brooke, drawings by H. Bellingham Smith and others (von Portheim, c. 1888). Details concerning H.B.S., his painting of Edith and his brother Eric's memories of the Blands in a letter from Eric Bellingham Smith to Vere Bellingham Smith (Hugh's wife), 3 August 1966, now in the possession of Mrs Shirley Colqhoun.

9 Griffith to D.L.M., n.d. [soon after 26 November 1931].

10 *Salome and the Head* (1909), pp. 58, 60. E.N. to H. G. Wells, n.d. [1905], warns: 'I can't remember whether you were told that our Inn at Yalding is "*The George*" – It would be dreadful if you were to seek us vainly at the "*Bull*" or the "*Anchor*".'

11 *Salome and the Head*, pp. 62–3.

12 *Ibid.*, pp. 65–70; *The Incredible Honeymoon* (1916, repr. London, 1921). Page references are for the 1921 ed., pp. 112–116.

13 Between January 1884 and 1885 the price of *To-Day* changed from sixpence to one shilling and then back to threepence, where it remained. 'Fabian Bland' took over as editor in May 1886 and Hubert was still editing it in 1889.

14 Notebook 4, interview with G.B.S.; E.N. to G.B.S., 29 June 1886, among the Shaw Papers, in the British Library.

15 'The Cleon is a society of drawing-room reformers, and Mr Huntley [Bland] took as much interest in that as he did in anything. Indeed, it was rather a pet of his, chiefly because Gottheim [Hyndman] abhorred this same Cleon, and spoke of it cuttingly as the "Micawber Club".' Fabian Bland: *Something Wrong*, ch. VI, *The Weekly Dispatch*, 28 March 1886, p. 12.

16 H.B. to G.B.S., 23 September 1885, in the Shaw Papers in the British Library (Add. MSS 50557).

17 There are numerous accounts of 'Bloody Sunday' and the match girls' strike – see, for example, Norman and Jeanne MacKenzie: *The*

First Fabians (1977), pp. 88–9, 91. Bernard Shaw: *The Diaries 1885–1897*, ed. Stanley Weintraub (1986), vol. 1, pp. 314–5, 394, 396 (entries for 13 November 1887, 14, 21 July 1888).

18 'Billy the King', in *Oswald Bastable and Others* (1905), pp. 272–3.

19 Notebook 3, interview with Griffith. See also *The New Treasure Seekers* (1904), 'The Golden Gondola', pp. 192–5.

20 H.B. to G.B.S., 25 September 1886, among Shaw Papers in the British Library (Add. MSS 50557).

21 Mrs Wilson expressed her opinion of the Fabians in her letters to Karl Pearson, cited by Hermia Oliver in *The International Anarchist Movement in Late Victorian London* (1983), p. 33. I have drawn on her second chapter, concerned with Mrs Wilson, for my account.

22 E.N. to Ada Breakell, n.d. [c. summer 1885].

23 Shaw: *The Diaries: 1885–1897*, vol. 1, pp. 353–4, 368, 399–400, entries for 29 February, 4 March, 20 April, 31 July, 6 August 1888. E.N. to Ada Breakell, n.d. [after 23 August 1885], records: 'On Saturday Mr Marson (clergyman) and Mr Sidney Webb (foreign office) are coming to dinner. Both are very clever so I expect we shall have a nice evening.' Sidney Webb (Lord Passfield) to D.L.M., 4 November 1931, adds that Olive Schreiner was also present. For her visit to England, her association with Eleanor Marx, etc., see Ruth First and Ann Scott: *Olive Schreiner* (1980), esp. ch. 4, pp. 108–188.

24 Olive Schreiner's letter to E.N. was shown to D.L.M. by Havelock Ellis; though undated, he conjectured that it was written in 1888. O.S. to Edward Carpenter, 20 July 1888, among Carpenter's Papers in the Sheffield City Library.

25 O.S. to E.N., n.d., [?early autumn, 1888].

26 O.S. to Havelock Ellis from Alassio, 22 October 1888, in *The Letters of Olive Schreiner 1876–1920*, ed. by S. C. Cronwright-Schreiner (1924), pp. 143–4. O.S. to Edward Carpenter, 17 December 1888, among Carpenter Papers at Sheffield.

27 O.S. to E.N., 17 May 1890.

28 She contributed to a series of such books produced by Raphael Tuck in the early 1890s, many of them under the editorship of Edric Vredenburg, as well as to *Nister's Holiday Annuals*. The story 'The Oak Panel' (from *Listen Long and Listen Well*, Raphael Tuck, 1893), while feebly constructed, seems to spring from a real memory of being abandoned, rather than from a fictional stereotype.

29 Alice Hoatson's memoir.

30 On the Lewisham Literary Society, E.N. to Ada Breakell, 30 March 1884. A note to John Lane invites him to a meeting of 'It' at Birch Grove, when Mr Carr is to open a discussion of 'Thackeray's

estimate of our great humorists', 19 February 1890, among the John Lane Papers now at the Harry Ransom Research Centre, Austin, Texas. On the demise of 'It', Noel Griffith to D.L.M., n.d. [soon after 26 November 1931]; G.B.S. in interview, Notebook 4.

31 Mrs A. J. Moore to D.L.M., 6 June 1931 and 1 July 1931.

32 Noel Griffith in interview recalled: 'They would run up their butcher's bill to £60 or £70 and clear it off when she sold a book.' Mrs A. J. Moore remembered '*great* difficulties to pay tradesmen and Mrs Bland remarking, "How can I let the Deptford children starve to pay butchers, bakers, etc.!"' (to D.L.M., 1 July 1931).

33 Berta Ruck, *A Story-Teller Tells the Truth* (1935), p. 147; *A Smile for the Past* (1959), p. 115. Iris described her mother's domestic economies in a letter to D.L.M. accompanying correction slips of her proofs, n.d. [between 26 October and 18 November 1932].

34 The Deptford treats described in Alice Hoatson's memoir, and Rosamund Sharp to D.L.M., 23 and 26 July 1931.

35 From 'The Criminal', first published in *The Neolith*, no. 1, November 1907, p. 21, and subsequently in *These Little Ones* (1909), p. 116.

36 Housman's letter quoted in D.I.M.: *E. Nesbit* (1933), pp. 108–9 (the copy taken of it has not survived). Rosamund Sharp to D.L.M., 23 July 1931 and in interview, Notebook 1. In 1909 E. Nesbit published a play of *Cinderella*, with songs to popular tunes, in a series designed for schools, possibly a version of the play she had written for the Deptford treat.

37 Laurence Housman to D.L.M. on his first meeting with E.N., 12 July 1931.

38 Housman to E.N., 19 October [1904]; Housman to D.L.M., 12 July 1931. R. P. Graves: *A. E. Housman* (1979) also gives some account of Laurence.

39 The badminton incident was the subject of a birthday postcard, first reproduced in D.L.M.'s biography, opposite p. 128; Housman to D.L.M., 12 July 1931.

40 Housman to D.L.M., 12 July 1931.

41 *Ibid.*; L. Housman: *The Unexpected Years* (1937), pp. 128, 129.

42 On the Steeles' poverty, Iris Philips to D.L.M., n.d. [between 26 October and 18 November 1932]; Steele referred to himself as a 'Professor of Elocution' in a letter to John Lane, n.d. [1909], among the Lane Papers, as is E.N. to John Lane, 25 June, 1890; Griffith's comment in interview, Notebook 3.

43 The Emerson volumes, the birthday poems for 1892, 1894, 1897, 1898 and 1911 plus a further three, undated (probably 1893, 1895, 1896) were shown to me by Anne Excell. The two for 1917, 1918 are

in the scrapbook made by Mavis Carter for E.N. when she was dying (JNA). The letter concerning E.N.'s biography was sent from Three Gables (1894–9) to Mr Colles – presumably Morris Colles, her agent from c. September 1897 to c. April 1901. It is in the possession of S. J. Robinson and was on exhibition at Eltham in May 1974. Alice Hoatson's memoir recalls Steele taking over E.N.'s political verse spot in *The Weekly Dispatch*. Steele's stories for children are *Mostly in Mischief* (1899).

44 Richard le Gallienne to D.L.M., 26 August 1931.

45 G.B.S. to Pakenham Beatty, 4 January 1893 in his *Collected Letters 1874–1897*, ed. Dan H. Laurence (1965), p. 375; Shaw referred to Richard as 'twaddly enough' in a letter to William Archer, p. 401. Le Gallienne's versified 'squeak of pain' was also published in *The Star* where he too was a regular reviewer, reprinted *ibid.*, p. 374.

46 Le Gallienne to John Lane, 25 May, 18 November, 10 and 13 December 1888 among the John Lane Papers. My account of le Gallienne derives from his biography by Geoffrey Smerdon and Richard Whittington-Egan: *The Quest of the Golden Boy* (1960).

47 Arthur James Bennett was the editor of *The Dawn: A Monthly Magazine of Progress*, published at Warrington. Volume 1, no. I, January 1901 began to serialize a novel, *Harold Wolfgang* by Arthur James [i.e. Bennett]; this account from ch. 1, p. 2. E.N. to Lane, n.d. [early 1889] among the Lane Papers. The dedication of *Volumes in Folio* is dated 19 March 1889 (JNA).

48 Le Gallienne's phrase about 'Mrs B.'s anathema' to Lane, 14 April 1889, among the Lane Papers. E.N. to le Gallienne, n.d. [before 14 April 1889?] is one of two letters held at the Harry Ransom Research Centre, Austin, Texas.

49 Le Gallienne to Lane ('I went to Dorville Road yesterday as arranged . . .'), 22 April 1889, among the Lane Papers.

50 D.L.M.'s filecard on le Gallienne includes a private note: 'After a bad scene she was once stopped from running away with him by Miss Hoatson. Whether he would have acquiesced in such an impulsive scheme is perhaps doubtful. Miss H. stopped her on the stairs, and was violently resisted.' The information was probably supplied by Rosamund. The phrase describing Mildred is Arthur Bennett's, from *Harold Wolfgang*, ch. XII, *The Dawn*, vol. 1, no. 9, September 1901, p. 101.

51 *Harold Wolfgang*, book III, ch. XV, *The Dawn*, vol. V, no. 12, December 1905, p. 135.

52 *Ibid.*, ch. XVII, p. 138.

53 *English Poems* (1892), p. 31.

CHAPTER 7

1 Details of Fabian elections from the Minute Books, among the Fabian Papers at Nuffield College. Noel Griffith was born on 24 March 1864. Richard William Reynolds was born on 4 February 1867, educated at King Edward's School, Birmingham, and Balliol, 1886–1890, where he took a second in Mods. and a First in Greats; E.N. conferred his (then very prestigious) college on the Bastables' father, also called Richard. Bower Marsh, son of a solicitor of that name, was born at Rochester, 25 January 1866 and educated at Christ's Hospital and Exeter, 1885–1889. Arthur Oswald Barron was born on 3 January 1868 (he shared a birthday with Hubert – E.N. must have liked Capricorns); he did not go to university.

2 Noel Griffith in interview, Notebook 3; Griffith on Marsh, to D.L.M., 23 February 1931; postcard, 5 December 1932; 19 February 1936; Marsh's stories about Barron in interview D.L.M., Notebook 3.

3 Marsh on the Blands in interview, Notebook 3; H.B.'s letters to Edward Pease refer to tours of the Midlands in June 1892, December 1892, 1893 and 1894, and are among the Fabian Papers at Nuffield College. On H.B.'s column for the *Sunday Chronicle*, see the preface to his posthumous *Essays* (1914). Iris's account of her father's article-writing, to D.L.M., n.d. [early March, 1932].

4 Bower Marsh in interview, Notebook 3; W. E. Henley to E.N., 17 April 1899. (The sequence was 'Via Amoris', *The Rainbow and the Rose* (1905), pp. 112–4.)

5 Bower Marsh in interview; E.N. refers to 'the Discobolus, whom we all love, and who is exactly like Mr Graham Wallas in youth' in *Wings and the Child* (1913), p. 50.

6 A group of books given by E.N. to Bower Marsh now belong to Keith Thomas, who kindly lent them to me; further details from Marsh's interview, Notebook 3.

7 D'Arcy Reeve's acts of patronage are described in Alice Hoatson's memoir and confirmed by Noel Griffith in interview; E.N. to Lane, n.d. [? summer, 1890], among the Lane Papers at the Harry Ransom Research Centre, Austin, Texas.

8 Their journey described in A.H.'s memoir, and later (and more amusingly) by E.N. in her novel *Dormant* (1911), pp. 116–118.

9 A.H.'s memoir; May Bowley to D.L.M., 11 November 1931; letters from H.B. to Edward Pease indicate that he arrived at Antibes a few days before 13 March, having met the Bowley girls in Paris and brought them down, that he visited Nice and Avignon while there and expected to return to town on 10 April, Fabian

Papers at Nuffield College; E.N. on 'Picnics' in *The Daily Chronicle*, 11 June 1910, p. 7.

10 H.B.'s article 'In the South' (1892) reprinted in his *Essays* (1914), pp. 234–242; see also May Bowley to D.L.M., 11 November 1931. H.B. describes Grant Allen as 'novelist, man of science, and Fabian'. Possibly he was one of his converts; an earlier letter from Allen to Bland in the Bodleian Library (MSS Eng. Lett. e.120), explains his reasons for not joining the Fabian.

11 The dance described in May Bowley to D.L.M., 11 November 1931; the text of E.N.'s rondeau is taken from the MS sent to Bower Marsh; a less personal version was quoted in H.B.'s article, 'In the South'.

12 Jepson, *Memories of an Edwardian and Neo-Georgian* (1937), p. 24; interviews with Bower Marsh and Noel Griffith; Kropotkin to E.N., 4 September 1890; N.G.'s diary in letter to D.L.M., n.d. [soon after 26 November 1931]; E.N.'s poem 'New College Gardens, Oxford' in her *Songs of Love and Empire* (1898), pp. 135–6.

13 Griffith's diary in letter to D.L.M., n.d. [soon after 26 November 1931] mentions Angmering; Basil de Sélincourt exchanged affectionate verses with E.N., but resented D.L.M.'s enquiry about them and refused to allow her to publish his – see his letter to her of 4 March 1932; E.N. to John Lane from Sheerness, n.d. [1889] and from Worthing, 11 September 1894, in Lane Papers at the Harry Ransom Research Centre, Austin, Texas; H.B. to Pease, 8 July 1895, among Fabian Papers at Nuffield College.

14 Florence R. Simpson to D.L.M., 23 May 1931.

15 Paul Bland to D.L.M. on Dymchurch, 9 March 1932, and on a slip attached; Mrs F. Ethel Ringland wrote of E.N. at Dymchurch to D.L.M., esp. 3 June 1931.

16 H.B. to Pease on the death of his mother, n.d. [between 9 and 16 August 1893]; note from Dymchurch, 31 October 1893, both among Fabian Papers at Nuffield College.

17 *The New Treasure Seekers* (1904), 'The Flying Lodger', p. 214.

18 Rosamund Sharp to D.L.M., 16 June 1931; John Bland and Stephen Chant in interview, Notebook 2.

19 Letters from E.N. to Lane from 1891 onwards enquire, 'What about the new book?' The collection of poetry that eventually became *A Pomander of Verse* was provisionally entitled 'Love Lyrics'; her letters are among the Lane Papers at Austin, Texas; John Lane on E.N., quoted in D.L.M.'s *E. Nesbit* (1933), p. 288 (information from Russell Green).

20 Among the Lane Papers at Austin, Texas.

21 W. E. Henley to E.N., n.d. ['Monday'] informs her: 'I am afraid that, on perusal, I did not like Mr Barron's verses as well as I did at first. But I will read them again, and give them the benefit of any doubt I may have about them'; another from Henley to the same effect, 15 October 1897; Bower Marsh in interview, Notebook 3; Barron to D.L.M., 26 May 1931; 17 December 1931.

22 Information taken from his *Who's Who* entry.

23 Edgar Jepson, *Memories of an Edwardian and Neo-Georgian*, pp. 19, 25, 26. E.N.'s enthusiasm for old oak is evident in *The Red House* (1902), ch. X, pp. 232.

24 Edgar Jepson in interview, Notebook 1.

25 Edgar Jepson, *Memories*, pp. 19, 24–25.

26 'The Nobleness of Oswald', later ch. XII of *The Treasure Seekers*, was first published in *The Windsor Magazine*, vol X, October 1899, pp. 550–6.

27 *The Treasure Seekers* (1899), ch. XII, p. 212.

28 *Ibid.*, pp. 214–5.

29 Allardyce Nicoll: *A History of English Drama 1660–1900*, vol. 5, Late Nineteenth Century Drama 1850–1900 (1959), p. 502; Griffith sent D.L.M. details of *The Butler in Bohemia* for her bibliography taken from Bower Marsh's copy (since disappeared) on a postcard, 5 December 1932.

30 For example, 'The Life-Lamp', *Atalanta*, vol. VI, June 1893, pp. 562–4; 'The Secret of Monsieur de Roche Aymon', *Atalanta*, vol. viii, October 1894, pp. 34–36; 'Peter with the Fist', *Atalanta*, vol. X, February 1897, pp. 288–291.

31 Barron to D.L.M., 26 May 1931.

32 Shaw's letter to Pakenham Beatty, 23 January 1896, *Collected Letters 1874–1897*, ed. Dan H. Laurence (1965), p. 588; David Garnett: *The Golden Echo* (1953), pp. 19–20. Stepniak's death also inspired the episode in Conrad's *Under Western Eyes*, in which the deaf Razumov is run down by a tram.

33 'The Treasure Seekers' by Ethel Mortimer, *Father Christmas*, 1897, p. 25; see Roger Lancelyn Green: *Tellers of Tales* (1969), p. 210. E.N. complained to her agent Morris Colles that it had been 'miserably mutilated', n.d., Berg Collection, New York Public Library.

34 'The Treasure Seekers', *Father Christmas*, 1897, p. 30.

35 *The Treasure Seekers* (1899), ch. I, p. 4.

36 See Jacqueline Rose: *The Case of Peter Pan* (1984), p. 21.

37 This was 'Noel's Princess', the second episode to appear in the *Pall Mall Magazine*, vol. XV, June 1898, p. 178–184.

38 *The Treasure Seekers*, ch. XII, pp. 198–9.

39 *Ibid.*, ch. I, pp. 3–4.

40 Charles Dickens's *Holiday Romance*, a series of stories each told by a different child, first appeared in the magazine *All the Year Round* in 1868. Its influence on E.N. and her (anonymous) contributions to *Nister's Holiday Annuals* are discussed by Roger Lancelyn Green, *Tellers of Tales*, pp. 195, 207. *Nister's Holiday Annuals* for 1894, 1895 and 1896 included episodes of 'The Play Times': the pages are unnumbered and the pieces unsigned but they are undoubtedly by E.N., who reworked material from them for ch. VIII of *The Treasure Seekers*. One of the children here is already called 'Noel', but oddly he is not the aspiring poet (who is Jack).

41 *The Treasure Seekers*, ch. XVI, pp. 293–4.

42 *Ibid.*, ch. VI, p. 82.

43 *The New Treasure Seekers* (1904), 'The Conscience-Pudding', pp. 37–61; (this story first appeared in the *Illustrated London News* for Christmas 1900).

44 *The Wouldbegoods* (1901), ch. VIII, p. 188.

45 *The Phoenix and the Carpet* (1903), ch. V, p. 144; ch. XI, p. 294.

46 *The Wouldbegoods*, ch. VII, p. 167.

47 She wrote to Frederic Chapman: 'I'm glad you like Lord Tottenham and the Divining Rod. I wonder whether Mr Lane would be inclined to pay fifty pounds down, as an advance on royalty, for the child's book of which these stories are part?' The letter, n.d. (' '98' is pencilled in), is in the Lane Papers at the Harry Ransom Research Centre, Austin, Texas; all other information from E.N.'s letters to her agent Morris Colles, 1898–9, quotations in E.N. to M.C., n.d. and 7 February 1898; Garnett's reports for Fisher Unwin, 27 October 1898, 30 January 1899. Letters and reports in the Berg Collection, New York Public Library.

48 E.N. to Morris Colles, 30 September 1897, n.d. [16 July 1898], in Berg Collection. Information on *The Marden Mystery* based on an unidentified reader's report in D.L.M.'s archive.

49 *The Secret of Kyriels* (1899), pp. 172–3: 'Over one wall a great vine was trained, a vine long past bearing, but still beautiful with many red and yellow leaves, and under the shadow of the fruitless vine, seated on a stone bench that ran along the wall, wrapped in costly furs, sat the object of their search.' Edith had once been 'the merriest, most light-hearted, most delightful girl on God's earth. That first day in the boat I remember she sang little Spanish songs to her guitar . . .' (p. 216). My discussion of this novel is indebted to feminist criticism of romance modes, and in particular to Sandra M. Gilbert and Susan Gubar: *The Madwoman in the Attic* (1979).

50 *The Secret of Kyriels*, p. 325: ' "It holds nothing, you fool, and you know it," he said to himself . . .'

CHAPTER 8

1 E.N. to Sarah Nesbit, n.d. [15 August 1898], signed 'from your loving child Daisy'.

2 'Via Amoris' was published in *The Rainbow and the Rose* (1905), pp. 112–114. Henley to E.N., 13 March 1898, does not identify the poems by name, but since she sent 'Via Amoris' with some other poems to Colles at the same date, it is a natural inference, as is the poems' connection with Barron, and his marriage in the following year. Perhaps she indicated something of this to Henley, though it seems unlikely. For whatever reason, Henley added 'What you told me about your latest trouble makes me rather wonder if it be not their true motive, and (if I be right) why you do it wrong by turning it to other issues. But of this I have scarce the right to speak. And I hope you will believe me when I say that my first thought is always for the verses'. E.N. to Morris Colles, 7 March 1898, tells him to 'Do what you like with the other verses. The ones I care most about are "After Death", "Via Amoris" and "The Guest" '. This and other letters to Colles are in the Berg Collection, New York Public Library.

3 *A Story-Teller Tells the Truth* (1935), p. 147.

4 *Wings and the Child*, pp. 6–7.

5 E.N. to Sarah Nesbit, n.d. [autumn 1898]. Information about Paul's illness and the ensuing circumstances, including her own illness, from Alice Hoatson's memoir, though she misremembers the year as 1900. E.N. to Morris Colles, 4 October 1898 (in the Berg Collection), refers to Paul having typhoid. Adeline Sergeant to E.N., 7 December 1898, asks, 'And how is Paul getting on? I hope he is now beginning to pull round. Are you going to send him away for a change? Let me recommend Bournemouth'. E.N.'s 'Poem for Paul Recovering from Typhoid', 22 October 1898, in JNA. The dog-cart accident is referred to in a letter from E.N. to her (second) agent J. B. Pinker, n.d. [late December 1898?] in the Berg Collection, New York Public Library.

6 E.N. to John Lane, 22 February 1899, carries the postscript: 'I am so sorry to be so blotted. I have been planting roots all day, and my hand shakes like a telegraphic needle' (which, incidentally, suggests that, as she wrote, she had no immediate plans to move) – among the Lane Papers at the Harry Ransom Research Centre, Austin, Texas.

7 E.N.'s account of the ghosts in a memoir written by Mavis Carter for D.L.M.

8 These disasters are described in her novel *The Red House* (1902). May Bowley to D.L.M., 11 November 1931, explained: 'They

moved to Well Hall because it was picturesque . . . The disasters of *The Red House* mostly really happened at Well Hall . . . The staircase fell down before they had fairly got the bedroom furniture in place'. Slips with Paul Bland's letter to D.L.M., 9 March 1932, give details of Lamert as tenant.

9 Charlotte Perkins Gilman: *The Living of Charlotte Perkins Gilman: An Autobiography* (1935), pp. 198, 203, 211.

10 C.P.G. to E.N., 22 May 1899, in JNA; passage cited from *The Living of C.P.G.*, p. 268; Bland (mainly Paul's) family photograph album in JNA.

11 For E.N.'s stillbirth, see D.L.M.'s filecard on 'Her Children'; *The Red House* (1902), ch. XII, p. 273; John Bland to D.L.M., 15 March 1932, remarks, 'My passport tells me that the date of my birth was 6 October 1899, otherwise I should have forgotten it. I always keep, my birthday on the twenty-first' (his birth certificate, like Rosamund's, could not be traced); Mrs Ringland (of Dymchurch) to D.L.M., 27 February 1933, referred to village gossip about John 'who never came there unless with Miss Hoatson'.

12 E.N. to the Rev. C. Grinling, 22 May 1896, explains that 'all the money we can spare has to go to my sister-in-law and her children . . .', in a collection of letters from the Blands to Grinling at Greenwich Local History Library, Woodlands, Mycenae Road, S.E.3. Rosamund's story about her underwear in interview, Notebook 1, redated by Iris on a corrective slip with her letter to D.L.M., n.d. [between 26 October and 18 November 1932].

13 'In Memory of Saretta Deakin', *The Rainbow and the Rose* (1905), pp. 139–142.

14 Iris Philips to D.L.M., 23 May 1932.

15 Housman to D.L.M., 24 May 1931.

16 E. M. Forster in interview, Notebook 2; H. G. Wells: *Experiment in Autobiography* (1934, 1984), vol. ii, p. 624; Berta Ruck: *A Story-Teller Tells the Truth* (1935), p. 143.

17 This account is based on Alice Hoatson's memoir. His death certificate records the post-mortem verdict: 'Syncope following administration of chloroform properly administered for perform-ance of necessary operation.'

18 Iris on Fabian's death on a correction slip with letter, n.d. [between 26 October and 18 November 1932]; Paul Bland on a slip with a letter, 9 March 1932 (he added '[Fabian] died just when he was beginning to be a companion to me on walks and all kinds of expeditions'); Rosamund Sharp to D.L.M., 12 December 1931.

19 Helen Macklin to D.L.M., 4 and 9 June, 1933.

20 H. R. Millar in interview, Notebook 3; 'The Criminal' in *The*

Neolith, no. 1, November 1907, p. 22, and later in *These Little Ones* (1909), p. 116.

21 Hubert Bland: *Letters to a Daughter* (1906), p. 4. The passage is ostensibly about his daughter's absence, but the paragraph ends, 'Oh, the deathly chill of an empty and tidy nursery!'

22 Rosamund Sharp in interview, Notebook 1 ('She could not help dramatizing all her emotions . . . always played up to a situation that was dramatic'); 'In the Queen's Garden' was published in *The Neolith*, no. IV, August 1908, pp. 1–11; John Bland to D.L.M., 16 November 1932, identified a play about which Shaw had advised E.N. on copyright (in November 1908) as '"Absalom" a play in verse mainly about David. The censor banned it because of its Biblical characters.'

23 Paul Bland in interview, Notebook 2; Rosamund Sharp in interview, Notebook 1; Paul's slip in letter to D.L.M., 9 March 1932, explains that Fabian was first educated at a prep school in Lee with Paul, then, c. 1896, was sent as a pupil to Warren Farm, Telscombe, Sussex, where he was taught by a Miss Anne Verrall (a cousin of Noel Griffith's), and afterwards at Erringham Farm, Shoreham. He was then at St Dunstan's for a short time and Loretto for six months; he may have been educated at home latterly. Paul himself was sent, at one stage, to an experimental school run by the Rev. Cecil Reddie on spartan lines at Abbot's Holme, Derbyshire; he left after six months and an attack of pneumonia (in interview, Notebook 2).

24 Mrs A. T. Moore to D.L.M., 1 July 1931; Helen Macklin to D.L.M., 9 June 1933; Bower Marsh in interview, Notebook 3; Ada Breakell in interview, Notebook 2.

25 Mrs Ringland to D.L.M., 27 February 1933; Iris Philips to D.L.M., 23 May, 1932.

26 On Iris and Rosamund, Berta Ruck to D.L.M., 13 January 1933; Mrs Ringland to D.L.M., 27 February, 1933; Berta Ruck in *A Story-Teller Tells the Truth* (1935), p. 146; Elsa Courlander, and several other later friends described E.N. as 'aloof', and Mrs Courlander told D.L.M. that Rosamund and E.N. 'together created an atmosphere of embarrassment' (in interview, Notebook 3).

27 D.L.M.'s filecard on 'Her Children' gives many of these details; also John Bland in interview, Notebook 1.

28 Hubert's slamming down the piano related by Mrs Paul Bland to Doris Ker; on her mother's cruelty, Rosamund to D.L.M., 15 December 1931; John Bland in interview, Notebook 1.

29 Berta Ruck to D.L.M., 11 May 1931.

30 Maria Louisa Charlesworth: *Ministering Children* (1854). Oswald's view is that 'Being good is so much like being a muff, generally.

Anyhow I'm not going to smooth the pillows of the sick, or read to the aged poor, or any rot out of *Ministering Children*.' It is Daisy's favourite reading – see *The Wouldbegoods* (1901), ch. II, p. 32; ch. IV, pp. 68, 70; ch. XIII, p. 286. Susan Coolidge: *What Katy Did* (1872) is taken as a model by Dora when she has hurt her foot (*The Wouldbegoods*, ch. II, p. 45).

31 *The Wouldbegoods*, ch. II, p. 23.

32 These episodes became chapters V and VI.

33 Paul Bland in interview, Notebook 2; Fisher Unwin's letter offering her differential royalties on her books is referred to in E.N.'s correspondence with G. H. Thring of the Society of Authors, February 1920, in the British Library (Add. MSS 56762).

34 William de Morgan to E.N., 12 June 1907: '[*The Red House*] is charming, idyllic and original in structure – and what an accumulation of photographic detail'; Andrew Lang to E.N., 18, 20 February 1903; Richard Whiteing to E.N., 9 February 1903.

35 *Letters to a Daughter* (1906), pp. 184–5.

36 *The Red House* (1902), ch. X, pp. 225–6.

37 *The Daisy Chain* suggested ch. X ('The Sale of Antiquities', esp. pp. 221–3) of *The Wouldbegoods* and probably the disguises adopted in 'The Golden Gondola', *The New Treasure Seekers*; *The Golden Age* is alluded to in ch. VI ('Noel's Princess') of *The Treasure Seekers* and ch. XIII ('The Dragon's Teeth') of *The Wouldbegoods*. *The Jungle Book* inspired ch. I of *The Wouldbegoods*.

38 *The New Treasure Seekers*, 'The Young Antiquaries', p. 125.

39 Harold Robert Millar was born in February 1869 (in Thornhill, Dumfriesshire) and died in December 1942. He was trained at the Birmingham School of Art, and also, he claimed, as an engineer. His drawings appeared in the very first issue of *The Strand*, but later on his illustrations came to be closely associated with E.N. and so disappeared after 1913. His work after the First World War is, in any case, disappointing. An account of his first meeting with E.N. in H.R.M. to D.L.M., 26 July 1931. I am grateful to Louisa Smith for information about H.R.M.

40 *The Book of Dragons* (1900), 'The Book of Beasts', pp. 12–13.

41 *Nine Unlikely Tales* (1901), 'The Blue Mountain', p. 87; 'The Town in the Library in the Town in the Library', p. 245.

42 H. R. Millar in interview, Notebook 3; Millar's second son, Donald, died unexpectedly in 1905.

43 *Five Children and It* (1902), ch. I, p. 5. The same house provides the setting for her short story 'The Hermit of "The Yews"', *Man and Maid* (1906), here described as an ugly stucco villa between Rochester and Felsenden, almost at the edge of a disused chalk quarry.

44 *Ibid.*, ch. I, p. 14; H. R. Millar to D.L.M., 26 July 1931.
45 'The Tale of the Three Wishes' in Iona and Peter Opie's *The Classic Fairy Tales* (1974), pp. 151–4; Bruno Bettelheim in *The Uses of Enchantment* (1976), Part One: Transformations, p. 71.
46 *Five Children and It*, ch. III, p. 102.
47 *Ibid.*, ch. XI, p. 299.
48 Berta Ruck: *A Smile for the Past* (1959), p. 115.
49 *Five Children and It*, ch. XI, pp. 298–9.
50 These verses, in DLMA, were transcribed from a scrapbook belonging to Iris. 'Esmond' has not been identified.
51 In all the photographs of Kennedy, he appears in a wheelchair. After the publication of D.L.M.'s biography, he sent her a letter enclosing the (undated) note cited here, and promising to reveal 'the circumstances connected with' his many other letters, 13 February 1933, though he did not apparently do so. He may be identical with the writer of that name, working in the twenties.
52 E.N. to her agent J. B. Pinker asks him to place Dorothea's novel *Georgie*, 13 July 1905 (in the Berg Collection of the New York Public Library); the relevant filecards are 'Her Love Affairs' and 'Richard Reynolds' – the source of the second note is given as 'various members of the family'.
53 Paul's note on a slip with his letter to D.L.M., 9 March 1932.

CHAPTER 9

1 John Bland on his parents' Catholicism, to D.L.M., 24 May 1932; Iris on H.B.'s parents on a correction slip with letter to D.L.M., n.d. [between 26 October and 18 November 1932]; H.B.'s Protestant upbringing endorsed, John to D.L.M., 16 November 1932; H.B.'s claims to have 'come of excellent North Country stock' were widely accepted – see D.L.M.'s *E. Nesbit* (1933), pp. 43, 50; H. G. Wells was more sceptical – see *Experiment in Autobiography* (1934, 1984), vol. ii, p. 604.
2 Gerald Gould to D.L.M., 30 May 1932.
3 Alice Hoatson's memoir; Paul Bland in interview, Notebook 2; John Bland to D.L.M., 24 May 1932.
4 Gould to D.L.M., 30 May 1932; H.B. on 'Hegel's Theory of the State' in *Essays* (1914); H.B.'s paper 'Socialism and Orthodoxy' was read to the London Society for the Study of Religion, 1 March 1910, and reprinted as a pamphlet, *Socialism and the Catholic Faith* (n.d.) by the Glasgow Catholic Socialist Society.
5 On R. H. Benson, see Elsa Courlander's memoir of E.N., sent with

a letter to D.L.M., 17 October 1931. Rolfe to the Secretary of the Fabian, from Jesus College, Oxford, 15 February 1906; Rolfe to H.B., 4 May 1906; Rolfe to John, 10, 20 October 1907, 27 February 1909.

6 See Brocard Sewell: *Cecil Chesterton* (1975), esp. pp. 18–19, 20–21, 23–24.

7 Mrs Cecil Chesterton: *The Chestertons* (1941), pp. 58–9.

8 Iris on H.B. to D.L.M., n.d. [between 26 October and 18 November 1932]; H. G. Wells, *Experiment in Autobiography*, p. 605; Rosamund on E.N. as hostess in interview, Notebook 1; Laurence Housman in memoir with letter to D.L.M., 24 May 1931.

9 H. G. Wells in interview, Notebook 1; Nina Griffith's account, sent with a letter to D.L.M., 19 November 1931, is reproduced in D.L.M.'s *E. Nesbit* (1933), pp. 184–7.

10 According to her death certificate Mary Margaret Ann Doran was the daughter of Thomas Doran, dyer, of 31 High Street, Beckenham. Her age was given as 47, so she was born on 22 December 1855 (or 1856 – the 1881 census gives her age as 24 and her birthplace as Leeds); Iris Philips on a correction slip with a letter to D.L.M., n.d. [between 26 October and 18 November 1932].

11 Iris in interview, Notebook 1.

12 E.N. to J. B. Pinker, 1, 2, 8 March 1904, in the Berg Collection, New York Public Library; photographs in the Bland family album show Paul and Hubert in Paris, with E.N., Rosamund, Iris, Dorothea and friends; H. G. Wells to E.N., 5 March 1904; *The Journals of Arnold Bennett 1896–1910*, ed. Newman Flower (1932), p. 170.

13 Berta Ruck: *A Story-Teller Tells the Truth* (1935), pp. 73–5, 143–4.

14 Arthur Watts, who with Berta Ruck, figures in Bland photographs taken in Paris, is, as 'Oswald in Paris', the dedicatee of *The New Treasure Seekers* (1904); he illustrated her story about the Musée Grevin, 'The Power of Darkness', for *The Strand* (April 1905), vol. XXIX, pp. 441–9; details of his friendship with E.N. given in interview, Notebook 4; he was born in 1883 and celebrated his twenty-first birthday during E.N.'s stay in Paris (he died in an aircrash in 1935).

15 The Griffiths' visit to Paris in 1904 recorded in his diary – see his letter to D.L.M., 8 February 1932; on the meeting with Hermann Webster and Justus Miles Forman, Rosamund Sharp to D.L.M., 'Thursday' [between 2 and 5 November 1932]; Berta Ruck to D.L.M., 'Sunday' [between 27 and 31 May 1932].

16 E.N. to J. B. Pinker from 49, Boulevard Montparnasse, n.d.: 'I have been ill ever since I came to this detestable city'; n.d., 'Paris is a

hateful place. I do *loathe* cities' in Berg Collection. The holiday at Grez was described by Berta Ruck, *The Story-Teller Tells the Truth*, and letters to D.L.M., between 27 and 31 May 1932; *The Incomplete Amorist* (1906), p. 269. Though E.N. wrote much of this novel in France in the spring of 1904, it was conceived late in the previous year, E.N. to J. B. Pinker, 11 December 1903, in the Berg Collection of the New York Public Library.

17 Berta Ruck, pp. 144–5; Arthur Watts in interview, Notebook 4.
18 *The New Treasure Seekers* (1904), 'The Flying Lodger', pp. 210–11; E.N. to Ada Breakell, 'Sunday' [6 April 1884], wrote: 'I've just been reading *Jessica's First Prayer* to my maid (who is a treasure) and I felt my eyes smart and my throat grow lumpy towards the finish. Pathetic simplicity is a grand gift in writing.'
19 *The New Treasure Seekers*, 'Over the Water to China', pp. 99–100.
20 *The Wouldbegoods* (1901), chs. III, XI, esp. pp. 58, 253–5; *The New Treasure Seekers*, 'The Poor and Needy', p. 318, 319–20. On E.N.'s treatment of the poor, see Barbara Smith: 'The Expression of Social Values in the Writing of E. Nesbit', *MLAA Children's Literature* (1974), vol. III, pp. 153–164; Alec Ellis: 'E. Nesbit and the Poor', *The Junior Bookshelf* (April, 1974), pp. 73–8.
21 *The Railway Children* (1905), ch. V, pp. 114–5; later editions change the text of this passage so that Mother speaks of the Czarist regime as a thing of the past.
22 *Ibid.*, ch. VI, p. 123; ch. V, p. 117.
23 E.N. to J. B. Pinker, 7 April, 7 May 1905, correspondence with Pinker in the Berg Collection, New York Public Library. Details of the plays E.N. wrote with Dorothea from Allardyce Nicoll: *English Drama 1900–1930* (1973), p. 854. *The Amulet* (1906), chs. I, II, pp. 17, 18, 41.
24 Letters from E.N. to J. B. Pinker indicate that she was trying to sell *The Amulet* from 19 August 1903 to Greenhough Smith of *The Strand*, but the serial had not been completed by 7 May 1905 – correspondence in the Berg Collection, New York Public Library. Wallis Budge is described by John A. Wilson: *Signs and Wonders upon Pharaoh* (1964), p. 88; his first encounter with E.N. described in his interview, Notebook 2.
25 John A. Wilson, *Signs and Wonders upon Pharaoh*, pp. 88–92; Wallis Budge: *Egyptian Magic* (1901), pp. 26–7, 43–4; I am grateful to Helen Whitehouse of the Ashmolean Museum for her translation of the words of power and for advice on Wallis Budge and Egyptology.
26 *The Amulet*, ch. VIII, p. 191.
27 Wallis Budge in interview, Notebook 2.

28 *The Amulet*, ch. X, p. 240; ch. VIII, pp. 195–6; Ruskin on 'the signs of a slavery in our England' in *The Stones of Venice* (1853), vol. ii, ch. 6, p. 193 (*Complete Works*, ed. Cook and Wedderburn, 1904).

29 *The Amulet*, ch. VI, pp. 136–7; Plato's Dialogues *Timaeus* and *Critias* provided sources for the description of Atlantis in ch. IX; H. G. Wells: *A Modern Utopia* (1905), p. 244.

30 *The Amulet*, ch. XII, pp. 307–8.

31 E.N. to H. G. Wells, n.d. [? summer, 1905], among the Wells Papers at the University of Illinois, Urbana-Champaign; *A Modern Utopia*, pp. 354–8.

32 E.N. to H.G.W., 2 January 1906, among the Wells Papers; Introduction to the *Barrack-Room Ballads* in 'The Seven Seas', *Rudyard Kipling's Verse* (1940), p. 351.

33 Kipling to E.N., 15 November 1896, responds to a request for a contribution and hopes 'to have the pleasure of meeting you over a chafing-dish which I take it is the inner meaning of crabs with cream' – this letter (a transcript of which is in DLMA) is reproduced in *The Kipling Journal* (July 1948), vol. XV, no. 86, p. 13; Bernard Shaw in interview, Notebook 4, mentions Beresford as having known the Blands; a note from Kipling's secretary to D.L.M., 7 May 1931, states that they never met.

34 Transcripts of this letter in DLMA and (with slight variants) in *The Kipling Journal* (December 1947), vol. XIV, no. 84, pp. 15–16, where Elsie (by then Mrs Bambridge) commented, 'I remember the stories mentioned quite well, and how much we enjoyed them as children.'

35 Transcripts of this letter, 20 October 1904, both incomplete (presumably because sections were illegible) in DLMA and *The Kipling Journal* (July 1948), vol, XV, no. 86, p. 13. This text is a composite of the two.

36 Transcript of a letter from Kipling to E.N., 15 November 1905, JNA.

37 See Roger Lancelyn Green: *Kipling and the Children* (1965), pp. 200–2.

38 *The Amulet*, ch. X, p. 255.

39 *Something of Myself* (1937), ch. VII, pp. 187–8.

40 Roger Lancelyn Green, *Kipling and the Children*, pp. 205–6.

41 Berta Ruck: *A Smile for the Past* (1959), pp. 117–8; the verses themselves are quoted from the original MS, in Miss Ruck's possession when I saw it.

42 The 'blight' over Hester Radford and Spencer Pryse's absence described by Gerald Gould in interview, Notebook 2 – he later wrote a ballad about the incident to amuse E.N. Her visit to the Rucks referred to by Berta in interview, Notebook 2, and described

by E.N. herself in *The Incredible Honeymoon* (1921), ch. XVI, esp. pp. 216–9 (Colonel Ruck has become 'Colonel Bertram').

43 E.N. to J. B. Pinker, n.d. [? April 1905], in the Berg Collection of the New York Public Library.

44 Gerald Gould in interview, Notebooks 1, 2; 'E. Nesbit' by Gerald Gould, *Week-End Review*, 28 January 1933; the underground episode recalled by Graily Hewitt, Notebook 3: 'E.N. was very fond of mothering young genius. She mothered G. Gould to such an extent that once . . .'

CHAPTER 10

1 'The Fantastic Imagination', *A Dish of Orts* (1893), pp. 314–5.

2 See above, pp. 8–9, 13–15.

3 On their similarities, see Iona and Peter Opie: *The Classic Fairy Tales* (1974), pp. 137–8.

4 'Man-Size in Marble' in *Grim Tales* (1893), and *Fear* (1910); *The Enchanted Castle* (1907), ch. X, p. 292.

5 Mrs Ethel Ringland to D.L.M., 20 May 1931: 'On one occasion, being short of actors, Mrs Bland improvised some out of coats and hats with paper faces . . . These figured later in one of her children's stories as the "Ugly-Wuglies"'.

6 *The Enchanted Castle*, chs. VI–VIII, XII, esp. pp. 185–6, 206–7, 352.

7 *Ibid.*, chs. X, XII, pp. 286–7, 304, 350.

8 John Austin Philips (1875–1947) worked for the post office, but wanted to be a writer. He began writing verses for magazines, but, with E.N.'s encouragement, turned to short stories, and got his work into *The Strand*. Later he resigned his job to become a full time (and very prolific) novelist.

9 E.N. to H. G. Wells, n.d. [2 January 1906], among the Wells Papers at the University of Illinois at Urbana-Champaign; Iris to D.L.M., 27 May 1932; Rosamund to Mrs Wells, 4 March 1908, among the Wells Papers at Illinois.

10 Berta Ruck to D.L.M., 13 January 1933; Iris to D.L.M., 23 May 1932.

11 *The Magician's Heart*, is referred to in David Devant's autobiography, *My Magic Life* (1931), p. 133. E.N. later rewrote it as a short story and included it in *The Magic World* (1912).

12 Ambrose Flower to D.L.M., 15 June 1932.

13 Clifford Sharp to D.L.M., 17 December 1931; Arthur Watts to E.N., n.d. [?1906].

14 Arthur Watts in interview, Notebook 4; Watts and John Bland described her as quite definitely 'prudish', whereas Berta Ruck thought her 'naturally chaste ... fastidious and dainty' (see D.L.M.'s filecard on 'Her Prudery'). E.N. had grown up a Victorian; her inhibitions were more evident in her attitudes than in her actions.

15 Arthur Watts in interview, Notebook 4.

16 Nina Griffith posed as Sandra for Spencer Pryse's illustrations to *Salome*, Nina Griffith to D.L.M., 25 May 1932; Spencer Pryse also illustrated E.N.'s story 'The Princess and the Hedge-Pig', included in *The Magic World* (1912).

17 Ernest Jackson in interview, Notebook 4; Graily Hewitt to D.L.M., 19 May 1931. E.N. wrote to Kipling and Kenneth Grahame eliciting contributions for a projected children's magazine late in 1896: Kipling's reply, 15 November 1896; Grahame's reply, 28 and 30 October 1896 (in the Bodleian Library, MSS Eng. Lett. e. 129); nine years later she made a similar request of Wells in a letter to him, n.d. [11 February 1905], among the Wells Papers at the University of Illinois.

18 *Dormant* (1911), pp. 28, 29–30 (with real names substituted); the furniture expresses E.N.'s own taste, and most of the items here mentioned survive in her last home.

19 Graily Hewitt in interview, Notebook 3; Ernest Jackson in interview, Notebook 4.

20 Graily Hewitt in interview, Notebook 3; Hewitt to D.L.M., 8 February 1933.

21 E.N. to Evelyn Sharp, n.d. [?1907] (in the Bodleian Library, MSS Eng. Lett. d. 277).

22 Hewitt and Jackson in interviews, Notebooks 3 and 4.

23 Lord Dunsany in interview, Notebook 1; Mark Amory: *Lord Dunsany* (1972), p. 71; Lord Dunsany: *Patches of Sunlight* (1938), p. 141.

24 Andrade to D.L.M., 14 January 1933; Edward N. da C. Andrade, 1887–1971, later Quain Professor of Physics at the University of London, was twenty when he first met E.N.

25 H. G. Wells: *Experiment in Autobiography* (1934, 1984), vol. ii, p. 605.

26 Andrade to D.L.M., 9 June 1932; my account of E.N.'s Baconianism is based on his, and amplified from S. Schoenbaum's *Shakespeare's Lives* (1970), esp. part 6, chs. I–III.

27 E.N. in *The Incredible Honeymoon* (1921), p. 182; Henry James in a letter to Violet Hunt, 26 August 1903, quoted by Schoenbaum, p. 571.

28 Andrade in interview, Notebook 2; Andrade to D.L.M., 28 June 1932.

29 *The Incredible Honeymoon* (1921), pp. 182–5.

30 *Ibid.*, pp. 185, 189.

31 Andrade to D.L.M., 9 June 1932; in interview, Andrade told D.L.M., 'She was victimized by a Baconian who practically lived on her', Notebook 2; Iris to D.L.M., n.d. [between 22 February and 11 March 1932]; her letter identifies the tenant as 'Mrs Patrick Campbell's brother – I know he was mad on the subject – gave all his time to it and had no money'.

32 *Baconiana*, Third Series, vol. vii, July 1909, no. 27, p. 208 (also p. 149).

33 Information about E. V. Tanner from Margot Peters: *Mrs Pat – The Life of Mrs Patrick Campbell* (1984) (she gives no indication of his Baconian interests).

34 E.N. to her brother Harry Nesbit in Australia, 24 February [?1915].

35 Andrade called it 'dreary nonsense' in a letter to D.L.M., 9 June 1932; Iris in interview, Notebook 1; Andrade wrote to D.L.M. 'the fact is that after Bacon-Shakespeare came she was finished as a writer. Her socialism, which was intellectually of the same stamp, remarkably enough never seems to have taken hold of her sufficiently to stop everything else, as B-S did', 14 January 1933.

36 Shaw in interview, Notebook 4; Shaw to E.N., 5 June 1910, in his *Collected Letters 1898–1910*, ed. Dan H. Laurence (1972), p. 927; *The Magic City* (1910), ch. V, p. 149.

37 Graily Hewitt to D.L.M., 19 May 1931.

38 *The House of Arden* (1908), chs. II, XIV, pp. 51, 341–2.

39 'Oh, my daddy, my daddy!' also ends 'Justnowland', *The Magic World* (1912), p. 205; *The House of Arden*, chs. XIV, II, pp. 349, 53.

40 Its power over white things recalls E.N.'s early story 'The White Messengers', published in *Father Christmas*, the *Illustrated London News* supplement for 1897, but the pigeons are borrowed from Mrs Molesworth: *The Wood-Pigeons and Mary* (1901).

41 *The House of Arden*, ch. II, p. 54; *Harding's Luck* (1909), ch. VII, p. 180.

42 *The House of Arden*, chs. IV, VIII, XIII, pp. 100, 205–9, 312–3. The preparations made for Napoleon's invasion are very much in evidence at Dymchurch, and on Romney Marsh more generally, in the form of the Martello Towers and the Royal Military Canal.

43 Hurstmonceux was dismantled in 1777 when building materials were taken from the castle to build a new house within its walls; it remained derelict until restoration began in 1913 (see *The Incredible Honeymoon*, pp. 266–7).

44 'Hurst of Hurstcote' was published in *Something Wrong* (1893) and *Fear* (1910); its title and theme owe something to Vernon Lee's 'Oke of Okehurst' (*Hauntings*, 1890). Hurstmonceux's inclusion in *The Incredible Honeymoon*, a fictionalized sentimental journey, suggests that it had a special emotional significance for her – my guess is that she had visited it with Oswald Barron.

45 *The House of Arden*, ch. XIII, pp. 319–20; cf. *Harding's Luck*, ch. VII, p. 183, where the witch tells Dickie that even though they don't burn witches in the twentieth century, 'they let them live such lives in their ugly towns that my life here with all its risks is far better worth living.'

46 *The House of Arden*, ch. X, p. 240; this scene is replayed in *Harding's Luck* from Dickie's point of view, ch. VII, p. 175.

47 *Harding's Luck*, ch. 1, p. 9 (the incident recalls Johnny's going to hospital in Dickens's *Our Mutual Friend*).

48 *Ibid.*, ch. 1, pp. 7–8.

49 This lecture, first given in 1877, is reprinted in *Political Writings of William Morris*, ed. A. L. Morton (1973), p. 39.

50 'The Hopes of Civilization', *ibid.*, p. 164.

51 *The Magic City* (1910), ch. XII, p. 326; cf. *The Wouldbegoods* (1901), ch. IV, p. 72: 'I remember mother telling Dora and me when we were little that you ought to be very kind and polite to servants, because they have to work very hard, and do not have so many good times as we do.'

52 *Harding's Luck*, ch. IV, p. 100. There is another stagey Jew, Moses Mosenthal, in *Salome and the Head* (1909).

53 E.N. to Lady Dunsany, n.d. [1913]: 'Any success my stories have had is due I think to a sort of light-hearted outlook on life'; the sermon on *Harding's Luck* was preached by the Rev. R. J. Campbell, according to T. T. Tucker in interview, Notebook 2.

54 For example in *The Social Cobweb*, ch. VI, *The Weekly Dispatch*, 10 February 1884, p. 12. The sick or crippled child was a favourite subject for sentimental Victorian paintings or stories – compare Mrs Craik: *The Little Lame Prince* (1875).

55 D.L.M. suggested the novel's connection with Maude Allan, *E. Nesbit* (1933), p. 243; an article on E. Nesbit by Mary E. Breakell in *The Literary Post*, 6 July 1910, links it with the Well Hall legend; E.N. to Harry Nesbit in Australia n.d. [November or December 1912].

56 *Salome* (1909), p. 134: 'And even Mr Stewart Hedlam [sic], the staunch, unswerving upholder of the old teetotum-skirted, pigeon-winged *première danseuse*, clapped his hands sore from the stalls, and cheered [her] . . . by the sight of his beautiful silver hair and his fine, kind, mellow, approving face.'

57 E.N. to Lord Dunsany, n.d. [September or October 1909].

CHAPTER 11

1 For Wells's life, see Norman and Jeanne MacKenzie: *The Time Traveller* (1973), David C. Smith: *H. G. Wells – Desperately Mortal* (1986); Mrs Wells to E.N., 23 November 1902, n.d. ('Sunday'); there are photographs of Mrs Wells and of Henry Hick in the Bland family album.

2 H.G.W. to E.N., 17 September 1903, 17 December 1904 (the latter reproduced from D.L.M.'s *E. Nesbit* (1933), pp. 192–3); interview with H.G.W., Notebook 1.

3 E.N. to H.G.W., n.d. [8 January 1905], among Wells papers at the University of Illinois at Urbana-Champaign.

4 E.N. to H.G.W., n.d. [11 February 1905], among Wells Papers.

5 E.N. to H.G.W., n.d. among Wells Papers (copy in DLMA).

6 Rosamund and H.G.W. in interviews, both Notebook 1. H.G.W. to E.N., 3 August 1905, in Yale University Library (bought under the misapprehension that 'Yale' referred to the university rather than to the Blands' dog?).

7 Mrs Wells to E.N., n.d.; H.G.W. to E.N., 13 August 1905.

8 E.N. to H.G.W., n.d. [between 14 and 30 August 1905], among Wells Papers.

9 E.N. to H.G.W., n.d. [before 21 October 1905], among Wells Papers (and a copy in DLMA).

10 *H. G. Wells in Love* (Postscript to an *Experiment in Auto-biography*), ed. G. P. Wells (1984), p. 68; *Experiment in Auto-biography* (1934, 1984), vol. ii, p. 605.

11 Almost all E.N.'s letters to Wells that have survived (among the Wells Papers at Illinois) were written between January 1905 and January 1906. This suggests that earlier letters were thrown away (that they existed is implied by earlier replies from H.G.W. to E.N., e.g. 5 March 1904, in DLMA). Later 'insulting letters to Jane' (*H. G. Wells in Love*, p. 69) must also have been destroyed. E.N. to Mr and Mrs Wells, 23 October 1905 ('Very late at night: really some way into Oct. 24'), among Wells Papers.

12 E.N. to H.G.W., n.d. [17 November 1905], among Wells Papers; a letter from Arthur Watts (who shared rooms with Horsnell) to E.N., n.d., refers to Horsnell spending three weeks with the Wellses (JNA).

13 E.N. to Mrs Wells, n.d. [29 November 1905]; E.N. to H.G.W., n.d. [1 December 1905, 7 December 1905, 30 December 1905, 1 January 1906], among the Wells Papers.

14 E.N. to Mrs Wells, n.d. [29 January 1906]; Rosamund to Mrs Wells, 28 January [1906]; Iris to Mrs Wells, 23 March 1906, all among Wells Papers.

15 Ford Madox Ford: *Mightier than the Sword* (1938), p. 160, cited by the MacKenzies, *The Time Traveller*, p. 195.

16 H.G.W. on Well Hall in his *Autobiography*, p. 607; several admiring notes from Cecil Chesterton to E.N. are in the Notre Dame University Library.

17 H.G.W. to G.B.S., 26 March 1906, among Shaw Papers in the British Library. (Add. MSS 50552).

18 *The Diary of Beatrice Webb*, ed. Norman and Jeanne MacKenzie, vol. III 1905–1924 (1984), 1 March 1906, p. 31; Shaw to H.G.W. in *Collected Letters 1898–1910*, ed. Dan H. Laurence (1972), 24 March 1906, pp. 612–4; 11 September, pp. 648–49; undated [14 September 1906], pp. 650–3; 22 September 1906, pp. 653–5.

19 The MacKenzies: *The Time Traveller*, p. 208; Bland to Pease, 14 October 1906, among Fabian Papers at Nuffield College, Oxford.

20 Shaw: *Collected Letters 1898–1910*, 10 December 1906, p. 666.

21 *The Diary of Beatrice Webb*, vol. III (1984), 15 December 1906, p. 62; accounts of the meeting of 14 December in the MacKenzies, *The Time Traveller*, pp. 217–8; Anne Fremantle: *This Little Band of Prophets* (1960), p. 154, gives details of Shaw's speech, concluding, 'Wells was squelched by a joke.'

22 Shaw to H.G.W., *Collected Letters 1898–1910*, 17 December 1906, pp. 667–8; Ensor's remarks to Anne Fremantle, p. 155.

23 Clifford Dyce Sharp, 1883–1935; *The Diary of Beatrice Webb*, vol. III (1984) gives a vivid character sketch of him (while dismissing Rosamund as 'a charming little person, a fellow Fabian, without money or influence, but with literary tastes and housewifely talents'): entry for 22 September 1917, pp. 286–7. Sharp was the founder of the Fabian Nursery and a talented journalist. He became political editor for Orage's *New Age*, editor of *The Crusade* and in 1913, editor of the *New Statesman*, started by the Webbs. He later became an alcoholic.

24 *H. G. Wells in Love* (1984), p. 69; H.G.W. to Violet Hunt, 9 March 1907, among Violet Hunt's Papers at Cornell University Library and cited by the MacKenzies, *The Time Traveller*, p. 225; Rosamund to H.G.W., dated 26 January, refers to 'twenty years of married life', so was written in 1929 or 1930.

25 Rosamund's account to D.L.M. is on the filecard 'H. G. Wells' but is incomplete and probably misdated; Rosamund to Mrs Wells, 4 March 1908, among Wells Papers.

26 The date is bounded on one side by Rosamund's letter to Jane (4

March 1908), on the other by Wells's affair with Amber Reeves which began in the late spring or early summer of 1908. Accounts of this episode were given by Robert Ensor to Anne Fremantle, *This Little Band of Prophets*, pp. 155–6, and by the MacKenzies, *The Time Traveller*, p. 247, whose source was partly Berta Ruck; the 'family version' was given by Mrs Paul Bland to Doris Ker – she thought Wells had been taking Rosamund to Paris for 'a dirty weekend'. Bland on his punching muscles, *Letters to a Daughter* (1906), p. 129.

27 Berta Ruck told the MacKenzies that 'what angered Hubert most . . . was that, as part of his seductive ploy, H.G. told Rosamund the details of her father's sex life', *The Time Traveller*, p. 246, and Robert Ensor made the same point independently to Anne Fremantle, *This Little Band of Prophets*, p. 158.

28 Rosamund to D.L.M., 12 December 1931.

29 *H. G. Wells in Love* (1984), p. 69; H.G.W. to G.B.S., n.d. (but obviously written in the immediate aftermath, i.e. spring 1908), among Shaw Papers in the British Library (Add. MSS 50552).

30 H.G.W. to G.B.S., n.d., among the Shaw Papers.

31 *Shaw: An Autobiography, 1898–1950*, ed. Stanley Weintraub (1970), pp. 176–7.

32 *H. G. Wells in Love* (1984), p. 68.

33 *Letters to a Daughter*, p. 2; *Experiment in Autobiography* (1934, 1984), p. 607.

34 *Ibid.*, pp. 606–7.

35 *H. G. Wells in Love* (1984), p. 69; *The Diary of Beatrice Webb*, vol. III (1984), entry for early August 1909, pp. 120–1.

36 *The New Machiavelli* (1911), book 4, ch. 2, part 2, p. 461.

37 *Ibid.*, book 4, ch. 2, part 2, p. 465; on Bland's high voice and wide shoulders, see Bernard Shaw: *Collected Letters 1898–1910*, ed. Dan H. Laurence (1972), G.B.S. to Archibald Henderson, 3 January 1905, p. 496.

38 *The New Machiavelli* (1911), book 4, ch. 2, part 2, pp. 462–3; on Horsnell's refusal to be mentioned as E.N.'s secretary or indeed anywhere in the book, see John Bland to D.L.M., 16 November 1932 and her reply, 19 November 1932.

39 *The New Machiavelli* (1911), book 2, ch. 4, part 4, pp. 267–8.

40 *Experiment in Autobiography* (1934, 1984), pp. 603, 602, 604.

41 *Ibid.*, pp. 603–4.

42 *Ibid.*, p. 607.

43 E.N. to H.G.W., 12 November 1915, n.d. [but a successor to the previous note]; Rosamund to H.G.W., 3 September [no year], all among Wells Papers.

CHAPTER 12

1 E. M. Forster in interview, Notebook 2; Elsa Courlander in interview, Notebook 3.
2 H. R. Millar in interview, Notebook 3; 'The Challenge of Our Time' in Forster's *Two Cheers for Democracy* (1951).
3 In *Nine Unlikely Tales* (1901), pp. 205–6.
4 *Wings and the Child* (1913), p. 52; John Ruskin: 'Fiction, Fair and Foul', Essay 1, *Nineteenth Century* (1880–1).
5 *The New Machiavelli* (1911), book 1, ch. 2, part 1, pp. 13–14. On its dating, see Norman and Jeanne MacKenzie: *The Time Traveller – The Life of H. G. Wells* (1973), pp. 267–8.
6 Lord Dunsany in interview, Notebook 1; see also Mark Amory: *Lord Dunsany* (1972), p. 71.
7 In *Wings and the Child*, p. 124. E.N. claims to have invented magic city building, but as an adult – her childhood building games required less patience (see pp. 144–7). She was always wonderfully skilled with her hands, sewing, making paper flowers, doing pokerwork and arranging decorations.
8 Early drafts of *The Magic City* (as 'The Temple City') are in the Greenwich Local History Library, Mycenae Rd., S.E.3; Wells's *Floor Games* (1911), p. 45.
9 *The Magic City* (1910), ch. VI, p. 164; ch. XI, p. 305; ch. I, pp. 22–3.
10 *Wings and the Child*, pp. 124–5, 146–9.
11 'The Town in the Library . . .', *Nine Unlikely Tales* (1901), pp. 245, 253, 254.
12 *Ibid.*, p. 259; Forster to E.N., 22 May 1911, thanked her for sending 'the Other Omnibus', i.e. 'The Cockatoucan', in her volume *Nine Unlikely Tales* (1901). She had sent it to him in return for his book *The Celestial Omnibus* (1911), the title story of which recalled her own (earlier) omnibus story in several respects. He added 'of the other stories [I] was particularly delighted with "The Town in the Library, in . . .".'
13 'The Palace on the Floor' in Evelyn Sharp's *The Other Side of the Sun* (1900), pp. 129–45; I am grateful to Gwen Watkins for pointing out the similarities.
14 According to an obituary, Bland's 'cast of mind was singularly akin to that of Mr Balfour and Lord Haldane, for both of whom he had a great – and, as some of his friends thought, an immoderate – intellectual admiration. But he had worked with both statesmen on Royal Commissions and other bodies, and knew their qualities at first hand.' *Manchester Evening Chronicle*, 15 April 1914.

15 Typed notes for *The Magic City* and letters to Philip Bursill from E.N., 13 May 1913 and 16 June 1913, at Greenwich Local History Library.

16 *The Magic City*, ch. III, p. 84.

17 *Ibid.*, ch. VI, p. 165, ch. X, p. 274; *The Last Cruise of the Teal* (1893) by Leigh Ray (identified by Gwen Watkins) describes a yachting adventure, which takes in Hythe (near Dymchurch). 'Leigh Ray' is undoubtedly a pseudonym; the real author was probably known to Edith and may have been the prolific writer H. Gordon Stables.

18 *The Magic City*, ch. VI, p. 171; ch. III, p. 89 (cf. *Alice in Wonderland*, chs. 1, 2); ch. XII, p. 326, 327.

19 *Ibid.*, ch. IV, p. 118; Gerald Gould, reviewing D.L.M.'s biography in *Week-End Review*, 28 January 1933.

20 Details of the Fabian women's group meetings, and of their executive committee (esp. 4 April, 9 May, 3 June and 16 July 1908 – Dr Fry spoke at the latter) among Fabian Papers at Nuffield College.

21 E.N. to Evelyn Sharp, 13 June 1910, in Bodleian Library (Eng. Lett. d. 277).

22 See above, pp. 228-9.

23 E.N. to Harry Nesbit, 17 April 1911; details of Crowlink interior from *The Incredible Honeymoon* (1921), where it appears as 'Crow's Nest', esp. pp. 275, 277; pinning up charms, from interview with Stephen Chant and John Bland, Notebook 1.

24 E.N. to Mavis and Kathleen Carter, n.d. [late 1909?], in collection of Mrs Strange (née Mavis Carter).

25 DLMA includes a number of letters from child admirers; Paul Bland in interview, Notebook 2; Charles Bastable is first mentioned in a letter from E.N. to Mr Ratcliffe, 16 December 1912, and writes to Ratcliffe on her behalf, 14 January 1913, – both letters in the Macmillan Archive of the British Library (Add. MSS 54964).

26 Extract from a diary kept by Mavis Carter in 1910 (owned by Mrs Strange); extract from 'Notes on E. Nesbit by Mavis Carter' (MS in DLMA).

27 E.N. to Mavis Carter, 18 January 1911.

28 Account from Mavis Carter's 'Notes on E. Nesbit'; *The Incredible Honeymoon* (1921), chs. XIII, XIV; E.N. to Mavis Carter (dictated to Paul), 16 December 1923 (owned by Mrs Strange); both in her notes and in conversation Mavis Carter recalled her last meeting with E.N. (and her embarrassment about paying).

29 Mavis Carter in conversation; Rosamund Sharp in interview, Notebook 1; *The Magic City* (1910), ch. X, p. 275, ch. VI, p. 166.

30 A letter and part of the enclosed précis from E.N. to H. R. Millar, n.d. [early 1911?].

31 *Dormant* (1911), p. 287.

32 *Ibid.*, pp. 96, 99, 115, 119, 250.

33 E.N. to Harry Nesbit, n.d. [1911?]; n.d. [spring 1912?].

34 E.N. to Harry Nesbit, n.d. [October 1912?]; the agent was presumably J. B. Pinker, who had been acting for her for some years.

35 See letters to her agents, Morris Colles and J. B. Pinker (in the Berg Collection of the New York Public Library) and her correspondence with Macmillan, and with the Society of Authors, to which she belonged and to whom she constantly appealed for advice on business affairs (both in the British Library).

36 E.N. to Harry Nesbit, n.d. [October 1912?].

37 E.N. to Mr Ratcliffe of Macmillan, esp. 4 July, 5 August, 16 December 1912, in Macmillan Archive in the British Library (Add. MSS 54964).

38 *Wings and The Child*, pp. vii, 127–9.

39 E.N. to Mr Ratcliffe, 16 December 1912, 17 January 1913; n.d. [October 1912] (and cf. *Wings and the Child*, pp. 5–7); E.N. to Sir Frederick Macmillan, 15 April 1913 – letters in Macmillan Archive.

40 *Wet Magic* (1913), ch. I, pp. 13–17, 9; ch. II, p. 29.

41 *Ibid.*, ch. VI, pp. 119–121; ch. VII, p. 132.

42 E.N. to Harry Nesbit, 1 December 1913.

43 E.N. to Lady Dunsany, n.d. [December 1913?].

44 Quotations from three letters to A. P. Watt, all headed 'Crowlink', but undated. They are accompanied by eight deciphered fragments, three in verse, and three apparently worked out from 'The Phoenix and the Turtle', all in the Berg Collection, New York Public Library.

45 One passage reads: 'We kissed her hand and vowed to let no man know the truth, lest the Queen might be known to have been with child by Earl Leicester before they were married by a priest on the XIX of March, MDLV.' Another reads: '[Guy] Fawkes said that Elizabeth bore two boys F. Bacon and Lord Essex . . . but Glory loved them not, because F. Bacon . . . (etc.)'. The theory that Elizabeth was Bacon's mother was held by some Baconians, including Dr O. W. Owen – see S. Schoenbaum: *Shakespeare's Lives* (1970), pp. 553, 575.

CHAPTER 13

1 E.N. to Mavis Carter, 2 February 1914, in Mrs Strange's possession.

2 This account of the events surrounding Hubert's death is based on

Alice Hoatson's memoir and John Bland and Stephen Chant in interview, Notebook 1.

3 Details of the funeral are given in Hubert's obituary in the Woolwich local paper, *The Pioneer and Labour Journal*, 24 April 1914. It was edited by C. H. Grinling, a friend of the Blands – their letters to him are now in the Greenwich Local History Library at Mycenae Rd., S.E.3.

4 *The Sunday Chronicle* (Manchester), 19 April, 1914; Alice Hoatson's memoir.

5 As she showed it to George Seaver, according to his 'Memories of E. Nesbit' (at the Greenwich Local History Library).

6 Elsa Courlander in interview, Notebook 3.

7 A.H.'s memoir.

8 George Seaver's 'Memories of E.N.'.

9 John Bland and Stephen Chant in interview, Notebook 1.

10 E.N. to G. H. Thring of the Society of Authors, 3 June 1914, 20 August 1914 (cited) – her correspondence with them is in the Society of Authors archive at the British Library (Add. MSS 56762).

11 A.H.'s memoir.

12 Iris Philips to D.L.M., 23 May 1932; A.H.'s memoir.

13 John Bland in interview, Notebook 1; *Wings and the Child* (1913), pp. 6–7.

14 E.N. to G. H. Thring, 14 December 1914, in her Society of Authors' correspondence; E.N. to Edward Andrade, n.d. [summer 1915?]; Paul Bland in interview, Notebook 2.

15 Interview with John Bland and Stephen Chant, Notebook 1; E.N. to Harry Nesbit, 24 February 1915; E. M. Forster in interview, Notebook 2; Lord Dunsany in interview, Notebook 1; E.N.'s rebuke to Alice on the filecard on Alice Hoatson, attributed to Iris Philips; Joan Evans de Alonso: 'E. Nesbit's Well Hall, 1915–1921 – A Memoir', *Children's Literature* (MLAA), Vol. III, 1974, p. 152.

16 The wreath story from Mrs Paul Bland in interview, Notebook 2; E.N. to Harry Nesbit, 24 February 1915.

17 E.N. to Edward Andrade, 28 March 1915; n.d. [summer 1915?], E.N. to G. H. Thring, 12 May 1915, in her correspondence with the Society of Authors.

18 E.N. to Edward Andrade, 12 July 1916; A.H.'s memoir; Joan Evans de Alonso (E. Nesbit . . . A Memoir), p. 147.

19 *Ibid.*, pp. 147, 148.

20 *Ibid.*, pp. 148–152; John Bland and Stephen Chant in interview, Notebook 1.

21 *Ibid.*, pp. 147, 151; A.H.'s memoir.

22 T. T. Tucker in interview, Notebook 2; E.N. to Edward Andrade, 12 July 1916.

23 A.H.'s memoir; the phrase 'Like a little fat Cockney robin' was used by Margaret Furse (daughter of Arthur Watts) in her account of E.N., now at Greenwich Local History Library.

24 E.N. to Paul Bland, n.d. [June 1916?] (JNA).

25 E.N. to Harry Nesbit, [late] February 1917.

26 E.N. to Edward Andrade, 7 February 1917.

27 Berta Ruck to D.L.M., 13 January 1933; Arthur Watts in interview, Notebook 4; Rosamund's response to E.N.'s second marriage is recorded on the filecard 'Mrs Rosamund Sharp'.

28 Iris Philips to D.L.M., n.d. [between 18 November 1932 and 2 January 1933]; she added, 'I fear his in-law relations have made him worse than he was – they are of the most prim.'

29 T. T. Tucker to D.L.M., 8 June 1932 and in interview, Notebook 2; Iris Philips to D.L.M. (2 letters), n.d. [between 28 May and 20 June 1932]; on her spirituality, see Athene Seyler in interview, Notebook 2, Russell Green in interview, Notebook 3; Berta Ruck to D.L.M., 13 January 1933.

30 E.N. to Edward Andrade, 7 February 1917.

31 Elsa Courlander in interview, Notebook 3; E.N. to Harry Nesbit, 12 June 1918.

32 Berta Ruck to D.L.M., 13 January 1933; T. T. Tucker in interview, Notebook 2.

33 Elsa Courlander in interview, Notebook 3.

34 Paul Bland in interview, Notebook 2, said that she suffered from bronchitis during the last eighteen years of her life but the evidence suggests that it was for most of her adult life – she gave up smoking near the end; A.H.'s memoir.

35 T. T. Tucker in interview, Notebook 2.

36 These verses and a note written to Gertrude on the eve of her wedding, making the same point ('You'll have to find a nicer name for me than Mrs Tucker, won't you?') are in JNA.

37 E.N. to Gertrude Bland, 11 November 1918 (JNA): Russell Green in interview, Notebook 3; Rosamund Sharp told D.L.M., 15 November 1932, 'We all feel Russell Green's contribution is pretty awful, but perhaps we are prejudiced . . .'.

38 Russell Green in interview, Notebook 3; E.N.'s verses for the bathroom in DLMA.

39 T. T. Tucker in interview, Notebook 2; according to a letter to the Society of Authors, Fisher Unwin offered her a 25 per cent royalty (after sales) on *The Treasure Seekers*, *The Wouldbegoods* and *The New Treasure Seekers*, 20 per cent on *Five Children and It*, *The Amulet*, *The Enchanted Castle* and *The House of Arden* and 16 per cent on *The Phoenix and the Carpet* and *Nine Unlikely Tales* in

February 1920 – her correspondence with the Society of Authors is in the British Library.

40 Bernard Shaw in interview, Notebook 4; Andrade's loans recorded in a private note on the filecard 'Prof. E. N. da C. Andrade'.

41 E.N. to Berta Ruck, 5 December [1923].

42 *Daily Mail*, 5 November 1917.

43 According to John Bland in interview, Notebook 1.

44 E.N. to Mavis Carter, n.d. [Spring 1923], in Mrs Strange's possession.

45 *The Lark* (1922), p. 246.

46 Athene Seyler in interview, Notebook 2; T. T. Tucker in interview, Notebook 2; John Casson: *Lewis and Sybil – A memoir* (1972), pp. 97, 98.

47 Noël Coward in interview, Notebook 3; Cole Lesley: *The Life of Noël Coward* (1976), p. 68; Noël Coward: *Present Indicative* (1938), pp. 12, 176, 177 (cited).

48 G. B. Stern in interview, Notebook 3.

49 E.N. to Berta Ruck, 20 June 1923.

50 Berta Ruck: *A Story-teller Tells the Truth* (1935), pp. 149, 150.

51 Iris Philips in interview, Notebook 1; T. T. Tucker in interview, Notebook 2; a filecard on 'Her Last Illness' says she was suffering from lung trouble, heart trouble and a tumescent growth, probably cancer; her death certificate gives the cause of death as 'bronchiectasis and cardiac dilatation'.

52 Mavis Carter's 'Notes on E. Nesbit'.

53 E.N. to Mavis Carter, 16 December 1923; letters concerning the scrapbook are dated 24 January, 1, 10, 11, 19 February, 5, 10 March 1924 (all dictated); it was completed by 10 April 1924, when the Skipper wrote to thank her – letters in Mrs Strange's possession.

54 Berta Ruck: *A Story-Teller Tells the Truth* (1935), p. 151.

55 E.N.'s letters to Berta Ruck in DLMA; correction slip by Iris Philips, attached to letter, n.d. [between 26 October and 18 November 1932]. Paul also claimed that she died in his arms, but Iris's version sounds more plausible.

56 Details of the mourners from her obituary in *The Kentish Express*, 10 May 1924; on her friendship with the Rev. Cooke and her final views on religion, see T. T. Tucker to D.L.M., 6, 8 June 1932, *Dormant* (1911), p. 312.

AFTERWORD

1 Iris Philips in interview, Notebook 1; T. T. Tucker and Olive Hill in interview, Notebook 2.

2 Lord Passfield to D.L.M., 4 November 1931; E.N. to Berta Ruck, 21 April 1924.

3 Iris Philips to D.L.M., n.d. [between 26 October and 18 November 1932]; D.L.M. referred to Paul's distress in her 'Retrospective Introduction' to the second edition of *E. Nesbit* (1966), p. xiii; Rosamund Sharp to D.L.M., 15 November 1932.

4 John Bland to D.L.M., 23 November 1932, 15 March 1932; *E. Nesbit* (1966), p. xxvii.

5 T. T. Tucker was 79, and died 17 May 1935; Paul Bland was 60, and died on 9 October 1940 (information from their death certificates).

6 The poem was 'The Things That Matter', from *The Rainbow and the Rose* (1905), a very unexpected choice. In her lifetime her most frequently anthologized poems were 'The Baby-Seed Song' and 'The silver birch is a dainty lady . . .'

7 Lord and Lady Dunsany in interview, Notebook 1.

8 Nina Griffith to D.L.M., 25 May 1932; E.N. to Morris Colles, 7 February 1898, in the Berg Collection, New York Public Library.

9 See *The Treasure Seekers* (1899), ch. III, p. 31; ch. IV, p. 57; ch. VI, p. 82; ch. XII, p. 197; *The Wouldbegoods* (1901), ch. I, pp. 7, 11; ch. II, pp. 32, 45; ch. IV, p. 68; ch. V, pp. 94, 95; ch. VIII, p. 180; ch. X, pp. 215, 221. This by no means exhausts the list of books referred to in these two volumes alone; the total number of literary allusions occurring in her children's books is exceptionally high.

10 'Bigwardrobeinspareroom' appears in 'The Aunt and Amabel', *The Magic World* (1912), pp. 224–5; C. S. Lewis: *Surprised by Joy* (1955), p. 21; Charles Williams: *The Image of the City* (1958), p. 171; *The Amulet*, ch. XII, p. 293.

11 See Chapter 1 of Freeman Dyson's *Disturbing the Universe* (1979). Two recent appreciations of E.N. are Gore Vidal's 'E. Nesbit's Magic' in *Collected Essays 1952–1972* (1974), pp. 174–180, and Alison Lurie's 'Riding the Wave of the Future', *The New York Review of Books*, vol. XXXI, no, 16, 25 October 1984, pp. 19–22.

12 Edward Garnett, reading some of the stories that later made up *The Treasure Seekers* for Fisher Unwin, made this point about her Englishness: 'a vey charming picture of English family life – the best characteristics, the best in the English temperament and manner of educating children is here . . .' – his report is in the Berg Collection, New York Public Library; Clemence Dane's letter, dated 'March', in DLMA; Noël Coward's letter quoted from Cole Lesley's *The Life of Noël Coward* (1976), pp. 370–1.

A NOTE ON THE ILLUSTRATIONS

The clover leaf sign used under the chapter headings was Edith's decorative way of signing her initials, E.B. She also used it in her book of MS poems, apparently to designate poems that she particularly liked.

Family tree designed by Alan Clark.

Chapter 1: at end, Edward Ardizzone's illustration of E.N. at her desk at Halstead, from the reprint of her memoirs, 'My School-Days', retitled *Long Ago When I Was Young* (1966, 1974).

Chapter 2: at end, E.N.'s marriage certificate.

Chapter 3: at end, Leonora Bowley's illustration 'We are going to make our fortunes,' to E.N.'s 'The Story of the Golden Apple, the Enchanted Water and the Magic Rose', from *Father Christmas*, the children's supplement to the *Illustrated London News* (1895–6), p. 16.

Chapter 4: at end, vignette of drowned lovers by May Bowley, to illustrate E.N.'s short story '*The Poor Lovers*', *Atalanta* (1982), vol. V, p. 224.]

Chapter 5: in text, Fabian card for 1886–7; at end, illustration from *Lilies and Heartsease*, a selection of poems made by E.N. and Robert Ellice Mack, illustrated anonymously (1888).

Chapter 6: in text, Laurence Housman's birthday card for E.N. shows him accidentally hitting her nose at badminton; at end, the bookplate Laurence Housman designed for her.

Chapter 7: in text, the MS of the poem E.N. sent to Bower Marsh from Antibes; Gordon Brown's illustration 'She sat very upright on the grass, with her fat little hands in her lap' (the Bastables discovering Noel's princess) for *The Treasure Seekers* (1899), facing p. 86.

Chapter 8: in text, H. R. Millar's illustration ' "Poof, poof, poofy," he said, and made a grab', from *Five Children and It* (1902), facing p. 82.

Chapter 9: in text, the amulet and its inscription (as written by Wallis Budge) from *The Amulet* (1906), pp. 46, 53; at end, H. R. Millar's illustration to introduce *The Amulet* as serialized in *The Strand* (1905).

Chapter 10: in text, part of the programme for E.N.'s play *The Magician's Heart*; at end, Gerald Spencer Pryse's illustration 'The Last Rehearsal' (Nina Griffith as the model) for *Salome and the Head* (1909), facing p. 182.

Chapter 11: in text, Bland looking every inch the poseur in a portrait by George Phoenix, 1909; at end, Wells's cartoon of himself being inspired by the Mind of the Race – it was intended for *Boon* (1915) but not used.

Chapter 12: in text, 'The Guard-Room', an illustration by George Barraud for *Wings and the Child* (1913), p. 149; H. R. Millar's illustration 'Philip felt that it was best . . .' for *The Magic City* (1910), p. 307; at end, Leonora Bowley's illustration 'The Whole Court Fled,' to E.N.'s story 'The Prince, Two Mice, and Some Kitchen Maids' from *Father Christmas*, the children's supplement to the *Illustrated London News* (1896–7), p. 31.

Chapter 13: at end, the church of St. Mary in the Marsh, drawn by F. Hibbert, 1971.

Afterword: at end, decoration from *Winter Songs and Sketches*, selected by E.N. and Robert Ellice Mack, various illustrators (1886).

Below: anonymous illustration (signed G.L.) to Amy Levy's essay 'Readers at the British Museum', *Atalanta* (1889), vol. II, p. 450.

BIBLIOGRAPHY

Compiled by Selwyn Goodacre

1885

The Prophet's Mantle (in collaboration with Hubert Bland, under the pseudonym 'Fabian Bland'). Henry J. Drane & Co., London, pp. vi, 322; Bedford Clarke, Chicago, 1889. Reprinted 1888, 1889.

1886

Spring Songs and Sketches; *Summer Songs and Sketches*; *Autumn Songs and Sketches*; *Winter Songs and Sketches*. Illustrated books of verses, selected and arranged by E.N. and Robert Ellice Mack. Griffith, Farran, Okeden & Welsh, London; E.P. Dutton, New York. (Produced and printed by Ernest Nister, Nuremberg.) Each contains poems by E.N.

Lays and Legends. Longmans, Green & Co., London, pp. viii, 197. (Reprinted as 'First Series', 1892.)

1887

Morning Songs and Sketches; *Noon Songs and Sketches*; *Eventide Songs and Sketches*; *Night Songs and Sketches*. Illustrated book of verses, selected and arranged by E.N. and Robert Ellice Mack. Griffith, Farran, Okeden & Welsh, London; E.P. Dutton, New York. (Produced and printed by Ernest Nister, Nuremberg.) Each contains poems by E.N.

River Sketches, words selected and written by E.N. Illustrated by Charles G. Noakes. Von Portheim & Co., London; E.P. Dutton, New York. (2 poems by E.N.)

The Lily and the Cross. Griffith, Farran, Okeden & Welsh, London; E.P. Dutton, New York. (Produced and printed by Ernest Nister, Nuremberg.)

The Star of Bethlehem. Ernest Nister, London; E.P. Dutton, New York. (Produced and printed by Ernest Nister, Nuremberg.) (Reprinted in 1894.)

1888

The Better Part, and other poems. Henry J. Drane & Co., London, pp. 16.

Easter-Tide (with Caris Brooke). Henry J. Drane & Co., London; E.P. Dutton, New York.

The Time of Roses (with Caris Brooke and others). Henry J. Drane & Co. (1 poem by E.N.)

By Land and Sea, poems selected by E.N. Henry J. Drane & Co., London.

Landscape and Song. Henry J. Drane & Co., London; E.P. Dutton, New York, pp. 16.

The Message of the Dove. Henry J. Drane & Co., London; E.P. Dutton, New York.

Autumn Leaves, selected and arranged by E.N. With pen and ink drawings by H. Bellingham Smith. Henry J. Drane & Co., London; E.P. Dutton, New York. (Printed in Germany.)

Winter Snow, selected and arranged by E.N. With pen and ink drawings by H. Bellingham Smith. Henry J. Drane & Co., London; E.P. Dutton, New York. (Printed in Germany.) (It seems likely that there were also volumes for Spring and Summer).

Lilies and Heartsease, songs and sketches arranged by E.N. and Robert Ellice Mack. Griffith, Farran, Okeden & Welsh, London; E.P. Dutton, New York. (Printed by Ernest Nister, Nuremberg.)

Falling Leaves, songs and sketches arranged by E.N. and Robert Ellice Mack. Griffith, Farran, Okeden & Welsh, London. (Printed by Ernest Nister, Nuremberg.)

Daisy Days, with verses by E.N. and others. Griffith, Farran, Okeden & Welsh, London.

All Round the Year, by E.N. and Caris Brooke. With drawings by H. Bellingham Smith and others. Von Portheim & Co., London. (Printed in Germany.)

Leaves of Life. Longmans, Green & Co., London and New York, pp. x, 185.

1889

Evergreen from the Poet's Corner, selected and arranged by Robert Ellice Mack. Ernest Nister, London; E.P. Dutton, New York (2 poems by E.N.).

The Lilies Round the Cross (with Helen J. Wood). Ernest Nister, London; E.P. Dutton, New York.

Corals and Sea Songs. Ernest Nister, London; E.P. Dutton, New York.

1890

Life's Sunny Side (poems by E.N. and others). Ernest Nister, London; E.P. Dutton, New York.

Songs of Two Seasons. Illustrated by J. McIntyre. Raphael Tuck & Son, London.

Told by the Fireside (short stories by E.N. and others). Illustrated by Marie Seymour Lucas. Griffith, Farran, Okeden & Welsh, London, pp. 88. (1 story by E.N., in rhyme: 'The Excursion'.)

Songs of Scotland (selected by E.N.). Ernest Nister, London; E.P. Dutton, New York.

1891

Twice Four (short stories by E.N. and others). Griffith, Farran, Browne & Co., London, pp. 50. (1 story: 'Finding a sister'.)

The Poets and the Poetry of the Century, ed. Alfred H. Miles. Hutchinson & Co., London, pp. 714. Vol. 8, 'Robert Bridges and Contemporary Poets'. (11 poems by E.N., and a short appreciation by Alex H. Japp – pp. 579–592.)

1892

The Voyage of Columbus, a narrative in verse. Illustrated by Will and Frances Brundage, and J. Pauline Sunter. Raphael Tuck & Son, London. (A souvenir of the 400th Anniversay.)

Story upon Story, and Every Word True (by E.N. and others). Raphael Tuck & Son, London. (1 story: 'Allie's House-Keeping'.)

Sweet Lavender (verses). Ernest Nister, London; E.P. Dutton, New York. (Printed in Bavaria.)

Lays and Legends (verses). Longmans, Green & Co., London. Second Series, pp. 160.

1893

Contributions to the following books of verse and prose, all published by Raphael Tuck & Son, London:

Flowers I Bring and Songs I Sing. (7 poems written under the name E. Bland; other poems by H.M. Burnside and A. Scanes.)

Our Friends and All About Them. (Poems, and 3 stories: 'The Self Respecting Pussies', 'Down at Grannie's', 'Mabel's Pussy'.)

Listen Long and Listen Well. (2 stories: 'Midsummer Day', 'The Oak Panel'.)

Sunny Tales for Snowy Days. (1 story: 'Ella's Adventure'.)

Told by the Sunbeams and Me. (2 stories: 'Dorothy's Birthday', 'Being Bandits'.)

What Really Happened. (1 story: 'The Babe in the Wood, or What Happened at Kitty's Party'.)

We've Tales to Tell. (2 stories: 'How Jack came to tea', 'A Crooked Tail'.)

Grim Tales. A.D. Innes & Co., London, pp. 167. (Short stories originally published in *Longman's Magazine, Temple Bar, Argosy, Home Chimes,* and *Illustrated London News.*)

Something Wrong. A.D. Innes & Co., London, pp. 158. (Short stories originally published in *Longman's Magazine, Temple Bar, The Sketch, The Victorian,* and *The Sunday Chronicle.*)

1894

Contributions to the following books of verse and prose, all published by
Raphael Tuck & Son, London:
Hours in Many Lands. (2 stories: 'The Little Heroine', 'Effie's Birthday'.)
Tales that are True for Brown Eyes and Blue. (1 story: 'Lonely Mabel'.)
Tales to Delight from Morning till Night. (1 story: 'Mother's Present'.)
Fur and Feathers, Tales for All Weathers. (1 story: 'More Haste, Less Speed'.)
All But One, Told by the Flowers. (1 story: 'Hot Pies'.)
Lads and Lasses. (Stories not individually signed.)

The Girls' Own Birthday Book, selected and arranged by E.N. Henry J.
    Drane & Co., London, pp. 252.
Nister's Holiday Annual (1894). (Includes 'The Play Times, Vol, 1 No. 1' and
    1 story: 'The Tiger's Story'.)
The Butler in Bohemia (short stories, written in collaboration with Oswald
    Barron). Henry J. Drane & Co., London, pp. 142.
The Marden Mystery (a novel). Bedford Clarke, Chicago.

1895

Contributions to the following books of verse and prose, all published by
Raphael Tuck & Son, London:
Tick Tock, Tales of the Clock. (1 story: 'The Glordy John'.)
Stories in a Shell. (1 story: 'The Rainbow Queen'.)
Treasures from Storyland. (1 story: 'Linda and the Prince'.)
Friends in Fable, A Book of Animal Stories. (1 story: 'A House of Her Own'.)

Dulcie's Lantern, and other stories. Griffith, Farran, Browne & Co., London.
    (1 story: 'Finding a Sister'.)
Pussy Tales. Illustrated by Lucy Kemp-Welch. Marcus Ward & Co. Ltd.,
    London.
Doggy Tales. Illustrated by Lucy Kemp-Welch. Marcus Ward & Co. Ltd.,
    London.
Rose Leaves (verses). Ernest Nister, London. (Printed in Bavaria.)
Poets' Whispers, a Birthday Book (quotations selected and arranged by E.N.,
    and with introductory poem by E.N.) Henry J. Drane & Co., London,
    pp. 252.
Nister's Holiday Annual (1895). (Includes 'The Play Times, Vol. 1 No. 2' and
    1 story: 'Dolly's Voyage'.)
Holly and Mistletoe, a book of Christmas Verse (with Norman Gale and
    Richard le Gallienne). Marcus Ward & Co., London.
A Pomander of Verse. John Lane, London; McLury, Chicago, pp. 88.

1896

As Happy as a King (children's story in verse). Illustrated by S. Rosamund Praeger. Marcus Ward & Co. Ltd., London.

Nister's Holiday Annual (1896). (Includes 'The Play Times, Vol. 1 No. 3'.)

In Homespun (short stories). Vol. 22 in the 'Keynote Series'. John Lane, London; Robert Bros., Boston, pp. 189.

1897

Once Upon a Time, The Favourite Nursery Tales, E.N. and others. Ernest Nister, London; E.P. Dutton, New York. (Printed in Bavaria.)

Dinna Forget. (2 poems by G. Clifton Bingham and E.N.) Ernest Nister, London; E.P. Dutton, New York (1898). (Printed in Nuremberg.)

Tales Told in the Twilight (very short stories by E.N. and others). Ernest Nister, London; E.P. Dutton, New York, pp. 120. (Printed in Bavaria.) (20 stories by E.N.)

The Children's Shakespeare, ed. Edric Vredenburg. Illustrated by Frances Brundage, M. Bowley, J. Willis Grey, etc. Raphael Tuck & Son, London; Altemus, Philadelphia (1900). pp. 96.

Romeo and Juliet, and other stories. Illustrated by Frances Brundage and J.W. Grey. Raphael Tuck & Son, London, pp. 64.

Royal Children of English History. Illustrated by Frances Brundage and M. Bowley. Raphael Tuck & Son, London, pp. 94.

Nister's Holiday Annual (1897). (Includes 'The Revolt of the Toys'.)

1898

Dog Tales, and other Tales (with A. Guest and Emily R. Watson), ed. Edric Vredenburg. Illustrated by R.K. Mounsey. Raphael Tuck & Son, London.

A Book of Dogs, being a discourse on them, with many tales and wonders gathered by E.N. With original pencil drawings by Winifred Austin. J.M. Dent, London; E.P. Dutton, New York.

Nister's Holiday Annual (1898). (Includes 'The Pen Fairy', 'The Rat Princess', 'Prince Feather-Head and the Mer-Princess', 'No Good'; several verses.)

Songs of Love and Empire. Constable & Co., London, pp. 168. (Verses previously published in the *Daily News*, *Pall Mall Gazette*, *Daily Chronicle*, and *Athenaeum*.)

1899

Pussy and Doggy Tales. Illustrated by Lucy Kemp-Welch. J.M. Dent, London; E.P. Dutton, New York (1900), pp. 132. (A combined edition of the two 1895 volumes, with new material.)

The Story of the Treasure Seekers, Being the Adventures of the Bastable Children in Search of a Fortune. Illustrated by Gordon Brown (15) and Lewis Baumer (2). T. Fisher Unwin, London; Frederick Stokes, New York, pp. 296.
(Previously published in *Pall Mall Magazine*, *Father Christmas*, *Nister's Holiday Annual* 1894 and 1895, *Windsor Magazine*).
(15 impressions by 1928, then reissued both separately, and by Ernest Benn in 1929 as the first part of *The Complete Story of the Bastable Family* and reprinted regularly thereafter.)

The Secret of Kyriels, a novel. Hurst & Blackett, London; Lippincott, Philadelphia, pp. 391.

The Book of Dragons. Illustrated by H.R. Millar, with decorations by H. Granville Fell. Harper & Bros., London and New York. pp. 290.
(First published as *The Seven Dragons* in *The Strand Magazine*, March–September 1899.) (Reprinted 1901.)

Father Tuck's Annual (1900). (1 story: 'The Fairy Godmother'; 1 poem: 'Fairies'.)

1901

Nine Unlikely Tales for Children. Illustrated by H.R. Millar (8), Claude Shepperson (20), frontis, M. Bowley. T. Fisher Unwin, London; E.P. Dutton, New York, pp. 297.
(Previously published in *The Strand Magazine*, *Father Christmas*, *The Sphere*, *Black and White*, and elsewhere.)
(14 impressions by 1928, then taken over by Ernest Benn and further reprinted.)

The Wouldbegoods, Being the Further Adventures of the Treasure Seekers. Illustrated by Arthur H. Buckland (17), and John Hassell (2). T. Fisher Unwin, London; Harper & Bros., New York, pp. 331.
(Previously published in *Pall Mall Magazine*, and *Illustrated London News*, July 1900–July 1901.)
(14 impressions by 1928, then taken over by Ernest Benn and further reprinted.)

To Wish You Every Joy. Raphael Tuck & Son, London.

Thirteen Ways Home (short stories). Anthony Treherne & Co., London, pp. 306.

1902

The Revolt of the Toys, and What Comes of Quarrelling (2 stories). Illustrated by Ambrose Dudley. Ernest Nister, London; E.P. Dutton, New York, pp. 32. (Printed in Nuremberg.)

Five Children and It. Illustrated by H.R. Millar. T. Fisher Unwin, London; Dodd, Mead & Co., New York (1905), pp. 301.
(First published as *The Psammead* in *The Strand Magazine*, April–December 1902.)
(4 impressions by 1912, then taken over by Ernest Benn, and further reprinted.)

The Red House, a novel. Illustrated by A.L. Kellar. Methuen & Co., London; Harper & Bros., New York, pp. 274. (5th edition by 1911.)

1903

The Rainbow Queen, and other stories. Illustrated by E. and N.R. Taylor, M. Bowley, etc. Raphael Tuck & Son, London, pp. 64.

Playtime Stories. Raphael Tuck & Son, London.

The Literary Sense (short stories). Methuen & Co., London; Macmillan, New York, pp. 299.

1904

Cat Tales (with Rosamund Bland). Illustrated by Isabel Watkin. Ernest Nister, London; E.P. Dutton, New York. (Printed in Nuremberg.)

The Phoenix and the Carpet. Illustrated by H.R. Millar. George Newnes, London; Macmillan, New York. pp. 236.
(Previously published in *The Strand Magazine*, July 1903–June 1904.)
(9 impressions by 1929, taken over by T. Fisher Unwin by 1920, and later by Ernest Benn and further reprinted.)

The New Treasure Seekers. Illustrated by Gordon Browne (31) and Lewis Baumer (2). T. Fisher Unwin, London; Frederick Stokes, New York, pp. 328.
(Previously published in *The London Magazine*, *Black and White*, and *Illustrated London News*, mainly December 1903–November 1904.)
(9 impressions by 1929, then taken over by Ernest Benn and further reprinted.)

The Story of the Five Rebellious Dolls. Ernest Nister, London; E.P. Dutton, New York. (Printed in Nuremberg.)

1905

Pug Peter (a dog story. Pictures by Harry Rountree, vignettes by John Hassall. Alfred Cooke, Leeds and London, pp. 63.

Oswald Bastable and Others. Illustrated by C.E. Brock (7) and H.R. Millar (13). Wells, Gardner, Darton & Co., London, pp. 369.
(Previously published in *Crampton's Magazine*, *The London Magazine*, *The Windsor Magazine*, *Sunday Strand*, *Woman at Home*, *The Strand Magazine*, *Black and White*, and *The Jabberwock*, between February 1902 and December 1905.)

The Rainbow and the Rose (poems). Longmans, Green & Co., London and New York, pp. 143.

1906

The Story of the Amulet. Illustrated by H.R. Millar. T. Fisher Unwin, London; E.P. Dutton, New York, pp. 374.
(Previously published in *The Strand Magazine*, May 1905–May 1906.)
(6 impressions by 1926, then taken over by Ernest Benn and further reprinted.)

The Railway Children. Illustrated by C.E. Brock. Wells, Gardner, Darton & Co., London; Macmillan, New York, pp. 309.
(Previously published in *The London Magazine*, January 1905–January 1906.)
(Reprinted a number of times.)

The Incomplete Amorist, a novel. Illustrated by Clarence F. Underwood. Constable & Co., London; Doubleday, Page & Co., New York, pp. 311.

Man and Maid (short stories). T. Fisher Unwin, London, pp. 312.

1907

The Enchanted Castle. Illustrated by H.R. Millar. T. Fisher Unwin, London; Harper & Bros., New York, pp. 352.
(Previously published in *The Strand Magazine*, January–November 1907.)
(7 impressions by 1929, then taken over by Ernest Benn and further reprinted.)

Twenty Beautiful Stories from Shakespeare, 'a home study course, being a choice collection from the World's greatest classic writer, William Shakespeare, retold by E.N., beautifully illustrated with many new colour plates and fine pen drawings by Max Binn'. ed. and arranged by E.T. Roe. Hertel Jenkins & Co., Chicago.
(Reprinted in 1926, by D.E. Cunningham & Co., Chicago.)

1908

The Old Nursery Stories. Illustrated by W.H. Margetson. Henry Frowde, and Hodder & Stoughton, London, pp. 165.
(This is No. 1 of 'The Children's Bookcase' series; later books in the series were by other authors.)

The House of Arden, a story for children. Illustrated by H.R. Millar. T. Fisher Unwin, London; E.P. Dutton, New York (1909), pp. 349.
(Previously published in *The Strand Magazine,* January–November 1908.)
(5 impression by 1929, then taken over by Ernest Benn and further reprinted.)

Jesus in London, a poem, with seven pictures by Spencer Pryse. A.C. Fifield, London, pp. 14 (in folio).

Ballads and Lyrics of Socialism, 1883 to 1908 (published for the Fabian Society). A.C. Fifield, London, pp. 80.

1909

Harding's Luck. Illustrated by H.R. Millar. Hodder & Stoughton, London; Frederick Stokes Co., New York (1910), pp. 281.
(Previously published in *The Strand Magazine,* January–November 1909.)
(Taken over by T. Fisher Unwin in 1923, and in 1930 by Ernest Benn, reaching a 6th impression by 1944.)

These Little Ones (short stories). Illustrated by Spencer Pryse. George Allen & Sons, London, pp. 210.

Cinderella, a play with twelve Songs to popular airs. Sidgwick and Jackson, London.

Daphne in Fitzroy Street, a novel. George Allen & Sons, London; Doubleday, Page, and Co., New York, pp. 417.

Salome and the Head, a modern melodrama. Illustrated by Spencer Pryse, Alston Rivers, London; Doubleday, Page & Co., New York (as *The House with No Address*), pp. 309.
(Reprinted in London by George Newnes in 1914 with the revised title.)

Garden Poems. Collins, London and Glasgow, pp. 95.

1910

The Magic City. Illustrated by H.R. Millar. Macmillan & Co., London, pp. 333.
(Previously published in *The Strand Magazine,* January–November 1910.)
(Later taken over by Ernest Benn and further reprinted.)

Days of Delight, ed. Edric Vredenburg. (Tales by E.N., M.A Hoyer, etc.) Raphael Tuck & Son, London, pp. 71. (In 'Father Tuck's Golden Gift Series'.) (1 story: 'The Fairy Godmother'.)

Children's Stories from English History, told by E.N. and Doris Ashley. Illustrated by John H. Bacon, Howard Davie, M. Bowley 'and other popular artists'. Raphael Tuck & Son, London, pp. 144.
(Reprinted material from *Royal Children of English History*, 1897; reissued in 1914.)

Children's Stories from Shakespeare, by E.N., with 'When Shakespeare was a boy' by Dr. F.J. Furnivall. Illustrated by John H. Bacon and Howard Davie, and 'many interesting black and white drawings' by Harold Copping. Raphael Tuck & Son, London; McKay, Philadelphia (1912).
(Later reprinted with a revised title, *Shakespeare Stories for Children*.)

Fear (short stories). Stanley Paul & Co., London, pp. 318.

1911

My Sea-side Story Book, by E.N., with G. Manville Fenn. Illustrated by W. Rainey, A. Well, and others. Ernest Nister, London; E.P Dutton, New York. (Printed in Bavaria.) (1 story: 'Prince Feather-Head and the Mer-Princess'.)

The Wonderful Garden, or the Three C's. Illustrated by H.R. Millar. Macmillan & Co., London, pp. 402.
(Previously published in *The Strand Magazine*, January–November 1911.)
(Taken over by Ernest Benn in 1930 and further reprinted.)

Ballads and Verses of the Spiritual Life. Elkin Matthews, London, pp. 105.

Dormant, a novel. Methuen & Co., London; Dodd, Mead, New York (1912) (as *Rose Royal*).

1912

The Magic World (short stories). Illustrated by H.R. Millar (21) and Spencer Pryse (3). Macmillan & Co., London and New York, pp. 280.
(Previously published in *The Strand Magazine*, *Pall Mall Magazine*, *Black and White*, *Sunday Strand*, and *Blackie's Christmas Annual*, 1908.)
(2nd impression, 1924, taken over by Ernest Benn in 1930, and further reprinted.)

1913

Our New Story Book. Illustrated by Elsie Wood, Louis Wain, etc. Ernest Nister, London; E.P. Dutton, New York. (Printed in Nuremberg.) (2 stories: 'Our Black Cat' and 'The Likeness'.)

Wet Magic. Illustrated by H.R. Millar. T. Werner Laurie, London, pp. 274.
(Previously published in *The Strand Magazine*, December 1912–August 1913.)

(Taken over by T. Fisher Unwin in 1926, and by Ernest Benn for the 4th impression in 1929, and further reprinted.)

Wings and the Child, or the Building of Magic Cities. Illustrated with photographs and diagrams by George Barraud. Hodder & Stoughton, London; Doran, New York, pp. 197.

1914

Battle Songs (chosen by E.N.). Max Goschen, London, pp. 96.

Essays, by Hubert Bland, ed. 'E. Nesbit-Bland'. Max Goschen, London, pp. 284.

1916

The Incredible Honeymoon. Harper and Bros., New York, pp. 315.
  (First published in England in 1921, by Hutchinson & Co., pp. 286.)

1920

Children's Annual 1920. (Includes short story, 'The Doll's House'.)

1921

The New World Literary Series, Book Two (10 short stories and 10 poems for children), ed. Henry Cecil Wylde. Collins Clear Type Press, London & Glasgow. pp. 164.

1922

The Lark, a novel. Hutchinson & Co., London, pp. 286.
  (Went to a 2nd edition).

Many Voices (poems). Hutchinson & Co., London, pp. 94.

1923

To the Adventurous (short stories). Hutchinson & Co., London, pp. 286.

1925 (posthumous)

Five of Us, and Madeleine (short stories, linked together by Rosamund Sharp). Illustrated by Norah S. Unwin. T. Fisher Unwin, London; Adelphi Co., New York (1926), pp. 310.
  (Previously published in *Hulton's Children's Annual*, 1920, *Time and*

Tide, The Jolly Book, 1917, *The Strand Magazine, The Pall Mall Magazine*, and *Collins Children's Annual*, 1914.)
(Taken over by Ernest Benn for the 3rd impression, 1928, and further reprinted.)
The Bastable Children (a reprint of the three Bastable books), preface by Christopher Morley. Coward-McCann, New York.
(Went to a 5th impression by 1932.)

UNDATED

Fading Light. Illustrated by A. Warne Browne, W. Hagelberg, London and New York.
Apple Pie. pp. 12.
Miss Mischief. Ernest Nister, London; E.P. Dutton, New York, pp. 12.
Off to Fairyland. Ernest Nister, London; E.P. Dutton, New York. (3 stories: 'Our Black Cat', 'The Blue Bird' and 'Multiplication is Vexation'.)
My Farmyard Story Book by E.N. and others. Ernest Nister, London; E.P. Dutton, New York. (1 story: 'Our Pony'.)
Stories for All Times by E.N. and others. Ernest Nister, London; E.P. Dutton, New York. (1 story: 'The Suitor's Suit'.)
Fairies, painted by Pauline Sunter. Raphael Tuck & Son, London.
(A shaped book, 'designed at the Studios in England and printed by the "Rafolith" process at the Fine Art Studious in Saxony'.)

PLAYS

E.N. wrote the following plays, of which only the first appears to have been published. Further details of their performance are given in the main text:
Cinderella (see 1909).
A Family Novelette (written in collaboration with Oswald Barron).
The King's Highway and *The Philandrist, or the London Fortune Teller* (both written in collaboration with Dorothea Deakin).
The Magician's Heart.
In the Queen's Garden (or *Absalom*).
Unexceptionable References.

PERIODICAL PUBLICATIONS

E.N. contributed extensively to periodicals of all kinds. The above list includes material later collected in her published books, but much remains that was never gathered in this way. Most of the uncollected work is now unidentifiable. (There is, for example, a scrapbook compiled by E.N. which has several hundred cuttings of poems, with little or no indication of their place of publication.) Certain substantial serial writings are listed below:
The Social Cobweb (signed 'B').
    The Weekly Dispatch, 6 January–23 March 1884.
Something Wrong, by 'Fabian Bland' (E.N. and Hubert Bland).

The Weekly Dispatch, 28 March 1886–4 July 1886.
The Hour before Day, by Fabian Bland.
The Weekly Dispatch. 20 September 1885–4 October 1885.
A series of short stories.
    The Weekly Dispatch, 17 April 1887, 1 May 1887, 15 May 1887, 21 August
    1887, 28 August 1887, 25 December 1887.
    E.N. continued to contribute weekly poems and/or short stories, virtually
    without a break from 1888 to the end of 1891, and sporadically thereafter,
    until 1894.
My School-Days. Girl's Own Paper, October 1896–September 1897.
Unsigned poetry criticism for the *Athenaeum* – 1896.
The Neolith, published quarterly under the direction of E.N., Graily Hewitt,
    F. Ernest Jackson, and Spencer Pryse. 4 issues published:
    November 1907: includes 'The Criminal'.
    February 1908.
    May 1908: includes 'The Ashpits'.
    August 1908: includes 'In the Queen's Garden'.
Weekly articles for children
    The Daily Chronicle, 11 contributions between 23 April–16 July 1910.

CRITICAL ACCOUNTS
Three books concerned exclusively with E. Nesbit, followed by three that
include interesting discussions of her work. The magazine *Junior Bookshelf*
produced an 'E. Nesbit issue' for her centenary, October 1958, (22, 4).
Doris Langley Moore: *E. Nesbit: A Biography*, Ernest Benn, London 1933.
    Revised edition, Chilton, Philadelphia 1966; Ernest Benn, 1967.
Noel Streatfeild: *Magic and the Magician: E. Nesbit and Her Children's
    Books*, Ernest Benn, London; Abelard Schumann, New York, 1958.
Anthea Bell: *E. Nesbit*, Bodley Head Monographs, London, 1960; Walck,
    New York, 1964.
Roger Lancelyn Green: *Tellers of Tales: Children's Books and Authors from
    1800 to 1968*, Kaye and Ward, 1969 (a revised and expanded version of the
    study first published in 1946).
Marcus Crouch: *Treasure Seekers and Borrowers: Children's Books in Britain
    1900–1960*, The Library Association, London, 1962.
Stephen Prickett: *Victorian Fantasy*, Harvester Press, Brighton, 1979.

E.N. was the subject of a television play shown on BBC television in 1973 in
the series *The Edwardians*. The play was written by Ken Taylor, and starred
Judy Parfitt as E. Nesbit. A version of the series was published in book form:
Peter Brent: *The Edwardians*, BBC, London, 1972 (pp. 147–167).

INDEX